IMMIGRANTS IN TWO DEMOCRACIES

IMMIGRANTS IN TWO DEMOCRACIES
French and American Experience

Edited by
Donald L. Horowitz and Gérard Noiriel

An American Academy of Arts and Sciences Book

NEW YORK UNIVERSITY PRESS
New York and London

Library of Congress Cataloging-in-Publication Data
Immigrants in two democracies : French and American experience /
edited by Donald L. Horowitz and Gérard Noiriel.
p.   cm.
"An American Academy of Arts and Sciences book."
Includes bibliographical references and index.
ISBN 0-8147-3479-0 (acid-free paper)
1. Immigrants—United States.   2. United States—Emigration and
immigration.   3. Immigrants—France.   4. France—Emigration and
immigration.   I. Horowitz, Donald L.   II. Noiriel, Gérard.
JV6450.I554   1992
304.8'73—dc20   91–27545
                                                                CIP

This collection of essays was prepared under the auspices of the American
Academy of Arts and Sciences with the support of grants from The Lynde
and Harry Bradley Foundation and, in France, from the Ecole Normale
Supérieure and La Mission Interministérielle Recherche Expérimentation
(MIRE). Opinions, findings, conclusions or recommendations expressed herein
are those of the individual authors and do not necessarily reflect the views
of the American Academy or the supporting foundations.

New York University Press books are printed on acid-free paper,
and their binding materials are chosen for strength and durability.

C 10 9 8 7 6 5 4 3 2 1

CONTENTS

PREFACE

In spite of heightened awareness of issues of immigration and ethnicity in the Western world, there have been relatively few efforts to compare the experiences of Western countries. The present volume is an effort to redress this deficiency. It arose out of a sense that there was much to be learned—and learned reciprocally—from a focused, carefully conceived comparison of two countries sharing many common traditions and responding to rather similar questions. The project was a joint venture of the American Academy of Arts and Sciences and the Ecole Normale Supérieure, culminating in an intensive, three-day conference held at the Abbaye de Royaumont, outside Paris.

The conference was preceded by nearly three years of planning, designed to make the project genuinely comparative. The results are visible in this volume, which contains parallel French and American treatments.

In organizing the comparison, we were particularly concerned to emphasize ideas as well as institutions. All along, we have been much impressed by the profound impact of divergent conceptions of immigration and group identity on such matters as historical memory, the behavior of immigrant groups in the political process, antidiscrimination law, education, and even statistical practices. While the papers survey a wide array of subjects, they are heavily informed by a sense that ideas and history are important determinants of the way countries deal with these issues.

In planning this venture, we were fortunate to have unusually acute and well-informed colleagues. On the French side, an informal planning group consisting of Gérard Noiriel, Jean-Louis Fabiani, and Roxane Silberman met with us on several occasions in the United States and France. The American Academy planning committee for the project, consisting of Walker Connor, Nathan Glazer, Lance Liebman, Corinne Schelling, Stephan Thernstrom, Myron Weiner, and myself, met on numerous occasions, with and without our French colleagues. We were aided throughout by Robert Wood, who first conceived the idea of a Franco-American comparison on this theme, among others, and introduced us to the Ecole Normale group with whom we worked on this study.

The planning phase was facilitated by funds from the Research and Planning Committee of the American Academy of Arts and Sciences. At every stage we have had encouragement from Joel Orlen, Executive Officer of the Academy. The conference itself was made possible by a generous grant, on the American side, by The Lynde and Harry Bradley Foundation, and by contributions, on the French side, from the Ecole Normale Supérieure and La Mission Interministérielle Recherche Expérimentation (MIRE). We are particularly grateful to Hillel G. Fradkin and Michael S. Joyce at the Bradley Foundation for their interest. In France, Patrick du Cheyron of MIRE provided invaluable assistance to us prior to and during the conference.

All the French papers have been translated for this American edition by The French Library in Boston. We are especially appreciative of the translation work of Tiane Donahue. We also are grateful for the assistance from Professor Alain A. Levasseur with the translation of legal terminology in the chapter by Danièle Lochak.

The American Academy of Arts and Sciences has had a long history of involvement in the serious study of racial and ethnic pluralism, both in the United States and abroad. Much of this work has been pursued as a result of the interest and efforts of Corinne S. Schelling, Associate Executive Officer of the Academy. This venture is no exception. It could never have been begun or brought to fruition without her unique combination of initiative, insight, and persistence. Everyone who has touched this project in any way knows how much is owed to the work Corinne Schelling put into it.

DONALD L. HOROWITZ

ONE

IMMIGRATION AND GROUP RELATIONS
IN FRANCE AND AMERICA

1

IMMIGRATION AND GROUP RELATIONS IN FRANCE AND AMERICA

Donald L. Horowitz

International migration is often thought of as something new in world history. In receiving countries, the immigrants, their place in the new society, and their ties to the old are rediscovered by each generation as issues to be faced afresh. Since World War II, there has been a new surge of movement across international boundaries. The need for labor in industrial countries, the gap in standards of living, turbulence and warfare in many newly independent countries, and the greater ease and reduced cost of transportation have all contributed to increased migrant flows, particularly increased flows over longer distances. Yet, despite ebbs and flows, the world-wide movement of peoples is of long standing.

So, too, are the characteristic issues raised by international migration in the receiving countries. How do the immigrants fit into and affect the receiving polity and society? What changes can or must the receiving country make to accommodate them? What changes do immigrants and their descendants experience, in culture and ethnic identity? What are the relations of immigrant groups to the mix of peoples already present in the receiving country? What determines the policies that govern the reception and treatment of immigrants? What determines the success and satisfaction of immigrants over time? Everywhere questions such as these have been asked.

All translations from the French are by the author.

Uniform questions, however, do not elicit uniform answers, even among countries with relatively similar institutions, ideologies, and histories of immigration. Two of the world's oldest democracies, the United States and France, have traditionally welcomed immigrants. With strongly entrenched official doctrines of equality, traceable to common sources in the European Enlightenment, both countries have long received immigrants seeking economic opportunity, and both pride themselves on their hospitality to political refugees and dissidents. Both experienced large immigrant flows in the late nineteenth and early twentieth centuries, followed by a hiatus and then resumed flows from different source countries in recent decades. Both have become home to large numbers of immigrants from countries outside of Europe and North America. Both need to accommodate greater racial and religious heterogeneity than they were previously accustomed to accommodating.

France and the United States are attempting to come to grips with the effects of immigration on the economy, on political integration, and on culture. France has experienced an anti-immigrant backlash and a debate on the place of immigrants and ethnic minorities in French society. In France, as elsewhere in Europe, immigrant groups are now perceived as a major "problem." In the United States, passage of the Immigration Reform and Control Act of 1986 and of the Immigration Act of 1990 has by no means ended debate on such matters. On the contrary, the United States may be in the process of redefining the nature of its society and polity—a process prompted by the conjunction of large-scale immigration with the increased economic and political participation of preexisting racial minorities. In both countries, immigration has wrought profound change. In neither has the process of change run its course.

The many similarities between France and the United States make a comparison of the two countries particularly feasible and intriguing. Despite the similarities, what is striking is how different many of the results of immigration have been thus far. In both countries, there is an interplay of popular conceptions about immigrants (and about the pluralism they engender) with national history and ideology, as well as with official policy and thought about the nature of the society being created. Yet, whereas the United States is overtly a country of immigrants, France is only covertly and partially such a country. The French do not regard themselves, in the way that Americans do, as the descendants of immigrants. Subtle differences in doctrines of equality yield different relations of citizens to the state, and a different configuration of political institutions also produces divergent conceptions of the role of immigrant and minority groups in the polity. Many of the same roots grow into quite different branches.

IMMIGRATION: PARALLEL HISTORIES

About 7 percent of the United States population and about 8 percent of the French population were born in foreign countries. Although the French percentage is the highest in Europe, other countries of immigration, such as Australia, have much higher percentages. Perhaps as much as one-third of the population of France can trace its origins to the immigration of a grandparent (Girard 1971). *"France, terre d'accueil"*—"a welcoming country"—is a boast with considerable historical validity. Moreover, as previous generations of immigrants became "just Americans" (Lieberson and Waters 1988), their counterparts became just French, to the point where Gérard Noiriel (1988, 19) speaks of a "collective amnesia" about immigrant origins.

In the United States and in France, immigration has come in discernible waves, each wave from varying source countries. The great migrations from Europe to the United States ended, for the most part, with the restrictive legislation of 1924. Four decades later, in 1965, Congress opened the door to immigration once again. The results have been dramatic and unexpected. Legal immigrants grew from about a half-million in the 1940s to more than four million in the 1970s.[1] Perhaps an additional six million entered illegally during the latter decade. In the 1950s, Europeans comprised 59 percent of all legal immigrants to the United States. In the 1970s, Europeans were only 18 percent of all immigrants. Instead, Latin Americans, who in the 1950s comprised only 22 percent of all legal immigrants, were, by the 1970s, 41 percent. Asians, 6 percent in the 1950s, were 36 percent by the 1970s. Germany, Italy, and Ireland were the largest sending countries between 1821 and 1930. Following the passage of the 1965 act, Mexico, the Philippines, and various Caribbean countries became the largest source countries (Warren 1980, 3). Between 1980 and 1990, the Latino population of the United States grew by more than 50 percent, and the Asian population more than doubled. In short, both the size and composition of the flow of immigrants into the United States have changed sharply.

The consequences are striking. To take just one set of revealing figures, the population of California in 1960 was 87 percent non-Hispanic White. In 1980, it was only 67 percent White, 19 percent Latino, 8 percent Black, and 5 percent Asian. By the year 2010, according to some estimates (Cain and

Kiewiet 1986a), non-Hispanic Whites will comprise less than half of California's population.

The effects of such immigrant flows can hardly be overestimated. Around the turn of this century, more immigrants entered the United States than do now, but more also left.[2] There is much less back migration today. The United States is once again a country of mass immigration.

France, too, has a population traditionally enriched by immigration. Mass immigration to France began in the mid–nineteenth century. Among the main source countries were Belgium, Italy, and Poland. By 1930, France had the world's highest rate of immigration, 515 per one hundred thousand inhabitants, higher than the United States, with 492 (Noiriel 1987, 3). Following World War II, immigration resumed, putting France near the top of the world's countries in terms of foreign-born population. To the earlier central European immigrants who staffed the mines and factories in which French peasants were reluctant to work was added a new wave of Iberian, Asian, and North African immigrants. In 1901, nearly two-thirds of the foreign population in France was Belgian or Italian. During the interwar period, a good many Slavs came as well: Poles, Czechs, and Ukrainians. By 1975, a year after the French border was closed to most immigration, more than four-fifths of all foreigners had come from North Africa or the Iberian peninsula, with more than a fifth each from Portugal and Algeria. Like the United States, France has its old immigrants and its new, and by some estimates (*Figaro*, 16 October 1989) nearly a million illegal immigrants. In both countries, restrictions on immigration have increased the numbers of those seeking entry in special categories: refugees in the United States, asylees in France (OECD 1990, 37).

In France, as in the United States, immigrants are not distributed randomly across the country. As the favored American destinations of central and eastern Europeans were the industrial cities of the Midwest, so the favored destination of Mexicans has been California, that of Cubans has been Florida, and that of a great many other groups has been New York City and its environs. Belgians congregated in nineteenth-century French factory towns, and Poles sought work in the mines of Lorraine and Languedoc. North Africans have been heavily concentrated in and around several major cities: Paris, Lyon, and Marseilles.

Americans like to think that the United States is distinctive in its creation through immigration. In this, of course, they are quite mistaken. Not only have Canada, Australia, and Argentina been equally affected by immigration, but so have several European countries, none more than France. The difference between France and the United States has not been so much in immigration but in ideas about immigration—and hence about ethnicity—and in the institutions that govern the reception of immigrants and their descendants.

NATIONAL IDEAS: DIVERGENT HISTORIES

Both France and the United States share a conception of open admission to the political community. The French census and other officially gathered statistics divide the population into "French" and "foreigners." Earlier generations of immigrants, especially European immigrants but not merely Europeans, have moved over into the "French" column, in much the same way as previous immigrants to the United States were "Americanized"—and by many of the same methods. In both countries, the public schools were taken to be important vehicles of acculturation. Mastery of the French and English languages also played roughly similar roles in the transformation of immigrants into citizens. Although France has not had the same liberal *jus soli* rules of citizenship that the United States has had, it nevertheless has made naturalization liberally available to immigrants and their children, and there are forces working for further liberalization of citizenship rules (see the report of the so-called *Commission des Sages*: Long 1988).

At the same time, the division of the population into French and foreign implies something that goes to the heart of differences between France and the United States. The dichotomization of identity means that immigrants who are no longer "foreigners" are presumed to exchange their former identity for a French identity. Hyphenation, the hardy perennial of American ethnic studies, is logically foreclosed in France (with exceptions to be noted later). It is possible to be an Italian in France, but it is not possible to be an Italian-Frenchman in the same easy way as it is possible to be an Italian-American.

Right at this point, one can glimpse some central differences in French and American thought. These relate to the concept of a core identity, the relation of people to the land and the community, and the relative spheres of the state and civil society.

At the time of the French Revolution, the French language and French identity certainly did not occupy the same geographic space that they do today. Both have spread out from the center to most parts of the periphery. Still, the core identity has not been in doubt. There was a French nation, defined largely by blood and later by conceptions of "our ancestors, the Gauls"—a conception taken a bit more literally than the rather metaphorically invoked "pilgrim fathers" in the United States. After the Revolution, to be sure, powerful doctrines of equality bonded citizens to that nation, irrespective of blood. The concept of the nation was not, however, wholly drained of its organic character (Safran 1989a)—as Gérard Noiriel points out in this volume, 1789 was said to mark the victory of the Gauls over the aristocratic Franks—and immigrants were often greeted with a considerable measure of xenophobia. Anti-Belgian feeling ran very strong in northern France in the mid–nineteenth century (Noiriel 1988, 258). In the 1870s, Italians were viewed as "parasites on the economic system" and thought to be utterly unassimilable (Morsy 1984, 33). The same objections are raised today for the Maghrébins.

In the United States during the revolutionary period, the various colonies were composed of differing ethnic and religious mixes. Often, there was mutual enmity within colonies, as between, for example, Scots-Irish Presbyterians and English Quakers in Pennsylvania. Political positions taken toward the American Revolution were frequently explicable in terms of such ethnic and religious rivalries (Alger 1974). No doubt, earlier migrants from Great Britain often were acknowledged as a founding population, but the fact that the Revolutionary War was fought against Britain diluted any stronger claims that might have been made over the long term. Ultimately, the sense of the United States as a country formed and re-formed by immigration precluded the creation of a permanent core identity to which outsiders could only aspire.

There were, to be sure, powerful waves of nativist sentiment, triggered by each new wave of immigration (see Higham 1968). At various times, those who arrived earlier pursued conflict against foreigners, against Catholics, against Irish, and against eastern and southern Europeans. These conflicts were punctuated by lethal episodes of ethnic violence (Horowitz 1983). As Italians were killed in a southern French city in 1893, they were also lynched in a southern American city in 1891 (Higham 1968, 91). Yet, in the end, yesterday's immigrants became today's natives, precisely because there was no fixed notion of who—among Whites—could claim indigenous status. A study in a small Vermont city in the 1930s found that more recent immigrants accorded a mild form of deference toward the established "Yankee" families of the city, who were acknowledged by their Irish and French Canadian neighbors as a "Charter Group," people associated with the founding (Anderson 1937). Beyond that, at least for Whites, the society could make no permanently fixed distinctions between indigenes and immigrants. It had no strongly organic conception of Americanness.

The United States was also conceived as a great adventure in the conquest and taming of a vast land. It was a country in the making, and immigration was essential to settling it. Gérard Noiriel (1988) points out that immigration was encouraged not in order to settle France, but to provide labor. Still, in

France, there was—and is—some notion, however fictitious, that immigrants may actually return to their countries of origin, and there has been no notion that immigrants have been in any sense creating the country. The nation and the republican polity were created by 1789. Unlike the American Revolution, which was a beginning, the French Revolution was a culmination. Immigrants could cleave to a France already established, but they could neither make nor remake it.

Equally republican, France and the United States nevertheless entertain diametrically opposed conceptions of state and society. French revolutionary norms provide for a direct relationship between the citizen and the state. Jacobin ideals are hostile to organizations that mediate this relationship. Hence the suspicion of ethnic interest groups. Until 1981, there was actually in force a statute that prohibited formation of organizations of foreigners. There is no denying that various interest organizations exist and that they sometimes lobby government, but the phenomenon gives rise to theoretical discomfort. Interests, which are inevitably partial, are a contradiction of Rousseauean notions of the general will (Ehrmann and Schain 1991, 165). In such an ideological climate, ethnic pluralism does not flourish easily. It is not surprising that even the term *ethnicity*, with its connotations of competing, substate loyalty, is regarded with considerable suspicion.

The United States, on the other hand, is beholden more to Montesquieu than to Rousseau. Madison, too, was suspicious of interests, but he saw them as inevitable, indeed natural, and his response was to balance them rather than to delegitimize them (Hamilton, Jay, and Madison 1888, nos. 10, 51). There has always been a legitimate place in American political thought for mediary institutions between the citizen and the state. Speaking of the multitude of American voluntary associations, Alexis de Tocqueville (1945, 198) aptly linked them to "mistrust" of "social authority." American theorists often regard a rich array of interests as supportive of democracy (Key 1956, 10–11; Diamond *et al.* 1988), partly because they help to limit state power. Traditional American liberalism has been thoroughly hostile to state power (and "big government"), which it placed in opposition to the popular will (Hartz 1955, 211–18). For this among other reasons, voluntary associations are not suspect. The assortment of American ethnic organizations active in lobbying on policy matters seems thoroughly bewildering in France (see Weiner, 1989).

As William Safran (1989a, 6) has well said, the United States favors civil society against the state, whereas France favors the state over civil society. Is it any wonder that France habitually forgets its previous waves of immigration and provides little or no space for ethnic groups, whereas the United States has made the recollection of immigration and the exaltation of ethnicity something of a cottage industry?

IMMIGRATION: THE COMPARATIVE SPECTRUM

To emphasize that we are comparing within a fairly narrow range, it is instructive to broaden the comparison somewhat by taking a brief look at Germany and Britain as well as the United States and France. Germany is at one end of the Western immigration continuum, and the United States is at another.[3]

Polities differ in the extent to which they divide ethnic groups into natives and immigrants. In some states, a sense of indigenousness creates strong claims to priority over those who come later, whereas in others immigrants can quickly become natives. To be an immigrant is, in some measure, to lack legitimacy in the state and to lack entitlement to the panoply of rights and opportunities afforded by the state. If there exists an immigrant group, there also exists, implicitly, a more legitimate indigenous group. Some of the most extreme cases of ethnic conflict in Asia and Africa revolve around sharp distinctions between indigenes (or "sons of the soil") and immigrants. In some cases, immigrants who have been in the country for generations are told that they are there on sufferance, that they are guests who must yield pride of place to their indigenous hosts. In Fiji, Malaysia, Assam in India, and to some extent Sri Lanka, indigenousness is ideologized into an elaborate claim to priority.

In the most extreme version of the host-guest model, the prospect of integrating migrants into the host society is rejected altogether. Rights to citizenship, political participation, property ownership, welfare benefits, and the immigration of family members are severely restricted or denied altogether. This is the situation of long-term guest workers from Asia in the Persian Gulf states (Weiner 1990, 144–49), and it was roughly the position from which *Gastarbeiter* began more than a generation ago in several northern European countries, including Germany.

A few basic questions about the relations of immigrants to citizens reveal considerable differences across countries. First, what is the size of the sector regarded as "foreign," relative to the actual number of people of foreign origin? Second, how easy is it to change one's legal status from foreigner to citizen? Third, what changes in social identity follow from such a change in legal status?

In the United States, whatever lingering claims to priority were entertained by those whose ancestors came from Great Britain have been eroded to the point of disappearance. World War II had an important effect of emphasizing the common Americanness of those who fought in it, and the "G.I. Bill of Rights," which provided free education for war veterans, facilitated university education for the children and grandchildren of a good many working-class immigrants. The Immigration Act of 1965 and—especially—the indirect effects of the Civil Rights Movement of the 1960s heightened the emphasis on racial and ethnic equality. In social practice, the category of immigrant, except in the literal sense of someone who has arrived very recently, has largely been eliminated. The idea of speaking of "Americans," on the one hand, and of "foreigners" or "immigrants," on the other, would be regarded as a form of not-very-subtle bigotry. Whereas one can be an immigrant even intergenerationally in France and elsewhere in Europe, this is not possible in the United States. Conversely, whereas there is little space for ethnic groups in France, in the United States that space is nearly unlimited.

It is not surprising that, in such a society, the main problem for immigrants is to gain lawful entry into the country. Once admitted lawfully for long-term employment, citizenship is, ultimately at least, not a major problem; it will, in most cases, be forthcoming. A country with a national ideology that equates "Americanness" not with blood but with adherence to a set of ideals, or perhaps only with lengthy lawful presence in the territory, will increasingly regard the grant of citizenship by naturalization not as a privilege accorded the recipient but as a formality. Such a state will also have the most liberal *jus soli* rules of citizenship.

In all of this, I do not mean to imply that there is not a strong fear of immigration. There is, indeed, especially on the southern border. But the national ideology has constrained the United States in its ability to act once immigrants are in the territory. By judicial decision, even illegal immigrants are entitled to certain benefits, and their children, born in the United States, are citizens.

The contrast with Germany could not be sharper. The German practice of *jus sanguinis* citizenship; the most restrictive naturalization practices and the possibility of administrative arbitrariness in the decision to confer citizenship (Fijalkowski 1989); the idea that the third generation of Turks or Yugoslavs could still be considered immigrant; the notion that, at least in theory, such people might really return to their ancestral home countries and that policy might be geared to such a prospect—all of this is truly at another pole from where the United States is now. To take just one point of contrast with third-generation *Gastarbeiter*, there is evidence from a careful study in Los Angeles that, by the third generation, English is the main language of the home for 84 percent of Mexican-Americans (Lopez 1978).

If being American is now a status devoid of blood content, one major implication is that citizenship and membership in the nation are essentially the same. (Indeed, *nationality* is a term hardly ever used, for citizenship is so much more important.) In some ways, this is a remarkable achievement, given the immigration of the last quarter-century. The non–blood-based definition of Americanness survives and is even strengthened in a period of radical change in the sources of immigration. For a recent immigrant to become American does not entail relinquishment of ethnic identity. On the contrary, the growing inclusiveness of the overarching identity has been accompanied by an accentuation of some ethnic differences within the American polity, a kind of hyper-hyphenation.

To be German has a completely different connotation. As Rogers Brubaker (1988) has explained, the German conception of nationhood and citizenship was the product of the nineteenth-century unification of Germany, with roots in Romanticism rather than the Enlightenment. Blood origins play a large role in identifying who belongs to the political community. The line between the foreign sector and the German sector of the population is firm and sharp. For those few who do change legal status, there is no hyphenate group to which they may adhere. Turko-German is an oxymoron. The most one can be is a Turk in Germany. The Turks in Germany have networks of organizations, but these typically reflect home-country divisions and are directed at Turkish problems in Turkey, rather than Turkish problems in Germany (Wilpert 1988).

France and Britain are not properly placed in either the German or the American category. If being German implies being German by descent, being French or British is more ambiguous. As I have suggested, there are some blood connotations to Frenchness, but there has long been, even in France's African and Asian colonies, the possibility of *assimilation*. French citizenship is not based exclusively on *jus soli* or *jus sanguinis*. A good many Maghrébins are French citizens. Annually, France naturalizes three times as many immigrants, and Britain naturalizes four to five times as many, as Germany does (OECD 1990, 187, 190). Being a Black Briton is not the same enormous contradiction as being a Turko-German. In both Britain and France, advocacy of repatriation of the immigrant populations is regarded as radical and extreme. In both countries, the immigrant communities have turned their attention to politics in Britain and France, and not primarily to politics in the home country. There are several Black members of the British Parliament, and there are local councils controlled or heavily influenced by immigrants. The emergence of S.O.S. Racisme, France Plus, LICRA, and MRAP (the Movement against Racism and for Friendship among Peoples) and of far more numerous and militant groups in Britain finds no parallel in Germany. Not surprisingly, perhaps, the two main excolonial powers exhibit the greatest ambiguities regarding immigration and integration, whereas the two countries with the most traumatic histories of racial and ethnic relations (Black slavery and Jewish extermination, respectively) anchor the ends of the spectrum.

If we examine what happens to those who are admitted to the national community, the spectrum appears again. In Germany, individuals may acculturate and conceivably merge into the German population, but more likely their new citizenship will not change their social identity. They will technically no longer be foreign, but they will remain "immigrant." By contrast, American society is filled with ethnic affiliations to which individuals can adhere; the United States is a patchwork quilt. Britain is not, because it is not historically a country of immigration. It is mainly an ethnically undifferentiated society, which also contains discrete minorities separated socially from other Britons by fairly firm lines. France has similarly firm social boundaries for some minorities, notably the Maghrébins and Black Africans, but others, such as Italians, appear to be melting a bit in the French *creuset*.

In short, immigrant status in the United States is short-lived; the boundary between aliens and citizens is porous; the status of "American" is open; and being American is not incompatible with being a member of an ethnic group. In Germany, immigrant status is long standing and intergenerational; the boundary between aliens and citizens is relatively impermeable; it is difficult to become a German; and being German is incompatible with being anything else. In Britain and France, noncitizen status may be, but need not be, intergenerational; the boundary between aliens and citizens is modestly permeable; and there is some loose sense of contradiction between being British or French and being something else. In France, however, unlike Britain, the voyage from being something else to being French has been made by many people, albeit not usually in the first generation. In this respect, the French identity, like the American, has a universalistic aspect to it that derives from both eighteenth-century thought and a long history of immigration.

THE *FOULARD* AFFAIR: IMMIGRANTS AND TWO SECULAR RELIGIONS

I said earlier that ethnic pluralism is not in favor in France, largely because of long-standing ideas about the relationships of citizens to the state. There are other forces that point in the same direction, most notably the singular secularism of the French state, with its origins in the thought of Voltaire and the *philosophes* (see, e.g., Cobban 1961, 83–84).

A revealing example of the powerful challenge immigrants are thought to present to some fundamental conceptions of French nationhood is provided by the great *foulard* controversy of 1989. A furor was created when three North African students in a state school north of Paris refused to remove the head coverings *(chadors)* worn by Muslim women, in order to attend class. School authorities prevented their attendance. In a compromise, the students then agreed to remove the head coverings in class but not at recreation, but they subsequently reneged. Muslim students elsewhere in France took a similar position, and the matter quickly became a *cause célèbre* (see, e.g., the several articles in the right-wing newspaper *Figaro*, 20 October 1989). Eventually, French educational authorities relented, but it was widely agreed that the episode epitomized serious tensions.

For many North African Muslims, the issue was religious freedom and the reception of immigrants in France. Studies of Maghrébin acculturation show strong differences by generation and a good deal of attitudinal convergence between French and Maghrébin youth, but Maghrébin attitudes toward religion exhibit significantly less change than do attitudes in other areas (Malewska-Peyre and Zaleska 1980; Muxel 1988). Such findings obscure important changes in religious practice among Maghrébin youth, particularly a rather strong secular trend, in behavior and attitudes, among young Maghrébin women, most of whom have abandoned the *chador* (Muxel 1988, 938–39; Begag 1988; Begag 1990, 7; cf. Grillo 1985, 146–59). Islamic practice is thus an important symbolic issue, even as it is in the course of change.

Islam and the *chador* were of equal and opposite symbolic importance for influential sectors of French opinion, which placed the *foulard* controversy in the context of the Iranian revolution and the threat posed by Islamic doctrine to a secular France (e.g., Max Clos in *Figaro*, 16 October 1989). Recounting a number of disturbing tales of the allegedly excessive accommodation of French authorities to exotic immigrant practices, Annie Kriegel put her finger on what was disturbing about the *chador* in schools. To fail to adhere to the central principles of the public philosophy, she argued, and to move the law toward something other than a unitary conception of the relations of individuals to the state—"on the pretext of tolerance"—is "to retribalize a country whose civilization and Revolution had appropriately contributed to detribalization" (*Figaro*, 17 October 1989). And so a local tempest touched two nerves at once: secularism and the conception of a citizen as being stripped of cultural particularism before the state.

The *foulard* dispute had a concrete aftermath. The *Front National*, with a strong anti-immigrant platform, scored a number of immediate electoral gains. A month after the *foulard* dispute arose, the *Conseil d'Etat* upheld the determination of the Minister of Education that the *chador* was permissible clothing in schools, provided it was not worn for "pressure, provocation, preaching, or propaganda" (*Reuters Library Report,* 27 November 1989). Shortly thereafter, the government declared that France "can no longer be a land of immigration" (*Washington Post,* 7 December 1989); it announced strict border controls and intensified measures to integrate immigrants already in the country. Surveys showed French public opinion strongly hostile to the immigrant presence, intolerant of cultural difference, and favorably disposed to expelling immigrants with irregular status while "integrating" the rest (*Paris Match,* 14 December 1989).

Then, in October of 1990, a suburb of Lyon experienced a riot by immigrants that resembled the American urban riots of the 1960s and the British riots of the early 1980s (see Horowitz 1983). Triggered by an incident that symbolized police harassment, the violence took place in a model redevelopment area and involved attacks on police, looting of shops, and arson in the new commercial district (*New York Times,* 19 October 1990). By then the *foulard* affair had passed, but the violence suggested to the government the urgency of integrating immigrants. To the *Front National,* it suggested the urgency of repatriating them.

In the United States, the *foulard* dispute would quickly have been perceived to implicate only the right to religious freedom. That is not to say that the courts would under all circumstances have upheld the right to wear the *chador* (cf. *Employment Division v. Smith* [1990]), only that the matter would have been cast instantly in the discourse of rights. The *chador* might make a variety of groups uneasy, for a variety of reasons, none of which—certainly not the secularization of the schools—could compete with a formulation in terms of rights. A public school that excluded a student on grounds of religiously motivated costume would have been widely denounced as bigoted. If France worships at the shrine of the undifferentiated citizen, the United States worships at the shrine of constitutional rights.

This is particularly so in ethnic and racial relations, where rights discourse furnishes strong support for the entrenchment of heterogeneity. The Constitution and several civil rights statutes have produced an elaborate jurisprudence of ethnic and racial equality, about which I shall say more later. An important illustration of the reach of such doctrine is the decision of the United States Supreme Court that aliens are a "protected class," so that legal classifications based on alienage receive "close judicial scrutiny" for their conformity to the principles of equal treatment embodied in the Constitution and in a plethora of judicial decisions (*Graham v. Richardson* [1971]).

Although, as I shall suggest, the influence of American law on the relations among immigrant groups, other groups, and the state is in some measure a secondary effect of the formidable role played by law in the Black civil rights revolution, it is by no means just that. Rather, the law was invoked in the 1950s and 1960s because it already provided powerful but untapped resources to help in the struggle for equality. Some proof of this proposition lies in the xenophobic 1920s, a decade in which the Supreme Court vindicated the rights of immigrant and religious minorities on no fewer than three occasions. One case involved German language instruction in the schools; another, compulsory enrollment in public schools; and the third, schools to inculcate Japanese language and values.[4] Legal recognition of cultural pluralism was already deeply embedded, and so was the notion that law and the courts were the ultimate arbiters of ethnic and racial relations.

To be sure, the law is not silent on such matters in France. There are ongoing efforts to make legal procedures affecting immigrants more fair (see, e.g., *Libération,* 14 October 1989, on stays of deportation), and there are statutes prohibiting ethnic and racial discrimination in employment, provision of goods and services, including housing, and treatment by public authorities (Costa-Lascoux 1990). But discrimination is difficult to prove, the law has been effective only "where the discrimination is manifest and specific," and the number of cases remains small: well under one hundred that reach final adjudication each year (Costa-Lascoux 1990, 17, 18).

Moreover, the scope of the interests protected by French law is relatively narrow. Foreigners are excluded from French civil service employment and membership in the professions—both areas opened up to aliens by the Supreme Court of the United States (*Sugarman v. Dougall* [1973]; *In re Griffiths* [1973])—and immigrants are frequently subject to arbitrary police action. The range of matters conceived in legal terms is completely different, as indeed the remedies are as well. Whereas the British Race Relations Act of 1976 makes limited provision for positive discrimination (affirmative action), French law has no such provision.

More to the point, however, is the judicialization of the whole subject in the United States in a way that is completely unheard of in France or anywhere else. If Congress passes an act forbidding discrimination in employment, as indeed it has in Title 7 of the Civil Rights Act of 1964, the cases number annually in the many thousands. Title 7 law is voluminous and elaborate; it engages the attention of thousands of lawyers and administrators in the private and public sectors. If there are thought to be too few television programs catering to minority tastes, then the Federal Communications Commission may set aside a certain share of television licenses for applicants who are "Black, Hispanic Surnamed, American Eskimo, Aleut, American Indian and Asiatic American," and the courts will decide whether the set-aside is lawful (*Metro Broadcasting v. FCC* [1990]). It was, again, Tocqueville (1945, 290) who first noted the powerful impact of law and legal thinking on Americans. In the United States, he said, everyone speaks "the language of the magistrate." Tocqueville's insight applies to immigration, race, and ethnicity, as much as it does to any other field.

The result is that rights discourse often displaces other modes of conceiving and communicating about intergroup relations in the United States. Take, for example, the question of political power. In 1965, Congress enacted the Voting Rights Act. The act outlawed devices designed to deprive Blacks of their exercise of the franchise. Within a few years, Black voter registration and then office holding increased dramatically (Horowitz 1983, 202–3). The act was soon interpreted by the Supreme Court to forbid electoral arrangements that might subtly "dilute" the voting power of minorities rather than simply deny them the right to vote (*Allen v. Board of Elections* [1969]). In 1975, "language minorities," including "persons who are American Indian, Asian American, Alaskan Native or of Spanish heritage," were added to the coverage of the act; and in 1982, the act was amended to prohibit not merely intentional discrimination but "discriminatory effects" (Thernstrom 1987). There followed a plethora of lawsuits challenging an array of electoral practices, from run-off elections to at-large elections to multimember constituencies. In many cases, constituencies were redrawn and electoral systems were revamped by the courts in order to favor minority candidates, mainly Black and Hispanic. To a greater extent than anywhere else in the world, the electoral process has been placed in the framework of legal rights and in the custody of the courts.

In the United States, then, ethnic and racial politics wears the clothing of the law. This means, first of all, that ethnicity and ethnic politics are legitimate —indeed, legally protected—in ways that are inconceivable in France. There is, for example, a role for ethnic groups in American foreign policy toward Northern Ireland, Israel, Cyprus, South Africa, and Cuba, among others, that would be anathema in France (see Glazer 1987). It also means that the law and often the Constitution are on the side of ethnic pluralism, and those who question the rights of immigrants and minorities start out at a considerable disadvantage. The children of illegal immigrants, for instance, have a right to free public education that cannot be withdrawn by the local authorities that provide the education (*Plyler v. Doe* [1982]). Despite the widespread public perception of uncontrolled immigration as a serious policy problem, there are, in contrast to France, few votes to be had on this issue at the national level of politics. There is no nativist equivalent of Jean-Marie Le Pen, leader of the *Front National*. Equally, there is no longer an echo of the 1968 presidential campaign of George Wallace, with its overtones of resistance to civil rights. Rather, there is good evidence that attitudes toward racial minorities have become steadily more favorable in recent decades, accelerating particularly from the 1960s onward, the period during which the law has been most active (Schuman et al. 1988). How all this happened is an interesting question, to which I shall return.

None of this implies that the United States is a happier multiethnic society than France is. It does suggest that quite different paradigms are at work.

The most direct manifestation of the two paradigms is the different meaning of equality in the two countries, despite the common sources of the very concept of equality. In France, the attainment of equality implied erasing blood privileges and therefore more generally erasing traces of origins.[5] In the United States, with no aristocracy, stripping citizens of birth origins before their encounter with the state was a less pressing task. It is thus possible to say that Americans are equal despite remaining differences (and, more recently, that the differences, irrespective of their content, are enriching). If the *bête noire* of ethnic activists in the United States is "Anglo conformity," much of the society—even much of what remains of discernible Anglo-Saxon society—opposes that conformity. But if an equivalent *bête noire* should emerge in France—call it "Franco conformity"—the mainstream population is unlikely to understand why this should be regarded as any kind of beast at all. The very epithet sounds highly improbable. When the French government speaks of "integration," it is safe to assume that something like conformity to French cultural norms forms a major part of such a program. Americans, on the other hand, no longer speak of either "Americanization" or integration.

THE INTERPLAY OF GROUP CATEGORIES

There are subtle connections among immigration, religion, and language in France. The fact that several major groups of immigrants to France—Italian, Slavic, and Iberian—were largely Roman Catholic may well mark the contrast with the Muslim Maghrébins more strongly than it would otherwise be marked. On the other hand, the main peripheral ethnolinguistic minorities—the Bretons, the Basques, the Corsicans—make it a bit harder to claim that to be a first-class citizen of France one must be unambiguously French by descent. The conceptual relationship between the peripheral ethnolinguistic groups and the immigrant groups is badly neglected in France (see the excellent inventory of Safran 1989b, 115–16). In a sample survey, Basques conceived their identity variously: only 20 percent called themselves French; 25 percent, Basque; and 55 percent, hyphenated Basque-French or French-Basque (Jacob 1978).

Such peripheral identities were previously suppressed (especially during the Third Republic) by a French state that conflated political unity with cultural unity, saw "cultural particularism . . . as a serious threat to national unity," and felt a need to "struggle against centrifugal forces" (Schnapper 1989, 100, 106). The greater legitimacy of hybrid formulations today is a contradiction of the otherwise strong, if informal, French rule against hyphenation.

Relations among the immigrant groups themselves are an important but neglected issue. In 1990, there were some lethal clashes between Black African and North African gangs, but their significance is underexplored. Among certain categories of immigrants, there are new ventures in cooperation, such as the construction of a mosque in Lorraine by Maghrébins and Turks, using Moorish and Ottoman architecture.

There are more Algerians in France than Moroccans and Tunisians combined (see Cordeiro 1987, 60), and it is often remarked that relations between French people and Algerians are more tense than with other North Africans (e.g., Grillo 1985, 18–19). Cultural difference is not the reason; for example, fewer Algerians than Moroccans and Tunisians can read Arabic. In a moment, I shall suggest that the timing of the new immigration into the United States was conducive to a good reception for the immigrants. The timing of the Maghrébin immigration to France was much less propitious. It straddled the Algerian war (1954–1962) and therefore coincided with the immigration of French colonists from Algeria *(pieds noirs)*, who are hostile to Algerians in France, and of Harkis, Algerians who sided with the French. Apart from everything else, the Algerian youth who decides to identify with France, electing French citizenship at eighteen, as many can, will then be identified by other Algerians "with the despised Harkis" (Grillo 1985, 164). The Algerian Beurs (a colloquial term for the second generation) thus appear to have special reasons to stay aloof and act out their alienation. By most accounts (Lapeyronnie 1987; Muxel 1988), the alienation and frustration are considerable.

There is no doubt that, of immigrant groups, Maghrébins are the target of greatest French enmity. Asked in a survey which category of immigrant poses the greatest difficulty for integration, 50 percent of French respondents identified North Africans, far more than the 19 percent who named Black Africans or the 15 percent who named Asians (*Paris Match*, 14 December 1989). Among the Maghrébins, the Algerians are perceived as the furthest group in French social distance studies, followed by the Moroccans and Tunisians, then the Portuguese, Spanish, and Italians (Caillot 1969). A study from the 1960s found Algerians stereotyped as "underhanded, lazy, aggressive, dirty, vicious, touchy, having a bad character, and cruel" (Nouschi 1984, 47). Black Africans and Portuguese were not characterized in such terms.

The connections among immigration, race, and ethnicity are greater and more direct in the United States. As I mentioned earlier, there is some mystery about the decline of American nativism. The United States had experienced wave after wave of anti-immigrant sentiment, well into the twentieth century, with peaks in the 1850s, the 1890s, and "the tribal twenties" (Higham 1968, 264). Pseudoscience was deployed in elaborate efforts to prove some "races," mainly northern Europeans, more fit for immigration than others, mainly southern and eastern Europeans. By 1965, however, public opinion was strongly favorable to more liberal immigration, and later surveys showed Americans overwhelmingly well disposed toward the immigration of groups previously despised (Fuchs 1990, 362–63).

What explains these changes? The early notion of a core population ultimately gave way to an American identity that was quite porous, partly because the core kept expanding. The changes actually came in series, and they were propelled by several forces.

One source of the permeability of the founding group identity was the continuing volume but shifting sources of immigration. Pre–Civil War immigrants were assuredly "foreigners," as mobs in Philadelphia and Louisville in the 1840s and 1850s made very clear. The Civil War, however, crosscut this antagonism with a different, regional juxtaposition, superseding for a time the native-immigrant juxtaposition. The post–Civil War immigration made it hard to assert the former distinctions with quite the same force, because the identity of the sending countries had changed. By the 1890s, the battle lines were defined differently. By then, it was northern Europeans against those arriving in large numbers from other parts of Europe. Germans, a century earlier regarded (by Benjamin Franklin, among others) as doubtful candidates for good citizenship, had come to be considered the "most assimilable and reputable of the immigrant groups" (Keller 1979, 1). Although some group was always excluded, the boundaries of the American community kept expanding.

Another important reason the native-immigration or Protestant-Catholic cleavage did not become ascendant in the United States over the long run is that it was preempted by the White-Black cleavage. The amalgamation of White groups was fostered by the contrast provided by Blacks (for the mechanism, see Horowitz 1975, 122–23). The Black migration to the North coincided roughly with the last major wave of nativism there, and it triggered many violent episodes. White mobs in northern and midwestern cities gathered to wage brief race wars in which dozens of people might be killed (see, e.g., Tuttle 1972; Rudwick 1964). Racial issues displaced immigrant issues in the North from this point forward. With immigration suspended for forty years, Americans could concentrate on race rather than being diverted by new waves of foreigners. Paradoxically, the United States owes to Black Americans much of the ease of relations among White Americans of various origins.

Before the hiatus in immigration had ended, the Civil Rights Movement had come along. It was armed with the Constitution, and it produced important changes in White-Black relations. Fortuitously, the Civil Rights Movement achieved many of its legal goals before the greatest impact of the new immigration was felt. The 1965 immigration legislation was enacted a decade after the school desegregation decisions and a year after the Civil Rights Act of 1964. In a major way, the movement against discrimination ultimately washed over the new immigrants, who otherwise might well have met a good deal of nativist resistance. Instead, immigrant categories were soon added by amendments to the protected categories of several major civil rights statutes, as we have already seen. And as the new immigration began, new racial attitudes were already manifest in sample surveys.

The importance of sequencing can be tested by asking what would likely have happened, had the new immigration *preceded* the new tolerance. There seems little doubt that, with its Asian and Latin American sources, the new immigration would have had an unfriendly reception that might also have put the civil rights project that was about to be launched very much in doubt, in the same way as nativism was easily converted to racial hostility earlier in the century. Not only is the sequence that occurred evidence of the powerful influence of capricious timing, but it makes clear just how interdependent the relations of various groups are in the United States.

The fortuity of this timing does not, however, imply ineluctably conflict-free relations among various ethnic and racial groups in the United States. On the contrary, there are some new patterns of conflict—between Blacks and Koreans in New York and Atlanta, between Blacks and Cubans in Miami, between Asians and groups benefitting from affirmative action in elite California high schools and universities (*Far Eastern Economic Review*, 24 March 1988, 42–44; Gibney 1988). Immigration, ethnicity, and race can hardly be disentangled.

Nor can the society be divided easily into a few neat categories, such as White, Black, Hispanic, and Asian. It certainly cannot be reduced to the dichotomy of Whites versus all "people of color."

Despite heterogeneous origins, the "White" identity is a reasonably coherent one. Many recent studies document the emergence of a "just American" or "White" or, least likely, "European-American" category (Gans 1979; Alba

1990; Waters 1990). Declining cultural differences, increasingly equal life chances, and high rates of intermarriage have all helped to reduce the significance of subgroup identity among Whites.

It seems unlikely that the same will soon happen for all the component groups in the Latino and Asian categories. To be sure, official categorizations are often important influences on subjective identification, and so, too, are outgroup perceptions of commonality among ingroups. As French society brackets all Maghrébins, American society—and certainly government—brackets all "Hispanics," persons of "Spanish origin" or with a "Spanish surname," as it also groups "Asian-Americans" together. Yet the economic circumstances of the various Asian and Hispanic groups are very different, as we shall soon see.

So, too, are their histories in the United States and their political and social propensities. Koreans and Vietnamese tend to be Republicans, as do Cubans—and for similar reasons related to relations between the United States and the home country. Several other Asian groups are divided in party loyalty, but most other Latinos are Democrats.

Those groups that have been in the United States longer often have high rates of exogamy. Notwithstanding the enormous hardships borne by Japanese during their initial immigration, the California anti-Japanese campaign in the early twentieth century, and the internment during World War II (see Kikumura 1981; Daniels 1973; Houston and Houston 1973), Japanese families carried on a long-term process of cultural change in the United States. In many ways, the Japanese-American family came to resemble other American families more than it did Japanese families in Japan (Kikumura 1981, 127–30; Connor 1977). And Japanese-Americans married other Americans, particularly Whites. Japanese exogamy rates have been at or above the 50 percent range since the late 1960s (Kikumura 1981, 134). Vietnamese, Chinese, and Koreans all intermarry at much lower rates (Jiobu 1988, 158–62).

Both the Asian and Hispanic categories are extremely heterogeneous. Both categories embrace much earlier and much more recent migrants. The mass Mexican migration began about 1910, a half-century before the Cuban migration. Similar differences divide early Japanese from late Vietnamese immigrants. Motives for migration, the socioeconomic configuration of the groups, and relations among themselves all vary.

Moreover, there are many different patterns of ethnic and racial relations with Whites. Compare, for example, the situation of Mexican-Americans with that of Black Americans. A careful study conducted in Houston, Texas, found that non-Hispanic Whites ("Anglos") were determined to maintain more social distance between themselves and Blacks than between themselves and

Mexican-Americans (Antunes and Gaitz 1975). More than that, however, Blacks perceived Anglos to be even more strongly determined to maintain social distance than they in fact were. The perceptions of Mexican-Americans ran in the opposite direction; they actually exaggerated positive Anglo attitudes slightly. Likewise, Mexican-Americans are spatially better distributed in cities than Afro-Americans are; they have relatively high rates of intermarriage, particularly in California; they display strongly positive orientations toward the political system (Mexican-American students often outdo Anglo students on some such indicators); they report much less discrimination than Blacks do; and they have policy preferences that are often close to Anglo preferences (see the studies summarized in Horowitz 1985; see also de la Garza and Weaver 1985; Rose Institute 1988). Some surveys show most Mexican-Americans unwilling to build local political coalitions with Blacks (Meier and Stewart 1989, 2)—a not surprising result, considering the different issue positions occupied by the two groups.

And so, on the one hand, the Hispanic and Asian groups have benefitted from the civil rights struggle and the renewed, more inclusive emphasis on equality that it produced. On the other hand, the groups have made their own, disparate adjustments to American society. Black Americans pioneered a civil rights path, but that path does not lead to a consolidation of a single "minority" political identity.

If we put France back in this mirror, it is clear that Maghrébin immigrants do not benefit from any major, prior civil rights struggles. By and large, the earlier and contemporaneous European immigrants to France have made their adjustment to French society by acculturation rather than by demands for the society to accommodate them as minorities. The Italians in France overcame the prejudice against them in the same way as the Italians in the United States did. To put the point dramatically, in America the racial issue and the immigrant issue came separately. In France, the two issues are the same, and they are equally unresolved.

THE CONFIGURATION OF INSTITUTIONS

In any inventory of French-American differences bearing on immigration and group relations, the political institutions of the two countries must rank high. To some extent, of course, the institutions are the product of the national ideologies. The importance of the central government in France reflects the *étatisme* of France (Wilson 1989); federalism in the United States reflects the desire for complex institutions to prevent the concentration of power in any one of them. Yet institutions structure the way groups relate to the polity.

For the United States, federalism historically meant that ethnic groups that opposed each other in one state did not necessarily meet the same antagonists in the next. Federalism compartmentalized tensions and made identities relevant at the state level that could never have been relevant at the national level. It reinforced the fragmented character of ethnic cleavages and precluded the ultimate ascendancy of any one of them, save the White-Black cleavage. It also permitted groups to attain a measure of satisfaction by attaining local power when national power was far from their grasp.

Lacking federalism, France's immigration problems are national—in many ways, uniform—problems. The decentralization of power beginning in 1982 has, however, allowed some scope for local management of minority problems (Ireland 1989, 323), not always felicitous management. The same was true historically in the United States, for state control made possible the maintenance of racial segregation in the southern states until the issue of racial equality was nationalized, first by the Supreme Court and then by Congress.

Political party systems are crucial to patterns of immigrant and ethnic politics. French parties are centrally directed; voter identification with parties is not overwhelming; voters can be volatile; and the party system is fragmented across a wide spectrum, so that no party approaches a majority. The party system is therefore "susceptible to single-issue movements, such as the *Front National*" (Hollifield 1989, 7). As established parties sense the saliency of the immigrant issue, they respond by making it their issue, as the Socialist government did soon after the *foulard* controversy. Indeed, the Communists, who controlled some local authorities with heavy concentrations of immigrants, began to implement anti-immigrant policies in the late 1970s and early 1980s (Schain 1988, 605). That the left proved soft on xenophobia despite its class commitments is testimony to the power of the immigrant issue in electoral politics. The decline of the Communist vote was indeed paralleled by the growth of the *Front National,* often in the same urban areas.

In certain areas heavily populated by immigrants, the FN has gained seats overwhelmingly, by winning a majority of the vote. Nowhere else in Western Europe does anti-immigrant sentiment, strong though it may be, have such a promising electoral foothold. With two relatively strong parties, Germany has some extremist parties as well, but none with such an exclusive focus on immigrant groups or with as much electoral appeal. The FN has no strong electoral counterpart in two-party-dominant Britain. The anti-immigrant cause has been taken up in Italy by regional parties, such as the Lombardy League, their national strength limited by their parochial appeal. In France, the combination of a spectrum of opinion, concomitantly weak parties, and a strong center undiluted by Italy's pervasive regionalism provides no barrier to the power of the immigrant issue.

The American system is, of course, completely different. Parties are decentralized, and candidates operate as sovereign political entrepreneurs, which means that they are open to ethnic and racial interest groups on an individual basis. Two parties are dominant, and plurality elections pull both of them to the center. Occasionally, extreme candidates can win elections, but it is difficult to imagine an ethnically or racially extremist party with power at the polls. In the United States, where ethnic and racial politics pervades the system, the issues still do not quite have the clarity that they have in France. Some issues are localized, and others find their way to the courts. In France, immigration issues ebb and flow, but the politics of integration or exclusion has a bluntness and a resonance denied to it by the complexity of American institutions as well as by American ideology.

CONVERGENCE: THE COMMON QUESTION OF GROUP SUCCESS

So far this has been a tale of ideological, historical, and institutional contrasts —so much so that even terminology must be watched: one cannot speak of ethnicity in France, even for third-generation Maghrébins, and one cannot speak of immigrants in America, even for first-generation naturalized citizens or long-term residents. The contrast begins to look almost too perfect.

At one point, however, the connections between the two countries are clear and firm. They show that international diffusion is undermining even the most distinctive national approaches to these questions. The point of connection can be illustrated by an example.

In the late 1960s and early 1970s, when French social scientists turned in earnest to immigration issues, one place they looked was to race relations in the United States.[6] In a well-known article (Girard 1971), the case was made for what was called a "tolerance threshold," the point at which the French would leave an urban area or a housing project if the immigrant percentage of occupancy was too high. Based on such notions, quotas were sometimes used to keep immigrant families to specified levels (Grillo 1985, 125–27). By the same token, urban planners attempted to design low-rise, low-density housing. In all of this, the example of the United States was on the French mind. The tolerance threshold was a version of the "tipping point" concept introduced in the United States in the 1950s and 1960s with regard to White flight from residential neighborhoods. Low-rise, low-density housing was a reaction to high-rise, high-density public housing, believed to create slums in the United

States. The aim was to avoid ghettoization, to prevent French cities from becoming what seems generally to be referred to in France as "Chicago."

What such images suggest is the great fear of creating an underclass. Wherever ethnic or racial differences exist, so, too, do differences of education, occupation, and income. And, on this point, general Western norms of achievement converge with both French and American conceptions of equality to create a powerful focus on success, social mobility, and the relative position of immigrant, ethnic, and racial groups in the occupational and class structure. If the earlier, celebrated opportunity for immigrants to "make it in America" eventually gave rise to careful investigations of which groups really were succeeding in the United States, there is now a similarly pointed curiosity virtually everywhere (for France, see, e.g., Noiriel 1988, 191–98).

Everywhere, the results are disparate by group. In Britain, Indians and Pakistanis succeed in school at higher rates than West Indians, but Bangladeshis succeed at lower rates than West Indians; among West Indians, Barbadians and Trinidadians outperform Jamaicans (*Economist*, 4 July 1987, 61). In Germany, Turks are far less well represented in grammar and middle schools than are Yugoslavs and Spaniards, and Turks are much less likely than any other group to leave school with a certificate that opens the way to vocational training (Castles 1984, 181–82). Everywhere, too, there is the familiar debate about whether the sources of disparate achievement are to be found in group cultures, ethnic discrimination, or social class differences.

If the United States is any guide, the fear of creating an ethnic underclass is well founded. Even as civil rights law and affirmative action facilitate the emergence of a Black middle class, nearly half of all Black children live in poverty, and the size and minority share of the urban underclass grew rapidly in the 1970s (Gephart and Pearson 1988). The minority composition of the underclass was highly variable by group, however. This was particularly true for the Hispanic groups. Proportionately twice as many Puerto Ricans as Mexican-Americans were living in poverty as of 1980, and by 1987 twice as many Puerto Ricans were living in the female-headed households that are associated with poverty (Fuchs 1990, 489–91). Puerto Rican per capita income is below Afro-American per capita income (Bonilla and Campos 1981).

The socioeconomic situation of minorities needs to be disaggregated, for it is far less homogeneous overall than is the situation of non-Hispanic Whites. Whereas Blacks and Puerto Ricans are residentially segregated, Mexican-Americans encounter fewer housing barriers and are far more dispersed (Massey and Mullen 1984; Cain and Kiewiet 1986b). Indeed, there is evidence that many Hispanics, like Whites, avoid residential contact with Blacks (Massey and Mullen 1984, 869–70). The same pattern of heterogeneity applies to education and income. Of the Hispanic groups, Cubans are highest on both dimensions (Bean and Tienda 1987; 234, 346–47). Mexican-Americans have significantly less education than African-Americans but significantly greater income (Horowitz 1985, 71–73). Mexican-American families are more intact, less frequently in poverty, and less dependent on public assistance (Rose Institute 1988, 13; Shastri 1986, 5–19). Younger Mexican-American cohorts show strong gains in income and education and high rates of intermarriage (Murguia and Frisbie 1977). For Mexican-Americans, there are fairly strong signs of intergenerational social mobility, as there are not for Puerto Ricans.

The same themes can be sounded for the various Asian groups. American-born Japanese, Chinese, and Korean men earn more than Whites (U.S. Commission on Civil Rights 1988). They also complete more years of schooling. Such conspicuous success masks the enormous differences between, for instance, a population such as Asian Indians, among whom about three-quarters have postgraduate education (Leonhard-Spark and Saran 1980), and refugees from Southeast Asia, more than half of whom have only education at the primary level or below (Whitmore, Trautmann, and Caplan 1989, 125). With low levels of education, it is not surprising to find very high rates of unemployment among groups such as Laotians and Cambodians (Strand 1989, 114). Despite common images of uniform Asian success, two of the fastest-growing groups in the United States, Filipinos and Vietnamese, are well below White levels of median income.

It has been argued that post-1965 immigrants are, overall, more educated and more skilled than earlier waves of immigrants were (Portes and Rumbaut 1989). On the other hand, there is evidence that less skilled immigrants are increasingly attracted to the United States (Borjas 1990). In the main, these immigrants do not compete economically with natives (Borjas 1990, 19), which may help explain why the new immigrants have not attracted more hostility. Over the long term, however, in an achievement-oriented society with a heightened emphasis on ethnicity, ethnically demarcated islands of conspicuous lack of success will signal increased conflict.

France also has such islands, and they are overwhelmingly North African. The islands are physical as well as social. "The *bidonville* has become, for most families, the place of welcome in France" (Cordeiro 1987, 51).

As in the United States, schools perform an important credentialing function, and they have traditionally helped perform the function of assimilating immigrants (Boulot and Boyzon-Fradet 1988). That function is much in doubt today. There is, in French schools, a good deal of ability grouping, generally based on examinations, often at a fairly early age. Immigrant students, especially Maghrébins and Portuguese, are usually found in the lowest streams, and rarely found in the highest (Begag 1990, 12; Grillo 1985, 169–76). Once the social class of parents is controlled, many differences in performance between French and immigrant students disappear (see Boulot and Boyzon-Fradet 1985), but of course the immigrants are at least twice as likely to be of working-class background as the French (OECD 1987, 60).

Again, the Algerians seem particularly disadvantaged in school. They are far more likely than French students, and somewhat more likely than Tunisian or Moroccan children, to be enrolled in vocational rather than academic streams; and the Maghrébin proportion in vocational streams grows as students arrive at secondary level (OECD 1987, 65–68). Maghrébin students are "often perceived as prone to unruliness, difficult to control," unwilling to conform to expectations, slow to learn, quick to engage in mischief, and good at sports (Hamonet and Proux 1984, 106). These are not the stereotypes of educational success.

In employment, Moroccans and Portuguese are particularly likely to be found in the manual and unskilled categories (OECD 1987, 59). In the Moroccan case, this may be attributable to slightly more recent immigration, on average. Beyond this, there are merely anecdotes. Tunisians, for example, are said to be more upwardly mobile than other North Africans. The serious study of the ethno-occupational structure in France is just beginning, and official French statistics make the job difficult,[7] but it promises to be a growth business. In this matter, France and America are of one mind.

WHAT KIND OF SOCIETY?

Both France and America may be on the verge of redefining the relationships of groups to each other and possibly to the state. But the differing directions of the redefinition are suggested by two French events. In September 1989, French demonstrators protested plans to build a mosque in Lyon. The mayor declined to retract the building permit, but he did say that no call to prayer would be allowed from the minaret. A year later, a mosque was built in Lorraine, with an eighty-foot minaret, from which, the mosque's builders volunteered at the outset, no amplified call to prayer would issue, for fear of drowning out church bells nearby (*New York Times*, 29 November 1990). There have been Maghrébin protest marches, but at bottom the cautious etiquette of group relations in France reflects deference of the immigrants to the indigenous population and a model that still differentiates, in some measure, hosts and guests.

To be sure, there are many proposals by distinguished students of French immigration for a new French pluralism. But what is emphasized in such proposals is, first of all, to redress the failure to remember the long French history of immigration and to acknowledge France as the home of xenophobia as well as of the Rights of Man, not merely for historical accuracy but to ameliorate the plight of today's immigrants, who suffer from a debilitating sense of difference (Noiriel in *Le Monde,* 20 October 1989). Beyond that, the demand for a *"multiculturalisme à la française"* is generally an argument for the integration of "foreign origin populations by universal institutions" (Schnapper 1989, 107)—which is to say that it is an argument for liberal equality and against balkanization along ethnic lines. Here, too, the American experience enters, for differential treatment, including what are seen in France as ethnic "quotas," is believed to produce only a "false equality." The United States provides again a contrast for France to avoid.

Now, however, as France moves haltingly to a recognition of pluralism, with a strong admixture of integration and acculturation, the United States may be moving to something different: a more truly plural or mosaic society, with many compartments.

Such an impetus derives, above all, from a combination of subjective and objective developments in race relations. There is a gap between White and Black attitudes. In recent years, Whites increasingly believe a great deal of progress has been made in race relations. Blacks decreasingly believe that (Schuman et al. 1988, xiv, 141–42). At the same time, there has been some tendency toward separate Black institutions—some separately run schools based on voucher plans and a certain elite enthusiasm for so-called Afrocentric curricula. All of this is concurrent, of course, with increasing representation of Blacks in formerly White institutions, from universites to corporations, professions, and governmental bodies. As the society has moved from racial subordination, the claim has increasingly been made by Black elites that the United States is a truly "multicultural society." In place of the previous horizontal cleavage, one or more vertical cleavages may be emerging.

Here, again, the connection between the Afro-American experience and the recent immigrant experience becomes crucial. It is open to Hispanics and Asians to take up this invitation for a reconstruction of American society along genuinely plural or multicultural lines. Presumably, the implication of such a formulation is that groups would have considerable autonomy in regulating their own affairs, and there would be shares of rewards and oppor-tunities apportioned in advance by a political process involving negotiations among group representatives and doubtless by a legal process involving new rights. Needless to say, there are societies organized along such lines, but the United States has not been one of them.

Whether it will become such a society depends on many things, including political and legal institutions. One thing it also depends on is the emerging perceptions and social constructions of the Hispanic and Asian groups. Thus far there is little in the ideology or behavior of these groups that would suggest that such a formulation is congenial to them (see, e.g., Horowitz 1985, 77–92). But if anything like such a conception should prevail, France will observe this experience with keen interest, the French-American contrast will be extended, and French fears of "ethnicity" will undoubtedly be confirmed.

NOTES

1. In this paragraph, I am drawing on an earlier memorandum by Nathan Glazer and myself for the American Academy of Arts and Sciences.
2. As Stephan Thernstrom notes in his contribution to this volume.
3. This section draws heavily on Horowitz 1989.
4. As Lawrence Fuchs reminds us in his contribution to this volume. See *Meyer v. Nebraska* (1923); *Pierce v. Society of Sisters* (1925); *Farrington v. Tokushige* (1926).
5. See particularly the contribution of André-Clément Decouflé to this volume.
6. That tradition continues. See Wieviorka 1991.
7. See Roxane Silberman's contribution to this volume.

CASES CITED

Allen v. Board of Elections, 393 U.S. 544, 549 (1969).
Employment Division v. Smith, 108 L. Ed. 2d 876 (1990).
Farrington v. Tokushige, 284 U.S. 298 (1926).
Graham v. Richardson, 403 U.S. 365 (1971).
In re Griffiths, 413 U.S. 717 (1973).
Metro Broadcasting v. FCC, 110 S. Ct. 2997 (1990).
Meyer v. Nebraska, 262 U.S. 390 (1923).
Pierce v. Society of Sisters, 268 U.S. 510 (1925).
Plyler v. Doe, 457 U.S. 202 (1982).
Sugarman v. Dougall, 413 U.S. 634 (1973).

STATUTES CITED

Civil Rights Act of 1964, Title 7, as amended, 42 U.S.C. §§ 2000e et seq.
Immigration Act of 1990, Pub. L. 101–649, 104 Stat. 4978 (29 November 1990).

Immigration Reform and Control Act of 1986, Pub. L. 99–603, 100 Stat. 3359.
Voting Rights Act of 1965, as amended, 42 U.S.C. §§ 1971 et seq.

BIBLIOGRAPHY

Alba, Richard. 1990. *Ethnic Identity: The Transformation of White America*. New Haven, CT: Yale University Press.

Alger, Janet Merrill. 1974. "The Impact of Ethnicity and Religion on Social Development in Revolutionary America." In *Ethnicity and Nation-Building*, edited by Wendell Bell and Walter E. Freeman, 327–39. Beverly Hills, CA: Sage.

Anderson, Elin. 1937. *We Americans: A Study of Cleavage in an American City*. Cambridge, MA: Harvard University Press.

Antunes, George, and Charles M. Gaitz. 1975. "Ethnicity and Participation: A Study of Mexican Americans, Blacks, and Whites." *American Journal of Sociology* 80, no. 5 (March): 1192–1211.

Bean, Frank D., and Marta Tienda. 1987. *The Hispanic Population of the United States*. New York: Russell Sage.

Begag, Azouz. 1988. "Les filles Maghrébines et les Symboliques de la Mobilité." *Hommes et Migrations Documents*, no. 1113: 9–13.

———. 1990. "The 'Beurs,' Children of North-African Immigrants in France: The Issue of Integration." *Journal of Ethnic Studies* 18, no. 1 (Spring): 1–14.

Bonilla, Frank, and Ricardo Campos. 1981. "A Wealth of Poor: Puerto Ricans in the New Economic Order." *Daedalus* 110, no. 2 (Spring): 133–76.

Borjas, George J. 1990. *Friends or Strangers: The Impact of Immigrants on the U.S. Economy*. New York: Basic Books.

Boulot, Serge, and Danielle Boyzon-Fradet. 1985. "L'échec scolaire des enfants de travailleurs immigrés (un problème mal posé)." In *L'immigration Maghrébine en France*, 212–24. Paris: Denoël.

———. 1988. "L'Ecole Française: Egalité des chances et logiques d'une institution." Unpublished paper presented at the Conference on the Politics of Immigration in Europe and the United States, Centre d'Etudes et de Recherches Internationales, 21–22 April.

Brubaker, [William] Rogers. 1988. "Immigration and the Nation-State in France and Germany." Unpublished paper.

Bryce-Laporte, Roy Simon, ed. 1980. *Sourcebook on the New Immigration*. New Brunswick, NJ: Transaction Books.

Caillot, R. 1969. *L'insertion des étrangers dans l'aire métropolitaine Lyon-Saint-Etienne*, 64–145. Paris: Hommes et Migrations Etudes no. 113.

Cain, Bruce, and D. Roderick Kiewiet. 1986a. "California's Coming Minority Majority." *Public Opinion*, March 1986, 50–52.

———. 1986b. "Minorities in California." California Institute of Technology, Division of Humanities and Social Sciences. Mimeographed.

Castles, Stephen. 1984. *Here for Good: Western Europe's New Ethnic Minorities*. London: Pluto Press.

Cobban, Alfred. 1961. *A History of Modern France*. Vol. 1. Baltimore: Penguin Books.

Connor, John W. 1977. *Tradition and Change in Three Generations of Japanese Americans.* Chicago: Nelson-Hall.

Cordeiro, Albano. 1987. *L'immigration.* 3d ed. Paris: Editions la Découverte.

Costa-Lascoux, Jacqueline. 1990. "Anti-Discrimination Legislation: Belgium, France, Netherlands." Council of Europe, Strasbourg, Committee of Experts on Community Relations (mimeo., EMG-CR 2.90).

Daniels, Roger. 1973. *The Politics of Prejudice: The Anti-Japanese Movement in California and the Struggle for Japanese Exclusion.* New York: Atheneum. Originally published 1962.

de la Garza, Rodolfo, and Janet Weaver. 1985. "Chicano and Anglo Public Policy Preferences in San Antonio: Does Ethnicity Make a Difference?" *Social Science Quarterly* 66: 576–86.

Diamond, Larry, et al. 1988. *Democracy in Developing Countries.* Vol. 2, *Africa.* Boulder, CO; Lynne Rienner.

Ehrmann, Henry W., and Martin A. Schain. 1991. *Politics in France.* 5th ed. New York: Harper Collins.

Fijalkowski, Jurgen. 1989. "Les obstacles à la citoyenneté: Immigration et naturalisation en République fédérale d'Allemagne." *Revue européenne des migrations internationales* 5, no. 1 (2ème trimestre): 33–46.

Fuchs, Lawrence H. 1990. *The American Kaleidoscope: Race, Ethnicity, and the Civic Culture.* Hanover, NH: University Press of New England.

Gans, Herbert. 1979. "Symbolic Ethnicity: The Future of Ethnic Groups and Cultures in America." *Ethnic and Racial Studies* 2, no. 1 (January): 1–19.

Gephart, Martha A., and Robert W. Pearson. 1988. "Contemporary Research on the Urban Underclass." Social Science Research Council, *Items* (June): 1–10.

Gibney, James S. 1988. "The Berkeley Squeeze." *The New Republic,* 11 April 1988, 15–17.

Girard, Alain. 1971. "Attitudes des Français à l'égard de l'immigration étrangère." *Population* 26, no. 5: 827–76.

Glazer, Nathan. 1987. "New Rules of the Game." *The National Interest,* no. 8 (Summer): 62–70.

Grillo, R. D. 1985. *Ideologies and Institutions in Urban France: The Representation of Immigrants.* Cambridge: Cambridge University Press.

Hamilton, Alexander, John Jay, and James Madison. 1888. *The Federalist.* New York: G.P. Putnam. Originally published 1788.

Hamonet, France, and Michèle Proux. 1984. "L'enfant maghrébin en milieu scolaire." In *Les Nord-Africains en France,* edited by Magali Morsy, 105–8. Paris: Centre des Hautes Etudes sur l'Afrique et l'Asie Modernes.

Hartz, Louis. 1955. *The Liberal Tradition in America.* New York: Harcourt, Brace & World.

Higham, John. 1968. *Strangers in the Land: Patterns of American Nativism, 1860–1925.* New York: Atheneum. Originally published in 1955.

———. 1977. "Disjunction and Diversity in American Ethnic History." Unpublished paper presented at the Woodrow Wilson International Center for Scholars, April.

Hollifield, James F. 1989. "Migrants into Citizens: The Politics of Immigration in France and the United States." Unpublished paper presented at the Annual Meeting of the American Political Science Association.

Horowitz, Donald L. 1975. "Ethnic Identity." *Ethnicity: Theory and Experience*, edited by Nathan Glazer and Daniel P. Moynihan, 111–40. Cambridge, MA: Harvard University Press.

———. 1983. "Racial Violence in the United States." In *Ethnic Pluralism and Public Policy: Achieving Equality in the United States and Britain*, edited by Nathan Glazer and Ken Young, 187–211. London: Heinemann.

———. 1985. "Conflict and Accommodation: Mexican-Americans in the Cosmopolis." In *Mexican-Americans in Comparative Perspective*, edited by Walker Connor. Washington, DC: Urban Institute.

———. 1989. "Europe and America: A Comparative Analysis of 'Ethnicity.'" *Revue européenne des migrations internationales* 5, no. 1 (2ème trimestre): 47–61.

Houston, Jeanne Wakatsuki, and James D. Houston. 1973. *Farewell to Manzanar*. New York: Bantam Books.

Ireland, Patrick R. 1989. "The State and the Political Participation of the 'New' Immigrants in France and the United States." *Revue française d'etudes américaines* 14, no. 41 (Juillet): 315–28.

Jacob, James E. 1978. "Two Types of Ethnic Militancy in France." Unpublished paper presented at the Annual Meeting of the International Studies Association.

Jiobu, Robert M. 1988. *Ethnicity and Assimilation: Blacks, Chinese, Filipinos, Japanese, Koreans, Mexicans, Vietnamese, and Whites*. Albany: State University of New York Press.

Keller, Phyllis. 1979. *States of Belonging: German-American Intellectuals and the First World War*. Cambridge, MA: Harvard University Press.

Key, V. O., Jr. 1956. *Politics, Parties, and Pressure Groups*. 3d ed. New York: Thomas Y. Crowell.

Kikumura, Akemi. 1981. *Through Harsh Winters: The Life of a Japanese Immigrant Woman*. Novato, CA: Chandler & Sharp.

Lapeyronnie, Didier. 1987. "Assimilation, mobilisation, et action collective chez les jeunes de la seconde génération de l'immigration maghrébine." *Revue française de sociologie* 28: 287–318.

Leonhard-Spark, Philip J., and Parmatma Saran. 1980. "The Indian Immigrant in America: A Demographic Profile." In *The New Ethnics: Asian Indians in the United States*, edited by Parmatma Saran and Edwin Eames, 136–62. New York: Praeger.

Lieberson, Stanley, and Mary Waters. 1988. *From Many Strands: Ethnic and Racial Groups in Contemporary America*. New York: Russell Sage.

Long, Marceau. 1988. *Etre français aujourd'hui et demain*. Paris: Documentation française.

Lopez, David E. 1978. "Chicano Language Loyalty in an Urban Setting." *Sociology and Social Research* 62:267–78.

Malewska-Peyre, Hanna, and M. Zaleska. 1980. "Identités et conflits de valeurs chez les jeunes immigrés Maghrébins." *Psychologie française* 25, no. 2.

Massey, Douglas S., and Brendan P. Mullen. 1984. "Processes of Hispanic and Black Spatial Assimilation." *American Journal of Sociology* 89:836–73.

Meier, Kenneth J., and Joseph Stewart, Jr. 1989. "In Search of Rainbow Coalitions: Racial/Ethnic Representation on Public School Boards." Unpublished paper presented at the Annual Meeting of the American Political Science Association.

Morsy, Magali. 1984. "La migration: dimension et révélateur de la vie nationale." In *Les Nord-Africains en France,* edited by Magali Morsy. Paris: Centre des Hautes Etudes sur l'Afrique et l'Asie Modernes.

Murguia, Edward, and W. Parker Frisbie. 1977. "Trends in Mexican American Intermarriage." *Social Science Quarterly* 58:374–89.

Muxel, Anne. 1988. "Les attitudes socio-politiques des jeunes issus de l'immigration maghrébine en région parisienne." *Revue française de la science politique* 38, no. 6 (Décembre):925–39.

Noiriel, Gérard. 1987. "Proposals for a Comparative Research Program on Immigration in France and the United States." Unpublished paper, Paris.

———. 1988. *Le Creuset Français.* Paris: Seuil.

Nouschi, André. 1984. "Esquisse d'une histoire de l'immigration maghrébine." In *Les Nord-Africains en France,* edited by Magali Morsy. Paris: Centre des Hautes Etudes sur l'Afrique et l'Asie Modernes.

OECD (Organization for Economic Cooperation and Development). 1987. *Immigrants' Children at School.* Paris: OECD Directorate for Social Affairs, Manpower and Education.

———. 1990. *Continuous Reporting System on Migration, SOPEMI, 1989.* Paris: OECD Directorate for Social Affairs, Manpower and Education.

Portes, Alejandro, and Rubén G. Rumbaut. 1989. *Immigrant America: A Portrait.* Berkeley: University of California Press.

Rose Institute. 1988. "Selected Cross-Tabulations: A Survey of California Latinos, 1988." Claremont: Rose Institute of Claremont McKenna College.

Rudwick, Elliot. 1964. *Race Riot in East St. Louis, 1917.* Carbondale: Southern Illinois University Press.

Safran, William. 1989a. "Nationality and Citizenship in France and the United States: Concepts of Membership in the Political Community." Unpublished paper presented at the Annual Meeting of the American Political Science Association.

———. 1989b. "The French State and Ethnic Minority Cultures: Policy Dimensions and Problems." In *Ethnoterritorial Politics, Policy, and the Western World,* edited by Joseph R. Rudolph, Jr., and Robert J. Thompson. Boulder, CO: Lynne Rienner.

Schain, Martin A. 1988. "Immigration and Changes in the French Party System." *European Journal of Political Research* 16:597–621.

Schnapper, Dominique. 1989. "Un pays d'immigration qui s'ignore." *Le genre humain* (printemps):99–109.

Schuman, Howard, et al. 1988. *Racial Attitudes in America.* 2d ed. Cambridge, MA: Harvard University Press.

Shastri, Amita. 1986. "Social Welfare and Social Service Recipients in California by Ethnic Origin." California Institute of Technology, Division of Humanities and Social Sciences. Mimeographed.

Strand, Paul J. 1989. "The Indochinese Refugee Experience: The Case of San Diego." In *Refugees as Immigrants: Cambodians, Laotians, and Vietnamese in America,* edited by David W. Haines, 105–20. Totowa, NJ: Rowman & Littlefield.

Thernstrom, Abigail M. 1987. *Whose Votes Count? Affirmative Action and Minority Voting Rights.* Cambridge, MA: Harvard University Press.

Tocqueville, Alexis de. 1945. *Democracy in America.* Vol. 1. Translated by Francis Bowen. New York: Knopf. Originally published 1835.

Tuttle, William M., Jr. 1972. *Race Riot: Chicago in the Red Summer of 1919.* New York: Atheneum.

U.S. Commission on Civil Rights. 1988. *The Economic Status of Americans of Asian Descent.* Washington, DC: U.S. Government Printing Office.

Warren, Robert. 1980. "Volume and Composition of U.S. Immigration and Emigration." In *Sourcebook on the New Immigration,* edited by Roy Simon Bryce-Laporte, 1–14. New Brunswick, NJ: Transaction Books.

Waters, Mary C. 1990. *Ethnic Options: Choosing Identities in America.* Berkeley: University of California Press.

Weiner, Myron. 1989. "Asian-Americans and American Foreign Policy." *Revue Européenne des Migrations Internationales* 5, no. 1 (2d trimestre):71–112.

———. 1990. "Immigration: Perspectives from Receiving Countries." *Third World Quarterly* 12, no. 1: 140–65.

Whitmore, John K., Marcella Trautmann, and Nathan Caplan. 1989. "The Socio-Cultural Basis for the Economic and Educational Success of Southeast Asian Refugees (1978–1982 Arrivals)." In *Refugees as Immigrants: Cambodians, Laotians, and Vietnamese in America,* edited by David W. Haines, 121–37. Totowa, NJ: Rowman & Littlefield.

Wieviorka, Michel. 1991. *L'espace du Racisme.* Paris: Seuil.

Wilpert, Czarina. 1988. "Associations of Turks in the Federal Republic of Germany: Between Guestworker Policy, European Integration and Ataturk's Aspiration to a Secular and Monocultural Nation State." Paper presented at the Conference on the Politics of Immigration in Europe and the United States, Centre d'Etudes et de Recherches Internationales, Paris, 21–22 April.

Wilson, Frank L. 1989. "France: Group Politics in a Strong State." Unpublished paper presented at the Annual Meeting of the American Political Science Association.

TWO

CONCEPTS AND NUMBERS

2

THINKING ABOUT IMMIGRATION AND ETHNICITY IN THE UNITED STATES

Lawrence H. Fuchs

To understand how most Americans thought about immigration and ethnicity in the United States in the 1980s, it is necessary to examine the
evolution of four ideas—asylum, assimilation, race, and ethnic diversity—
and to see what happened to them after World War II, especially since the
civil rights revolution of the 1960s and 1970s.

ASYLUM

The founders of the republic created a unique national myth to justify revolution and the establishment of a new nation—the myth that the United States
was created by God as an *asylum* in which liberty, opportunity, and reward
for achievement were possible, and in which equal rights would be guaranteed
to newcomers. That myth provided an ideological rationalization for the
selfish interest Americans had in recruiting European immigrants to claim the
land, fight Indians, and expand capital and labor. Territorial and capital
expansion drove immigration policy; the founding myth rationalized it.

The very idea of a nation as an asylum for permanent settlers was invented
by Americans. No one before had described their *nation,* as George Washington did, as "an Asylum . . . to the oppressed and needy of the Earth" (Rischin
1966, 44).[1] Thomas Jefferson asked, "shall oppressed humanity find no asy-

lum on the globe?" when he argued for a short period of residency for aliens to become eligible for citizenship, signifying that asylum in the United States was no temporary refuge but an opportunity for permanent settlement (Franklin 1969, 97). In the first debate over a new naturalization law in 1790, one of Jefferson's allies from Virginia in the House of Representatives argued that "we shall be inconsistent with ourselves, if, after boasting of having opened an asylum for the oppressed of all nations . . . we make the terms of admission to the full enjoyment of that asylum so hard as is now proposed. It is nothing to us, whether Jews or Roman Catholics settle amongst us; whether subjects or kings, or citizens of free states wish to reside in the United States, they will find it in their interest to be good citizens" (Ringer 1983, 109, 110). Not only was "the bosom of America," in Washington's maternal phrase, "open to receive . . . the oppressed of all Nations and Religions," but they were "welcome to a participation of all our rights and privileges" (Ringer 1983, 43).

Enormous hypocrisy underlay the hyperbole about asylum, since it was applied only to whites from Europe, and also because it was driven primarily by capital seeking labor in pursuit of wealth and by the desire to clear Indians from their own lands. The term fell into disuse, particularly in the last quarter of the nineteenth century and the first sixty years of the twentieth, as Americans became more restrictive toward immigration. But it was revived again in the 1980s, as Americans liberalized their immigration policies. Following the civil rights revolution, it was applied (and not just expressed) in universal terms without regard to color or nationality, as when Ronald Reagan accepted the Republican nomination for the presidency on 18 July 1980 and asked, "Can we doubt that only a Divine Providence placed this land, this island of freedom here as a refuge for all those people in the world who yearn to breathe freely, Jews and Christians enduring persecution behind the Iron Curtain, the boat people of Southeast Asia, of Cuba and Haiti, victims of drought and famine in Africa . . ." (*Congressional Quarterly* 1980, 2066). There was much hypocrisy in Reagan's question, as there often is when American political leaders use the asylum theme, and there certainly was inconsistency in the Reagan administration's implementation of the principle. Those fleeing Communist countries, for example, fared much better than refugees in Africa or asylum applicants from Central America; but Reagan's question drew upon an idea that had never died entirely because it had been an essential part of the founding myth of the republic. Once again, Americans were ready to use in public speech a term that many of them thought gave particular meaning to their national identity.

CULTURAL ASSIMILATION

The founders needed and wanted European immigrants to master a continent, but they wanted them, in the phrase of John Quincy Adams, "to cast off the European skin" (Rischin 1966, 47). They probably found it comforting to assume the inexorability of the cultural assimilation of the newcomers. It also was politically advantageous to emphasize the unity of Americans. Whatever the reasons, the authors of *The Federalist,* John Jay, James Madison, and Alexander Hamilton, did not even mention what we would now call ethnic diversity in their famous essays. Even though the first census would show that the English and their descendants constituted just under one-half of the population, Madison said nothing about what is now called ethnicity in his two famous essays on diversity, and John Jay wrote that "Providence has been pleased to give this one connected country to one united people—a people descended from the same ancestors," even though his paternal grandfather was a French Huguenot and he was Dutch on his mother's side (*Federalist* 1937, 9). Intermarriage was extensive among the children and grandchildren of European immigrants, a phenomenon described by Michel Guillaume Jean de Crèvecoeur, an eighteenth-century French Catholic farmer, who called Americans a "promiscuous breed," arisen from "a mixture of English, Scotch, Irish, French, Dutch, Germans and Swedes" (Rischin 1966, 24).

Crèvecoeur was writing about what later would be called the American melting pot. It was not until well into the twentieth century that "melting pot" implied ethnic diversity. As used earlier, as in Emerson's "smelting pot," it meant either that the newcomers and their descendants would tend to become more and more like the founding Anglo-Europeans who dominated the national politics and culture of the early republic or that they would in some way create "a new race," in Emerson's phrase, out of "the energy of Irish, Germans, Swedes, Poles and Cossacks, and all the European tribes" (Gabriel 1986, 46). Nearly a century later, the Jewish immigrant playwright Israel Zangwill made the term popular when he wrote of the United States as "God's crucible, the great melting pot" (Zangwill 1922, 184–85).

Zangwill's play was in praise of asylum and intermarriage, not ethnic diversity. It was not until World War II and the decades that followed that the term "melting pot" would be inaptly used to imply diversity.

POLITICAL ASSIMILATION

There was another idea implicit in the view of many of the founders about the nature of American unity that allowed for ethnic diversity. That view—that

Americans were held together by shared political beliefs, principles, and practices regardless of national or religious background—could be inferred from the statements and actions of Thomas Jefferson and his followers (Peterson 1977, 125).

At the Constitutional Convention in 1787, Jefferson's friend James Madison acknowledged that it might be dangerous to have immigrants easily naturalized who had "foreign predilections," but that he thought it wise "to invite foreigners of merit and republican principles" (Kettner 1978, 27). Jefferson and Madison wanted to make certain that immigrants with aristocratic backgrounds would convert to the political ideology of republicanism before admitting them to citizenship. Later, they pushed through a naturalization bill requiring that any applicant must "make an express renunciation of his title or order of nobility." By making American citizenship virtually synonymous with American identity and by making the test of citizenship ideological, the Congress put American identity theoretically within the claim of anyone, regardless of national background. Understandably, a great many Anglo-Americans, particularly in New England, assumed that their cultural characteristics were linked to the political principles of the republic. Anglo-Americans, after all, had led the Revolution and written the state and federal constitutions. The assumption of a link spurred the rise of the Native American movement and its success in Massachusetts and other New England states in the 1850s in reaction to Irish Catholic immigrants, who were alleged to be incapable of participating in a self-governing republic because of their slavish adherence to an authoritarian church.

That point of view held sway at the centennial celebration of the beginning of the American Revolution at Concord and Lexington, Massachusetts, on 19 April 1875. In sharp contrast to the celebration of ethnic diversity that took place one hundred years later in Massachusetts, the ceremonies in 1875 included speeches by illustrious Anglo-Americans, including Ralph Waldo Emerson, James Russell Lowell, John Greenleaf Whittier, and Julia Ward Howe, but none from an Irish-Catholic American, a German-American, a Jew, or an African-American. The largely Anglo-American audience, including President Ulysses S. Grant and key members of his cabinet, was reminded by the president of the day in Lexington, Thomas Merriam Stetson, that the fallen heroes of Lexington and Concord all had English names. Speaking of the martyrs of the Revolution, Stetson called their courageous stand against the larger British force "the flower and consummation of principles that were long ripening in the clear-sighted, liberty-loving, Anglo-Saxon mind" (Little 1974, 56).

Abraham Lincoln held a different view from those who assumed that political and cultural assimilation were tightly connected. He argued that even though the immigrants of his time could not link their families by blood to the heroes of the Revolution and the early days of the republic, they felt "a part of us" because "when they look through that old Declaration of Independence, they find those old men say that 'We hold these truths to be self evident, that all men are created equal,' is for everyone." Then, said Lincoln, "they have a right to claim it as though they were blood of the blood and flesh of the flesh of the men who wrote the Declaration of Independence," and, Lincoln concluded, "so they are" (Eastland and Bennett 1979, 53).

POLITICAL ASSIMILATION PERMITS CULTURAL DIVERSITY

It was Jefferson's and Lincoln's thinking that individuals who comported themselves as good citizens were free to differ from each other in religion and other aspects of their private lives. The idea that American identity is based solely on political beliefs and practices permitted and even encouraged ethnic-Americanization, in which immigrant settlers from Europe and their progeny were free to maintain affection for and loyalty to their ancestral religions and cultures while claiming membership in the American polity at the same time. The Germans—the first large non-English-speaking immigrant group—provided a paradigm for the process of ethnic-Americanization that applied to all subsequent immigrant-ethnic groups. An early nineteenth-century German visitor to the United States, Francis J. Grund, wrote extensively on the process (Grund 1837). He saw that Germans wanted to retain their ties to the German culture, observing that "there are now villages in the states of Pennsylvania and Ohio, and even in the new state of Illinois, where no other language is spoken" but German (Grund 1837, 68). The Germans, Grund noted, "hardly feel that they are strangers in the land of their adoption," because they developed the habit "of remaining together, and settling whole townships or villages," making "their exile less painful" and enabling them "to transfer a part of their own country to the vast solitudes of the New World" (Grund 1837, 212–13).

The Germans had more in common in the United States than they had in their homelands, where they were divided by religion, dialect, and politics. They found that it was to their advantage to establish a new identity as ethnic-Americans (the term had not been invented). The process of reconfiguring one's ancestral identity to some extent was one that other groups would go through, too, including various Filipino and Chinese dialect groups, Italian *paisani*, and Jews from many national backgrounds. For all of them, the reconfiguration of identity became and still is a mechanism for bridging differences and enlarging common interests, loyalties, and sensibilities. It was and is also a way of gaining protection against the surprises and dangers of the new environment, and of making claims within it.

Even as the Germans became ethnics, they became Americans. Grund noticed the obvious affection and loyalty that many Germans quickly gave to the United States. By holding out to all persons (meaning white persons) "without distinction of birth or parentage" the hope of acquiring property, the United States bound its newcomers to the national polity, just as Crève-coeur explained happened in the late eighteenth century. But Grund wrote much more about rights than economic opportunity. Like Alexis de Tocque-ville, Grund was fascinated by the American preoccupation with politics. "Every town and village in America has its peculiar republican government, based on the principle of election . . . freedom takes its root at home, in the native village or town of an American . . . in every place, in every walk of life, an American finds some rallying point or centre of political attachment." Grund wrote, "The Americans present the singular spectacle of a people united together by no other ties than those of excellent laws and equal justice" (Grund 1837, 148, 209–10). Since patriotism consisted of love of principle, the main one being liberty, what Grund called "the essence of their common-wealth," and since foreign-born citizens and native-born citizens were placed on a footing of equality, it was not surprising to find that Germans rallied "cheerfully round the banner of the American republic" (Grund 1837, 69, 152–153). They could use politics to express themselves as German-Ameri-cans. In this way, ethnic mobilization was not only compatible with patriotism but was an expression of it, as they made their claims in the name of liberty and equal rights.

The individual who most eloquently proclaimed the possibilities of ethnic-Americanization in Lincoln's time was his friend Carl Schurz, a German immigrant who helped to organize the new Republican party in Wisconsin in 1856, only four years after he had arrived in the United States. Schurz almost was elected lieutenant governor of that state in 1857, even though he still was not a citizen. Having won a reputation for political and oratorical skills, Schurz, who would later serve as a diplomat, general, U.S. senator, and secretary of the interior, was invited in 1859 to give a speech in Boston's Cradle of Revolution, Faneuil Hall, where the German immigrant spoke as a newly naturalized citizen on the audacious topic of "True Americanism."

Speaking in a thick German accent in the heartland of Know-Nothingism and aware of the hostility of Massachusetts Protestants toward Catholic immigration, Schurz repudiated the idea that had been born in Massachusetts that political membership must be based on religious identity or some other ancestral attribute. Praising the founding myth of the United States as an asylum for those seeking freedom and opportunity regardless of their nationality or religion, Schurz proudly claimed the heritage of Bunker Hill, Charlestown, Lexington, John Hancock, and Benjamin Franklin as his own. The United States, he said, was founded as "a great colony of *free humanity* which has not old England alone but the *world* for its mother country." "True Americanism," Schurz asserted, is based on the belief in "that system of government, which makes the protection of individual rights a matter of common interest" (Rischin 1966, 124).

Not all immigrants claimed to be "true Americans." Large numbers returned to their homelands, and many who stayed in the United States had no desire to identify as Americans. Cultural and ethnic conflicts among immigrants themselves—the common phenomenon of older ethnic groups putting down new ones—and narrow, parochial political agendas in some cases belied romantic talk of being "real Americans." The claim made by Schurz and other Americans often was rebuffed by native-born Americans who held to the old idea that political and cultural assimilation were inextricably linked. During World War I, there were massive, hysterical attacks on expressions of German language and culture in the United States, probably advancing by one generation the decline of ethnic maintenance and mobilization in the German-American community. But what is extraordinary about the American experience is not that there were such periodic outbursts of xenophobia or that large numbers of immigrants felt exiled emotionally as well as physically in the United States until they died, but that so many of them, and especially their children, claimed an American identity successfully.

One of the boldest of the ethnic group leaders in the twentieth century was James Michael Curley, the Irish Catholic mayor of Boston, who rose to popularity among his Irish constituents by attacking the descendants of those who made the Revolution, the Brahmins of Boston. Yet Curley, a parochial Irish politician, was an ardent and eloquent spokesman for the civic culture. Like Carl Schurz, he identified with the Yankee heroes of the Revolution, praising them as if they were his own. Many of those he praised, such as John Hancock and John Adams, shared the hatred of papism common to Boston in their day. But Curley appropriated them and their ideals, even as he did battle with Yankees who tried to exclude the Irish from the banks, businesses, and social clubs of Boston. Curley felt no embarrassment in telling visitors that after they had drunk "from freedom's fountain in Boston" they should "go forth as zealous missionaries determined to teach by individual example the lesson of the [founding] fathers."[2]

Explaining how the hyphen unites an old identity with a new one, Slovenian-born journalist Louis Adamic told of returning to the village in which he was born and being asked, " 'Do you consider yourself an American or a Slovenian?' " The answer came swiftly that Adamic believed himself to be an American, "not only legally and technically but actually," adding, "I sometimes think I am more American than a great many of them." Then Adamic said something that must have confused many of the villagers, when he remarked, "I am also a Slovenian . . . and I would say that I am an American of Slovenian birth; but, if you like it better, you can consider me as a Slovenian who went to America when he was not quite fifteen and became an American . . . there is no conflict in me between my original Slovenian blood or background and my being an American." Adamic reveled in his Slovenian roots. Even though he lost fluency in his mother tongue, *slovenstvo* (which means deep love for and loyalty to Slovenian traditions) had become a powerful part of his being. It was the genius of America, he said, to give room for him to find and give "the essentials of it *[slovenstvo]* wider and fuller expression than I could probably ever have found had I remained at home" (Adamic 1938, 126–28).

It was easy for Adamic and other immigrants to celebrate American holidays such as Thanksgiving and Independence Day in an ethnic way. In the 1880s in Worcester, Massachusetts, the Ancient Order of the Hibernians, an Irish nationalist society, held a picnic on July Fourth, American Independence Day, where the exuberance of the Irish served "both as a preservation of Irish customs and a defense of American freedoms" (Rosensweig 1983, 77). Similarly, the Swedes of Worcester celebrated Independence Day in the 1890s with picnics that attracted about forty-six hundred participants out of a total Swedish-American population of approximately eleven thousand. They began the day with services at one of the eight Swedish Protestant churches and ended at a picnic where they heard patriotic pro-American speeches, spoken sometimes in Swedish, as in 1896, when the minister of the Swedish Evangelical Lutheran Church talked about both love for the old country and loyalty to the United States. All of the ethnic groups of Worcester "used the Fourth as an occasion to assert their particular identity and values," even as they celebrated their American freedoms (Rosensweig 1983, 77).

THE CONSTITUTION AND ETHNIC DIVERSITY

Religion, language, and ancestral customs constituted the major expressions of ethnicity. The First Amendment to the Constitution clearly protected religious diversity. The issue of language and customs was raised by cultural conformists in the first few decades of the twentieth century as a result of large-scale immigration from eastern and southern Europe. In 1919, the state of Nebraska passed a law forbidding the teaching of modern foreign languages to children between the ages of eight and sixteen. The special intention of the law, like others passed in South Dakota and Iowa, was to eliminate the German language, particularly in church-related schools run by German-Americans. The supreme courts of Iowa, Ohio, and Nebraska upheld such acts as constitutional on the broad ground that the legislature could decide what the common welfare demanded, but Justice James C. McReynolds, speaking for the Supreme Court, overruled them.

The Supreme Court, he wrote, was sympathetic to the desire of the legislature "to foster a homogeneous people with American ideals, prepared readily to understand current discussions of civic matters." It was cognizant of the fact that "the foreign born population is very large, that certain communities use foreign words, follow foreign leaders, move in a foreign atmosphere, and that the children are thereby hindered from becoming citizens of the most useful type." However, a law to prohibit the teaching of foreign languages in the schools, while possibly acceptable in other societies, was inimical to basic rights in the United States. McReynolds wrote for the majority that in the United States parents were free to engage teachers to instruct their children in whatever subject matter they chose, even if that tended to encourage the maintenance of old-country languages and customs, because the Constitution "belongs to those who speak other languages as well as those born with English on the tongue" (*Meyer* v. *Nebraska* 1923, 401–3).

Two other decisions followed that strengthened the idea that American identity was essentially civic and not religious, linguistic, or in some other way characteristic of a tribal culture. In 1922, the state of Oregon passed a law requiring all students to attend the public schools, with the intention of stamping out Catholic and other parochial religious schools. The Society of Sisters, a Catholic order conducting parochial schools, lost their case in the Oregon Supreme Court and then took it to the U.S. Supreme Court, where Justice McReynolds wrote the majority opinion upholding the right of Americans to send their children to private or parochial schools. In what are essentially private matters, the Court said, diversity is protected by the Constitution of the United States. The freedom given to all Americans prevents the state from taking actions "to standardize its children . . . the child is not the mere creature of the state; those who nurture him and direct his destiny have the right, coupled with the high duty, to recognize and prepare him for additional obligation" (*Pierce* v. *Society of Sisters* 1925).

In 1926, the Supreme Court heard arguments on a law in the territory of Hawaii as to whether or not private language schools were free to shape their own curricula as long as they also complied with the requirements of the public schools. A majority of Japanese-American children went to Japanese-language schools, sometimes getting up as early as 4:00 A.M. to attend school, where they learned Japanese values, customs, and history; some were even taught to venerate the emperor of Japan as a semi-deity. These things were so troubling to the leading Americanizers in the territory that the state legislature attempted to regulate the language schools through strict examinations for the teachers and through oversight of the curriculum. But the U.S. Supreme Court held that the laws regarding the language schools were unconstitutional. After noting that there were 163 foreign-language schools in the territory (nine Korean, seven Chinese, and the remainder Japanese), Justice McReynolds, while once again personally sympathetic to efforts to assimilate newcomers culturally, spoke for the Court in deciding that the territory could not constitutionally take away from parents the right to sponsor schools that taught an understanding and love of foreign, ancestral languages and cultures (*Farrington* v. *Tokushige* 1926).

RACE

From the earliest days of the republic, most Americans thought of Indians and blacks as outsiders. The authors of the Declaration called the Indians "merciless savages" in a document that criticized the king for putting obstacles in the way of immigration and easy naturalization for Europeans. Andrew Jackson, hero of the Scotch-Irish-Americans on the frontier, promised Euro-Americans in his second inaugural address "The Continued Blessings of Liberty, Civilization and Religion" if they pushed the Indians out of lands that whites could usefully occupy (Forbes 1964, 100). The opening of land for white newcomers was the attraction that made their participation in the civic culture so easy. One Norwegian settler, writing home in 1835, spoke of moving to the interior of New York State in 1832, where he had great success in planting "Indian corn." Because he could purchase public land in Illinois at $1.25 an acre, he was planning to move there. In the United States, he wrote, "whether native born or foreign, a man is free to do with it [land] what he pleases." Urging his friend to emigrate, he wrote, "Even if many more come, there will still be room for all" (Ifkovic 1975, 173–74).

As the United States expanded westward, the frontier became a symbol of the American myth of a nation founded to provide freedom and opportunity for white Europeans such as the Norwegian immigrant on his way to Illinois. Between 1810 and 1821, more than half a million Euro-American settlers poured into Kentucky, Tennessee, Alabama, Mississippi, and Louisiana, and almost another half-million into Ohio, Indiana, Illinois, and Missouri. Many were squatters or, as they were also called, "pre-emptors," who found land, farmed it, and claimed it as their own. So widespread was the practice that in 1841 Congress legalized it through the Preemption Act, virtually ensuring a continuation of the policies of removal and extinction of Indians. One hundred thousand Indians were removed from the East before the Civil War, obliging western tribes to give up hunting grounds to make room for them and eventually for more whites. The land hunger of Euro-Americans, rationalized in large measure by feelings of racial superiority, also were fed by the millions of acres given to them by many land acts, including the Homestead Act (1862), and indirectly through land grants to the railroads following the Civil War.

Even more than the Indians, the position of blacks in American society had a profound impact on the way in which Euro-Americans and immigrants from Europe thought about immigration and ethnicity. From the seventeenth century on, when fundamental distinctions in law were made between white and black indentured servants, blacks (including those who were not slaves) were generally locked into a system of caste. Three hundred years later, Malcolm X bitterly summed up the view that many African-Americans had about immigration and Americanization. White immigrants, he pointed out, did not have to struggle to become Americans. "Those Hunkies that just got off the boat," he said, "they're already Americans; Polacks are already Americans; Italian refugees are already Americans. Everything that came out of Europe, every blue-eyed thing, is already an American ... being born here in America doesn't make you an American. . . . they don't have to pass civil-rights legislation to make a Polack an American" (Breitman 1965, 26). By emphasizing race exclusively, Malcolm ignored the resistance that nativist Americans had to Irish Catholics and Jews and the differences in the experiences of the children of immigrants from Asia or Mexico from those of native-born black Americans. But, like other black leaders before him, he was painfully aware that immigrants, including blacks from the Caribbean, seized opportunities that were kept from native-born blacks.

To judge from the African-American press prior to World War II, black Americans were particularly hostile to Mexican and Asian immigrants, not just because they took jobs away from blacks but also because they were seen as people with strange, foreign ways who were given privileges and opportunities invariably denied blacks (Schenkman 1982, 16, 72–73). Mexican and Chinese immigrants knew blacks were at the bottom of the American ethnic pecking order and that the bottom was determined by the kinds of jobs that were assigned to them. One Chinese immigrant from the United States told of working in France in World War I, where he saw Chinese laborers who had been imported to work on the railroad and who were assigned to the worst jobs. After work, he said that they were pushed into a stockade where they had no freedom but were simply locked up "sort of like a bunch of cattle or a bunch of horses and probably when their contracts are finished, they'll load them onto freight boats and ship them back." They were, he said, "like the colored people, they were nothing but scavengers, they were doing scavenger work" (Nee and Nee 1972, 79–80).

What was not emphasized in the African-American press was that Asian and Mexican immigrants were themselves often the victims of racism. During the congressional debate on the naturalization law in 1870, which provided for the first time that persons of African descent could be naturalized, Republican Senator Charles Sumner of Massachusetts proposed an amendment that would permit naturalization for other nonwhites. But senators from the western states, determined to continue excluding alien Chinese from citizenship, persuaded enough of their colleagues to defeat Sumner's motion overwhelmingly (Ringer 1983, 628). To most Americans, naturalization for the Chinese was unthinkable. The Democratic party platform of 1884, after calling the United States "the land of liberty and the asylum of the oppressed of every nation," made an explicit exception for the Chinese, who were "unfitted by habits, training, religion or kindred . . . for the citizenship which our laws confer" (Porter and Johnson 1969, 67). A large number of single white males, say Italians, who smoked opium and worked under "coolie" conditions would have offended middle-class Americans, too. But there was something else besides "habits, training, religion or kindred" that kept the Chinese as outsiders. It was race. Popular literature, political speeches, and government reports tended to stigmatize the Chinese as inherently immoral. Called "Celestials," "Mongolians," "Coolies," and "Chinks," they were portrayed as inured to filth, disease, and immorality, themes stressed in a half-dozen popular magazines in the 1850s and 1860s (Miller 1969). In an 1865 editorial, the *New York Times,* warming to the subject of Chinese exclusion, said, "We have four million of degraded negroes in the South . . . and if there were to be a flood-tide of Chinese population—a population befouled with all the social vices, with no knowledge or appreciation of free institutions or Constitutional liberty, with heathenish souls and heathenish propensities," then, warned the *Times,* "we should be prepared to bid farewell to republicanism and democracy" (Miller 1969, 170).

Their ineligibility for citizenship as nonwhites made the Chinese immigrants particularly vulnerable. At the same time that police authorities and immigration inspectors chased the Chinese in the West, German and Scandinavian aliens in Wisconsin, Wyoming, and Nebraska were being urged to vote (seven states had laws permitting alien suffrage up to the outbreak of World War I). At the very time that the California Constitution of 1878–1879 stipulated that "no alien ineligible to become a citizen of the United States shall ever be employed on any state, county, municipal or other public work in this state" (Ringer 1983, 592), there were more than fifty Irish Catholics on the Boston police force; and in five years, the immigrant Hugh O'Brien would be elected for the first of five terms as mayor. Asian immigrants were thought of as rotating units of work, no more than "that of cattle on the ranges," according to one plantation representative in Hawaii in 1910 (Mead 1910).

Mexicans also suffered from racial prejudice, but unlike the Asians, they were eligible for citizenship. Also unlike the Asians, their situation was complicated by the history of the Southwest. For decades after the American conquest of northern Mexico, many Mexicans saw the Anglos as usurpers of the land; and near the border in Texas, violence was common between the two groups. By the early twentieth century, particularly after the Mexican revolution, when large numbers of Mexican immigrants came to work in the United States, the issue of the conquest had receded. But Mexican immigrants often were not seen by Anglos as intending immigrants. Frequently, they were thought of as temporary workers to be dispensed with when no longer needed, a perception encouraged by a contract-labor program negotiated with the Mexican government during World War I, two subsequent *bracero* programs, and the growing movement of illegal aliens from Mexico to the United States seeking temporary work.

Growers in the Southwest and in California were able to rely on the motivation of poor Mexican workers—often undocumented—and on the cooperation of government in helping to manage their labor needs. The willingness of government to help turn the spigot that controlled the flow of cheap labor from Mexico to the southwest was not the only factor that made the situation of Mexican sojourners different from that of sojourners on the East Coast. The French-Canadian workers who came to New England throughout the late nineteenth and early twentieth centuries were most like the Mexicans in the ease with which they moved back and forth across the border, their reluctance to put down roots in American life, their strong sense of cultural identity with their homeland, and their lack of progress in acquiring English literacy and fluency. But there also were differences between the two groups in addition to the role that government played in explicitly serving employer interests in the West, the main one being race. Dark skin color made it easy for whites to think of Mexicans as stoop labor or "wetbacks" and not as immigrants or even persons. Thinking of them in a depersonalized way, one could feel more comfortable with sudden roundups, deportations, and con-tract-labor programs, and could ignore the conditions under which Mexicans and Mexican-Americans actually lived and worked.

The system had a particularly brutal aspect in Texas, where at the turn of the century and into the twentieth century vigilante bands carried out attacks against Mexicans and Mexican-Americans (de Leon 1983, 101–5). By the early part of the twentieth century, the Texas Rangers had replaced the local police in Texas as the main enforcers of the system of sojourner pluralism; and later, the Border Patrol of the Immigration and Naturalization Service and local police forces took over from the Rangers. Although the Border Patrol was not brutal, it developed informal arrangements of cooperation with agricultural employers from the 1920s on through the 1950s. The I.N.S. would go easy on enforcement until picking time was over, making only a few raids to indicate that it was doing its job in order to justify federal appropria-tions. Sympathetic to the needs of the local economy and amenable to political pressures, it stepped up enforcement when laborers became difficult, as in the I.N.S. crackdown following the so-called wetback strikes of 1951 and 1952 (Berrera 1979, 125–27).

Turning the spigot that controlled the labor supply on and off with the cooperation of the authorities had become a well-established pattern of labor control by the 1920s. The revolving door turned with the seasons to some extent. At crop-picking time, workers would go north from Mexico; at slack periods and especially at Christmas, they would go home. But more impor-tantly, the revolving door turned with economic cycles. When employer de-sires for Mexican labor waned in 1928, U.S. authorities cooperated in keeping the Mexicans out by applying the literacy test that had been enacted by Congress in 1917 but that had been ignored for Mexicans for years. With the onset of the Depression between 1929 and 1934, more than four hundred thousand (perhaps more than five hundred thousand) Mexicans were sent home without formal deportation proceedings, including thousands of U.S. citizens of Mexican descent who were deported illegally (Samora 1971).

Such actions were either supported or ignored by a large majority of Americans, who shared racist assumptions about Asians and Mexicans. Yet, the children of Mexicans who settled in the United States were Mexican-Americans, and children of Asians were Asian-Americans. They often behaved as ethnic-Americans, catching the spirit of the civic culture and using its rhetoric to defy the exploitation of their people. Despite the obstacles of racism, their situation was in many respects more like that of Euro-Americans than that of blacks, who, before the civil rights revolution, were still limited by the coercive characteristics of caste. By the early 1900s, when Jim Crow laws were being enforced vigorously against African-Americans in the South, attempts to segregate Mexicans in the Southwest had ambiguous results. The African-American press noticed that Mexicans (and Asians) were permitted to ride in white-only streetcars and trains and attend first-class theaters in the white sections, while well-educated, prominent blacks could not (Schenkman 1982, 156). Although segregation of Mexican-American children in the public schools of California and the Southwest was fairly well established by the mid-1920s, it was done through assignment of school districts rather than by state law, and it was never uniformly applied. In California, some districts chose not to separate children of Mexican descent, and even in segregated districts, some Mexican children were allowed to attend white schools (Wollenberg 1976, 116–17). The 1876 Texas Constitution established separate schools for "white" and "colored" children, but the state never legislated separate schools for Mexican-Americans, although in Texas, where discrimination against Mexicans was the most severe of any place in the country, the vast majority of Mexican and Mexican-American children went to segregated schools in a tri-ethnic school system (von der Mehden 1984, 55).

The realities of informal or unofficial segregation were cruel: Mexican-American children were turned away from white swimming pools; Mexican-Americans were sometimes denied service at good Anglo restaurants; and Mexican-Americans were discouraged from moving into better neighborhoods. But when these established patterns of discrimination against Mexicans and Mexican-Americans in Texas conflicted with American war goals in 1944, the Texas legislature passed the Caucasian Race Resolution, indicating that Mexicans and Mexican-Americans officially were to be considered as Caucasians and that all Caucasians, including the Mexicans, should have equal rights in public places of business and amusement (Meier and Rivera 1972, 210). Twenty-five years later, it would be shown that except for Puerto Ricans, the level of segregation of Hispanics from Anglos generally was much lower than between blacks and whites, and was reduced over time. Whereas a rise in socioeconomic status was associated with a weakening of residential segregation nationally for Mexican-Americans, it was not for blacks (Massey 1970; Lopez 1981; Denton and Massey 1988).

The children of Asian immigrants were even less segregated in schools and neighborhoods than those of Mexicans. In Hawaii, extensive intermarriage between whites *(haoles)* and Hawaiians made virtually impossible the establishment of racially segregated public schools. With the introduction of the normal schools to train teachers in Hawaii in the early twentieth century, many Chinese and Japanese parents urged their children to attend and become teachers. By the mid-1920s, Asian-American youngsters were attending schools in largely integrated settings, and almost 15 percent of the schoolteachers in Hawaii were Chinese-Americans, more than double the proportion of the Chinese population in the islands.

Efforts by whites to segregate the Japanese-Americans in California and other mainland states were unsuccessful. By 1905, the policy of the board of education in San Francisco to segregate Chinese high school students broke down when Chinese parents threatened to boycott the elementary school and cause a significant loss of state financial aid. In the following year, President Theodore Roosevelt, under pressure from the imperial government of Japan, condemned San Francisco's policy of keeping Japanese students from the public schools. Within several years, many were attending integrated schools, and by 1920 most of them went to schools with whites (Wollenberg 1976, 44, 65–66, 72). As early as 1915, only one-third of the nisei respondents in one study lived in predominantly Japanese-American neighborhoods. The proportion of nisei living in mixed neighborhoods or mainly non-Japanese neighborhoods increased in every subsequent decade (Montero 1980, 36–39).

For the most part, Asian- and Mexican-Americans followed the path of ethnic-Americanization despite the obstacles placed in their path, including the internment of Japanese-Americans during World War II. They also produced their share of protagonists for the civic culture, their apostles of "true Americanism." One of them, Carlos Bulosan, a young Filipino immigrant, wrote an autobiography in 1943 called *America Is in the Heart* (Bulosan 1943). That theme had always been implicit in the founding myth of the United States, but it was still tarnished by racism. The young Filipino saw the darkest side of America. He knew how employers, sometimes with the cooperation of the police, engaged in a pattern of exploitation of Filipinos and other dark-skinned workers. He watched organizations with patriotic names, such as the Liberty League of California, the Daughters of the Golden West, and the Daughters of the American Revolution, try to deprive Filipinos of their rights. Yet, he identified with the immigrant saga, asserting pride in his Filipino identity while proclaiming his love for the United States and the principles that he believed gave Americans their identity.

THE CIVIL RIGHTS REVOLUTION AND ETHNIC DIVERSITY

In the years following World War II, Americans radically changed the way they thought about race, a development that profoundly affected thinking about immigration, immigrants, and ethnic diversity. Large numbers of blacks in the armed services traveled all over the country and much of the world to defend American liberty; abhorring the racism of the Nazis, Americans revived the ideology of equal rights; previously entrenched theories of eugenics and race were thoroughly discredited by scholars; the G.I. Bill ·of Rights exposed hundreds of thousands of ex-servicemen to an education that enlarged their tolerance of others; the Cold War forced American leaders to emphasize the theme of freedom for all; the Supreme Court, responding to the social and intellectual currents of the time, steadily eroded the doctrine of separate but equal; and finally, the civil rights revolution firmly established discrimination based on race or ethnicity as an anathema to the American ethos.

To continue an immigration admission system based on discrimination by nationality was no longer tenable. The national origins system, blatantly inconsistent with the emerging civil rights consensus, was abandoned in 1965, resulting by the mid-1970s in a tremendous shift in the composition of lawful immigrants, most of whom were neither white nor European. Negative concerns about immigration focused openly not on the new composition of the immigrants but on the increase in the number of illegal aliens. As a result of those concerns and also to reassess all aspects of immigration and refugee policy, the Congress and President Jimmy Carter established the Select Commission on Immigration and Refugee Policy in 1978. The commission (which consisted of four senators, four members of the House of Representatives, four cabinet members, and four public members appointed by the president) addressed the question of race and nationality at its second meeting. Then, all of its members strongly endorsed the statement by one of them, then Secretary of Health, Education and Welfare Patricia Roberts Harris, a former civil rights leader, that the issue of race should never again become an "implicit or explicit" basis for selecting immigrants to the United States (*Select Commission on Immigration and Refugee Policy Newsletter* 1979).

When the Select Commission made its report in the spring of 1981, it praised immigrants, now mostly nonwhite, as a source of strength in the American nation and called for an increase in numerically restricted immigration from 270,000 to 350,000 and for a program to legalize a substantial number of illegal aliens along with measures to curtail their number in the future. It would take five years for Congress to pass legislation focused primarily on the question of illegal aliens and eight years before the Senate would pass many of its recommendations concerning lawful immigration. During that time, the nation's political leaders, journalists, and other opinion makers embraced the ideal of ethnic diversity more enthusiastically than ever before. The insistence by blacks on black pride during the civil rights revolution gave new emphasis to the significance of ethnicity in American life. But a racial definition of pride was no longer acceptable because it contradicted the antiracist premise of the civil rights revolution. Even the black pride and power movement lost its racial emphasis, as black leaders such as Martin Luther King, Jr., and Jesse Jackson spoke of blacks as an ethnic group and as black immigrants and their children called themselves Ghanaian-Americans, Ethiopian-Americans, Jamaican-Americans, etc.

EXPANDING IMMIGRATION AND CELEBRATING DIVERSITY

As immigrants arrived from all over the world, the old American ideas of asylum and diversity were used with increasing favor in public rhetoric. There was obvious danger in assertions of ethnic chauvinism and power and considerable controversy over specific public policies such as affirmative action and bilingual education. There also was concern over the low naturalization rates of Mexican immigrants and over the school dropout rate for Hispanic children. Xenophobia erupted in attacks on immigrants and refugees. Yet, there emerged a widespread public agreement on the value of ethnic diversity that extended to conservatives as well as liberals. Jeane Kirkpatrick, a leading conservative intellectual and member of the Reagan administration, wrote that "only those who do not understand America think it is 'un-American' for Cuban-Americans to have a special interest in Cuba, or black Americans to have a special interest in Africa, or Polish-Americans in Poland, or Jews in Israel" (Kirkpatrick 1986). In Ronald Reagan's presidential campaign in 1980, he explained to the Spanish International Television Network that Americans were special because they "came from every corner of the world." Praising ethnic diversity, he said, "we've all kept our pride . . . whether it was our parents or grandparents or great-grandparents who came from somewhere else . . . we've kept alive the culture . . . I've been to many ethnic festivals recently—Ukrainian, Lithuanian, Polish—and seen how they've kept alive the customs of the country, and yet they are Americans" (Spanish International Network 1980). In his 1984 acceptance speech to the Republican National Convention, Reagan spoke of the "golden door" that continued to welcome new immigrants from all over the world. Speaking about the athletes representing 140 countries at the Olympic Games in the United States, he praised the United States as "the one country in the world whose people carry the blood lines of all of those 140 countries and more" (*Congressional Quarterly* 1984).

It is hard to imagine a conservative leader of any other nation praising ethnic diversity and new immigrants without suffering political damage. But by 1983, ethnic diversity had become so central to the way Americans looked at themselves and presented themselves to the world that after *Time* magazine ran an Independence Day feature praising ethnic diversity in Los Angeles, it did not publish a single letter that warned against the dangers of such diversity (*Time* 1983).[3] The *Time* story was a special feature, but the daily newspapers also presented ethnic variety not as different from mainstream America but as typically American, as when the *New York Times* published a story and a picture about American students (ages ten through thirteen), two of whom were black, two Asian, and two white, who visited the Soviet government's compound in New York to discuss their hopes for peace (*New York Times* 1983). A full-page picture showing a representative group of American youth in *U.S.A. Today* presented a San Diego fifth-grade class of about thirty youngsters, of whom eight were black and nine or ten from Asian and Hispanic backgrounds (*U.S.A. Today* 1983). A widely used advertisement of the *Wall Street Journal* in 1986 showed a picture of immigrants debarking at Ellis Island captioned with the headline: "They Didn't Bring Riches. They Brought Something Better." In a widely distributed comic strip, "Fun Facts with Nikki, Todd and Randy," the three youngsters debated whether or not they should buy only American cars, as Todd, the young black boy, suggested. Randy, the Asian-American youngster, demurred, reminding the blonde girl, Nikki, that her great-grandfather came from Ireland and Todd that his great-great-grandfather came from Africa. "And my parents came here from Cambodia . . . so in a way, aren't we all imports?" asked Randy (*Boston Sunday Globe* 1985).

The folkways of Americans on Thanksgiving showed how they expressed ethnic identities in relation to their American identity. In 1976, the *New York Times* told of an Italian family who ate a Thanksgiving meal as they imagined Columbus might have eaten it. A Russian-American family featured a Russian dessert made from cranberries; a Chinese-American family ate Peking Duck instead of turkey; and an Austrian-American family feasted on braised turkey and white beans (*New York Times* 1976). A *Boston Globe* story in 1985 told of Kampucheans, Vietnamese, and Laotians celebrating Thanksgiving at a feast sponsored by the Jewish Vocational Service. There, the refugee families ate fiery Nuk Chow sauce and Cha Gio eggrolls along with their roast turkey, cranberry sauce, and pumpkin pie. At the end of the day, a Kampuchean refugee remarked, "It is good to learn of this Thanksgiving Day. When we hear of all the many immigrants who came before us we do not feel so much alone" (*Boston Globe* 1985).

By 1986, a writer for the *New York Times* concluded that "as an American holiday, Thanksgiving's universality must lie in its ability to welcome succeeding generations of immigrants to these shores." She wrote of Haitians, Barbadians, Jamaicans, Panamanians, and Trinidadians sitting down with family members for dinners that merged the culinary traditions of their homeland cultures with those of the more traditional Thanksgiving. "For me," reported one second-generation American of West Indian background, "Thanksgiving is a mixing of the black-American traditions with the Caribbean" (Alexander 1986).

In the 1980s, the centennial celebration of the Statue of Liberty and the bicentennial of the Constitution also became occasions for emphasizing immigration and ethnic diversity as central to American identity. On the eve of the statue's centennial, eighty Americans from forty-two different ethnic groups were honored with the Ellis Island Medal of Honor for what news anchorman Tom Brokaw, the host for the occasion, called their dedication "to the American way of life while preserving the values or tenets of a particular heritage group." One of the speakers, Senator Daniel Patrick Moynihan (D–New York), called the event "an unabashed celebration of ethnicity" (*New York Times* 1986). While fireworks were going off in New York City's harbor on 4 July to honor Miss Liberty, Hispanic members of the Local 23-25 of the Blouse, Skirt, and Sportswear Workers of the International Ladies' Garment Workers' Union in New York sponsored a "dance for liberty" featuring two live bands, and the Chinese members of Local 23-25 held a "Chinatown Liberty Fair" even as Jewish-Americans and Italo-Americans held their own special celebrations (Local 23-25 1986).

Underlying the consensus on the value of ethnic diversity was a widespread acceptance of the view of Jefferson and Lincoln that immigrants became Americans when they embraced the political ideals of the republic. Some contemporaries thought that immigrants were particularly good exemplars of those ideals. Conservative author and columnist George F. Will wrote in 1980 that "the newest citizens have the clearest idea of what we are celebrating when we raise a red, white and blue ruckus on the Fourth of July" (Will 1980). Jeane Kirkpatrick wrote six years later that the values of the republic receive "continual renewal by new citizens, who bring to us a special personal sense of the importance of freedom. . . . Perhaps it is the immigrants' function from generation to generation to remind them [native-born Americans] of what a treasure it is they own" (Kirkpatrick 1986). President Reagan expressed that view in 1984 at a naturalization ceremony for 1,548 new citizens from eighty-two countries—a common American cultural display—when he told the about-to-become citizens that although some Americans had doubted the meaning of the American dream and had lost confidence in American destiny, the immigrants proved that American ideals and values were still powerful. "They have wondered if our nation still has meaning. But then we see you today, and it's an affirmation," he concluded (Weinraub 1984).

Such thinking reflected and encouraged a growing sentiment in the Congress in favor of liberalizing immigration and refugee legislation, beginning with the passage of the Refugee Act of 1980, which for the first time provided a system for admitting refugees to the United States each year outside of the numerically restricted immigration preference system and without having to resort to the passage of special refugee legislation for each emergency. Four years later, a public opinion poll revealed that Americans generally accepted the view that immigrants and refugees should be admitted to the United States without consideration of race or nationality (Simon 1985, 34–36).[4] When Congress passed the Immigration Reform and Control Act of 1986, not a single member of either house spoke in complaint against the vastly changed composition of immigrants. In supporting measures to curtail illegal immigration, many senators and congressmen argued that it was important to protect the legal immigration system. Although much of the media attention to the Immigration Reform and Control Act centered on the employer sanctions law to deter illegal migration, several other provisions of the act were strongly proimmigration, following the recommendations of the Select Commission. In addition to its comprehensive legalization program (1.77 million applicants), Congress also passed a special legalization program for illegal aliens who had worked in agriculture for ninety days in the previous year and for another group who could persuade the I.N.S. that they had worked for ninety days in each of three successive previous years (a total of 1.3 million additional applicants). These special agricultural workers represented a concession to the old immigration tradition of the southwest and California, in which low-cost workers were supplied to employers with the help of the government. But the program also signaled a fundamental departure from that tradition by specifying that the workers would not be confined to agriculture or to any section of the country and that they could become eligible for permanent residency. The repudiation of any version of a guest worker program represented a triumph for the principle that anyone who worked in the United States, regardless of national background, should be entitled to the fundamental protections of the Constitution.

In addition to these major increases in lawful immigration, the Congress in 1986 took other steps to open the front door: it increased the immigration ceilings for colonies and dependencies from five hundred to six thousand. It provided for the adjustment of the status of nearly one hundred thousand special entrants who came from Cuba and Haiti in the early 1980s to that of permanent resident alien; and it added five thousand immigrants annually for two years to be chosen from persons who were nationals of thirty-six countries with low rates of immigration attributed to the emphasis in the 1965 amendments on family reunification. The last provision was extended to bring fifteen thousand additional immigrants in 1989 and in 1990; and in 1988 Congress also increased immigration by providing ten thousand additional visas annually for 1990 and 1991 for would-be immigrants from 162 countries, who were chosen by lottery in the summer of 1989 from 3.2 million individual applicants who mailed or delivered typewritten letters to the State Department in March of that year. (The twelve leading countries of immigration in 1988 were excluded from the lottery, and the largest numbers of winners came from Bangladesh and Pakistan.)

Three years later, the Senate, continuing the debate on immigration reform proposed by the Select Commission, passed by a vote of eighty-one to seventeen legislation that would establish a floor on legal immigration of 630,000. (The assumption of continued demand was obviously realistic.) If the Congress passed the Senate bill, it was likely that immigration would rise in a few years from the 1987 and 1988 levels of six hundred thousand to about 650,000 (both figures include unrestricted numbers of immediate relatives of U.S. citizens and refugees who adjust their status to that of immigrant). In the Senate debate, one conservative Senator, Rudi Boshowitz (R—Minnesota), and one liberal, Paul Simon (D—Illinois), referred proudly to the fact that fourteen of seventeen valedictorians in Boston city high schools in June of 1988 were immigrants (*Congressional Record* 1989, S7863, S7897). Even Senators who voted against the bill, such as Robert Byrd (D—West Virginia), praised immigrants for the "wonderful strength and diversity brought to this nation" (*Congressional Record* 1989, S7902).

Many Senators referred to their own immigrant backgrounds. Senator Arlen Spector (R—Pennsylvania) spoke of his immigrant father coming to the United States by steerage without money and not knowing how to speak English. Spector proudly reported that out of his father's loins and those of his mother's immigrant grandparents came doctors, lawyers, a scientist, and an artist (*Congressional Record* 1989, S7967). In arguing for an amendment to increase the numerically restricted immigration of brothers and sisters of U.S. citizens by an additional forty thousand (the only liberalizing amendment to fail), Senator Phil Gramm (R—Texas) said America became a great nation because of the immigration of "ordinary people who have been inspired and activated and energized by freedom" (*Congressional Record* 1989, S7896).

Positive thinking about immigration in 1989 resulted from many factors: continued economic growth in the United States; the continued low fertility of Americans and the fear of labor shortages in the future; the 1986 attempt by Congress to curtail illegal immigration; the growing political influence of immigrant-ethnic constituency groups; the reported success of many of the new immigrants, who tended to be better educated and more highly skilled than those who arrived at the turn of the century (Portes and Rumbaut 1989, 28, 78–79);[5] and the celebration of the American civic culture and its founding myth of asylum in ceremonies commemorating American independence, the Statue of Liberty, and the Constitution in the late 1980s. Confidence in the new immigration led President Bush to sign the most sweeping revision of American immigration law since 1924, a law passed overwhelmingly by Congress in late October 1990 that would increase annual immigrant admissions, including refugees and asylees who adjust their status, from about six hundred thousand to approximately eight hundred thousand. Most immigrants would continue to come from Asia and Latin America, not because the policy favored such nationals but because the United States no longer based its immigration policy on discrimination by nationality or race. The new law was immigrant-friendly in many ways: increasing immigration to reunify families, reducing the waiting time for spouses and minor children of resident aliens; almost tripling the number of immigrants admitted for those coming to work independent of family in the United States; establishing a safe haven for those in the country fleeing civil war and natural disasters, applicable immediately to Salvadorans; providing fifty-five thousand visas annually for three years for the spouses and minor children of recently legalized aliens under the 1986 program for illegal aliens; vastly enlarging the number of visas for persons from Hong Kong; setting aside forty thousand visas a year for thirty-three countries that had low rates of immigration in recent years; and giving more time for newly legalized aliens to apply for permanent residency.

The positive mood toward immigration might be changed by sharp economic reversals. But it is unlikely that Americans will stop celebrating diversity as a feature of American identity as long as ethnic claims are not asserted on the basis of group rights and expressions of ethnic pride do not spill over into chauvinistic hatred. Nor is it likely that Americans will return to an immigration policy governed by racist considerations, religious bigotry, or even nationality preferences. Asian immigrants, perhaps more than any other group, symbolized the dramatic shift that had taken place in the twentieth century with respect to American thinking about immigration and ethnicity. Once ineligible for citizenship and then barred from immigration altogether, they constituted over 40 percent of all immigrants and, of the different continental immigrant groups—European, Hispanic, and Asian—they had the highest rates of naturalization (Barkan 1983). Almost entirely buried was the old assimilationist view that held up Anglo-Americanism as a model to which others were expected to assimilate, or at least as a kind of ethnic-Americanism superior to any other. The view of "true Americanism" preached by Carl Schurz and so many other immigrant leaders, implicit in the thinking of Jefferson and explicit in that of Lincoln, had prevailed.

NOTES

1. I want to thank Philip Gleason for bringing to my attention Cecil B. Eby's article "America as 'Asylum': A Dual Image," *American Quarterly* (Fall 1962):483–89. Eby confirms the view that asylum was a quite popular public term in the first half-century of the nation's history.

2. Curley's speech is on a tape recording in the author's possession. Stephan Thernstrom pointed out to me after reading this section that not all of the opposition to Germans and Irish in the early part of the twentieth century came from Anglo-Protestants intolerant of diversity. Much of it originated with other ethnic groups, growing out of old-world conflicts or new battles in the American cities. There is no question that the parochialism of the Germans and the Irish also accounted for some of the hostility felt toward them by others, including the Anglo-Americans. Nevertheless, when looked at from the perspective of other multiethnic societies, a surprising proportion of immigrants and nearly all of their children succeeded in their claim of "true Americanism."

3. Of the five letters printed concerning the article, two came from Korean-Americans and one from a Mexican-American congressman, each emphasizing the positive aspects of diversity. Another was from a Protestant minister in a small town in Illinois who wrote that "America has grown by accepting and appreciating the gifts and contributions of all our minorities and ethnic groups." The fifth was from a second grade schoolteacher in La Habra, California, who boasted about her multiethnic class, which included children from Jordan, Egypt, Mexico, Peru, Cuba, the Philippines, Korea, Thailand, and Lebanon. Proudly she wrote, "I have Irish and Polish and English-Americans, a first generation Italian, and a child from Sri-Lanka. . . . America is blessed by these immigrants. We can learn so much from them."

4. When the Gallup poll asked Americans in 1965 if they would favor changing the immigration law "so that people would be admitted on the basis of their occupational skills rather than on the basis of the country they came from," 51 percent favored such a change, with only 30 percent against it. When respondents in one 1984 survey were asked whether "a man from Taiwan who wants to come to the United States to be with his daughter, who immigrated here ten years ago," should be admitted, only 16 percent said no, compared to 75 percent who said yes. When the sample was asked if "a Jew from the Soviet Union facing persecution because he is Jewish should be admitted," only 14 percent said no and 79 percent yes. Sixty-six percent believed that "a man from El Salvador who comes from a town in which many people were killed by fighters from both sides of that country's civil war and who fears that if he is forced to return he will be in danger" should be admitted, while only 24 percent said no. Most surprising of all, perhaps, while

52 percent said that they would admit a man from England "who wants to start a new life for himself in this country," 57 percent said that they would admit a man from Mexico with the same intention. See United States Committee for Refugees, "Public Attitudes on Refugees," 7 June 1984. This national public opinion poll was conducted in 1984 by the firm of Keene, Parsons, and Associates, Inc., and was accurate to within four or five percentage points.

5. The proportion of professionals and technicians among immigrants in the 1980s consistently exceeded the average among U.S. workers. Immigrant professionals represented around 25 percent of the total, compared to 18 percent professionals and technicians in the American labor force. Immigrants had slightly more education than the average for natives. Of course, there were differences among groups. Among the foreign-born, Mexicans had the lowest level of schooling and immigrants from south Asia the highest. Fifty percent or more of the foreign-born of the best educated groups (Indians, Iranians, Taiwanese, and Nigerians) arrived in the late 1980s.

REFERENCES

Books and Articles

Adamic, Louis. *My America, 1928–1938.* New York: Harper, 1938.

Alexander, Daryl Royster. "A Spicy Blend of Caribbean and Black-American Flavors." *New York Times,* 19 November 1986, C-1.

Barkan, Elliott R. "Whom Shall We Integrate?: A Comparative Analysis of Immigration and Naturalization Trends of Asians before and after the 1965 Immigration Act (1951–1978)." *Journal of American Ethnic History* 3 (Fall 1983):48.

Berrera, Mario. *Race and Class in the Southwest: A Theory of Racial Inequality.* Gary, Ind.: University of Notre Dame Press, 1979.

Boston Globe. 27 November 1985, 1, 8.

Boston Sunday Globe, 31 March 1985, comics.

Breitman, George, ed. *Malcolm X Speaks.* New York: Grove 1965, 26.

Bulosan, Carlos. *America Is in the Heart: A Personal History.* Seattle: University of Washington Press, 1943.

Congressional Quarterly. Washington, D.C.: Congressional Quarterly, Inc., 19 July 1980.

———. Washington, D.C., Congressional Quarterly, Inc., 25 August 1984.

De Leon, Arnaldo. *They Called Them Greasers: Anglo Attitudes toward Mexicans in Texas, 1821–1900.* Austin: University of Texas Press, 1983.

Denton, Nancy A., and Douglas S. Massey. "Residential Segregation of Blacks, Hispanics, and Asians by Socioeconomic Status and Generation." *Social Science Quarterly* (1988):797–817.

Eastland, Terry, and William J. Bennett. *Counting by Race: Equality from the Founding Fathers to Bakke and Weber.* New York: Basic, 1979.

The Federalist, by Alexander Hamilton, James Madison, and John Jay, with an introduction by Edward Mead Earle. New York: Modern Library, 1937.

Forbes, Jack D., ed. *The Indian in America's Past.* Englewood Cliffs, Prentice-Hall, 1964.

Franklin, Frank G. *Legislative History of Naturalization.* New York: Arno, 1969.

Gabriel, Ralph Henry. *The Course of American Democratic Thought.* New York: Greenwood, 1986, 46.

Grund, Francis Joseph. *The Americans in Their Moral, Social, and Political Relations.* Boston: March, Capen, and Lyon, 1837.

Ifkovic, Edward, ed. *American Letter: Immigrant and Ethnic Writing.* Englewood Cliffs, N.J.: Prentice Hall, 1975.

Kettner, James H. *The Development of American Citizenship, 1608–1870.* Chapel Hill: University of North Carolina Press, 1978.

Kirkpatrick, Jeane. "We Need the Immigrants." *Washington Post,* 30 June 1986, A-11.

Little, David B. *America's First Centennial Celebration.* Boston: Houghton Mifflin, 1974.

Local 23-25, International Ladies' Garment Workers' Union, 35, no. 3 (October 1986):4.

Lopez, M. M. "Patterns of Interethnic Residential Segregation in the Urban Southwest, 1960 and 1970." *Social Science Quarterly* 62 (1981):50–63.

Massey, Douglas S. "Residential Segregation of Spanish-Americans in United States Urban Areas." *Demography* 16 (1970):553–63.

Mead, Royal D. "The Sugar Industry in Hawaii." *San Francisco Chronicle,* 18 July 1910.

Meier, Matt S., and Feliciano Rivera. *The Chicanos: A History of Mexican-Americans.* New York: Hill and Wang, 1972.

Miller, Stuart Creighton. *The Unwelcome Immigrant: The American Image of the Chinese, 1785–1882.* Berkeley: University of California Press, 1969.

Montero, Darryl. *Japanese-Americans: Changing Patterns of Ethnic Affiliation over Three Generations.* Boulder, Colo.: Westview, 1980.

Nee, Victor G., and Brett Debarry Nee. *Longtime Californ'.* New York: Pantheon, 1972.

New York Times, 22 November 1976, C-8.

———. 10 December 1983, B-1.

———. 28 October 1986, B-3.

Peterson, Merrill D., ed. *The Portable Thomas Jefferson.* New York: Penguin, 1977.

Porter, Kirk H., and Donald Bruce Johnson, eds. *National Party Platforms, 1840–1968.* Urbana: University of Illinois Press, 1969.

Portes, Alejandro, and Ruben G. Rumbaut. *Immigrant America: A Portrait.* Berkeley: University of California Press, 1989.

Ringer, Benjamin R. *We, The People, and Others.* New York: Tavistock, 1983.

Rischin, Moses. *Immigration and the American Tradition.* Indianapolis, Ind.: Bobbs-Merrill, 1966.

Rosensweig, Roy. *Eight Hours for What We Will: Workers and Leisure in an Industrial City, 1870–1920.* New York: Cambridge University Press, 1983.

Samora, Julian. *Los Mojados: The Wetback Story.* Gary, Ind.: University of Notre Dame Press, 1971.

Schenkman, Arnold. *Ambivalent Friends: Afro-Americans View the Immigrant.* Westport, Conn.: Greenwood, 1982.

Simon, Rita J. *Public Opinion and the Immigrant: Print Media Coverage, 1880–1980.* Lexington, Mass.: Lexington Books, 1985.

Spanish International Network. Interview with Ronald Reagan, 1980. Unpublished transcript in author's files.

Time. 4 July 1983, 8.

U.S.A. Today. 11 July 1983, 8-A.

von der Mehden, Fred R., ed. *The Ethnic Groups of Houston.* Houston: Rice University Studies, 1984.

Weinraub, Bernard. *New York Times,* 2 October 1984, A-22.

Will, George F. *Newsweek,* 18 July 1980, 76.

Wollenberg, Charles. *All Deliberate Speed: Segregation and Exclusion in California Schools, 1855–1975.* Berkeley: University of California Press, 1976.

Zangwill, Israel. *The Melting Pot: Drama in Four Acts.* New and rev. ed. New York: Macmillan, 1922.

Government Documents

Congressional Record 135, no. 92. 101st Cong., 1st sess., 11, 12, 13 July 1989.

Farrington v. Tokushige et al. 284 U.S. 298 (1926).

Meyer v. State of Nebraska. 262 U.S. 390 (1923).

Pierce, Governor of Oregon, et al. v. The Society of Sisters. 268 U.S. 510 (1925).

Select Commission on Immigration and Refugee Policy Newsletter, no. 1 (November 1979):1.

3

DIFFICULTIES IN FRENCH HISTORICAL RESEARCH ON IMMIGRATION

Gérard Noiriel

In this chapter I shall review French historical research on immigration in order to explain why until now this subject has been so neglected by French historians. Then I will show the consequences of this neglect for the problem of assimilation of immigrants. In conclusion, I will propose a few hypotheses that I hope will help stimulate a program of comparative French-American research.

THE "FRENCH PATTERN" OF IMMIGRATION: THE REJECTION OF HISTORY

French-American comparative approaches to immigration cannot escape an immense paradox. At the level of what the Durkheimian sociologist Maurice Halbwachs called "real-life history," based on individual and family recollection (Halbwachs 1964), the memory of immigration (meaning the process of definitive displacement of a group of people from one country to another) today concerns, proportionally, the French more than the Americans.[1] And, yet, at the level of "collective memory"—that which is conveyed, maintained, and celebrated by all forms of communication and dissemination (school texts, monuments, official ceremonies, etc.)—the situation is completely reversed. We are reminded by Lawrence Fuchs in his chapter in this volume that the American myth of a "melting pot," that is, the myth of the United States as a place of "refuge" for all people, is still so prevalent in American consciousness that even a conservative president like Ronald Reagan dutifully referred to it in his speeches. In contrast, the role played by immigration in the makeup of present-day French society remains completely repressed in the French national memory.[2]

These contrasting uses of "memory" reflect the radical difference between the French and the American "patterns" of immigration. In all countries, a nation-state's creation is accompanied by a certain number of "myths of origin" or founding myths that reinforce the cohesion of a population composed of different groups. In countries where immigration played a decisive role in the initial settlement, the theme of "immigrants" often occupies an important place in the "myths of origin" (for example in Australia, where collective memory sanctifies English convicts as those who formed the basis of the current population).

Immigration in France cannot be explained historically by the need for population. Until the end of the eighteenth century, France was the most populated country in Europe. The first statistical studies of population bemoaned the fact that although French districts existed in most of the large European cities, foreigners were scarce on French soil.[3] But, recent Anglo-Saxon studies have noted that the French pattern of immigration foreshadowed by a half-century, perhaps even a century, a process that would become widespread in Europe following World War II:[4] general recourse to immigrant labor as an exploited work force used in the most devalued sectors of the industrial labor market.

By the Second Empire, it became strikingly clear that the immigration curve closely traced that of industrial development. The "boom" of the 1850s–1870s was accompanied by a doubling of the foreign population (which bordered on a million individuals around 1880). Marked by severe depression, the following decades saw the number of foreigners stagnate. During the twentieth century, each cycle of expansion/economic crisis almost mechanically provoked a corresponding cycle of immigration (flux/reflux).[5] Also, as of the Second Empire, foreign workers were particularly numerous in the most mechanized industrial sectors (textile industry), as well as in the most physically arduous sectors (mining, agriculture). Finally, the sectors in which immigrant labor was extensively employed were frequently also those that had the most striking rates of development (for example, heavy industry between 1900 and 1930), without a doubt thanks to the profits earned by firms with a dual labor force: French workers (stable and skilled)/foreign workers (unstable and unskilled).

Historically, it is thus indisputable that the French pattern is identified as a "work-related immigration." However, to understand this pattern completely, the sociological reasons that explain the economic situation must be analyzed. How could a country that enjoyed an overabundant supply of labor at the beginning of the Industrial Revolution overwhelmingly and continually resort to foreign labor to develop successfully for the next 150 years? The answer illustrates two other decisive aspects of the French pattern of immigration found, and not by accident, in most European countries following World War II: the democratization of the political system and demographic Malthusianism.

Without tarnishing the recent celebrations of the French bicentennial, we must stress the significant influence the French Revolution had on immigration.[6] As Karl Marx pointed out, one of the major effects of the Revolution was the strengthening of the peasantry's roots in the land,[7] making this social group numerically significant. The adoption of universal suffrage in 1848 furnished this peasant mass with the peaceful means of blocking massive rural exoduses and radical proletarianization such as occurred in Great Britain. The restriction of births across the French countryside during the nineteenth century limited the dispersion of property (another classic factor of proletarianization).

By the end of the nineteenth century, Malthusianism in France was so strong that all great European countries were able to surpass France in population. A demographic deficit (aggravated by the slaughter of World War I) made large industry's recourse to immigration inevitable. The very fact that immigration was conceived as a solution to overcome any obstacles created by the rigidity of the labor market explains (in part) another characteristic of the "French pattern": the premature and almost obsessive use of police and administrative means to channel the flux of immigrants toward the sectors of the labor market dependent on their presence (for example, the complicated bureaucracy of "identification papers," work contracts, police surveillance . . .).

This cursory presentation of the French historical pattern of immigration explains why, unlike in other countries where immigration played an important role, immigrants have practically no place in the French national memory. For a century, at each period of influx of immigrants, French public opinion has consistently viewed immigrants as transient workers destined to return "to their country" (an opinion shared at the outset by the majority of immigrants themselves). Only the ordinary "populationists" (who appeared at the end of the nineteenth century at the initiative of demographers, such as Jacques Bertillon), haunted by the theme of the decline of the French "race" (or people) and supported by the nationalist and xenophobic parties, conceived the question of immigration in terms of "assimilation" or "integration," thus, in historical perspective, as a lasting, irreversible phenomenon. We must not underestimate the strength and the influence of this view.[8] As we will see later, the assumptions on which it was developed by its proponents are too alien to republican values and myths to be widely accepted.

I have touched upon the central political problem posed by the comparative study of immigration in France and in the United States: the question of the founding myth and its role in modern societies. Contrary to superficial analyses that consider a myth an "illusion," or at least a "veil," I believe that we must stress the influence of the founding myth. This requires a serious analysis of its genesis. A comparison of France and the United States cannot avoid Tocqueville: "a people," he affirms, "is always affected by its origins. The circumstances surrounding its birth and development influence the rest of its existence" (Tocqueville [1835] 1981). This remark is fundamental for those who wish to understand the radically different manner in which Americans and French have, until now, understood the role of immigration in their history. In the case of the French, neither the "ethnic" nor the immigration issue played a role in the birth of their republic.

Mass immigration only began in the second half of the nineteenth century, at a time when the French nation's framework had already been in place for quite some time. Even though, as Eugene Weber has shown (1976), regional diversity remained significant in France until the end of the nineteenth century, the beginnings of political centralization date from the sixteenth century; the origins of linguistic unification and codification date from the seventeenth century, etc. This explains why, when the Republic of France developed its own instruments of political control (judicial system, administration, statistics, etc.), there were no racial problems like those that existed in the United States at its birth, and no large-scale linguistic battle (like that which has always pitted the Flemish against the Walloons in Belgium), etc. Furthermore, unlike in the United States, where republicans were able to develop their constitution without opposing an aristocratic "ancien régime," in France the political system imposed by the French Revolution was profoundly marked by the desire to discredit and eliminate the values and norms of the nobility and the clergy, both principal supporters of the monarch. This antiaristocratic and anticlerical sentiment explains, far beyond the philosophy of the Enlightenment, the essential aspects of the Declaration of the Rights of Man and Citizen.

Behind the haunting theme of equality is a violent rejection of all privilege (and all stigmatization) based on *origin*. Whereas under the monarchy legitimacy of social position depended on birth and demanded the display of a genealogy and a degree of noble lineage, under the Republic only personal merit and technical qualification (acquired at school and measured by competitive examinations) defined hierarchies. This taboo of origins, in the spirit of the revolutionaries, most significantly includes class origin, but does not exclude ethnicity, religion, or national origin. In effect, this taboo is combined with another decisive aspect of revolutionary ideology: the struggle against the religious beliefs conveyed by the Catholic clergy. The entire struggle concerning Jews, Protestants, or Blacks from the colonial world at the beginning of the Revolution shows that, beyond the fight for human rights, at stake was a definitive separation between "public" life (the universe of "politics" in the true sense of the term) and "private" life (in which the individual is sovereign and which includes religion, race, family culture). That is to say, it took from the Church all essential elements that had allowed it to exercise its hold on the population.

The rejection of the criterion of origin in order to increase the social value of the individual and the confinement of religion to the sphere of "private life" constitute two innovations of the French Revolution that are of decisive importance for the history of immigration. Every society invents its own social classifications. The initial weakness of ethnic and racial criteria (due to the long process of political homogenization mentioned above), supported by revolutionary action, in turn assigned an exaggerated importance to judicial criteria for nationality as the fundamental principle of social classification. We see once again how heavily initial circumstances weigh on a nation's history. In his chapter, Fuchs notes the importance of the frontier theme (moveable and changeable) in American mythology—another symbolic reminder that in time, as in space, the American nation has not yet been completely formed. In French mythology, the question of a frontier plays an equally significant role, but in a radically different sense from the role it plays in the United States. In fact, for the French, since 1792 (the significance of the Battle of Valmy) the border is first and foremost to be defended and preserved against attacks from invaders. In contrast to the United States, France is a small country, a complete world, whose territory is totally "cleared" and settled and has been for some time. The French nation is a *state* (State) and not an *"evolution."* This rigid concept of the frontier is paramount in the republican right of nationality. Since the Revolution, the fundamental line of demarcation between men is between the citizen (or at least the "national") and the foreigner. Whereas under the monarchy of the ancien régime, a foreigner could occupy high public posts (and even lead armies), as of 1793 only the French had access to the "public sector"; only the French could be electors and elected.[9] On the other hand, those who wish to enter the "French Club" are no longer, at least officially, discriminated against because of race and religious or ethnic origin. In sum, in republican logic everyone has the right to universalism, provided he is French.[10]

The rejection of origins brought about by the nascent Republic, combined with this vigorous notion of a fixed frontier seen as a rampart between "them" and "us," is essential in understanding why, in France, we speak of "immigration" ("others coming to our land") and not "ethnicity." Thus we see how profoundly dependent we still are today, in thought and actions,[11] on the initial circumstances in which our two republican revolutions unfolded.

Nevertheless, to break with certain of Tocqueville's metaphysical interpretations, we must say a word regarding the ways in which a nation perpetuates certain of its original traits. That which has often been analyzed in terms of the "soul of the people," or more recently "national identity," should be conceived much more concretely. As Emile Durkheim knew, what we "inherit" (often without knowing it) are words, judicial norms, classification statistics, which have perpetuated some of the initial circumstances surrounding the nation's creation. Take, for example, language. The entire "French" attitude toward immigration has been affected by both the resources and the gaps in the French language for defining social realities.

I believe the difficulty of grasping immigration as a historical process is, to begin with, based on linguistic peculiarities. We must return to the seventeenth century to understand why, in French, we do not have an equivalent of the English term "making" to describe both a social construction and a social movement. Likewise, as the German sociologist Norbert Elias (refugee in France and then in Great Britain) demonstrated, the French notion of "civilization," which according to him was not easily understood by foreigners, designates the result of a cultural process more than the process itself. "It expresses the self-satisfaction of a population whose national frontiers and specific characteristics are no longer questioned, and have not been for centuries, because they are permanently fixed" (Elias [1939] 1973). Such words are only obstacles to thinking of immigration in terms of contributing to French culture.

Another powerful instrument that has successfully transmitted these republican principles of origin is the law. As we will later see, when we try to define the impossible, an immigration "policy," the most important part of the Declaration of the Rights of Man of 1789 is not the Declaration itself (thrown together and imperfect as everyone knows it is), but the great principles embedded in legal clauses (notably in the constitution). These clauses have never really been challenged at any point, at least not in France (except under the Vichy regime): the separation of "public" and "private" life and the refusal to segregate according to origins have made it possible to limit the racist tendencies of French thought.

Statistics provide another major illustration of how the founding principles of a nation perpetuate themselves from generation to generation. As pointed out in Fuchs' chapter, the question of race (Blacks and Indians considered as foreigners) haunted American democracy from its beginning up until at least the 1960s. National origin and racial and ethnic background played a fundamental role in the taxonomy of the American census, and as a result, in the American perception of the social world. Conversely, from the beginning in France, official administrative classifications were based on "socioprofessional categories" and on nationality.[12] From the Third Republic on, all questions concerning religion, language, etc., were definitively forbidden in the census. From this stems the extreme difficulty for historians to undertake, for example, the history of Jews in France, and the tendency to limit research on immigration to the facts made available by the census. The accent is thus on the history of "foreigners" (defined by their nationality), who disappear from the historical scene as of the moment they or their children become legally French.

In addition to language, law, and statistics, another essential instrument by which nations transmit their original worldview is the way they convey their collective memory; here, I will limit my study to books that explain the history of France. We must return to the prerevolutionary period, the eighteenth century, to grasp how the issue of the legitimate "ancestors" of the French people came about. In the struggle that pitted the nobility against the "Third Estate," historians from the two camps quarreled over this subject. Whereas the nobility affirmed its affiliation with the Frankish aristocracy that conquered Gaul at the beginning of the Middle Ages, the "Third Estate" claimed the Gauls, the vanquished of the medieval contest, as their proper ancestors. This resulted in a presentation of the history of France in which "racial struggle" closely mirrored "class struggle"; the most famous historian of the Restoration, Augustin Thierry, drew the final conclusion: the French Revolution marks, for him, the victory of the people of Gaul over the Frankish aristocracy. Thus we see that the myth of "our ancestors, the Gauls," conveyed for more than a century by history books (even in African and Asian colonies), is an eminently republican myth. However, it wasn't until Michelet that republican mythology acquired its definitive identity. In the name of the universalist values held by the Republic, Michelet challenged the ethnic version of history developed by Thierry. He proposed instead the theme of the French people as the product of "fusion," of a "melting pot" in which were merged all the ethnic backgrounds of the people of Gaul. For Michelet, the "fuel" that permitted this "fusion" was the French nation itself, seen as both a nourishing and an assimilating land and as an abstract democratic principle that, with the Revolution of 1789, triumphed over all enemies, both internal and external.

At the end of the nineteenth century, when the Third Republic settled into power over French society, Michelet's message was interpreted in light of the political strategy of national reconciliation between aristocracy and the "middle class." The historian Ernest Lavisse, author of the historical works that constituted, until World War II, the veritable "Bible" of republican ideology, drove the point home by teaching even those in the smallest village school the theme of a "melting pot" of people (even if the "gaulist" component was given a special position).[13] This rapid summary shows that although there is a common thread between French and American mythologies, the "melting pot" (the concept of a people as a product of a "fusion," as compared to, for example, the German myth that identifies the populace as of a single ethnic group), a radical difference distinguishes the two: in the American case, the Revolution *inaugurated* the "melting pot" and the process has continued throughout the entire contemporary era; in contrast, in the French mythology, the process of a fusion of peoples *came to an end* with the French Revolution, rendering totally impossible all "redefinitions" of the French people that might arise from the subsequent waves of immigration.

THE POLITICAL AND SCIENTIFIC CONSEQUENCES OF THE HISTORY OF IMMIGRATION

Language, law, statistics, and the myth of origins thus combined to render unthinkable the idea of immigration as a historical problem. This repression of collective consciousness provoked a veritable century-long blindness in social-science research on the question. Considering the role of historians in producing the myth of origins mentioned above, we should not be surprised that until the 1970s–1980s, they paid no attention to the question of immigration. But even if we look at other disciplines, in which the practical aspects of immigration should have, at the very least, appeared in their work on assimilation, the same neglect exists. Since the end of the nineteenth century, the disciplines that have given the most attention to immigration are economics and law. But they have exclusively conceived of it as a current problem (problems of food supply, labor market, mobility, or of the right of nationality). After having ignored the question during the Durkheimian[14] period, starting with the 1960s sociological research on immigration proliferated, in an intellectual atmosphere dominated by Marxism; but even here it focused on the "workforce" and economic exploitation. Until recently, the only two fields that integrated history into their study of immigration have been anthropology (primarily physical anthropology) and demography, two disciplines that, given their purpose, could not avoid being preoccupied by problems of origin and genealogy. But the manner in which they approach this problem is surprisingly an extremely pessimistic and negative view, highlighting apocalyptic predictions for the future to the detriment of a dispassionate analysis of the past.

From the end of the nineteenth century, the question of assimilation was posed in terms that would not change until the 1950s. All discussion of the subject centered on one dilemma, a veritable squaring of the circle: either the waves of immigrants "flooding" into France would integrate themselves, thus causing the French population to lose its "identity"—"A population that recruits from abroad will quickly lose its character, its morals, its own force; it will lose with time that which is most precious: its nationality" (Rochard 1883)—or the immigrants would not be assimilated, thus putting the political unity of France at risk by the formation of "national minorities." This view was stressed by Jacques Bertillon, one of the most influential French intellectuals at the end of the last century, who even today is considered the "Founding Father" of demography. Bertillon predicted the forthcoming appearance in France of a *Fremdenfrage* (a "foreign question"), comparable to that in Russia or Austria-Hungary, "aggravating our fear for the future, that foreigners of the same nationality will group themselves in certain corners of the country: Italians along the Mediterranean, Spaniards along their border, Belgians in the North, Germans in the East" (Bertillon 1911). Fifty years later, anthropoligist Robert Gessain and the historian-demographer Louis Chevalier (professor at the Collège de France), developed the same argument in the first INED (National Institute for Demographic Studies) workbooks devoted to the question of immigration.[15] But it is in the writings of André Siegfried, published just following World War II, that we can best assess the influence of this logic and its internal contradictions.

In a French-American comparative context, it seems appropriate to evoke the name of André Siegfried. Like Tocqueville (to whom he was often compared), Siegfried, the foremost French connoisseur of America in his time, was elected to the Collège de France and was considered as the great forerunner of French "political science." He was the first to approach the question of immigration from a comparative French-American viewpoint. Beginning with the premise that immigration in these two countries is an ancient historical reality, Siegfried concluded that the assimilation that occurred in both countries did so according to the same laws: at least three generations must pass in order to complete assimilation, but in fact, it depends on the races involved. In the United States, the "nordic races" assimilate themselves more quickly. In contrast, "when dealing with exotic races such as the Chinese, the famous melting pot of races no longer functions." Similarly, in France, the integration of Italians and Spaniards is relatively easy, "but the Chinese always live as foreigners." In the case of France, adds the author, assimilation is even more difficult than in America because "our country has been settled, closed, almost completed (in the broadest sense of the term), for more than two centuries" and old organisms have more difficulty assimilating new elements (Siegfried 1946). In this argument we rediscover, strikingly, all of the republican mythology mentioned above, making the French Revolution an end result and not a beginning, and making the French people a fixed, static entity for eternity. But when we examine Siegfried's proposed solutions to the problem of immigration, we see that they are irreconcilable with the great principles of 1789. According to him—and to Louis Chevalier, who said the very same thing at the same time—the remedy is that in the end the French government must develop an immigration policy. The latter must be examined from the point of view "of the preservation of the traditional national character"; it should thus "admit the elements capable of assimilation and exclude the others." Consequently, Siegfried is an affirmed partisan of the policy of ethnic quotas similar to that in the United States during the 1920s, "even if," he adds, "from the point of view of principles, it can be contested because it is tainted with racism."

We are now at the heart of a decisive contradiction that, in large part, explains why an immigration policy in France could not exist until recently. French intellectuals are incapable of thinking of assimilation other than in terms of "ethnic compatibility" (what is now called "cultural distance"). From Adolphe Landry's speech in Parliament in 1915 (Landry was a demographer and minister of the population between the two wars) until 1945 when General de Gaulle wrote his "recommendations" aimed at limiting the naturalization of Mediterranean immigrants (especially Italians), the leitmotif of French political thought on immigration was that in order to preserve the identity of the French people, a policy of ethnic selection must be applied. However, it was impossible to do so officially without publicly contradicting the fundamental principles of the Republic that are fixed in republican law.

In the following decades, the intellectual situation was profoundly transformed. The struggles for decolonization, the hegemony of Marxism in the social sciences, the increasingly significant role played by militant sociology in immigration research, and a new phase of industrial development that again focused attention on problems of recruitment and management of the immigrant work force all helped to downplay thoughts of assimilation and discredited the questions that had dominated the French intellectual scene for decades. In fact, the very term "assimilation" became taboo as of the 1960s.

Now, following the stabilization of the last waves of immigrants on French soil, integration has once again become a current problem. The dominant question is whether France can consider assimilation without being trapped in the circle described above, and how the American experience and philosophy can help us to do so. At the risk of stirring controversy, I would say that a good part of the relevant literature in the social sciences is still caught in this circle. Some Frenchmen, skeptical about the notion of a "French melting pot," refuse—as did many generations of good republicans before them—to see this as an intellectual problem. Instead, they see a myth hiding the "real problems," protecting the existing political structure, as if in explaining the sociology of crime, the crime itself would be vindicated. Others continue to analyze the question of integration of immigrants in terms of "cultural distance" (with the current theme of Islam as an "obstacle" to integration). I am convinced that a program of comparative research would permit us to contemplate these questions in a different manner, notably by offering us the opportunity to escape a far too French approach. We could reexamine the proposal by Siegfried in the article quoted above, concerning the "long-term" assimilation of immigrants in France and in the United States, approaching it, however, with radically different conceptual tools.[16] As I attempted to show elsewhere (Beaud and Noiriel 1989), the three great theoretical "traditions" of sociology, the German tradition (Max Weber, Norbert Elias), the American tradition (the Chicago School) and the French tradition (Durkheim), can be mobilized towards this goal. This assumes that two preliminary conditions can be met. On one hand, scientific research on immigration must once again distance itself from political stakes and controversies. And, on the other hand, we must contemplate the problem of assimilation of immigrants, not as a problem in and of itself, but as a particular case within the problem of "social assimilation" that is at the heart of our contemporary history.

NOTES

1. I will not deal here with the statistical problems posed by attempts to classify the French population according to criteria of national origin; nor with the proofs that allow us to say that after three generations, the French with immigrant ancestors are proportionally greater today than Americans (Noiriel 1988).
2. On this subject, I want to underline my disagreement with the presentation of my

works made by Roxane Silberman (1989). Far from presenting the "French melting pot" as a "founding myth," in the image of the American "melting pot," I was endeavoring to show the contrary, apparently without success, that the "melting pot" (that is to say, the concept of social assimilation in scholarly language) was a "blank," an "unthinkable" in French ideology and thought.

3. Cf. for example Moheau, *Recherches et considérations sur la population de la France* ([1778] 1912).
4. Cf. the article by D. Dignan, "Europe's melting pot: a century of large-scale immigration into France" (1981) and the thesis of G. Cross, *Immigrant Workers in Industrial France (The Making of a New Laboring Class)* (1983).
5. The long-term similarities between the economic cycle and the cycle of immigration explain the cyclical waves of xenophobia in French politics. By underlining this relationship—which cannot be found on such a scale in other old countries of immigration, except, perhaps, in Switzerland—I only sought to underscore an element of the "French model" of immigration and not in the least to intervene in the debate for or against "economic determinism."
6. I go deeper into the question in G. Noiriel, "La France aux Francais! Etrangers et immigrés dans la mémoire nationale," in P. Nora, ed., *Les lieux de mémoire* (forthcoming).
7. Cf. K. Marx, *Le 18 Brumaire de Louis Bonaparte* ([1852] 1876).
8. French nationality law of 1889 (combining the jus soli and the jus sanguinis) reflects the compromise that arose, as of that era, between those who saw the immigrant as a foreigner whose presence was temporary, and those who saw in him, and especially in his children, a future Frenchman, who thus must be assimilated with haste.
9. On this subject, I would like to refer to the old, yet essential work, A. Mathiez, "La Révolution et les étrangers" (1918).
10. It is known that Jean-Jacques Rousseau anticipated the dilemma that the Republic of France was never able to resolve, the contradiction between the universal (man) and the particular (the citizen, the national). I am not tackling the colonial question, which would complicate the outline presented here. Since the French nation has always been strongly tied to a territory, to a fixed space (the hexagon), the colonial world has never really been considered an integral part of the nation. That is why the rejection of ethnic or racial principles in the "home country" was imposed at a much slower rate in colonial law.
11. Nathan Glazer recently conjectured that one of the major obstacles in the United States in curbing clandestine immigration stems from the collective sentiment that America is still an "unfinished country," precluding all rigid barriers.
12. The first census worthy of the name appeared in the middle of the nineteenth century. From the start, in place of the basic distinction between French/foreigners was categorization by nationality enriched by statistics on "naturalized" immigrants who even today constitute an essential part of our information on the subject. Regarding the dominance of "socioprofessional categories," again, republican power only restated the principles of classification used by the monarchy; cf. the first "statistical scale" of Vauban and the role of the Physiocrats.
13. Addressing all the young school children of France, he wrote in the introduction to his textbook: "Your ancestors the Gauls were valiant. Your ancestors the

Franks were valiant. Your ancestors the French were valiant." On this question, see G. Noiriel, "Une histoire sociale du 'politique' est-elle possible?" (1989).

14. Although he wrote his principal works at a time when the question of foreigners dominated the French political scene, Durkheim wrote practically nothing on immigration. Between the two wars, his students Marcel Mauss and Maurice Halbwachs no longer considered this question unworthy of sociological research; however, they saw it only as an American problem at a time (1930) when France actually had the highest rate of immigration in the world! (Halbwachs 1932).

15. Louis Chevalier (1947) wrote: "Recent developments have sufficiently underlined the dangers that organized minorities bring to a country, from the point of view of domestic policy, foreign policy and even the economy," and Robert Gessain would like to see an "anthropological science" capable of "defining more or less ethnically homogeneous zones."

16. Recent works (extremely few in France, it is true) have not called Siegfried's position into question. He suggested that the French process of assimilation was, for the most part, identical to that of the United States, despite the contrast between the political systems (decentralized on one side, "Jacobin" on the other). Considering only the most objective criteria (spoken language, practiced religion, number of mixed marriages), assimilation over three generations seems to operate at the same pace in both.

REFERENCES

Beaud, S., and G. Noiriel. 1989. L'assimilation: un concept en panne. *Revue Internationale d'Action Communautaire.*

Bertillon, J. 1911. *La dépopulation de France.* Paris: Alcan.

Chevalier, L., ed. 1947. *Documents sur l'immigration.* Book ne2. INED.

Cross, G. 1983. *Immigrant Workers in Industrial France.* Philadelphia: Temple University Press.

Dignan, D. 1981. Europe's melting pot: a century of large-scale immigration into France. *Ethnic and Racial Studies.*

Elias, N. [1939] 1973. *La civilisation des moeurs.* 2d ed. Paris: Calmann-Lévy.

Glazer, N., ed. *Clamor at the Gates: The New American Immigration.* San Francisco: ICS Press.

Halbwachs, M. 1932. Chicago expérience ethnique. *Annales d'histoire économique et sociale.*

———. 1964. *La Mémoire collective.* Paris: PUF.

Marx, K. [1852] 1876. *Le 18 Brumaire de Louis Bonaparte.* 2d ed. Paris: Editions Sociales.

Mathiez, A. 1918. *La révolution et les étrangers. Cosmopolitisme et défense nationale.* Paris: La Renaissance du livre.

Moheau,—. [1778] 1912. *Recherches et considérations sur la population de la France.* Paris: P. Geuther.

Noiriel, G. 1988. *Le creuset francais.* Paris: Seuil.

———. 1989. Une histoire sociale du 'politique' est-elle possible? *Vingtième Siecle.*

————. (forthcoming). La France aux Francais! in *Les lieux de mémoire*, ed. P. Nora. 5 vols. Paris: Gallimard.

Rochard, J. 1883. *Bulletin de l'Académie de Médecine.*

Siegfried, A. 1946. La France et les problemes de l'immigration et de l'émigration. *Les Cahiers du Musée Social,* nos. 2–3.

Silberman, R. 1989. Statistiques, immigration, et minorités. In *L'immigration à l'université et dans la recherche,* nos. 6–7, ed. P. Vielle.

Tocqueville, A. de. [1835] 1981. *De la démocratie en Amérique.* 2d ed. Paris: Flammarion.

Weber, E. 1976. *Peasants into Frenchmen.* Stanford: Stanford University Press.

4

AMERICAN ETHNIC STATISTICS

Stephan Thernstrom

Americans have long been a statistically minded people. An amazing number of American males today walk around with their minds cluttered with the batting averages of their current and past baseball heroes. And the United States, of course, has long been the strongest magnet for immigrants in world history, the recipient of more newcomers from abroad than any other society: more than 53 million since 1820, slightly less than the current population of France (see table 4.1). In addition, British North America was a multiracial society from its beginnings, as a result of the presence of peoples indigenous to the area and the large-scale importation of black people from Africa. Among the facts we have gathered most diligently are those concerning who we are in the sense of what racial and ethnic subgroups we belong to. A review of the rich body of statistics we have compiled about the changing ethnic composition of our population reveals not only how our society has changed but also how our conceptions of which distinctions are meaningful and which are not have altered over the centuries.

The British colonies in North America that eventually became the United States were ethnically heterogeneous from the start. In the early seventeenth century, newly arrived English settlers confronted and displaced the indigenous peoples already there, the Indians. Just how many Indians there were at the time of first contact is the subject of current debate, with estimates running from the once-standard figure of somewhat under 1 million to no less than 18

TABLE 4.1

Immigrants Admitted and Immigration Rate per
1,000 Residents per Decade, 1820–1988

	Immigrants (1,000)	Rate
1821–30	152	1.2
1831–40	599	3.9
1841–50	1,713	8.4
1851–60	2,598	9.3
1861–70	2,315	6.4
1871–80	2,812	6.2
1881–90	5,247	9.1
1891–1900	3,688	5.3
1901–10	8,795	10.4
1911–20	5,736	5.7
1921–30	4,107	3.5
1931–40	528	.4
1941–50	1,035	.7
1951–60	2,515	1.6
1961–70	3,322	1.7
1971–80	4,493	2.1
1981–88	4,711	2.5
TOTAL	54,367	3.3

Source: U.S. Bureau of the Census 1990, 9.

million, three times the estimated population of the British Isles at the opening of the seventeenth century (Snipp 1989, 5–23). When estimates vary by such a wild order of magnitude, the sensible reader will throw up his or her hands in despair. All that we can be sure of is that the native population of North America declined disastrously after contact with Europeans, partly as a result of warfare but more from their lack of immunity to European diseases. The disease environment in the entire western hemisphere was less complex than in Europe (and Africa, for that matter); even mild childhood diseases such as measles, mumps, and whooping cough take a death-dealing epidemic form in a "virgin" population (McNeill 1976, ch. 5; Crosby 1972).

The next element of heterogeneity was provided by Africans, who first landed in Virginia in 1619 but did not become a significant demographic presence or a major source of labor until late in the seventeenth century. Thereafter their numbers multiplied rapidly, partly from the international slave trade but also because, unlike most slave populations in the western hemisphere, they had a strikingly high rate of natural increase. There were fewer than seven thousand blacks in the colonies in 1680 and almost six hundred thousand a century later. Although the United States did not ban the import of new slaves from abroad until 1808, from 1720 on the slave population grew more from natural increase than from the international slave trade. Slave births exceeded slave deaths by a large margin. By the opening of the nineteenth century there were a million blacks in the U.S. If the colonial black population had had the same low birth rates and high death rates of slaves in the British West Indies, there would have been only 186,000 (Fogel 1989, 32–33).

The sporadic censuses conducted by the various colonies took pains to distinguish between the three groups. Thus the Virginia census of 1624–1625 counted 1,202 whites, twenty-three Negroes, and two Indians (U.S. Bureau of the Census 1975, 1171). The Indian figure is obviously preposterously low, considering the fact that Chief Opechancanough was able to enlist enough followers to kill off more than a quarter of the white settlers in the unsuccessful uprising he led in 1622. The two enumerated Indians were apparently those who remained within the pale of English civilization, not the vast majority who fled into the interior beyond the line of white settlement after their attack on Jamestown was repelled. Similar problems plague all Indian population data until after the last Indian wars in the closing decades of the nineteenth century. Until 1890, the only Indians counted by the census taker were those "living in the general population of the various states"; those living on reservations were ignored, as were those still roving free. Most Indians were not regarded as members of the community but rather as citizens of distinct "domestic nations," and accordingly no need was felt to enumerate them (U.S. Bureau of the Census 1975, 3–4).

Black people, though subordinate, were members of the community, increasingly necessary in the southern plantation colonies that became dependent upon a slave labor force. All colonial censuses, not just those in the South, distinguished blacks from whites. The Connecticut census of 1755, for example, enumerated 123,334 whites, 3,019 Negroes, and 617 Indians. The Maryland census that same year distinguished whites from mulattos and mulattos from blacks, and subdivided the latter two categories into free persons and slaves. Having some white blood was a crucial advantage; 40 percent of the mulattos but less than 1 percent of the Negroes were free. The Massachussetts census a decade later recorded whites, Indians, Negroes, and mulattos together, and a curious category of "French neutrals" (presumably Acadian residents in northern Maine, then part of Massachussetts, who had not aligned themselves with France during the recently concluded French and Indian War). This is the first and sole instance in American colonial statistics of a classification based upon national origin or ethnic allegiance rather than race (U.S. Bureau of the Census 1975, 1169–70). Racial differences were what counted, and what hence were counted.[1]

The population of British North America became increasingly heterogeneous in the eighteenth century as a result of the large-scale immigration of Scottish, Welsh, Scotch-Irish, German, Dutch, Huguenot, and Sephardic Jewish newcomers. Immigration was easy and was encouraged by authorities in a country that had a superabundance of land and a paucity of settlers (Thernstrom 1980, 486–88, 734–36). The prevailing attitude was well expressed in the directions the Dutch West India Company gave to Peter Stuyvesant, the governor of New Netherlands (soon to become New York), when he asked whether he should admit Jewish and Quaker immigrants: "Although we heartily desire that these and other sectarians remained away from there, we very much doubt whether we can proceed rigorously against them without diminishing the population and stopping immigration. You may therefore shut your eyes and allow everyone to have his own belief" (Handlin 1967, 62). European newcomers were regarded as different from blacks and Indians, but were not sharply distinguished from the original English settlers or from each other. Where you came from and what your religious beliefs were, so long as you were white, did not matter in a society committed to the most rapid possible growth. It is revealing that none of the censuses conducted sporadically by the various colonies distinguished the foreign born from the native born, much less people from English, German, or Dutch backgrounds. It was assumed—and indeed proved largely correct—that all white groups would blend in rapidly. There were ethnic tensions in the colonies, to be sure —between the Dutch and English in New York, and the Germans, English, and Scotch-Irish in Pennsylvania, for example. But the German pietist sects that created their own little island communities, isolated from the melting pot around them, were the rare exception (Thernstrom 1980, 406–8).

Following the Revolution, the Constitution that went into effect in 1789 placed immigrants on equal footing with the native born, with the sole exception that the president had to be a "natural-born" citizen or a citizen of the United States by the time the new frame of government was ratified. It empowered Congress to "establish a uniform rule of naturalization" to specify how alien newcomers were to be incorporated into the national community. The residence period prior to eligibility for citizenship was initially set at two years. It was then raised to five, briefly increased to fourteen in the late 1790s when the reigning Federalist party was fearful of the influx of French and Irish immigrants favorable to Jeffersonian Republicans, and then returned to five, where it has remained ever since (Thernstrom 1980, 736–37).

The Founding Fathers were as eager to encourage immigration as their predecessors, and one of the principal incentives to attract newcomers was full membership in the political community after a short probationary period. The desire was not simply to recruit a needed labor force, as was the case with indentured servants in early Virginia or later in Australia. It was more generally to populate the land. Another striking indicator of the prevailing faith in the absorptive capacity of the society was that for the first three decades of the nation's existence, until 1819, no record was made of the number of aliens entering the country. The volume of immigration in the period was quite low, due to the disruption of transatlantic shipping caused by the Napoleonic wars, but it is nonetheless suggestive that no effort was made to count entrants.

In one respect the Constitution was a giant step towards the modern statistical age. It required a decennial census of the population of the nation, making the United States the first country in the world to commit itself to a regular, systematic enumeration of its inhabitants. Its prime purpose was to reallocate representation in Congress in accord with shifting population patterns. One of the chief points of contention in the quarrels leading up to the Revolution had been American rejection of the British concept of "virtual representation," which held that the apportionment of seats in a legislature need not be closely tied to population distribution (Bailyn 1967, 161–70). A regular census would prevent the appearance of British-style "rotten boroughs," areas that had lost population relative to other places but retained the same political weight they had had when much larger demographically. The mandating of a census also suggests that the Founding Fathers agreed with Adam Smith that "the most decisive mark of the prosperity of any nation is the increase in the number of inhabitants," and were eager to have precise information about how well the United States was doing (Anderson 1988, 7).

In its first half-century, from 1790 to 1840, the U.S. census was a barebones population count that offers few data of interest to the student of immigration and ethnicity. Although the range of questions expanded over the period, these inquiries provided only the sparsest information about the characteristics of the population, distinguishing only whites, slaves, free blacks, and Indians (very imperfectly enumerated), and subdividing these groups into broad gender and age categories.

By the time of the 1850 census, the population of the nation had multiplied spectacularly—from under 4 million in 1790 to over 23 million—and a far more complex, nationally integrated economy had emerged. These developments created a need for a more elaborate national accounting system, and led to the decision to gather individual-level data about a host of social characteristics that had been neglected by early censuses. One of them was country of birth, about which a question first appeared in the census of 1850. This new interest in finding out more about who the American people were in terms of national origins was doubtless dictated by the fact that the flow of newcomers from abroad had risen from a trickle to a flood by midcentury (see table 4.1). An average of about fifteen thousand immigrants a year, almost all from Europe, entered the United States in the 1820s; by the 1840s it was more than ten times that, roughly 170,000 a year.

Of course the receiving population had grown greatly in the interim as a result of the high rate of natural increase of the native population. The significance of an immigrant influx, however large, obviously depends upon how many people are there to receive them. Thus we must look at the immigration rate per one thousand residents, which soared sevenfold from the 1820s to the 1840s (table 4.1). By this measure, the 1840s rank just a shade behind the 1850s, the 1880s, and the first decade of the twentieth century as record decades. (The 8.4 per thousand rate for the 1840s, it might be noted, was more than triple that for the 1980s).

The decision to enumerate the foreign born for the first time in the census of 1850 reflected the unease that some Americans were beginning to feel about this invasion, which stemmed not only from the unprecedented volume of immigration but also from the fact that the two largest flows were from Ireland and the German states, the vast majority of the former and a sizeable minority of the latter being Roman Catholics. The United States was already exceptional in its religious diversity and religious tolerance, but it was still an almost entirely Protestant nation, and Catholics were widely regarded as a menace. These newcomers clustered in the largest American cities, the Irish in the Northeast and the Germans in the Midwest, where they formed voting blocs that often tilted the balance of political power (Ward 1971). Nativist hostility against the newcomers mounted in the 1840s and reached a crescendo in the early 1850s, when the American or "Know-Nothing" party became the dominant political force in a number of states, before the sectional rivalry between the slave South and the free North became the overriding issue and brought the newly founded Republican party (1854) to power (Handlin 1959, ch. 7; Gienapp 1987).

Although the Know-Nothings fanned the flames of prejudice, their platform did not call for a ban on further immigration nor for the creation of a permanent *gastarbeiter* status. There were no demands for mass deportation of the foreign born like those heard in some European states today. The Know-Nothings sought only a lengthening of the naturalization period to twenty-one years and a bar against Catholics holding political office. The beliefs that immigration was on the whole beneficial to America, even if some particular immigrants were undesirable, and that opportunity to become incorporated into the political community should be made available, were too widely held for stronger exlusionary measures to gain significant support.

Although concern over the volume and characteristics of the growing immigrant stream lay behind the decision to distinguish the foreign born in the 1850 census, country of birth was a regrettably crude measure of the ethnic affiliations of the population. A substantial fraction of the almost 1 million Irish born living in the United States in 1850 were Ulster Protestants, who not only failed to blend with their Catholic countrymen as fellow Irishmen but who in fact detested them and were at the forefront of anti-Catholic nativist movements until late in the century. In popular thought, though not in the census, the concept "Irish" quickly was narrowed to Irish-Catholic, while the Protestant Irish disappeared into the melting pot. Likewise, the more than 350,000 immigrants from England and Scotland living in the United States at midcentury included many Irish Catholics who had been born in Liverpool or Glasgow. They assumed not an English or Scottish but an Irish identity. Similarly, the country-of-birth figures that identify almost six hundred thousand German immigrants residing in the United States in 1850 fail to distinguish German Jews from Catholics and Protestants, even though the former tended to associate with themselves more than with their fellow countrymen, and the Catholic-Protestant cleavage divided the German community. Still, country-of-birth data allow us to map the ethnic composition of the population with considerably greater accuracy than is possible prior to 1850.

When the children of that prewar immigrant stream came of age after the Civil War, it became apparent that in may ways they were more like their parents than like "plain Americans"—in their voting and fertility patterns, for example. They stood out, and the census takers recognized this by adding a new question on the 1870 census, about parental nativity as well as nativity. The tabulations showed that there were 5.5 million immigrants in the United States that year, over 14 percent of the population; another 5.3 million persons were the American-born children of immigrant or mixed parentage (the second generation), 13 percent of the total (table 4.2).

It is noteworthy that there was no parallel expansion of census categories when the grandchildren of the first great immigration wave at midcentury came of age. Until very recently, no attempt was made to gather data on the ethnic background of American whites beyond the second generation (see note 4). The prevailing assumption was that, after two generations, whites would be so melted that it made no sense to attempt to distinguish third- and later-

TABLE 4.2
Percent of U.S Population Foreign Born or of Foreign Stock,
1850–1980

	Foreign Born	Native Born Foreign Parentage	Foreign Stock
1850	9.7	NA	NA
1860	12.8	NA	NA
1870	14.4	13.3	27.7
1880	13.3	16.5	29.8
1890	14.7	18.3	33.0
1900	13.7	20.6	34.0
1910	14.8	20.5	35.3
1920	13.2	21.5	34.7
1930	11.6	21.1	32.7
1940	8.8	17.6	26.4
1950	6.9	15.6	22.5
1960	5.4	13.2	18.6
1970	4.7	11.4	16.1
1980	6.2	10.9	17.1

Source: Bureau of the Census 1975, 19; U.S. Bureau of the Census 1990, 41. Since the second generation was not enumerated in 1980, the 1980 figures for the native born of foreign parentage and the foreign stock are from the 1979 Current Population Survey; U.S. Bureau of the Census 1982, 10.

generation immigrants. This stands in sharp contrast with truly multiethnic societies like the Soviet Union (perhaps we should say multiethnic empires), in which the various "nationalities" vigorously and successfully strive to preserve their separate identities. Despite strenuous efforts to create a "new Soviet man," the inhabitants of the U.S.S.R. continue to identify as Latvians, Armenians, or Russians (Connor 1984; Connor 1978; Silver 1974; Silver 1978; Anderson and Silver 1983). Likewise in Canada, the census has long inquired into the "racial origin" of the population beyond the second generation, defined as the ethnicity of the first paternal ancestor to have come to Canada. Doubtless this was due to the unmistakable presence of an unmelted French minority comprised largely of the descendants of settlers who preceded the English in the area (Ryder 1955; Porter 1965, ch. 3).

To emphasize the rapid assimilation of European white immigrants by the third generation, and the consequent lack of interest in gathering data about more than nativity and parental nativity, is not to minimize the extent to which immigrants and their children aroused hostility on the part of old-stock Americans. In a country of 40 million in 1870, the presence of over 10 million people either born abroad or brought up in households headed by immigrants was bound to attract some unfavorable attention. Furthermore, these strangers were not randomly scattered across the land. By the late nineteenth century, men and women of "foreign stock" (the first and second generation together) comprised *two-thirds* or more of the population of virtually every large city in the industrial center of the economy, the manufacturing belt running from Boston to Baltimore in the East and from St. Louis to Milwaukee in the West. In the cities of the industrial heartland, the immigrant minority was in fact the majority—a large majority. Conversely, only one immigrant group was less strongly concentrated in cities of twenty-five thousand or more than were native-born whites of native percentage—Mexican-Americans, employed largely in southwestern agriculture. Every other foreign group was more urbanized than old-stock natives, and some of them—Irish, Italians, Poles, Germans— were urbanized at triple the rate of the native born of native percentage (Ward 1971). This pattern of concentration made them highly visible, and an easy target for those looking for scapegoats.

In the late nineteenth century, the census returns became an important source of—or at least rationalization for—nativist concerns about the immigrant invasion. From 1790 to 1860, the decennial growth of the population had averaged a bit over 35 percent per decade, a stunningly high figure. Thereafter, despite continued massive influxes from abroad, the decennial growth rate declined substantially. For the years from 1860 to the turn of the century, it averaged a bit under 25 percent, a drop of 29 percent from the antebellum average. With American fertility levels falling steadily, immigration became increasingly important as a source of population growth. In the 1820s, natural increase was responsible for 96 percent of the population increase, net immigration only 4 percent. By the 1850s, immigration accounted for 31 percent of the growth; by the 1880s it was 38 percent (Thernstrom 1980, 476).

Many contemporary observers, though still devoted to the gospel of growth, did not see immigration as a welcome force offsetting the fertility decline of native families. Not at all. Francis A. Walker, a leading statistician and the superintendent of the censuses of 1870 and 1880, worried that natives were committing "race suicide." Immigration was not the solution to the "problem" of declining rates of population growth; it was, he insisted, the cause of the problem. Why were native Americans having smaller and smaller families? It was all the fault of the immigrant. The sight of immigrant families living in squalor and misery provided old-stock Americans with "sentimental reason strong enough to give a shock to the principle of population":

The American shrank from the industrial competition thus thrust upon him. He was unwilling himself to engage in the lowest kind of day labor with these new elements of the population; he was even more unwilling to bring sons and daughters into the world to enter into that competition (Walker 1891).

This fear that traditional American culture was being undermined, that those with the strongest claim on the American past were destined to become an impotent minority in the near future, lay behind the immigrant restriction movement that took shape in the economically troubled 1890s and triumphed with the passage of anti-immigrant legislation between 1917 and 1924.

The treatment of black Americans in official statistics was more or less consistent between the time of the first census and the Civil War. As in the various colonial censuses, blacks were distinguished from whites and were divided into the categories "Slave" and "Free Colored." Very little information was gathered about slaves, roughly nine out of ten blacks. In 1850 the free population was counted as "White," "Black," or "Mulatto"; the figures for mulattos were not published, but were instead merged with those for blacks, out of a desire to deny public recognition of the unmistakable fact that racial mixing had taken place on a fairly large scale. Powerful southern white congressmen also successfully resisted proposals for more detailed coverage of slaves, fearing that evidence revealing that they typically lived in families vulnerable to being torn apart by the slave trade would provide valuable ammunition to the antislavery forces. Hinton Rowan Helper's 1857 volume, *The Impending Crisis of the South,* employed aggregate census statistics to demonstrate that the South lagged well behind the North in economic and social development. Additional census information about the condition of the slaves might have been even more embarrassing and dangerous (Anderson 1988, ch. 2).

After the war and emancipation, the slave category naturally disappeared. In the 1880 census, blacks and mulattos were recorded as "Colored," reflecting the prevailing societal assumption that having any visible traces of non-white origins was the decisive desideratum. "One drop of black blood," it was believed, "makes you black." The 1890 census seemed to break from this binary assumption by displaying great interest in gradations of blackness; it painstakingly distinguished 6.3 million Negroes, 957,000 mulattos, 105,000 quadroons, and 70,000 octoroons. However, the published tables ignored these fine gradations of blackness and lumped all Negroes together as a subdivision of the general category "Colored," alongside Indians, Chinese, and Japanese. In 1910 there was again an attempt to divide Negroes into "Black" (7.8 million) and "Mulatto" (2.1 million). If these figures are meaningful—which is questionable—there had been a good deal of race mixing between the 1890 and 1910 canvasses. While the Negro population had increased 24 percent, that of mulattos had doubled (U.S. Bureau of Census

1918). Thereafter, "Mulatto" disappeared as a census category, although a mulatto elite continued to occupy the upper rungs of the social ladder within the black community in such cities as Boston, Philadelphia, and Washington, D.C. for decades to come (Williamson 1980, ch. 3–4).

The first Asian immigrants to enter the United States—Chinese indentured servants and a small group of merchants who arranged for their passage and employment—came to California with the Gold Rush of 1849. In the 1850 census, the 758 Chinese immigrants in the country were classified by country of birth, like other immigrants. By 1860, however, the group, then grown to thirty-five thousand, was given its own category as members of a distinct "Oriental" race. The "Yellow Peril" aroused much deeper fears than the invasion of European immigrants, hence Asians were classified separately within a decade of their first arrival. Unlike nativity and parental nativity, race was a category one could not escape with the passage of time and the succession of generations. After two generations, European whites were just plain Americans, at least from the census taker's point of view. Even after three or more generations, it was assumed, the Chinese, like Indians and blacks, would still be Chinese, and consequently different in ways that had to be counted. Similar treatment was accorded Japanese immigrants, who arrived in the closing decade of the nineteenth century and the opening decade of the twentieth. Other Asian newcomers, of whom Filipinos and Koreans were the most numerous, were subsequently registered as members of the Oriental race. Asians were singled out as special in immigration law as well—especially unwelcome—with a series of restrictive measures like the Chinese Exclusion Act of 1882, the 1907–1908 "Gentlemen's Agreement" with Japan, and the 1917 creation of an "Asiatic Barred Zone." Movement from the Philippines, an American possession, was the exception.

Some recent scholarship on the history of Mexican-Americans emphasizes parallels between their experience and that of Asians and blacks, and various federal affirmative action programs in the past two decades have rested on the assumption that Mexicans—or more broadly and even more questionably, all "Hispanics"—have suffered comparable discrimination and disadvantage (Camarillo 1981). It is significant, though, that the compilers of the U.S. census did not identify Mexicans along with blacks, Asians, and Indians as a separate racial group when they first became a significant element of the population. The first sizeable cluster of Mexicans to reside in the United States appeared as a result of American territorial acquisitions following the Mexican War (1846–1848). An estimated eighty thousand former Mexican citizens (many of whom prided themselves on their Spanish rather than their Mexican identity) living in the Southwest from Texas to California chose to remain there after Mexico ceded the territory to the United States by the terms of the 1848 Treaty of Guadalupe Hidalgo. And yet the 1850 census reported only 13,317 foreign-born Mexicans in the country. Apparently these thirteen thousand were Gold Rush immigrants; the eighty thousand people annexed in 1848 were evidently classified as native born, strangely, on the grounds that they had been born on what by 1850 had become American soil!

From 1840 to 1930, Mexican-Americans were identified by the same criteria as those used with European whites—nativity and (from 1870) parental nativity. By 1930, however, the sharp rise in immigration from Mexico in the preceding decade and the outburst of tribalism that led to severe restrictions upon European immigration prompted the creation of a new census category —persons of Mexican "race." Mexican-Americans had previously been considered white. The enumerator's instructions for 1930, however, declared that Mexicans were "of a racial mixture difficult to classify, although usually well recognized in the localities in which they are found." Persons of Mexican descent who were not "definitely white," or Negro, Indian, Chinese, or Japanese, were to be counted as of "Mexican race," whatever their nativity and parental nativity (Jaffe, Cullen, and Boswell 1980, ch. 5). In practice, this seems to have meant that lighter, middle-class Mexican-Americans of whatever generation were not categorized as of the Mexican race; conversely, darker-skinned Mexican laborers, even those whose families had been living in the United States for three or more generations, were demoted to nonwhite status. In 1930, unlike today, there were no advantages in being officially categorized as nonwhite; far from it. Thus Mexican-American groups and the Mexican government protested vigorously against the action. The 1930 data were accordingly retabulated in accord with the traditional criteria of nativity and parental nativity, and the Mexican race question was dropped in the 1940 census. As a result of political pressures, Mexican-Americans rejoined the white race.

At the turn of the century, the data on American ethnic groups provided by the Bureau of the Census and other federal agencies grew in volume and became considerably more refined. Beginning in 1899, immigration officials went beyond the crude compilation of figures by country of origin and began to distinguish newcomers by "race or people," allowing the student of immigration to separate Armenians from Turks, and to distinguish the many peoples from the Russian and Austro-Hungarian empires, for example. Thus it can be determined that a mere 2 percent of the more than six hundred thousand immigrants from Russia who arrived in the years 1899–1904 were actually ethnic Russians; 42 percent of them were Jews, 27 percent Finns, and 10 percent Lithuanians (Thernstrom 1980, 1036–37).

The census takers, though, did not follow the lead of the immigration authorities and provide similarly refined information about immigrants and their children already in the United States in a census year, as opposed to just those entering (and often subsequently leaving) the country. The Bureau of the Census, however, did add one extremely useful question to the census schedules—one on "mother tongue," defined in slightly different ways over the years but always with a core meaning of the language spoken in the respondent's home when he or she was a child (Thernstrom 1980, 1039–40, 1053–58, 1067). These have been useful to scholars attempting to sort out various immigrant groups coming from the same country of origin.[2]

Although more refined data about the multitude of ethnic groups flocking to American shores in the late nineteenth and early twentieth centuries were becoming available, they did not enter significantly into the popular debate over immigration policy that took place then. Evidence was there to reveal quite striking differences in the adjustment to America among the most recent arrivals—among, for example, East European Jews, Greeks, Slovaks, Hungarians, and Italians. Natives who had contact with these various groups certainly recognized distinctions among them, as is indicated by the proliferation of such individious labels as "hunkey," "kike," "wop," and "greaser." However, the "we-they" distinction that became politically salient was that between the "old" immigrants—supposedly all sturdy individualists who accepted democratic principles and contributed to the country's rapid economic advance—and the "new" immigrants, alleged to be unassimilable and a grave menace to society. The conventional wisdom was summed up in *The Passing of the Great Race,* by Madison Grant, a prominent anthropologist of the day:

The new immigration . . . contained a large and increasing number of the weak, the broken, and the mentally crippled of all races drawn from the lowest stratum of the Mediterranean basin and the Balkans, together with hordes of the wretched, submerged populations of the Polish ghettos. Our jails, insane asylums, and almshouses are filled with this human flotsam and jetsam, and the whole tone of American life, social, moral and political, has been lowered and vulgarized by them. (Grant 1916, 89)

Census data on country of birth made it possible to divide the immigrant population into "old" (pre-1880s) and "new" (post-1880s) arrivals. The Bureau of the Census itself did not provide summary tabulations of data in these crude categories. They were instead developed and made relevant to policy in the massive forty-one–volume report of the U.S. Immigration Commission (1907–1910). The commission might more accurately have been named the Immigration Restriction Commission. It approached the issue with the preconceptions embodied in the Madison Grant passage quoted above, and manipulated the evidence—some of it from the census, some gathered through its own inquiries—to make it fit those preconceptions. More than three decades ago, Oscar Handlin subjected the commission's report to a withering critique that has never been refuted, and there is no need to repeat it here (Handlin 1957). Suffice it to say that this huge "study" lent the authority of science to nativist prejudices against strangers in the land that were growing ever stronger.

America's traditional open door to immigrants was closed—or at least narrowed to a crack—by the quota system enacted in the 1920s. The leaders of the restrictionist movement made plain that their target was not immigrants in general but the new immigrants specifically. They found it politically awkward to write their prejudices into law in such a naked form, however, and sought to develop a seemingly neutral statistical formula that would in fact cut back radically on the entry of the groups they found most distasteful (Anderson 1988), ch. 6). The first major restrictive bill, signed into law in 1921, set an annual quota on immigration from each country at 3 percent of the size of the group as determined by the 1910 census. That discriminated against the new immigrants, to some degree, because many earlier northern and western European newcomers were still alive to be counted in 1910, even though those countries were no longer major sources of incoming immigrants.

The discriminatory impact of the 1921 law upon immigration flows, though substantial, was not great enough for the most ardent restrictionists. Hence another much more radical measure was passed in 1924. The 1924 National Origins Act set new temporary quotas on the basis of the number of immigrants residing in the United States in *1890*, before all but a handful of newcomers from eastern and southern Europe had begun to arrive. The only possible rationale for the choice of the 1890 baseline was that it preceded the arrival of the new groups who were thought to be so troublesome. By this device they could be kept out without going so far as to name them explicitly.

The 1924 law also enjoined the Census Bureau to calculate the "national origins" of the entire white population at the time of the 1920 census. Once developed, these figures would replace the 1890 census figures as the basis for the quotas. Newcomers would be admitted in numbers proportional to their contribution to the growth of the American population since the beginning of the republic. It was a clever ploy. While the 1890 standard was patiently biased, there was a specious fairness in the principle that newcomers should be admitted to the United States in numbers that would keep the current ethnic mix of the population unchanged. When carried out, the required calculations, as expected, resulted in quotas that were about the same as those derived from the 1890 figures. That the English had been in the country for many more generations than the Poles and thus had much more opportunity to leave descendants in the American population pool was too complicated an objection to this device to carry much weight.

Census officials were not altogether enthusiastic about the assignment, but had no choice in the matter. Restrictionists were well aware of the advantages of having an objective, quantitative standard, however spurious, to appeal to. When one of the few congressional critics objected to the principle of freezing the ethnic shape of the nation via quotas, the rejoinder was that "the gentleman does not agree with the census." Even with the aid of eminent population experts named by the American Council of Learned Societies, the task of determining the "national origins" of the population proved exceedingly difficult, and the calculations that were finally developed rested upon a series of highly dubious assumptions (American Council of Learned Societies 1932; MacDonald and MacDonald 1980; *William and Mary Quarterly* 1984).[3] They went into effect in 1929, however, and set the basic framework of American immigration law until the major reform enacted in 1965.

The triumph of immigration restriction was not altogether surprising. Certainly there were grounds for abandoning the old faith that the capacity of the country to absorb newcomers was unlimited, and for imposing a ceiling on the total admitted. The United States was no longer an underpopulated nation with an open frontier. The old laissez-faire faith in the beneficent workings of the free market was under heavy attack by Progressive reformers who called for state intervention in the public interest. American trade unions argued with some plausibility that workers should be protected from the vicissitudes of the international labor market, just as manufacturers were protected by tariff barriers. The resort to the country-of-origin quotas that were so biased, however, reflected the triumph of racist propaganda that blamed all of America's social ills not on such internal forces as urbanization and industrialization but on external ones—the supposed inferiority of the new breed of immigrant.

The restrictionist legislation of the 1920s achieved its ends. Given the ardent conviction of some students of contemporary immigration that legislative prohibition can never significantly cut the flow of job-hungry migrants across international borders, it is noteworthy that there seems to be no historical debate at all over whether the national-origins quota system did what it was supposed to do. Apparently it did. It cut the number of new arrivals per year to about three hundred thousand by the late 1920s, very few of them the eastern and southern Europeans who had been pouring in in such large numbers. Entries by "new" immigrants plunged to a mere 3 percent of their average prewar level. Arrivals now were mostly from either the "old" immigrant countries or from Canada or Mexico, the latter because the quota laws did not cover immigration from the western hemisphere.

The Great Depression that began in 1929 made entry into an America of breadlines and soup kitchens far less attractive. Only half a million immigrants arrived in the entire decade of the 1930s, and somewhat more than that number returned home. Net immigration for the decade was actually negative. Immigration resumed on a large scale after World War II, however. Although the restrictive quota system remained in force, special exemptions were made for refugees and displaced persons who would otherwise have been barred, Hungarians and Czechs fleeing oppressive Communist regimes, for example. And then in 1965 a radically new immigration law increased the ceiling on newcomers and discarded the discriminatory national-origins quotas altogether. Immigration rose from 1 million in the 1940s to 2.5 million in the 1950s, 3.3 million in the 1960s, 4.5 million in the 1970s, and will total about 6 million for the 1980s (table 4.1). (In addition, there has been an unknown but undoubtedly quite large flow of illegal immigrants.)

In absolute numbers these figures are extremely high. The 1980s saw the entry of more immigrants than any previous decade in American history except 1901–1910, quite possibly more if one includes illegal arrivals. But considered as a *rate* relative to the receiving population, current levels of immigration are low by historic standards. The 1980s immigration rate of 2.5 per thousand residents is below the average for the entire period since 1820 (3.3), less than a third of what it was in the two decades before the Civil War, and not even a quarter of what it was for the peak 1901–1910 decade (10.4). The absolute numbers are very large, but the size of the receiving population is far larger than earlier.

In looking at current immigration flows we see that the absolute numbers are large, and the rate is relatively low. The size of these flows may be looked at from a third vantage point as well. How many of the world's immigrants are coming to the United States as compared to other countries? In the nineteenth-century era of mass immigration, about two-thirds of the world's immigrants made the United States their destination. It is striking that the figure is about the same today. No other country rivals the United States in its attractiveness to newcomers and its willingness to accept a great many of them. The era of completely unrestricted immigration is long over, but something of the old American confidence in society's capacity to absorb and benefit from the presence of people born in other lands has been restored.

The character of immigration to the United States has shifted dramatically as a result of the 1965 law. The hostility towards Asian newcomers that had marked American immigration law since the Chinese Exclusion Act of 1882 at last came to an end in 1965. Since then over 4 million Asians, 41 percent of total immigration, have entered the country, with the Philippines, China, Korea, and Vietnam being the leading countries of origin (table 4.3). Latin America is the other major source of contemporary immigration, accounting for another 41 percent of the total since 1971. Mexico alone has sent 1.2 million legal immigrants, as well as an uncounted number of illegal ones.

In terms of their educational and occupational backgrounds, recent immigrants fall into two classes. Most Asians are well educated, with 73 percent of them high school graduates and over a third (36 percent) with college degrees. Many move into professional or managerial occupations; there are currently twenty thousand physicians from India practicing medicine in the United States. Newcomers from Latin America, especially Mexico and Central America, resemble typical immigrants to the United States before World War I, arriving with very little in the way of human capital. Some 77 percent of immigrants from Mexico have less than a high school education, and only 3 percent are college graduates. For entrants from the Dominican Republic the figures are 70 and 4 percent; for those from El Salvador, Nicaragua, Guatemala, and Panama, 74 and 4 percent (U.S. Bureau of the Census 1990, 41). They are able to gain entry because since 1965 American immigration law has given enormous priority to "family unification" considerations, and these groups have an abundance of relatives already in the country. Whether they still play the positive role their predecessors did, in an economy radically different from that of an earlier America, is an open question (Borjas 1990).

Three issues in the politics of ethnic statistics in the current period stand out — the treatment of Asian groups, the creation of an Hispanic ethnic group, and the issue of the definition and enumeration of the Indian population. Although Asians have been as free as Europeans or others to move to the United States for the past quarter-century, they continue to be treated in a special way in official statistics — as a permanent racial group rather than as one that merits enumeration because they or their parents were born in another land. The grandchildren or great-grandchildren of Chinese arriving in the United States in 1855 or of Japanese landing in 1895 are still counted separately. The only changes are the substitution of the term "Asian" for the now-invidious "Oriental," and a shift in how individuals are placed in the category. Up through the 1950 census, racial classification was made on the basis of the enumerator's observation: "she looks Chinese to me." In 1960 the enumerator's judgment was supplemented by the self-classification of the

TABLE 4.3
Sources of Immigration, 1971–1988

Total entrants (1,000)	9,204
Percent from	
Europe- 14.3	
Asia- 41.3	
Canada- 2.2	
Latin America- 41.2	
Other- 1.0	
Leading countries (1,000)	
Mexico- 1,206	
Philippines- 735	
China*- 589	
Korea- 544	
Vietnam- 495	
Cuba- 415	
India- 377	
Dominican Republic- 331	
Jamaica- 306	

Source: U.S. Bureau of the Census 1990, 10.
* Includes Taiwan and Hong Kong.

individual respondent, though how the balance was struck in case of discrepancies is not clear. In 1970 the Census Bureau made self-classification the determining criterion.

This was a very important conceptual shift, making ethnicity a matter of choice, a state of mind rather than a matter for genealogists to determine: "It doesn't matter if you don't think I look Chinese. I feel Chinese; ergo I am Chinese." Why this might seem desirable is obvious, but, as we shall see below, it was problematic when certain ethnic choices but not others brought official rewards. By 1970, only 40 percent of the 429,000 Americans of Chinese race and a mere 20 percent of the 593,000 of Japanese race were foreign born, and a good many were third generation or more. Why the race of their remote ancestors should still be regarded as a datum worthy of recording was hard to discern, particularly in light of the fact that about half of native-born Asians were marrying whites. However, being singled out as nonwhite, once an invidious distinction, had become advantageous in the age of affirmative action. That groups with educational and income levels well above the national average still qualify as disadvantaged racial minorities seems quite anomalous. It does, though, help colleges and universities fill their quotas for "minority" students and faculty members, since there are so many Asian academic high achievers.

Statistics on the socioeconomic status of an Asian group comprised partly of people resident in the United States for generations and partly of people who have arrived within the past two decades are obviously of very limited value, and summary data on "Asians" in general that mix Cambodian tribesmen in the United States for only a few years with third-generation Japanese-Americans are virtually useless. The problem has been compounded by the Census Bureau's highly unfortunate decision to drop the century-old parental nativity question from the 1980 census, a decision not rescinded in 1990 despite many complaints from researchers. The loss of information on second-generation Asians precludes the systematic investigation of patterns of assimilation from generation to generation.

Current data on "Hispanics" also need to be approached with caution. Although protests from the group itself prevented Mexicans from becoming a distinct race as a result of the census of 1930, they have since been treated in a quite special and rather curious fashion. Some group spokesmen now insist, somewhat ironically in light of that earlier history, that they are not white but "people of color." In 1950 the Census Bureau attempted to enumerate all "white persons of Spanish surname" residing in the five southwestern states with the heaviest concentrations of Mexican-Americans (Grebler 1970, 601–4). This assumed that, at least in the Southwest, Mexicans were distinctive even unto the third and fourth generations. The resulting data were open to challenge, since many Mexican-Americans lacked common Spanish surnames, especially women who had married out of the group, and possibly even more non-Hispanics had such names, including non-Hispanic women who had married Hispanic males (Petersen 1987, 223–29).

Beginning in the late 1960s the Census Bureau came under pressure from Hispanic activists who naturally wished to claim maximal numbers for their constituents. That pressure resulted in the creation of a new ethnic group, "Hispanics," where before there had been Mexican-Americans, Puerto Ricans, Cuban-Americans, and more than a dozen others from various Spanish-speaking countries. The number of Americans in this new-born umbrella category, which includes peoples who differ radically in their education, incomes, fertility, geographical concentration, political leanings, and on virtually every other social indicator, has grown enormously in the past three decades, from less than 7 million to almost 20 million (table 4.4). In the 1970–1980 decade, the period of its most rapid apparent growth, the Hispanic population increased at *seven times* the rate for non-Hispanics. Some of this growth was doubtless real, the result of heavy immigration and of the high fertility of many, though

TABLE 4.4
Growth of the Hispanic Population

	Number (millions)	Percent Change
1960	6.9	NA
1970	9.1	32
1980	14.6	60
1990 (est.)	19.9	36

Source: Bean and Tienda 1987, 59; estimation, U.S. Bureau of the Census 1990, 14.

by no means all, Hispanic groups. A substantial part of it, though, was an artifact of changes in census procedures in counting Hispanics.

In 1970 the Census Bureau made estimates of the "Spanish heritage" population, based upon the traditional, more or less objective criteria of birthplace, parentage, Spanish surname, and Spanish mother tongue. In addition, it added a new, much more subjective question — whether individuals considered themselves of Spanish/Hispanic "origin or descent." This was a more expansive definition of the group, and one highly susceptible to shifting political currents that made it appealing and perhaps advantageous to choose such an identity. It was not employed as the major identifier of the Hispanic population in 1970, but would be in 1980.

Pressures for a better — defined, it appears, as a larger — count grew with the political mobilization of Hispanic groups. The 1975 appointment of a Census Advisory Committee on the Spanish Origin Population for the 1980 census reflected those pressures. Unlike advisory committees that had assisted the bureau in the past, this one included several members who had no social-science expertise; their credentials were only that they held office in Hispanic organizations (Choldin 1986). (Similar committees of black and Asian-American activists were also created.)

The stakes in the business of ethnic enumeration became increasingly important with the growing national commitment to affirmative action. If Hispanics in general were taken to be "disadvantaged" and in need of special efforts to insure their "full representation," in order to set appropriate "goals and timetables" one needed to know how many there were, and the larger the estimate the greater the benefits assigned to the group. A 1978 directive of the Office of Management and Budget codified current common practice in specifying that all federal statistics must categorize the American population into five groups: whites, American Indians or Alaskan Natives, Asians or Pacific Islanders, Blacks, and Hispanics, defined as persons "of Mexican, Puerto

Rican, Cuban, Central or South American or other Spanish culture or origin, regardless of race" (Lowry 1982).

The 1980 census used the Spanish/Hispanic origin question developed for 1970, and employed it as the basis for its Hispanic count. The desire for a maximal estimate is suggested by the fact that it asked every American the question, "Is this person of Spanish/Hispanic origin or descent?" — despite the presence in the census of another question about ancestry.[4] If you were a German-American or Polish-American, you had one chance to indicate it. Hispanics, it seems to have been assumed, needed to have two in case they missed the first opportunity (Petersen 1987; Bean and Tienda 1987, 45–47; Lowry 1982). Politics rather than logic explains the anomaly. The separate query was a success, if getting a larger body count was the criterion — as it was. Responses to the Spanish/Hispanic origin question yielded a million (13 percent) more Mexicans, half a million (39 percent) more Puerto Ricans, and two hundred thousand (35 percent) more Cubans than answers to the general ancestry query (Lowry 1982). Why the larger numbers could be assumed to be more accurate than the smaller ones was not evident. But the Census Bureau found it politic to err on the side of perhaps inflated rather than possibly deflated figures.[5] Its advisory committee on the Spanish-origin population fervently believed the more the better, and no organized group had a strong interest in more modest estimates.

The question of the racial composition of the Hispanic group is interesting and unresolved. A number of spokesmen maintain that they are not white, but not black either — not quite. They are of a unique mixed race *(La Raza)*, the argument goes, but are definitely "people of color" who suffer disabilities comparable to those of blacks (Camarillo 1981). This seems dubious, given the fact that many have lighter complexions than many Italians, Greeks, or other Mediterranean peoples, and given that they frequently marry whites. It is far from clear how many Hispanics actually consider themselves "people of color."[6] The 1970 census classified them as white.[7] On the 1980 census, a solid majority of them — 55 percent — classified themselves as white on the race question, and only 3 percent reported themselves as black (U.S. Bureau of the Census 1983, 1:21). Almost all of the remaining 42 percent wrote in "Spanish" or "Hispanic," leaving it unclear whether they actually considered themselves nonwhite or simply had not understood what information the elusively worded race question was seeking.[8]

The American Indian component of the population has grown even more rapidly than that of Hispanics in recent decades, having almost quintupled since 1950 (table 4.5). None of this rise, obviously, can be attributed to immigration. Some of it is due to natural increase; Indian fertility rates are

TABLE 4.5

The American Indian Population, 1930–1988

	Number (1,000)	Percent Change
1930	343	NA
1940	345	1
1950	357	3
1960	524	32
1970	793	51
1980	1,367	72
1988	1,699	24

Source: Snipp 1989, 64; U.S. Bureau of the Census 1990, 17. Figures are for persons who claimed to be of Indian "race"; the numbers claiming at least partial Indian ancestry are much larger (see text).

high and mortality rates have declined sharply. In 1940, Indian life spans were 24 percent below those of whites; by 1980 the gap was only 5 percent. However, a close demographic study indicates that only 39 percent of the dramatic Indian population gains in the 1970s could be attributed to changing vital forces (Snipp 1989, 71–72). Most of it was due to changes in self-identification. Until 1960, when the Indian population began to soar at an unprecedented rate, census enumerators made racial designations on the basis of their own judgment, and may have decided that many people of Indian blood didn't "look Indian." Since 1960, it has been up to the individual respondent to claim whatever racial identity he or she prefers, and some Indians previously missed accordingly now show up in the Indian category. The tendency to claim Indian identity was doubtless accentuated in the 1970s by affirmative action policies that provided special educational and job benefits to those so identified.

The problem of determining who is an Indian and who is not is greatly complicated by the little-known fact that the extent of intermarriage between Indians and whites has long been very high, and the offspring of mixed unions accordingly have options as to their ethnic identity. Historical studies of the phenomenon are lacking, but in 1980 only *48 percent* of the married males classified as Indian on the census had Indian spouses, and for married females the figure was *46 percent* (Snipp 1989, 157). Indians are actually more likely to marry whites than they are fellow Indians! (In-group marriages are more common among those dwelling on reservations, not surprisingly, but another little-known fact is that only a quarter of all Indians now live on reservations, with another 15 percent living on lands close to reservations. Almost half — 49 percent — live in metropolitan areas.) The level of black marriages with whites at the same time, by contrast, was under 2 percent. That a very high level of marital mixing also took place in the past as well is suggested by the fact that no less than *6.7 million* people claimed to be of at least partial Indian ancestry on the 1980 census. Thus, the number who claim some biological basis for identification as Indians is almost *five times* the 1.4 million the Census Bureau so classified in 1980.

This suggests a general problem with assigning benefits to people in particular ethnic categories when they themselves determine in which category they belong. For example, there was the 1989 case of two Boston men, apparently white, whose claims to be black were challenged after they were appointed to the police force on the basis of examination scores too low to qualify them had they been white but high enough for members of a group that was "underrepresented."[9] There are now powerful incentives to dredge up, or even make up, an Indian, Hispanic, or black grandmother and claim status as a member of a disadvantaged minority. The problem could become especially acute with the American Indian category, because there are so many people not presently classified as of the Indian race who maintain that they have some Indian blood.

If benefits are to be provided to people on the basis of the ethnic identity they claim, it may follow that we need gatekeepers to check credentials and accept or throw out the claim. If what group one belongs to determines what is a passing score, it seems anomalous to leave it to the individual to choose that group. In many societies, ethnic identity is not chosen but assigned on the basis of proven bloodlines. In the Soviet Union, for example, every citizen is designated to be of a particular "nationality," which is stamped upon his or her internal passport. The only people who have a choice as to nationality are the products of mixed marriages, who may opt for the group identity of one or the other parent. It would be difficult to introduce such a system in the United States, where ethnicity — except for nonwhites — has had such a strongly voluntaristic character, and where the mixing of the population through intermarriage has been very great not only for Europeans but in recent times for Indians, Hispanics, and Asians as well (Alba 1981; Gurak and Fitzpatrick 1982; Horowitz 1985, 81–84; Lieberson and Waters 1988, ch. 6–7).

It is a telling comment on ethnic relations in the United States today that a recent fanciful prediction about the impending emergence of a nonwhite population majority — a "minority majority" — has been accepted uncritically, and indeed with a certain amount of relish. Although no competent demographer has endorsed the claim, the belief that whites will be outnumbered by "people of color" by the year 2050 has gained surprisingly widespread credence since a cover story, "Beyond the Melting Pot," appeared in an April 1990 issue of *Time* magazine (*Time* 1990). Before long, the argument runs, native whites will be outnumbered by blacks, Asians, and Hispanics, therefore, the ebbing white majority must act now to improve the current lot of ethnic minorities. If whites empower the new majority before it takes over, once in the driver's seat it will be nicer to whites.

The theory of the emerging minority majority is simply the race suicide theory reborn, with a new spin. The fear-mongering race suicide theory incited Americans to guard the gates more vigilantly, to keep out the rabble. Now, similar population projections are being brandished as evidence of the need for their inclusion through bigger and better social programs.

Whatever the merits of particular programs advocated on the basis of the premise of an impending minority majority, the theory is built on sand. The Census Bureau has not been so incautious as to endorse this wild claim. It knows that population projections far into the future are of little value because the determinants of growth — fertility, mortality, and immigration — cannot be predicted accurately. Its most remote projection of the ethnic composition of the population is for 2025, at which time it expects that the proportion of Americans who are black or of "other race" will rise from today's 15.8 percent to 21.1 percent, hardly a dramatic gain. (We might note, for comparison's sake, that in 1910 immigrants, their children, and blacks together made up 46 percent of the population, and immigrants then were widely perceived as being a threatening alien presence.) And the bureau is far from certain, properly so, about the size of the total population of the United States at that date, its lowest projection being 262 million and its highest 349 million (U.S. Bureau of the Census 1990, 15). Any guess as to the size of the minority component of the population must be equally uncertain.

A brief look at current growth rates of blacks, Asians, and Hispanics offers little support for the minority-majority theory. The fertility rate for black women is currently about 30 percent higher than for white women, with an average of 2.3 expected births per woman compared with 1.8 for whites (U.S. Bureau of the Census 1990, 65). This differential has recently been shrinking a little. It was 33 percent in the late 1950s, and 37 percent as late as 1965. A 30-percent fertility differential on the part of a small minority does not result in dramatic changes in group size, particularly when the group also has above-average mortality rates.

The black share of the population has not been growing rapidly over the past several decades. It was 9.9 percent in 1920, 10.0 percent in 1950, 11.1 percent in 1970, and is expected to be a bit over 12 percent when the returns of the 1990 census are in, an extremely modest rise over a period almost as long as an average lifetime (U.S. Bureau of the Census 1990, 17). (Of course we know that the census takers are unable to provide a fully accurate count of blacks, but there is no reason to believe that the undercount was less in earlier enumerations. If anything, the undercount was probably smaller in recent censuses, since the problem has been recognized and efforts have made to overcome it.) The diminution of black-white fertility differentials reflects the rising educational level of blacks and the growth of a black middle class (Farley and Allen 1987, 89–102), and is likely to continue if those trends continue. Even if they do not, at their current growth rates blacks will remain a small fraction of the population even a century hence.

The spectacular growth of the Asian population of the United States since 1965 has been almost entirely attributable to immigration. The major Asian groups in the United States — Chinese, Japanese, Koreans, and Filipinos — are not notably fecund. If the proportion of Asians in the population were to rise so precipitously as to constitute a "problem" in the eyes of most Americans, the solution would be quite simple. The flow could be cut back as easily it was begun, by modifying the immigration law.

The striking growth of the Hispanic population over the past three decades has been the result of heavy immigration from Latin countries, the generally high fertility of Hispanic immigrants and their children, and changes in census enumeration procedures designed to maximize the size of the group. It is questionable whether most Hispanics in the future will be any more persuaded that they are "nonwhite" than are those today. Furthermore, the popular impression that Hispanic fertility is extraordinarily high is exaggerated. Cubans have a lower fertility rate than native American whites, and many other Hispanic groups do not have conspicuously large families. According to the 1980 census, the most fecund Hispanics — Mexicans and Puerto Ricans — had fertility rates that exceeded those of whites by 39 and 35 percent, respectively, and those of blacks by 9 and 6 percent — significant differential, but hardly an earth-shaking one, and far smaller than the gap between the fertility of natives and many European immigrant groups at the turn of the century. Furthermore, Hispanics born in the United States have fewer children than their immigrant parents, and their children have fewer still. In 1980 the fertility rate of native-born Americans of Mexican parentage was 15 percent below that of Mexican immigrants; for Puerto Ricans born on the mainland the generational fertility drop was 37 percent. With rising levels of education Hispanic distinctiveness diminishes further. The fertility of second-generation Mexican-American high school graduates is only 6 percent above that of non-Hispanic whites with equal schooling. For those with some college, the difference is only 1 percent, and second-generation Mexican-Americans with college degrees have 7 percent *fewer* babies than non-Hispanic white women with the same educational attainments (Bean and Tienda 1987, 216–32).

Thus there are two glaring flaws in the minority-majority theory. Projecting current fertility differentials far into the future ignores the wealth of evidence, historical and contemporary, that with assimilation, high-fertility immigrant groups adopt native patterns. Theorists of "race suicide" assumed that once a Ukrainian always a Ukrainian, even unto the third and fourth generations. They were utterly wrong, not least because with each passing generation a growing proportion of the descendants of the immigrants married people of different backgrounds. It continues to happen with Asians and Hispanics today.

The second fallacy in the projection of a minority majority is the assumption that immigration will continue at its present high levels and will be governed by the same entry criteria that have produced the current mix of groups. Since 1965 our immigration law has given overwhelming priority to "family unification"; nine out of ten entrants now come in on that basis. This, in effect, strongly discriminates against prospective entrants from countries that have been behind the Iron Curtain for a generation, and favors groups like Mexicans, who have many relatives already on the scene. Giving less priority to family considerations and more to the possession of skills in short supply in the American economy would bring in fewer Mexicans and more Czechs, Poles, and East Germans. That may or not be desirable. The point is that the system could easily be changed if there were a will to do so.

If today's immigrants assimilate to American ways as readily as their predecessors at the turn of the century, as seems to be happening, there won't be a minority majority issue. Whatever their origins, these immigrants will have joined the American majority, which is not determined by bloodlines but by a commitment to the principles for which this nation stands.

However, what happens to today's and tomorrow's immigrants will be shaped by societal expectations, and today the conception that assimilation is desirable finds little support among ethnic activists and the liberal community generally. The thrust of federal policy has been towards dividing the population into closed, ascriptive tribal compartments in order to allocate resources more equitably.

The government of France has traditionally been much less assiduous in gathering data about the ethnic composition of its population than has that of the United States. This policy may have been wise. American researchers are naturally happy to have more information to work with than their French counterparts. However, official statistics can have important *effects* upon how people think about themselves and their society. The collection and dissemination of ethnic data may itself heighten group consciousness, harden group lines, and accentuate differences that would otherwise be more manageable.

NOTES

1. William Petersen's otherwise excellent "Politics and the Measurement of Ethnicity" (1987) errs in suggesting that slaves and Indians were classified separately from whites in the first U.S census merely because the Constitution specified that they did not have the same weight as whites for purposes of political representation. This neglects the fact that both groups were consistently distinguished from whites in all censuses taken in British North America before 1790, and the further point that free Negroes — who were supposed to be counted like whites for political representation — were nonetheless carefully distinguished from whites.

2. In 1910 and 1920, the mother-tongue question was asked of all first- and second-generation immigrants. In 1930 it was asked only of the foreign born residing in cities of twenty-five thousand or more. In 1940, for the first time, the native born of native parentage were included in the mother-tongue inquiry. No mother-tongue question was asked in 1950. In 1960, it was asked only of immigrants. The 1970 census provides the richest body of material for analysis. Comparing mother-tongue figures with those on language currently used in the home offers important insights into the assimilation process. It provides overwhelming evidence of the extent to which second-generation immigrants growing up in households with mother tongues other than English themselves employed English as their "usual language," a profoundly important shift. For Chinese and Japanese it was 90 percent; for Germans 96 percent; for Greeks and Poles 98 percent; for Russians and Italians 99 percent. The exception was Mexicans, and even in that case a large majority — 63 percent — had shifted to English as their usual language in the home. For a fascinating international comparison of the rates at which immigrants in societies around the world have shifted from their mother tongue to the dominant language in their new homeland, see Lieberson and Curry (1971). The authors conclude that the rate of shift to the national language in the United States stands out as exceptional and "rather phenomenal."

3. The American Council of Learned Societies' estimates of the "nationality" of the population of the United States in 1790, developed in accord with the 1924 quota law, have been uncritically reproduced by a surprising number of scholars ever since, and are included in the generally reliable *Historical Statistics of the United States*. Since its publication in 1975, historians have subjected the figures to withering criticism. The whole enterprise was fraught with error. Forrest and Ellen MacDonald argue forcefully that the ACLS overestimated the proportion of the population that was English and underestimated the share of Celtic stock. Other specialists are equally skeptical (MacDonald and MacDonald 1980; *William and Mary Quarterly* 1984).

4. The new question about the "ancestry" of the population asked in 1980 was supposed to tap distinctive group identities beyond the second generation, but it is questionable whether it offers as much information of interest as the parental-nativity question, which was dropped to make room for it. (There would have been room to retain it but for the inclusion of a separate Spanish/Hispanic origin question, whose only raison d'être was that it would yield larger numbers.) Stanley Lieberson and Mary Waters have written an excellent volume analyzing the results (Lieberson and Waters 1988.) There are interesting nuggets to be gleaned from this material. However, answers to ancestry questions have a dismally low level of consistency and other serious flaws (Thernstrom 1989). Perhaps the most striking finding of the inquiry was an unintended one that the Census Bureau ignored in its analysis of the findings (U.S. Bureau of the Census 1983, "Ancestry"). Despite strong prodding from the census taker to answer in terms of some origin outside the United States, 6 percent of respondents insisted that their ancestry was simply "American" and another 10 percent answered "don't know." Plain Americans constituted the fifth largest ancestry group when defined as only those who gave "American" as a response, and were considerably larger still if the "don't knows" are included with them (Lieberson and Waters 1988).

5. It is curious that Bean and Tienda's exhaustive analysis of the 1980 census data (1987) fails to mention and evaluate these conflicting estimates, even though the authors cite the Lowry paper that raises the issue forcefully (Lowry 1982). They do mention that the March 1980 Current Population Survey estimated the total Hispanic population at 1.4 million (10 percent) less than the census count only one month later, but somehow see this, rather oddly, as evidence that "the Hispanic population was underestimated throughout the 1970s" (52). It could more easily be interpreted as evidence that it was overestimated in the 1980 Spanish-origin item. Bean and Tienda reassure us that answers to the origin question square well with more objective indicators like place of birth, surname, and language spoken in the home (51), which they say "supports earlier evidence" presented in Johnson (1974). In fact the Johnson study showed that over a fifth (21.1 percent) of the people who identified with a Spanish-origin group on the 1971 Current Population Survey gave a *different* origin on the CPS just one year later. About half of these inconsistent identifiers named another Hispanic group the second time around, but 12 percent of all those in the Hispanic category had abandoned it altogether within twelve months. This suggests that Hispanic identity is not as clear-cut and immutable as is sometimes believed.

6. Given the widespread currency of the argument that Hispanics are "people of color," it is surprising and disappointing that the Bean and Tienda study (1987) does not explore the issue, and indeed barely mentions race in its more than four hundred pages. Furthermore, a question fundamental to any consideration of Hispanics as a racial group or even a distinct ethnic group is that of patterns of endogamy and exogamy. Do they largely marry within the group? When they marry out, do they marry "people of color," with whom they allegedly have so much in common, or do they marry whites? There is extensive evidence of high rates of Hispanic exogamy, and the majority of those exogamous marriages are to whites (Horowitz 1985, 81–84; Gurak and Fitzpatrick 1982; Lieberson and Waters 1988, 173–76). Bean and Tienda offer only one sentence on the issue of intermarriage

(94). This contrasts with Grebler's major earlier study of Mexican-Americans, which includes an entire chapter on "intermarriage as an index of assimilation," showing it taking place on a very large scale (Grebler 1970, ch. 17). Likewise, the Lieberson and Waters volume in the same Russell Sage Foundation 1980 Census Monograph series in which Bean and Tienda appears devotes two of its eight chapters to the issue of ethnic intermarriage. The companion volume on blacks (Farley and Allen 1987) safely neglects the topic of black-white marriages because they are still so rare. Readers of Bean and Tienda will unfortunately be left with the mistaken impression that the same holds true for Hispanics.

7. Apparently some Hispanics did not classify themselves as white on the 1970 race question but instead checked "other" and specified Mexican, Puerto Rican, Cuban, etc. How many did this we don't know, because the Census Bureau considered that such responses indicated persons of "Indo-European stock" and hence tabulated them as white (U.S. Bureau of the Census 1972, sec. 2, app. 15).

8. The 1980 census race question was very curiously framed, making the results for some groups extremely ambiguous. Although the bureau was committed to racial classification of the population, for some reason it delicately shied away from the term "race" on the enumeration forms. Instead of asking respondents, "What is your race?" item 4 of the schedule was worded, "Is this person . . . ?", with choices beginning with White, then Black or Negro, then Japanese, Chinese, Filipino, etc. — a total of fourteen choices plus an "other" category. Only one answer was allowed, forcing people of mixed race to make a choice. The list of options began with two traditionally recognized racial groups, but quickly shifted into identifications having more to do with national or territorial origins, most of them subdivisions of what used to be called the Oriental racial group. "Hispanic" was not given as an option. Did the 42 percent of Hispanics (as measured by the Spanish/Hispanic origins question) who opted for "other" on the race item mean to declare that they were not white, the first choice given? Or were they cued by the several national-origins choices that followed to look for their national group, and, not finding it, to choose "other" and write in "Mexican," "Puerto Rican," or some other Hispanic label? When challenged, a spokesman for the bureau explained that the word "race" was omitted from the question because "it didn't apply to all the alternatives listed" (Lowry 1989). It didn't indeed. But why was this strange laundry list of alternatives provided in the first place? This belongs in the introductory sociology textbooks as a classic example of how not to pose a question.

9. The practice of "race norming" job tests is very common; no less than forty state employment bureaus were doing it as of 1986. The percentile ranking of candidates by test scores is computed comparing blacks only to other blacks and Hispanics to other Hispanics. A score that placed a white candidate in the fiftieth percentile would put a black in the eighty-fourth percentile. Top scorers from each group are then referred for jobs, without it being made clear to employers that bonus points have been awarded to blacks and Hispanics to inflate their performance level (Blits and Gottfredson 1990).

REFERENCES

Alba, Richard M. "The Twilight of Ethnicity among American Catholics of European Ancestry." *Annals of the American Academy of Political and Social Science* 454 (March 1981):86–97.

American Council of Learned Societies. "Report of Committee on Linguistic and National Stocks in the Population of the United States." In *Annual Report of the American Historical Association, 1931.* Vol. 1. Washington, D.C., 1932.

Anderson, Barbara, and Brian Silver. "Estimating Russification of Ethnic Identity among Non-Russians in the U.S.S.R." *Demography* 20 (November 1983):461–89.

Anderson, Margo J. *The American Census: A Social History.* New Haven: Yale University Press, 1988.

Bailyn, Bernard. *The Ideological Origins of the American Revolution.* Cambridge: Harvard University Press, 1967.

Bean, Frank D., and Marta Tienda. *The Hispanic Population of the United States.* New York: Russell Sage Foundation, 1987.

Blits, Jan H., and Linda Gottfredson. "Employment Testing and Job Performance." *The Public Interest* 98 (Winter 1990):18–25.

Borjas, George J. *Friends or Strangers: The Impact of Immigration on the U.S. Economy.* New York: Basic Books, 1990.

Camarillo, Albert. "Blacks and Chicanos in Urban America: Some Comparative Perspectives." Unpublished paper. 1981.

Choldin, Harvey M. "Statistics and Politics: The 'Hispanic Issue' in the 1980 Census." *Demography* 25 (August 1986):403–18.

Connor, Walker. *The National Question in Marxist-Leninist Theory and Strategy.* Princeton: Princeton University Press, 1984.

Connor, Walker. "A Nation is a nation, is a state, is an ethnic group, is a . . ." *Ethnic and Racial Studies* 1 (October 1978):377–400.

Crosby, Alfred W. *The Columbian Exchange: Biological and Cultural Consequences of 1492.* Westport, Conn.: Greenwood Press, 1972.

Farley, Reynolds, and Walter R. Allen. *The Color Line and the Quality of Life in America.* New York: Russell Sage Foundation, 1987.

Fogel, Robert W. *Without Consent or Contract: The Rise and Fall of American Slavery.* New York: Norton, 1989.

Gienapp, William E. *The Origins of the Republicans Party: 1852–1856.* New York: Oxford University Press, 1987.

Grant, Madison. *The Passing of the Great Race.* New York: Scribner, 1916.

Grebler, Leo, et al. *The Mexican-American People: The Nation's Second Largest Minority.* New York: Free Press, 1970.

Gurak, Douglas T., and Joseph P. Fitzpatrick. "Intermarriage among Hispanic Groups in New York City." *American Journal of Sociology* 87 (January 1982):921–34.

Handlin, Oscar. *The History of the United States.* Vol. 1. New York: Holt, Rinehart, and Winston, 1967.

———. *Boston's Immigrants: A Study in Acculturation.* Rev. ed. Cambridge: Harvard University Press, 1959.

———. *Race and Nationality in American Life.* Boston: Little, Brown, 1957.

Horowitz, Donald L. "Conflict and Accommodation: Mexican-Americans in the Metropolis." In *Mexican-Americans in Comparative Perspective,* edited by Walker Connor. Washington, D.C.: Urban Institute Press, 1985.

Jaffe, A. J., Ruth M. Cullen, and Thomas D. Boswell. *The Changing Demography of Spanish Americans.* New York: Academic Press, 1980.

Johnson, Charles E., Jr. "Consistency of Reporting of Ethnic Origin in the Current Population Survey." *Current Population Survey,* Technical Paper #31. Washington, D.C.: GPO 1974.

Lieberson, Stanley, and Timothy J. Curry. "Language Shift in the United States: Some Demographic Clues." *International Migration Review* 5 (1971):125–37.

Lieberson, Stanley, and Mary C. Waters. *From Many Strands: Ethnic and Racial Groups in Contemporary America.* New York: Russell Sage Foundation, 1988.

Lowry, Ira S. "Counting Ethnic Minorities in the 1990 Census." Unpublished paper, 1989.

———. "The Science and Politics of Ethnic Enumeration." In *Ethnicity and Public Policy,* edited by W. A. Van Horne and T. V. Tonnesen. Milwaukee: University of Wisconsin System American Ethnic Studies Coordinating Commitee/Urban Studies Consortium, 1982.

MacDonald, Forrest, and Ellen MacDonald. "The Ethnic Origins of the American People, 1790." *William and Mary Quarterly* 37 (1980):179–99. 3d series.

McNeill, William H. *Plagues and People.* Garden City, N.Y.: Anchor Doubleday, 1976.

Petersen, William. "Politics and the Measurement of Ethnicity. In *The Politics of Numbers,* edited by William Alonso and Paul Starr. New York: Russell Sage Foundation, 1987.

Porter, John W. *The Vertical Mosaic: An Analysis of Social Class and Power in Canada.* Toronto: University of Toronto Press, 1965.

Ryder, Norman B. "The Interpretation of Origin Statistics." *Canadian Journal of Political and Social Science* 21 (November 1955):466–79.

Silver, Brian. "Ethnic Intermarriage and Ethnic Consciousness among Soviet Nationalities." *Soviet Studies* 30 (January 1978):107–16.

———. "Levels of Socioeconomic Development among Soviet Nationalities." *American Political Science Review* 68 (December 1974):1618–37.

Snipp, C. Matthew. *American Indians: The First of This Land.* New York: Russell Sage Foundation, 1989.

Thernstrom, Stephan. "Counting Heads: New Data on the Ethnic Composition of the American Population." *Journal of Interdisciplinary History* 20 (Summer 1989):106–16.

Thernstrom, Stephan, ed., *Harvard Encyclopedia of American Ethnic Groups.* Cambridge: Harvard University Press, 1980.

Time. 9 April 1990. "Beyond the Melting Pot," 28–35.

U.S. Bureau of the Census. *Statistical Abstract of the United States.* Washington, D.C.: GPO, 1990.

———. *1980 Census of the Population: General Population Characteristics, U.S. Summary.* Washington, D.C.: GPO, 1983.

———. *1980 Census: Supplementary Report,* "Ancestry of the Population by State," PC80-SI-10. Washington, D.C.: GPO, 1983.

————. "Ancestry and Language in the United States, November 1979." *Current Population Reports: Special Studies*. Series P-23, no. 116. Washington, D.C.: GPO, March 1982.

————. *Historical Statistics of the United States: From Colonial Times to 1970*. 2 vols. Washington, D.C.: GPO, 1975.

————. *1970 Census of Population: Characteristics of the Population, U.S. Summary*. Washington, D.C.: GPO, 1972.

————. *Negro Population of the United States*. Washington, D.C.: GPO, 1918.

Walker, Francis A. "Immigration and Degradation." *Forum* 11 (1891):637–44.

Ward, David. *Cities and Immigrants: A Geography of Change in Nineteenth-Century America*. New York: Oxford University Press, 1971.

William and Mary Quarterly, "The Population of the United States in 1790: A Symposium." *William and Mary Quarterly* 41 (1984):85–135.

Williamson, Joel. *New People: Miscegenation and Mulattoes in the United States*. New York: Free Press, 1980.

5

FRENCH IMMIGRATION STATISTICS

Roxane Silberman

French literature on immigration has not been much concerned with statistical methodology, even though in France these statistics are relatively old and sound, compared with examples in other European countries of immigration.

This "taking of inventory" of foreigners is practically contemporary with the adoption of modern censuses (1851) because from the second half of the nineteenth century on, France was aware of a significant stream of immigration. From census to census, statistics have proliferated, resulting recently in publication of special reports just for this population. The first feature of the census is thus its long history.

The second feature is that it is linked to the state's central administration: almost all population statistics originate in the census and the complementary studies were based on censuses of the settled population (supply) and the data produced by immigration control organizations: border crossings and registration with the Office National d'Immigration (ONI), today called OMI. Quantitative studies, carried out by independent research bureaus, are rare. The information produced by the state dominates the field and is relied on, for better or for worse, by researchers.

I say "for better or for worse" because the literature is punctuated with critical remarks about the validity of statistics about foreigners. The emphasis is thus put on the problem of taking stock of a population that, when it arrives, is more transient than the native population and more likely to live in the types of housing (reception centers, dormitories at worksites, rooming houses) that are difficult for the census to identify. The emphasis is also on the inappropriateness of the categories that were designed for the French population, for example, the socioprofessional categories or those based on education and qualifications that do not easily apply to transient foreigners. These criticisms do not, however, prevent the writers (most often sociologists, sometimes economists) from reasoning on the basis of these statistics. Deeper but less open criticism comes primarily from anthropologically oriented research, which depends less on quantitative data. Anthropologists, interested in kinship and in daily and cultural practices, and who study subjects such as endogamy or the fabric of a community, work with populations that are not legally "foreigners" or "immigrants" (individuals born elsewhere). But this type of research doesn't really affect statistical method, since it doesn't rely on quantitative data.

The xenophobic movement, which orchestrates the political debate about potential changes in certain clauses of the Nationality Code, targets not only foreigners but also people who have acquired French nationality and children born in France to foreign parents (thus generally French at adulthood). Xenophobia shows up in the "inventory" stage with the "rough" estimates of the number of foreigners in France that double or even triple the number reported in the official census (Front National, an anti-immigrant political party of the Right).

Neither the xenophobic movements nor reappraisals of the Nationality Code are new in France. Nonetheless, the public reaction to these movements over the issue of statistical categories is remarkable.

When the "Committee of Wise Men," composed of members from many political groups, is given the responsibility for a report on the acquisition of French nationality and complains about the "lack of statistical data" (Commission de la Nationalité 1988), when studies (contractual research financed by the administration) about the population previously unexplored by census categories (second generation) suddenly multiply, and when INSEE is being asked about the possibility of introducing a supplementary question in some questionnaires about the birthplace of the applicant's parents, it would seem that we have a crisis in statistical methodology.

Quantification certainly plays an increasing role in the statistical expression of social and political tensions, but it is by no means the driving force. The appearance on the political scene of young people descended from immigrants (the second generation), in the form of a civil rights movement, also plays a decisive role. The thought that current social tension among communities might differ from tensions in the past, or that methods of integration, considered in France as assimilation, might not function any more resurfaces in every debate. These concerns have stimulated an interest in history (Noiriel 1988) that shows that existing categories and statistics do not reflect the actual outcomes for populations that arrived in the migratory waves that France experienced in the past; they have also caused a sudden interest in the United States and in Anglo-Saxon research about "minorities."

The methodological debate about immigration that is starting to appear in French research is thus strongly affected by the recent character of immigration and its political context, which underlie what is now a very muffled, almost embarrassed debate. This situation has not given rise to sound literature on the subject, although, in other areas, there is significant interest in France about the methodological issues related to statistical categories.[1]

The debate has resulted in a critical approach to statistics on foreigners, which had been perceived as immutable for more than a century. I will show how a certain number of long-accepted *practices* reflect a tradition, and that the political consequences of this tradition weigh heavily on the current methodological debate.

I. FRENCH STATISTICAL METHODOLOGY ON IMMIGRATION: ITS OBVIOUS STABILITY

The 1851 census is the traditional starting point for the first head count taken of foreigners; the French Revolution is the traditional source of certain population categories that count. But it is interesting first to linger for a moment on the earlier period. The 1851 count was linked to the existence, even prior to the Revolution, of a significant stream of immigrants into France. The category and the enumeration of foreigners existed before then, but within a very special perspective.

While the head counts carried out for fiscal and economic reasons from Colbert on don't mention foreigners, this category does appear in two particular "enumerations" (INSEE 1976): those of a few towns with strategic or military concerns (such as ordered by Vauban, 1678–1680) and those carried out in the colonies (for example 1648 in the Antilles), where next to "Europeans" and "Natives" we find the "Foreigners" category. The race to control the colonies played a decisive role in this: settling was connected to ruling, and foreigners threatened French sovereignty.

The first modern census, in 1801, was carried out by a specialized office that initiated a periodic publication. It was preceded by two other efforts during the Revolution, in 1790–1791 and 1793–1794, which gathered information only about gender and legal status. In 1836 an age question was introduced. The 1851 census, which identified nationality, was also the first census to produce, over and above simple head counts, a more complex presentation of statistical data. The appearance of statistics about foreigners was thus truly contemporary, in France, with the birth of modern statistical methodology; it is thus all the more surprising how little attention has been paid to the role of immigration in France's social and economic history, since the relevant categories were not unknown.

The first censuses, in fact, did capture immigration through the legal-nationality category. As obvious as this category may seem to a Frenchman, it is not obvious to others, and indeed the first censuses hesitated, before tipping decidedly towards a political solution.

Even before the 1851 census, the Prefecture reports were interested in foreign presence in France from a different perspective than simple policing (Mauco 1932). The domestic movements and short and long seasonal migrations of labor were the context in which the Prefectures were interested in the presence of a foreign workforce in certain regions. The first censuses demonstrate the same demographic and economic preoccupation with domestic workforce movements. The criterion of nationality thus emerged in a picture that described the population based on origin: in this case birthplace, in or out of France, of French citizens by birth or by naturalization, under the heading of population according to birthplace and nationality. Comments on the presentation of data suggest a connection between domestic migration, the population deficits of certain departments, and foreign immigration. This was the picture in the early censuses before it was replaced by a profile of the population solely identified by nationality.

Between the two types of scenarios, the questions in the census form were not modified. In both cases we find a question about birthplace and another about nationality. But while the hierarchical order of treatment of the two questions was uncertain at the start, it later leaned decidedly in favor of nationality. Foreigners were separated more clearly both from the rest of society and from their own entry into French society as naturalized French citizens. To favor the birthplace (place of origin, according to the terminology used) would have been to override permanently the nationality categories.

Why did statistical methodology focus on the legal-nationality category? Unquestionably for political reasons, which have been exposed elsewhere in this collection, and about which we will not go into detail here. The French mode of integration being in fact a mode of assimilation, the political individual resides entirely in the citizen, an abstract and universal category that owes nothing to the private sphere of origins and roots. We cannot have Breton citizens any more than we can have citizens of foreign origin. In theory[2] there are only either French citizens or foreigners. Demographic concerns (France was the first European country to have a drop in birthrate) and military preoccupations (providing French males for military service) move in the same direction.

This choice was expressed in statistics by the three categories set up by the Nationality Code: French by birth, naturalized French (who acquired the nationality), and foreigners. These categories would continue to appear in every census, giving the impression of agreement and stability. We will see, however, that further along the difficulties linked to this classification gave way to practices quite different from the theories.

Two interpretations of this choice are possible. The first, "French," reflects the desire not to make a distinction among citizens. In this perspective, retaining the memory of origins is equivalent to a denial of citizenship, to a second-class citizenship.

The second interpretation suggests in this choice an expulsion from French society of all who are not citizens even if they live in France, which creates a latent schizophrenia in the system: foreigners find themselves separated from their natural extension in French society — naturalized citizens and the generations, born of foreign parents, who are French at birth. Foreigners remain totally outside of French society, without a French history to look forward to, because to become French is to forget that one was ever a foreigner or had foreigners for parents. We will see that the first reading prevailed, while the second was rendered "impossible" by the political history of efforts to identify the origins of the French. It is clear that the impossibility of tracing the history of the outcome of immigration in France is inherent in this statistical methodology. The "French melting pot" (Noiriel 1988) is synonymous with the absence of an immigrant history.

While preoccupation with demographics came early and is recurrent in France's immigration politics, and while France has transformed a significant portion of the foreigners settled in France into French citizens, no category that keeps track of the number of people entering into the territory really corresponds to a category of "immigration," that is, of permanent settlement on French soil. But in the population data under the categories of the Nationality Code, we find data about "entry flow," linked to the administrative categories of French immigration policies.

Statistics on the immigrant stream are produced by the Office National d' Immigration, which in 1945 took over for employers the recruitment of foreign laborers, and also by the border patrol. The categories correspond to the procedures for entry and are entirely controlled by role in the labor market and migratory status. None of the categories of tourist, student, businessman, seasonal laborer, laborer, family, or refugee corresponds to the concept of permanent settlement. The seasonal laborer and laborer categories are only different degrees of the same thing, and correspond in reality more to the American H_2 program than to the "immigration" category. The family category is entirely dependent on the labor category; it refers to directly dependent members (spouse and minor children with dispensation for other relatives) of "active workers." Even if the families become settlers, the category under which they are classified remains strictly related to work status. In particular, it has nothing to do with the criterion of "family preference" in the American system, which qualifies candidates for settlement as individuals, but can bring "extra credit points" for those with family ties with someone already living but not necessarily working in the United States.

Here too the history of immigrants is partly erased. The dominance of the labor category not only suggests a short-term vision of foreign entry, migratory in nature and outside of French society, but also artificially divides populations that are fundamentally the same: a woman entering as a spouse is not classified as a laborer even if she immediately starts to work; the family ties of a brother, a cousin, a nephew, or an adult son who enters as a laborer disappear, even though these ties play a primary role; a refugee who will have to work is not a "migrant" and not really an "immigrant" since he had no choice but to come. The French categories for keeping track of stocks and flows are thus categories with neither a past nor a future.

Using these categories results in:

- *A static view:* The category for "foreigners" covers successive migratory waves that tend to be mixed together in the same way that a rapid succession of strongly lifelike images produces one image on the retina, giving a static image.
- *Dominance of the labor category:* The work dimension already applied to the entry categories equally dominates the analysis of the settled population, in the sense that it underlies most of the records maintained and published about this population. The data on foreigners' work is the most abundant, with information about lifestyles (consumption, savings, recreation) being much rarer — almost nonexistent.
- *The absence of any indication about role or function in the community:* Items such as spatial concentrations, community functions of certain labor markets, or endogamy are extremely poorly defined for a population that does not fit into the existing legal categories. Thus, the marriage of a child

born in France but of foreign parents with another child also born in France but of foreign parents is considered a marriage of two French citizens, like any other, when in fact it represents a strong endogamy.

• *Separation from other statistics:* The treatment of nationality indicators, never systematic and often inconsistent from one census to the next, is the subject of specialized data. The special documents for all these scenarios perpetuate the exclusion of foreigners from French society.

II. UNCERTAINTY, THE UNSPOKEN, THE PRACTICES: ABOVE AND BEYOND OFFICIAL PHILOSOPHY OR THE BASES OF THE PRESENT DEBATE

The outcome of the statistical procedures thus described appears simple and clear-cut. From one census to the next the principles are the same and the continuity appears strong. However, closer examination of the actual classification process reveals something much hazier, more complex, and less stable, and reveals a tradition that is in conflict with the official philosophy.

The many difficulties fall into three groups:

1. The complexity of the Nationality Code engenders uncertainty on the part of both the individuals being questioned and the questioners. At least three situations bring out these difficulties: first, mixed marriages and their effect on the nationality of the spouses; second, the different procedures for acquiring French nationality, some automatic, some by declaration, and some by decree; and finally, the classification of children born of foreign parents, depending on whether they are born on French territory or not, and on whether or not they are declared French by their parents, some of whom are foreigners until adulthood and then become French afterwards.
2. The modifications made several times in one century in certain parts of the Nationality Code — for example, the effect on nationality of spouses in mixed marriages — increase the uncertainty, and modify, from one census to the next, the size of the populations classified in each category.
3. Finally, the history of decolonization by several stages changed the status of individuals and moved them into different categories.

Faced with these difficulties, the classifying practices of the French census are normally controlled by two simple principles that can conflict, leaving a place for other practices that arise from another tradition altogether.

With respect to nationality, as with other matters, the census relies on the statements of the individuals being questioned. The uncertainties, the voluntary or involuntary errors in the answers, linked to the complexity of the system but also to the discrepancy between the legal situation of the interested parties and their perception of their situation (for example, naturalized citizens who forget their naturalized status as the years pass) are thus numerous. But, in theory, it is individual statements that prevail, even though elsewhere the census states that the principles of the Nationality Code, carefully referenced back to the Nationality Article in the methodological chapters containing the census results, provide the rules for classification. Depending on the information about birthplace, the error or the uncertainty can be more or less evident.

The very principle of resorting to the Nationality Code opens a certain area of uncertainty itself each time the clauses of the code are modified from one census to the next. The census is supposed to stick vigorously to the Code without accounting for the individuals who were classified differently in the preceding census. This is true also for modifications linked to changes in status of a territory (decolonization, status of departments, status of overseas territories).

Thus, in principle, the opportunities for "reclassification" by the questioner are extremely limited. It is the "insufficiency, sometimes even the total lack of responses" that allows "interpretation during the perusal, with the help of other information appearing in the individual questionnaire" (note in the introduction of the 1954 census).

Apparently, however, interpretation turns into "reclassification," because the numbers of foreigners shown by the surveys and those resulting from the simple tabulation of summary forms prepared by towns themselves and given to INSEE before transmission of the questionnaires differed by 104,081 individuals, or 6.7 percent of the total foreign population (1954 census).

In fact, we realize that the practice of reclassification varies enormously with the historic situation and the individuals involved. Thus residents of Alsace and Lorraine who declared themselves German were reclassified French by birth notwithstanding their formal declaration. On the other hand, the latest census (1982) produced an estimate of Algerians who should have declared themselves French but did not follow through with their reclassification.

These reclassification procedures thus not only reflect a simple application of the Nationality Code but affect other underlying ethnic categories as well. It is in the gap attributed to "insufficient or missing" responses that practices go beyond interpretation to become reclassification. This was most notably the case with the French Muslims at the time of Algerian decolonization.

The disguised existence of ethnic categories is diffused throughout all the censuses, discreet in the case of combining some groups, more open in certain periods with problems linked to decolonization and to overseas territories and departments.

The historic origin of ethnic categories in France is of fundamental interest if we want to appreciate the current methodological debate about populations that has resulted from immigration.

The ethnic head counts in *Metropolitan France* are limited and are not within the jurisdiction of official statistics. The existence of regional minorities, for example, partially emigrated outside their department of origin, is only rarely estimated quantitatively and is based on the data provided by local associations or monographs.

The same is true for estimating religions. Taking inventory of the religions in France was initiated by the regime instituted by the Concordat: the state responsibility for paying people who conducted religious services was proportional to the number of people in each religion and thus presupposed an inventory. This head counting disappeared with the end of the Concordat; only in Alsace, remaining under this rule, did this counting persist. Elsewhere the estimates were based on data provided by religious authorities or "unauthorized" cross-checking with certain nationalities (i.e., Muslims).

On the other hand, outside of the home-country areas, the ethnic categories blossomed in official censuses. After colonization, head counts of the "natives" were required, with categories based on nationality (European, French, foreigner), race (white, black, mulatto), and status (slaves, free men, domestics, women, children). On the eve of decolonization and when certain colonies had already made possible the emigration of "natives" to the home country, the situation was the same. We distinguished the native from the European French national in the colonial empire, depending on the status of the territory (colony, protectorate, etc.). The natives could be of French or foreign nationality, depending on the territory's status, and could be French citizens, admitted to French citizenship, or even French subjects. What to call natives took on varied forms that tried to focus "as closely as possible" on subjugated ethnic minorities: members of native tribes, Muslims, etc.

The modifications in access to French citizenship for natives of overseas territories following wartime promises, the change in status of colonial empire territories in 1946, and then decolonization, progressively confused the issue of ethnic labeling. Once eliminated, not without resistance, in the territories remaining French, it reappeared insidiously in the home country with migration from former territories that had become foreign, or from overseas departments.

For Algeria the changes in status introduced in 1946 were not taken into account by the 1946 census, on the pretext that this census took place before the new clauses were operative. The sounds of names (European or Arab) were used to reclassify individuals who "anticipated" the new rules and declared themselves French. In the home-country territory, however, the Muslims of Algerian origin were listed separately. The 1954 census indicated that "even if the Muslims of Algerian origin were French citizens, they received a *special code number,* because they made up a group about which it was helpful to know separately the results of the census, especially with regard to professional activities." Note that the results of this breakdown were published in the part of the report about the working population *devoted to foreigners.*

With independence and the right to choose between French and Algerian nationality, the common law of the home country was again reaffirmed, although not without expressions of regret about the impossibility of keeping the abovementioned breakdown. The category of repatriates without ethnic indication rapidly disappeared. On the other hand, the practice of grouping together Maghreb nationalities in census results was reaffirmed. Moreover, and in contrast to what was done for the Alsatians, individuals declaring themselves or their children Algerian, when in fact they were French, were not reclassified.

The issue of D.O.M.-T.O.M. (Overseas Departments-Overseas Territories) is equally interesting. The much earlier transformation of these territories into overseas departments and territories ended the ethnic-classified census long ago. But at the point where a massive emigration, especially "of natives," towards the home country becomes obvious, use in the home country of the indication of birthplace is authorized, but only for the individuals originating from the D.O.M.-T.O.M countries, just as in low-income, subsidized housing we see quotas for the populations from D.O.M.-T.O.M. countries, as well as for foreign populations.

Thus there exists a tradition of ethnic categories in France with a strong racist and colonial character. This tradition appears clearly, although less openly, in a certain number of secondary practices in relation to the nationality category. They are of two types: on the one hand, a regrouping of nationalities, and on the other, a conjunction of birthplace with nationality.

Regrouping or aggregation of nationalities permits, as a result of apparently technical modifications, the creation of an ethnic category. This practice affects nationalities that are as a rule separately classified in more detailed presentations, in alphabetical order in each continent. In the summary charts (like the one on working population), selected nationalities experience interesting peregrinations, as in the case with Turks who are frequently classified with the Maghrebs. Similarly, the nationalities within the jurisdiction of the European Community are grouped together.

This practice of regrouping affects the three broad categories defined by the Nationality Code. Changes in the category of French by acquisition affects differently, from one census to another, the categories of French by birth and foreigners. In certain censuses, we find almost no breakdown of "French" according to whether they arc French by birth or by acquisition. The widespread reappearance of French by acquisition is accompanied generally by a parallel presentation of these figures with those for foreigners. This almost always corresponds to a rise in xenophobia. From this point of view it is significant that the last census gave rise to an entire volume on the census results concerning the French by acquisition (the volume on nationality). In this volume one sees the emergence of another practice: associating the nationality of French by acquisition with birthplace. The question on birthplace existed from the first census, but was used sporadically and in various ways. We saw it used, in the beginning, equally for French by birth, French by acquisition, and foreigners (see table on origin and nationality in the first censuses). Then it was used for the French by acquisition and, as we have just seen, the populations originating from the D.O.M.-T.O.M. The history of this use, strongly related to the political context, is of interest in connection with the methodological debate that is taking place today in France.

The historic context in which the current debate is taking place does not appear to be neutral. On the one side we find an official tradition that calls for not distinguishing among the French and is solidly buttressed by legal categories; on the other side we find a clearly political history of ethnic labeling linked to xenophobic movements. Thus a certain embarrassment marks the debate in France.

The introduction of a supplementary criterion, the birthplace of parents, in certain studies linked to censuses, appears to be a technical matter, discussed behind the closed doors of the concerned bureaucracies. From the researchers' point of view, the embarrassment is obvious. The "scientific" concern about the future of immigration-based populations, beyond giving them a legal status, contrasts with the perception of a political context in which the debate takes place, and with the political history of French census categories.

The debate remains relatively restrained on this point. It has more impact on the problems of policy and technical feasibility (perception of the questions, reliability of responses) than on the definition of a minority: decisions about how to categorize (children born of mixed marriages), time (how many generations must we go back?), language criteria, religious criteria, and cultural practices in general. It is as if we were witnessing a scientific debate or reappraisal of the policy issue of jus soli (law of the soil): a reappraisal for one generation that lengthens the relevant time span but does not call for a reappraisal of the fundamental relationship between the community of origin and the nation-state.

We can summarize the French case by describing it as a constantly renewed effort, although muffled and hidden, to identify minorities without wanting to reconsider the general structure, which implies a nonrecognition of communities of origin. It is a one-way view of minorities, uniquely linked to the needs of the administration to deal with them. The European Community, however, in which France will find itself reduced to a minority among others within Europe, may totally upset this concept.

NOTES

1. This was the case, for example, with the socioprofessional categories.
2. In theory at least, because although all citizens are French, all French were not always citizens; there was a waiting period for naturalization until recently, and we also have the case of native French citizens of the colonial empire who were subjects, not citizens.

REFERENCES

Commission de la Nationalité. 1988. *Etre français aujourd'hui et demain*. Paris: INSEE (Institut National de la Statistique et des Etudes Economiques) *Pour une histoire de la statistique*. Paris: Imprimerie Nationale. Ed. Christian Bourgeois

Mauco, G. 1932. Les migrations ouvrières en France au début du dix-neuvième siècle. Paris: A. Lesot

Noiriel, G. 1988. *Le creuset français*. Paris: Seuil.

THREE

IMMIGRANT EXPERIENCES: SCHOOL, CHURCH, AND LITERATURE

6

IMMIGRANTS AND SCHOOLING IN THE UNITED STATES

Maris A. Vinovskis

Most Americans are either immigrants or the descendants of immigrants. As successive waves of immigrants came to the New World, they and their children encountered problems of adjusting and adapting to a different environment. Many scholars and the public believe that schools may have played a key role in that transition by either facilitating or hindering the assimilation of immigrants into American life.

This essay will explore the relationship between immigrants and schools in four different time periods: (1) colonial America, (2) antebellum America, (3) the late nineteenth and early twentieth centuries, and (4) the post–World War II period. As will become evident, the relationship between immigrants and schools varied considerably not only according to the characteristics of different groups of immigrants but also according to the changing nature of the American society and economy when they arrived.

Although this essay focuses specifically on immigrants and schools, much of the general education of immigrants often occurred outside any formal institutions in areas such as neighborhoods and workplaces. Nevertheless, by seeing the changing role of schooling in the lives of immigrants over time, we can develop a better appreciation of the diversity of immigrant experiences in the settling of America.

1. IMMIGRANTS AND SCHOOLS IN COLONIAL AMERICA

Many analysts of immigration ignore the early settlers of colonial America. For them immigration is almost exclusively a nineteenth- or twentieth-century phenomenon. This is unfortunate because individual and societal responses to the colonization of the New World provide a useful context for understanding the experiences of immigrants after the American Revolution.

Nearly thirty years ago Bernard Bailyn (1960) provided the classic analysis of the relationship between immigrants and schools in colonial America. Bailyn portrayed the English family as stable, extended, and patriarchal. Children received almost all of their education in the household and the rest was supplied by their neighbors.

The early English settlers brought with them the expectation that children and servants would be educated in a household rather than in a school. But the colonial family was fragmented and disrupted by the wilderness, according to Bailyn. As a result, the colonial authorities, particularly in Puritan New England, demanded the creation and maintenance of schools to educate and discipline the second generation.

Bailyn's provocative statements about the immense problems facing the first immigrants and their frantic attempts to create schools have not gone unchallenged. Recent studies of sixteenth- and seventeenth-century English families conclude that they were more nuclear and less geographically stable than had been suggested (Laslett 1965). Similarly, the extent of schools in England appears to have been underestimated (O'Day 1982; Stone 1964). Nevertheless, Bailyn's emphasis on the importance of household education, particularly among the English Puritans, has been sustained (Houlbrooke 1984).

Just as English families were more nuclear and more geographically mobile than Bailyn envisioned, so too New England families were more stable and cohesive. Indeed, American demographic historians portray New England families as more prosperous and less endangered than their English counterparts (Greven 1970; Lockridge 1970). Furthermore, other immigrants, such as the Pilgrims, never shared the Puritan obsession with education and schools even though they presumably experienced the same rigors of the transatlantic crossing and of making a living in the wilderness as did their northern neighbors (Demos 1970). Finally, the settlers of the Chesapeake, who faced the most severe and disruptive demographic conditions, also do not appear to have placed as much emphasis on providing schooling for their children as did the New England Puritans (Rutman and Rutman 1984).

If Bailyn exaggerated the demographic and geographic disruptions of New

England family life, he did not overstate their anxiety about socializing the next generation. Concern about the perpetuation of their religious ideals and doubts about the ability of the households by themselves to catechize their children and servants encouraged greater reliance on schools and churches (Vinovskis 1987).

Though there is little evidence so far that the schools played a major role in socializing the children of the immigrants throughout most of the colonies, at least in the North they complemented the efforts of families and churches in preparing the next generation. Even in colonies such as New York and Pennsylvania, where the population was much more ethnically and religiously heterogeneous than in either New England or the Chesapeake, schools were not frequently or extensively used as major instruments for assimilating immigrants or helping them to preserve their cultural heritage.[1] Instead, most immigrants received most of their education and guidance in their own households, churches, and local communities, with only limited exposure to formal schooling (Cremin 1970). Furthermore, for the large numbers of African slaves who were brought to the New World, schools played no part in helping them to cope with their destinies in the new land (Boles 1983).

2. IMMIGRANTS AND SCHOOLS IN ANTEBELLUM AMERICA

During the colonial period, most Americans were either farmers or closely tied to agriculture. Children anticipated following in the occupational footsteps of their fathers and most of them saw little need for education and training away from the home. Major changes after the American Revolution in the economy, political system, immigration, and schools transformed the experience of natives and newcomers in the antebellum period.

The first half of the nineteenth century witnessed changes in where many Americans lived and worked. The percentage living in towns of over twenty-five thousand people rose from 5.1 percent in 1790 to 19.8 percent in 1860.[2] Even more significant was the increase in nonagricultural workers, from 28.1 percent of the labor force in 1820 to 41.0 percent in 1860.[3] While only a small proportion of the increase in nonagricultural occupations was due to industrialization, the general commercialization of the economy provided antebellum children with many more occupational choices than their colonial predecessors.

As the economy expanded, the relationship between the employer and the employee was also altered. Particularly significant was the demise in the early nineteenth century of apprenticeship, which had provided some colonial youth with the training and experience necessary to become skilled artisans and craftsmen (Rorabaugh 1986). Workers in the 1820s and 1830s were forced gradually to seek additional schooling for their children to prepare them for the new employment opportunities since apprenticeship was no longer a viable alternative.[4]

Simultaneous with these economic developments was the change in the political system. Following the American Revolution and the ratification of the U.S. Constitution, an increasingly large proportion of the white male electorate became enfranchised and politically active. As a result, while many political conservatives in England questioned the wisdom of schooling for workers, there was a growing consensus in the United States that more education was essential as a means of preserving the republic from mobs and political demagogues (Kaestle 1983; Kaestle and Vinovskis 1980).

Into this changing economic and political situation, about 5 million people moved to the United States between 1820 and 1860. Most of these immigrants were poor and desperate and competed with native workers for unskilled and semiskilled jobs. Since a large proportion of these immigrants were Catholic, many native Protestants saw them as a grave threat to the existing political and social order. Not surprisingly, schools were often enlisted in the crusade to attempt to change the religion and culture of the children of these immigrants (Taylor 1971).

Whereas relatively few elementary schools existed in seventeenth-century America, by the mid–nineteenth century schools became commonplace throughout the North. Though the so-called revisionist scholars argue that the rise of mass schooling was the direct result of the activities of capitalists and manufacturers in the 1830s and 1840s who created these institutions to foster a more docile workforce during industrialization, these schools were developed in the late eighteenth and early nineteenth centuries — well before industrialization had occurred in the United States. Furthermore, the greatest increases in school attendance in the 1830s and 1840s were not in the more industrialized and urbanized Northeast, but in the more rural and agricultural Midwest (Vinovskis 1983).

But did schooling really help individuals in antebellum America to succeed economically? And did the children of immigrants attend these new schools or were they forced by poverty to enter the labor force prematurely? There is little consensus among historians on these important questions.

Nineteenth-century Americans agreed on the importance of education in general, but did not always associate it with economic success and mobility. Classical British economists such as Adam Smith mentioned the value of schooling, but mainly as a means of promoting social stability and harmony rather than fostering occupational mobility (Blaug 1986). Similarly, American antebellum political economists praised the value of education for enhancing the political and social well-being of the nation, but also did not emphasize the role of schooling in promoting social mobility (Phillips 1828). In part this was because in the early nineteenth century most occupational training and advancement was more associated with the practice of apprenticeship than with schooling.

The one individual who did directly link schooling and increases in economic productivity was Horace Mann, the first secretary of the Massachusetts Board of Education in 1837. In his widely circulated and publicized *Fifth Annual Report,* Mann reported that textile manufacturers in Lowell believed that education made workers more productive. Although Mann's analysis is seriously flawed, it was unchallenged at the time and contributed to the growing popular association between schooling and social mobility (Vinovskis forthcoming).

If nineteenth-century educators such as Mann saw a strong, causal relationship between schooling and occupational attainment, the recent "revisionist" scholars deny it altogether or even see schools as a deliberate impediment to social mobility. Harvey Graff (1979), for example, even argues that literacy was not an important or essential skill for nineteenth-century workers. Michael Katz (1975) adds that schooling did little to promote antebellum social mobility since poor immigrants could not afford to send their children to these schools. Furthermore, many of these scholars question the existence of social mobility in American society anyway and see the schools as institutions designed to promote and justify the reproduction of the existing capitalist system (Bowles and Gintis 1976).

There are very few methodologically sound studies of antebellum occupational mobility and most of these do not address directly the importance of education. Stephan Thernstrom's (1964) classic study of social mobility in mid–nineteenth-century Newburyport, Massachusetts, found modest gains in occupational status or property acquisition among the children of unskilled laborers. The Irish were particularly disadvantaged because they removed their children from school by the age of ten, and this presumably contributed to their lower rate of upward social mobility as compared to their native counterparts.

Studies of other antebellum communities such as Poughkeepsie, New York, found somewhat greater upward social mobility than in Newburyport, but confirmed Thernstrom's observation that the children of immigrants were particularly disadvantaged (Kaeble 1985). Unfortunately, most of these studies failed to test explicitly the relationship between schooling and subsequent mobility. Indeed, even Thernstrom's assumption that the children of unskilled parents had only limited occupational mobility because of their lack of education needs to be reexamined, as it appears that he underestimated the amount of education they received (Vinovskis 1985).

If there is little agreement on just how important antebellum schooling was in fostering social mobilty, everyone agrees that public schools were perceived and used as a means of acculturating Irish and German immigrants. Before the development of large-scale parochial school systems after the Civil War, most Catholic children in the Northeast attended public schools that tried to inculcate them with middle-class, Protestant values (Jorgenson 1987). In some areas, such as St. Louis, public schools found it politically necessary to offer German-language instruction, but most immigrant students receiving public schooling elsewhere attended English-speaking classes (Troen 1975).

While much has been written about the intentions of public school officials in trying to assimilate antebellum immigrants or of the immigrants resisting those efforts, little systematic evidence of the cultural impact of the schools on the children of the newcomers exists. Perhaps their acceptance and partial assimilation into antebellum society was influenced more by their neighborhood and work experiences than the training and socialization they received in the public schools. Certainly the Civil War may have played an important role in integrating immigrants into northern society and reduced at least temporarily the nativist attempts of the 1850s to use public schools to recast the immigrant population into a middle-class, Protestant mold (Higham 1955; Jones 1960).

Thus, the relationship between immigrants and schools in antebellum society was more complex than in most of colonial America, where schools were scarce and rarely intended to assimilate immigrants. Though the scholarly literature on the effects of schools on immigrants is mixed and inconclusive, my own suspicion is that schools did contribute to the limited occupational mobility of their students and helped to expose them to the prevailing cultural norms of that society. Nevertheless, this process of adjustment and partial assimilation was moderated by the local control of public schools, which allowed certain large immigrant groups such as the Irish and Germans to exercise some control and guidance over the education of their children and which was cut short by the Civil War. While free blacks migrating to the North during this period gained some access to public schooling, the even stronger racial prejudice and discrimination against them as compared with the other immigrants in the North probably meant that their newly acquired literacy and education had less of an economic value than that received by the children of either native-born whites or immigrants (Horton and Horton 1979).

3. IMMIGRANTS AND SCHOOLS IN THE LATE NINETEENTH AND EARLY TWENTIETH CENTURIES

Though the Civil War had a devastating impact on the participants, most of the antebellum social and economic changes continued unabated (Vinovskis 1989). The urbanization of the population increased steadily. By 1920 almost one out of every ten Americans lived in a city with over a million inhabitants (U.S. Bureau of Census 1975, series A57 and A69). Similarly, the percentage of the labor force in nonagricultural work rose from 48.7 percent in 1880 to 74.1 percent in 1920 (Lebergott 1964, 510).

The growth of the American economy attracted large numbers of immigrants. Nearly 24 million immigrants came to the United States between 1880 and 1920—though many of them eventually returned. The characteristics of the immigrants changed as the proportion from Northern and Western Europe declined while those from South, Central, and Eastern Europe increased (Taylor 1971). Many of these immigrants were either Jewish or Catholic and most of them did not speak English. Rather than being equally distributed throughout the country, most of them settled in cities (Lieberson 1980). Concerns about their social and political behavior led to efforts through the public schools to assimilate these new immigrants.

The public schools were also undergoing significant changes in the late nineteenth and early twentieth centuries. Although the growth of cities created shortages of public schools and teachers, urban school systems expanded rapidly. Urban schools became increasingly specialized and age-graded and centrally controlled by professional educators and local politicians (Angus, Mirel, and Vinovskis 1988; Cremin 1988).

The proportion of 5-17-year-olds in schools nationally rose slightly, from 78.1 percent in 1890 to 83.2 percent in 1920, despite the great influx of immigrants (U.S. Bureau of Census 1975, series H419). A sizable minority of these attended private schools that tried to preserve the ethnic and religious heritage of immigrant and second-generation children (Olneck and Lazerson 1980; Sanders 1976). Perhaps even more important in the long run was the growth in high school attendance. Although high schools existed in some parts of antebellum New England, these institutions now became more commonplace in other areas of the country and efforts were made to attract students who did not plan to go on to college (Vinovskis 1988). The percentage of 17-year-olds who graduated from high school rose from 2.5 percent in 1880 to 16.3 percent in 1920 (U.S. Bureau of Census 1975, series H599).

Nativist fear of the new immigrants prompted efforts to assimilate their children through Americanization programs both within and outside the public schools. But did the children of immigrants attend schools, and did that experience have any impact on them?

Earlier social historians such as Thernstrom (1973) saw the schools as an important factor in helping immigrant children succeed in America. But, as pointed out earlier, the revisionist education historians reject this positive interpretation of education and argue that schooling did not facilitate social mobility. Colin Greer (1972), for example, argues that schools deliberately frustrated and failed immigrant children in order to reproduce the existing social order. Public schools were designed not to help lower-class children but to control them.

During the period from 1880 to 1920, there was great variation in the school attendance pattern of immigrant children or of second-generation children. In general, immigrant children received much less education than those of the second generation (Angus and Mirel 1985; Olneck and Lazerson 1974). Some immigrant parents, such as those from southern Italy or Hungary, did not place much value on extended schooling and therefore their children did not receive as much education as others (Barton 1975; LaGumina 1982; Stolarik 1977). Jewish immigrants, on the other hand, placed great stress on education and their children stayed in school much longer (Dinnerstein 1982). Compared to the children of native-born whites in the North, second-generation children generally attended less school. However, that difference was not very large and decreased over time. Indeed, since white children in the South were disadvantaged educationally, the overall educational attainment of many groups of second-generation children equaled or sometimes even exceeded that of children of native white parents. Thus, while immigrant children were clearly disadvantaged educationally in the United States, many of those in the second generation were able to be competitive with if not equal to the children of the native-born population (Lieberson 1980).

Even if second-generation children attended public schools, this does not mean that they were treated equally. Several revisionist scholars contend that these children were denied opportunities for advancement within the schools. Unfortunately, we do not have any detailed statistical studies of the classroom experiences of immigrant children in elementary schools, but a recent analysis of the Central High School in Philadelphia suggests that students from disadvantaged backgrounds could compete with those from middle-class families (Labaree 1988).[5]

But did a high school education provide social mobility for immigrant and second-generation children? Until now most scholars have been forced to speculate on the basis of indirect evidence—usually from data on the occupational mobility of immigrants but without any direct information on their schooling. Reed Ueda's (1987, 179) analysis of intergenerational mobility in late–nineteenth-century Somerville, Massachusetts, found that children of blue-collar workers who enrolled in a high school were more successful occupationally than those who did not attend.

Similarly, Joel Perlmann's (1988, 38) detailed study of secondary schooling in Providence, Rhode Island, between 1880 and 1925 found that high school attendance greatly increased chances for upward occupational mobility—even after controlling for the effects of family background.

While second-generation immigrants were able to use their high school training to help them get ahead, the severe racial discrimination even in the North against blacks seeking employment greatly diminished the value of any additional schooling for them. Over time, this differential in the rates of return to education between blacks and second-generation Americans contributed to a growing gap between the two groups in the amount of education they sought for themselves and their children (Lieberson 1980).

If recent studies of the relationship between social mobility and education seem to suggest a positive role for schooling in helping the children of immigrants, what about cultural changes? Did the Americanization programs in the public schools succeed in helping to assimilate the children of immigrants into American society?

Most studies of the Americanization efforts have focused on the attempt to influence adult immigrants through special programs rather than on activities directed at their children in the public schools. These adult Americanization programs flourished particularly after World War I, as native Americans became anxious about the perceived threats posed by unassimilated immigrants. Public schools were frequently used as sites for adult citizenship classes and about 750 to one thousand communities participated in this effort in the early 1920s, with at least 1 million immigrants enrolling in formal public-school Americanization classes. What impact these classes actually had on the adult immigrants is still open to debate and only a small, though significant, proportion of all immigrants ever attended one. In addition, less than half of those who did enroll actually completed the course, and there was little agreement among educators on how to teach these courses. Nevertheless, many adult foreigners in the early twentieth century received at least some exposure to the English language and to white, Protestant, middle-class values even if most immigrants were unprepared to repudiate their old-world heritage, as many of the Americanizers wanted (McClymer 1982).

While some have argued that the Americanization programs emphasized conformity above all else, Michael Olneck (forthcoming) sees their importance more in terms of the symbolic reconfiguration of American civil culture with an emphasis on individualism and a delegitimation of collective ethnic identity. Though he is skeptical of the impact of Americanization programs on individual consciousness, he stresses its importance in fixing the public meanings of what constitutes a "good" American citizen.

Unfortunately, we do not have any rigorous or detailed analyses of the impact of schools on the assimilation of immigrant or second-generation children.[6] Certainly over time the educational level of more recent European immigrants has become almost indistinguishable from the rest of the white population, and schools obviously played a key role in this change. Changes in education probably also helped to decrease any occupational or income differences between these groups. On the other hand, fertility levels of the more recent European immigrant groups and their descendants now approximate that of the general white population, but it is not clear whether schools played a key role in this particular aspect of assimilation. Similarly, while intermarriage rates among white ethnics has been steadily increasing and a sizable proportion of the white population in 1980 no longer remembers or seems to care about their specific ethnic heritage, it is not clear what role, if any, schools played in this process (Lieberson and Waters 1988).

If socioeconomic and cultural differences have diminished significantly between the children of the late–nineteenth- and early–twentieth-century European immigrants and the rest of the white population, there remains a sizable gap between the white and black populations on a variety of indices. Despite the improved educational opportunities for the children of black migrants to the North in this period, they still faced severe racial discrimination in the labor force and in the housing market. If public schools in the North exposed blacks to white, middle-class, Protestant values, white society refused to accept them as equals even if they adopted those values. In the South blacks faced even more discrimination in the schools and were further handicapped by the overall inadequate educational facilities and offerings in the South (Kusmer 1976; Lane 1986; Perlmann 1988).

Thus, while the European immigrants and their children who came to the United States between 1880 and 1920 faced substantial discrimination and hardship, their descendants were able to better themselves economically. Schools appear to have played a key role in their upward social mobility, but without the economic opportunities available to them in the larger society, that additional education would have been much less useful. Certainly the children of black migrants to the North significantly improved their education without reaping the same occupational or income rewards. As a result, while the value of increased schooling became more apparent over time to the descendants of European immigrants, among disadvantaged minorities such as blacks it was not always clear that further education was worth the additional personal effort and family sacrifices that had to be made. Therefore, the gap in schooling between the descendants of late–nineteenth- and early–twentieth-century European immigrants and black migrants to the North increased and continues to disadvantage the latter group today.

4. RECENT IMMIGRANTS AND THE SCHOOLS

The situation in the United States has changed since the early twentieth century. Almost three-fourths of the population in 1980 lived in a community of twenty-five hundred or more people, though the proportion in cities of 1 million or more population was only about 8 percent (U.S. Bureau of Census 1989, tables 18 and 38). The percentage of the labor force in nonagricultural work had risen to 97 percent and 19 percent were in manufacturing while 32 percent were in services (U.S. Bureau of Census 1989, table 645). Increasingly workers are in jobs that require considerable education—often at least some college training (U.S. Bureau of Census 1989, tables 642 and 643).

Large changes have also occurred in schooling. The median years of education for the 25-29-year-old population rose from 10.3 years in 1940 to 12.8 years in 1987. The percentage of that population who had graduated from high school increased from 38.1 percent in 1940 to 86.0 percent in 1987; the percentage with at least four years of college rose from 5.9 percent in 1940 to 22.0 percent in 1987 (U.S. Bureau of Census 1989, table 211).

There were some differences in educational attainment by race, with the median years of school completed in 1987 for 25-29-year-olds overall being 12.8 years, 12.7 years for blacks and 12.3 years for Hispanics. Since minority children, especially among the Hispanics, were likely to be in grades below their expected ages, the differences in the percentage of 25-29-year-olds having graduated from high school were greater, with 85.9 percent of everyone, 83.4 percent of blacks, and 59.8 percent of Hispanics having completed high school (U.S. Bureau of Census 1989, table 213).

Just as schools were becoming more used by children, they were also better funded, larger, and more age-segregated in the classrooms (Cremin 1988). Increasingly, special federally funded programs such as Headstart and bilingual education were introduced in order to help disadvantaged children.[7] More efforts have been made to introduce into the curriculum information about the experiences and past accomplishments of minorities.[8] Nevertheless, there is growing concern in recent years that the quality of public education may have deteriorated even though the dollar amounts spent per pupil have increased substantially (Chubb 1988; Ravitch 1983).

The distribution of the sources of immigration to the United States has also changed dramatically since the early twentieth century. Approximately six hundred thousand legal immigrants entered the United States in 1987, but only 10 percent of them were from Europe. The bulk of legal immigrants came from Asia (43 percent), the Caribbean (17 percent), Mexico (12 percent), South America (7 percent), and Central America (5 percent) (U.S. Bureau of Census 1989, table 7). Although it was hoped that the Immigration Reform and Control Act of 1986 (Amnesty Law) would curb illegal immigration, it is estimated that the number of illegal immigrants crossing our southern border are about two hundred thousand per year—though a sizable proportion of these illegal aliens will eventually return or be returned.[9] Thus, most legal and illegal immigrants to the United States today are from non-European countries, often do not speak English, and usually are poor.

Since the bulk of immigrants today are either Asians or Hispanics, we need to consider how minority children in general have fared in American schools. Some minority children, such as blacks, continue to be disadvantaged in terms of school attendance or high school completion, but they recently have made sizable gains in closing some of the educational gap between themselves and the white native-born population (Farley and Allen 1987). Others, such as the second-generation children of Japanese or Chinese parents, have excelled educationally and often do better in American schools than the rest of the population (Hsia 1988). Overall, Hispanic children have not done as well educationally, but there are significant differences among them. Cuban-American children, for example, do relatively well educationally as compared with Puerto Rican or Mexican-American children (Bean and Tienda 1987).

Various theories have been advanced to explain the difficulties that many minority children encounter in American schools. Four of the more prominent explanations are (1) biological determinism; (2) cultural deprivation; (3) discontinuity between the minority and majority culture; and (4) psychosocial factors (Suarez-Orozco 1989).

Although the attempts at a biological explanation of the inferiority of school performance by certain minority children attracted considerable attention in the late 1960s and early 1970s, today these studies have been largely discredited as an adequate explanation (Gould 1981; Jensen 1969). Similarly, the argument that the inadequacies of the cultural background of minority children explain their problems in school flourished in the 1960s, but has few advocates today (Bloom, Davis, and Hess 1965; Ogbu 1978).

A more recent and persistent explanation for the problems of minority youth is the "cultural conflict" or "discontinuities" between the minority student and the school environment, which reflects the dominant culture

(Johnson 1970). Nevertheless, critics of this approach point out that some minority children from very different and distinct cultures, such as second-generation Japanese or Chinese, have done remarkably well in American schools despite their cultural differences (Hsia 1988).

Perhaps the most popular current explanations for the difficulties of minority students in American schools are psychosocial ones, which stress that any educational deficits are only a reflection of the larger overall problems facing these minorities in the United States today. John Ogbu (1986) argues that castelike minorities, such as blacks, Puerto Ricans, and Mexican-Americans, fare much worse educationally than the rest of the population because they were incorporated in the United States against their will and have faced a job ceiling regardless of their individual talents or school achievements. As a result, there is little incentive among castelike minority youth for further education—especially when schooling becomes identified with the majority, hostile culture.[10]

Other psychosocial explanations focus on the problems of the family, which are seen as particularly severe among many minority populations. Some studies have suggested that even after controlling for socioeconomic factors, children from single-parent homes do worse in school than those from two-parent families (McLanahan and Bumpus 1988). While some scholars dismiss the importance of the family as a factor in educational attainment, much of the general scholarly literature on schooling suggests that the role of the parents is crucial in predicting the amount of schooling received by their children (Coleman, Hoffer, and Kilgore 1982).

Given the diversity among immigrants today, one would expect considerable variety in the adjustment of their children to American schools. One might hypothesize that immigrant children whose parents were relatively affluent and well educated would fare reasonably well in the public schools. Those whose parents were poor and uneducated, however, might be expected to do much less well in the public schools—particularly if they were nonwhite minorities. Studies of recent immigrants and schooling in the United States challenge this conventional wisdom.

An anthropological study of Central American legal and illegal refugees in two inner-city high schools in California found that despite the impoverished condition of the El Salvadorian, Guatemalan, and Nicaraguan youth studied, they did surprisingly well academically. Though confronted with violence and hostility in these two heavily minority high schools, the immigrant children succeeded more than many of the other minority children attending. The author pointed out that despite the obvious initial handicaps faced by these non–English-speaking students, they succeeded in large part because of their particular cultural and familial situation. Having escaped to freedom from the terror and poverty of their homelands, the United States appeared as a land of unlimited opportunity for those with education and personal drive. In addition, the sacrifices made by their parents encouraged these youth to succeed in school as a means of repaying those who helped them. Furthermore, even when conditions in the United States did not live up to their previous, unrealistic expectations, the situation in their homelands was even worse and therefore not a viable alternative (Suarez-Orozco 1989).

Another larger and more detailed statistical, five-site study of the Indochinese Boat People who left their homes in the late 1970s for the United States suggests that the children do well in the public schools despite the seemingly insurmountable odds against them. Though many of the parents of these children were able to find employment, their jobs were low-skilled, with little prospect for future upward social mobility. Yet they sent their children to the public schools and encouraged them to get ahead in this country by acquiring a good education. Though the children initially usually lacked literacy in English, they eventually managed to earn a decent overall grade point average and scored high on the California Achievement Test (Caplan, Whitmore, and Choy 1989).

In trying to explain the unexpected academic success of the children of the Boat People, the study concluded that it was not due to the quality of the public schools, which were not very good, nor to the special English-language classes. Instead, they point to the cultural and familial values that encouraged and facilitated academic achievement. The parents, having accepted limited occupational mobility for themselves in the United States, placed their hopes on improving the situation of their children through education. As a result, despite the relatively poor quality of the public schools in these low-resource urban areas and the hostility that these Indochinese children frequently encountered both within and outside those schools, they excelled academically because they were highly motivated to learn. The study suggests,

We have probably gone too far, however, in the direction of believing that low-SES, single-parent homes with large numbers of children cannot succeed in school. The critical issue is not the number and relationship of the adults in the household to the children but rather what dominates and who determines the nature and character of the milieu, its beliefs and behaviors. It means that the values and aspirations linked to student learning have to be instilled early and that an environment promotive of learning must be supported by families in a society concerned with the well-being of all its members. (Caplan, Whitmore, and Choy 1989, 176).

If many of the Central American and Indochinese immigrant children appear to be succeeding in school, others whose parents are undocumented aliens from Mexico may not be faring as well (Suarez-Orozco 1987). Even though many immigrant children may do well in elementary or secondary school, they may lack access to higher education because of inadequate financial resources, lack of knowledge about higher education, or fear that undocumented aliens cannot attend a college or university. Since a high school education is no longer adequate for the best jobs in this country, the long-term occupational mobility of these seemingly successful immigrant children may be in jeopardy.[11] In addition, if the immigrant children who become more educated are unable to translate that advantage into better jobs and higher incomes because of discrimination, their own children may be discouraged from pursuing more schooling.[12] Finally, successful students appear to have become only partially assimilated into American society by accepting the values of hard work and more education while rejecting the strong individualism and materialism that characterize many of their native-born classmates. If these immigrant children or their offspring adopt the more individualistic and consumer-oriented ways of American society at large, perhaps some of their comparative advantages in these schools will disappear.

5. CONCLUSION

The role of the schools in the integration and assimilation of immigrants into American society varies greatly over time and is conditioned by the nature of the society and of the educational system in any given period. In colonial America, the family was the central institution for educating children, and the few primary schools that existed were only intended to supplement those efforts at home. Despite concerns about immigration, colonial communities did not turn to schools as a means of socializing and assimilating immigrants. Since most of the population was engaged in farming or related agricultural activities, extensive schooling was not viewed as essential for preparing most children for earning their livelihood.

In antebellum America, the importance of formal schooling increased as the number of these institutions multiplied rapidly and as they were seen as a means of preparing children for the growing diversity of employment opportunities. As apprenticeship declined, education was increasingly viewed by educators and the general public as necessary for upward social mobility.

The large influx of Irish and German immigrants before the Civil War led to nativist efforts to use public schools to assimilate these newcomers to white, Protestant, middle-class values and practices. While we lack adequate studies of the actual impact of these schools on the subsequent life course of the students, it does appear that they helped to foster at least some limited occupational mobility as well as exposure to the predominant American culture.

In the late nineteenth and early twentieth centuries, American society had become more urbanized and industrialized and public schools more centralized and professionalized. The new wave of immigrants from Southern, Eastern, and Central Europe alarmed many of the native-born population and led to a sense of urgency in the promotion of Americanization programs both within and outside the public schools. Most European immigrant and second-generation children seemed to benefit from the education they received and improved their position in society until today it is hard to distinguish occupationally or educationally among the descendants of these immigrants. Severe racial discrimination, however, prevented black migrants to the North from utilizing their schooling effectively and contributed to the growing educational gap between blacks and white immigrants in the first half of the twentieth century.

Today, immigrants to the United States are predominantly from Asia or Latin and Central America. Although many of them are disadvantaged in terms of their socioeconomic backgrounds and personal resources in the United States, many of their children are doing surprisingly well in school. Particularly interesting is the important role that familial and cultural values seem to play in facilitating the acquisition of schooling by these recent immigrants. Whether this pattern of school achievement will continue and whether their educated children will be given full and equal access to good job opportunities remains to be seen.

Overall, schooling in the nineteenth and twentieth centuries has provided many immigrant and second-generation children with the skills and credentials necessary for success in America. Though many of these European immigrants and their descendants initially faced substantial hostility and discrimination from the native population, over time much of that has disappeared. Unfortunately, for many minority populations such as blacks and Mexican-Americans that discrimination was more severe than for white immigrants and to some degree continues to deny their educated children equal access to advancement in the United States. Thus, while schooling can contribute and has contributed to the gradual integration and partial assimilation of immigrants into American society, it cannot succeed by itself without the concomitant acceptance of these newcomers by the larger society. Furthermore, while schools are essential for providing the training and credentialing necessary for advancement, they cannot accomplish their tasks without the active support and encouragement of the family and local community.

NOTES

1. In their efforts to Anglicanize the Dutch population in early eighteenth-century New York, the Society for the Propagation of the Gospel did establish English schools in some communities such as Albany and New York City. Nevertheless, the extent of their school building appears to have been limited, especially in the countryside, and was only a small, though important, part of the overall efforts to switch the inhabitants from the Dutch Reformed churches to Anglican churches (Balmer 1989).
2. Calculated from U.S. Bureau of Census 1975, part 1, series A57 and A69.
3. Calculated from U.S. Bureau of Census, part 1, series D152-166.
4. Whereas apprenticeship declined sharply in the United States in the nineteenth century, it endured longer in Britain because of its efficiency advantages and because of customs that favored training certification for job entry into skilled positions (Elbaum 1989).
5. Similarly, Joel Perlmann (1985) found that grades were a better predictor of staying in school than social class background.
6. For a useful discussion of the efforts to Americanize children in the public schools, see Mohl 1981.
7. There is a great debate over the value of bilingual education in helping disadvantaged students (Glazer 1981; Bean and Tienda 1987). For a review of the literature on bilingual education from the perspective of child development, see Hakuta and Garcia 1989.
8. Although some initially questioned the introduction of ethnic materials into the curriculum, most have now accepted the value of this information in the classroom (Glazer 1988). The debate is now, however, over whether or not courses on ethnic differences and racism should be mandated for all students.
9. The commissioner of the Immigration and Naturalization Service estimated that the number of illegal immigrants entering each year is between 1.7 million and 2.5 million. This figure seems much too high compared with most other estimates (*New York Times,* 18 June 1989, 1).
10. Ogbu sees immigrant children faring better than the castelike minorities who were brought here against their will. But he understimates the fact that many of the recent nonwhite immigrants to the United States also face racial opposition (Spencer 1988).
11. Nevertheless, a high school education still provides a substantial advantage over those who have dropped out of high school. For an estimate of the rates of return to schooling in 1962 and 1973, see Olneck and Kim 1975.
12. Some scholars maintain that the current educational system relegates immigrants only to low-paying jobs (Spener 1988; Bowles and Gintis 1976). Therefore, one would not expect any real upward mobility for the recent immigrants despite their efforts in the schools. I do not find this line of reasoning persuasive even though minority adults appear to continue to receive fewer rewards for their education than the rest of the population (Olneck and Kim 1975).

REFERENCES

Angus, D. L., and J. E. Mirel. 1985. From spellers to spindles: Work-force entry by the children of textile workers, 1888–1890. *Social Science History* 9:123–43.

Angus, D. L., J. E. Mirel, and M. A. Vinovskis. 1988. Historical development of age stratification in schooling. *Teachers College Record* 90:211–36.

Bailyn, B. 1960. *Education in the forming of American society.* New York: Vintage.

Balmer, R. H. 1989. *A perfect babel of confusion: Dutch religion and English culture in the middle colonies.* New York: Oxford University Press.

Barton, J. J. 1975. *Peasants and strangers: Italians, Rumanians and Slovaks in an American city, 1890–1950.* Cambridge, MA: Harvard University Press.

Bean, F. D., and M. Tienda. 1987. *The Hispanic population of the United States.* New York: Russell Sage Foundation.

Blaug, M. 1986. *Economic history and the history of economics.* New York: New York University Press.

Bloom, B. S., A. Davis and R. Hess. 1965. *Compensatory education for cultural deprivation.* New York: Holt, Rinehart, and Winston.

Boles, J. B. 1983. *Black southerners, 1619–1869.* Lexington: University Press of Kentucky.

Bowles, S., and H. Gintis. 1976. *Schooling in capitalist America: Educational reform and the contradictions of economic life.* New York: Basic Books.

Caplan, N., J. K. Whitmore, and M. H. Choy. 1989. *The boat people and achievement in America: A study of family life, hard work, and cultural values.* Ann Arbor: University of Michigan Press.

Chubb, J. E. 1988. Why the current wave of school reform will fail. *Public Interest* 90:28–49.

Coleman, J. S., T. Hoffer, and S. Kilgore. 1982. *High school achievement: Public, Catholic, and private schools compared.* New York: Basic Books.

Cremin, L. A. 1970. *American education: The colonial experience, 1607–1783.* New York: Harper and Row.

———. 1988. *American education: The metropolitan experience, 1876–1980.* New York: Harper and Row.

Demos, J. 1970. *A little commonwealth: Family life in Plymouth Colony.* New York: Oxford University Press.

Dinnerstein, L. 1982. Education and the advancement of American Jews. In *American education and the European immigrant, 1840–1940,* ed. B. J. Weiss, 44–60. Urbana: University of Illinois Press.

Elbaum, B. 1989. Why apprenticeship persisted in Britain but not in the United States. *Journal of Economic History* 49: 337–49.

Farley, R., and W. R. Allen. 1987. *The color line and the quality of life in America.* New York: Russell Sage Foundation.

Featherman, D. L., and R. M. Warner. 1978. *Opportunity and change.* New York: Academic Press.

Glazer, N. 1981. Ethnicity and education: Some hard questions. *Phi Delta Kappan:* 386–89.

————. 1988. Education for American citizenship in the twenty-first century. *Education and Society:* 5–10.

Gould, S. J. 1981. *The mismeasure of man.* New York: Norton.

Graff, H. J. 1979. *The literacy myth: Literacy and social structure in the nineteenth-century city.* New York: Academic Press.

Greer, C. 1972. *The great school legend: A revisionist interpretation of American public education.* New York: Basic Books.

Greven, P. J., Jr. 1970. *Four generations: Population, land, and family in colonial Andover, Massachusetts.* Ithaca, NY: Cornell University Press.

Hakuta, K., and E. E. Garcia. 1989. Bilingualism and education. *American Psychologist* 44:374–79.

Higham, J. 1955. *Strangers in the land: Patterns of American nativism, 1860–1925.* New Brunswick, NJ: Rutgers University Press.

Horton, J. O., and L. E. Horton. 1979. *Black Bostonians: Family life and community struggle in the antebellum North.* New York: Holmes and Meier.

Houlbrooke, R. A. 1984. *The English family, 1450–1700.* London: Longman.

Hsia, J. 1988. *Asian Americans in higher education and at work.* Hillsdale, NJ: Lawrence Erlbaum.

Jensen, A. R. 1969. How much can we boost I.Q. and scholastic achievement? *Harvard Educational Review* 39:1–123.

Johnson, K. R. 1970. *Teaching the culturally disadvantaged: A rational approach.* Palo Alto, CA: Science Research Associates.

Jones, M. A. 1960. *American immigration.* Chicago: University of Chicago Press.

Jorgenson, L. P. 1987. *The state and the non-public school, 1825–1925.* Columbia: University of Missouri Press.

Kaeble, H. 1985. *Social mobility in the nineteenth and twentieth centuries: Europe and America in comparative perspective.* Leamington Spa, England: Berg Publishers.

Kaestle, C. F. 1983. *Pillars of the republic: Common schools and American society, 1780–1860.* New York: Hill and Wang.

Kaestle, C. F., and M. A. Vinovskis. 1980. *Education and social change in nineteenth-century Massachusetts.* Cambridge: Cambridge University Press.

Katz, M. B. 1975. *The people of Hamilton, Canada West: Family and class in a mid–nineteenth century city.* Cambridge, MA: Harvard University Press.

Kusmer, K. L. 1976. *A ghetto takes shape: Black Cleveland, 1870–1930.* Urbana: University of Illinois Press.

Labaree, D. F. 1988. *The making of an American high school: The credentials market and the Central High School of Philadelphia, 1838–1939.* New Haven, CT: Yale University Press.

LaGumina, S. J. 1982. American education and the Italian immigrant response. In *American education and the European immigrant, 1840–1940,* ed. B. J. Weiss, 61–77. Urbana: University of Illinois Press.

Lane, R. 1986. *Roots of violence in black Philadelphia, 1860–1900.* Cambridge, MA: Harvard University Press.

Laslett, P. 1965. *The world we have lost: England before the industrial age.* New York: Scribner's.

Lebergott, S. 1964. *Manpower in economic growth: The American record since 1800.* New York: McGraw-Hill.

Lieberson, S. 1980. *A piece of the pie: Blacks and white immigrants since 1880.* Berkeley: University of California Press.

Lieberson, S., and Mary C. Waters. 1988. *From many strands: Ethnic and racial groups in contemporary America.* New York: Russell Sage Foundation.

Lockridge, K. A. 1970. *A New England town: The first hundred years: Dedham, Massachusetts, 1636–1736.* New York: Norton.

McClymer, J. F. 1982. The Americanization movement and the education of the foreign-born adult, 1914–1925. In *American education and the European immigrant, 1840–1940,* ed. B. J. Weiss, 96–116. Urbana: University of Illinois Press.

McLanahan, S. S., and L. Bumpus. 1988. Comment: A note on the effect of family structure on school enrollment. In *Divided opportunities,* ed. G. D. Sandeur and M. Tienda, 195–201. New York: Plenum.

Mohl, R. A. 1981. Cultural assimilation versus cultural pluralism. *Educational Forum:* 323–32.

O'Day, R. 1982. *Education and society, 1500–1800: The social foundations of education in early modern Britain.* London: Longman.

Ogbu, J. U. 1978. *Minority education and caste: The American system in cross-cultural perspective.* New York: Academic Press.

———. 1986. The consequences of the American caste system. In *The school achievement of minority children: New perspectives,* ed. U. Neisser, 19–56. Hillsdale, NJ: Lawrence Erlbaum.

Olneck, M. R. Forthcoming. Americanization and education of immigrants, 1900–1925: An analysis of symbolic action. *American Journal of Education.*

Olneck, M. R., and K. Kim. 1975. The relationship between education and income among American men: Some revisions and extensions. Unpublished paper. Wisconsin Center for Education Research, University of Wisconsin.

Olneck, M. R., and M. Lazerson. 1974. The school achievement of immigrant children: 1900–1930. *History of Education Quarterly* 14:453–82.

———. 1980. Education. In *Harvard encyclopedia of American ethnic groups,* ed. S. Thernstrom, A. Orlov, and O. Handlin, 303–19. Cambridge, MA: Harvard University Press.

Perlmann, J. 1985. Who stayed in school? Social structure and academic achievement in determination of enrollment patterns, Providence, Rhode Island, 1880–1925. *Journal of American History* 72:588–614.

———. 1988. *Ethnic differences: Schooling and social structure among the Irish, Italians, Jews, and blacks in the American city, 1880–1935.* Cambridge: Cambridge University Press.

Phillips, W. 1828. *A manual of political economy with particular reference to the institutions, resources, and condition of the United States.* Boston: Hilliard, Gray, Little, and Wilkins.

Ravitch, D. 1983. *The troubled crusade: American education, 1945–1980.* New York: Basic Books.

Rorabaugh, W. J. 1986. *The craft apprentice: From Franklin to the machine age in America.* New York: Oxford University Press.

Rutman, D. B., and A. H. Rutman. 1984. *A place in time: Middlesex County, Virginia, 1650–1750.* New York: Norton.

Sanders, J. W. 1976. *The education of an urban minority: Catholics in Chicago, 1833–1965.* New York: Oxford University Press.

Spener, D. 1988. Transitional bilingual education and the socialization of immigrants. *Harvard Educational Review* 58:133–53.

Stolarik, M. M. 1977. Immigration, education, and the social mobility of Slovaks, 1870–1930. In *Immigrants and religion in urban America,* ed. R. M. Miller and T. D. Marzik, 103–16. Philadelphia: Temple University Press.

Stone, L. 1964. The educational revolution in England, 1560–1640. *Past and Present* 28:41–80.

Suarez-Orozco, M. M. 1987. Hispanic Americans: Comparative considerations and educational problems of children. *International Migration* 25:141–63.

———. 1989. *Central American refugees and U.S. high schools: A Psychosocial study of motivation and achievement.* Stanford, CA: Stanford University Press.

Taylor, P. 1971. *The distant magnet: European emigration to the U.S.A.* New York: Harper and Row.

Thernstrom, S. 1964. *Poverty and progress: Social mobility in a nineteenth-century city.* Cambridge, MA: Harvard University Press.

———. 1973. *The other Bostonians: Poverty and progress in the American metropolis, 1880–1970.* Cambridge, MA: Harvard University Press.

Troen, S. K. 1975. *The public and the schools: Shaping the St. Louis system, 1838–1920.* Columbia: University of Missouri Press.

Ueda, R. 1987. *Avenues to adulthood: The origins of the high school and social mobility in an American suburb.* Cambridge: Cambridge University Press, 1987.

U.S. Bureau of the Census. 1975. *Historical statistics of the United States, colonial times to 1970, bicentennial edition.* Part 1. Washington, D.C.: U.S. Government Printing Office.

———. 1989. *Statistical abstract of the United States: 1989.* 109th ed. Washington, D.C.: U.S. Government Printing Office.

Vinovskis, M. A. 1983. Quantification and the analysis of American antebellum education. *Journal of Interdisciplinary History* 13:761–86.

———. 1985. Patterns of high school attendance in Newburyport, Massachusetts, in 1860. Unpublished paper presented at the American Historical Association Annual Meeting.

———. 1987. Family and schooling in colonial and nineteenth-century America. *Journal of Family History* 12:19–37.

———. 1988. Have we under-estimated the extent of ante-bellum high school attendance? *History of Education Quarterly* 28:551–67.

———. 1989. Have social historians lost the Civil War? Some preliminary demographic speculations. *Journal of American History* 76:34–58.

———. Forthcoming. Schooling in nineteenth-century America: Some economic considerations. In *Education for a new age and a different world,* ed. S. Berryman.

7

THE FRENCH EDUCATION SYSTEM: SPRINGBOARD OR OBSTACLE TO INTEGRATION?

Danielle Boyzon-Fradet

The most frequent reproach to the French school system since its creation has been that it is a formidable assimilationist machine, denying regional minorities and immigrants their cultural and linguistic identities on French soil. However, during the hearings before the Nationality Code Commission, appointed by Jacques Chirac's administration in 1987 to redefine the criteria for access to French nationality, the integrating role of schools with respect to immigrant children, especially from non-European countries, was challenged for the first time. Until that time, critics had only reproached them for not having programs that acknowledged the specific cultural and linguistic attributes of these groups, and thus of being assimilationist.

Witnesses before the "Committee of Wise Men" unanimously recognized that school is one of the most powerful vehicles for providing mastery of the French language and instilling republican and secular civic values: "what seems most important . . . is not so much the time period, but the schooling. . . . There is no more integrating factor than schooling, especially primary and secondary schooling" (Commission de la Nationalité 1988). This led the committee, contrary to what everyone expected, to propose that lengthy schooling in France should be added to the factors fostering access to French nationality (Boulot and Boyzon-Fradet 1988).

Certainly, school is not the only place where integration into society occurs, but it is the only institution responsible for children from the age of three (sometimes even two) at least up to sixteen, "no matter what their social, cultural, or geographic origin" (Loi d'Orientation sur l'Education 1989). This is why I will examine the intrinsic reasons that have given the school system such a strong integrating role for more than a century; the negative effects of policies introduced since the 1970s favoring children of immigrants; and the pressures exercised by the other sectors of society on integration through the schools.

1. PRINCIPLES AND OBJECTIVES

Well before the creation of a secular, mandatory public school system in 1881–1882, the Revolution stressed the role of educational institutions in instilling its values in citizens. Thus the decree of the thirtieth Vendemaire An II, 21 October 1793, entrusted to the schools the task of developing in children "republican morals, love of one's country, and the desire to work."

The avowed objective of the introduction of education as a public service at the end of the last century was described as follows: "The Republic created school, school will create the Republic." The still precarious Republic planned to strengthen its foundations through education.

Despite the many political changes from this period on, this objective was never modified, except during the Vichy regime, which tried to introduce religious education into the public schools, profoundly challenging their secularism. The most recent pedagogic directives and the laws about education of 1 July 1989 illustrate the permanence of this philosophy of instilling republican principles through education as a public service. The 1985 directives of the National Ministry of Education are explicated in the introduction to a volume devoted to elementary school (six to eleven years old), which reads:

The school level called "elementary," because it covers the fundamental elements of knowledge, plays a decisive role in the progress of democracy. School, in instructing, educates for liberty. In daily life at school and in the teaching at school, the virtues which form the basis for a civilized and democratic society will be cultivated: the search for truth and faith in human reason, intellectual rigor, the meaning of responsibility, respect for oneself and others, the spirit of solidarity and cooperation, the rejection of racism, the understanding of the universal element present in diverse cultures, the love for France which merges with a devotion to liberty, equality, fraternity.

In addition, the instructions concerning individual subjects detail exactly what they have in common with the general objective: "Mastery of the French language determines success in elementary school. It is . . . the prerequisite to all other learning . . . that is why it is the first instrument of liberty. . . . For children whose first language is not French, school provides a means of integration into the French community, and encourages a culture which remains open to diversity." "The understanding of our history, the assimilation of the French political and cultural heritage, the discovery of our people's and our country's riches, are indispensable to the formation of the French citizens. History and geography also give the student a national consciousness; he can thus appreciate other cultures' contributions, which he discovers through studies, trips, or visits to immigrant communities." "The republican state is made up of free, responsible people, sensitive to general concerns. We are born citizens, we become enlightened citizens. . . . Eminently moral, civic education develops honesty, courage, rejection of racism, love for the Republic."

The law, even though it adopts a less militant style, is nonetheless just as clear about the role of schools in the formation of citizens:

Education is the first national priority. Education as a public service is conceived and organized for students. It contributes to equalizing opportunity. The right to education is guaranteed to all people in order to permit them to develop their personalities, to raise their level of basic and ongoing training, to integrate themselves into social and professional life, and to exercise their citizenship.

The institutional mechanisms for putting these goals into practice and the wide range of people with whom schools must deal have certainly changed under the dual influence of economic necessity and social needs, but the fundamental principles of the schools have never been challenged; quite the contrary, they have been incessantly reinforced by the need for more equal opportunity.

The French educational system, although consisting of two parts (public and private), operates according to identical rules in almost every case. The private sector, which educates 20 percent of the students at the primary and secondary levels, is more than 90 percent contractual (99 percent for the primary and 90 percent for the secondary level). The contract with the state requires schools to admit children no matter what their religious affiliation; and to adopt the state goals, curriculum, schedules, and teacher-training equivalent to that of public-school teachers. In return the state covers salaries and, depending on the contract, part of the operating costs of the institution.

Despite the decentralization law of 1982, which assigns primary and elementary schools to town control, junior high schools to departmental control, and high schools to regional control, the content of courses, diplomas, and the pedagogic orientations remain under the control of the National Ministry of Education, and thus under central control.

Any child living on French soil is subject to the same rules:

- required schooling between the ages of six and sixteen. This is a given, with the exception of a few marginal cases. Time spent at school has increased considerably during the last decade: 100 percent of all children are being educated from the age of four on; 95 percent of all three-year-olds are being educated; 63 percent are still in school at eighteen years old;
- equal treatment in terms of hours, subject matter, and type of teacher training. This is almost absolute in elementary school, but more for appearance in secondary school;
- teaching only in the official national language, French, except in the very few bilingual institutions;[1]
- a secular education (in the public sector). "Secularism, a constitutional principle of the Republic, is one of the building blocks of public schooling. At school, as elsewhere, the religious beliefs of each person are personal and thus a matter of free choice. But at school, where all the young people, without discrimination, end up together, the exercise of freedom of conscience, the respect for pluralism, and the neutrality of public institutions require that the whole educational community be free from all ideological or religious pressure" (Circulaire de Ministre de l'Education 1989). This secularism implies no religious education, no religious observance, and no proselytizing within school grounds;
- free schooling until the age of sixteen (in the public sector and in certain private establishments).

Thus the French school system is based on the hypothesis that equal opportunity requires uniform treatment: education, to be a liberating influence, must offer the same mold for everyone, and must allow each, according to merit, the opportunity to advance in the social hierarchy. Of course, these principles, objectives, and programs hide significant disparities that in fact exist once children have gone beyond elementary school. The choice of institutions, options, and languages permits informed parents to act as "school consumers" as soon as their child enters junior high school; and their choices lead to unequal education. Since the system is not understood by the less privileged, the egalitarian philosophy favors the better informed.

Elementary school, which reflects the basic political philosophy and dispenses the fundamentals, resists efforts to destroy egalitarian logic. At this level, efforts to accommodate the specific features of regional minorities or immigrants, which led to sporadic redesign of schedules and programs and even to introducing people from outside the public service into the school system, never really succeeded. The resistance is clear in the teaching of regional languages or the national languages of immigrants.

Since 1851, the Falloux Law for primary teaching has prevailed: "French will be the only language in use in school"; at that time, the purpose was to eliminate regional dialects and unite France, which was split up into territories. As F. Brunot points out in his *Histoire de La Langue Francaise,* for political leaders, "language is surely what makes patriotism" (1967). Teaching regional languages and cultures conflicts with the desire for achieving national unity through schooling, and, it follows, with political differences (centralization vs. regionalism), philosophical differences (equal treatment vs. respect for differences), and substantive differences (rigidity of content and teaching, schedules, etc.) (Brunot 1967). Distinguishing measures according to linguistic, cultural, social, or geographic origins, within public elementary schools, contradicts the constitutional principles of the state-nation and are bound to fail.

It is important, however, to be aware of the practical problems of putting the Orientation Law of 1989 into practice. This law anticipates a profound modification in the organization of nursery and elementary school: "Cyclical" operations, grouping by achievement "levels" (tracking), institutional autonomy, financing of specific plans by groups in certain areas, awarding of bonuses to teachers in sectors with reputations for being difficult. Doesn't the effort to satisfy all the participants in the educational project risk increasing the inequalities between privileged geographic areas and other areas? The revival of Priority Educational Zones, created in 1981,[2] should go beyond the initial objectives of compensating for inequalities solely by providing supplementary credits. To reestablish a positive image for these "ghettos" will require turning them into favored areas to attract successful students, as well as competent, stable teachers, from other zones.

2. IMMIGRANT CHILDREN IN SCHOOL

French schools have always been confronted with diversity. At the end of the last century, schooling transformed little Bretons, little Provençals, and little Basques into French citizens, and converted the rural areas into one nation, while integrating the children of the first great immigration waves in the national melting pot. In fact, foreign children in the schools is an old phenomenon. Although the requirement that foreigners enroll their children in school was not explicit until the 1936 law, which required schooling up to fourteen years of age, many foreign children were in the schools before this date. Georges Mauco, in *Les Etrangers en France* (Foreigners in France, 1932) cites a study showing percentages of foreigners in the educational system equivalent to what we have today: in 1927 8.4 percent of the students aged six to thirteen were foreigners.

These percentages changed according to migratory waves and family relocation policies. Thus, during the 1950s, we see only 3 percent foreign children in the elementary level of public-sector schools. After the 1970s, there is a growth in number of foreigners, with family relocation or reunification policies contributing significantly to these numbers.

Considering the profound changes in the education system since the 1960s, in the growth of the stakes of education for the whole population, and in the transformation of the foreign population, it is exceedingly difficult to make comparisons with the past. In fact, only the 1970–1990 period allows rigorous analysis because there are no equivalent statistics for earlier periods (Boulot and Boyzon-Fradet 1988).

The statistics provided by the National Ministry of Education are based on legal nationality. Thus, the census accounts only for "foreign" children and not "immigrant" children. These are almost one and the same from the 1976–1977 school year on. In that year, the foreign students in primary and secondary levels were 6.6 percent of the total—a percentage that grew constantly until 1986–1987 and is now stabilized at a little less than 9 percent (8.74 percent in 1988–1989, just over a million students; see table 7.1).

In 1985, the official policy was clearly affirmed: immigrants and their children must be integrated into French society. Integration happens in many ways, but as far as children are concerned, education is the most important. From 1985 on, successive ministers unanimously acknowledged the dangers of the positive discriminatory policies promoted by their predecessors.

Following incidents in the fall of 1989, stemming from certain schools' refusal to accept foreign children and from the wearing of "Islamic scarves" by young girls in class in a Picardie junior high school, the government was obliged to submit the immigration issue to parliamentary debate. An interministerial committee on integration submitted a report in early 1990 about the various public agencies involved in integration. The inspector-general of national education, A. Hussenet, in charge of the report on school policies (Hussenet 1990), confirmed and clarified the principles adopted during the ministry of J. P. Chevènement (1985): "The mission of the schools is thus, from now on, to welcome and integrate foreign children, as all other children in difficult situations. This is what will ultimately condition their integration into French society." He also clarified his concept of integration: "to integrate

TABLE 7.1

1988–1989 School Year. Number of French and Foreign Students, by Nationality and Level in School, Public and Private.

Nationality	Number in Primary		Number in Secondary		Total Number	
	#	%	#	%	#	%
Total	6680516	100.00	5506764	100.00	12187280	100.00
French	6014851	90.04	5106969	92.74	11121820	91.26
Foreign	665665	9.96	399795	7.26	1-65460	8.74
French African	10502	0.16	2643	0.05	13145	0.11
Non–French African	40645	0.61	18789	0.34	59434	0.49
Algerian	167433	2.51	97381	1.77	264814	2.17
Spanish	12667	0.19	16276	0.30	28943	0.24
Italian	10109	0.15	13220	0.24	23329	0.19
Moroccan	162276	2.43	72624	1.32	234900	1.93
Portuguese	91659	1.37	35592	1.55	177251	1.45
Southeast Asian	33683	0.50	19442	0.35	53125	0.44
Tunisian	51444	0.77	22474	0.41	73918	0.61
Turkish	47680	0.71	22081	0.40	69761	0.57
Yugoslavian	6457	0.10	5784	0.11	12241	0.10
Other Common Market Countries	6942	0.10	7579	0.14	14521	0.12
Other	24168	0.36	15910	0.29	40078	0.33

Source: M. E. N.

is to establish a closer interdependence among members of a society, which implies both that the Republic's schools transmit to all their students a common body of knowledge, and of values of humanism, equality, liberty, and solidarity, and that these schools allow access to rational thought, highlighting French culture's openness to the world."

These principles were accompanied by a reminder of the measures that should be taken and by suggestions for complementary measures. First, enrollment: a 1984 memo states clearly that no matter what their parents' legal status, foreign children must submit to the educational requirements. Registration requirements in the educational institutions are no different than for the French. Neither ethnic background nor cultural background nor the parents' status or length of stay in France can prevent a child's registration in a school, junior high school, or high school, if he is under sixteen. Nonetheless, discrimination is practiced every year by certain communities, which use this as a weapon to win votes or to exert pressure in other political arenas, especially housing, even though they are given notice that they may not carry out such policies. These discriminatory practices, condemned by the central administration, affect the integration of the students in question.

Hussenet's report stresses the necessity of early schooling: "Enrollment into nursery school of foreign as well as disadvantaged children from two years old seems to be the best prevention of failure in school."

New non–French-speaking arrivals, if there are enough of them, enter into special temporary programs (one year maximum for elementary school, two year's maximum for secondary school) whose principal goal is intensive training in the French language to enable as rapid integration as possible into the normal curriculum. Since their experimental adoption in 1970 for six-to-eleven-year-olds and in 1973 for twelve-to-sixteen-year-olds (Ministry of Education 1970, 1973, 1986), these programs have educated over two hundred thousand students, but have not been evaluated: no serious data allow us to say whether they ultimately help or hinder good education.

Foreign children enrolled in initiation and adaptation classes account for less than 1 percent of all foreign children enrolled in elementary and first-level classes. The report requires these programs to "be maintained as long as they are justified by family relocations," to be "evaluated," and to be entrusted to "teachers with training in French as a second language in France."

Foreign children born in France or arriving before they are seven years old are educated in standard programs and receive the same education as their French classmates.

The only measure of positive discrimination within the school system itself is classes offered during school hours, designed for children of natives of certain foreign countries, in the language and culture of their country of origin.

The opportunity for children to receive an education in the language and culture of their country of origin, in response to a long-standing immigrant demand, is part of the economic agreements between France and certain immigrant countries. As early as 1925, the authorization to teach "modern languages by foreign instructors" in public school buildings *after* school hours resulted in a memo from the Ministry of National Education.[3] This was in fact a concession by the government, facilitating the renewal of labor agreements between the French Committee of Coalminers and the Agricultural Confederation of Devastated Regions, on the one hand, and the Polish government on the other hand (Ponty 1977). It wasn't until 1973 that foreign language instruction was introduced (sporadically and experimentally) in the public school system, for three hours weekly out of the twenty-seven hours of normal scheduled activities for the children. It replaced three hours of subjects such as history, geography, science, music, and plastic arts; since 1985, it has

TABLE 7.2

School Year 1988–1989. Classes for Foreign Children Recently Arrived in France (Public Schools). Percentage of Students in Different School Levels.

Nationality	Total Elementary	Initiation Classes		Total first level	Adaptation Classes	
		#	%		#	%
Total	3556957	4003	0.11	2687058	3561	0.13
French	3132736	512	0.	022422999	816	0.03
Foreign	424221	3491	0.82	264059	2745	1.04
French African	4569	132	2.89	1691	77	4.55
Non–French African	23702	136	0.57	10967	90	0.82
Algerian	107736	398	0.37	67401	225	0.33
Spanish	8475	104	1.23	8526	27	0.32
Italian	7039	13	0.18	7289	16	0.22
Moroccan	105465	692	0.66	52306	4894	0.93
Portuguese	62612	223	0.36	54648	286	0.52
Southeast Asian	19445	379	1.95	11885	349	2.94
Tunisian	31462	122	0.39	16175	72	0.45
Turkish	31917	689	2.16	17067	650	3.28
Yugoslavian	4522	75	1.66	3891	90	2.31
Other Common Market Countries	3661	60	1.64	3814	109	2.86
Other	13616	468	3.44	8399	360	4.29

replaced all or part of one of the regular curriculum subjects at the discretion of the teachers. The classes are only for the children of natives of countries with agreements with France. The first bilateral agreements were with Portugal and Italy in 1973, the last with Algeria in 1982. In all, eight countries are involved: Algeria, Spain, Italy, Morocco, Portugal, Tunisia, Turkey, and Yugoslavia. Classes are given by foreign teachers, not in the French public service, recruited and paid by their country of origin.

The guidelines regulating this teaching referred to the economic situation and migration policies and cited ambiguous and sometimes contradictory goals, for example, to facilitate the student's return to his/her country of origin or to integrate him/her into the school system; and to maintain a supposed heritage or to permit better acquisition of the French language. Practical difficulties (coordinating schedules, finding sites), ambiguous goals, the influence of the countries of origin, but above all the stigma of special treatment within a totally unified system, in particular in elementary school, lead us to wonder about the contribution of this program toward the goal of integration that has been officially proclaimed by the administration. In fact, elementary school operates on a simple principle: a group of children of a certain age range and a given educational level = a class and teacher. Foreign language classes require that at certain times the group must be separated from certain members who must go to another location (often nonexistent or meant to be used for something else—the cafeteria, the lobby . . .) with children from other classes, other levels, other age groups, under a foreign teacher, with pedagogic methods that are often very different from those of French teachers. Sometimes the course content goes against the secular, neutral principles of public school, as the control of French academic authorities often is hampered by the language barrier (Boulot and Boyzon-Fradet 1985).

The interministerial committee is definite on this point: "we can observe that this teaching program constitutes, in the current state of affairs, a factor for discrimination rather than for integration." Their proposals suggested ways to correct the negative aspects, essentially those that are infractions of the principle of secular education, to evaluate the quality and relevance of these courses, and to reexamine the bilateral accords in order to move these classes, currently held during the school day, to a time after school hours.

For a few years, the number of students benefiting from their native language courses during school hours has been diminishing; only 17.3 percent of the students potentially eligible for these courses in 1989–1990 participated —that is, only about sixty thousand students (see table 7.3).

At the junior high school level, students' choice of "immigration languages" is unexpected; English and German monopolize up to 98 percent of the first choice. And this cannot just be attributed to the absence of alternatives. The dominant cultural model weighs heavily in favor of English. Immigrant children can be put at a disadvantage by choosing their parents' maternal language as the first modern language to study, opening careers destined only for immigrants. Or courses in these languages may not be available. According to the studies from 1980, in seventh grade only 5 percent of Maghreb students studied Arabic, only 15.6 percent of Portuguese studied Portuguese, only 19.4 percent of Spanish studied Spanish, and only 2 percent of Italian students studied Italian.

As a result of recent research findings, foreign consular authorities have adopted different policies with respect to integration of classes during school hours. Aware of the difficulties, sensitive to the risks of marginalizing students, and sometimes at the request of the immigrant communities themselves, some prefer to hold the language courses after school, and others prefer cultural

TABLE 7.3

Classes in Maternal Language and Culture in Elementary School Public Institutions. Evolution from 1981–1982 to 1989–1990.[1]

Language	81/82	82/83	83/84	84/85	85/86	86/87	88/89	89/9
Arabic[2]								
Algerian	6232	9549	25668	30559	27289	23340	18745	16754
Moroccan	3775	4195	6723	4740	3813	5339	12279	12378
Tunisian	3131	3501	3506	4011	3639	3212	2854	2316
Spanish	996	905	1452	813	494	411	345	387
Italian	8149	8216	8503	12519	10335	10142	11138	11100
Portuguese	16644	17409	18166	19585	16881	14735	11547	9900
Turkish	4382	3880	5209	7029	7802	8047	8104	7932
Yugoslavian	143	44	71	104	107	108	176	69
Total	43452	47699	69298	79360	70360	65334	65188	60836
%[3]		12.36%	17.74%	20.24%	19.32%	17.52%	18.14%	17.26

Notes: 1. Data only available from 1981–1982 on.
    2. No data available.
    3. Percentage of students taking these courses as compared to potentially eligible students.
Source: M.E.N.

activities to linguistic training, aimed at entire classes where foreign and French children are mixed together with French teachers. This becomes a way of promoting an intercultural pedagogy.

However, this direction, born from the pilot project of the Commission of European Communities (1976–1979),[4] quickly deviated from its original concept. The idea was supposed to be to circumvent the insurmountable difficulties encountered in teaching maternal languages and cultures during school hours by replacing language courses with activities shared with all the children, under the joint responsibility of foreign and French teachers—activities requiring multiple and complementary approaches to develop the critical minds of children and to fight stereotypes (Boulot, Fradet, and Obispo 1980). Instead, the intercultural concept went totally astray and the class activities generally proposed are often reduced to folkloric or culinary demonstrations! In addition, no one questioned the psychological effects on children whose "culture" (whatever this "culture" of "origin" is) is being exhibited before the class.[5]

It becomes quickly apparent that the transformation of language courses, financed by the countries of origin, into cultural activities aimed at a mixed group of native French children and foreigners, has not always been appreciated by foreign authorities. Doubtless, the contradictions between the goals of these programs and their effect has accelerated awareness of the French schools' need to open their curriculum to foreign cultures and to integrate the history of immigration into it.

Thus, in 1985, Professor J. Berque, in his report on immigration in the Republic's schools (1985) declares, "Cultural openness, necessary for all students, given the irreversible evolution of our societies, must systematically and decidedly find its place in the general education given to everyone. It must become a normal part of school life at both the elementary and secondary levels."

This approach implies recasting the entire teaching program and providing adequate teacher training, a long and difficult process!

In order to accelerate the process, in September 1989 the minister of education published a memo encouraging institutions to organize Projects of Educational Action (PEA) about "foreign contributions to French heritage" (Operation Composition Française)—projects encouraged and financed jointly by the Ministry of Education and the Fonds D'Action Sociale.[6] A few interesting programs were filmed and shown on television in order to encourage new initiatives.

The interministerial committee's report of December 1989 suggests three measures for broadening the contents of the curriculum and the teacher-training programs:

- "Putting the contributions of immigration to France's culture into perspective." The study of immigration appears in history programs in a diffuse way; it is appropriate to go further and train teachers to "illuminate their teaching with pertinent literary, artistic, scientific, or technical references."
- Objectively studying the beliefs and rites of the great religions found in Europe (Christianity, Judaism, Islam), following the same perspective and modes as the first measure.
- "Extending instruction about civilizations, cultures, and current conditions in immigrant countries and the particular ways their peoples behave." These actions should be reinforced by the "development of exchanges of all kinds between our schools and institutions and foreign institutions."

It is clearly a case, as conveyed in the report, of the French educational system taking into account, within its normal operations and its fundamental principles, the heterogeneous nature of the country's population.

Teaching the language and culture of immigrant children's "origins" has aroused, during the past fifteen years, impassioned debate about the purpose of the French educational system, but also an awareness of the values of both the administrators and users of the schools. Secularism, political neutrality, and the philosophy of equal opportunity have been reinforced through this debate.

"Controlled experimentation with a foreign language in elementary school," begun in certain schools at the start of the 1989–1990 school year, barely opened the way for languages of countries of immigration. Ninety percent of the eligible classes chose English, 58 percent German, 8.8 percent Spanish, 0.75 percent Portuguese, 0.5 percent Italian, 0.3 percent Russian, 0.09 percent Polish, and 0.05 percent Arabic. These results are not in the least surprising when we consider the (legitimate) constraints: Sometimes there is only one choice for a class as a group, or only some instruction available at the school, or there are no available teaching personnel. When we know the choice of the parents and see the language options offered, we cannot see how diversification can really be brought about.

The creation of international sections in areas with a high percentage of immigrants will help those that are already deficient, as recommended by recent reports. But is this responsive to the wish of parents? Choice of language involves more than education policy. It requires training teachers who can teach children who are foreign or of foreign origin. This requirement— imposed by a European Community Directive in 1977 (Directive 77/486/CEE) —was the concern of the Ministry from 1975 on, and included sessions of teacher training, the creation of CEFISM,[7] and training for trainers. Today a coherent system concerning initial and ongoing training of teachers at all levels has been put in place; it has doubled operations to train the managers and nonteaching partners in the educational system. However, since 1986, only the teachers are subject to any initial required training course (twenty-seven hours out of the eighteen hundred hours of their degree program). In principle the creation of the University Institutes of Teacher Training[8] should fill the gap by introducing this dimension in the degree program for all future teachers. Ongoing training is a voluntary option, which limits its effectiveness; in addition, available financial means are insufficient to satisfy the needs.

The plan adopted in 1970 was not established until December 1989 as part of a universal, coherent immigration policy. There was no debate in the National Assembly about the goals for educating immigrant children—it is the executive branch that, with the help of administrative guidelines, has regulated the recruitment and the education of these children. This is why it is hardly surprising that the goals have fluctuated, contradicting themselves from one circular to the next and putting teachers in an uncertain situation that hampers efficient operations.

Fundamental changes in the migratory phenomenon and especially the birth of most immigrant children in France, but also and above all the political debate stimulated by the right and far-right parties, have led the ministers of national education since 1965 to clearly affirm the goal to give absolute priority to the integration of immigrant children into the normal school system and, more recently, to integrate educational policy into an overall immigration policy.

The state of mind of the early 1980s about the "right to be different" gave way, in the face of evidence of the negative effects of discriminatory measures, to a unanimous declaration in favor of integration. Would practical measures achieve this goal?

3. THE FRENCH EDUCATION SYSTEM: SPRINGBOARD OR OBSTACLE FOR INTEGRATION?

For our purposes, to be integrated into French society means to find a social and professional place and to adhere to its fundamental values, without denying the identity of the individual.

Measuring the influence of schooling on the integration of immigrant children is not easy. Before the 1960s, integration of youths of foreign origin occurred through other routes (training with an employer, early membership in a labor union). These modes of integration into society were also the most common routes for native populations. Today the situation has changed considerably and it is very difficult to single out the many integrating factors. In fact, since all the children are educated at least between the ages of three and sixteen, we have no reference population for comparisons. In addition, the role of academic qualifications in professional integration has increased and the labor market today essentially recruits on the basis of diplomas rather than specific professional qualifications. Schooling has become the required rite of passage, and its role, positive or negative, is thus reinforced.

Studies of French and foreign students, sociological givens being the same, that were carried out by the Bureau of Statistics of the National Ministry of Education on representative samples of the school population, allow us to make comparative analyses of the processes that lead to success or failure. From them, we can draw the following conclusions:

• Integration into the work force is directly correlated with the level of education: the higher the level, the lower the unemployment rate (see table 7.4), the higher the position in the professional hierarchy, and the higher the salary.
• The dominant factor in school success or failure remains the socioprofes-

TABLE 7.4

Unemployment Rate of Young Beginning Workers (18–24 Years Old) by Diploma Level.

| | Year | | | | | | | | |
| | 1973 | | | 1977 | | | 1980 | | |
	M	F	Total	M	F	Total	M	F	Total
No Diploma	12%	18%	15%	31%	46%	38%	42%	63%	52%
BEPC (Grade school diploma)	5%	16%	11%	22%	20%	21%	29%	43%	37%
CAP-DEP	6%	10%	8%	17%	26%	21%	21%	42%	32%
BAC (High school diploma)	9%	10%	10%	15%	22%	20%	19%	28%	25%
Short-term higher education	3%	4%	4%	7%	9%	8%	12%	13%	13%
Long-term higher education	10%	12%	11%	14%	14%	14%	11%	21%	16%
Total	9%	13%	11%	20%	26%	23%	26%	39%	36%

Source: INSEE (Institut National des Statistiques et des Etudes Economiques).

sional status of the parents. In spite of the will to democratize, education reinforces the social hierarchy.

Future of Students Entered into 7th Grade in 1972/1973/1974 According to C.S.P. (Socio-Professional Categories) (base 1,000)

Level	Workers	Liberal Professions and Upper Management
7th grade	1,000	1,000
10th grade	549	943
11th grade	269	855
BAC (high school diploma)	166	641

Source: Ministry of National Education

- For socioprofessional categories with equivalent backgrounds, school results of foreign students are identical to those of their French classmates, and slightly better than the most disadvantaged among them. Only late arrival in France, often accompanied by poor schooling in the original country, is a certain handicap for successful integration.

Rate of enrollment in senior year for disadvantaged CSP students according to nationality.

French	19.8%
French-born foreigners	20.5%
Foreigners born outside of France	14.5%

Source: Ministry of National Education

- Foreign families' behavior in relation to school is almost identical to that of French families, and the older the immigration, the less the difference: earlier and earlier preeducation, majority choice of English in high school, demands for a complete education . . . However, few foreign children are directed towards private education (20 percent of the total school population are in private schooling and only 5 percent of foreign children are there); the best represented of foreign nationalities are the oldest communities.

If massive membership of immigrant children in the most disadvantaged parts of the population puts them first in the line for educational failure, it is obvious that this failure is not in any way a result of their ethnic origin but rather of the inability of the educational system to reduce social inequalities. Thus, if we analyze the factors blocking paths to success, we see that they are identical no matter what the nationality of the student, with certain factors, such as being held back, sometimes having less disastrous consequences for a child of foreign origin than for a native French child since the first is credited with a language handicap that permits him to benefit from a supplementary year in his education.

Another feature of integration is the rising social mobility of young people of foreign origin as compared to their parents. This was brought out by Jean-Louis Borkowski's study, published in January 1990 in *Données Sociales.* Youths from immigrant families who have succeeded in integrating recognize the dominant role of schooling, and also the influential role of the family investment.[9] Among these youths we find the strongest defenders of this society's democratic and secular values, their awareness having been heightened by their struggle. On the other hand, young people who failed in school attribute this failure to the educational system, but in this respect they are exactly like their French classmates.

We often refer to the Gypsy population as a perfect example of resistance to integration through schooling. In fact, when this population is nomadic, the education of the children is sporadic and includes only the basic skills: reading, writing, arithmetic. However, the sedentary part of this population tends to follow a normal educational pattern, but finds itself socially outcast because of a tendency to concentrate in certain locations. This issue is complex and will require research.

It is not our intent to draw an idyllic picture of the educational situation of immigrant children, but it does appear that the integrating power of school cannot be challenged, no matter what profound changes it has undergone since 1881. The educational system produces both elites and rejects, among natives and "foreigners" alike. The recent incidents, when young Maghreb girls wore "Islamic scarves" to school, were interpreted by some as an indication of their opposition to being integrated. In fact, a careful analysis of this "scandal"[10] showed that this was not at all the case: excessive media attention to a minor incident, reports of political pressure, crystallization of latent problems in a particularly sensitive region, efforts of religious integration movements to become visible, efforts to destabilize the schools—many reasons placed this debate in the public eye!

In the end, the administration found itself required to call upon the Conseil d'Etat to resolve the conflict and organize a debate on migration policies. The founding principles of the Republic, and thus of the public schools, came out of the debate stronger than ever, but the political effects of this "scandal" were negative for immigrants (reinforcement of the National Front). This school year (1990–1991) inaugurates the first application of the 1989 Orientation Law on teaching. We shall see the recommendations of the interministerial committee applied to immigrant integration, not only in schools but in all the sectors involved in integration. A recent opinion poll (*Nouvel Observateur* 1990) shows the extent to which the French are worried about integration of immigrants, even while demonstrating support for the governmental goals and the French "melting pot" tradition.

The challenge to our society requires an answer to certain questions:

- In a period of economic crisis, will the desire to succeed in school maintain its strength despite the ethnic discrimination that occurs when two people with equivalent diplomas enter the work market?
- Housing policies, especially renovation of urban centers, which leads to relegation of the most disadvantaged people (hence populations of foreign origin) to the outskirts, transform the schools in these areas into real ghetto schools. Contact with the French population is limited. Doesn't the accumulation of difficulties risk leading a good many of the young, especially those who are failing, into delinquent activities or to withdrawal from their identity? (We should also ask about specific types of delinquency among

foreign youths and about the consequences of this denial of their own identity on their adherence to the principles of the receiving society.)

It is difficult in this period of change, to make predictions about the integration into our society of young foreigners. Don't we risk negative effects on the most disadvantaged populations as a result of the increasing independence of institutions, the decentralization of their management, and the development within the educational system of a business ethic, which seem inevitable in a period of improving the productivity of education and trimming its operations? Market criteria in education may be consistent with the strategies of the best-informed people. But, is the development of consumerism in education a democratizing factor?

NOTES

1. In 1984–1985, the bilingual sections included a total of thirty thousand French and foreign students. Only one thousand among them were in sections where immigrant-country languages, including Spanish, a language with a cultural tradition in France, were being taught. As for international sections, there were six in the elementary schools, ten in the junior high schools, and seven in the high schools during the same year.
2. The creation of Priority Education Zones was one of the first educational measures adopted by the Left in 1981. They were trying to reduce inequality by following three basic principles:

   — regulate "the increase in resources available for democratizing schooling"— that is, "give the most to those who have the least";
   — grant means to "define and then pursue realistic pedagogic goals"; and
   — include in these activities not just teachers but also local elected officials and all other interested parties, so as to unite all their efforts.

   After a difficult start in 1981, the movement was launched in 1982–1983 (6 percent of elementary schools, 10 percent of junior high schools, only 1 percent of high schools), but then collapsed in 1984. In 1989, the Ministry relaunched this program.
3. Memo of 25 July 1925: Foreign instructors of modern languages.
4. Reports on the Pilot Project of the European Communities; 2 volumes prepared by CREDIF, unpublished (1977, 1978, 1979, 1980).
5. We should point out that the Center for Research and Innovation in Teaching in O.C.D.E. had voiced serious doubts about these multicultural educational policies for immigrants. See, on this subject, the report of the 1985 colloquium about "Educational Policies and Minority Social Groups."
6. Fonds d'Action Sociale for immigrant workers and their families, a public institu-

tion created in 1958. It has three key intervention points: training, social and cultural activities, and housing.

7. CEFISM: Centres de Formation et d'Information pour la Scolarisation des Enfants des Migrants. These are the pedadogic sections of teacher-training schools whose goal is to train personnel involved in the education of immigrant children. Twenty-three academies out of twenty-six provide this in metropolitan France.

8. From the 1991–1992 school year on, first and second level teachers, recruited after obtaining their licenses, will be trained in these University Institutes for Training Teachers.

9. This is attested to by autobiographical accounts of authors of foreign origin, notably François Cavanna, *Les Ritals* (Paris; Belfond, 1978); Azouz Begag, Le Gône du Chaâba (Paris: Le Seuil, 1986).

10. See also *Hommes et Migrations* 2 1129–1130 (February–March 1990); *Herodote*, no. 56 (first trimester 1990); *Le débat*, no. 58 (January–February 1990).

REFERENCES

Berque, Jacques. 1985. *L'immigration à l'école de la République*. Report to Ministry of Education. Paris: La Documentation Française.

Borkowski, Jean Louis. 1990. "L'insertion sociale des immigrés et de leurs enfants." *Données Sociales*. Paris: La Documentation Française.

Boulot, S., and D. Boyzon-Fradet. 1988. Français par le sang. *Plein Droit* 3 (April). 29–32.

———. 1988. *Les immigrés et l'école*. Paris: L'Harmattan.

———. 1987. Un siècle de reglementation des langues à l'école. In *France, pays multilangue*. Paris: L'Harmattan.

———. 1985. L'apprentissage de leur langue maternelle. In *Le citoyen de demain et les langues*.: Les Langues Modernes.

———. 1984. *Autour des Ritals de Cavanna*. Paris: Didier.

Boulot, S., D. Fradet, and S. Obispo. 1980. Napoléon, la conquête de l'Espagne. In *Une année d'enseignement de la langue et de la culture espagnoles*. Vol. 2. Paris:CREDIF.

Brunot, F. 1967. *Histoire de la langue française*. Vol. 9. Paris: Colin.

Commision de la nationalité. 1988. *Etre français aujourd'hui et demain*. Paris: Commission de la nationalité.

Hussenet, A. 1990. *Une politique scolaire d'intégration*. Unpublished report to Ministry of Education.

Mauco, Georges. 1932. *Les étrangers en France*. Paris: Colin.

Ministère de l'Education Nationale (M.E.N.) Memoranda of 13 January 1970; 25 September 1973; and 13 March 1986.

Nouvel Observateur. 13 September 1990.

Ponty, J. 1977. Les problemes soulevés par la scolarisation des enfants polonais. *Relations Internationales* 12.

8

IMMIGRATION, RELIGION, AND INTERGROUP RELATIONS: HISTORICAL PERSPECTIVES ON THE AMERICAN EXPERIENCE

Philip Gleason

Although most historical studies of immigration take some note of religion, relatively few have systematically analyzed its role in the adjustment of immigrants to their new life; until recently, scholars of American religious history were even more neglectful of immigration (Dolan 1988). In fact, religion played too vast and complex a role in the history of American immigration for comprehensive treatment here. What follows offers only the barest outline of two dimensions of the topic. Part 1 sketches the way historians have dealt with the issue. My purpose here is not to provide a full survey of the literature, but simply to suggest the scope of the topic and indicate the principal interpretive approaches adopted by earlier scholars. Part 2 ventures into more speculative territory by focusing on education as a locus of interaction among immigration, religion, and American civil religion. For our purposes, most historical treatments can be grouped under two broad headings: those that focus on the *positive* role of religion in helping immigrants to adjust to American life, and those that stress its *negative* aspects, especially its divisiveness. We will begin with the former.

1.

It says something about the neglect of this subject that George M. Stephenson's *The Religious Aspects of Swedish Immigration* (1932) remains the single most comprehensive study of the place of religion in the life of an American immigrant group. Stephenson provides detailed coverage of religious conditions in the homeland and of ecclesiastical developments in the United States between the 1840s and the 1920s. What justifies calling his approach positive, however, is his insistence that the Lutheran church (Augustana Synod) constituted the essential institutional nucleus around which the group life of Swedish immigrants structured itself. The same could be said, mutatis mutandis, of most other immigrant groups and their churches and, as historians have recently emphasized, of African-Americans as well.

Stephenson did full justice to the bitter doctrinal quarrels and organizational splits that disrupted the religious life of Scandinavian immigrants. In that sense, his work documented the negative as well as the positive role of religion. But taken as a whole, Stephenson's study illustrates the theoretical point made earlier by the great sociologist and student of Polish immigration, W. I. Thomas, namely, that ethnic institutions such as churches, far from isolating newcomers from American life, actually provide the organizational vehicles that allow them to participate in it (Thomas 1966, 206–10).

Besides illustrating this fundamental point about the positive role of religion, Stephenson alluded in his preface to the similarity between the religious concerns of his subjects and those of the New England Puritans. This effort to integrate the immigrant story with the dominant national tradition was developed more systematically by another historian of Scandinavian background, Marcus Lee Hansen. In an essay entitled "Immigration and Puritanism," Hansen argued that moral rigor (which is what Puritanism primarily connoted in the 1920s and 1930s) was the clergy's natural reaction to the disruption of social norms and community controls brought on by emigration in the case of colonial New Englanders and nineteenth-century immigrants alike. Hansen thus linked immigrants firmly to the nation's mythic past, *and* used their experience to throw new interpretive light upon it (Hansen 1940, 97–128).

Neither Stephenson nor Hansen developed a point implicit in their discussions of religion—that it played a positive role *psychologically,* as well as institutionally, by providing emotional anchorage for persons undergoing the traumatic shock of dislocation and resettlement in a strange land. The explication of this phenomenon was left to Oscar Handlin (1951), whose *The Uprooted* shaped a whole generation's understanding of the immigrant experience. Religion, in his poignant account, was what gave meaning to life in the ancestral village; after migration, it took on even greater significance as the one feature of old-world culture that seemed capable of being transplanted into the new world. But—as M. Oriol has likewise found in the case of recent Catholic immigrants to France (see chap. by M. Oriol)—the church of the homeland could not be reconstituted in its old form in the new society; the effort to do so was inevitably attended by frustration, disappointment, and strife. Even so, the conflicts over religion that erupted among Handlin's urban immigrants (as among Stephenson's Swedes) could be understood in a positive way, for they required the newcomers to reflect on their novel situation and to forge a new kind of self-definition (Skardal 1974, 183–85).

Will Herberg likewise stressed the psychological angle in his *Protestant-Catholic-Jew,* a work that undertook to explain how the midcentury "revival of religion" could occur in a society growing ever more secularized. The key to the puzzle was to be sought in the social psychology of an immigrant-derived people. Appealing to what he called "Hansen's law"—what the son wishes to forget the grandson wishes to remember—Herberg argued that third-generation Americans were "returning" to the churches and synagogues as a means of reestablishing contact with their ancestral heritages. Besides constituting a link with the past, religion met the much-talked-of psychological need for "belonging" by providing an answer to the "aching question" of identity, "Who am I?" (Herberg 1955; Gleason 1990).

Herberg thus assigned great social and psychological importance to the interaction between immigration and religion. But as a believing Jew, he was troubled by his findings. Americans, he feared, valued religion for the social and psychological functions it served, not because it offered a message of transcendent intrinsic worth. Protestantism, Catholicism, and Judaism might be hailed as "the three great faiths of democracy," but only because they embodied the "spiritual values" underlying "the American Way of Life," which was the *real religion* of Americans. This aspect of Herberg's analysis anticipated the late-1960s discovery of "civil religion," but he gave much greater prominence to immigration as a factor in its development than any other commentator.

Herberg also popularized the notion of the "triple melting pot." This interpretation—introduced by Ruby Jo Reeves Kennedy (1944) in a study of ethnic intermarriages in New Haven, Connecticut—held that the assimilation of immigrants tended to follow broadly religious lines rather than taking place in an undifferentiated fashion. Thus Protestantism, Catholicism, and Judaism constituted three distinct "melting pots," and religion became an important analytical tool for understanding American society at midcentury. Although forgotten in the racial and ethnic upheaval of the 1960s and 1970s, the assumption that Protestants, Catholics, and Jews—along with Blacks—constituted the principal social groupings in the American population is still to be found in two works that attained the status of classics: *Beyond the Melting Pot,* by Nathan Glazer and Daniel P. Moynihan (1963); and *Assimilation in American Life,* by Milton M. Gordon (1964).

In terms of assigning analytical importance to the religious factor, Herberg's work represents the high point in the literature. But the so-called revival of ethnicity, along with the upsurge of interest in social history, has since combined to produce an outpouring of scholarship on immigration, ethnicity, and religion. The most recent comprehensive history of American Catholicism (Dolan 1985) gives unprecedented attention to immigration; and since its publication two other general studies of Catholic immigration have appeared (Olson 1987; Liptak 1989). Although predominantly descriptive, virtually all of the new historical work assumes that "pluralism" is desirable and deprecates "assimilation" implicitly if not explicitly. Much of it also exhibits a more diffuse tendency to treat "religion" as merely an aspect of "ethnicity," that is, as an epiphenomenon or function of something more basic (Miller and Marzik 1977).

At least in part as a reaction to the erosion of religion's status as an independent variable, Timothy L. Smith (1978) vigorously reaffirmed its causal potency in an essay entitled "Religion and Ethnicity in America." He makes three important claims. First, he maintains that religion was the key element in the process by which immigrants who were strangers to each other, and who lacked a common "national" identity, molded themselves into relatively coherent groups, each with its own distinctive sense of peoplehood. It does not stretch categories unduly to think of this as an elaboration of the institutional-nucleus function noted earlier.

Secondly, Smith calls immigration a "theologizing experience" because it intensified "the psychic basis of religious commitment," personalized it by requiring new choices, gave it an ethical slant ("How should we live our new lives?"), and provided resources (e.g., Biblical images of hope and redemption) that nourished a forward-looking, progressive outlook on the part of immigrants. This goes much further than Handlin's psychologism, but it too focuses on the personal rather than the institutional dimension of religion. In his third point, which is less fully developed but more a genuine novelty, Smith draws attention to religious universalism, the "idea of a common humanity [that] stands at the center of all major western religions." By affirming this idea, he suggests, all the "ethnosectarian versions of Jewish and Christian faith in America" contributed to America's "integrative pluralism."

Something of a tour de force, Smith's essay is the most systematically developed and explicitly positive analysis of the interaction between religion and immigration known to me. Taking it as the capstone of that interpretive tradition, we turn now to treatments that focus on the negative dimensions of the interaction. These accounts concern themselves, not with the unifying and stabilizing functions of religion, but with its *divisiveness*. Religion can create or exacerbate ill feeling in two ways: within and among immigrant groups themselves; and between immigrants and the host society. The former we have already noted in passing, and there is no room here to discuss the literature in detail; the latter, which falls under the heading of "nativism," requires brief discussion.

Given the salience of nativism as a theme in immigration historiography, it is remarkable that two works published many years ago still dominate the field: *The Protestant Crusade,* by Ray Allen Billington (1938), a study of the origins of nativism in the antebellum period; and *Strangers in the Land,* by John Higham (1955), which covers the period 1860–1925. The former identifies religion—specifically the anti-Catholicism of the Protestant majority—as the central element in American nativism; the latter takes religion into account, but its interpretive scheme is more complex.

An intellectual historian sensitive to the dangers of nationalism, Higham portrayed nativism as an inverse form of nationalism directed against groups that seemed to threaten the well-being of the republic from within. It varied in intensity according to the degree of confidence or anxiety felt by the cultural majority, and was guided in its selection of targets by three ideological principles—anti-Catholicism, antiradicalism, and racialism. Religion thus remained central to Higham's analysis, but it was no longer the primary element in nativism.

Although it allowed him to deal fully with anti-Catholicism, Higham's approach was less well suited to an exploration of the anti-Semitic dimension of American nativism. Hence he devoted several later essays to that subject, the most important of which are included in *Send These to Me: Jews and Other Immigrants in Urban America* (Higham 1975). Catholic and Jewish historians also dealt with nativism as it affected the two groups, but the timing of their studies differs. Catholics produced many monographs on nativism in the era when Billington's book appeared, but interest in the topic has slackened in the more recent past. Just the opposite tendency is discernible among Jewish historians: anti-Semitism has become a major focus of scholarly attention only in the past two decades (Gerber 1986).

After the appearance of *Strangers in the Land,* scholarship on matters related to nativism took a different turn, probably because that book seemed definitive on the subject as traditionally understood. Higham himself signaled the new direction when he pointed out that his "ideological" interpretation was but one approach to the problem. Nativism also reflected genuine conflicts—for material advantage, for prestige, and over "real issues of faith"—among different segments of society, and had to be seen as part of the "total complex of ethnic tensions in American society." The new task, therefore, was "to analyze the historical composition of American society in ethnic terms" (Higham 1958).

Higham's prescience in this matter is noted by James Bergquist (1986) in a survey of recent work on nativism that provides an admirable review of the new literature. In politics, the "ethnocultural approach" highlighted the importance of religious, linguistic, and other immigrant-related issues in the party battles of the past. Social historians explored the relation of ethnicity and religion to mobility patterns and their accompanying tensions, while labor historians featured the linkages between ethnicity and working-class culture. Historians of education showed how often ethnoreligious factors were at work in conflicts over school reform, and the same applies to other areas of reform as well.

Although this literature has given new prominence to ethnic-religious issues, most historians would probably agree with Higham that the term "nativism" should not be applied "to all or even most of this recent scholarship." Nativism, he goes on to say, is "a one-sided word, pinpointing exclusionary impulses expressed in the name of the native population," and its use should be confined to that "traditional meaning" (Higham 1986). The point is well taken, and Higham might have added that historians still conventionally regard nativism in this sense as an unqualified evil. For despite mounting evidence that ethnoreligious conflicts are complex, and may involve legitimate concerns on the part of "nativists," historians still tend almost automatically to side with the "victims." Indeed, this disposition is the most powerful, most widely held, and least critically examined attitude—not to say prejudice—that shapes historical work in the field of immigration and religion.

As broadly as it has been applied, the positive/negative classification does not compass all the works that demand notice even in this schematic overview. A highly relevant work that escapes these (or any other) categories is *Religious Outsiders and the Making of Americans*, by R. Laurence Moore (1986). Here Moore pursues a problem he encountered in an earlier study of spiritualism: What constitutes "the mainstream" in American culture and why are certain groups (insiders) considered part of it, while others (outsiders) are not? The immigrant dimension as such is present in only two of the groups Moore examines (Catholics and Jews), but the profoundly "ethnic" question of how group boundaries are established and maintained is likewise involved in his discussion of Mormons, Christian Scientists, and several varieties of Protestant fundamentalists.

A series of related essays rather than a systematic historical treatise, Moore's book sparkles with insights but resists easy encapsulation. He argues that the metaphor of "the mainstream" distorts reality and should be dropped, pointing out again and again that groups regarded as outsiders shared the same values and assumptions as insiders even though they employed the rhetoric of outsiderhood for purposes of boundary maintenance. He also urges historians to look more deeply at the conflicts among these groups because they played so essential a role in forging the religious identities through which men and women invested their lives with significance.

If Moore's message is hard to pin down, that is even more true of the literature on American civil religion; but it demands attention as relevant, particularly to the second part of this essay, since it involves the question of American "identity." The general idea—namely, that religion and politics had somehow blended together to impart a sacred dimension to American ideology and institutions—long antedated the appearance of Robert Bellah's landmark essay, "Civil Religion in America" (Bellah 1967). Why that piece set off such a flood of publications, both popular and academic, is a subject deserving of analysis in its own right (Mathisen 1989). In any case, the notion—elusive at best—had assumed such protean form by 1980 that Bellah himself described it as having lost all conceptual coherence "or at least . . . anything I ever meant by the term" (Bellah and Hammond 1980, 1).

For Bellah, who can fairly be called a theologian of this form of faith, civil religion is the spiritual bond that unifies Americans and, as it were, sanctifies their common life. This obviously suggests that American civil religion is a kind of super-religion with which immigrant groups professing various "particularistic" faiths must somehow come to terms. Even though Bellah later conceded that "two different types of civil religion" might be distinguished, "both [were] operative in America" and the unifying function seemed unaffected (Bellah 1976, 237). But if civil religions continued to multiply, what would that do to national unity? Martin Marty did not address the question when he explained that America really had "Two Kinds of Two Kinds of Civil Religion" (Marty 1971). Neither did Michael Novak, although he brought immigration decisively into the picture by asserting that there were at least four Protestant, three Jewish, three Irish Catholic, and an unspecified number of other ethnic civil religions (Novak 1976). But these formulations unquestionably complicated civil religion's unifying role, and Laurence Moore was unkind enough to suggest that, like the other faiths he studied, civil religion probably "split Americans into separate camps as often as it has brought them together" (Moore 1986, 202).

The only work known to me that attempts to explain just *how* civil religion promotes national unity by moderating interreligious strife is *No Offense: Civil Religion and Protestant Taste,* by John Murray Cuddihy (1977). In what he calls a willful misreading of Bellah's work, Cuddihy converts civil religion into the "religion of civility." He then proceeds to show how the American imperative of civility—showing respect for others; at its blandest, "being nice" —requires the believers in different religious faiths to moderate their public claims to exclusive possession of the truth, extend de facto recognition to others, and thereby implicitly acquiesce in the reduction of their own faith-position to one among many, all of which must abide by the prescriptions of the secular religion of civility. Cuddihy's brilliant analysis not only "operationalizes" civil religion but also explains why the ideal of pluralistic tolerance is emotionally unsatisfying, for civility does not promise genuine solidarity, much less salvation. Mutual forbearance, necessary and admirable though it is, fails to stir the soul.

Cuddihy also contributed to a volume entitled *Uncivil Religion: Interreligious Hostility in America* (Bellah and Greenspahn 1987). Although Bellah is a coeditor and contributor, the book has little to say about civil religion as such. It presents, rather, a useful survey of tensions affecting a wide range of religious groups, and between society at large and "cults" such as the Reverend Sun Myung Moon's Unification church. In his concluding commentary, Bellah focuses on the issue of group boundaries. While rejecting rigid exclusivity, he sees greater danger at present from the "radical individualism" that threatens to dissolve group boundaries entirely, relativize all judgments, and undermine "the moral norms that provide the terms for our democratic conversation." Bellah prescribes maintaining "group identities and group boundaries while remaining open to knowledge of and cooperation with others, including those of different faiths." He calls this position "authentically biblical and authentically American" (Bellah and Greenspahn 1987, 219–32). It might even be an authentic expression of American civil religion, although Bellah does not make that claim; but as the long history of controversy over religion, education, and Americanism demonstrates, the reconciliation of conflicting group identities and group boundaries is a perennial problem.

2.

Group identities and group boundaries are inescapably involved in education because its primary purpose is to inculcate in children and young people the knowledge, beliefs, and values of the groups of which they are a part. In the Christian west, this activity was traditionally carried out under religious auspices, suffused with religious assumptions, and oriented toward religious goals. But in the era of modern nationalism that dates from the French Revolution, the traditional arrangement came into conflict with, and was progressively displaced by, state control of education. The new system was promoted by political leaders who perceived the crucial role the schools could play in molding national unity, and whose outlook often had a strongly civil-religious cast. Conflicts over secular (political) versus religious (church-related) control of education were more embittered in Europe, particularly France, than in the United States (Moody 1978). But those that occurred here are particularly relevant to our interest because religious diversity arising from immigration was so centrally involved and because civil religion, broadly understood, has been so prominent a theme. Although the discussion must be schematic in the extreme, looking at the school question over time will give us a more concrete sense of the issues.

Few difficulties arose in the colonial era because formal education at the elementary level, which was religious in inspiration, operated in localized fashion and on a small scale (Lowe 1986–1987). After independence, there was a gradual shift toward greater reliance on the state, but church-related schooling continued strongly into the early decades of the nineteenth century. Although various schemes of "national education" were floated as early as the 1790s, they resembled the educational projects of revolutionary France too closely to gain much support. Only in the late 1830s did a groundswell of opinion begin to build up in favor of state control of education—which in this country meant, of course, control by the states, not the national government. Many factors were at work in this transition, but it could not have occurred at all if it had not been perceived as a necessary, *and authentically religious,* modification of church-related schooling (Jorgenson 1987, chs. 1–2; Glenn 1988, ch. 4).

Horace Mann, other aspects of whose influence are discussed in Vinovskis's chapter in this volume, was the key figure in articulating the religious rationale for the shift (Glenn 1988, 79–82, 158ff.; Michaelsen 1970, 70–79). Mann believed fervently in using the powers of the state to elevate the condition of humankind, but his policies as secretary of the Massachusetts Board of Education also reflected his deeply held religious beliefs. Mann was a Unitarian whose religion was primarily ethical: he looked upon Jesus as the exemplar of human perfectibility, the Bible as a treasury of spiritual inspiration, and Christianity as a summons to work for moral improvement in oneself and others. This kind of religion—Mann called it the "religion of heaven"—*belonged* in the schools, for without it they could not effectively carry out their primary task, moral formation. Nor could the task be adequately performed in any but a statewide, publicly supported system of "common schools," in which children of all social and religious backgrounds were brought together and molded into good citizens along lines suggested by Mann's understanding of religion, pedagogy, and civic virtue. Hence Mann opposed more traditional forms of church-related schooling.

His opposition was powerfully reinforced by the repugnance he felt for the content of the religious instruction carried on in such schools. This too reflected his Unitarianism, a religion that developed as a reaction against traditional Calvinism and repudiated its teachings as the worst kind of religious error. Mann shared passionately in this aspect of his faith; he objected almost violently to the inclusion of Calvinist beliefs in any educational program. Such "sectarian" teaching, besides being wrong, was socially divisive; his "religion of heaven," besides being true, brought young people together on a "nonsectarian" basis and formed them into good Christians and good citizens. Hence it served patriotic as well as religious purposes. By midcentury, the dominant cultural majority had swung behind this position, rejecting church-related schools in favor of "common schools" in which moral and civic formation took place in an atmosphere of nondenominational Protestantism (Jorgenson 1987, chs. 3–4; Smith 1967).

Mann's emphasis on classroom reading of the Bible—the moral efficacy of which he regarded in almost magical terms—helped immensely in rallying support to his plan and overcoming the resistance of Protestant traditionalists, which was at first considerable. Even more important, however, was the terrific growth of the Catholic population, which affected the public-school issue in two ways. On the one hand, the vast increase in Catholic immigration heightened the perceived need for "common schools" to assimilate the newcomers and thereby mitigate the strain on national unity that their very presence was thought to entail. On the other hand, Catholic espousal of the church-related plan of education—to say nothing of demands for public funds to support *their* schools—discredited the older system in Protestant eyes and converted all but a few foreign-speaking conservatives (most notably the Missouri Synod Lutherans) into supporters of public schools and "common school religion" (Jorgenson 1987, ch. 5; Glenn 1988, ch. 8; Curran 1954; Beck 1939).

The controversies set off by massive Catholic immigration forged an ideological outlook that assimilated Protestantism to Americanism. This view, which dominated the public mind through the second half of the nineteenth century, may be summarized as follows: 1) It was indeed possible for public schools to teach those elements of the Christian religion essential to personal morality and civic virtue without transgressing on the doctrinal territory disputed among the various churches; hence Catholics had no valid religious grounds for objecting to public-school education. 2) Since the public schools were—as they should be—teaching this kind of religion, the charge of "godlessness" leveled against them was unfounded. 3) Because such religious education, rooted in the nation's historic Protestant heritage, was an essential constituent of American nationality, Catholics inevitably brought their civic loyalty into question by criticizing and refusing to patronize the public schools. 4) Despite earlier precedents to the contrary, the kind of tax-supported denominational schools Catholics demanded were out of the question because they would frustrate the nation-building mission of public education, encourage sectarian strife, and benefit a church that was basically anti-American in its inherent structure and in the policies it pursued (Jorgenson 1987, chs. 6–9; Gleason 1987, 115–34).

The same controversies that produced this Protestant consensus convinced Catholics that they would have to go it alone in respect to schooling. Hence they built up a vast educational system of their own, financed entirely from private resources (Dolan 1985, ch. 10; Sanders 1977; Perko 1988). Three points about it are especially pertinent to this discussion: the religioethnic mix of motivations; the Catholic view of the public-policy issue; and their understanding of the relationship between religious education and civic loyalty.

As to the first, language was the most obvious "ethnic" factor involved. Among non–English-speaking groups, such as the Germans and Poles, the desire to preserve the mother tongue as well as religion was unquestionably a strong motivating factor in the founding of Catholic schools. Indeed, German Catholics often contrasted their zeal for parochial schools with what they regarded as the lukewarmness of Irish Catholics. But most Irish Catholics were, in fact, equally committed to parochial schools, in part because religion served for these immigrants as the chief symbol of group identity and focus of ethnic loyalty (Barry 1953, 184–200; Weisz 1976). Catholic "Americanizers" often criticized their coreligionists on this very point: Orestes Brownson protested in the 1850s against using "the pretext of providing for Catholic education" to preserve what he called "Irishism"; thirty years after Archbishop John Ireland of Saint Paul lodged the same basic complaint against

German Catholics (Gleason 1987, 161; Reilly 1943, 256–57; O'Connell 1988, chs. 13–15).

The undeniable significance of linguistic-cultural factors should not, however, mislead us into dismissing religion as the chief motivation for the founding of Catholic schools. Such an interpretation, which reflects the tendency noted earlier to demote religion from the status of an independent variable, reads too much of the present back into the past. As George F. Theriault showed in a brilliant but neglected study of Franco-Americans in New England, language, religion, and nationality were not discrete elements in the thinking of nineteenth-century immigrants (Theriault 1951, 378–79, 538ff). Rather, they were intermingled in—or, more precisely, had not yet been differentiated as parts of—a complex cultural whole that also included local and familial traditions. Religion was thus centrally involved in the heritage Catholic immigrants founded schools to preserve; it provided the institutional vehicle for realizing this aim; and as the constituent elements of immigrant heritages were gradually differentiated, religion proved the most enduring.

With respect to the issue of public policy, the Catholic view derived from a more fundamental conviction that the personal formation essential to true education had to be based on religion in its dogmatic fullness, not on a least-common-denominator moralism (which was actually, as Catholics saw it, a diluted form of Protestantism). The only way the Catholic prescription could be realized in a religiously diverse society was for each religious group to have its own schools; and if the state supported any, it should in justice support all of them equally. Catholic spokesmen, liberals as well as conservatives, advanced this argument from the 1840s through the 1880s. But it was doomed by midcentury because Protestants regarded the common schools as essential to the survival of the republic. Even maintaining their own schools on a purely voluntary basis branded Catholics as un-American. As Cardinal Gibbons explained to Rome, the school question more than anything else persuaded Americans "that the Catholic church is opposed by principle to the institutions of the country and that a sincere Catholic cannot be a loyal citizen of the United States" (Ellis 1952, 1:664–65).

Catholics of course rejected this view of the relation between education and civic loyalty. They could not deny that their schools were, in a sense, divisive; the criticism of the Americanizers testified to internal disagreement about how severe that drawback was and what could be done to mitigate it. But the dominant opinion among Catholics held that the need for religious schooling outweighed the negative effects of having a system that kept their children apart from other young people. And not even the Americanizers would concede that social divisiveness implied civic disloyalty. On the contrary, Catholics claimed to be as good Americans as anyone else. Their schools taught that love of country, respect for her institutions, and obedience to her laws were moral duties. And those schools themselves had come into being through the free exercise of religion—a right guaranteed by the Constitution. By the time the issue was explicitly formulated as "divisiveness" (around 1950), Catholics were learning to turn it aside by appealing to "pluralism" (Gleason 1984, 235–41). Neither that term nor "civil religion" was available to them in the nineteenth century. Had they been, Catholics might well have responded that the charge of disloyalty could only seem convincing to people who identified Americanism with the acceptance of civil religion in its public-school Protestant form.

In the twentieth century, this form of civil religion underwent a process of secularization. That, along with the persistence of the Catholic issue and the emergence of Jews as a major factor on the religious/educational scene, require brief notice.

Secularization is, of course, a complex and controversial concept. I use it here in the loose vernacular sense to designate the process by which public education lost most of its nonsectarian-Protestant coloration, but retained certain vestiges that merged with elements from other sources to form a fuzzier and more generalized version of public-school civil religion associated primarily with unifying Americans on the basis of commonly shared "moral and spiritual values" (Michaelsen 1970, ch. 2). The continuities in this process are clearly observable in the thinking of John Dewey, the philosopher whose ideas dominated American public education in the first half of the twentieth century.

Dewey abandoned the Protestantism of his New England ancestors but not their moralism and concern for social betterment. In 1908, just as immigration reached its climax, he published an essay entitled "Religion and Our Schools," in which he affirmed that the public schools were "performing an infinitely significant religious work" by taking young people of diverse backgrounds and "assimilating them together on the basis of what is common and public in endeavor and achievement." By teaching both self-respect and respect for others, the schools promoted a social unity that was truly religious in character. While properly eschewing the formalism of traditional religious instruction, which could inhibit the development of "state-consciousness," they were nevertheless providing education genuinely "religious in substance and in promise" (Dewey 1908).

Dewey's revisionist understanding of religious education was, as it were, expanded and generalized in his book *A Common Faith* (Dewey 1934). Here he sought to emancipate "the religious"—by which he meant those dimensions of our experience that elevate, inspire, and unite us with others—from its stultifying identification with "religion"—by which he meant formal religion, the creeds and cults of the organized churches. According to this view of things, the public schools ought definitely to engage in "religious" education; but to teach "religion" would militate directly against the success of "religious" education, rightly understood. The terminology confuses, but a close analogy can be drawn between Dewey's position and that of Horace Mann. Where Mann prescribed "the religion of Heaven," Dewey prescribes "the religious"; where Mann rejected "sectarianism," Dewey rejects "religion." In respect to their understanding of the broadly "religious" aims of public education—personal development of the individual meshing with social improvement and national cohesion—there is not just analogy but straightforward continuity between the positions of the two men.

Dewey was not alone in viewing the public schools from a civil-religious perspective. Ellwood P. Cubberly, an educational historian whose remarks on assimilating immigrants are regularly exhibited as a nativistic horror, also observed that the work of the public schools was "to a large degree" religious (Cubberly 1909, 68). Denis Brogan likewise emphasized their religious quality in his well-known delineation of *The American Character* (Brogan 1944, 136–37). The crisis brought on by World War II, which linked democracy to "our Judeo-Christian heritage," prompted J. Paul Williams, a professor of religion at Mount Holyoke College, to speak of the public school as "a veritable temple for the indoctrination of democracy," which should be taught explicitly *"as religion* [sic]" (Williams 1952, 371). This kind of talk embarrassed most public-school spokesmen, who were strict separationists on the church-state issue, but it was taken seriously by the prominent church historian Sidney E. Mead and other commentators on civil religion (Mead 1963, 68–71). And the programs to "teach about religion" that sprouted in the public schools after the Supreme Court outlawed prayer and Bible reading in the early 1960s were permeated by civil-religious goals such as deepening students' appreciation for national values, promoting intergroup harmony, and contributing to the moral renewal of society (Gleason 1977).

Since separation of church and state, religious neutrality, and the "secularity" of the schools are fundamental postulates of the whole system of public education, willingness to recognize its religious quality, even in the Deweyan sense, has been rare. Such willingness as exists is important, however, for the testimony it gives to the substratum of religious seriousness with which Americans regard public education, particularly in its function—which is closely related to immigration—of integrating the diverse elements of the population around the values of freedom, equality, and other elements of the national ideology. It is this underlying concern with unity that continued to make the existence of a separate system of Catholic schools problematic—particularly since Catholics were widely regarded by important opinion leaders, both religious and secular, as committed by their religion to principles incompatible with Americanism (e.g., Young 1932, 499–500).

Concern for national unity and doubts about the civic loyalty of Catholics were both involved in the Oregon School Law of 1922 that would have put Catholic schools out of business by requiring all students to attend public schools. In the nativistic atmosphere of the time, several other states were considering similar legislation, but the U.S. Supreme Court struck down the Oregon statute, denying that the state's regulatory authority included the power "to standardize its children by forcing them to accept instruction from public teachers only" (Jorgenson 1987, ch. 10). Extremely important in itself, the Oregon case also gave a hint of what was to come, for it marked the Supreme Court's entry into a constitutional area that was to become increasingly active after World War II, namely, church-state questions involving the schools.

The issue of aid to parochial schools, which was seen by non-Catholics as part of a Catholic campaign to subvert the principle of church-state separation, figured very prominently in this post–World War II development, but we cannot enter upon its complexities. Two observations will have to suffice. The first is that the Court's educational decisions have defined separation more and more stringently, with the result that public funds are available to Catholic schools only for quite marginal types of assistance (except at the level of higher education, where a more flexible interpretation permits public support for nonreligious purposes). Secondly, moving this key aspect of the Catholic question to the sphere of constitutional adjudication has helped to contain intergroup friction by bringing it within a framework of settlement that everyone regards as legitimate, disappointing as the outcomes may be to one or another party in any given case.

American Jews, who resemble Catholics in their character as immigrants, take a very different position on matters relating to religion and education. In the nineteenth century, German Jews maintained a few full-time day schools; more recently, Orthodox Jews have established them. But these are exceptions to the general rule. Most American Jews have always patronized the public schools, relying on various types of supplemental education to provide the specifically Jewish content of their children's formation. Besides being strongly committed to secular public schools, Jews have also championed strict separationism on church-state issues. So deeply rooted is this complex of attitudes that even during the "ethnic studies" boom of the 1970s, Jews remained "wary of encouraging the teaching of Jewish studies" in the public schools (Sklare 1983, 367; Gartner 1969; Moore 1981, ch. 4).

The process by which "Jews transformed themselves from a group which gave primacy to sacred learning into one which gave primacy to secular learning" may be, as Marshall Sklare observes, imperfectly understood (Sklare 1983, 366), but the congruence between Reform Judaism and the public-school ideology, both of which emerged in the mid–nineteenth century, goes far to explain their original acceptance of the American system. Reformism envisioned Jews as "fully integrated citizens of the modern secular state, differentiated only by religion," and with all outmoded or discordant features of the Jewish religious tradition trimmed away. In the words of Lloyd P. Gartner, Reform Jews looked upon religiously neutral public schools as "a blessing and a necessity, for they were a microcosm of the society in which Jewish children would find a place as adults. . . . The public school was viewed as the symbol and guarantee of Jewish equality and full opportunity in America" (Gartner 1969, 8–9).

The commitment to public education intensified with the coming of the East European Jews, who immigrated in massive numbers around the turn of the century. Heavily concentrated in New York City and "overwhelmed," as Gartner says, by "modern secular culture" (Gartner 1969, 10), many East European Jews simply abandoned Judaism, while others reintegrated the religious elements of their tradition with more modern ways of thinking. Theorists of Jewish education were naturally involved in this ferment; several of the most important were in contact with, and influenced by, John Dewey, who had moved to Columbia University in 1904. One such was Mordecai M. Kaplan, and echoes of Dewey's ideas—including the distinction between "the religious" and "religion"—are clearly discernible in the Reconstructionist Movement, of which Kaplan was the founder (Moore 1981, 107–9; Berkson 1971, 57–59; Kronish 1987).

Reconstructionism holds that "Jewishness" is broader and more basic than "Judaism," for the former designates a "religious civilization" while the latter refers to the "religion" that has historically given expression to the civilization, but that does not exhaust its spiritual potentialities. The Reconstructionist program of integrating the Jewish heritage with the best in the modern world had an obvious affinity with civil religion. "Indeed," writes Charles S. Liebman, "Kaplan's belief that church and state must be separate, but that every civilization must have its own religion to assure social cohesion and unity, makes a civil religion a necessity" (Liebman 1970, 22). Hence it is not surprising that Kaplan collaborated with J. Paul Williams in editing *The Faith of America,* a devotional anthology of "prayers, readings, and songs for the celebration of American holidays," and that his son-in-law and successor, Ira Eisenstein, took satisfaction in noting that the country seemed to be ready for a civil religion in 1976 (Kaplan, Williams, and Kohn 1961; Eisenstein 1976).

Commitment to American civil religion is an equally prominent motif in certain varieties of Jewish "secularism." For our purposes, the key figure here is Horace M. Kallen, formulator of the theory of "cultural pluralism," which has become a kind of shibboleth among commentators on education, as well as those who write on ethnicity and religion (Konvitz 1987; Sollors 1986). Kallen's active career spanned more than half a century (he was ninety-two when he died in 1974) and covered a wide range of topics. A pragmatic philosopher like John Dewey, with whom he was closely acquainted, Kallen shared Dewey's quasireligious understanding of democracy, his enthusiasm for public education, his opposition to public aid for Catholic schools, and his hostility to Catholic "authoritarianism" in general.

Kallen's views on ethnicity, religion, and American nationality, which were first set forth in strongly antiassimilationist terms (in 1915 and 1924), represented his personal integration of Jewish and American elements. His cultural pluralism originally envisaged American society as a kind of federation of ethnic nationalities; but the concept took on a life of its own, and by World War II had converged with the kind of assimilationism that stressed the acceptance by all groups of American ideals, especially "tolerance for diversity" (Gleason 1984, 223–29). When Kallen himself returned to the subject in the 1950s, cultural pluralism had become indistinguishable in his thinking from "the American Idea," which he capitalized and invested with explicitly religious authority. Yet his version of American civil religion was in its own way quite "sectarian." He described it as a distinctive "apprehension of human nature and human relations" that *everyone* ("every sort and condition of Protestant, Catholic, Judaist, Moslem, Buddhist, and every other communion") had to accept and live by in order to be a good American (Kallen 1956, 204–5)!

Kallen made his sweeping assertion in response to a Catholic critic who had objected to his elevating the American Idea into a "surrogate religion." We should not, of course, make too much of a single episode, but this one is highly symptomatic of the quite different ways Catholics and Jews—the two major immigrant religions in the United States—have understood the relation between religion, ethnicity, and civic loyalty. It is too early to say what additional differences will come to light as a result of recent immigration that has augmented the strength of religious traditions (Islam, Hinduism, Buddhism, and others) that have not hitherto played a significant role in American developments. For that matter, we are still far from really understanding the interaction between immigration and religion among the groups that did figure prominently in our past. But the little that we know, although not necessarily transferable to France or any other country, strongly suggests that education is likely to be a flash point of conflict and that "civil religion" needs to be taken into account along with the traditional faiths of both immigrants and host society.

WORKS CITED

Barry, Colman J. 1953. *The Catholic Church and German Americans*. Milwaukee, WI: Bruce.

Beck, Walter H. 1939. *Lutheran Elementary Schools in the United States*. St. Louis, MO: Concordia.

Bellah, Robert N. 1967. Civil Religion in America. *Daedalus* 96:1–21.

———. 1976. Civil Religion and the American Future. *Religious Education* 71:235–43.

Bellah, Robert N., and F. E. Greenspahn, eds. 1987. *Uncivil Religion: Interreligious Hostility in America*. New York: Crossroad.

Bellah, Robert N., and P. E. Hammond. 1980. *Varieties of Civil Religion*. San Francisco: Harper & Row.

Bergquist, James. 1986. The Concept of Nativism in Historical Study since *Strangers in the Land*. *American Jewish History* 76:124–41.

Berkson, I. B. 1971. Jewish Education—Achievements and Needs. In *The American Jew: A Composite Portrait*, edited by Oscar I. Janowsky, 56–91. Freeport, NY: Books for Libraries Press.

Billington, Ray Allen. 1938. *The Protestant Crusade: A Study of the Origins of American Nativism*. New York: Macmillan.

Brogan, Denis W. 1944. *The American Character*. New York: Knopf.

Cubberly, Elwood P. 1909. *Changing Conceptions of Education*. New York: Houghton Mifflin.

Cuddihy, John Murray 1977. *No Offense: Civil Religion and Protestant Taste*. New York: Seabury Press.

Curran, Francis X. 1954. *The Churches and the Schools: American Protestantism and Popular Elementary Education*. Chicago: Loyola University Press.

Dewey, John. 1908. Religion and Our Schools. *Hibbert Journal* 6:796–809.

———. 1934. *A Common Faith*. New Haven, CN: Yale University Press.

Dolan, Jay P. 1985. *The American Catholic Experience: A History from Colonial Times to the Present*. Garden City, NY: Doubleday.

———. 1988. Immigration and American Christianity: A History of Their Histories. In *A Century of Church History: The Legacy of Philip Schaff*, edited by Henry W. Bowden, 119–47. Carbondale: Southern Illinois University Press.

Eisenstein, Ira. 1976. Is the U.S. Ready for a Civil Religion? *Religious Education* 71:227–29.

Ellis, John Tracy. 1952. *The Life of James Cardinal Gibbons, Archbishop of Baltimore, 1834–1921.* 2 vols. Milwaukee, WI: Bruce.

Gartner, Lloyd P., ed. 1969. *Jewish Education in the United States; A Documentary History.* New York: Teachers College Press.

Gerber, David A., ed. 1986. *Anti-Semitism in American History.* Urbana: University of Illinois Press.

Glazer, Nathan, and Daniel P. Moynihan. 1963. *Beyond the Melting Pot.* Cambridge, MA: MIT Press.

Gleason, Philip. 1977. Blurring the Line of Separation: Education, Civil Religion, and Teaching about Religion. *Journal of Church and State* 19:517–38.

———. 1984. Pluralism and Assimilation: A Conceptual History. In *Linguistic Minorities: Policies, and Pluralism,* edited by John Edwards, 221–57. London: Academic Press.

———. 1987. *Keeping the Faith: American Catholicism Past and Present.* Notre Dame, IN: University of Notre Dame Press.

———. 1990. Hansen, Herberg, and American Religion. In *American Immigrants and Their Generations: Studies and Commentaries on the Hansen Thesis after Fifty Years,* edited by Peter Kivisto and Dag Blanck, 85–103. Urbana: University of Illinois Press.

Glenn, Charles L., Jr. 1988. *The Myth of the Common School.* Amherst: University of Massachusetts Press.

Gordon, Milton M. 1964. *Assimilation in American Life.* New York: Oxford University Press.

Handlin, Oscar. 1951. *The Uprooted: The Epic Story of the Great Migrations That Made the American People.* Boston: Little, Brown.

Hansen, Marcus Lee. 1940. *The Immigrant in American History.* Cambridge, MA: Harvard University Press.

Herberg, Will. 1955. *Protestant-Catholic-Jew: An Essay in American Religious Sociology.* Garden City, NY: Doubleday.

Higham, John. 1955. *Strangers in the Land: Patterns of American Nativism, 1860–1925.* New Brunswick, NJ: Rutgers University Press.

———. 1958. Another Look at Nativism. *Catholic Historical Review* 44:147–58.

———. 1975. *Send These to Me: Jews and Other Immigrants in Urban America.* New York: Atheneum.

———. 1986. The Strange Career of *Strangers in the Land. American Jewish History* 76:214–26.

Jorgenson, Lloyd P. 1987. *The State and the Non-Public School, 1825–1925.* Columbia: University of Missouri Press.

Kallen, Horace M. 1956. *Cultural Pluralism and the American Idea.* Philadelphia: University of Pennsylvania Press.

Kaplan, Mordecai M., J. Paul Williams, & Eugene Kohn, eds. 1961. *The Faith of America.* 2d. ed. New York: Reconstructionist Press.

Kennedy, Ruby Jo Reeves. 1944. Single or Triple Melting Pot? Intermarriage Trends in New Haven, 1870–1940. *American Journal of Sociology* 49:331–39.

Konvitz, Milton R., ed. 1987. *The Legacy of Horace M. Kallen.* Rutherford, NJ: Fairleigh Dickinson University Press.

Kronish, Ronald. 1987. Horace M. Kallen and John Dewey on Cultural Pluralism and Jewish Education. In *Legacy of Horace M. Kallen*, 90–107. See Konvitz 1987.

Liebman, Charles S. 1970. Reconstructionism in American Jewish Life. In *American Jewish Year Book 1970*, 71:3–100. New York: American Jewish Committee.

Liptak, Dolores. 1989. *Immigrants and Their Church*. New York: Macmillan.

Lowe, John W., Jr. 1986–1987. Church-State Issues in Education: The Colonial Pattern and the Nineteenth Century to 1870. In *Church and State in America: A Bibliographical Guide*. 2 vols. 1:297–329. Westport, CT: Greenwood Press.

Marty, Martin E. 1971. Two Kinds of Two Kinds of Civil Religion. In *American Civil Religion*, edited by Russell E. Richey and Donald G. Jones, 139–57. New York: Harper & Row.

Mathisen, James A. 1989. Twenty Years after Bellah: Whatever Happened to American Civil Religion? *Sociological Analysis* 50:129–46.

Mead, Sidney E. 1963. *The Lively Experiment: The Shaping of Christianity in America*. New York: Harper & Row.

Michaelsen, Robert. 1970. *Piety in the Public School*. New York: Macmillan.

Miller, Randall M., and Thomas D. Marzik, eds. 1977. *Immigrants and Religion in Urban America*. Philadelphia: Temple University Press.

Moody, Joseph N. 1978. *French Education since Napoleon*. Syracuse, NY: Syracuse University Press.

Moore, Deborah Dash. 1981. *At Home in America: Second Generation New York Jews*. New York: Columbia University Press.

Moore, R. Laurence. 1986. *Religious Outsiders and the Making of Americans*. New York: Oxford University Press.

Novak, Michael. 1976. America as Religion. *Religious Education* 71:260–67.

O'Connell, Marvin R. 1988. *John Ireland and the American Catholic Church*. St. Paul: Minnesota Historical Society Press.

Olson, James S. 1987. *Catholic Immigrants in America*. Chicago: Nelson-Hall.

Perko, F. Michael, ed. 1988. *Enlightening the Next Generation: Catholics and Their Schools, 1830–1980*. New York: Garland Press.

Reilly, Daniel F. 1943. *The School Controversy (1891–1893)*. Washington: Catholic University of America Press.

Sanders, James W. 1977. *The Education of an Urban Minority: Catholics in Chicago, 1833–1965*. New York: Oxford University Press.

Skardal, Dorothy B. 1974. *The Divided Heart: Scandinavian Immigrant Experience through Literary Sources*. Lincoln: University of Nebraska Press.

Sklare, Marshall. 1983. *American Jews: A Reader*. New York: Behrman House.

Smith, Timothy L. 1967. Protestant Schooling and American Nationality, 1800–1850. *Journal of American History* 53:679–95.

———. 1978. Religion and Ethnicity in America. *American Historical Review* 83:1155–85.

Sollors, Werner. 1986. A Critique of Pure Pluralism. In *Reconstructing American Literary History*, edited by Sacvan Bercovitch, 250–79. Cambridge, MA: Harvard University Press.

Stephenson, George M. 1932. *The Religious Aspects of Swedish Immigration: A Study of Immigrant Churches*. Minneapolis: University of Minnesota Press.

Theriault, George F. 1951. The Franco-Americans in a New England Community: An Experiment in Survival. Ph.D. diss., Harvard University.

Thomas, W. I. 1966. *On Social Organization and Social Personality: Selected Papers*, edited by Morris Janowitz. Chicago: University of Chicago Press.

Weisz, Howard R. 1976. *Irish-American and Italian-American Educational Views and Activities, 1870–1900*. New York: Arno Press.

Williams, J. Paul. 1952. *What Americans Believe and How They Worship*. New York: Harper & Row.

Young, Donald. 1932. *American Minority Peoples: A Study in Social and Cultural Conflicts in the United States*. New York: Harper & Brothers.

9

ISLAM AND CATHOLICISM IN FRENCH IMMIGRATION

Michel Oriol

Two striking observations emerge from a review of the few available bibliographies[1] about the relationship between religion and immigrant groups in France (these observations are equally applicable to the sociological works in most of continental Europe): first, religion was taken into consideration remarkably late; and second, when it was dealt with, much of the research and discussion concerned Islam, even though (despite the most recent immigrant flow) most of the populations resulting from the immigration since the 1950s were of Catholic origin.[2]

Before considering the meaning of these observations, we can state that in France (but not only in France) research on this topic faces two obstacles at the theoretical level: in spite of the apparent decline of Marxist theories, religion is still rarely considered fundamental by sociologists; and it is only a problem in their view when it concerns cultural alienation. So wouldn't the provocative jibes of political analyst Bruno Etienne (1989), who calls France "papist *cesaro*," meaning that secular and religious spheres are under one authority, apply not only to social life but also to sociological works?

From 1981 on, we have seen that in subordinating research to political and administrative priorities, we ended up neglecting almost everything that was "cultural" (Oriol 1981). But at the same time, we must emphasize that most of the concepts that European experts tried to use to analyze the migratory process were borrowed from North American integration theories, which could have corrected this neglect. But, research went on as if the experts had little more to fall back on than opinion, confusing invisible practices or unobtrusive networks with their irreversible decline. We needed the response within French society to the widespread Middle East crises and the identity-related mobilizations of groups of Muslim origin at the end of the 1970s for immigrants to be seen as "homo religiosus" at least as much as "homo economicus."[3]

The difficult birth of the research we are reporting on here left important marks:

1. A large part of the publications is not intended so much for sociological elucidation of historic processes as for a debate between, on the one hand, social-science experts and, on the other hand, the views they are striving to fight against or the persistent prejudices they hope to rectify. The title of the special issue of the magazine *Autrement,* edited by Olivier Mongin and Olivier Roy, "Islam, the Big Misunderstanding" (1987), is quite characteristic of the orientation.
2. Even when epistemological distance is taken from ideological urgency, the political dimension of religious life is given priority. We can see the reinforcement of the paradox mentioned above: because being Catholic is not supposed to have direct effects on civic matters, it is only rarely and not even openly studied.
3. In the same way, anthropological study of daily or ceremonial practices is underdeveloped. In the terms we proposed earlier about dialectic opposition, everything is seen as if the institutional aggregate (groups united by institutional structures and their fundamental ideologies) is the most influential factor, or at least the predominant one, compared with the "existential aggregate" (group unity based on practices and symbols).
4. We do find the information necessary to view religion in relation to other categories of sociological analysis. But there are still syntheses to carry out, especially since at this level of research intercultural comparison clearly becomes possible and fruitful.

It is difficult to find exact correspondence between these four points, which I will illustrate here, and Philip Gleason's remarkably comprehensive statement about the relationship between immigration and religion in U.S. history.

We should not be surprised to observe that the problem treated by Gleason has long been closely connected with the definition of "Americanization," while in France the narrow, quasiobsessive public debates about integration, raised in relation to questions about admitting a Muslim community into France, are quite recent. Up until this point, the debate about the state's secular nature (an especially ardent debate with respect to education, as Gleason reminds us), separated the two concepts of national historic patrimony. (The anti-Semitic crises in France at the end of the nineteenth century expressed more an overall zenophobia than the concept of selective assimilation, as was the case with American immigration "quotas.") The recent consideration of compatibility of religion with citizenship has, all of a sudden, provoked reversals in France's political party platforms that were as rapid as they were surprising: the same people who supported the mass demonstrations in 1985, which obliged the leftist government to withdraw a proposed law inspired by secular influences, strongly criticized the Socialist minister of education when, in the "scarf scandal," he strove to downplay the incident by invoking tolerance.

Does this signify that henceforth the difference between the American situation and the French situation will be substantially reduced, so much so that political analysts find themselves fully justified in giving greater importance to their perspective? (This is a second theme, which I will develop later.) To accept this view would be, I believe, to forget that the symbolic systems of different national groups are rooted in very different histories.[4] Philip Gleason shows clearly that the concept of civil religion corresponds in the United States with legitimate national loyalty, according to which faithful members of diverse beliefs join together with mutual respect. French national identity corresponds to much more clearly "objective" historic and cultural symbols, such that citizenship is expected to internalize a history that transmits common values, rather than to give contractual support to a "new" country.[5]

STUDIES OF IMMIGRANT COMMUNITIES AS RELIGIOUS COMMUNITIES

If we put aside works reflecting ideological controversy, we see that the first important studies in the area we are exploring consider groups of Islamic origin in France (Krieger-Krynicki 1985, Weber 1985, Lamand 1986). Their purpose is first to inform the reader, in order to dispel the myths that feed racism. But it is important to recognize the problems that even the most elementary description poses. The concessions to "popularization" may not have been well advised.

For example, all these studies, but especially Krieger-Krynicki's, raise the question of actual numbers. But the argument Hervé Le Bras brought up (and rightly so) with regard to the census of "foreigners" (who will determine the criteria for "foreignness"?) is even more radically true for defining the category Muslim (Le Bras 1988).

If, as is usually done, we consider French nationals from Muslim countries, to which we add the community of Algerians loyal to France, we arrive at large numbers (one million, seven hundred thousand plus five hundred thousand) that are both approximate and arbitrary. The qualitative problems of categorization (administrative, formal and informal, defined by someone else or by oneself) and of family or community transmission of heritage influence the validity of quantitative estimates.

Krieger-Krynicki distinguishes the members of the community of pro–French Algerian soldiers (which she discusses in her second chapter, titled "Muslims *of* France") from people resulting from immigration ("Muslims *in* France") without considering the case of Muslims of French origin, who are actually the easiest to identify, even if their number, greatly overestimated by Islam publications, is uncertain (Fifty thousand? See the discussion of these estimates by S. Sellam 1987). But as of the 1982 census, most holders of French citizenship with a family name indicating Muslim origin in the PACA region are descended from immigrants. And Krieger-Krynicki herself insisted on the increasing unlikeliness of immigrants returning to the country of origin, and the greater improbability of their children doing so. It is thus dangerous to apply the "Muslims *in* France" category to these populations.

Krieger-Krynicki did, however, draw our attention to immigrant groups that are less well known because of their low numbers and their often irregular status, such as the Pakistanis. Subsequent studies (especially the essential book by Gilles Kepel 1984) highlighted the fact that in the group dynamics of Muslim communities in France, the influence of this group was much bigger than its actual size.[6]

Another conceptual difficulty in the "descriptive" studies rests in the uncertainty of the definition and description "Muslim culture." This problem is well illustrated by Edgard Weber (1985). Even though he prudently opens with a critique of culturalism, he nonetheless presents a large number of propositions that tend to "reify" Islam in their misunderstanding of the elementary principles of "methodological individualism."[7]

The references to the Koran, in a work dealing with the "Arab Maghreb," are presented as if they had inherent descriptive value or provided sociological explanation of behavior. They rarely escape two critiques: the more theoretical critiques, as made by Abdelmalek Sayad (1984, 1987) against those who make Islam out to be some sort of social force accounting for immigrant practices; and the more empirical critiques. These were stimulated by studies of popular Maghrébian Islam, dominant among immigrants and resistant for generations to "missionary" efforts, first of modernists and then of Islamists who were trying to straighten out its considerable inconsistencies with relation to scholarly (or orthodox) readings of the Book (used most often for its magico-religious virtues rather than for careful analysis and interpretation; see on this point all the contributions of Sossie Andezian, to which I will return).

As usually occurs with this type of debate, the term "intercultural" (the subtitle of E. Weber's work is "milestones for an intercultural renewal") was invalidated because the concept of culture had no epistemological status.

S. Sellam's work (1987), which retraces the history of ideologic and political relationships between France and Islam, is much more enlightening. Presented from the perspective of a Muslim author, without a systematic a priori, this information allows reconsideration of the current "misunderstandings" and presents a gallery of portraits of intellectuals of Islam in France, past or contemporary, who are often not well known.[8] Their influence, outside of the smaller circle of militant students, remains poorly understood.

At this level of empirical description, the comparison with studies of groups of Catholic origin is of little interest, except for historic works recounting the structuring role of the priests from the home countries, or the welcoming role carried out by missions or parishes of the Eglise de France (Noiriel 1988). The church is not only a social agent but also a producer of sociological studies. (The CIEMM, today called the CIEMI, directed by members of the Scalabrini Order, produced the first index of Islamic places of worship [1977].)

In this capacity, the church carries out, with unrivaled intensity, studies on many subjects likely to shed light on its pastoral vocation and thus, as a general rule, on the social and legal conditions of immigrants (Centro Studi Emigrazione 1984). But it maintains a normative tone reflecting its institutional purpose when the issue at hand is catechism exercises or confessional practices.

Most writings now put the accent on "pluralism," understood as respect for the cultural identity of a church-going believer of foreign origin, (as in G. Tassello's preface to Centro Studi Emigrazione (1984): "The ever growing flood in Europe of Islamic immigrants created a new challenge to society at the level of religious pluralism and social cohesion"; "Certain religious traits, when transformed, take on a new value, like feast days and popular religious practices, which are considered a means for defending and maintaining a specific cultural identity and distinguishing oneself from others" (translation from Italian mine).

The research of two Brussels priests shows clearly how migration displaces not only people but also the symbolic meaning of their practices (Pittau and Ducoli 1972–1973). According to them, it is equally unacceptable to reproduce the "sociological Christianity" of the home country and/or to impose on immigrants the style of the parishes of the receiving country.

We will find additional references to research in areas that confirm the presuppositions implicit in these pastoral prescriptions. The religious community is not unequivocably an integrating factor. Integration threatens the cohesion and the symbolic resources of primary groups. Surveys relevant to the history of groups of Polish or Italian origin confirm this observation (Dzwonkowski 1981 and 1982) and show how the "church of origin" and the "receiving church" and/or the immigrant communities developed profound conflicts (see the observations of Chanoine C. Kaczmarek 1928, about Poles; on the conflicts between the Italian state, the Holy See, and the immigrants themselves, for control of the Bonomelli Opera, dissolved by the Vatican in 1928, see P. V. Cannistraro and G. Rosoli 1979).

This brief review of descriptive or normative studies is not without theoretical value. The relative proximity of most countries of origin to France, and the strength of its ideology, make it particularly unlikely that religious membership as a system of cultural traits and established practices would have an "integrating" power.

This more or less explicitly functionalist interpretation has been challenged by today's most influential authors with a symbolic interpretation in which migration illustrates the relative flexibility of structures of influence and control.

2. POLITICAL ANALYSIS

The key merit of Bruno Etienne's work (1981–1989) was to see religion as an arena where symbols are created, untangling and interpreting it according to Max Weber's categories and Pierre Bourdieu's reformulation of those categories.

Among other advantages, such a conceptualization makes possible a comparison between very different populations or practices. Etienne effectively applied this approach to the comparison between the Islam of "Dar El Islam" and the Islamic "expatriate" (or as he says himself, the Islamic "minority"), as I will show later. We can, however, lament that the comparisons that Weberian epistemology made possible were only sketched out and concerned only the political dimension of integration of Jewish minorities or Black Muslims, even though the proposals advanced by the author of "radical Islamism" called for, among other things, rigorously comparing the futures of diverse groups of Muslim origin in Western Europe.

It is not always easy to identify the principal contributions of his writings, which, deliberately aimed at provoking controversy, do not always conform to academic norms. Among other themes, we find the following:

— analysis of the diversity of Islam. This is above all illustrated by the conflict, which Etienne began to clarify in his work on Moroccan Islam (1981), between "the legitimate experts" (in managing the benefits of the faith), in competition with the "small professional independent entrepreneurs," on the one hand, and the "fundamentalist Muslims" on the other.

— a reevaluation of the Islamists, who are "traditionalists through an excess of modernism" (Etienne 1987), whose ideology and disputes compete with the leaders in the home countries, and who often remain ideologically, culturally, and even linguistically unable to create an identity in the popular milieus they would like to influence.

— the weakness of observable (that is, measurable) ritual practice in a proletarianized milieu, in spite of the fact that Islam has been revitalized in response to diverse forms of economic and urban alienation. But Etienne insists that even the ritual dimension needs to be viewed in the context of all the other manifestations of religion (ideological, existential, consequential, cognitive).

Etienne thus focuses the problem of immigrant Muslims in France on the ability of groups to produce "clerics" recognized by their fellow Muslims, in France and in foreign states that are officially Muslim, rather than on "integration." This implies a triple debate, both positive and normative, on the status of domestic Islam (which Etienne says could not have become "private"), on the status of secularism in France, and on the international status of the Umma.

The value of G. Kepel's publications, based on a study by the Fondation Nationale des Sciences Politiques directed by R. Leveau and C. Withol de Wenden, is that they combined a considerable amount of field research with documentation, in a perspective that focused on the relative autonomy of groups and the international dimension of conflicts about legitimacy between states, movements, and brotherhoods. Kepel gathered and analyzed the most significant facts both about local associations (although sometimes with a national audience, as with Paris or Lyon) and the workplace by focusing on the establishment and functioning of places of worship (mosques, prayer rooms).

These studies, based on objective criteria, clearly establish the unquestionable rise of the recently "institutionalized" Islam. They relate it noticeably (especially through the analysis of the "fundamentalist intellectuals") to the surge of popular movements at the start of the 1980s, culminating in the reinforcement of the "demand for Islam" among the second generation.

Kepel's principal work abounds in precise information about the manner in which this demand is dealt with. It clashes with the misgivings (sometimes even the violent opposition) of French opinion, shaped or manipulated by elected officials. It is what is at stake in the rivalries between Muslim states (especially between Algeria, more or less direct manager of the Mosquée de Paris, and protagonists of a worldwide Islamic union, mostly Saudi Arabians) and the transnational movements, which can sometimes exhibit a fairly strong degree of independence (such as the Jama' at al Tabligh, criticized for its apolitical position by the nebulous Islam movements, whose networks arose out of the student milieu). What Sellam would call Islamic self-management ("autogestion") applies to exceptional cases (see the report of the creation of a prayer hall in a low-income housing project after a process characterized by voluntary association).

The decisive importance of methods or movements is illustrated in the Belgian case by F. Dassetto and A. Bastenier's research (1984), which undertook an "objective" study of institutionalization, management, and use of places of worship. This study, prompted by the fact that Belgian law recognizes and supports religious institutions, illustrates the difficulties of putting official status into practice. Turks and Maghrebs have their own places of worship for reasons linked to the'r dependence on their home countries, and to wide differences in religious or cultural tradition. Denominational teaching is the object of resentment or apprehension in the Belgian school system, where it is often seen as a force against integration.

Many of these places of worship had been proposed in the beginning, in both France and Belgium, by the Catholic or Protestant churches, in the spirit of pluralism mentioned earlier. On the other hand, paradoxically, we do not have a precise sociological assessment of the organization by Catholic or Protestant missions of groups of Italians, Polish, Spanish, or Portuguese. The records are abundant and available, but have not yet found any takers.

Here again, we will find much more diversity than we would expect from a common reference to "the church." M. A. Hily's interview with a Portuguese priest clearly illustrates national differences: "There is an extraordinary peculiarity about Catholic migration to France—the institutional church of the country of origin did not work . . . the Portuguese did not have any Portuguese priests, and it is the first emigration where the church did not follow the exodus" (Hily and Oriol 1988). Even if one has reservations about such a judgment (from the era of Salazar on, there were Portuguese priests in France), it also rightfully highlights the diversity of the fate of Catholic immigrants.

But this did not ipso facto mean that the Portuguese were more "assimilated" because they were unaware of the conflicts that had pitted French priests against the Polish, Italian, or Spanish parish priests who accompanied their flocks in a staunch national, moral, and religious spirit. The "blue collar" church with which they were involved often sidetracked them (Oriol 1984) as did the stripping of offices and ceremonies, in the spirit of Vatican II. Then, a whole series of differences were evident between what might be expected from a group united by its religious membership and what could be observed. Attendance at religious services remains weak (Hily and Oriol 1988). Most ceremonies are carried over from rituals specific to Portugal, but not without raising the misgivings of thc French clergy, which the Portuguese Pastors Collective for immigrants apparently tried to overcome with explicit injunctions:

> Instead of refusing these demands, we want to have a lucid attitude towards them . . . thus a pastoral attitude which will value the positive aspects of pilgrimages (especially the privileges given to the worshipers of Our Lady of Fatima) with the hopes of bypassing the danger of deviation. (Hily and Oriol 1988, 63)

We will see that the faithful resolve these contradictions by going to rural areas during their vacations and rediscovering the most meaningful practices of their religion.

But other outcomes are possible, such as a rupture with the Catholic church in order to affiliate with a sect (Pentacostalist, Jehovah's Witness). This route, taken more frequently than we might think, was studied in Belgium with groups originating from Sicily (Leman 1979). Such observations go beyond the usual domain of political analysts to call on the resources of anthropology: members of these groups demonstrate profound existential orientations, such that, paradoxically, the marginality of the chosen group offers a sense of security, allowing them to escape all the uncertainties of the demands of conforming to the majority.

But before evaluating the studies oriented towards anthropology, let us mention the studies of Serge Bonnet and his colleagues (Bonnet, Santini, and Barthelemy 1962), who tried to correlate the political expressions of Italian immigrants in Lorraine (the P.C.F. vote) with their religious attitudes. Bonnet and his colleagues observe that the labor movement plays a more determining role than does religious affiliation in integration (measured by the acquisition of an elective or bureaucratic status). Above all, they notice similarities between the two memberships: "When the Communist party becomes the electoral majority, there are at least three levels of political behavior: (a) the communist *voter*, who reminds us of (and is sometimes confused with) the seasoned Catholic conformist; (b) the *subscriber*, whom we can compare to the parish faithful; (c) finally, the *militant*, rare in the party as in the church" (Bonnet, Santini, and Barthelemy 1962).

"Communism as manifested in the region, like Christianity as it was and is perceived by someone who has been removed from it, calls on an identical psychology: devotion, daily actions, and generosity finally carried out in acts of fraternity and solidarity" (1962). Here we find the beginnings of a study that would retrace the genesis of forms of socialization based on traditional religious practice. They are worth pursuing in order to clarify the system of organization and communication brought by immigrants, and also to combine history and sociology in a theory of socialization (Oriol 1987).

3. STUDIES FROM AN ANTHROPOLOGICAL ORIENTATION

We have moved from studies focused on religious institutionalization to those more directly related to the individual's strategies (Dassetto and Bastenier 1979), orientations, statements, and practices because the impact of institutions depends on the process of internalization/objectification of personal faith. What is, for example, the effect of preaching, which Etienne and Kepel agree is often more positively accepted when pronounced at the mosque where it is in a language unfamiliar to the listeners?[9]

The limitations of our knowledge lead to views of doubtful value. This is the problem with "polls" such as the ones proposed by the *Nouvel Observateur,* designed to give readers a sense of "Muslim" attitudes after the "Rushdie affair" (1989). Without restating the difficulties raised earlier about the possibility of objectively defining this population (or even more, of creating a representative sample), we need hardly elaborate on the risks of generalization." To the question, 'Does it seem acceptable or unacceptable for a Muslim woman to marry a non-Muslim Frenchman?' 53 percent (of which 55 percent were men) answer in the positive; thus the definitive end to theories about the community of brothers and cousins" (Alia 1989).

However, Jocelyne Streiff-Fenart's observations (1989) show that the matrimonial plans of immigrant families radically exclude the thought of mixed marriage for women, which is seen not just as an illicit religious union but as an act of social treason. It is true that the continuous growth in the number of these marriages, usually carried out in the face of family opposition, demonstrates secularization in the younger generation, and its growing independence of community control.

Sossie Andezian's studies of prayer groups of the ISSAWA brotherhood show the value of observation linked to intimate knowledge of well-defined social milieus. They established a number of facts that run counter to both accepted ideas and macrosociological observations. Andezian underlines the fact that "the brotherhood" has been almost totally reappropriated by women.

She also shows that the networks thus constructed permit even better maintenance of the ties with the home country—not only a maintenance of a symbolic relationship with Zaouia, but also a process of various exchanges— more or less open trading. Finally, the fact that such activities are altogether disapproved of by Islamic officials does not prevent the members of the brotherhood from considering themselves excellent Muslims.

I am tempted to say that these observations only characterize marginal groups, maybe even on the verge of extinction. This objection could also be applied to Dassetto and Bastenier (1984), who use data from research in 1939, at which time 3.8 percent of Morocco's population belonged to a brotherhood. More scientifically, Etienne, who interprets Andezian's research as the reduction of Islam to a "private religion," reminds us that his own studies have shown unanimously unfavorable responses to such an outcome (Etienne 1989).

The debate continues, both because Islam as practiced at home may not be subject to a semantic public/private differentiation, and because, as pointed out earlier, it is possible that socialization as a result of the brotherhood experience is much more widespread than we are led to believe by the speeches of "fundamentalist intellectuals," who are quite hostile towards it.

Nadja Semra's study, combining ethnological observations with psychosocial techniques and conducted in Vallauris on young people of Maghreb origin, confirms that the correlation between affirmation of nationality and affirmation of religious membership, while statistically significant, is less strong than the correlation between affirmation of nationality, expression of a desire to "return" to one's home country, and regular use of the Arab language (Semra 1987). In the second generation we find young people serenely determined to practice their religion in France, even to the point of relying partly on the French education system to "Islamize their children." "I certainly won't be the one to teach them religion, I don't know much about all that. They will learn it at school or from an older person" (Semra 1987).

Practically speaking, all these young people, regardless of their investment in their communities, challenge the style of religious education they received. Isn't this a sure sign, observed in the field and outside the realm of ideological and institutional debates, of a step towards the "critical" component of secularization?

Here again, observations inform an important but difficult debate. Sayad, who sees the Islamic immigrants' expressions as stigmatization and a reversal of the stigma, interprets this situation as a quasi-insurmountable obstacle to all challenges. "The overdetermination of denial is such that it practically forbids all belonging to the heritage of the past, all ties to past tradition, if one is not a Muslim believer, or at least if one is not socially Muslim, if not a believer" (Sayad 1987).

Although the studies carried out with young Portuguese, using the same methodological tools as Semra, do not deal with religious practices or opinions, they demonstrate a weakening of the church's moral teachings. Only abortion continues to be the object of massive condemnation, but the signs of moral liberalization are strictly individual in nature, marked by the random distribution of response patterns to the questionnaires.

Anthropology confirms that, even in the absence of a moral role, religion still plays a powerful role in identity affirmation. M. A. Hily's observations in Portugal show that village holiday calendars are modified in order to maintain the "aggregating" function of the ceremonies, reunifying those who stayed with those who left. Immigrants compete, at great expense, in the prestige of the rituals, which are often reserved for sacraments tied to family life (communion and marriage).[10] Here, it is the diaspora that claims paradoxically to be "integrated."

4. WHAT IS RELIGIOUS AND WHAT IS NOT

These transnational movements signal a specific pattern that appears in religious movements in immigrant communities in France and in Western Europe, where the links among religious identity, social identity, and national identity are defined.[11] From an existential point of view, these movements frequently revitalize what I have called "periodic identity" (Oriol 1983).

From the global institutional point of view, these movements result in international strategies that can use, twist, or weaken national identities. We should thus be cautious about the conclusions proposed by A. Bastenier and F. Dassetto at the end of their analysis of "transplanted Islam": "What is currently happening is not without analogy to the role played by the ethnic-religious components in the future of immigrant communities in the United States during the first decades of this century" (Dassetto and Bastenier 1984).[12]

Organized in networks rather than in geography-based communities, in Europe Catholics and the Muslims of foreign origin will find the means of consolidating and expanding their contacts, which will not be simply symbolic or denominational.

For legislators, they will pose difficult problems about policies relevant to the status of religion. As the law establishes common legal arrangements, future discussion will probably forbid the reinforcement of official discrimination.[13] But there will doubtless be strong pressures from the legitimate religious authorities of the home countries.

Must we then expect that these political and legal developments will reinforce cultural differences between Catholic groups, who separate their confessional practices from the rest of their social affiliations, and Muslim groups, for whom the separation of faith and social relationships remains meaningless or inadvisable?

We lack sufficient field work to answer such questions. Analysis of immigrants' religious practices has revealed how little we know about the future of popular religion and its relation to official churches. What Etienne calls "Grandpa Islam" is little known because it avoids visibility. The same is true of almost all the Portuguese communities, which may yet have a role in the revitalization of Catholic action movements that is difficult to foresee.

Just as the European debate on citizenship mobilizes political passions that correspond very little with the concerns of interested parties about their civic options, it seems as though the content of religions will be increasingly altered by the forms of religious organization and the modes of worship that develop.

A particularly important task for social sciences is to develop a "cultural perspective" (Le Bras 1988) that will create a pluralist concept[14] linked to relationships between nations and denominational groups, not as an abstract principle, a purely rhetorical exercise, or an ideological evasion, but as the principal resource for enlightened decisions.

NOTES

1. M. Oriol (1981), CSER (1984), IREMAM (1986), REMESIS (1984–1989).
2. This report was drafted before the "Scarf Scandal," which aroused and divided French public opinion, had fully broken out. It was about the right of a Muslim schoolgirl publicly to state her membership in a faith by the clothes she wore to school. For the most part, it seems to me that the extraordinary dramatization of a minor event confirms my position.
3. See S. Sellam (1987) on this point. As I have already said, the same blindness appeared in general in Europe. In 1980, when I suggested that the Fondation Europeene de la Science organize a colloquium on Islam in Europe, all the members of the Social Science Commission hesitated, citing various objections: What is there in common between a Birmingham Pakistani and a Frankfurt Turk? Why not give priority to more "concrete" themes such as the changing family or urban integration?
4. See on this point the argument presented at the Sorbonne in Oriol, M. 1989. *Identités culturelles et identités nationales. Théorie et étude de cas.* (Université de Paris V, June 1989). Nice: IDERIC.
5. The ever-increasing influence of the "American model" of citizenship leads us to certain paradoxes. Many politicians (especially right-wing ones) are beginning to wish that naturalization in France would return to the American procedure of

oaths. Doesn't this mean casting France in the image of the United States as a nation founded on the voluntary oaths of immigrants? It is true that the sharpness of our ideological debates menaces the solidity and the stability of our cultural heritage.

6. Other than Jacques Baron's excellent articles, work on "Black Muslims" in France remains very limited. B. Etienne (1987) did, however, highlight the considerable role of their brotherhoods in the influence or initial development of mosques.

7. See p. 1551: "Faced with this reality, specific to Europe and especially to secular France, Islam must honestly think: Can it renounce its militant universalism?"

8. Sellam's detailed account of the election of Dr. Philippe Grenier, who converted to Islam in 1896 at Pontarlier, to the Chamber of Deputies (279–297) of course challenges any simplistic representation of political, cultural, or religious traditions in France.

   To understand the role of assumptions, it is interesting to see the difference between the portrayals on the one hand by S. Sellam, and on the other hand by G. Kepel, of the militant anticolonialist Malek Bennabi, who was very influential in immigrant milieus either through direct contact (1930–1956) or through his writings. Sellam writes, " 'biculturalism' (attachment to Islam, adherence to Western culture); the "two cultures" as defined by Snow (scientific and literary culture); life at Dreux and trips to Tebessa permitted him to make the syntheses that were the source of the originality of his writings" (Sellam 1987). G. Kepel (1984) writes, "Member of FLN, refugee in Cairo during the Algerian War, he devoted himself to reflection on the problems of Muslim society, in a way that received a flattering mention in Sayyid Qutb's book, *Signes de piste,* a manifesto about contemporary Islamic movements. He has had a variety of responsibilities in his country since 1962, and has spiritual authority over many students he is helping to bring back to Islam." The term "Islamist" appears to be at least as variable in interpretation as "Muslim."

9. Jocelyne Cesari points out that the unavoidable recourse to anthropology is unwarranted in the case of Islam, which does not fit well into the Durkheimian theory of the religion:

   > The very distinctiveness of Islam, which is not just a religion but a way of life and a cultural system, obliges us to rethink the opposition of the sacred and the profane, and no longer permits us to treat the sacred as a group of dogmatic beliefs and obligatory rites. Because of the individual nature of each believer's faith, it is no longer enough to list the number of faithful, or the regularity of their meetings and practices; we must also appreciate the nature of their commitment, whose direction is as significant as their intensity or their fervor.

   > Considering only the institutions or doctrinal and historic approaches does not allow us to perceive the distance, the manipulation—even the redefinition by the actors themselves—of doctrinal codes and practices (Cesari, personal letter).

10. Similar observations for Spain can be found in *Don Quixote*, by Graham Greene, and in a film produced by P. Pascon in R.I.F.

11. The propositions of Sayad, for whom the social identity of Muslim immigrants is mingled with religious identity in order to be readopted by the faithful only to gain a "pseudonational identity," seem to minimize the considerable role of movement across national borders of symbolic messages. New diasporas are not

in my view condemned to the status of "pseudonations." They demonstrate only the growing complexity of managing collective identities that try to restore the religious dimension in the global context of symbolisms of all types (political, cultural, linguistic) that contribute to preserving or modifying common memberships *from a distance.*

12. Simple thought: if the transnational networks of communication did not constantly put the country of origin and the country of immigration in a close relationship, would the Rushdie affair have exploded?

13. B. Etienne is completely justified in devoting the very important last chapter of *France and Islam* to the effects of European community.

14. I didn't know about Philip Gleason's paper when I drafted this conclusion. It is only all the more remarkable to note that our two contributions conclude with the same question: What status should be given to the plurality of memberships in the structure of a society of laws? However, our definitions and formulations are quite different: Gleason poses, in terms of harmony among the different faiths, a question that I characterize as the harmony of relationships between public powers and civil society. But our difficulty in finding adequate answers is the same. The need to clarify and make concrete the relationship between political society and "existential" communities is the same. It would be opportune and helpful to pool our concerns.

REFERENCES

Andezian, Sossie. 1981. Appartenance religieuse et appartenance communautaire. In *L'annuaire de l'Afrique du Nord*, 266–89. Paris: Centre National de Recherches Scientifiques

———. 1983. Pratiques féminines de l'Islam en France. *Archives de sociologie des religions* 55:53–66.

———. 1985. Emergence des rôles religieux féminins dans l'immigration algérienne en France. In *L'interculturel en éducation et en sciences humaines*, 639–50. Toulouse: Travaux de l'Université Le Mirail.

Arkoun, M., and H. Sanson. 1989. *Religion et laïcité*. L'Arbresle: Dossiers du Centre Thomas More.

Barou, J. 1985. L'Islam, un facteur de régulation sociale? *Esprit* 102:207–15.

Bonnet, S., C. Santini, and H. Barthelemy. 1962. Appartenance politique et attitude religieuse. *Archives de sociologie* 13:45–71.

Cannistraro, P. V., and G. Rosoli. 1979. *Emigrazione, chiesa, e fascismo*. Roma: Studium.

Centro Studi Emigrazione. 1984. Religione ed emigrazione: una selezione bibliografica. *Studi Emigrazione/Etudes Migrations* 21, no. 76 (December): 439–534.

C.I.E.M.M. 1978. *L'Islam en France*. Paris: unpublished.

Coste, A. 1988. L'église catholique dans le débat sur l'immigration. *Revue européene des migrations internationales* 4:29–45.

Costes, A. 1983. Les immigrés dans la société française. *Documents Episcopats* 17:12–20.

Culture-religion et citoyenneté. 1985. Paris: Centre Sèvres.

Dassetto, F., and A. Bastenier. 1979. Hypothèse pour une analyse des stratégies religieuses au sein du monde migratoire en Europe. *Social Compass: Revue Internationale de Sociologie de la Religion.* 26:145–70.

⸻. 1984. *L'Islam transplanté: vie et organisation des minorités musulmanes de Belgique.* Brussels: EPO.

Dzwonkowski, R. 1981. Les recherches sur la vie religieuse des Polonais en France. *Studi Emigrazione/Etudes Migrations* (18)62:243–54.

⸻. 1982. Observations sur la vie religieuse des Polonais en France au vingtième siècle. *Studi Emigrazione/Etudes Migrations* (18)67:405–18.

Etienne, B. 1981. Magie et thérapie à Casablanca. In *CRESM, Le Mahgreb Musulman,* 263–84. Paris: Centre National de Recherche Scientifique.

⸻. 1985. La mosquée comme lieu d'identité communautaire. In *Les Nords africains de France,* 131–50. Paris: Publications du CHEAM.

⸻. 1987. *L'islamisme radical.* Paris: Hachette.

⸻. 1989. *La France et l'Islam.* Paris: Hachette.

Gril, D. 1986. L'Islam dans les prisons. *Sociologie du Sud-Est. Revue des sciences sociales* 49–50:71–74.

Hily, M. A., and M. Oriol. 1988. *Activités culturelles et insertion urbaine de la communauté portugaise dans le Sud-Est de la France.* Nice: IDERIC.

Les immigrés maghrébins et l'Islam en France. 1986. *Hommes et Migrations* 1097:43–63.

IREMAM. 1986. *L'émigration maghrébine de 1962 à 1985.* Aix-en-Provence: Travaux et documents de l'IREMAM.

Kaczmarek, C. 1928. *L'émigration polonaise en France après la guerre.* Paris: Berger-Levrault.

L'Islam de France et de Belgique. 1987. *Hommes et Migrations* 1102:23–49.

Kepel, G. 1984. *Les banlieues de l'Islam.* Paris: Seuil.

Kepel, G., and R. Leveau. 1988. *Les Musulmanes dans la société française.* Paris: Presses de la Fondation Nationale de Sciences Politiques.

Krieger-Krynicki, A. 1985. *Les Musulmans en France.* Paris: Maissoneuve et Larose.

Lamand, P. 1986. *L'Islam en France: les Musulmans dans la communauté nationale.* Paris: A. Michel.

Le Bras, H. 1988. Prospective démographique de l'immigration. In *Prospective Culturelle,* 55–65. Brussels: IRFEC/Europe/IDERIC.

Leman, J. 1979. Jehovah's Witnesses and Immigration in Continental Western Europe. *Social Compass: Revue Internationale de Sociologie de la Religion* 26.

⸻. n.d. Leuven: Centrum voor Sociale en Culturelle anthropologie. Ford Foundation Report. 1979. n.p.

Mongin, O., and O. Roy, eds. 1987. Islam, le grand malentendu. *Autrement* 95:213. Special issue.

Noiriel, G. 1988. *Le creuset français.* Paris: Seuil. *Nouvel Observateur.* 1989. No. 1272.

Oriol, M. 1981. *Bilan des études sur les aspects humains et culturels des migrataions internationales en Europe occidentale.* Strasbourg: European Science Foundation.

⸻. 1983. L'effet Antée ou les paradoxes de l'identité périodique. In *"Peuples*

Mediterranéens-Mediterranean peoples" 24, n. Spécial (sous la direction de M. Oriol). "L'identité déchirée: formes instituées et expressions subjectives": 45–60.

———. 1987. Sur la Transposabilité des cultures "populaires" (ou "subalternes") en situation d'émigration in (sous la direction de C. Camilleri, A. Sayad et I. Taboada-leonett). *L'immigration en France: le choc des cultures.* L'Arbresle: Centre Thomas More. Recherches et documents 51:43–50.

———. 1989. *Identités culturelles et identités nationales. Théories et étude de cas.* Thèse de Doctorat sous la direction de G. Balandier, Université Paris V, 1989. Nice: IDERIC.

Oriol, M., ed. 1984, 1988. *Les variations de l'identité.* 2 vols. Final report of ATP Centre National de Recherche Scientifique 054. Nice-Strasbourg: Institut d'Etudes et de Recherches Interethniques et Interculturelles: Fondation Européene de la Science.

Pittau, F., and B. Ducoli. 1972–1973. *Pour une pastorale des immigrés.* Brussels: Centre International Lumen Vitae.

REMESIS. 1984–1989. *Revue bibliographique sur les migrations internationales.* Paris: Centre National de Recherches Scientifiques.

Sayad, A. 1984. Islam et immigration. In *L'Islam en Europe à l'époque moderne,* 29. Paris: Association pour l'avancement des études islamiques.

———. 1987. L'islam immigré. In *L'immigration en France, le choc des cultures,* 109–29. L'Arbresle: Centre Thomas More.

Sellam, S. 1987. *L'Islam et les Musulmans en France.* Paris: Tongui.

Semra, N. 1987. *Approche psychosociologique de l'identité chez les jeunes issus de l'immigration maghrébine.* 3d-cycle thesis, Université de Nice.

Social Compass: Revue Internationale de Sociologie de la religion 26. 1979. Special issue on "Immigrés et religion," containing articles by L. Favero, G. Tassello, H. Mol, C. Hames, D. Boardman.

Streiff-Fenart, J. 1989. *Les couples franco-maghrébins en France.* Paris: L'Harmattan.

Weber, E. 1985. *Maghreb arabe et Occident français.* Toulouse: Publications de l'Université de Toulouse-Le-Mirail.

10

"OF PLYMOUTH ROCK AND JAMESTOWN AND ELLIS ISLAND;" OR, ETHNIC LITERATURE AND SOME REDEFINITIONS OF "AMERICA"

Werner Sollors

The changes that have occurred in the position of "ethnic" literature in the United States in the past hundred years are remarkable: whereas a century ago, "ethnic" writers were largely on the fringes, the outer edges of the publishing industry, they have since visibly moved to the center.* In 1896, for example, the Russian Jewish immigrant Abraham Cahan published his interesting novel *Yekl: A Tale of the Ghetto* in English (he later serialized a Yiddish version under the title *Yankele the Yankee*). As Jules Chametzky has shown, in some of his other stories he varied the plot lines in the English and Yiddish versions, excising the Socialist editor's voice and adding a happy ending as well as more caution in matters of sexual frankness for the "American" audience.[1] Even though William Dean Howells reviewed Cahan praisingly,

* I am grateful to Maxine Senn-Yuen for her superb research assistance, and to Donald Horowitz, the members of the 1989 colloquium at Royaumont, LaVonne Brown Ruoff and the 1990 *MELUS* conference in Chicago, as well as to David Blight, Catherine Clinton, Rhonda Cobham-Sander, Geneviève Fabre, Robert Gooding-Williams, Anne Halley, Corinne Schelling, and John Seelye for comments. Some examples and passages have been taken from my study *Beyond Ethnicity: Consent and Descent in American Culture* (1986), from my contributions to *Reconstructing American Literary History*, ed. Sacvan Bercovitch (1986) and to *The Columbia Literary History of the United States*, ed. Emory Elliott (1988), as well as from the introduction to the reprint of Hamilton Holt's *Life Stories of Undistinguished Americans as Told by Themselves* (1990).

and later ethnic writers such as James T. Farrell or Jerre Mangione were influenced by Cahan's English-language novel *The Rise of David Levinsky* (1917), he was hardly considered an "American" writer. It is telling that *Levinsky* is discussed in the chapter on "Non-English Writings" in *The Cambridge History of American Literature* (1917ff.). Half a century later, by contrast, such Jewish writers as Saul Bellow or Philip Roth were at the very center of the literary mainstream.

The fortunes of black American literature were similar to some extent. Thus the exciting Afro-American writers Charles Chesnutt and James Weldon Johnson published without adequate public recognition, though Chesnutt's short stories of the 1890s and Johnson's novel *The Autobiography of an Ex-Colored Man* (1912) received modest revivals during the Harlem Renaissance years of the 1920s. Yet in the 1950s and 1960s Ralph Ellison and James Baldwin received wide national and international recognition. The perhaps most striking examples of the changes come from the writings by Toni Morrison, Rita Dove, or Adrienne Kennedy, contemporary "women of color" (as they are again called today) who have not only received the high literary honors of Obies, National Book Awards, and Pulitzer Prizes, but also (especially in the cases of Alice Walker and Maxine Hong Kingston) a broad public success and high national and international sales figures.

Ethnicity may have been transformed from a liability into an asset on literary and academic markets;[2] and the ethnic dimension of popular culture, from Spielberg films to rap music, may now even be extremely profitable. Robert Christopher cites *Forbes* magazine, according to which "entertainment exports—television programming, movies, videocassettes, and musical recordings—earned a bigger net profit for the U.S. in 1986 than the exports of any other industry except the defense-aerospace complex," yielding nearly a 5 billion dollar trade surplus (Christopher 1989, 194). What were once truly fringe cultural enterprises thus seem to have become national art forms, commodities that can be exported more easily than other American products.

Ethnic and national identities are interrelated in ways that are important for an analysis of minority as well as majority cultures. Thus the different developments of migrants in various points of the globe cannot easily be explained by going back to their common origins: Italian emigrants, for example, have moved along different trajectories in Brazil, Canada, or the United States. Julius Lester has made a similar case for the intellectual among the descendants of African slaves in the New World:

[He] must realize that his blackness has been acted upon and has reacted to forces that are peculiarly American. Thus, his black experience is different from that of the Jamaican, Brazilian, or Guinean. (Brown 1969)

For this reason the historical nature of categories such as "American" deserves close scrutiny in investigations of immigrant, ethnic, and black cultural issues. The terms "American" and "American culture" have undergone some dramatic transformations that are indicative of the changing ethnic composition of the United States. The diverse answers to the question of who was (and who was *not*) "American"—at times formulated in reaction to various ethnic groups—played their parts in reconceiving the social issues in an increasingly polyethnic society. Cultural symbols and texts are often particularly appropriate vehicles for containing and transporting different and even mutually exclusive interpretations; and America's national symbols are no exception. They could be read in dramatically different ways depending upon who interpreted them; and writers and intellectuals could make attempts at manipulating or changing them.

It is well known that modern geographers named the New World "America," honoring the Italian explorer Amerigo Vespucci; Martin Waldseemüller's map of 1507 is sometimes considered the first instance. Initially the term "American" referred to the Indians; in Puritan New England, however, it was increasingly adopted to refer to the British colonists (as when Nathaniel Ward, in 1647, spoke of an "American Creed"—and meant the religious beliefs of the English settlers). In the American Revolution the term was used to emphasize less the British origin than the new makeup of the settler population of the United States. Crèvecoeur's famous answer to the question "What is an American?" in the third of his *Letters from an American Farmer* (1782) included the often-repeated (and at times misquoted) formula: "He is either an European, or the descendant of an European, hence that strange mixture of blood, which you will find in no other country" (Crèvecoeur 1957, 39). For Crèvecoeur, the term "American" referred to the ethnic diversity of at least the white colonists in the New World. Yet as Earl Jeffrey Richards has shown, anchoring national identity in mixing goes back to Daniel Defoe's English model that he advanced in *The True-Born Englishman* of 1701: "I would examine all Nations of Europe and prove, that those Nations which are most mix'd, are the best, and have least of Barbarism and Brutality among them" (Richards 1989). The hyphenated Anglo-Saxons thus provided a prototype for Crèvecoeur's supposedly uniquely mixed Americans.

In the course of the nineteenth century the population of the United States changed so dramatically that the definition of "America" became more and more debatable, a development that came to full fruition in the twentieth century. In 1800 the United States population was approximately 5 million: among them were 1 million Afro-Americans and an estimated half-million of diverse nations of original inhabitants ("Indians"). Nearly 80 percent of the white population was descended from British colonists. In 1900 there were 76 million Americans, among them about 9 million blacks and only 237,000 surviving Indians. Eleven million were foreign born, mostly in Europe. (The number goes up to 25 million if one includes the second-generation children of foreign-born Americans.) More than half a million had come from Russia, a million from Scandinavia, a million and a half from Ireland, and well over 3 million from Germany and Austria. The majority of the newcomers were arriving during what is termed the "new immigration," the wave that peaked in the years from the 1880s to the 1920s (Pitkin 1975, 65–109; Brownstone 1979, 4–5). There were also twenty-three thousand Japanese and eighty-five thousand Chinese immigrants (the number declined once Chinese exclusion took effect) as well as many people of Spanish and some of French descent who had been incorporated into the United States by annexation and territorial expansion. In the course of the nineteenth century the United States grew from a British-dominated provincial country into a large, modern, polyethnic, and also increasingly urban world power.[3]

This development was accompanied by a flood of literature, both from the "American" and from the various "ethnic" sides. From the time of the first arrivals, American settlers were particularly print-hungry for published tracts, sermons, historiography, as well as other genres such as poetry and satire. The people living in the United States who were excluded from the term "American" in the nineteenth century also wrote prolifically, not only diaries and letters (the famous "America letters" that encouraged Old World friends and relatives to come to the New) but also published autobiographies, poetry, drama (probably more than English-descended Americans), and, perhaps most particularly, a broad variety of literature in newspapers and periodicals that flourished in many languages and helped to establish generalized immigrant and ethnic identities in the German, Spanish, Yiddish, Polish, Russian, Japanese, Chinese, American Indian, and Afro-American press as well as in English- and foreign-language papers of many other groups (Elliott 1988, 568–88). Robert Park estimated that the American foreign-language press alone had a circulation of 10 million copies in 1922. Philippe Lejeune comments that there are few lower-class autobiographies in nineteenth-century France and nothing comparable to the American slave narratives (Lejeune 1989, 200); he might also be interested in the many life stories published in the American ethnic press. Such literature helped to establish what Benedict Anderson has called "communities by reverberation," imagined 'new national and ethnic identities among readers who might previously have thought of themselves as defined by a family, a kinship system, or a town—but not by belonging to a group of people most of whom they would never meet and with whom they had no blood ties (Anderson 1985, 74).

Nineteenth- and twentieth-century American ethnic literature included a wide generic variety and expressed many themes that are of interest to immigration historians and sociologists of ethnicity: genealogical reconstructions and generational confrontations, religious adaptations and crises, language loyalties and changes, interethnic and intraethnic conflicts, positive ingroup images and outgroup stereotypes, themes of gender and ethnicity, romantic love across ethnic and religious boundaries and despite parental prohibitions, double-consciousness and issues of identity, changes from premodern to modern and often urban ways, experiences with industrial, agricultural, and other work situations, nostalgia or hatred for a past, and representations of melting-pot experiences, expectations, fears, from many points of view—all figure prominently in much of the literature. Writing was published in many languages, and some texts were even written in a hodgepodge of different tongues: Luigi Donato Ventura's *Peppino* (1885), for example, an early Italian-American novel, was published in French, interspersed with Italian and English phrases; the anonymous German-American play *The Emigrants* (1882) was written in a highly English-infused German, while contemporary Chicano (Mexican-American) writers in the Southwest and Puerto Rican poets in New York ("New Yorican") expressly draw on the literary possibilities of bilingualism.

Around 1900 traditional associations with the term "American" had often become problematic. In 1907 Henry James asked:

Who and what is an alien . . . in a country peopled from the first under the jealous eye of history?—peopled, that is, by migrations at once extremely recent, perfectly traceable and urgently required. . . . Which is the American, by these scant measures?—which is *not* the alien, over a large part of the country at least, and where does one put a finger on the dividing line? (James 1968, 124)

"American" could mean all sorts of things: the ethnic fault line (or James's "dividing line") could be drawn on linguistic or religious grounds, making the English language and protestantism touchstones of America.[4] Americanness could also be determined by juxtaposition against such terms as "aristocratic" and "anarchist," or the broad catch-all neologism "un-American," defined by the *Oxford English Dictionary* as "not in consonance with American characteristics." (The first example given comes from 1818: "Ninety marble capitals have been imported at vast cost from Italy . . . and shew how un-American is the whole plan.") Even the Americanness of the first group of people who were called "Americans" could now become questionable. Thus the author of the early Indian novel *O-Gî-Mäw-Kwĕ Mit-I-Gwä-Kî (Queen of the Woods)* (1899), Chief Simon Pokagon, whose tribe had once owned the land on which Chicago was built, described in disbelief the question a white American woman asked him at the 1893 Chicago Columbian Exposition: "How do you like our country?" Nearly a century later, the hero of Maxine Hong Kingston's novel *Tripmaster Monkey: His Fake Book,* the Chinese-American beatnik tellingly named Wittman Ah Sing, mentions the same question as one that white Americans should never ask him (Kingston 1989, 317).

At the center of the debates about the nature and future of America was the problem of ethnic heterogeneity: how inclusive and how exclusive could America be? An extreme example of the method with which whole groups could categorically be excluded from "America" was provided by the political journalist David Goodman Croly, the author of the *Miscegenation* hoax of 1863, Democratic campaign biographer, and father of the *New Republic*'s Herbert Croly. In 1888, David Croly published *Glimpses of the Future, Suggestions as to the Drift of Things.* Contemplating the future American, Croly's mouthpiece "Sir Oracle" comes to the following conclusion:

> We can absorb the Dominion . . . for the Canadians are of our own race . . . but Mexico, Central America, the Sandwich Islands, and the West India Islands will involve governments which cannot be democratic. We will never confer the right of suffrage upon the blacks, the mongrels of Mexico or Central America, or the Hawaiians. . . . I presume the race of mulattoes is dying out. . . . If the blacks left to themselves become as degraded as in the West India Islands, the time may come when they will be treated as badly as the Chinese and Red Indians are now, even to the extent of depriving them of their political privileges. Practically this is the case to-day over a large section of the South. The white race is dominant and will keep their position, no matter how numerous the negroes may become. (Croly 1888, 22–24; see Kaplan 1949)

According to Croly's view, "American" meant "white"—hence nonwhite and mixed races were not considered "absorbable" or eligible for full citizenship rights. Croly himself was an Irish immigrant but did not wish to extend the melting-pot metaphor to nonwhites. Of all the fault lines, "race" (or, more precisely, the decision whether a person was "white" and thereby a potential American or "nonwhite," hence "nonabsorbable") has remained the most persistent dividing line.

On the other side were reformers, such as the newspaper editor Hamilton

Holt, who early in the century ran a series of about seventy-five first-person singular accounts by people of many racial and ethnic backgrounds in the *Independent.* When he published sixteen of those "lifelets" in book form in 1906, he chose the programmatic title *The Life Stories of Undistinguished Americans: As Told by Themselves* (reprinted in 1990), stressing the compatibility of the elastic term "American" with a very broad spectrum of the populace: Rocco Corresca, an Italian bootblack; Sadie Frowne, a Jewish sweatshop worker from Poland; Amelia des Moulins, a French dressmaker; Ann, an Irish maid; Agnes M., a German nurse girl; Axel Jarlson, a Swedish farmer; a Syrian journalist, L. J. A.; Antanas Kaztauskis, a Lithuanian butcher; an anonymous Negro peon, a Japanese manservant, a Greek peddler, a midwestern farmer's wife, and a handicapped Southern Methodist minister; a Chinese laundryman and businessman, Lee Chew; Fomoaley Ponci, a foreign nonimmigrant Igorrote chief from the recently conquered Philippines who was on display at Coney Island; and an Indian, Ah-nen-la-de-ni. Holt includes everyone in his notion of the "American": black, white, Indian, Asian, native born, immigrant, refugee, temporary migrant, sojourner—people from all walks of life. Their voices cover a broad ethnic spectrum, making the book one of the most inclusive "American" texts early in the century; and some reviewers had no difficulty accepting Holt's open-ended definition of "American," which virtually transformed the whole world into potential Americans.[5]

The contrast between Croly's exclusive and Holt's inclusive "America" was pronounced. On such a contested terrain, attempts at symbolizing *one* America had to yield contradictory and problematic results.

"AMERICANS ALL!" was the title of a poster designed by Howard Chandler Christy in 1917, used to promote Victory Liberty Loans, employment opportunities for soldiers, and other war efforts. It depicts a scantily clad young blond woman in front of an American flag and holding a laurel wreath under which an "honor roll" of ethnic names appears: Du Bois, Smith, O'Brien, Cejka, Haucke, Pappandrikopolous, Andrassi, Villotto, Levy, Turovich, Kowalski, Chriczanevicz, Knutson, and Gonzales—they were all to be Americans at a time when World War I made undivided loyalties mandatory. At first glance this may have seemed to constitute an invitation to foreigners who were thus honored to become eligible as Americans—in the vein of Holt's *Undistinguished Americans.* Yet the allegorical figure who was meant to signal the incorporation of various ethnic groups into "America" is not a Mulatto madonna with an Indian headdress but "the American girl," an English-looking white woman, not sturdy like the Statue of Liberty—for which the

Alsatian sculptor Frédéric Auguste Bartholdi's mother had posed (Gilder 1943, 17; Trachtenberg 1977, 60)—but with a glitzy Christy-style look. As Martha Banta suggested, a contemporary pamphlet by George Barr McCutcheon, "What Is It to Be an American?" (1918) seems to verbalize Christy's visual rendition of the theme: "Our backbone is Anglo-Saxon; the sinews of our vast body may come from a hundred hardy races, but our backbone comes from but one" (Banta 1988, 125).[6]

In the historical context of the debate about "America" the poster did not simply honor ethnic diversity: Christy's image contains a double message as ethnics are asked to assimilate to an Anglo-Saxon norm (its origins in mixing forgotten) that is constituted precisely in opposition to them. They are told to be "Mr. American" by conforming to something that they might never become physically. The representative American body of 1917 does not include their features; and their names sound like those of many Hollywood actors and actresses *before* they changed them into more palatable ones:

Betty Joan Perske > Lauren Bacall
Anna Maria Italiano > Ann Bancroft
Anthony Benedetto > Tony Bennett
Dino Crocetti > Dean Martin
Margarita Casino > Rita Hayworth
Bernard Schwarz > Tony Curtis
Doris von Kappelhoff > Doris Day

Incidentally, if Hollywood once exported an Anglo-American image, it now also propagates an openly ethnic look. Most performers and producers have stopped camouflaging their ethnic names behind Anglicized stage names: Martin Scorsese and Sissy Spacek stand for the new generation; and an Anglicized name may now be an ironic comment on the old status quo—as when a transvestite appears under the name "Holly Woodlawn."[7]

Christy's World War I poster could be read both inclusively (as in Holt's *Life Stories*) and exclusively (as in Croly's *Glimpses*); and it is interesting to consider how important the manipulation of such symbols can be for the establishment of a national identity as well as for various ethnic identities. A very famous example is the Statue of Liberty. The dedication of the statue on 28 October 1886 inspired the aging political poet John Greenleaf Whittier—whose career had climaxed before the Civil War with his widely cited antislavery verses—to compose the poem "The Bartholdi Statue" (1886). Whittier stresses Franco-American liberty as an enlightening force:

O France, the beautiful! to thee
  Once more a debt of love we owe:
In peace beneath thy Colors three,
  We hail a later Rochambeau!

Whittier concludes with the following stanza:

Shine far, shine free, a guiding light
  To Reason's ways and Virtue's aim,
A lightning-flash the wretch to smite
  Who shields his license with thy name!

Whittier thus presents the official "Franco-American" interpretation of the statue as advanced during the dedication ceremony, which included only very brief references to immigrants;[8] yet the poet also celebrates especially the abolition of slavery as the realization of the dream of American liberty:

Unlike the shapes on Egypt's sands
  Uplifted by the toil-worn slave,
On Freedom's soil with freemen's hands
  We rear the symbol free hands gave.

(Whittier 1904, 295–96)

Whittier's national and "official" reading thus also contained his own political cause (the memory of the abolition of slavery), an issue that was not to remain in the foreground of later interpretations of the statue, despite the inviting presence of the broken shackles of tyranny on the monument.

The Jewish poet Emma Lazarus saw a different statue in her sonnet "The New Colossus," which was written in 1883, three years *before* the dedication, for a literary auction in aid of the Bartholdi Pedestal Fund (Hurwitz 1975, 379); her poem constituted a recasting of the statue's officially intended meaning. Lazarus alludes to Matthew 11:28, a biblical verse frequently cited in ethnic and immigrant literature (among them, most notably, Israel Zangwill's 1908 Jewish-Gentile intermarriage melodrama *The Melting-Pot,* in which the lines of Matthew are quoted in order to suggest the meaning of the Statue of Liberty).[9] Addressed as "Mother of Exiles" (and compared with the "beacon" that one associates with John Winthrop's Puritan adaptation of Matthew for his New English "Citty vpon a Hill" rather than merely with enlightening liberty), Lazarus's statue speaks:

"Keep, ancient lands, your storied pomp!" cries she
With silent lips. "Give me your tired, your poor,
Your huddled masses yearning to breathe free,
The wretched refuse of your teeming shore.

Send these, the homeless, tempest-tost to me,
I lift my lamp beside the golden door!"

(Lazarus 1888, 202–3)

Whittier's apostrophe "shine far" contrasts markedly with Lazarus's well-known motto "send these to me." The poet James Russell Lowell seems to have been among the first to recognize the significance of Lazarus's poem; when he was ambassador in England, he reportedly wrote her that he liked her poem better than Bartholdi's statue: "But your sonnet gives its subject a *raison d'être* which it wanted before quite as much as it wanted a pedestal" (Handlin 1971, 61, 63; Jacob 1949, 179). A plaque with Lazarus's sonnet was affixed to the Statue of Liberty in 1903; and though this was noted in a famous travel guide (Baedeker 1909, 72) and in some immigrant writing, it remained, according to John Higham's book, significantly entitled *Send These to Me*, relatively unnoticed until the mid-1920s, when the immigration restrictions were legislated (Higham 1975, 82–83). While the overt message of Lazarus's poem seemed to be foremost an invitation to immigrants ("From her beacon-hand / Glows world-wide welcome") and thus offered a reinterpretation of the Statue of Liberty that was offbeat enough to remain ignored or at least of secondary importance for some time, the reference to the newcomers as "wretched refuse" also permitted a reading that the immigration historian James P. Shenton convincingly paraphrased as "welcome, garbage!" (see also Higham 1975, 85–86). Even the proimmigrant interpretation was multivalent.

Lazarus's voice opposed not only the sentiments that Whittier was to express but also opinions like those of Croly that were later put into poetry by the New Englander Thomas Bailey Aldrich in his once-famous "Unguarded Gates" (1892), a work venting anti-immigration feelings freely. One may look at his poem as another reinterpretation of "Liberty."

> Wide open and unguarded stand our gates,
> And through them presses a wild motley throng—
> Men from the Volga and the Tartar steppes,
> Featureless figures of the Hoang-Ho,
> Malayan, Scythian, Teuton, Kelt, and Slav,
> Flying the Old World's poverty and scorn;
> These bringing with them unknown gods and rites,
> Those, tiger passions, here to stretch their claws.
> In street and alley what strange tongues are these,
> Accents of menace alien to our air,
> Voices that once the Tower of Babel knew!
> O Liberty, white Goddess! is it well
> To leave the gates unguarded? On thy breast

Fold Sorrow's children, soothe the hurts of fate,
Lift the down-trodden, but with hand of steel
Stay those who to thy sacred portals come
To waste the gifts of freedom. Have a care
Lest from thy brow the clustered stars be torn
And trampled in the dust. For so of old
The thronging Goth and Vandal trampled Rome,
And where the temples of the Caesars stood
The lean wolf unmolested made her lair.

(Aldrich 1892; cf. Zangwill 1910, 199–200)

Aldrich's liberty is not imagined as a "Mother of Exiles" but, in exactly opposite terms, as a "white goddess" who should guard freedom *against* the menace of the rather beastly invaders. It is clear that Aldrich did not believe in the message "send these to me," but he also had little faith in liberty's ability to enlighten the whole world.

It is a measure of the transformation of public memory that Lazarus's voice clearly won out over Whittier's and Aldrich's. A 1950s guidebook by the National Park Service, for example, calls the statue "the most symbolic structure of the United States," notes that with "the passing of the years its significance has deepened," and gives the fullest account of Lazarus's vision with the complete text of her sonnet (Levine 1957, 1). Despite the obvious differences between American and French public acts of commemoration, there are some similarities in the ways in which multicultural variety was incorporated both into the American Statue of Liberty centennial festivities of 1986 and into the French revolutionary bicentennial of 1989, during which the 14 July parade organizer Jean-Paul Goude described his intention "to show that races, tribes and countries can mix together."

"A nation may reason, 'Why burden ourselves with the rearing of children? Let them perish unborn in the womb of time. The immigrants will keep up the population.' A people that has no more respect for its ancestors and no more pride of race than this deserves the extinction that surely awaits it" (Ross 1914, 304; see Kallen 1924, 69–70). This sentiment, emphatically expressed by the University of Wisconsin sociologist Edward Alsworth Ross at the end of his work *The Old World in the New,* was not unusual at the time. At the peak of the new immigration, some "old-stock" American intellectuals perceived themselves as outnumbered by the "invasion" of "strangers" in the country their ancestors, real or adopted, had founded. I say "real or adopted" even in thinking of the group of intellectuals who were dubbed "Brahmins" by Oliver Wendell Holmes (as if they were a caste) because in fact many of them were, as William Taylor reminded us, not old-stock descendants but upwardly mobile young men, several of whom had married into old families (Taylor 1979, 43–44). Such "Boston-plated" intellectuals—this is Aldrich's term (Samuels 1965, 16)—also adopted and increasingly stressed the symbols of the *Mayflower* and Plymouth Rock as mythic points of origin. (In America, "origin" may denote the point of arrival in the New World.) The invention of Plymouth (and especially Plymouth Rock) as an exclusivist ethnic symbol replaced earlier ideological readings in revolutionary, religious, or abolitionist contexts at the end of the nineteenth and the beginning of the twentieth centuries.

The Pilgrims had landed in 1620 at the Pamet Sound near Truro (Cape Cod); and leaving the *Mayflower* at Provincetown they sailed on to Plymouth a month later; the rock that commemorates this second landing is of dubious authenticity (Bradford 1952, 72n). The Federal Writers' guidebook to the Bay State comments: "Historians have for the most part exploded the landing myth, but popular sentiment clings to the long-hallowed stepping-stone" (*Massachusetts* 1937, 324). Prior to the Civil War the overwhelming significance of the settlements in the northern colonies was, it appears, not yet commonplace: William Bradford's Pilgrim Fathers were still in competition with Sir Walter Raleigh's and John Smith's Virginians. Even within Massachusetts regional history, the Pilgrims were at times considered less important than John Winthrop's Bay Colony; and nineteenth-century American writers described the seventeenth-century New Englanders more frequently as somber and haughty than as ideal ancestors. To be sure, James Kirke Paulding wrote an "Ode to Jamestown" before the Civil War, in which he celebrated America as the peaceful synthesis of Plymouth and Jamestown, North and South:

> Jamestown, and Plymouth's hallowed rock
>   To me shall ever sacred be,—
> I care not who my themes may mock,
>   Or sneer at them and me.
> I envy not the brute who here can stand
> Without a thrill for his own native land.
>
> And if the recreant crawl her earth,
>   Or breathe Virginia's air,
> Or in New England claim his birth,
>   From the old pilgrims there,
> He is a bastard if he dare to mock
> Old Jamestown's shrine or Plymouth's famous rock.
>
> (Stevenson 1922, 46–47)

This was apparently the special interest of a northerner with strong sympathies for the South (and slavery) who wanted to reconcile Puritans and Cavaliers and defy abolitionist readings of the rock.[10] In the world of widely shared national public memorialization, however, Plymouth Rock still seems to have played only a minor role (see, e.g., Lossing 1873, 36).

Of course, there was a long tradition of local references to the Pilgrim Fathers and their *Mayflower* (a North American equivalent for Columbus and his *Niña, Pinta,* and *Santa Maria*), which was imagined present at the landing in Plymouth. The Plymouth centennial of 1720 was commemorated, and starting in 1769 the Old Colony Club celebrated the arrival of the Pilgrims annually. In 1741, Elder John Faunce, then ninety-five years old, had identified a boulder as the "place where the forefathers landed," a phrasing that was probably misunderstood as referring to the "first landing" (Bradford 1952, 72n); and in 1774, at an attempt to consecrate the rock, it split—which was interpreted as an allegory of the division of the British Empire (Thacher 1835, 199). For the bicentennial in 1820 the Pilgrim Society was founded (*Pilgrim* 1823) and, in 1834, received a painting by Henry Sargent depicting the arrival (Barber 1839, 518–23); also in 1834, on the Fourth of July, a piece of the rock "was carried in procession" from the Liberty pole in town square to Pilgrim Hall (Burbank 1916, 34). In a footnote to *Democracy in America,* Tocqueville observed:

> This rock has become an object of veneration in the United States. I have seen bits of it carefully preserved in several towns of the Union. Does not this sufficiently show how all human power and greatness are entirely in the soul? Here is a stone which the feet of a few poor fugitives pressed for an instant, and this stone becomes famous; it is treasured by a great nation, a fragment is prized as a relic. But what has become of the doorsteps of a thousand palaces? Who troubles himself about them? (Tocqueville 1951, 34n8; see Sears 1985, 16).

And in 1852 Lydia Huntley Sigourney viewed Plymouth Rock as a sacred stone, similar to the Muslim Kaaba:

> Recount their deeds of yore,
>   Sons of the ancient sires,
> And kindle in this sacred shore
>   True freedom's beacon fires;
> And give him praise, whose Hand
>   Sustained them with His grace,
> Making this Rock, whereon ye stand,
>   The Mecca of their race.
>
> (Sigourney 1852)

A canopy over the site of Plymouth Rock was commissioned and erected from 1859 to 1867; the two major pieces of rock were united, without ceremony, on 27 September 1880, at the suggestion and expense of Joseph Henry Stickney, a "wealthy Baltimore merchant of Boston nativity" who had also renovated Pilgrim Hall (Burbank 1916, 34–35, 13). The Society of Mayflower Descendants was founded in 1894 (Baltzell 1966, 115). While the first edition of William Bradford's *Of Plimoth Plantation* had appeared in 1856, the most influential one was published in 1912 (Bradford 1952, xxvii–xlii). Only the 1920 tercentenary inspired the National Society of the Colonial Dames (a women's association constituted in 1891, incorporated in 1899, and dedicated to preserve shrines of Anglo-American history under the motto "Not Ancestry but Heredity") to erect the present memorial by the famous architects McKim, Mead, and White, completed in 1921 (Lamar 1934, 19–44, 132–43).

It seems likely that the new immigrants and their reinterpretation of the Statue of Liberty helped to strengthen the Brahmins' consciousness of Plymouth: at least the toga-clad allegorical figure representing "Faith," sculpted in granite after a more grandiose design by Hammatt Billings (Gomes 1971, 14–17) that crowns the National Monument to the Forefathers in Plymouth, dedicated on 1 August 1889, three years after the Statue of Liberty (though plans for the Plymouth monument go back to 1855), does resemble her much larger sister on Bedloe's Island in New York harbor; Faith's left "foot rests upon Forefather's Rock [supposedly an actual piece of Plymouth Rock]; in her left hand she holds a Bible; with the right uplifted she points to heaven" (Burbank 19165, 8).[11] Horace Kallen argued in 1915 that it was the new presence of vast non-English populations, the feared "barbarian hordes," in the United States that had the effect of throwing back "the Brito-American upon his ancestry and ancestral ideals," a development that manifested itself in the heightened public emphasis upon "the unity of the 'Anglo-Saxon' nations" and in the founding of societies such as the Sons and Daughters of the American Revolution (we might add, the Colonial Dames) "that have arisen with the great migrations" (Kallen 1924, 98–99).

The public function of "Plymouth" changed in the debate about the meaning of America against the challenge of the new immigration: the more heterogeneous the country became, the more the supposedly common origins in a Plymouth arrival came to be stressed. This tension erupted in the controversy about the Russian Jewish immigrant Mary Antin, the author of the popular autobiography *The Promised Land* (1912). Antin's claim to a full American identity was a cause célèbre in the second decade of the century. She had startled some readers of her autobiography (originally serialized in the *Atlantic Monthly*) by thinking of herself as an Emersonian new being who had made herself anew in the New World, leaving her medieval-seeming background behind and regarding herself simply as one U.S. citizen and George Washington as another (Antin 1912, xi–xv, 223–29). In her book *They Who*

Knock at Our Gates (1914) she took on the invasion metaphor of Aldrich's poem when she voiced the question she felt in the air: "Did the founders of the Republic foresee the time when foreign hordes would alight on our shores, demanding a share in this goodly land that was ransomed with the blood of heroes?" (Antin 1914, 24). Her answer was to invoke America's (and thereby also *her*) revolutionary ancestors against the prophets of invasion: "If our Fathers did not foresee the whole future, shall we therefore be blind to the light of our own day?" (Antin 1914, 24). The Jewish immigrant Antin's use of the phrase "our Fathers," chosen here and elsewhere in order to describe Franklin and Jefferson, her speaking of "our faith as Americans" or "our American sensibility" (Antin 1914, 8–9) caused some consternation. No matter how patriotic her sentiments were, who was *she* to claim such Americanness, some citizens asked. (To them Antin may have anticipated Peter Sellers's parodistic psychoanalyst character in Stanley Kubrick's Nabokov film *Lolita* [1962] who says, unforgettably and hauntingly, "veee Amerrickans.")

Antin went on to suggest the compatibility of Jewish and American identity, viewing the transatlantic crossing as a new exodus (as the Puritans had done), and supported Lazarus's reinterpretation of the Statue of Liberty as a symbol of welcome to immigrants (dedicating *The Promised Land* to Emma Lazarus's sister Josephine):

Let it . . . be repeated that the Liberty at our gates is the handiwork of a Frenchman; that the mountain-weight of copper in her sides and the granite mass beneath her feet were bought with the pennies of the poor; that the verses graven on a tablet within the base are the inspiration of a poetess descended from Portuguese Jews; and all these things shall be interpreted to mean that the love of liberty unites all races and all classes of men into one close brotherhood, and that we Americans, therefore, who have the utmost of liberty that has yet been attained, owe the alien a brother's share. (Antin 1914, 25–26)

What Antin did for the Statue of Liberty (depicted on the covers of both of her cited books), she boldly extended to the core symbols of Brahmin descent: "The ghost of the Mayflower pilots every immigrant ship, and Ellis Island is another name for Plymouth Rock" (Antin 1914, 98). Antin courageously equated the Pilgrim Fathers' increasingly enshrined American beginnings with the modern clearing center (opened 1 January 1892 and closed 3 November 1954) in which approximately 12 million immigrants were processed from 1892 to 1924 alone and about three thousand committed suicide (Bolino 1985; Perec 1980, 16). Thereby Antin attempted to subvert the point of view from which a Plymouth Rock and *Mayflower* ancestry gave a speaker the right to reject an Ellis Island immigrant as a potential citizen. For Antin, *any* arrival in America after a transatlantic voyage was thus comparable; and the formula "Plymouth Rock = Ellis Island" as well as her use of the possessive pronoun were to become centerpieces of the expansion of the term "American" that supported the integration of minorities. In developing her elaborate analogy between Puritans and immigrants, she invokes the Brahmin James Russell Lowell and finds that he is a writer who chips

away the crust of historic sentiment and show[s] us our forefathers in the flesh. Lowell would agree with me that the Pilgrims were a picked troop in the sense that there was an immense preponderance of virtue among them. And that is exactly what we must say of our modern immigrants, if we judge them by the sum total of their effect on our country. (Antin 1914, 69)

Melvin Tumin accused Antin of adhering to a "cult of gratitude" (Rose 1969, 69–82). Antin's attitude toward assimilation and America was, indeed, largely positive. Yet her works, and the controversies they generated, also illustrate the complications of national integration in a polyethnic immigrant country: nations often need founding myths and stories of origins, beginnings in the past that authenticate the present. Those who do not share such pasts (or at least their myths) can then be excluded from the concept of the nation: if they mean "foreigners" when they say "our forefathers" they define themselves as aliens; if they mean the Puritan and Revolutionary heroes, they "forget who they are." (By contrast, a myth of origin in a mésalliance may stimulate polyethnic integration as ever newly combining mixed marriages can then be regarded as the fulfillment of a prophecy in the national past, and not as a threatening penetration by foreigners; the children of such unions may combine memories of different, even antithetical pasts. Thus immigrants and ethnic minorities can become directly related and affiliated with the national past.)

In 1918, the New York trial of the Russian Jewish anarchist immigrant Jacob Abrams, who had arrived at Ellis Island in 1908, illuminated the problem. At the point in the trial when he was about to defend himself for having distributed English and Yiddish leaflets against Wilson's war policies by invoking American revolutionary beginnings, saying, "When our forefathers of the American Revolution—" the Alabaman, federal judge Henry DeLamar Clayton, Jr., interrupted, "Your what?" When Abrams repeated, "My forefathers," the judge asked in disbelief, "Do you mean to refer to the fathers of this nation as your forefathers?" In the course of the trial Abrams, who was not even a citizen, was asked twice, "Why don't you go back to Russia?" Later the judge recalled responding to Abrams's phrase, "our forefathers": "What? You were born in Russia and came here four or five years ago and not a citizen, an anarchist, who can never become a citizen. Our forefathers . . . why, just look at it." Abrams received a twenty-year sentence (Polenberg 1985, 397, 407; Fuchs 1990, 68).

Antin's reception similarly shows how difficult the process of becoming "American," of adopting another country's past, could be. As in the Abrams case, some American-Americans were not pleased. (In using this term, I am thinking of "French-French" as used in Joseph Losey's film *Mr. Klein* [1976] in order to denote "non-Jewish" during the Occupation.) The New Englander Barrett Wendell, for example, who was among the first professors of English to teach American literature at Harvard University, wrote in a letter of 31 March 1917 to his friend Sir Robert White-Thompson that Antin "has developed an irritating habit of describing herself and her people as Americans, in distinction from such folks as [Wendell's wife] Edith and me, who have been here for three hundred years" (Howe 1924, 282). Edith Greenough Wendell served, incidentally, as president of the Colonial Dames' Plymouth Executive Committee in 1920; she also participated in the Jamestown project and was secretary of the Colonial Dames from 1919 to 1925 (Lamar 1934, 135, 119, 14). Wendell continued his reflections on Antin's position:

Whether she has children I don't know. If she has, their children may perhaps come to be American in the sense in which I feel myself so—for better or worse, belonging only here. And that is the kind of miracle which America, for all its faults and its vulgarities, has wrought. (Howe 1924, 282)[12]

Wendell thus claimed Americanness by seniority of ancestry and by the exclusiveness of his allegiance, tested over generations; yet he did concede the possibility (or the "miracle") that a grandchild of Antin's—born in America of American-born parents—might one day be entitled to citizenship in the same sense that his family was. Wendell's look into the future marked one rhetorical resolution to the problem of immigrant national identity: "American" became a term descriptive of process. Several immigrant autobiographies did describe Americans "in the making." For example, Jerre Mangione's novel *Mount Allegro* (1942), a book that evokes the author's experience of growing up in an Italian-American (or more precisely, Sicilian-American) family in a mixed neighborhood of Rochester, New York, starts with this passage:

"WHEN I GROW UP I WANT TO BE AN AMERICAN," Giustina said. We looked at our sister; it was something none of us had ever said.

"Me too," Maria echoed.

"Aw, you don't even know what an American is," Joe scoffed.

"I do so," Giustina said.

It was more than the rest of us knew.

"We're Americans right now," I said. "Miss Zimmerman says if you're born here you're an American."

"Aw, she's nuts," Joe said. He had no use for most teachers. "We're Italians. If y' don't believe me ask Pop."

But my father wasn't very helpful. "Your children will be *Americani*. But you, my son, are half-and-half. Now stop asking me questions. You should know those things from going to school. What do you learn in school, anyway?" (Mangione 1982, 1)

Americanness was imaginatively placed in the future.

In 1916 the conservative *Atlantic Monthly* journalist Agnes Repplier was troubled (as was Wendell) by Mary Antin's presumptuousness in calling the Pilgrim fathers "our forefathers" as well as by her critical attitude.

Why should the recipient of so much attention be the one to scold us harshly, to rail at conditions she imperfectly understands, to reproach us for . . . our slackness in duty, our failure to observe the precepts and fulfill the intentions of those pioneers whom she kindly, but confusedly, calls *"our* forefathers." (Repplier 1916, 226–27)

Worried by Antin's reference to the numeric strength of immigrants in elections (Repplier 1916, 205), Repplier failed to see any parallels between Plymouth Rock and Ellis Island:

Had the Pilgrim Fathers been met on Plymouth Rock by immigration officials; had their children been placed immediately in good free schools, and given the care of doctors, dentists, and nurses; had they found themselves in infinitely better circumstances than they had ever enjoyed in England, indulging in undreamed-of luxuries, and taught by kind-hearted philanthropists,—what pioneer virtues would they have developed, what sons would they have bred, what honours would history have accorded them? (Repplier 1916, 219–20)

Reviewing some evidence of the new ethnic heterogeneity, Repplier concluded with the question that gives away her restrictive sense of a national identity: "It is all very lively and interesting, but where does the American come in?" (Repplier 1916, 205). Repplier (incidentally, not of Brahmin New English but of Franco-German background) resented Antin's use of Lowell as a misquoting of the dead (Repplier 1916, 197–201; Lowell 1892, 220–54) and, in turn, invoked the antiassimilationist Kallen in order to support her dislike of "Mrs. Amadeus Grabau (Mary Antin)," alluding publicly to the fact that Antin had married a non-Jewish German-American professor: "Mr. Horace Kallen," Repplier writes approvingly, "has put the case into a few clear conclusive words when he says, 'Only men who are alike in origin and spirit, and not abstractly, can be truly equal, and maintain that inward unanimity of action and outlook which makes a national life' " (Repplier 1916, 198–99, 203; see Kallen 1924, 115). Kallen had criticized Antin earlier when he considered her —as well as the immigrant autobiographers Jacob Riis and Edward Steiner—

"intermarried, 'assimilated' even in religion, and more excessively, self-consciously flatteringly American than the Americans" (Kallen 1924, 86); yet Kallen had also partly adopted Antin's line of argument and, for example, compared Polish immigrants with the Pilgrims when he wrote: "the urge that carries [the Poles] in such numbers to America is not so unlike that which carried the pilgrim fathers" (Kallen 1924, 106). Repplier recognized the danger that Antin's "cult of gratitude" could not cover up: assimilation, full American identity (even if adopted unilaterally by declaration of will rather than by birth or acceptance from old-stock Americans), and the notion of equal merit of Plymouth Rock and Ellis Island origins entitled Antin to criticize her adopted "promised land" quite openly.[13]

The function of assimilation as the basis for a potentially critical position has been articulated by a number of ethnic writers, among them, most recently, Richard Rodriguez, who wrote in his widely debated autobiography *Hunger of Memory:* "Only when I was able to think of myself as an American, no longer an alien in *gringo* society, could I seek the rights and opportunities necessary for full public individuality" (Rodriguez 1982, 27). By contrast, his parents adhered to another definition of "American": "They regarded the people at work, the faces in the crowds, as very distant from us. They were the others, *los gringos.* That term was interchangeable in their speech with another, even more telling, *los americanos*" (Rodriguez 1982, 12). Judging by the testimony of Slovenian-born American writer Louis Adamic, Rodriguez's parents may be more representative of ethnic attitudes toward the term "American":

I find that most of the new people, when they say "we," don't mean "we Americans" or "we the people in this town," but "we who live in this section and are of Polish or Armenian, etc., origin or background." When they say "Americans," they don't mean themselves. (Adamic 1940, 297)

For some ethnic intellectuals, the adoption of an "American" identification strengthened their public voice, at least toward the majority; hence they may emphatically say "our country," mean America—and criticize it.

As Higham has argued, young intellectuals among old-stock Americans also found ethnicity useful for their purposes and invoked the promise of a future multiethnic intelligentsia in their battle against the "Anglo-Saxon" genteel tradition, which they could thereby reject as the result of a British colonial mentality (Higham 1989, 23–26). The most outstanding representative of this tendency was the important culture critic Randolph Bourne. A true American blue blood, Bourne was acutely aware of the political implications of the New Englanders' reaction to Mary Antin and took the opportunity to advocate a new radical cosmopolitanism, envisioning a new American culture on the basis of ethnicity. "We have had to watch," Bourne wrote in the famous essay of 1916, programmatically entitled "Trans-National America," "hard-hearted old Brahmins virtuously indignant at the spectacle of the immigrant refusing to be melted, while they jeer at patriots like Mary Antin who write about 'our forefathers' " (Bourne 1977, 249). Ellery Sedgwick, the editor of the *Atlantic Monthly* (in which both Antin's autobiography and Repplier's critique had appeared) and a long-standing admirer of Bourne, wrote him apropos of "Trans-National America": "I profoundly disagree with your paper." Sedgwick sounded, as Thomas Bender has pointed out, the voice of an older gentility when he insisted that the United States was "created by English instinct and dedicated to the Anglo-Saxon ideal"—exactly the tenets Bourne sought to undermine. Sedgwick criticized Bourne by saying: "you speak . . . as though the last immigrant should have as great an effect upon the determination of our history as the first band of Englishmen" (Bender 1987, 246–49). Like Repplier, Sedgwick simply could not accept the parallel of Plymouth Rock and Ellis Island—though he thought, by the way, that Antin had written an important autobiography, comparable only with *Up from Slavery* (1901) by the African American Booker T. Washington (Handlin in Antin 1969, xiii), whom Barrett Wendell had also complimented for a "simple, manly" style and for telling the wonderful story of *per aspera ad astra* of someone who has had the "great, if disguised, opportunity" of being born to hardship, unlike Wendell, who "happened in this world to be singularly free from hardship" (Harlan 1977, 87; see Washington 1986, 35). For Sedgwick, Bourne's essay was simply a "radical and 'unpatriotic' paper" —though he did publish it in the *Atlantic Monthly* (Bender 1987, 246–49).

In the course of Bourne's essay, the "American" core definitions and their symbolizations were again revised:

Mary Antin is right when she looks upon our foreign-born as the people who missed the Mayflower and came over on the first boat they could find. But she forgets that when they did come it was not upon other Mayflowers, but upon a "Maiblume," a "Fleur du mai," a "Fior di Maggio," a "Majblomst." (Bourne 1977, 249)

Bourne perceived the tremendous cultural opportunity of creating a cosmopolitan culture that thrives upon the richness (linguistic and cultural) that ethnic variety brings to what he envisoned as a truly "Trans-National America" in which each American citizen (with unchanged name, one presumes from the *Mayflower* exegesis) could also remain connected with another culture (Matthews 1970). Bourne laid the foundation of the concept of a cosmopolitan intelligentsia that attempted to struggle free from an automatically English orientation in American culture and from the requirement that newcomers shed their cultural, religious, or linguistic pasts upon becoming Americans (Hollinger 1985, 56–73). He also did not think' that immigrants could remain fixed to their pasts in the manner of Kallen's static pluralism. Instead Bourne advocated the new ideal of "dual citizenship," both for immigrants who came to the United States and for the increasing number of internationally oriented individuals who, like American expatriates in France, were born in one country but live in another. In Bourne's hands the contemplation of Americanness in the face of diversity led to a reconsideration of the nationalist premises of citizenship.

In order to strengthen his argument Bourne also recapitulated the substance of Antin's plea to regard the new immigrants as latter-day Puritans, though without her apologetics, and with a touch of Henry James's perception of the difficulty of drawing a line between the "alien" and the "American":

We are all foreign-born or the descendants of foreign-born, and if distinctions are to be made between us they should rightly be on some other grounds than indigenousness. (Bourne 1977, 249)

It is this proposal, clearly a minority voice in 1916, that became the semiofficial core of a redefinition of America during World War II and, finally, the official line for celebrations from the bicentennial in 1976 to the dedication of Ellis Island in 1990. (It currently informs an advertising campaign by an American telephone company.) Philip Gleason has traced the way in which immigrants slowly became accepted as prototypical Americans after being considered among the problematic exceptions (Gleason 1980, 248–54).

As Higham stresses, however, the victory of multiethnicity may have been bought at a terrible price: the battle (Higham calls it a *Kulturkampf*) pushed the conservatives toward racism, anti-Semitism, nativism, and anti-intellectualism, and it alienated radical young intellectuals from people—except those people who belonged to distinct ethnic groups (Higham 1989, 25–29). It helped to create an atmosphere in American intellectual life in which many participants value various ethnic backgrounds more than the ideas that emanate from them, a trend that may have persisted to this moment. After the battles of the 1910s and 1920s (which resulted in the enactment of immigration restrictions), the change from monoethnic to polyethnic thinking gained ground in the period from the late 1930s to the 1950s.

In the late 1930s and early 1940s the Slovenian immigrant Louis Adamic was especially identified with the popularization of the formula "Plymouth Rock = Ellis Island," first in the section "Ellis Island and Plymouth Rock" in his book entitled, in the Antin tradition, *My America* (1938), and then in lectures to hundreds of audiences, a summary of which he reprinted under the title "Plymouth Rock and Ellis Island" in *From Many Lands* (1940). Both works also invoked Emma Lazarus's "New Colossus" (Adamic 1938, 195; Adamic 1940, 292; see Higham 1975, 85; and Gleason 1980, 244). Adamic wanted to

work toward an intellectual-emotional synthesis of old and new America; of the Mayflower and the steerage; of the New England wilderness and the social-economic jungle of the city slums and the factory system; of the Liberty Bell and the Statue of Liberty. The old American Dream needs to be interlaced with the immigrants' emotions as they saw the Statue of Liberty. The two must be made into one story. (Adamic 1940, 299)

Adamic—who also planned for a while to publish a book entitled "Plymouth Rock and Ellis Island"—was a moving spirit behind the Common Council for American Unity and its journal *Common Ground* (a telling title), which contained numerous contributions by a great variety of writers and intellectuals that supported Adamic's project, reiterated the parallels between "old" and "new" American symbols, exclaimed "Americans All!" (now with more varieties of body features), and invoked Walt Whitman's revived poetic formulation from the preface to *Leaves of Grass* (1855): "Here is not merely a nation but a teeming nation of nations" (Whitman 1982, 5). One of Adamic's many other works was also entitled *Nation of Nations* (1945). Comparisons and parallels between Plymouth Rock and Ellis Island became more and more widespread, from Caroline Ware's theoretical work (Ware 1940, 73) and Salom Rizk's immigrant autobiography (Rizk 1943, 317) to the present moment at which no satirists seem to comment on the strange fact that America's First Lady, Barbara Bush, paid one hundred dollars to commemorate her Puritan ancestor Thomas Thayer (who emigrated from England in 1630) by having his name put on a copper plaque on the Wall of Honor now surrounding the Ellis Island immigrant museum (Stanley 1990), a wall that displays nearly 200,000 other names, among them that of the prototypical Plymouth character Myles Standish. I also found it perfectly fitting that Pamela Berger's 1989 film *The Imported Bridegroom*, based on a story by Abraham Cahan, represents the Old World Jewish *shtetl* (to which the protagonist returns for a while) by what looks very much like the living history museum of Plymouth Colony. Plymouth Rock and Ellis Island seem to have become interchangeable indeed, in contemporary American culture.

The "old-stock"/"new immigrant" distinction on which much of the thinking about "America" and "ethnicity" rested did not, of course, apply to all ethnic

groups. Unless forced into the somewhat misleading notion that they constituted "America's first immigrants," American Indians may have an equally
problematic relationship to Plymouth Rock and Ellis Island; yet when during
the restoration work of Ellis Island skeletal fragments were found, they were
blessed in a public ceremony performed by Willy Snake of the Delaware
Indians ("Indian" 1987), a ritual that seemed intended to connect American
Indians with the new national core symbol of Ellis Island. (When Native
Americans occupied Alcatraz they may have wished thereby to create an
alternative symbol.)

Those Mexican-Americans whose ancestors became Americans by annexation and conquest are also likely to have a somewhat ironic relationship to the
"nation of immigrants" and its symbols of arrival as well as to the narrowing
of the meaning of "America" to stand for the United States rather than for the
whole continent. Among immigrant groups proper, American citizens of Japanese descent were, exactly at the time that Adamic popularized the reinterpretation of the immigrants as new Puritans, stripped of their rights as citizens
and property owners and interned in detention camps—as a *race* (unlike
German or Italian enemy aliens, who were generally detained only on the
grounds of individual affiliations or political acts).[14] And the 17,500 Chinese
immigrants who, from 1910 to 1940, were processed through the detention
center at Angel Island in San Francisco Bay, may have gone through a clearing
house modeled on Ellis Island; yet Angel Island, called "Devil's Pass" by the
Chinese migrants, undoubtedly treated immigrants worse than its model.
Several of the (recently published) Chinese poems that were scribbled on the
walls of Angel Island comment explicitly on the immigration procedure. For
example:

> I am distressed that we Chinese are detained
>   in this wooden building.
> It is actually racial barriers which cause
>   difficulties on Angel Island.
> Even while they are tyrannical, they still
>   claim to be humanitarian.
> I should regret my taking the risk of coming
>   in the first place.
>
> (Yin 1991; Lai 1980, 100)

Or:

> Alas, yellow souls suffer under the brute force of the white race!
> Like a homeless dog being cursed, we are forced into jail.
> Like a pig chased into a basket, we are sternly locked in.

> Our souls languish in a snowy vault; we are really not even the equal of cattle and
> horses.
> Our tears shower the icy day; we are not even equal to bird or fowl.
>
> (Yin 1991; Lai 1980, 92)

One also wonders what significance any of the old arrival points or symbols
can have for the new immigrants who have come to the United States since
the 1960s. I shall here, however, in conclusion, concentrate on the problematic
situation of black Americans, one of the "oldest" and most "indigenous" yet
most persistently excluded groups that consists mostly of descendants of
people who did cross the Atlantic, though involuntarily and as slaves.

Identifying himself in the *Atlantic Monthly* merely as "a peaceable man,"
Nathaniel Hawthorne wrote during the Civil War that there was a special
affinity between Puritans and southern Blacks:

There is an historical circumstance, known to few, that connects the children of the
Puritans with these Africans of Virginia, in a very singular way. They are our brethren,
as being lineal descendants from the Mayflower, the fated womb of which, in her first
voyage, sent forth a brood of Pilgrims upon Plymouth Rock, and, in a subsequent one,
spawned slaves upon the Southern soil,—a monstrous birth, but with which we have
an instinctive sense of kindred, and so are stirred by an irresistible impulse to attempt
their rescue, even at the cost of blood and ruin. The character of our sacred ship, I
fear, may suffer a little by this revelation; but we must let her white progeny offset her
dark one,—and two such portents never sprang from an identical source before.
(Hawthorne 1862, 50)

Hawthorne's appears to have been a lonely voice, and the relationship between Plymouth Rock and American slavery has more typically been drawn
as a contrast rather than as an affinity. *The Autobiography of Malcolm X,* for
example, formulated the relationship of a critically conceived black history
with the "old" American story most vividly: "We didn't land on Plymouth
Rock, my brothers and sisters—Plymouth Rock landed on *us!*" (Malcolm X
1966, 201). Malcolm X may have been thinking of Cole Porter's song "Anything Goes" (1934), which opens with the claim that if the Puritans were to
arrive today " 'Stead of landing on Plymouth Rock,/Plymouth Rock would
land on them."

The black writers' difficulties with Plymouth Rock become clear when one
considers Wendell's exclusive sense of "American" one more time. When the
black Harvard student Alain Locke—who later became famous as a philosopher and editor of *The New Negro* (1925)—was chosen by Pennsylvania as
America's first (and, until 1962, only) black Rhodes scholar at Oxford in
1907, Wendell held both Locke and the Pennsylvania board in error since the
terms of the scholarship included wide comprehensive representation of what
was "best in the state" that sent the scholar. Wendell wrote to Horace Kallen:

At least for many years to come, no negro can take just this position anywhere in America. Before he can, the kind of American which unmixed nationhood has made me must be only a memory. It is sad, I admit—not least so to me for the reason that I am passing, perhaps of the past altogether. (Wendell 1907)

Couched in Wendell's melancholy terms is a definition of "American" as meaning unmixed (New English) nationhood from which blacks (though they are English-speaking and predominantly Protestant) are categorically excluded, no matter how long their residence in the United State has lasted. No three-generation formula, no Old Testament parallel is offered as a bridge between "Negroes" and "Americans." Wendell was not alone in setting up different rules for African Americans and for immigrants. Those redefiners of "America" who wanted to make it more "ethnic" and "pluralistic," such as Kallen, Antin, and even Bourne, paid little or no attention to black Americans in their attempts at broadening American cultural categories. As Higham writes: "The pluralist thesis from the outset was encapsulated in white ethnocentrism" (Higham 1975, 208).

Was Ellis Island a more appropriate image than Plymouth Rock for those Americans whose ancestors had been forcibly transported to the New World as slaves? How would the American story have to change in order to accommodate black history? In his last writings the late historian Nathan Huggins took American historians to task for dealing with Afro-American history only too rarely (and then usually as an "exception" and "anomaly") in their generalizations about American history (Huggins 1990, xliv–xlvi) and called attention to African American writers who have, for a long time, taken on the special responsibility of questioning American national symbols by confronting them with the history of slavery and segregation. In the first novel published by an American Negro, William Wells Brown's *Clotel; or the President's Daughter* (1853), the author dedicated a whole page to the contrast between the two American beginnings of the "May-flower" and of Jamestown, of freedom and slavery (Brown 1970, 147). At the end of the novel, the titular heroine and slave woman dies, pursued by slave catchers, in the Potomac, "within plain sight of the President's house and the capitol of the Union" (Brown 1970, 177). Her father Jefferson was not only the "author" of the Declaration of Independence but also of unacknowledged slave children (whether or not this was literally the case is not important since it is "*symbolically* true" [Huggins 1990, xlvii]).

In his famous work *The Souls of Black Folk* (1903) W. E. B. Du Bois specifically mentioned the slave ship that "first saw the square tower of Jamestown" as an American beginning point (Du Bois 1986, 424; see also Griggs 1969, 197) and, near the end of the book, he says: "Your country?

How came it yours? Before the Pilgrims landed we were there" (Du Bois 1986, 545). For black writers "Jamestown" memorializes 1619, the first arrival of Africans in what is now the United States. This is, incidentally, an event not remembered much even in Jamestown itself. It has hardly played a part in the anniversaries of the founding of Jamestown—although Meta Vaux Warrick contributed a sculpture on the "advancement of the Negro since he landed" to the Jamestown tercentennial in 1907, and Duke Ellington in 1944 publicly claimed Jamestown descent (Hatch 1957, 23–24; *Anniversary* 1958, 78; *Jamestown* 1958; True 1983; Washington 1909, 293–94; Adamic 1945, 195).

A poetic example is James Edwin Campbell's "The Pariah," which makes an explicit case for the merger of Plymouth Rock and Jamestown through the union of the black-white couple that follows the formula: "She the Brahmin, I the Pariah." Speaking about the woman's father, the poem explicates:

> Traced he back his proud ancestry
>   To the Rock on Plymouth's shore,
> Traced I mine to Dutch ship landing
>   At Jamestown, one year before.
>
> (Campbell 1895, 82)

Whereas Paulding wanted to see a northern-southern merger of Puritans and Cavaliers, and immigrant enthusiasts such as Zangwill, Antin, and Adamic thought that the whole American synthesis was embodied in the fusion of Ellis Island and Plymouth Rock (leaving out the legacy of slavery that way), the black poet Campbell viewed the merger of the Pariah and the Brahmin (as in Paulding's "Ode to Jamestown," with echoes of the Pocahontas story, and as in Zangwill's *Melting-Pot,* with a focus on an intermarriage) as the hope for a casteless country of Jamestown *and* Plymouth Rock (ignoring the arrival point of immigrants). Both "Jamestown" and "Ellis Island" were, in different fashions, symbolic alternatives to the narrow interpretation of America as *Mayflower*-descended, yet alternatives that could also exclude each other.

With his exquisite sense of irony, Charles W. Chesnutt confronted white and black origins in his short story "Her Virginia Mammy" (1899) in which Clara Hohlfelder, an American orphan who had been adopted by German immigrants, is about to marry John Winthrop, a *Mayflower* descendant, and now wishes to discover a desired Cavalier ancestry for herself in order to be the perfect match. Yet despite many clues, she fails to recognize her own mother, a black woman, whom she interprets instead as her "dear Virginia mammy." Chesnutt's irony hinges on the heroine's misunderstanding of ambiguous terms such as the word "belong" in the revelation: "Your mother— . . . belonged to one of the first families of Virginia, and in her veins flowed some of the best blood of the Old Dominion." The union of southerner and New Englander is bought at the expense of masking the history of slavery and of the racially mixed identity of the country, while Chesnutt incorporates the immigration theme into the adoption story. Clara may be Chesnutt's allegory of America, as she includes only white New England and Virginia as *meaningful* ancestry for her family romance, while relegating the histories of black slavery and European immigration to the subordinate symbolic roles of adoptive parents and mammies (Chesnutt 1968, 53, 59).

In 1942 the black modernist poet Melvin B. Tolson contributed to *Common Ground* the poem "Rendezvous with America," in which he seems to have desired to represent America as the merger of *all* points of arrival. The poem opens with the lines:

> Time unhinged the gates
> Of Plymouth Rock and Jamestown and Ellis Island,
> And worlds of men with hungers of body and soul
> Hazarded the wilderness of waters,
> Cadenced their destinies
> With the potters'-wheeling miracles
> Of mountain and valley, prairie and river.
>
> (Tolson 1942, 3)

Tolson's critique of American symbols is directed against their exclusiveness, which he tries to break (unhinging Aldrich's "gates") by the addition of many points of entry. The Whitmanian conflation of old and new national symbols reaches a higher pitch when Tolson explicitly makes a special place for those groups (such as Indians) not automatically included by the "Plymouth Rock and Ellis Island" formula, when blind bigots are rebuked for their prejudices, or when the question "America?" is answered in the following way:

> America is the Black Man's country,
> The Red Man's, the Yellow Man's,
> The Brown Man's, the White Man's.
> America?
> An international river with a thousand tributaries!
> A magnificent cosmorama with myriad patterns and colors!
> A giant forest with loin-roots in a hundred lands!
> A mighty orchestra with a thousand instruments playing
> *America!*
>
> (Tolson 1942, 4–5)

Tolson worries about inadequacies in the image of the Statue of Liberty; yet his poem, written upon the occasion of Pearl Harbor, sees this inadequacy in a tranquilized Uncle Sam's lack of watchfulness: he "Pillows his head on the

Statue of Liberty" (Tolson 1942, 7). In his harmonic vision of a polyethnic America the shadow of one enemy—Japan—remains. Perhaps this enemy image may even have helped with the project of integrating Red, Black, and White (though Tolson does mention "Patriots from Yokosuka and Stralsund" in one of his melting-pot catalogues [3]).

The incorporating mode of the war years affected even politically radical writers such as Richard Wright. He did not publish American paeans but composed a publicity statement for his autobiography *Black Boy* (1945) that made a strong polyethnic pitch:

[To] those whites who recall how, in the early days of this land, their forefathers struggled for freedom, BLACK BOY cannot be a strange story. Neither can it be a strange story to the Jews, the Poles, the Irish, and the Italians who came hopefully to this land from the Old World. (Wright 1945)

This statement parallels Wright's famous quip that the Negro was "America's metaphor" (Wright 1964, 72) as well as Boris Max's defense of the black murderer Bigger Thomas in Wright's novel *Native Son:* "In him and men like him is what was in our forefathers when they first came to these strange shores hundreds of years ago. We were lucky. They are not" (Wright 1940, 332). When Wright was invited to go to France shortly after World War II and was repeatedly denied a passport, he sounded a different note. His friends, the journalist Michel Gourday and the painter Marc Chagall, appealed to the French cultural attaché Claude Lévi-Strauss, and Wright received an official invitation by the French government and, finally, after much more maneuvering, a U.S. passport, too. In a conscious rewriting of the classic Ellis Island scene the way Adamic would have liked it or the way in which Adolph Treidler's war bonds poster of 1917, "Remember Your First Thrill of American Liberty," had portrayed it (Banta 1988, 28), Wright described his emotions in the essay "I Choose Exile": "I felt relieved when my ship sailed past the Statue of Liberty!" (Wright 1948). The feeling is familiar, except that Wright was *leaving* the United States for France!

Exclusion of any group from national symbolism may generate not only the insistent argument for the group's compatibility with those symbols ("our forefathers") but also a rejection of such symbols (which may be undertaken with the intention of facilitating an ultimate integration on equal footing). Wright's ironic reversal of interpreting the Statue of Liberty was not a unique occurrence. Thus, Du Bois described in his *Autobiography* how, upon returning from Europe in 1894 on an immigrant ship, he saw the Statue of Liberty:

I know not what multitude of emotions surged in the others, but I had to recall that mischievous little French girl whose eyes twinkled as she said: "Oh yes the Statue of

Liberty! With its back toward America, and its face toward France!" (Du Bois 1968, 182)

Yet in our days the symbol of Ellis Island is used explicitly to incorporate Afro-Americans. Thus the black former congresswoman Barbara Jordan, together with Frank Sinatra, was awarded the Ellis Island Medal of Honor by the Statue of Liberty-Ellis Island Foundation ("Chronicle" 1990).

Having surveyed some voices engaged in the redefinition of who was "American" let me return one more time to the remarkable collection of 1906, *The Life Stories of Undistinguished Americans*. What emerges in that book is no single voice (be it inclusive or exclusive), but a chorus of different speakers and writers who narrate their own lives, sometimes with a tellingly unstable use of the pronoun "we." For some narrators America appears to be a utopia come true. Thus the Swedish farmer cherishes the American freedom not to have to take off his hat to aristocrats. Others express their desire to leave America. As the French dressmaker Amelia des Moulins puts it:

I am not to live here.
To one born in England, Germany, Austria, Holland or Scandinavia this
may appear fine, but not so to the French.
There is but one France and only one Paris in all the world, and soon,
very soon, [her roommate] Annette and I will be aboard some great ship
that will bear us back there.

(Holt 1990, 76)

Lee Chew, the Chinese businessman, concludes his narrative (which is also the ending of the book) with the strong statement: "how can I call this my home, and how can any one blame me if I take my money and go back to my village in China?" (Holt 1990, 185). A "Southern colored woman" who read the *Life Stories* responded with her story, which was published in the *Independent*. She particularly addressed the Swedish farmer and the Chinese laundryman: "There are 'aristocrats' to push me and mine down and say we are not worthy because we are colored. . . . Happy Chinaman! Fortunate Lee Chew! You can go back to your village and enjoy your money. This is my village, my home, yet am I an outcast" (Holt 1990, 220). *The Life Stories of Undistinguished Americans* is a text that shows how difficult it is to think of a single truly representative national generalization.

Many of the stories that focus on immigrants include arrival scenes, sometimes with reference to the Statue of Liberty. The Jewish sweatshop worker Sadie Frowne notes that upon arriving in New York she "saw the beautiful bay and the big woman with the spikes on her head and the lamp that is lighted at night in her hand (Goddess of Liberty)" (Holt 1990, 22), and the

Syrian journalist mentions that he "passed close by the grand Statue of Liberty" and saw in the distance the "beautiful white bridge away up in the blue sky and the big buildings towering up like our own mountain peaks" (Holt 1990, 154). Mike Trudics, a Hungarian peon, misread the statue's torch as a broom: "A well dressed man who spoke our language told us that the big iron woman in the harbor was a goddess that gave out liberty freely and without cost to everybody. He said the thing in her hand that looked like a broom was light—that it was to give us light and liberty too." Yet unfazed by that identification, he continued: "he told us a man could stand inside the broom" (Holt 1990, 201). The Hungarian's interpretation shows that Ellis Island immigrants, too, could try to reinterpret the statue in other ways than by stressing their own compatibility with America viewed as Plymouth Rock. The *Life Stories* thus foreshadow such famous and sinister misreadings of the Statue of Liberty as those in Franz Kafka's *Amerika* (1913) and in Henry Roth's classic American immigrant novel *Call It Sleep* (1934), in both of which the torch of the statue is described as a sword. The beacon of light of American freedom as a broom or a sword change the national symbol into a cleaning-lady or an avenging angel; and these are readings that, like Wright's and Du Bois's, cleared the way for recasting the national imagery in a broader, polyethnic way.

It was during World War II and in the Supreme Court decisions and civil rights bills of the 1950s and 1960s that the term "American" actually became intertwined with ethnicity and flexible enough to include—in widely accepted public usage—such groups as immigrants, African Americans, and American Indians. Minorities have moved into the center of the cultural industry; and the metaphor of the "invading hordes" seems to have fallen not only into disfavor but into oblivion. The growth of a more flexible term for an American national identity thus *seems* to be a success story. Yet it is not only that, and the hymnic synthesis invoked by some poets has hardly become an American reality. After all, the successful expansion of the term "America" came about only in the heated debates about national loyalty generated by two world wars, and after immigration had been severely limited along racial categories. The broad notion of "America" has never really included everybody, all the arguments for compatibility notwithstanding; especially in the case of blacks, the inclusive use of "American" remains ambiguous even today, as the Jesse Jackson campaigns repeatedly showed. Xenophilic cosmopolitanism may have helped to further alienate some liberal intellectuals from people other than those in distinct ethnic groups and encouraged some conservatives to embrace racism and anti-intellectualism more openly. The educational system confronts tough debates over *which* American culture should be taught to children and adolescents. The battle for "America" continues, and there are today more (and more contradictory) notions and definitions of what is or ought to be "American" than there are views of the Statue of Liberty.

NOTES

1. Chametzky 1977, 43–74. Comparisons of literary variants in linguistically differentiated media could offer a particularly fruitful approach to studying the differences between "national" and "ethnic" cultures, or at least to the way in which a specific author imagines these differences. Such studies could also continue Benedict Anderson's pioneering work (1985), according to which modern group identities are intricately intertwined with the imaginary world of print media.

2. How did the change come about? Of all factors, perhaps it was the cultural reaction to World War II that mattered most. (See Gleason 1980; and Thernstrom 1980, 31–58.) The postwar Beat generation artists were no longer considered ethnic (though Jack Kerouac, Allen Ginsberg, Lawrence Ferlinghetti, Frank O'Hara, and Diane DiPrima hardly denied their ethnic backgrounds); and Andy Warhol, for example, was, I think, rarely described as a Czech-American artist. In popular culture, too, World War II marks the divide, during which black music, or at least black-inspired music, could simply be regarded American music (which was still a dream for James Weldon Johnson); and "Jewish" Hollywood and comics were rarely regarded as the products of the ethnicities of their makers but as American national entertainment.

   The writings of American intellectuals illustrate the contested nature as well as some limits of these changes. This development is all the more significant since the terms "ethnic," "minority," "immigrant-descended," or "foreign-stock" may apply, in American usage, to several generations after the initial arrivals (unlike what some observers find true in France, where a very high threshold before becoming French is followed by an easier acceptance of immigrants' children as simply French-born French). See Kivisto 1990 for new essays on the important topic of generations.

3. Contemporary observers noted that in several American cities at the beginning of the twentieth century Americans of British descent were seriously outnumbered; one could read in the *Atlantic Monthly,* for example, that Baltimore "had 40 percent of foreigners with their children in 1900," Boston 70 percent, New York 80 percent, and the proportion "reaches a maximum in Milwaukee, with 86 percent thus constituted" (Ripley 1908, 748). Compared to the data from before World War I, all subsequent figures of ethnic population changes in the United States have been less significant. Even with the inclusion of the estimates for illegal immigrants, "immigration to the United States in the latter half of the 1980s was running at a yearly rate equal to only one-third of one percent of the national population . . . considerably less than one-third the rate prevailing in the first

decade of the twentieth century. As of 1986 . . . only 7 percent of the inhabitants of the United States were foreign-born—which was substantially smaller than the comparable figure for Australia (20%), Canada (16%), or even France (11%)" (Christopher 1989, 279).

4. James's statement deserves to be read against Fredrik Barth's notion of the boundary (Barth 1969). The writer Lafcadio Hearn, for example, felt compelled to defend the measures taken by the Louisiana legislature to encourage continued use of the French language on American soil against more powerful opponents who equated "American" with "English-speaking." Hearn wrote about "The French in Louisiana" in the *Item* (2 March 1880):

> It has been said that New Orleans is not a French city, but an American city; and that the use of the English language alone should be permitted in public affairs and public schools (Hutson 1926, 81–83).

Maintenance of languages other than English has remained relatively low in the United States, however, with a marked increase from 1960 to 1970, though issues of bilingualism continue to cause virulent debates up to the present (Thernstrom 1980, 619–38). Religion could become the dividing line, for example, when anti-Irish agitation manifested itself as anti-Catholicism. Thus Samuel F. B. Morse viewed "Popery" as "opposed in its very nature to Democratic Republicanism" and advocated a lifetime denial of suffrage to foreign immigrants (Morse 1835).

5. See, for example, the review in the *Annals of the American Academy* 28 (July 1906): 176. Interestingly, the reprint of the *Life Stories* in 1990 was reviewed without much attention to immigration or ethnicity (Morris 1990, 100–103).

6. Banta also notes that McCutcheon does not even mention Indians, African Americans, Asians, or Jews (126). On the ambiguity of nationalism and universalism in American representations of Liberty (that are iconographically derived from Britannia) see Higham 1990, 61–71. Cf. also the subtitle to Joseph Stella's realistic immigrant portrait that serves as Mary Antin's frontispiece: "THE SINEW AND BONE OF ALL THE NATIONS" (Antin 1914).

7. Many writers of non-English origins participated in this method of Americanization: Crèvecoeur had used the pen name Hector St. John and passed his narrator off as an English immigrant; Francesca Vinciguerra became Frances Winwar; and as recently as the 1970s, the French immigrant author (Sanche) de Gramont changed his name, in anagrammatic fashion, to "Ted Morgan." Integration could be imagined by the cultural participants as a marriage in which the newcomer plays the bride who gives up her ethnic maiden name for her English husband's. There were, of course, authors who chose different strategies: Louis Adamic refused to change his name to "Adams"—while he did get rid of the accent over the "c" (Adamic 1942, 11–23); and the recently rediscovered Jewish immigrant writer who published under the name "Anzia Yezierska" spent most of her childhood as "Hattie Meyer." See also the parallel development of surname choices such as Booker T. Washington and Frederick Douglass as opposed to Malcolm X and Amiri Baraka. For some general observations on name changes see Baltzell 1966, 46–48.

8. The Honorable Chauncey M. Depew briefly alluded to the statue's expression of "welcome" to "the poor and the persecuted with the hope and promise of homes

and citizenship" (*Programme* 1886, 33–34), and speaking for France, W. A. Lefaivre made a longer mention of the "thousands of Europeans who are daily conveyed to these hospitable shores," among whom "no one will pass before this glorious emblem without immediately perceiving its moral greatness, and without greeting it with respect and thankfulness" (*Inauguration* 1887, 36).

Whittier's poem was recited at the dedication (*Programme* 1886, 61–62); in the *Official Programme*, however, Lazarus's poem (*Programme* 1886, 24; see also Handlin 1971 and Trachtenberg 1977, 214n11) as well as the following, virtually unknown sonnet by Sydney Herbert Pierson were published:

Liberty

She stands upon the threshold of the sea,
   Emblem, in burnished bronze and carven stone,
   Of sister nations welded into one
By no long wars nor bloody tyranny
Of might made right and weakness slavery;
   But by the blood of brotherhood alone,
   And love of her whose immemorial throne
Is Peace, Equality, Fraternity.

As in the unborn centuries, the light
   Of her shall lead the world's unfortunate
From out the gloom of wrong and tyrant might—
   To-day the slaves of ancient scorn and hate
Behold across the waters and the night
   Her blazing torch flame through ocean's gate.

(Programme 1886, 43)

9. For various uses of Matthew 11:28 in American ethnic culture see Stowe 1982, 405 (ch. 32); Zangwill 1910, 35; Howells 1891, 90; Du Bois 1968, 410; Bennett 1967, 151; and the 1986 inscription on the Chinese Ling Liang (or Grace) Church housed in the original building of the *Jewish Forward* at 173–175 East Broadway in New York City. Antin at times resembles Zangwill (e.g., 1910, 91); and after 1915, Zangwill quoted Lazarus's poem in an appendix to *The Melting-Pot* (1925, 208–9).

10. These two stanzas appear at the end of a twenty-stanza poem at the center of which are the Indian-white encounter and the Pocahontas story:

And she! the glorious Indian maid,
   The tutelary of this land,
The angel of the woodland shade.
   The miracle of God's own hand,
Who joined man's heart to woman's softest grace,
And thrice redeemed the scourges of her race.

Sister of charity and love,
   Whose life-blood was soft Pity's tide,
Dear goddess of the sylvan grove,
   Flower of the forest, nature's pride,

He is no man who does not bend the knee,
And she no woman who is not like thee!

(Stevenson 1922, 46)

The poem is part of the literary tradition that places the origin of a nation in a mésalliance. For the connection between miscegenation and national myths see Huggins 1990, lxix, and Cagidemetrio 1989, 14–43.

Paulding's poem may have been directed against such interpretations as Daniel Webster's famous attack on the African slave trade, delivered at Plymouth on December 22, 1820: "If there be, within the extent of our knowledge or influence, ·any participation in the traffic, let us pledge ourselves here, upon the Rock of Plymouth, to extirpate and destroy it. It is not fit that the land of the pilgrims should bear the shame longer" (Pierpont 1835, 184). There were also abolitionist poems in this vein, such as Elizabeth Barrett Browning's "The Runaway Slave at Pilgrim's Point" (1848); or James Russell Lowell's "On the Capture of Fugitive Slaves near Washington" (1845), which sees in Plymouth the promise of the end of slavery: "When first the pilgrims landed on the Bay State's iron shore, / The word went forth that slavery should one day be no more" (Lowell 1897, 83). Lowell's poem was originally published in the *Boston Courier* (19 July 1845); see also Scudder 1901, 1: 174–75.

Oliver Wendell Holmes's poem "The Pilgrim's Vision," included in the famous *Cyclopedia of American Literature* (Duyckinck 1866, 516–17), ended with the legend of one "hoary rock," "HERE WAS THE PILGRIM'S LAND!" And an early local *Guide to Plymouth* also specifically celebrated the "Forefather's Rock" in poetry and prose (Russell 1846, vii, 176–77, and, in the appendix "Airs of the Pilgrims," 25, 47, 49, 53, and 57).

11. The description of the Plymouth statue's dedication is quite interesting. Former governor John D. Long spoke of 60 million Americans of "every race and color" that were prefigured by the pilgrims; John Boyle O'Reilly recited the poem "The Pilgrim Fathers," which included the lines "How sum their merits? They were true and brave; / They broke no compact and they owned no slave"; and William T. Davis, a former president of the Pilgrim Society, addressed O'Reilly as a "son of the Emerald isle" and continued: "I extend the right hand of a cordial friendship. An exile from Erin, I welcome you to the congenial air of the Pilgrim exiles' home" (*Old Colony* 1990, 2–4). In other words, it appears that there were more explicit references to ethnicity at the dedication of the Monument to the Forefathers than of the Statue of Liberty. One is reminded of Georges Devereux's illuminating concept of "antagonistic acculturation" (1943).

12. Wendell's genealogical consciousness drew strongly on the male line of descent. He says little about his mother's ancestors; and her middle name, Bertodi, is mentioned but not explained in the detailed genealogical account included in Howe 1924, 6–11.

13. Still, the formulaic comparison of immigrant and Puritan caught on; and it is interesting that even such a racial thinker as Henry Pratt Fairchild conceded that American nationality "is not a question of birth, ancestry, or race." He amplifies:

A person may be born within sight of Plymouth Rock, of old colonial stock, and be much less an American than one whose parents brought him here in an immigrant ship a quarter

of a century ago. American fellowship and affiliation are natural, easy, and largely unconscious for one who has always lived in America. They are an achievement for one whose
origin is foreign. But America is one and the same for all. (Fairchild 1926, 202)

14. It would be an interesting project to compare the detention-related works by
    Japanese-American writers such as Hisaye Yamamoto's "The Legend of Miss
    Sassagawara" with Jerre Mangione's account of Italian-Americans and German-
    Americans in "Concentration Camps—American Style" (Yamamoto 1988, 20–
    33; and Mangione 1978, 319–52). On the Japanese camp period see also Hane
    1990.

BIBLIOGRAPHY

Adamic, Louis. 1938. *My America, 1928–1938.* New York and London: Harper.
Adamic, Louis. 1940. *From Many Lands.* New York and London: Harper.
Adamic, Louis. 1942. *What's Your Name.* New York and London: Harper.
Adamic, Louis. 1945. *A Nation of Nations.* New York and London: Harper.
Aldrich, Thomas Bailey. 1892. "Unguarded Gates." *Atlantic Monthly* 70:57.
Anderson, Benedict. 1985. *Imagined Communities: Reflections on the Origins and
    Spread of Nationalism* (1983). London: Verso.
Anniversary. 1958. *The 350th Anniversary of Jamestown, 1607–1957: Final Report.*
    Washington, D.C.: National Park Service
Antin, Mary. 1912. *The Promised Land.* Boston and New York: Houghton, Mifflin.
Antin, Mary. 1914. *They Who Knock at Our Gates: A Complete Gospel of Immigra-
    tion.* Boston and New York: Houghton, Mifflin.
Antin, Mary. 1969. *The Promised Land,* ed. Oscar Handlin. Boston: Houghton,
    Mifflin (Sentry edition).
Baedeker, Karl. 1909. *The United States, with Excursions to Mexico, Cuba, Porto
    Rico, and Alaska.* Leipzig: Baedeker.
Baltzell, E. Digby. 1966. *The Protestant Establishment: Aristocracy and Caste in
    America* (1964). New York: Vintage.
Banta, Martha. 1988. *Imaging American Women: Idea and Ideals in Cultural History.*
    New York: Columbia University Press.
Barber, J. W. 1839. *Historical Collections Relating to the History and Antiquities of
    Every Town in Massachusetts.* Worcester, Mass.: Dorr, Howland.
Barth, Fredrik ed. 1969. *Ethnic Groups and Boundaries: The Social Organization of
    Culture Difference.* Boston: Little, Brown.
Bender, Thomas. 1987. *New York Intellect: A History of Intellectual Life in New
    York City, from 1750 to the Beginnings of Our Own Time.* Baltimore: Johns
    Hopkins University Press.
Bennett, Hal. 1967. *A Wilderness of Vines.* New York: Pyramid.
Bolino, August C. 1985. *The Ellis Island Source Book.* Washington, D.C.: Kensington
    Historical Press.
Bourne, Randolph S. 1977. *The Radical Will: Selected Writings, 1911–1918,* ed. and
    introd. Olaf Hansen. New York: Urizen.

Bradford, William. 1952. *Of Plymouth Plantation, 1620–1647,* ed. and introd. Samuel Eliot Morison. New York: Modern Library.

Briggs, Rose T. 1988. *Plymouth Rock: History and Significance* (1968). Plymouth: Pilgrim Society.

Brown, Sterling A. et al. ed. 1969. *The Negro Caravan* (1941), intr. Julius Lester. New York: Arno Press.

Brown, William Wells. 1970. *Clotel; or, The President's Daughter* (1853). New York: Collier.

Brownstone, David M. et al. 1979. *Island of Hope, Island of Tears.* New York: Rawson, Wade.

Burbank, A. S. 1916. *Guide to Historic Plymouth: Localities and Objects of Interest.* Plymouth: Burbank.

Cagidemetrio, Alide. 1989. "A Plea for Fictional Histories and Old-Time 'Jewesses.' " In *The Invention of Ethnicity,* ed. Werner Sollors. New York and Oxford: Oxford University Press, 14–43.

Campbell, James Edwin. 1895. *Echoes. . . . From the Cabin and Elsewhere.* Chicago: Donohue and Henneberry.

Chametzky, Jules. 1977. *From the Ghetto: The Fiction of Abraham Cahan.* Amherst: University of Massachusetts Press.

Chesnutt, Charles. 1968. *The Wife of His Youth and Other Stories of the Color Line* (1899). Ann Arbor: University of Michigan Press.

Christopher, Robert C. 1989. *Crashing the Gates: The De-WASPing of America's Power Elite.* New York: Simon and Schuster.

"Chronicle". 1990. *New York Times,* 8 December.

Crèvecoeur, J. Hector. 1957. *Letters from an American Farmer* (1782). New York: Dutton.

Croly, David. 1888. *Glimpses of the Future: Suggestions as to the Drift of Things.* New York and London: Putnam's.

Devereux, George(s) et al. 1943. "Antagonistic Acculturation." *American Sociological Review* 7:133–147.

Du Bois, W. E. B. 1968. *Autobiography.* New York: International Publishers.

Du Bois, W. E. B. 1986. *Writings.* New York: Library of America.

Duyckinck, Evert A., and George L. eds. 1866. *Cyclopedia of American Literature.* (1855). New York: Scribner.

Elliott, Emory ed. 1988. *Columbia Literary History of the United States.* New York: Columbia University Press.

Fairchild, Henry Pratt. 1926. *The Melting-Pot Mistake.* Boston: Little, Brown.

Fuchs, Lawrence H. 1990. *The American Kaleidoscope: Race, Ethnicity, and the Civic Culture.* Middletown, Conn.: Wesleyan University Press.

Gilder, Rodman. 1943. *Statue of Liberty Enlightening the World.* New York: New York Trust Company.

Gleason, Philip. 1980. "Americans All: Ethnicity, Ideology, and American Identity in the Era of World War II." In *The American Identity: Fusion and Fragmentation,* ed. Rob Kroes. European Contributions to American Studies 3. Amsterdam: Amerika-Instituut, 235–64.

Gomes, Peter J. 1971. *The Pilgrim Society, 1820–1970.* Plymouth: Pilgrim Society.

Griggs, Sutton. 1969. *The Hindered Hand; or, the Reign of the Repressionist* (1905). Miami: Mnemosyne.

Handlin, Oscar. 1971. *Statue of Liberty.* New York: Newsweek Book Division.

Hane, Misiko. 1990. "Wartime Internment." *Journal of American History* 77: 569–75.

Harlan, Louis et al. eds. 1977. *Booker T. Washington Papers.* Vol. 6, Urbana: University of Illinois Press.

Hatch, Charles E. 1957. *Jamestown, Virginia: The Townsite and Its Story* (1949). Washington, D.C.: National Park Service.

Hawthorne, Nathaniel. 1862. "Chiefly about War-Matters. By a Peaceable Man." *Atlantic Monthly* 10 (July): 43–61.

Higham, John. 1975. *Send These to Me: Jews and Other Immigrants in Urban America.* New York: Atheneum.

Higham, John. 1989. "The Redefinition of America, 1910–1930." ms.

Higham, John. 1990. "Indian Princess and Roman Goddess: The First Female Symbols of America." *Proceedings of the American Antiquarian Society* 100.1:45–79.

Hollinger, David A. 1985. *In the American Province: Studies in the History and Historiography of Ideas.* Bloomington: Indiana University Press.

Holt, Hamilton. 1990. *The Life Stories of Undistinguished Americans: As Told by Themselves* (1906). New York and London: Routledge.

Howe, M. A. DeWolfe. 1924. *Barrett Wendell and His Letters.* Boston: Atlantic Monthly.

Howells, William Dean. 1891. *An Imperative Duty.* New York: Harper.

Huggins, Nathan Irvin. 1990. "Introduction: The Deforming Mirror of Truth." *Black Odyssey: The African American Ordeal in Slavery.* New York: Pantheon.

Hurwitz, Samuel J. 1975. "Lazarus, Emma." In *Notable American Women* (1971), vol. 2, ed. Edward T. James, et al. Cambridge and London: Harvard University Press.

Hutson, Charles Woodward ed. 1926. *Editorials by Lafcadio Hearn.* Boston and New York: Houghton, Mifflin.

Inauguration. 1887. *Inauguration of the Statue of Liberty Enlightening the World by the President of the United States. Issued under the Authority of the Committee.* New York: Appleton.

"Indian" 1987. "Indian Ceremony on Ellis Island." *New York Times,* 29 June, B3.

Jacob, Heinrich Eduard. 1949. *The World of Emma Lazarus.* New York: Schocken.

James, Henry. 1968. *The American Scene* (1907). Bloomington and London: Indiana University Press.

Jamestown. 1958. *Significant Addresses of the Jamestown Festival, 1957,* ed. Ulrich Troubetzkoy. Richmond, Va. (With addresses by Queen Elizabeth, President Eisenhower, Richard Nixon, and others.) Printed by Garret and Massie, Richmond, Va.

Kallen, Horace M. 1924. *Culture and Democracy in the United States: Studies in the Group Psychology of the American Peoples.* New York: Boni and Liveright.

Kaplan, Sidney. 1949. "The Miscegenation Issue in the Election of 1864." *Journal of Negro History* 34.3:274–343.

Kingston, Maxine Hong. 1989. *Tripmaster Monkey: His Fake Book.* New York: Knopf.

Kivisto, Peter et al. eds. 1990. *American Immigrants and Their Generations: Studies and Commentaries on the Hansen Thesis after Fifty Years.* Urbana and Chicago: University of Illinois Press.

Lai, Him Mark et al. eds. 1980. *Island: Poetry and History of Chinese Immigrants on Angel Island, 1910–1940.* San Francisco: HOC DOI (History of Chinese Detained on Island), Chinese Cultural Foundation.

Lamar, Mrs. Joseph Rucker. 1934. *A History of the National Society of the Colonial Dames of America from 1891 to 1933.* Atlanta: Brown.

Lazarus, Emma. 1888. *Poems of Emma Lazarus.* Vol. 1. Boston and New York: Houghton, Mifflin.

Lejeune, Philippe. 1989. *On Autobiography,* ed. John Paul Eakin and transl. Katherine Leary. Minneapolis: University of Minnesota Press.

Levine, Benjamin et al. 1957. *Statue of Liberty: National Monument, Liberty Island, New York.* Washington, D.C.: National Park Service Historical Handbook Series No. 11.

Lossing, Benson J. 1873. *A Common-School History of the United States: From the Earliest Period to the Present Time.* New York: Sheldon.

Lowell, James Russell. 1892. *Literary Essays.* Vol. 3. Boston and New York: Houghton, Mifflin.

Lowell, James Russell. 1897. *The Poetical Works.* Boston and New York: Houghton, Mifflin.

Malcolm X. 1966. *The Autobiography of Malcolm X* (1965). With the assistance of Alex Haley. New York: Grove Press.

Mangione, Jerre. 1978. *An Ethnic at Large: A Memoir of America in the Thirties and Forties.* New York: Putnam's.

Mangione, Jerre. 1982. *Mount Allegro: A Memoir of Italian American Life* (1942). New York: Columbia University Press.

Massachusetts. 1937. *Massachusetts: A Guide to Its Places and People.* (Federal Writers' Project.) Boston: Houghton, Mifflin.

Matthews, F[red] H. 1970. "The Revolt against Americanism: Cultural Pluralism and Cultural Relativism as an Ideology of Liberation." *Canadian Review of American Studies* 1.1:4–31.

Morris, Edmund. 1990. "Short and Simple Annals." *New Yorker,* 11 June, 100–103.

Morse, Samuel F. B. 1835. *Imminent Dangers to the Free Institutions of the United States through Foreign Immigration.* New York: Trow.

Old Colony. 1990. *Old Colony Memorial: Plymouth Rock.* Old Colony Sentinel 68, no. 31 (3 August 1889).

Perec, Georges. 1980. *Récits d'Ellis Island: Histoires d'errance et d'espoir.* Paris: Editions du Sorbier.

Pierpont, John ed. 1835. *The American First Class Book; or Exercises in Reading and Recitation.* Boston: Carter, Hendee.

Pilgrim. 1823. *The Constitutional Articles of the Pilgrim Society, Incorporated February 24, 1820.* Plymouth: Danforth.

Pitkin, Thomas M. 1975. *Keepers of the Gate: A History of Ellis Island.* New York: New York University Press.

Polenberg, Richard. 1985. "Progressivism and Anarchism: Judge Henry D. Clayton and the Abrams Trial." *Law and History Review* 3.2 (Fall): 397–408.

Programme. 1886. *The Official Programme. The Statue of Liberty: Its Conception. Its Construction. Its Inauguration.* New York: Dinsmore.

Repplier, Agnes. 1916. *Counter-Currents.* Boston and New York: Houghton, Mifflin.

Richards, Earl Jeffrey. 1989. "European Literature and the Labyrinth of National Images: Literary Nationalism and the Limits of Enlightenment." Dissertation, Univ. Aachen.

Ripley, William Z. 1908. "Races in the United States." *Atlantic Monthly* 102: 742–59.

Rizk, Salom. 1943. *Syrian Yankee.* Garden City, N.Y.: Doubleday, Doran.

Rodriguez, Richard. 1982. *Hunger of Memory: The Education of Richard Rodriquez.* Boston: Godine.

Rose, Peter I. ed. 1969. *The Ghetto and Beyond.* New York: Random House.

Ross, Edward Alsworth. 1914. *The Old World in the New: The Significance of Past and Present Immigration to the American People.* New York: Century.

Russell, William S. 1846. *Guide to Plymouth and Recollections of the Pilgrims* (with an appendix "Airs of the Pilgrims"). Boston: George Coolidge.

Samuels, Charles E. 1965. *Thomas Bailey Aldrich.* New York: Twayne.

Scudder, Horace Elisha. 1901. *James Russell Lowell: A Biography.* Boston and New York: Houghton, Mifflin.

Sears, Charlotte. 1985. *The Peregrinations of Plymouth Rock.* Plymouth: Antiquarian Society.

Sigourney, L. H. 1852. *National Era,* no. 281 (20 May).

Stanley, Alessandra. 1990. "Ellis Island Will Reopen in a Subdued Mood." *New York Times,* 3 September, 1, 32.

Stevenson, Burton Egbert ed. 1922. *Poems of American History* (1908). Boston and New York: Houghton, Mifflin.

Stowe, Harriet Beecher. 1852. *Uncle Tom's Cabin; or Life among the Lowly.* In: *Three Novels.* New York: Library of America, 1982.

Taylor, William. 1979. *Cavalier and Yankee: The Old South and American National Character* (1957). Cambridge: Harvard University Press.

Thacher, James. 1835. *History of the Town of Plymouth.* Boston: Marsh, Capen, and Lyon.

Thernstrom, Stephan et al. eds. 1980. *Harvard Encyclopedia of American Ethnic Groups.* Cambridge and London: Harvard University Press.

Tolson, Melvin B. 1942. "Rendezvous with America." *Common Ground* 2, no. 4 (Summer).

Tocqueville, Alexis de. 1951. *Democracy in America* (1835). Henry Reeve text, ed. Phillips Bradley. Vol. 1. New York: Knopf.

Trachtenberg, Marvin. 1977. *The Statue of Liberty* (1976). Harmondsworth and New York: Penguin.

True, Ransom B. 1983. *Jamestown: A Guide to the Old Town.* Richmond: Association for the Preservation of Virginia Antiquities.

Ware, Caroline F. ed. 1940. *The Cultural Approach to History.* New York: Columbia University Press.

Washington, Booker T. 1909. *The Story of the Negro: The Rise of the Race from Slavery.* Vol. 2. London: Unwin.

Washington, Booker T. 1986. *Up from Slavery* (1901). New York: Penguin.

Wendell, Barrett. 1907. Letter to Horace M. Kallen, 3 November (manuscript, American Jewish Archives, Cincinnati).

Whitman, Walt. 1982. *Complete Poems and Collected Prose.* New York: Library of America.

Whittier, John Greenleaf. 1904. *Complete Poetical Works.* Boston and New York: Houghton, Mifflin.

Wright, Richard. 1940. *Native Son.* New York: Harper.

Wright, Richard. 1945. Publicity statement for *Black Boy* (manuscript, James Weldon Collection, Beinecke Library, Yale University).

Wright, Richard. 1948. "I Choose Exile" (manuscript, James Weldon Collection, Beinecke Library, Yale University).

Wright, Richard. 1964. *White Man, Listen!* (1957). Garden City, N.Y.: Doubleday.

Yamamoto, Hisaye. 1988. *Seventeen Syllables and Other Stories.* Latham, N.Y.: Kitchen Table: Women of Color Press.

Yin, Xiaohuang. 1991. "Gold Mountain Dreams: Chinese American Literature and Its Socio-Historical Context." Diss., Harvard University.

Zangwill, Israel. 1910. *The Melting-Pot* (1909). New York: Macmillan.

Zangwill, Israel. 1925. *The Melting-Pot* (with an appendix). New York: Macmillan.

FOUR

IMMIGRANT EXPERIENCES: IN THE CITY AND AT WORK

11

IMMIGRANT HOUSING AND INTEGRATION IN FRENCH CITIES

Véronique de Rudder

With respect to the integration of immigrants into French cities, neither general nor targeted housing policies are the major factor. Immigrants are primarily involved in the private housing sector, which is controlled by the free play of market supply and demand and only slightly affected by local or national public officials. We can best evaluate housing as a route to integration by considering social stratification and tendencies toward segregation in the housing market itself, on the one hand, and social and ethnic segregation —the stakes and circumstances of multiethnic or mixed housing—and social relationships within the neighborhood, town, and region on the other hand.

Since immigrants have benefited little from welcoming services during the period of their massive arrival, it is more relevant to talk about population relocation and management policies. But these policies are not based solely on social considerations. They are also linked to settling or mobilizing the labor force, to urban renewal and planning, and to efforts to rationalize or adapt the production of housing to economic changes. Legislative and regulatory measures concerning immigrant housing can be legitimately analyzed from any of these points of view. Moreover, approaching this problem from the point of view of housing policy as such is not the best way to understand what encourages or discourages residential integration for immigrants.

HOUSING POLICIES FOR IMMIGRANTS?

Since World War II, measures concerning immigrant relocation have vacillated between two opposing approaches that were in fact combined in several ways, depending on the period. The first approach relies on law to integrate immigrants, while the second targets specific action.

In fact, we find few direct measures before the 1950s. Until then, the priority given to construction at a time of housing shortages cut out the most destitute populations, especially immigrants (though they were relatively few at this point) (Ballain and Jacquier 1987).

Until the 1970s public housing construction, but even more, private construction, began to solve the inherited postwar quantitative crisis. But there continued to be a qualitative problem: those in poor housing, in substandard or dilapidated settlements and in shanty towns, were generally thought of as "the casualties of population growth." Immigrants, and their families who joined them, rarely obtained housing and swelled the ranks of inhabitants of haphazard settlements, such as illicit rooming houses.

Urban renewal and the expansion of relocation policies in subsidized housing—constructed on the outskirts of towns in order to minimize property costs—provoked the exodus of lower-income populations occupying small, uncomfortable housing in urban centers. The standards for housing for the working class varied according to the resources of the beneficiaries and according to social goals. The National Construction Association for Algerian Workers (SO.NA.CO.TRA) in 1957, and then the Group for Social Action for Muslim Algerian Workers in France (F.A.S.) in 1959 were originally created to respond specifically to the problems of immigrants from the colonies. Their scope progressively expanded during the 1960s, with the considerable growth of immigration, to include all workers and migrant families. They played a fundamental role in creating and managing hostels for individual workers and in subsidizing housing programs (at normal and reduced rates) —especially the "transitional cities" designed to encourage progressive adaptation to collective housing.

The fight against shanty towns and substandard housing (1964, 1966, and 1970 laws) was clearly successful when it came to shanty towns (the biggest ones will disappear in the next few years); there have been less clear results against substandard housing. This policy groups together reduction of substandard housing, land recovery, urban renewal, and relocation for the "fringe" populations.

Between 1965 and 1975, as a result of the combined effects of relaxation of the housing crisis, measures to gain access to property, and regulations requiring that 6.75 percent of new housing go to families from substandard housing (adopted in 1968 but not applied until 1971), the most underprivileged classes of society succeeded very gradually in infiltrating the "standard" low-income housing developments, progressively vacated by the middle classes who had occupied them. Immigrant families followed close on the heels of French working-class families.

The situation has not changed much since the mid-1970s, with the economic recession and the financial housing reform, adopted in 1977, which helps individuals (making demand creditworthy) rather than supporting construction (improving the supply). It is no longer a question of providing access to public housing for the working class—including immigrants—but of helping them achieve circumstances under which they can obtain and remain in decent housing.

Rehabilitating old housing and restoring deteriorated public housing has taken the place of urban renewal. But, when residential development is brought to a halt by the recession, construction slows considerably, public financing becomes hard to find, public housing deteriorates, and the homeless reappear. The housing market is once again strained, and competition sharpens. Social and sometimes ethnic segregation increases in urban and peripheral zones in both the private sector and public housing, bringing with it residential discrimination and, sometimes, tensions between immigrants and French native occupants.

A policy for resolving these crises, adopted in 1977 under the name "Operation Living and Social Conditions" and broadened in 1982 under the name "Social Development of Neighborhoods," tried to deal simultaneously with these related problems.[1]

The measures adopted for immigrant housing essentially follow general housing policy and its evolution. Some specific measures were adopted one by one[2] to deal with the situations caused by a lack of foresight, often after dramatic incidents (such as the death of five African workers in a substandard hostel on 1 January 1980) and sometimes as a result of public opinion and media pressure (Delcourt 1977).

We can see, however, a shift towards adopting specific measures during the 1960–1975 period: regulations, institutions, management, financing,[3] procedures, and types of specialized housing multiplied, although their results did not always match the effort invested, except in certain cases (well out of reach of immigrants or even poorly housed people) where the goal was urban renewal or the opening up of a new urban area, gradual elimination of shantytowns, creation of a service industry, or construction of new towns.

But the negative effects of these particular measures finally surfaced. The rent strike in migrant workers' housing settlements from 1974 to 1976 is particularly revealing. It was the result of residents' discontent with housing costs, but even more with the discriminatory social treatment they received. They protested the authoritarian methods of management and the control of managers, and demanded participation by resident representatives in management and normalization of residential status based on the model of landlord status. The strike can be considered the most important urban struggle of this period in France. In low-income subsidized housing, intended to help people adapt to "standard" subsidized housing, the "transition" often didn't work and families remained stuck in fairly precarious housing conditions that rapidly deteriorated. The correlation between maladapted and immigrant families contributed to a persistent marginalization and stigmatization of inner cities and their inhabitants.

Since the end of new immigrant workers' entry (July 1974) and the increase in family reunifications in spite of measures designed to hinder them, official orientation is towards normalizing treatment of immigrant housing and equalizing immigrant housing conditions with those of French citizens in the same socioeconomic categories (Secrétariat d'Etat aux Travailleurs Immigrés 1980). It is in this framework of efforts to place immigrants in normal situations (the fight against illegal immigration being its corollary) that the effects of economic recession on the residential real estate market and on the current housing situation for these populations can be seen.

2. IMMIGRANTS IN THE HOUSING MARKET

Improving housing conditions for the French, although obviously unequal for different social classes, was common enough to permit "the conquest of standard housing" by the working class, as Michel Verret says. Immigrants did not benefit from this movement at the same time, nor in the same way, as did the native French. The majority, especially those from underdeveloped countries or old colonies (in France just as in the rest of Europe), live "wherever they are tolerated" (Delcourt 1977).

First they occupied vacant spaces, either those abandoned by the French during residential development or those not yet developed. With time, and with the "settling process" of immigration, the gap diminished: general living conditions for immigrant workers, primarily laborers, progressively moved closer to the conditions for French laborers. But they were a long way from being equal.

As we have seen, immigrants are largely housed in the private sector, in particular in the rental sector. The influence of the private market on immigrant housing obviously mitigates the effects of both specific measures and general housing policies.

The impact of various immigration waves on the housing market is explained by a dual process of segregation:

— social segregation, which, for both immigrants and French nationals, links place of residence (location, type, size, comfort, conditions for occupation) to socioprofessional status. Thus, the socioprofessional background of each immigrant nationality helps explain its living conditions.
— ethnic (or "racial") segregation that places each immigration wave in an unequal position with respect to French nationals of the same socioprofessional category, and thus determines their place in the hierarchy.

Both these factors are in operation, but ethnic segregation is stronger as it is combined with social segregation. The gap between the living conditions of an unskilled native French laborer and an unskilled immigrant laborer is greater than the gap between a French native who is a supervisor or technician and his or her foreign colleague. In both cases, the difference is even greater when the immigrant is of an origin that is particularly discriminated against (see Section 3 following).

Immigrant housing conditions reveal a socioethnic hierarchy. Contrary to what is sometimes suggested, neither the history of migratory waves, nor the history of individuals, nor the cultural adaptation of those most discriminated against, nor even family migration—all of which tend to improve immigrant housing conditions—can alone explain this hierarchy, which clearly arises from distinctive social treatment.

Subsidized housing acts more and more as a competitive market. Immigrant penetration into this sector dates generally from the 1970s. It is, however, uneven, and varies locally, depending on the amount of available publicly assisted housing and its "desirability," linked, notably, to more central or more peripheral location, available public transportation, and proximity of shopping and cultural or recreational facilities, but also to the general social image of the neighborhood.

Access to subsidized housing and the criteria for its allocation are legally and officially blind to the origin of the applicants and unaffected by the constraints of private sector profits. However, for quite some time they have in fact been biased against immigrants. First, immigrants have to wait in turn for their housing applications to be considered, and sometimes they also have to fulfill a residency requirement in the department or county where they make the request. Then there is a wait because immigrant families do not have money for the rent and other expenses (which have all risen in recent years), especially in the most comfortable and best-established subsidized housing. This lack of resources is insufficiently compensated for by credit aid.

Even now, other factors continue to keep immigrants at a disadvantage:

— inadequate subsidized housing for people in categories who have a "right" to it (a reduction in construction over the past decade, and the arrival on the residential market of immigrants' children risk increasing this shortage);

— inadequate quality for many immigrant families because of the scarcity of large apartments;

— growing explicit or latent refusal to have immigrants share public housing because of images and stereotypes concerning the immigrant lifestyle, or the lifestyle of certain nationalities, and fear of reduction of status or image;

— politicization of immigrants' presence and an unofficial (because illegal) but often barely hidden (in the electoral process) use of quotas, limiting the burden of immigrants on society. The role of local elected officials, sensitive in varying degrees to pressure from their constituents, in managing and distributing subsidized housing, brought about a noticeable reduction in the number of immigrant families obtaining housing. The fact that foreigners in France continue to be deprived of citizenship at the local, regional, or national level has not yet been compensated for by naturalizations nor by the fact that many children of immigrants, French by birth or by choice, are voters.

Immigrant representation in subsidized housing is below what one would expect on the basis of their numbers in the lower classes of the population, for whom this housing was created. In all, 23.5 percent of foreign "households" living together, whether related or not, live in low-income housing[4] (INSEE 1982), as compared to 12.7 percent of "households" that are French by birth, but over three-quarters of employed foreigners are laborers or service workers. These differences are even more noticeable in some areas: when the stock of low-income housing is small and/or when it is attractive, it is still primarily occupied by families of moderate incomes (skilled workers, technicians, supervisors, employees) and immigrants have great difficulty gaining access. For example, in Paris, 7.5 percent of households of foreign laborers live in low-income housing, as opposed to 21 percent of households of French laborers; for households carrying out intermediary jobs, these percentages are 7 and 13 (Champion 1987); when the housing stock is more adequate—but the supply is not equal to the demand—it becomes a stratified market, with immigrants concentrated in the inferior sections of stock. In publicly supported housing, as in the private sector, a large number of immigrants has an effect on market stratification; it is a devaluating factor.

3. HOUSING CONDITIONS

Statistics that allow us to evaluate housing quality are in short supply. The descriptive criteria used, partly linked to administrative and regulatory norms, are based on "average" comfort standards. For a population usually "disadvantaged," it is often less the "quality" (in the positive sense) than the defectiveness of the housing that should be evaluated. We especially need to consider features such as humidity; natural lighting; general condition of the building; doors and window frames; the electrical, heating, and ventilation systems; infestation by bugs or vermin, etc. Certain studies, thorough but selective (and thus less representative than censuses), show that immigrants are clearly more exposed than French nationals to these faulty conditions.

Furthermore, the statistics supplied by INSEE are not informative about living conditions, by socioprofessional category and by nationality. This shortcoming hinders the analysis of the available data because it prevents us from pinpointing what arises from the socioeconomic situation, and what from ethnic discrimination.

"Standard housing," as a percentage of all housing occupied by immigrants, has grown since the 1960s with each census, while the share of "nonstandard housing" (dormitories, rooming houses and hotel rooms, buildings or locations not intended for long-term housing) has diminished. In 1975, 86 percent of foreigners (as opposed to 96 percent of French by birth) lived in "standard housing"; but this overall figure hides important disparities among nationalities; only 67 percent of the Turks, 72 percent of the Moroccans, and 75 percent of the Algerians were in standard housing. Italians and Spanish, who had immigrated in much earlier waves, were housed quite similarly to French nationals (INSEE 1975, 1982; Cealis and Jansolin 1983). Immigrants remain the primary, almost exclusive, clientele of inferior housing, and of housing supplied by employers (company dormitories, worksite camps, servants' rooms and lodges, and furnished hotels): 7.4 percent of foreign households are housed by their employers, and 5.9 percent live in a rooming house or a furnished room, as opposed to respectively 4 percent and 1.5 percent of all French households.

Immigrants live more frequently than native French—and than native French in the same socioprofessional category—in apartment buildings, which is related to their higher rental percentage (63 percent, versus 38 percent of households of French by birth, and 50 percent of all laborers). They are also found more often in poorly equipped dilapidated buildings. In the 1982 census, only 51.2 percent of foreign households had both a tub and a shower, indoor bathrooms, and central heat, as opposed to 63.4 percent of households of French by birth, and 60.7 percent of working households in general. Immigrants' houses or apartments are also, on the average, smaller than those of the native French: immigrant households have 3.06 rooms, versus 3.65 for households overall, while immigrant households average 3.34 people, versus 2.7 people in households overall. Consequently they have a much higher density rate: 42.7 percent of foreign households live in overcrowded housing; this percentage is 15.8 for households overall, and 21.8 in laborer-only households. We do not have a breakdown in the 1982 census by nationality, but in 1975, while 20.8 percent of the households of French by birth and 43.8 percent of the foreign households lived in overcrowded conditions, these percentages reached 71.5 percent in Algerian households, 64.6 percent in Moroccan and Tunisian households, 61.5 percent in Turkish households, and 59 percent in Portuguese households.

At the present time 52.7 percent of French households and 41.3 percent of workers' households are property owners, versus only 21 percent of foreign households, with great disparities depending on nationality. For example, 15.1 percent of Portuguese households were property owners, of Algerians only 10.6 percent, and of Moroccan only 5 percent. European immigrants, especially those from the early waves, bought property much more often than did immigrants from underdeveloped countries. But even among the immigrants from underdeveloped countries, the situation varies with the socioeconomic structure of each nationality. Groups of immigrants with a sizeable proportion of skilled workers, and especially groups including lower-middle and middle-class members, have a higher percentage of property owners than the groups made up primarily of unskilled laborers. For example, 20 percent of Yugoslavian households and 13 percent of Vietnamese households live in housing they own.

Immigrant access to property ownership doesn't seem to reduce the degree of overcrowding—on the contrary—but it seems to be correlated with a higher level of health standards and comfort, a bit closer to the level of the native French in the same social category.

4. MULTIETHNIC HOUSING

Interethnic relationships are rarely studied in France, perhaps because community membership and ethnicity have no institutional status and remain essentially without political expression. These relationships have been studied in housing and daily life, especially when coexistence seems to be potentially or actually causing conflict. Urban subsidized housing and housing developments on the outskirts, in particular, have been the object of investigations by public officials determined to intervene in favor of "social development" of these deteriorated, devalued areas. The economic crisis, which has pauperized the already underprivileged residents, doubtless has helped increase the tensions in multiethnic residential arrangements, which are imposed rather than chosen and which are constraining and for many have become a dead end. In addition to recurring discussion about cultural incompatibility and the differences among lifestyles, recent studies have clarified the material and status elements at stake by identifying and distinguishing among groups and class factions. Fear of social status depreciation and other aspects of "white racism," stimulated by living and economic difficulties, have in certain cases encouraged the extreme right to vote in protest and to call upon the state and political leaders to favor French nationals in employment or housing. However, these conflicts, whether latent or open, and although sometimes quite real, are often exaggerated by their own protagonists. In painting the picture of social conditions, they may mask the often numerous, dense, and interconnected networks of cooperation and multiethnic support.

The conditions of coexistence of French natives and immigrants are in fact quite diverse. For the working class, and especially laborers, multiethnic housing remains one feature, among others, of more general social interactions, which—despite residential segregation—bring together different groups. The characteristics specific to both majority and minority groups, in terms of social class, resources, means of socialization, and goals, induce both conflicts and alliances, depending on situations and circumstances. This leaves a margin of freedom for groups and individuals when it comes to the importance they give to affiliations, identities, boundaries, and ethnic stereotypes. The urban particularities of the community and the neighborhood, their history, the process of settlement and population changes, etc., create a context in which immigrants are both the actors and the stakes. Their socioeconomic integration, although limited mostly to unskilled jobs, is still enough to bring about diversely based relationships. Work, commercial exchanges, neighborhoods, and daily encounters thus give rise to a convergence or a divergence of concerns, complementarities or rivalries. These relationships depend on the economic, spatial, or social modes of integration, on behavior, and on other aspects of immigrants' presence. Depending on the type and degree of social, economic, and urban usefulness of these foreigners, and depending on whether they are seen as a danger or as a resource, attitudes of native French towards immigrants vary. In one and the same urban atmosphere, hostile, indifferent, ambivalent, and accepting French natives generally coexist. The balance among these determines the "climate" for immigrant integration, which encourages or hinders their activities, their efforts toward community or cultural preservation or affirmation, and their practical integration or assimilation, and which thus tends to define the limits of their autonomy. In spite of the diffusion of ethnic stereotypes, the ethnicization of mixed housing relationships, and a fortiori ethnic separation, is not the norm in residential areas. There is a diversity of equilibriums, in more or less stable "balance" or in conflict, that are achieved locally through the interaction between populations and social groups.

It is hardly possible, given the state of research, to propose a systematic classification of mixed housing situations. We can only try, on the basis of observations in Paris in the past few years, to show how urban conditions, class relations, and interethnic relationships are worked out in housing arrangements (Guillon and Taboada-Leonetti 1986; de Rudder and Guillon 1987; and Taboada-Leonetti and Guillon 1988).

In a "good neighborhood," where many immigrants (one-fifth of the population) work in service jobs for a French middle class long established in the area, class complementarity and employer/employee relationships overshadow the interethnic aspect of contacts. The immigrant presence is either not known or misunderstood, and is not perceived very differently from the presence of people from the provinces who at the beginning of the century carried out the same jobs. Immigrants develop an independent social and community life, parallel to the life of French nationals, but unnoticed by them.

In another area, the popular "urban village" dominated by craftsmen and commercial activities, native French and immigrants (representing one-fourth of the inhabitants) belong clearly to the same socioprofessional categories, and conflict and competition are limited by the complementary nature of their activities, which guarantees the prosperity of the area. The economic interconnections that give rise to many relationships and to constant ethnic intermingling establish the model for social relationships characterized by recognition (either acceptance or denial) of the presence of minorities, but also by avoidance of ethnic separation, and by individual, often personalized interaction.

In yet another area, renovated during the 1970s and 1980s, Southeastern Asian refugees (mostly Chinese) settled and developed an Asian commercial area, while the French who live there belong to the middle class (employees and middle management). The relatively close-knit Asian community structure induces a different type of social atmosphere, separate from that of French nationals. Social lifestyles are therefore largely parallel, and French nationals' attitudes are ambivalent: immigrants are seen as a resource that gives the area an economic liveliness and a certain exotic attraction, but their inward-looking organization is seen as a threat of minority autonomy to the dominance of French identity.

The case of a deteriorated area, with "an atmosphere of newly settled immigrants," through which, without any major objections from the native French, several waves of immigration have passed since the beginning of the century, illustrates an immigrant ethnic enclave and ethnic conflict. The decline of previous economic activities and above all the imminence of urban renewal made of this area, in a few months, a festering place for deviant activities (drug traffic, receiving of stolen goods, squatting in housing, etc.). The ethnic conflict arose when legal and illegal African residents were identified with the deviant activities, while with the help of the media, social and ethnic segregation of the area was reinforced, confirmed by fear. A series of police operations, including arrests and expulsions, preceded the total transformation of the area into a residential and commercial neighborhood. Geographic concentration of groups, which fulfilled typically urban functions (localization of minority or marginal practices, exoticism, etc.), and which allowed the conservation of a potential land reserve, facilitated, through manipulation of ethnic groups and ethnic images, the recovery of the space by deportation of the inhabitants.

5. ETHNIC GROUPING AND "GHETTOS"

In France, although it is not often admitted, there is the risk of creating sections, in effect "ghettos," of enforced housing by restricting the opportunity for residential choice for certain categories of the foreign population. Thus in the metropolitan Paris area, the tendency for foreigners to scatter over the entire area, observed during the between-census period of 1968–1975, seems to have slowed or even stopped in some areas between 1975 and 1982. But the French situation is not and never has been that of "segregated neighborhoods," as they are called by the Chicago School.

During crises caused by the decline in traditional urban activities, downtown residential concentrations often occur in obsolescent areas, which are abandoned by households with resources to flee uncomfortable, substandard housing. The age of the buildings is not the only problem because the decline in values sometimes also affects new buildings, both highrise and low buildings, characteristic of postwar architecture. On the other hand, many older buildings continue to be well kept up and improved, and remain in demand.

Contrary to what the public often believes—natives and immigrants alike—these neighborhoods never have an absolute majority of foreigners among their residents. Even today, there is no urban section with more than a 40 percent concentration of foreigners. Higher concentrations exist only in smaller areas: a building, a group of buildings, or at the very most, a block.

"Gentrification" and expansion of tertiary industries pushes the working classes out of central neighborhoods in which they have lived for a long time. We see the classic phenomenon of population succession, ending with the removal of the working class. The deterioration of a neighborhood and the lack of comfortable housing stock officially motivate these substitutions. Some studies show that urban renewal in the 1960s didn't always give priority to the most substandard sections, but rather to the most working-class or immigrant sections; and many neighborhoods were voluntarily abandoned to deterioration, or were purposely brought to the edge of decrepitude to justify the renewal. When poor-quality housing was removed, its residents were also removed because the relocation quarters offered were usually elsewhere, especially in peripheral areas. Even those who succeed in being relocated in the same area often end up having to leave because of the rent increases following the renovation, if the slow pace of the process does not hinder land speculation. Others, in spite of assurances that they will be relocated, do not benefit from this right, either because, as more or less precarious occupants without a lease, they are legally excluded, or because, tired of waiting in an insecure situation, they relocate on their own.

The economic recession and the criticism of "operation bulldozer" cut back the large-scale urban renewal projects in favor of more selective restoration of neighborhoods and building rehabilitations. The social consequences of these projects, although less brutal and less traumatic for the fabric of the neighborhood and its residents, are not always much different from the earlier ones, even if they sometimes take longer.

Working-class suburbs, old industrial outskirts, or zones on the edge of urbanization also sometimes have a concentration of immigrants, particularly in subsidized housing. The media, politicians, and public opinion focus these days on this issue of low-income housing, in a joint denunciation of "ghettos," social problems, and conflicts in mixed housing between native French and immigrants. These concentrations originated in the recovery of city centers, and the suburban construction development of the 1960s and 1970s. Relocation housing for a poor family, especially a large poor family, almost necessarily requires a move to the outskirts of town. Certain housing complexes were abandoned bit by bit by families able to continue climbing the residential ladder, especially by purchasing property, which was encouraged by the state. Others find hardly any French interested in living in them. The vacancy created by this absence of French demand has permitted immigrants to enter subsidized housing, but they enter from the bottom and are concentrated in the most deteriorated housing complexes.

The "spontaneity" of community groupings, through the organization of strong networks of diverse immigrations, stimulates much discussion of the tendency of certain nationalities or ethnic groups to gather together voluntarily, even to crowd together. This "popular" talk covers up "vulgar" or even out-and-out racist modes of discourse, as much as it swamps more informed discussion. These concentrations are interpreted as the fruits of cultural maladaptation and immigrant poverty, rising from a need for mutual support and a desire for joining with others of the same background.

However, this "culturalist" vulgate, widely spread by the administration as much as by the media and public opinion, overshadows the social mechanisms in play. These associations occur in the absence of native French demand and because of discrimination; family and previous village relationships of immigrants do not by themselves explain them, even though, without a doubt, these factors allow us to understand certain features, such as the attachments that contribute to reuniting the immigrants from the same region in a particular geographic area. Many groupings, sometimes even hardly noticed by inhabitants, operate like this. It is often the principal mode of residential settlement by migratory waves subject to the least discrimination, those whose image is not accompanied by fantasies of aggression and contamination.[5] But community support and exchange, although generally important for immigrants, does not necessarily create concentrations. These are more frequent for populations discriminated against or excluded; but in addition, the gathering of stigmatized populations is more "visible" and more worrisome for French natives.

In urban centers, immigrants often live together with the poor native French, among whom the proportion of older people and single people is significant. In the suburbs, on the other hand, they live alongside generally young French families, including a relatively large number of families that social service administrators classify as "in great difficulty" or "in some difficulty" (problems resulting from many children, single parenthood, uncertain or almost nonexistent resources, unemployment, sickness, handicapped status, alcoholism). Certain immigrant households also find themselves in this type of situation. But whatever the problem, the assemblage in one area of immigrant families and of families "in difficulty" contributes to the general confusion about immigrants and social problems.

Whether central or on the outskirts, these areas of immigrant concentration serve in varying degrees not only as real estate reserves, but even more as population stocks. Downtown, these populations insure a profitable transition between the departure of the previous population (a commercial or craftsman middle class, tradesmen) and installation of new activities and new social classes (service industry, middle and upper management). In the suburban outskirts, they render profitable real-estate projects requiring low investment and which cannot attract a clientele who can pick and choose. If initially it is not the arrival of immigrants that makes the French natives flee, but rather the natives' abandonment of an area that allows immigrants to settle, then maybe at a second stage the immigrant presence—which serves as a sign of neighborhood decline—hastens the process of French people moving out and deters others from moving in.

Among the populations most discriminated against in the deteriorated urban sections, we find an immigrant social category that supplies housing and services to other immigrants of the same origin, substituting for the lack of "standard" offerings. Alongside "official," legal furnished hotels and rooms, they create a parallel market, more or less substandard and illegal, and provide services "adapted" to their clientele. The competition in this market remains lively, and the drying up of the demand does not seem to be of concern.

The battle against such "slum landlords" or exploitative superintendents also hurts the renters, who must find other housing. Alternative housing is offered to some. They may accept or refuse it because of its cost or its location in relation to where they work. But those who occupy housing without title or illegally are obliged to relocate on their own. They will thus enlarge the ranks of clients of other buildings of the same nature. The struggle against slumlords has only a minimal effect when it is not accompanied by a relocation policy with good-quality and plentiful housing. It is also often perceived by the immigrants as persecution, since owners, superintendents, and renters keep the parallel market alive.

Indeed, the center-city zones of concentration also fulfill purposes other than simply residential: work location, transit availability, informal exchanges, specialized trade, particular recreational activities. They offer an ethnic infrastructure that also taps a nonresident population, often coming from well outside of the area, notably at the end of the week, on vacation days, or during holidays traditionally celebrated in the countries of origin. They are urban magnets, allowing affirmation and community and cultural autonomy, which restore a devalued identity

Be that as it may, the term "ghetto," which is often applied to neighborhoods with a relatively strong immigrant presence, turns out to be inappropriate here. In France, these neighborhoods never combine all the characteristics of the known ghettos of history. Not only are they not institutionalized, but they are also not homogeneous: immigrants are minorities, and even if they constitute a clear minority they are not all of the same national, ethnic, or cultural origin. We do find larger groups leaving an imprint on the neighborhood in terms of "lifestyle" and provoking an identification of the neighborhood as "Arab" or "Asian," but we never find a "major minority" among the minorities. Ethnic identities and characteristics in these areas are nowhere near as noticeable as in other countries. These "Arab neighborhoods" or "Chinatowns" are in fact a pale equivalent to the black, Chinese, or Puerto Rican neighborhoods of American cities. Finally, and perhaps above all, immigrants in France are rarely structured into relatively autonomous "microsocieties," organized defensively and offensively, made up of diverse social classes, with real territorial bases, and with organizations, institutions, leaders, and networks of political action or opinion capable of collective negotiation. The use of the term "ghetto" here seems to have a more ideological than descriptive function. The word causes fear—as does the reality, perceived as a "social evil" more or less absolute and mythical—among French natives as much as immigrants themselves. Thus both exclusion and social control (or even policing) over minorities are confirmed and even justified. Among other things, the stigmatization of a residential area as a "ghetto" facilitates removal and dispersal (de Rudder 1987).

6. THE SITUATION AND STRATEGIES OF THE PLAYERS

The diverse groups involved in the allocation of housing and in determining the conditions of immigrant life develop differentiated strategies, related to positions they themselves occupy in the social structure.

Private Landowners and Superintendents of Subsidized Housing

Undoubtedly, some private landowners, especially those who cannot count on any other income from their property and who lack means or the desire to work, will continue to offer housing to immigrants at a profit. Other landowners will try to conserve a higher status for their buildings or housing, which increases their return. This presupposes that they will avoid immigrant renters, or at least renters of certain nationalities, who could lower their status. The proportion of one to the other and its evolution depends on the available real estate and the tightening or loosening of the market, and thus on the economic resources that will be devoted to construction and improvements for housing in the coming years.

As far as subsidized housing is concerned, the situation is quite inconsistent.

The administration and elected officials are confronted with a growing demand from immigrants and from the most destitute of the French natives, which logically should bring about relocation of the poor, in conformity with the social purpose of public housing. But the officials are also under pressure from those already living there and, more generally, from local public opinion, which tends to object to immigrants and relocation of the poor in their neighborhoods.

An exclusion policy that contributes to segregated concentrations of immigrants or of marginalized citizens is, even as it is carried out, perceived as a social and a public problem, sometimes aggravated by the reactions of the native French. Integration is the only solution. But good integration is, in the end, the one we participate in as little as possible. Responsible administrators and elected officials are tempted, however, to adopt quotas and other limitations on the percentage of immigrants in buildings, neighborhoods, and communities. But the reasoning itself is contradictory. First, immigrants are supposed to integrate only when dispersed (which has the added advantage, and not a small one, of making them disappear as actual or potential collective players). Their integration requires that we prevent them from gathering together, and thus that we remove the segregationist causes of these concentrations. But if these causes are removed, there is hardly a reason for quotas. Next, because the conflicts between immigrants and native French appear when there are "too many" immigrants, it is a good idea to rely on the strength of numbers in favor of the native French in order to prevent conflict. This would tend to exclude some immigrants from subsidized housing to which they have a right, and to encourage their gathering in the housing areas where they are tolerated. Setting limits to immigrant settlement thus ends up hindering their access to housing and to the areas appropriate to their social category—housing, neighborhoods, and work communities—and reinforcing their relegation to the most devalued areas. We have "integration" by dispersion, in the first case, "passing the threshold of tolerance" in the second.

The decentralization plan, adopted in 1982, which gives more power and autonomy to local communities as opposed to the state, could, in the absence of efficient regulation, lead to a heightened aggravation of the process of segregation. Elected officials and bureaucracies, who are closer to the people they administer, risk of course being more sensitive to their pressure.

Immigrant Populations

Populations of foreign origin develop diversified strategies depending on where they came from, their migratory traditions, and their social structures. We often attribute different behaviors of immigrants to their cultural traditions, when international comparisons make it appear that the differences depend more on the receiving country (de Rudder 1985)[6] and its structures, ideologies, and opportunities. Immigrant strategies regarding integration are strategies of adaptation to local and national situations. This observation is more confirmed than contradicted by the fact that these strategies mobilize knowledge and savoir-faire that are acquired before migration or are transmitted by the community and ethnic networks. In addition, a study in progress about integration strategies is uncovering, at the heart of each migratory wave, a great diversity in attitudes and behaviors—a diversity that seems to grow as the immigrants' stay lengthens (de Rudder, Taboada-Leonetti, and Vourc'h 1988).

Immigrants are generally aware of the negative effects of concentrating groups of disfavored and segregated populations on themselves (they dread the possibility of "pogroms" that "ghettos" may offer), as well as on society as a whole. But that does not prevent them from demonstrating their opposition to dispersion policies. Local community support permits them to resist discrimination, and dispersion risks destruction and submersion of the group, which amounts to domination.

Young Adults

The strategies of young adults, born of immigrant families, are an unknown. Socialized in France, they do not have the same strong community attachments nor the resulting behaviors that their parents have. The egalitarian, individualist, and hedonist values that their country of residence has instilled in them are sometimes in violent contradiction with the social destiny reserved for them by that country, which makes them particularly sensitive to feelings of oppression and discrimination. Today employment seems the most important issue to be faced. And housing depends on employment. The risk of revived housing competition is great because of the slowing of construction and the decline in public financing for housing. If the segregational effects of these developments are not controlled, the situation will deteriorate.

Public Opinion

For some years now we have witnessed a resurgence of racism and of its expression in politics. Opinion polls reveal a radicalization of attitudes towards immigrants. Indifference becomes rare, giving way to more clear-cut positions. Alongside a trend favorable to immigration (even if it favors assimilation, denying cultural recognition) and to equalizing immigrants' rights and living conditions, which remains a minority view, there is a trend developing to reject immigrants that falls just short of nationalist, chauvinist, xenophobic, or racist positions. Immigrants are denounced as illegitimate competition at the heart of an uncertain economic situation; they are held responsible for problems or at the very least are considered a nuisance.

Even apart from the economic crisis, as immigrants move towards consolidating their positions in France, developing their claims for better integration, equal treatment, recognition of their identity and of cultural autonomy, etc., there has been a sharpening racism, which might have remained latent as long as the immigrants seemed to accept their precarious lot and "stay in their place." But (national) anguish, stirred up by the extreme right, now focuses on the loss of national identity that would be provoked by settlement of non-European families. At the same time, the French keep alive both a strong rejection of a racist social order—to the point where even the nationalistic extreme right paradoxically claims this view as its own—and their attachment to egalitarian values.

Housing: Cause and Consequence of Integration

The residential conditions of immigrants are not, on the whole, characteristic of what we often called "first settlement." The most marginal situations are generally slowly remedied, except, doubtless, for illegal immigrants.

The hierarchy between native French and immigrants and between immigrants from different points of origin, however, perpetuates itself. The universal factors that tend to improve living conditions, such as how long the individual immigrant has been there, how long ago the wave of immigration of which the individual was part occurred, whether the family joined the individual, how well he or she has mastered the French language, familiarity with social and administrative matters, knowledge of rights, improvement in earnings and professional skills, etc., have an effect, as does ethnoracial status. But these factors do not succeed in completely balancing out the influence of racial discrimination. Immigrant status also interferes when the individual tries to move upward, by blocking professional promotion, thus preventing the achievement of other characteristics that lead to better residential integration. Maghreb populations, and particularly Algerians, no matter how long they have been in France and/or how good their command of the language and the social system, continue to suffer segregation in both the private sector and public housing. This hinders their access to the older, more comfortable housing, and relegates them to the least desirable sections of subsidized housing.

Housing thus appears as both product and producer of integration or of marginalization, as both cause and consequence. We must not underestimate its role. However, no matter what its importance—undeniable as it is—housing is only one aspect of integration, because it is only one aspect of the relationship between immigrants and the receiving country. We should not minimize the effects of the contacts on other levels: in jobs, work relationships, school, but also in the street, the media, stores, unavoidable meeting places (offices, institutions, public urban spaces), and recreation facilities.

A mixed neighborhood, with French natives and immigrants, is not in itself a certain integrating factor, in the context of competition and insecurity. However, local life, daily interactions, interpersonal relationships and group activities made possible by living together often have a positive if sometimes unnoticed effect. Everyday reality is often more complex than inhabitants and observers would have us believe. And even conflict, when not focused on divisive ethnic factors, is part of a coexistence where inclusion and exclusion, rejection and cooperation, fear and support all occur in the same place. Local ethnic relationships can contribute to immigrant integration, as a result of functional contacts among the diverse groups.

While it may be true that bad housing conditions tend to have a negative influence, they also permit practical adaptations, "cultural tinkering," and diversified integration strategies, sometimes protected by a certain freedom from the dominant society's control. But in order for these practices to support real integration, the situation must not be closed; a margin of initiative must remain. The issue is not only housing conditions, but even more important, the residential freedom of immigrants. Housing is really only negatively connected to integration. The "dead end" or forced housing situation stigmatizes its inhabitants (to the point where people are refused jobs because of where they live), and brings about self-devaluation that breeds failure and apathy, but also weak, more or less unorganized revolt, and deviance—all well-known effects of social exclusion.

From this perspective, the vicious circle in which immigrant workers who want to bring in their families find themselves can also create integration problems. In an effort to avoid the creation and reproduction of slums, public officials justify acceptance of immigrant families with larger and more comfortable housing. But subsidized housing, even without quotas, takes a long time to obtain, and is never allocated when the family is not yet in France. A person is thus required to find housing in the private market that is too big and too expensive for one person before requesting that the family be allowed to join him or her, and sometimes the waiting period is long.

Immigrant adaptation and integration is also too often measured by immigrants' silence, submission, and social invisibility. However, individual or collective refusal of the social treatment they are subjected to in the form of resistance or struggle, bypassing the law, or confrontation is a demonstrable sign of integration, and of the desire to integrate. Social struggles have, in and of themselves, a certain integrating power because they entail debate, contact, search for solutions, mediators, and negotiations. They often permit accelerated socialization into the process of social regulation in France. They also bring out actors, leaders, and negotiators from the immigrant groups whose role is often important in achieving their integration.

It is true, however, that urban or housing struggles often have trouble surfacing: residential location, in France is not a framework where collective identity of adversaries is easily developed. Negotiations and conflict resolution concerning living conditions are poorly organized. Life outside of work atomizes individuals, sending them back to primary attachments rather than to local organizations that will fight for their claims.

NOTES

1. One hundred and thirty neighborhoods were affected by this policy aimed at coordinating diverse public services such as architectural restoration, economic development, revitalization of social and communal activity, prevention of academic failure and delinquency, etc.
2. Remember that the massive call for foreign labor during the expansion years was less controlled by the state than followed by it—79 percent of immigrants arriving in France in 1967 were legalized after their "illegal" entry into France.
3. Such as the allocations for immigrants of 0.2 percent, then 0.1 percent of employers' contributions to workers' housing, adopted in 1977, 1975, and 1979.
4. The term "household" defines, in census terms, a group of people living in the same house, whether relatives or not. For convenience, we call "French households" or "foreign households" those in which the person "referred to" (declared as such in the census forms) is French or foreign. Certain households are clearly multinational, but the general indications remain valid.
5. The racist image includes many animalistic comparisons and metaphors, mostly referring to harmful or predatory animals that reproduce quickly (rodents, insects, vermin, images of proliferation and invasion . . .). It is also frequently associated with bacteriological, microbic, or viral attacks, and insidious contaminations. We cannot analyze the racist's explicit or implicit fantasizing here, but we must not forget how widespread it is, extending well beyond openly acknowledged racists.
6. Thus, for example, the proportions of landowners among immigrants varies considerably from one country to the next, less for cultural reasons than as a function of the rental market.

REFERENCES

Ballain, R., and C. Jacquier. 1987. Quarante ans de mesures en faveur des mal logés. *Urbanisme* 220 (July):4–5.

Boumaza, N. 1989. Les immigrés en banlieue, habitants et citoyens. In *Banlieues, immigration et gestion urbaine*, 441–67. Grenoble: Université Joseph Fourier.

Cealis, R., and X. Jansolin. 1983. Le logement des étrangers en 1975. In *Le logement des immigrés en France*, 33–93. Lille: Ominor.

Champion, J. B. 1987. L'accès des étrangers au logement social. *Aspects économiques de l'Ile de France* 19 (September).

Delcourt, J. 1977. *Le logement des travailleurs migrants*. Brussels: Commission of European Communities.

de Rudder, V. 1984. Le logement des Maghrébins: Racisme et habitat. *Les temps modernes* 452, 453, 454 (March, April, May): 1956–74.

———. 1985. *Le logement des immigrés en Europe*. Strasbourg: Rapport au Conseil de l'Europe.

———. 1987. La peur et le ghetto. *Politique aujourd'hui*, report no. 2:24–37.

de Rudder, V., and M. Guillon. 1987. *Autochtones et immigrés en quartier populaire*. Paris: L'Harmattan.

de Rudder, V., I. Taboada-Leonetti, and F. Vourc'h. 1988. *Migrations et stratégies*. Paris: URMIS—LSCI—CNRS and the Direction Régionale de l'Equipement d'Ile de France.

Godard, F., et al. 1973. *La rénovation urbaine à Paris*. Paris: Mouton.

Guillon, M. 1988. *Les traductions spatiales des processus ségrégatifs en Ile de France*. Paris: Direction Régionale de l'Equipement.

Guillon, M., and I. Taboada-Leonetti. 1986. *Le triangle de Choisy: un quartier chinois à Paris*. Paris: L'Harmattan.

INSEE. 1975. Population Census.

———. 1982. Population Census.

Petonnet, C. 1982. *Ethnologie des banlieues*. Paris: Editions Galilée.

Pincon, M. 1981. *Les immigrés et les H.L.M.* Paris: C.S.U.

Secrétariat d'Etat aux travailleurs immigrés. 1980. Le logement des immigrés. *Revue des ingénieurs des travaux publics de l'Etat* 51 (February–March):8–44.

Taboada-Leonetti, I., and M. Guillon. 1988. *Les immigrés des beaux-quartiers*. Paris: L'Harmattan.

Verret, M. 1979. *L'espace ouvrier*. Paris: A Colin.

12

THE NEW IMMIGRATION AND THE AMERICAN CITY

Nathan Glazer

For the last three decades immigrants to the United States have settled overwhelmingly in cities. This is of course to be expected: the great majority of Americans live in cities. Only a few percent live on the land and make their living from the land. We can view the impact of immigration on American cities from many perspectives, but four specific considerations will channel this discussion.

First, the immigrants of recent decades have been sharply concentrated in a few major cities and metropolitan areas, and minor cities adjacent to them. If we consider the impact of recent and current immigration on American cities, we immediately think of Los Angeles, New York, Miami, and San Francisco. Chicago, our third largest city, is also a major focus of attraction for immigrants, but less so than the four mentioned. This concentration in a few major cities is in contrast to the distribution of the last great waves of immigration into the United States, the immigrants from Southern and Eastern Europe who flooded into American cities between the 1880s and 1920s, until sharply cut off by restrictive immigration policies in the 1920s. This immigration spread through all the industrial cities of New England, the Middle Atlantic States, and the Midwest: Chicago and Detroit and Cleveland and Buffalo were as much immigrant cities as New York, the major port of entry, and immigrants dominated the industrial work force throughout the industrialized Northeast and Midwest.

The location of the new immigration is rather different. The two great immigrant cities today are New York and Los Angeles. If one adds San Francisco, Chicago, Miami, and Houston, one has accounted for almost three-quarters of current immigration.

Second, recent and current immigration, the immigration made possible by immigration legislation of 1965, which abandoned national-origins quotas and racial restrictions, has been, in contrast to previous waves of immigration, predominantly and by now overwhelmingly non-European. Inevitably, if we think of the impact of recent and current immigration on the American city, we must consider the impact and significance of its rapidly changing racial and ethnic composition. The American city in the ages of the earlier great immigration was overwhelmingly white and European, though it was divided among Protestants and Catholics and Jews, among "old Americans" and Irish and Germans and Italians and many other groups. Black minorities were small in the cities of the Northeast and Midwest, until black migration to the northern cities began in World War I and the 1920s. The American city then became a city of blacks and whites, and many issues were contested between them. The cities of the new immigration are cities of blacks, whites, Hispanics, and Asians, a rather more complex racial and ethnic mix.

A third factor usefully channels and restricts our topic. When we say "city" in the United States, our attention is immediately drawn to a specific set of problems, to problems of decline: in population, wealth, power, amenity. They were at the heart of the attempt to create a subdiscipline of urban studies in the 1950s, which flourished in the 1960s and early 1970s, ran into trouble in the later 1970s, and is virtually defunct today. There were no "urban studies" in the contemporary sense in the United States during the heyday of the old immigration, through the 1920s. Then the cities boomed. Great investments were made in infrastructure—water supplies, bridges, tunnels, subways. Population rose sharply with each decade. Suburbs were annexed by strong and growing cities, and found it desirable to be part of cities and connected with their higher level of services. Cities were richer than the rest of the country.

This began to change after World War II. (Was one reason for the change the cut-off in immigration? A number of economists who believe the impact of immigration on the city is positive, such as Julian L. Simon [1989] and Thomas Muller [forthcoming], might think so.) There had been little building in the cities during fifteen years of depression and war. New housing was desperately needed; infrastructure had to be renewed. Meanwhile the heavy migration of blacks from the South into the cities, spurred by the war, continued during the postwar prosperity. Great numbers of city dwellers moved into new suburbs made accessible by a huge program of road building, into houses built under federal mortgage rationalization programs. The central city began to suffer from the loss of population and its replacement by a less educated and less qualified population; from the loss of industry, looking for newer facilities; and from the need to renew old, fixed infrastructure at a time when it was cheaper and easier—or so it appeared—to build new suburbs on open farmland around the city.

Central cities—the political unit around which the metropolitan areas grew, and in particular the inner city, the old areas of central cities inhabited increasingly by minorities—became the focus of concern. Thus when we speak of the impact of the new immigration on the city we ask such questions as these: Will it provide a well-qualified and trained labor force that permits the cities that are the main recipients of immigration to compete with their suburbs and with other cities? Will it impose budgetary costs for education, health, and welfare greater than its benefits? Will the new immigration, in other words, be an asset in dealing with problems of decline or a liability? During the periods of rapid urban growth and mass European immigration, this was scarcely an issue: of course, the city needed labor. The liabilities of immigration, for those who spoke of liabilities, were seen rather in the impact of immigration on the civil life of cities, its connection to urban political corruption, and its effects on the social life of cities.

Finally, when we say "urban problems" now, we mean not only problems of decline; we mean problems of race. The "urban problem" in the United States in the last thirty years has become indissolubly linked with the problem of race, or more specifically, of American blacks. Until World War I, 90 percent of the blacks were still in the South, on the land, in small towns, or in southern cities. The North, Midwest, and West had few blacks. Thus, the black population of New York City in 1900 was a mere 3 percent of the total, a small minority compared with the numbers of Irish, Germans, Italians, Jews. Black migration to the North swelled in World War I, drawn by labor shortages, continued at a high rate during the 1920s, was further spurred by World War II, and continued at a rapid rate for two decades after the war. The southern countryside was largely emptied of blacks, as they concentrated in cities in the South, the Northeast, the Midwest, and the West. The central city became the place of black habitation. Whereas blacks still form only 12 percent of the population, they make up two or three or four or five times that proportion of the population of most major American central cities.

Of course there were many urban problems in the 1960s and 1970s that seemed unconnected with the change in racial composition. But most were connected in some way with the change in central-city population. Cities, from being places with higher-than-average income, became places of lower-than-average income. From being places with strong tax bases able to support expanding urban infrastructure, they became places of diminishing tax bases, not able to maintain their urban facilities. From being places with what were considered strong school systems, they became places with weak school systems, unable to educate the children in their charge to a reasonable standard. From being places of growth, they became, almost universally in the 1970s and 1980s, places of declining or stable population. From being places in which central location was highly desirable and brought high rents, they became areas in which large sections of central-city land lay unused and needed huge subsidies for redevelopment.

These problems have no necessary connection with the change in population composition. In all societies, economies change, formerly strong cities lose their economic base, renewal of older fixed facilities is required, and central cities must draw on the national government's revenues. But in the United States it is fair to say that all these central-city problems were inextricably connected with racial problems. If schools declined, that seemed to be connected with the change of school population, or with the segregation of blacks, or alternatively with the attempt to desegregate blacks. If population fell, that seemed connected with a "white flight" from a central city that was becoming in large measure black. If tax revenues fell, that of course was connected with the decline of population, in turn connected with the racial change. If business left, that was connected in part with the change in the labor force and the tax burden.

One could ascribe all these changes to racism if one wished, and find in these changes a self-inflicted wound on American society arising from American racism. Indeed, many analysts would have it so, and insist that we must still strive to desegregate schools despite white flight, that banks must invest in black areas despite their fear that they will only experience losses, that public and private business must hire fixed proportions of blacks regardless of effects on efficiency (effects these analysts would deny, dismissing this concern as simple racism). But whether we deal with racism or something else, or racism combined with something else, urban problems immediately bring to mind in the United States racial issues, to the point where "urban" sometimes becomes a euphemism for "black."

Thus when we speak of the impact of the new immigration on the American city, we will have to consider its impact on American blacks in American cities. Does it weaken the already weak economic position of blacks? Does it offer blacks political allies with whom they can together remake the political and economic features of American cities to their advantage? Does it provide a labor supply of lower qualification and desirability than blacks, offering blacks the possibilities of economic advancement in the city, the same possibility that opened for nineteenth- and early twentieth-century immigrants as less qualified immigrant streams entered the city?

These factors focus our consideration of the impact of the new immigration on the American city.

The general picture of immigration into the United States since the change in law in 1965 is well known. It has risen from an average of 250,000 a year in the 1950s, to 330,000 a year in the 1960s, to 400,000 a year in the 1970s, to 600,000 a year in the 1980s. For the last two decades one must add an uncertain number of illegal immigrants who have settled more or less permanently, one hundred to two hundred thousand a year or more. More striking has been the shift in composition, with Europeans now making up less than 10 percent of immigrants, Asians almost half, Latin Americans and Caribbeans the rest.

Immigration has been sharply focused geographically. The North Central region and the South show a sharp underrepresentation of the foreign born, the Northeast and the Pacific region a strong overrepresentation. Using an index of representation, the Northeast has 50 percent more than its "expected" share of the foreign-born population, the Pacific region more than twice its "expected" share, on the assumption of random distribution. Illegal aliens are, it is believed, even more sharply concentrated in southern California, and in the Northeast around the New York metropolitan area. One-half of the illegals enumerated in the 1980 census (on the basis of a distinctive methodology to locate them) were in California. Immigrants are concentrated in metropolitan areas. (U.S. Department of Labor, Bureau of International Labor Affairs 1989, 49):

> Immigration and Naturalization Service data indicate that, initially, 86 percent of the immigrants admitted in 1984 stated their intention to settle in metropolitan areas. . . . Overall, 92 percent of the foreign born were found in metropolitan areas as of 1980, and it is estimated that 93 percent of the illegal population was also found in metropolitan areas. . . . This compares with an average of 75 percent of the total U.S. population living in metropolitan areas in 1980. (U.S. Department of Labor, Bureau of International Labor Affairs 1989, 51)

About a fifth of incoming immigrants settle in New York and New Jersey and a quarter to a third in California. Together these three states take generally about half of incoming immigrants (U.S. Department of Labor, Immigration and Naturalization Service 1983, 64). Within these states the immigrants concentrate overwhelmingly in New York City and the New York metropolitan area, and in the Los Angeles metropolitan area. New York City alone, with 3 percent of the American population, takes in about 15 percent of all immigrants a year. The Los Angeles metropolitan area takes a similarly disproportionate share of new immigration.

No such consequences were expected as a result of the immigration reform of 1965. Nor is it politically feasible to make any changes in basic immigration law under which six hundred thousand legal immigrants a year enter. Whatever other reforms are under consideration today can only increase the flow of immigration, not reduce it.[1]

The new immigration is driven much less than the old by economic considerations. It continues unabated through prosperity and recession. A chart showing the immigration history of the United States presents jagged peaks and deep abysses until the 1920s. Since substantial immigration resumed after World War II, the course has been evenly and steadily upward. Even the terrible financial crisis of New York City in 1975 and the huge loss of manufacturing jobs in the 1970s did little to stem immigration into New York City.

I concentrate in this paper on only two cities, New York and Los Angeles. This is justified by the large role they play in taking in new immigrants. Other cities also have large numbers of immigrants, and Miami, as a smaller city, has been affected by immigration even more radically than Los Angeles and New York. However, a concentration on Los Angeles and New York is indicated if one wants to consider the impact of the new immigration on the American city.

Two preliminary points on the statistics and categories I use should be made clear. Many of the statistics in the following discussion will refer to New York *City* and to the Los Angeles *metropolitan area* or, even more broadly, to southern California. Why not compare New York City and the City of Los Angeles, or the New York and Los Angeles metropolitan areas? The reason lies in the difference in the relationship of each city to its metropolitan area. New York City is a compact geographical form, consisting of five counties of New York State, and makes up a large part of its metropolitan area. New York City makes up 85 percent of the New York "Primary Metropolitan Statistical Area" (PMSA),[2] which consists of New York City and its northern suburbs, and 39 percent of the very large "Consolidated Metropolitan Statistical Area" (CMSA), which includes much of northern New Jersey, all of Long Island, and part of Connecticut. The political entity the City of New York is a powerful one, raising huge sums in taxation, and providing almost all the services in the city.

The City of Los Angeles is, in contrast, a large, irregular blob, with various nuclei and arms, which encompass other cities and villages, as well as unincorporated urban areas that are part of Los Angeles County. The County, which is also the Los Angeles-Long Beach PMSA, is politically as important as the City, or more important, in terms of the revenues it raises and services it provides. The City is only 40 percent of the PMSA, 26 percent of the large CMSA. Thus the contrast of New York *City* with the Los Angeles primary metropolitan *area* is meaningful, and captures the character of both as in effect the central cities of their CMSAs, despite their formal nonequivalence. It reflects this meaningfulness that other analysts whom I will lean on often also concentrate on New York *City* and the Los Angeles *metropolitan area* respectively, and present their data for these entities.

A second preliminary point on statistical categories is necessary. For Americans, whether specialists, politicians, officials, or ordinary people, the primary categorical distinction in dividing up the population of American cities is not natives and immigrants; rather, it is black, white, and Hispanic. That is how the census presents data on cities and metropolitan areas, with Asians becoming a significant fourth category in some cities. None of these categories is particularly satisfying to the logical mind, and they are particularly unsatisfying for our present purposes because they do not separate, within each of these categories, natives and immigrants, though that can be done with more detailed census data. The only explanation for these categories is historical. The odd term "non-Hispanic white" refers to all those of European descent. The term "white" used to be satisfactory in identifying them, as against "black" (who under one name or another have always been counted as a separate group in the census, regardless of state of freedom, nativity, or citizenship) and as against Asian groups, who have always been listed separately.[3]

The mass immigration of Mexicans to the Southwest and Puerto Ricans into New York introduced two new categories that it seemed important to distinguish. (Of course, there have been Mexicans in the Southwest since before the formation of the American Republic.) The census could have listed one or the other or both as a separate race, or it could have included them in the "white" race. There was the sense that they were "different," in a way European or Near Eastern immigrant groups were not different, and so they were listed separately. Mexican immigrants for one census were indeed called a "race," alongside blacks and the various categories of Asian "race." For an intermediate period, the census used the odd appellation "Spanish-surnamed" to cover Mexicans and Puerto Ricans. This included both native citizens (Puerto Ricans and some Mexicans) and immigrants (the rest of the Mexicans), and it also of course included all other Latin Americans, with the exception of those who might be surnamed O'Higgins or Timerman, and Spaniards. The census has finally settled on the term "Hispanic," which of course reflects a judgment of similarity or linkage among all groups of Spanish-language background, a judgment that confounds groups of higher educational attainment and social class, such as the first waves of Cuban refugees, with groups of lower educational attainment and social class (Mexicans and Puerto Ricans).

Concretely, in 1980 the number of Hispanics was determined by the census by asking persons whether they are of "Spanish/Hispanic descent." If so, they specified which subgroup of Hispanic they belonged to: these were listed as "Mexican, Mexican-American or Chicano" (since the terms of self-identification vary); "Puerto Rican"; "Cuban"; or "other." "Argentinean, Dominican, Nicaraguan, Salvadoran, and Spaniard" were listed as helpful examples. (Any Spaniard would have asked in wonder, how did I get in that galley?) The census also asked independently for "race," and the categories listed were "White; Black or Negro; Indian (Amer.); Eskimo; Aleut; or Asian and Pacific Islander," and for this last category "Chinese, Filipino, Hawaiian, Vietnamese, Japanese, Asian Indian, Samoan, Guamanian," and "other" are listed. The same procedure was used for the 1990 census. The conclusion of this extended excursus on ethnic-racial categories in the American census is that four large categories are generally distinguished when we speak of urban populations: non-Hispanic white (that is, European); black; Hispanic; and Asian. "Hispanic" overlaps with "white," and if one wants to distinguish the two groups one must subtract from "whites" those who are Hispanic, which leaves us with "non-Hispanic whites." American Indians, one may note, play no role in this division: they are too few in any large American city to make up a substantial category.

We find these groups in summary census statistics, as in the *U.S. Statistical Abstract,* and we also find the same distinctions made in newspapers and magazines when they describe the composition of a city, or of its school system, or of the voting population.

In the 1980 census, the populations of New York City and the Los Angeles "Primary Metropolitan Statistical Area" were roughly the same. The 7,100,000 population of New York was slightly over half "non-Hispanic white"—that is, Jews, Italians, Irish, Greeks, Ukrainians, Germans, and many other groups, including the oddly named "wasps" (white Anglo-Saxon Protestants); about one-quarter black; about 20 percent Hispanic; and about 3 percent Asian. The blacks included a large number of recent immigrants from Jamaica and other black Caribbean islands. The Hispanics were three-fifths Puerto Rican, the rest from Cuba, the Dominican Republic, and various countries of Central and South America.

In 1984, a typical year, ninety-two thousand immigrants, 17 percent of all, said they intended to live in the New York metropolitan area. New York City contained 12 percent of the nation's foreign born (1.7 million out of 14 million) in the 1980 census. The foreign born made up 24 percent of the city's population, and had increased from 18 percent in 1970. The census acknowledges a considerable undercount in New York City, and with the uncounted the foreign born may have been near 2 million. With the continuing flow of immigration, the foreign born were certainly more than 30 percent of New York City's population in 1990.

A listing of the foreign born in New York City by country still is strongly influenced by the survivors of the early decades of the century and the refugee and displaced-person inflows of the 1930s and late 1940s. If we consider only the foreign born who entered between 1975 and 1980, the ten leading countries are the Dominican Republic, the U.S.S.R., China, Jamaica, Guyana, Haiti, Korea, Colombia, Trinidad and Tobago, and India, an indication of the remarkable diversity of the New York City immigrant stream.

The Los Angeles PMSA in 1980 contained 7.5 million people, of whom about 53 percent were "non-Hispanic white"; 13 percent black, less than in New York City; a rather larger proportion of "Hispanics" than in New York City (some 28 percent); and a larger proportion of Asians, some 6 percent.

Puerto Ricans are the dominant group among New York Hispanics, Mexicans the overwhelmingly dominant group among Los Angeles Hispanics— almost four-fifths. The Asian mix in the two cities was also somewhat different. The first two Asian groups in size in Los Angeles were Japanese and Filipino, in New York, Chinese and Asian Indian.

In both cities, there were large numbers of the uncounted. New York City sued the Census Bureau to require it to adjust its numbers upwards by the four hundred thousand or so it claimed the census had missed. The undercount in Los Angeles was estimated to be as high, and the inclusion of those missed in both cities would have increased the numbers of blacks, of Hispanics, and of Asians (U.S. Bureau of the Census, as given in Sassen 1988, 73; Bogen 1987, 4, 5, 39, 56–57; Muller and Espenshade 1985, 16–17, 41, 42).

The impact of recent immigration on California is indicated by the Muller and Espenshade estimate that 4.7 million persons, about 20 percent of California's residents, were foreign born in 1983, and that the majority had arrived since 1970. Mexicans were the largest group in the post-1970 arrivals, about 37 percent, and with other Hispanics made up not quite half of the total. Asians constituted one-third of the recent arrivals, and the rest were

Europeans. Muller and Espenshade assert that "Los Angeles . . . now has a larger proportion of foreign-born residents in its population than New York City—close to one-third by conservative estimates—and nearly as large a proportion as New York City had at the height of European immigration in 1910" (Muller and Espenshade 1985, 42).

These two great immigrant cities were probably attracting nearly one hundred thousand immigrants a year each during the late 1980s. For New York, this has meant only a rearrangement of its population, as the flow to the suburbs and beyond continues, and the population of the city increased only slightly in the 1980s, by about 4 percent. Blacks have only modestly increased their proportion in the city's population—from 24 to 25 percent—but the foreign-born component among blacks has gone up. Asians were in 1990 almost 7 percent of the population, and increasing (*New York Times* 1990, B1, 2). In the geographically more ample Los Angeles PMSA, growth continued vigorously throughout the 1980s, with a 15 percent increase in overall population between 1980 and 1988, to 8.6 million (U.S. Department of Labor, Bureau of the Census 1989).

Despite the contrast between slow growth in population in New York and rapid growth in Los Angeles, as well as other differences that strikingly differentiate the two cities—one an old, dense city with a transportation infrastructure completed fifty years ago, the other a spread-out metropolis with a strikingly modern transportation system of multilaned and multileveled expressways completed only in recent decades—there are some basic common underlying trends. One would expect this from their common role as major magnets for immigrants.

Saskia Sassen argues that the huge loss of manufacturing jobs in New York City (down from 947,000 in 1960 to 430,000 in 1984) while manufacturing jobs were still rising in Los Angeles, should not obscure more significant common trends. In both, older manufacturing industries that had been mainstays of the city—printing and garment manufacturing in New York, automobiles and related industries in Los Angeles—were leaving or declining, and the proportion of unionized and high-paid manufacturing workers was declining. Their place was being taken by low-wage immigrants in both cities, working in many new small firms that were using low-cost labor to compete with overseas producers (garment manufacturing in both cities, high-tech industries in Los Angeles). In both cities, the major growth sectors are in services, in finance, insurance, and real estate ("FIRE," as the acronym dramatically has it). Producer-service industries, industries serving business primarily (computer services, management consulting, advertising, public relations, finance and banking, insurance, real estate, and the like), dominate the economic growth of both cities. The employment share in such industries in 1981 was 31 percent in New York and 25 percent in Los Angeles. Sassen sees similarities in the economic transformation that serves to attract and employ immigrants in both cities. She finds immigrants employed disproportionately in a downgraded manufacturing sector, in which trade unions and protection for employees are weak; a growing financial and services sector that includes both highly paid and poorly paid positions; and a growing "informal" economy, in which many immigrants work, in such fields as construction and renovation (Sassen 1988, 146–62).

Our central concern in considering this vast transformation taking place as the result of immigration is, what is the effect of the immigrant inflow on the economic fate of the city? The growth of a substantial "underclass,"[4] evident in the 1970s and receiving growing attention from journalists and academics in the 1980s, raises sharply the question of whether the American city has failed to incorporate properly the last great migration before the present one, that is, the migration of blacks and Puerto Ricans and Mexicans in the 1950s and 1960s, and how it will fare in integrating the new immigrants. Is the immigrant inflow yet another burden for the cities, or is it a boon offering the opportunity for economic renaissance?

This question is enormously complicated. Many perspectives—economic and sociological, ethnographic and econometric—can be deployed to try to give answers, and the research is voluminous and often enlightening, but when it comes to the ultimate question of whether the recent immigration has added to the problems of cities or mitigated them, the research is contradictory and ambiguous.

The question can be divided into many parts, none of which is decisive. Let us consider a few.

First, is the new immigration a drain on city services and thus an uncompensated charge on city finances? One will hear many complaints that this is indeed so. In Miami, schools are being built at a record rate to accommodate a huge increase in the school-age population as a result of immigration. In hospitals in some cities, there is great pressure on maternity facilities, even more pressure on emergency rooms. Since there is no general and universal health insurance in the United States, and immigrants are more likely not to be included in the health insurance plans linked to stable employment, they undoubtedly contribute to this pressure disproportionately. The sudden insurge of 125,000 Marielitos from Cuba in 1980, many released from jails and mental institutions, certainly added to the costs imposed by crime and mental illness in Miami, and in other cities to which they spread, including New York.

Nevertheless, a general accounting of social costs set against taxes collected seems to support the argument that immigrants do not impose a disproportionate burden. Julian Simon tries to develop such an accounting generally for recent cohorts of immigrants, and his conclusion is that immigrants use a below-average quantity of services, largely because of the youthful age and sex composition of the immigrant groups. Much of this favorable balance is accounted for by the fact that immigrants are concentrated in working ages, and not many draw Social Security (old-age pensions). Shortly after arrival they do begin to use more educational services than natives. He also argues that the taxes they pay more than pay for the services they use (Simon 1989, 117 and ch. 5). The problem of course is that different services are provided by different levels of government; the city, overwhelmed by the need to build more schools or pay for emergency services in public hospitals, is not helped much by the fact that immigrant workers are providing payroll taxes to the federal government and have not yet reached the age where they draw Social Security. Thus the impact on the city's finances may well be negative, even if the overall balance of public costs and taxes is positive.

It is just this point that comes out in what is perhaps the most meticulous attempt to account for fiscal impact, but one that is limited to impact on state and local government. Muller and Espenshade have carried through such an analysis for Los Angeles County, taking into account the costs for social services required by Mexican immigrants (the majority of immigrants into Los Angeles) and the taxes they pay to local and state government:

Our estimates indicate that, when state and local government are combined, each Mexican immigrant household received an average $4,842 in government services in 1980 but paid just $2,597 in taxes. Thus, benefits received outweighed taxes paid by a factor of nearly 2 to 1. . . .

The substantial gap between revenue and expenditure flows for Mexican immigrant households is traceable to several factors, but the two most important ones are low Mexican earnings and large Mexican families. . . . [E]ach Mexican immigrant household enrolled an average of 2.25 times the number of children in elementary and secondary schools as the average Los Angeles County household. (The number was 1.06 versus 0.47 per household.) (Muller and Espenshade 1985, 143).

Muller and Espenshade point out that their analysis is limited to Mexicans enumerated by the census. If one added the five hundred thousand undocumented persons whom they estimate the census missed, most of whom are single, do not draw on government services, and pay taxes, the cost of Mexican immigration to local government is reduced. If one takes into account further the fact that non-Mexican immigrants, that is, other Latin Americans, Europeans, and Asians, are of higher education and get higher-paying jobs than Mexicans, this deficit is even further overcome (Muller and Espenshade 1985, 43, 44, 142–44). I have not seen such an accounting for New York City, but it would probably come out not very different from Los Angeles. Indeed, the post-1965 immigrants, as we will see later, undoubtedly are less of a drain on city coffers than the previous waves of blacks and Puerto Ricans who settled in the city in the 1950s and 1960s (who are of course not immigrants but internal migrants).

George J. Borjas presents a gloomier picture, primarily because of the declining quality of recent immigrant cohorts in terms of education and skill and labor force participation rate. He presents evidence of this pattern of decline, contrasting the foreign born in 1940, 1960, 1970, and 1980. Clearly the foreign born of 1940 were very different from those of the later decades — they included both many more surviving immigrants from the great South and East European immigration, originally of low education but who had been in the United States a long time, and also more recent German Jewish immigrant refugees of high education and occupational attainment. One wonders how useful a contrast between the foreign born of 1940, who came under such very different conditions, and those of the 1970s can be. But even the contrast between the foreign born of 1970 and 1980 seems to support Borjas's argument, and it is probably the case that "chain migration," the migration of relatives who become eligible on the basis of the earlier migration of members of their families who are more likely to have entered the United States on the basis of occupational qualification, does lead to some decline in the quality of migration. This must affect the cost-benefit ratio of immigrants from the point of view of public costs and revenues, but even Borjas does not claim this should be an important concern in considering immigration policy (Borjas 1990, chs. 3 and 9).

Perhaps more important is a second question: the impact of immigrants on native workers, who may be displaced by immigrants willing to work for lower wages or put in longer hours, or less likely to be organized into trade unions, and possibly more fearful because of their illegal status of objecting to harsh conditions imposed by employers. The American city is afflicted with problems of crime and homelessness and drugs, with a large underclass whose major component is native blacks (though in New York Puerto Ricans are a very large proportion, and of course other ethnic elements are also included in it). Both New York and Los Angeles have high rates of unemployment among blacks — exceptionally high rates among black teenagers — and if one factor in producing these consequences is immigration, this is a serious matter indeed.

There are various ways of approaching this matter, and they come, unfortunately, to different conclusions. Attempts to show that there is a direct relationship between large immigrant flows and these particular problems do not come up with a clear and direct relationship:

For example, unemployment rates in 1984 for all blacks, black teenagers, and all teenagers in California, Florida and Texas (states with large immigrant populations) were below the national rates for these groups. In New York State, black teenage unemployment was above the national average, but black adults had a lower than average unemployment rate. . . . More complicated empirical research has failed to reveal strong displacement. The studies usually compare wage or unemployment levels of particular groups of natives in Standard Metropolitan Statistical Areas with large immigrant populations to those levels in SMSA's with few foreign-born workers. Some studies have concluded that there are moderate negative labor market effects for some natives. Other studies have found no relationship. . . . And still others have found evidence that the presence of immigrants strengthens the employment position of some native groups that tend to work for low wages. (Bailey 1987, 5)

As analyzed by Borjas, these studies seem to show a very small negative impact on the wages of natives (a 0.2 percent decline as a result of a 10 percent increase in immigrants), but a somewhat smaller negative impact on white wages, a slightly larger negative impact on wages of blacks and young Hispanics, and an even larger impact on manufacturing workers' wages, 0.4 percent. Surprisingly, increased immigration goes along with a positive impact on the wages of women. The increase in the demand for welfare and health services because of greater immigration may increase the employment and wages of persons who work in these sectors, who are disproportionately female and black.

The econometric analyses, then, show a very small effect of immigration on native workers, but a slightly larger one on those with whom they might be expected to compete directly, native Hispanics and blacks in manufacturing. We know that the effects shown by econometric models depend a good deal on their specifics. It does stand to reason that there should be such an effect, and in cities where immigration is large, a substantial one. But we must of course distinguish among the effects of different groups of immigrants. The chief differentiating characteristics affecting the role of recent immigrants in the labor market are education and occupation. In general Asians come with more education than American natives, Caribbeans and Latin Americans with somewhat equivalent education, Mexicans with considerably less. Thus, while 36.5 percent of Filipinos have a college-level education, only 3 percent of Mexicans do. The American average is 15 percent (Borjas 1990, table 5.1).

Language facility also affects strongly what immigrants can do. Twenty-nine percent of Koreans have college degrees, but they are disproportionately found among small entrepreneurs, such as in small retail stores. The reason (or at least one reason) is that they cannot translate their educational credentials into professional jobs as easily as can, say, Asian Indians, who have been educated in English.

When one learns that some twenty thousand Indian immigrants are doctors —3 percent of all doctors in the country, and concentrated in California and around New York City—one assumes there must be an impact on the earnings of American doctors. (In view of the earnings of doctors in general and the high cost of medical care in the United States this kind of competition from immigrants may be a boon, though doctors might not think so.) When one sees that Korean greengrocers have replaced Italian greengrocers in New York City and Jewish storekeepers in black areas, that Indian newsstand keepers have replaced whoever previously ran those stores, one can imagine that there has indeed been a specific impact, in certain places, on certain groups.

Our greatest concern of course is with impact on native blacks and native Hispanics, but in particular on native blacks. Clearly there has been change in the composition of manufacturing and service labor forces. One sees this both from observation and from studies. Those who clean office buildings, for example, are predominantly Hispanic and immigrant (and illegal immigrant?) where they were once black. The labor force in garment manufacturing has become predominantly Chinese and Hispanic women where it was once from Italian and other white ethnic groups.

But is this to be called "displacement," that is, do we find that natives who want these jobs are losing them, or are we rather to call it "replacement," as workers of one ethnic group find better opportunities, or get older, or retire? Bouvier and Martin, writing of California, argue forcefully that direct displacement does occur. A "pioneer" worker from an immigrant group is hired for some job. He is willing, energetic, works harder, is absent less. The employer finds him a desirable worker. He brings in a friend or relative because the employer thinks he will be similar to the first. In short order the language used on the job changes, and the work force becomes entirely immigrant. One might argue that these are not good jobs, but this is not necessarily so (Bouvier and Martin 1985, 28–30).

The tension has perhaps been strongest in Miami and Dade County, where the huge Cuban immigration has created a large Spanish-speaking enclave in which Spanish is not a hindrance to getting a job but a positive aid, and where native blacks feel frozen out by the dominant Cubans, as well as by incoming

Haitians who expect less and for whom American wages are a considerable advance over what they can earn in their homeland. Thus we find the phenomenon of large numbers of native blacks unemployed and on welfare, with a mass of attendant social problems, even when unemployment in general is low and jobs go begging. Admittedly we find the same in cities that have not been as sharply impacted by immigration as Miami, New York, and Los Angeles, but is this an argument that there has been *no* impact?

Bouvier and Briggs, writing on New York State, are convinced that there has been a substantial impact in New York City, as Bouvier and Martin are convinced there has been such an impact in Los Angeles:

Exactly how immigrants affect the labor market of New York City is a subject that is far from resolved. The political structure prefers not to confront the issue. As one public official . . . stated, "No one wants to talk about the big issue of the effects of immigration on the city, for to do so would immediately bring up charges of being 'insensitive' or worse, of 'racism.' " (Bouvier and Briggs 1988, 60)

But even if public officials try to avoid the topic in the somewhat hysterical ethnic-racial atmosphere of New York City, analysts cannot.

Bouvier and Briggs find it disturbing that ethnic immigrant groups are concentrated in certain lines of work:

Although post-1965 Asian immigrant males made up only 3.2 percent of the city's male labor force, they were 15.2 percent of all male workers in eating and drinking establishments; post-1965 Black immigrant women—mostly from the West Indies— were 5.5 percent of the city's female labor force but were 23.9 percent of the female household workers and 21.5 percent of female nursing home employees; post-1965 Hispanic male immigrants were 5.1 percent of the city's labor force but were 12.9 percent of all men employed in miscellaneous manufacturing. (Bouvier and Briggs 1988, 61)

On the other hand, isn't this just what we might expect? And how, if concentrated in the poorer jobs, do they affect native workers? Bouvier and Briggs argue:

Often denied access to the few industrial sectors of the city's economy that are expanding, many immigrants turn to direct competition with the city's considerable unskilled and poorly educated citizen population. . . . [I]mmigrants . . . will do whatever is necessary to survive . . . double up families in apartments, work dual jobs, have several family members in the labor force, and accept substandard wages and working conditions. . . . It should not be surprising that many citizen New Yorkers . . . cannot or will not compete for jobs on such demeaning and often unfair terms. For too many New Yorkers, the options are unemployment, or welfare, or participation in the city's enormous "irregular" economy.

It is true that some immigrants do create some new enterprises that are designed to serve the needs of people from the same ethnic background. . . . But . . . how important would their loss be if they were not there? Moreover, . . . immigrant-owned enterprises too often also means restricted job opportunities for others. They typically prefer to hire only workers of similar ethnic backgrounds. . . . Anti-discrimination laws typically do not apply to enterprises that hire fewer than 15 employees. (Bouvier and Briggs 1988, 63)

It stands to reason that displacement occurs, and yet when we consider some of the specific areas of immigrant concentration, the evidence that immigrants take jobs and opportunities that blacks would otherwise have is not strong. Would, for example, blacks become proprietors of small stores in black areas if Koreans and Chinese had not moved into these locations, replacing aging and frightened Jews? We find so few examples of black business enterprise that it hardly seems likely: some other group would serve blacks in black neighborhoods, as other groups have in the past. The argument that blacks have no access to capital is not a very strong one: neither do immigrants on the whole, and capital is not what is needed to run such stores successfully. The ubiquitous Korean-run greengroceries of New York City, which have expanded into general groceries and delicatessens, began with almost no capital, as it takes very little money to equip a fruit and vegetable store (one can sell from the boxes, if one spends enough time arranging the produce), nor, obviously, does it require much inventory. And these stores, to begin with, often rented for very little when Koreans suddenly emerged in this trade in the early 1980s. (Matters as far as rents are concerned have changed considerably since.) Ivan Light, writing about the Koreans of Los Angeles, describes the factors involved in the immigrant takeover in some areas of retail trade:

Koreans . . . worked sixty-hour weeks; saved one-half of their income by dint of painful thrift; accepted the risk of criminal victimization; passed business information among themselves; maintained expected patterns of nepotism and employer paternalism; praised a Calvinist deity; utilized family, alumni, congregational, and network solidarities; thought of themselves as sojourners; expressed satisfaction with poorly remunerated work; and utilized rotating credit associations in financing their small businesses. All of these culturally derived characteristics of the Korean immigrant community contributed to Korean entrepreneurship, but none required money. (Light 1985, 174)

One can say the same about the Korean storekeepers of New York.

The Koreans do have other resources, too: a large proportion are college-educated and had they stayed in Korea they would have been in professional, technical, or managerial occupations. They bring talents to storekeeping that are generally not found in this economic sector (Waldinger 1989).

When one examines in detail some of the cases of ethnic concentration reported by Bouvier and Briggs, evidence of direct ethnic competition for jobs is not very common. Blacks, for example, never went into the garment industry in great numbers, and it would be hard to say they were "displaced" by Chinese, Puerto Rican, and Dominican women in New York (Waldinger 1986). Thomas Bailey has done an intensive study of the restaurant industry in New York, an important and large industry there, and finds such a degree of ethnic specialization that, again, direct competition is not common. Fast food restaurants use teenage workers, not terribly reliable, with high turnover, who are often looking only for part-time jobs. They are not likely candidates for "full-service" restaurants, nor for the very large number of "immigrant" restaurants. "Full-service" restaurants now are heavily dependent for waiters and waitresses on young adults, many hoping to become actors and artists (or already actors and artists), who are young and attractive and are skilled in making a good impression. But part-time waiting is the only job *they* would take in the restaurant industry. They wouldn't work in the kitchen. Newer immigrants without English may not have the skills for waiting jobs. They take the kitchen jobs. They also open their own restaurants in profusion, because unlike the young native adults they do not have good opportunities outside the industry.

The main area in which Bailey finds some direct competition from immigrants in the restaurant industry is in the employment of women. Women play a much smaller role in the restaurant industry in New York City than in the nation generally, undoubtedly because of the profusion of immigrants available and eager to advance in the industry. Black men also are underrepresented in restaurants in New York, compared to the nation in general. The immigrant networks simply seem more effective, Bailey believes, in getting the skills that one needs in an industry where skills are acquired haphazardly and informally.

Do immigrants take jobs from blacks in construction? In construction the good jobs in New York have always been handed down from father to son or uncle to nephew, within ethnic groups, and are controlled by the unions. Despite long-sustained efforts to break these union-ethnic monopolies and make it possible for blacks to enter (for example, through the "Philadelphia plan" and its equivalents, specifying the number of blacks that every contractor doing public work has to employ), Bailey finds that black representation in the industry dropped in the 1970s. Immigrants are overrepresented: though if the explanation for employment is the family monopolies, one wonders how they get in to begin with. Bailey explains:

In construction, both as workers and as owners, blacks have had more success in gaining access to the more formal and institutionalized sectors of the industry. . . . In contrast, recent immigrants are found more in the open-shop sector where they appear to be better able than native blacks to use informal contacts and neighborhood networks to establish themselves. (Bailey 1987, 111)

Bailey believes there would be no great impact on native black employment if immigration were sharply restricted:

[I]t is unlikely that blacks could move in large numbers directly into many of the jobs vacated by immigrants even if the blacks were willing to work for low wages. . . . [I]n the past, the employment gains made by native blacks were not based in industries and jobs characterized by informal organization and employment processes. (Bailey 1987, 120)

Blacks find more opportunity in the organized and public sector, where, whatever the situation in the past, they now face little discrimination and are able to depend on formal protection. They also have the advantage of knowing English and being citizens. A surprising 34 percent of all New York City blacks work in the public sector, compared to 18 percent of all New York City residents (Bailey 1987, 115). Waldinger shows a similar preference (Waldinger 1987).

Where does one come out in this tortured question of immigrant impact on native workers, and in particular on native blacks (and, in New York City, on citizen Puerto Ricans)? It seems that two perspectives are in conflict. As we find in Bailey and Waldinger, one perspective emphasizes the specificity of immigrant niches, tends to minimize direct competition, and suggests that there would be no great impact if immigration were restricted. Along with the immigrant niche emphasis, one finds reference to worker expectations and desires and experience: immigrants compare wages and opportunities with those they have left behind, and the refugees and those who have come a long way in particular make a major commitment to make the best of things in the new land. Natives do not have such a contrast to make. Indeed, they may recall circumstances in which they held the very jobs immigrants now hold and they do not want to remain in them. They may also well feel, after the political upheavals and legislative revolutions of the 1960s and 1970s, that they deserve better, and would not want to take those jobs even if they were to become available. On the other hand, one could argue that if they were to become available because of immigrant restriction, the wages and working conditions they provide would have to improve to compete in a more restricted labor market, and they would become more attractive. This seems to be the point of view of Bouvier and Martin and Bouvier and Briggs.

The latter two studies also expand the debate to consider a larger question of impact. Even if the picture painted by Waldinger and Bailey is correct—

even if, as we are often told, the garment industry, for example, would not survive without cheap immigrant labor—is it a good thing that such industries survive? (One is fairly convinced that industries that are immobile, such as restaurants and hotels, would survive—they would only cost more.) It is true, Bouvier and Martin tell us, that immigrants

are willing to work long hours at low wages in hopes of eventually getting a higher paying job or forming a small business. This flexibility makes it less necessary for American businesses to embark on costly and risky strategies to replace low-wage workers in manufacturing, services and agriculture by restructuring work to attract American workers or by automating. (Bouvier and Martin 1985, 27)

Thus they expand the question of the economic impact of the immigrant on the American city to consider the impact of immigration on the American economy. Just as the local perspective may be too limited, and therefore too negative, when we consider immigration's fiscal impact only on city and state without considering its fiscal impact at the federal level, so it may be too limited, and too optimistic, to consider immigration's economic impact on the city alone without also considering its impact on the nation from a broader, international perspective. The city finds that even its old declining industries can be maintained through immigrant labor. Its tourist industries are not as expensive as they might be and thus draw tourists from abroad: among them, great numbers of Japanese tourists, who would not dream of allowing immigrants to enter in order to maintain labor-short but not high-value-added industries or to keep down the price of hotel rooms, restaurant meals, and vegetables and fruits. The city in some sense may be aided as immigrants pour into declining neighborhoods, opening stores and small manufacturing establishments, renting empty stores, filling and renovating apartments and houses, making the avenues bright with signs in Korean and Chinese and Russian. One truly feels the immigrants are invigorating the city—thus the delights of the enormous Koreatown in Los Angeles or of the Indian settlement in Flushing or the Russian Jewish concentration in Brighton.[5] But is this urban revival coming at a cost? The strict analysis of the dismal science comes into conflict with the urbanite's desire for a lively city texture, not to mention in conflict with some groups' economic interests. Immigration has certainly done a great deal to feed the huge increase in real-estate values in Los Angeles and New York in recent years. Crowding benefits some people. Does it benefit all?

Understandably, our discussion of immigration's impact on the native labor force has concentrated on those immigrants who may compete directly with native black and Hispanic workers. But a good number of immigrants come with more education and higher-level skills than either native blacks or Hispanics, or indeed the average native white worker. These, if the language barrier can be breached, go into the professions, into medicine and health services and engineering. There we are steadily made aware of the shortages of available labor: thus, the New York hospitals are desperate for nurses and scour the West Indies or the Philippines to find them. Competition among doctors does not bother most people: they can always take lesser paying jobs in the public sector (as many immigrant doctors do). Our own native supply of engineers does not generally keep up with demand. Thus, one can say immigrants aid the economy. But one can counter this with the same argument used in the case of lesser qualified immigrants: if the immigrants were not there, we would be forced to train our own nurses and engineers and doctors, and we would find a way, to the benefit of our own native workers.

I do not know at this point how research can resolve this question. Values must come into play, preferences as to the kind of society one wants and the degree of heterogeneity one finds tolerable or desirable.

It is clear that in various ways blacks and Puerto Ricans are being left behind in New York by the new immigrants. One can show that Puerto Ricans have higher rates on welfare, lower wages, more family breakup (which may be seen as a consequence or cause of the former) than non-Puerto Rican Hispanics. We can make the same contrast, to the advantage of immigrant blacks, between immigrant and native blacks. Compared with both groups, Asians, despite great differences among them, are best off. That, at least, is the case in New York (Glazer 1988). Whether something similar is the case in Los Angeles I do not know.

What political scenario can we expect on the basis of the demographic and economic facts in New York City? In 1989, a black mayor was elected for the first time, with the overwhelming support of black voters, considerable support among Hispanic voters, and modest but essential support among whites. (Los Angeles, with many fewer blacks, has for a long time had a black mayor, of the same equable temperament as the mayor elected in New York City.) But as we have seen, immigration has reduced the black percentage of the population in Los Angeles, and, despite the higher proportion of black immigrants into New York City, will not raise it there. The rising groups in both cities are Hispanic and Asian. Many of the Hispanics are of course not yet citizens, and they take out citizenship at a much slower rate than Asians. Thus, the age of Hispanic political domination in Los Angeles and New York, which one might on the basis of demography expect, is still far in the future.

One suspects that the blacks will hold the political kingdom in New York City, for a while. Meanwhile, the newer immigrants, the Asians in particular, the blacks and Hispanics to some degree, will concentrate in the private economy, because of the preferences already demonstrated, because they are faced with language barriers, and because they include fewer citizens. One sees a situation developing similar to the great age of immigration around the turn of the century, in which one group (Irish then, blacks now) is dominant politically, other groups (Jews then, along with Italians to some extent, Asians preeminently now) forge ahead in the economy and the professions. One can also expect that black political power will not be sympathetic to the private business interests in the city.

Blacks will for a while hold the political kingdom, and immigrants will join the older non-Hispanic whites in a more secure footing in the economic kingdom. One can expect that black political power will in some way be used to reduce immigrant (and white) economic advantage. One can also expect, following Thomas Sowell, and the pattern of American history, that a primary base in local political power, whatever its satisfaction in jobs gained and contracts granted, will not lead to economic power. That is what the Irish learned; it is what all developing countries that try to replace their entrepreneurial elements learn. Meanwhile, even the black hold in the political sphere is challenged by the demographic rise of Hispanics and Asians.

However the economic argument turns out, the political argument can only mean that the American commonwealth, which on the whole has done well in accommodating and integrating many ethnic and racial groups, is again put under strain as new groups enter and new lines of conflict emerge.

NOTES

1. Congress was given advice on the impact of the 1965 reforms that was wildly wrong (see Glazer 1985, 7). Congress has already seen its expectations regarding the 1986 reforms, designed to stem the flow of illegal immigrants, proven entirely wrong: "Congress expected that 250,000 undocumented agricultural workers would apply for amnesty under the SAW [Special Agricultural Worker] program, and agricultural employers expected that the number would not exceed 350,000. But by the time the application window for the SAW Amnesty program closed, over one million workers had applied for amnesty" (RAND and Urban Institute 1989, 9). In 1990, new legislation raised the maximum level of legal immigration to 750,000 a year.
2. This is a U.S. census term for a part of a "Consolidated Metropolitan Statistical Area" (CMSA), a very large "Metropolitan Statistical Area" (MSA).
3. A new "race" is started in the census as each East or South Asian group becomes large enough to be worth counting separately. By now every East Asian and South Asian group is listed as a separate "race" in the census, including Asian Indians, Pakistanis, and Bengalis—but other Asians, such as Iranians, Israelis, and Lebanese, are not considered separate "race." So much for logic.

4. This term, now in wide use, implies a group that is not incorporated in the ordinarily expected networks of family, school, and work and that places a disproportionate burden on city social, health, protective, and rehabilitation services. There is now a debate among American social scientists as to whether the term is useful at all, following on efforts to define the underclass empirically and to determine whether and how fast it is increasing. A forthcoming volume edited by Christopher Jencks and Paul Peterson, consisting of papers presented at a conference on the underclass at Northwestern University, will throw much needed light on these questions.

5. Since this was written, a study of one such neighborhood in New York City revived by new immigrants has been published: Louis Winnick, *New People in Old Neighborhoods*, New York, Russell Sage Foundation, 1990.

BIBLIOGRAPHY

Bailey, Thomas R. 1987. *Immigrant and Native Workers: Contrasts and Competition.* Boulder, Colo.: Westview.

Bogen, Elizabeth. 1987. *Immigration in New York.* New York: Praeger.

Borjas, George J. 1990. *Friends or Strangers: The Impact of Immigrants on the U.S. Economy.* New York: Basic.

Bouvier, Leon F., and Vernon M. Briggs, Jr. 1988. *The Population and Labor Force of New York: 1990–2050.* Washington, D.C.: Population Reference Bureau.

Bouvier, Leon F., and Philip Martin. 1985. *Population Change and California's Future.* Washington, D.C.: Population Reference Bureau.

Glazer, Nathan. 1988. "The New New Yorkers." In *New York Unbound*, ed. Peter Salins, 54–72. New York: Basil Blackwell.

———, ed. 1985. *Clamor at the Gates: The New American Immigration.* San Francisco: Institute for Contemporary Studies.

Light, Ivan. 1985. "Immigrant Entrepreneurs in America: Koreans in Los Angeles." In *Clamor at the Gates*, ed. Nathan Glazer, 161–78. San Francisco: Institute for Contemporary Studies.

Muller, Thomas. Forthcoming. *Immigration Reform from an Urban Perspective.* New York: Twentieth Century Fund.

Muller, Thomas, and Thomas J. Espenshade. 1985. *The Fourth Wave: California's Newest Immigrants.* Washington, D.C.: Urban Institute Press.

New York Times, 13 September 1990, B1, 2.

RAND Corporation and Urban Institute. 1989. *Program for Research on Immigration Policy: Research Mission and Initial Public Policy Agenda.* Santa Monica, California and Washington D.C.: RAND Corporation and Urban Institute.

Sassen, Saskia. 1988. *The Mobility of Labor and Capital: A Study in International Investment and Labor Flow.* New York: Cambridge University Press.

Skerry, Peter. 1989. "Borders and Quotas: Immigration and the Affirmative-Action State." *The Public Interest*, no. 96: 86–102.

Simon, Julian L. 1989. *The Economic Consequences of Immigration.* Cambridge, Mass.: Basil Blackwell.

U.S. Department of Labor, Bureau of the Census. 1989. News release of 8 September 1989.

U.S. Department of Labor, Bureau of International Labor Affairs, Division of Immigration Policy and Research. 1989. *The Effects of Immigration on the U.S. Economy and Labor Market*. Immigration Policy and Research report no. 1. Washington, D.C.: Division of Immigration Policy and Research.

U.S. Department of Justice, Immigration and Naturalization Service. 1983. *Statistical Year Book of the Immigration and Naturalization Service*. Washington, D.C.: The Service.

Waldinger, Roger. 1989. "Structural Opportunity or Ethnic Advantage? Immigrant Business Development in New York." *International Migration Review*. 23:1 pp. 48–72.

————. 1986. *Through the Eye of the Needle: Immigrants and Enterprise in New York's Garment Trades*. New York: New York University Press.

————. 1987. "Changing Ladders and Musical Chairs: Ethnicity and Opportunity in Post-Industrial New York." *Politics and Society* 15:4.

13

FRENCH CITIZENS AND IMMIGRANTS IN THE WORKPLACE: MARGINALITY OF THE SUBJECT, MARGINALITY OF THE RESEARCH?

Maryse Tripier

Not much is known about the place of immigrants in business, their relationship to work, their "careers," and the relationships they maintain with the management and friends at work. Studies are scarce for several reasons.

The problems considered crucial for French society from the postwar period to the 1960s were those posed by a massive rural exodus, industrialization, urbanization, and rising wages (Reynaud et al., 1965). Until the 1980s, when a series of historical works appeared, the role of immigrants in French industrialization was little known and generally underestimated (Noiriel 1988). Between the end of the 1930s and the 1960s, immigration went through a slow period of about twenty years; when the consequences of renewed immigration became clear, one whole generation thus believed that this was a "new" situation, but various factors showed how little we knew.

Statistics only imperfectly reflected the foreign presence in the workplace in the past, because some foreigners returned home, some were naturalized, or their descendants became French. In fact, as soon as immigrants become French, our statistics no longer identify them because it is the legal criterion of nationality that is the measure of foreign population, not birthplace or some "ethnic" criterion. Immigrant workers have never attained quantitative significance in the working class. In 1954, they represented 6.1 percent of the working C.S.P. and in 1982, 12.7 percent—but overall the distribution was unequal among economic sectors, regions, and types of jobs.

Foreigners remain concentrated in industry and in public works and building trades, with a growing importance in manufacturing industries since the last war, at the expense of the earliest industrialized sectors: textiles, mining, ironworks. In the last few years we have witnessed their growing role in service industries such as cleaning companies and shops.

On the whole, they have followed the evolution of industry and of available work. They remain concentrated in certain regions, especially the Paris region (Ile de France), where 40 percent of all foreigners settle. The first generation's social mobility, which remains weak, depends on two routes: saving money and improving skills. The social mobility of their children is very hard to measure (R. Silberman's chapter in this volume). For practical reasons, foreigners were excluded from all the important studies on social mobility (Thelot 1982; Bertaux 1985). In certain businesses, foreign workers make up the basic work force (as in some shops of automobile factories), but in many others, only a few or none are employed, as in public sector jobs that are reserved for French nationals. These imbalances, even considering small overall numbers, disappear as soon as we study national trends in wages, work conditions, and qualifications. Identifying and studying immigrants in the workplace depends on the sample of businesses studied or on a specific choice of research effort.

PREDOMINANCE OF ECONOMIC FACTORS

The strong resurgence of immigration has increased interest in foreigners' work conditions, but the view that their stay is temporary has weakened interest in their behavior as social beings. However, from the 1970s on there were plenty of reports testifying to the poor working and living conditions of the recently immigrated and not officially welcomed population. These descriptions appeared on the margins of sociology and especially of the sociology of work. They did not deal much with the work relationship between the French and the immigrants.

According to authors of "The French Worker in 1970," "The criterion of nationality thus eliminated the immigrants from the sample. Foreign workers present too many special features to be studied in the same way as workers of French nationality. . . . The study thus is cut off from a significant part of the working class (about 2 million wage earners who play a strong role in social conflicts and in the formation of workers' attitudes)" (Adam et al. 1971). The same reasoning was used by others.

P. Dubois and his colleagues reviewed the themes recently treated in the sociology of work (Dubois and Kastoryano 1985; Chave 1985). Among the studies in progress in 1984, immigration appeared as a subcategory under the heading "labor markets," which itself represents less than 10 percent of the total of research; economists studied this much more than sociologists.

Immigrants are considered as a labor force category in the economic system. This general orientation raises questions that are part of the scope of the sociologists of work: the management of foreign workers, their relation to work, hierarchical relationships, primary social contracts, and collective action. But the employment of foreigners has been mostly studied with respect to the following questions: Why reliance on foreign labor? Why in the 1960s? What are the effects on employment, wages, foreign exchange, or the stage of development in countries of origin?

We know today that employment of foreigners in the 1960s responded to both the worldwide labor imbalance and the need for unskilled, undemanding, and unprotected labor that provided important benefits to businesses, permitting them to fulfill their orders without confronting working conditions and social relationships. We also know that the state counted on the benefits of the already substantial presence of a labor force that it hoped would remain at the margins of society, thus avoiding the costs involved in settling families. With the recession this situation changed. Many foreigners had settled in France and in the labor market, and they appear today to be the principal victims of the economic downturn. As the unskilled workers grow old, they cannot fill the increasing need for more skilled workers, nor do they provide flexibility in the labor market (set-length contracts, interim work, subcontracts . . .). Foreign unemployment is higher than for French workers, and foreigners' children do not have access to stable employment (Merckling 1986). For sociologists to incorporate the "ethnic" variable into studies about social relationships, permanent settlement of foreigners and recognition that immigration had become a permanent political factor would have been necessary.

MANAGEMENT CATEGORIES AND SOCIOLOGICAL CATEGORIES

Beyond these problems, we face inherent difficulties that account for the weakness of studies bearing on immigrants in the workplace. This research clashes with the official ideology of the professional world, which is defined in terms of abstract categories. There are legitimate and illegitimate modes of designation and identification; someone can be designated by function, trade, or seniority, but cannot be officially "managed" in terms of nationality, sex, or opinions.

The dominant categories in industry are primarily in terms of work-related factors: services or shops, functions, qualifications, age, seniority, level of training. Sometimes we can add individual behavior labels, such as loyalty or competence, which are rarely used. This is why businesses most often refer to the components of the "immigrant" category, rather than defining the category itself.

Annual social assessments, for example, allow us to identify the different groups within the workplace. The number of foreign workers may be accounted for, but no breakdown of salaries, of absenteeism, or of work-related accidents is carried out according to nationality. We do not know the status of foreigners in relation to the French.

This universalist concept of the world of work reflects reality. We can legitimately wonder whether business, especially industry, is not one of the places where social relationships are the least "ethnicized." Isn't the other side of the depersonalization of workers, paradoxically, this merging into an organization that doesn't take "race" or past history into account? Doesn't the worker's role completely outweigh his or her private identity? Isn't this the basis for the creation of new identities?

This separation is not without advantages for immigrants, some of whom declare: "In the factory I am a worker; outside I am a foreigner." Knowing that work is essential for their presence in France, immigrants, in spite of their special situations, find their professional identities to be a positive resource. This is what I found in my studies, starting in 1970 in Parisian metallurgy companies and in small businesses in rural areas (Tripier 1977; 1986; 1987).

My work, reaffirmed by R. Linhart's experience in a Citroen factory (1978), made clear an informal but very well organized strategy of dealing with ethnic difference: either assignment to shops under the control of foremen of the same nationality, or the opposite, purposeful mixing of nationalities in production lines. Citroen may be unique, but in all the businesses surveyed I found some degree of special "treatment" of immigrants, although sometimes only for certain nationalities. Actual practice often contradicts the abstract policy of universality and in doing so creates an underground of social relationships.

Generally, foreigners are not promoted in businesses; nor do they have access to training. Skilled foreign workers are usually Europeans who were already educated or skilled before their arrival in France. Literacy or job training programs are not well adapted to immigrants, and bettering their salaries or work conditions has usually depended on collective action, carried out with the support of unions, without regard to ethnic factors, and applied to all workers. The union *(ouvriers specialisés)* strikes peaked after the May 1968 movement until 1976. The strength of the economy at that time allowed abandonment of the use of short-term contracts and extension of social and union rights to immigrants.

METHODOLOGICAL PROBLEMS

Observing and understanding the mechanisms of discrimination in the workplace require techniques to uncover discrimination and "signs" of unacknowledged or unconscious discriminatory practices.

Only elaborate statistical techniques permit us to trace immigrants' work experience and to compare them to others. On the other hand, anthropological observations are required to delve into the nature of day-to-day interpersonal relationships and to distinguish the effect of background factors.

This is particularly true with regard to social relationships among workers. For example, it was necessary for G. Wahlraff to disguise himself as a Turkish worker and share the work experience of Turkish immigrants for two years in order fully to grasp the depth of racism in the workplace, but also to see the solidarity among workers, both Turkish and German (Bernoux, Motte, and Saglio 1973).

If employers' and managers' statements often seem to be a denial of the distinctiveness of foreigners or else a folklorization of their qualities and faults, what is the case with unions, the other important player in work life?

PROFESSIONAL RELATIONSHIPS

Professional relationships in the workplace (at least in businesses with more than fifty employees) are organized through groups such as company committees, personnel delegations, and health and safety committees, which get their legitimacy from law. They then rely on a bureaucratic norm, in the Weberian sense of the term, that is, on impersonal relationships. This arrangement serves several goals, one of which is the integration of foreigners into the legal structure. Unions rightfully remind us of the long battles to end discrimination in law and in fact, and to integrate foreigners into common rules of the workplace (Tripier 1977). Quite a few personnel heads, and foremen as well, had been recruited from the former colonial army to develop personalized relationships with the immigrants, and to escape bureaucratic rules of the game and bypass the union, in a paternalistic management framework.

Focusing on foreign identity would challenge the universalist basis of union actions, weaken their negotiating capacities, and leave the field free for a return to paternalism. This is why we are witnessing a categoric refusal to develop nationality-based organizations within industry and the funneling of immigrants into either the internal affairs of unions or the development of cultural activities by company-based committees. Foreign "culture" is sometimes recognized, but is relegated to the "private" sphere, which, according to the unions, must not alter their broad representational role.

The description of conflict, such as Bulledor's, analyzed by D. Kergoat (1973), my own research, and more recent studies carried out by C. de Wenden and J. Barou (1986) show, however, a permanent tension between two goals: On the one hand, the recognition of worker individuality, and thus of foreign identity, without which the union cannot be firmly entrenched in its "base," i.e., its members; on the other hand, the elimination of ethnicity, age, and sex in the search for a broader legitimacy and representativeness. Here again, the researcher must identify the actual results of the union ideology of universality. In the past, unions did admit groups of militants of foreign origin, as soon as they had accepted the rules of the game.

SOCIALIZATION TO WORKER NORMS

A company that has been in existence for a long time and whose employees stay with it a long time is a center for the creation and transmission of worker values.

We have seen a similarity in the behavior of all immigrant workers in their first industrial work experiences: "an excess of zeal," withdrawal from social life, etc. The first years for all immigrants are years of transition, shaped by the initial migration process and the necessity for integration into the economic system.

As long as they still envision a return to their country, migrants live in a special time frame, a time between parentheses. French workers live in a different atmosphere, one that emphasizes their local and national destiny.

However, as time passes foreigners' behavior changes and becomes markedly different according to the group and the local and national environment. Italians did not become abstract "workers," but rather steelmakers of Lorraine or masons of the Midi. By the same token, Portuguese, Maghrebs, and Turks became "Renaults" and "Citroens."

More generally, my research has shown a conformity among foreigners who socialize themselves to working-class culture and to different businesses, depending on their workplace. They gain from not being rejected by the working-class group, a rejection that becomes intolerable when the immigrants' stays lengthen.

A FRENCH MODEL

In sum, in understanding relations between workers, the cultural differences appear less important than differences of past history and future strategies. The linguistic gap that accompanies the diversity of origins sometimes aggravates the bad hierarchical relationships; but we cannot describe business as a world compartmentalized by ethnic groups and administered accordingly.

No permanent associations to manage, express, or negotiate the collective interests of immigrant groups have been created. Even the Billancourt Islamic groups do not really extend their sphere of influence to life in the company or in unions. This fact is explained by the universalist reference of the workplace, which itself goes back to the all republican institutions.

Furthermore, the work community, although fragmented, remains unified by one employer. Even if it appears to be invisible or distant, the business is still a place of negotiation of work conditions, except in limiting cases of subcontracting (cleaning services, dressmaking at home), or black-market work and extralegal work, which are not affected. The business community remains critical to the worker's fate.

Labor law is an essential element of the universalist reference of companies. This law applies generally, except for forbidding access to certain jobs by foreigners (of which there are many in France). Thus immigrants have progressively become full participants in the world of work; they vote and are eligible to appear on ballots. Less and less do they have special status as they become formally identified with other private sector workers.

For a long period of time, professional unionism was the favored channel of communication for immigrants because it was the only legal and legitimate channel for their collective action; it thus permitted socialization into French working-class culture. This phenomenon was accentuated by the fact that unionism in France has, for twenty years, entrenched itself into business at the expense of regional organizations. Unions, because of class and international consciousness and the logic of efficiency, have produced an ideology that excludes organizations of workers separated by ethnicity. Nevertheless, the variety of the unions reflects specifically French groupings and complicates the choices of immigrants, who are worried about effectiveness, especially with respect to wages; thus immigrants tend to orient themselves most often towards the strongest unions in their sector.

In sum, ethnicity is taken into consideration, although only in an informal manner, by company management, and is handled internally by union organizations.

INTEGRATION INTO THE WORKPLACE, INTEGRATION INTO A CLASS

Based on my research results, I have proposed that the workplace is, for immigrants, a more integrating factor than the home.

If by integration we include social participation and, even more, integration into a value system, we observe, however, two weaknesses: the fragility of acceptance of foreigners by the French as soon as employment crises arise, and the fragility of foreign adherence to French worker values.

My monographic studies have in fact shown that outside of company walls, contact between first-generation immigrant workers and French workers is superficial. When the immigrant retires, he loses most of these ties; especially if he becomes unemployed, his legitimacy as a member of the work force is challenged.

The more strongly French workers are socialized in the work culture, the more they resist this reversal, especially if they have shared struggles with immigrants, because they relate not to abstract "immigrants" but to work comrades they know individually. This may explain the difference observed between the protectionist or racist views expressed by workers in opinion polls and the neutralization or weakening of these views in the workplace.

On the other hand, I observe that immigrant adherence to worker norms is often superficial and related to the length of the immigration period. But I must qualify this point. Certain French have the same attitude with regard to these worker norms; many workers aspire today to individual mobility and distance themselves from a collective concept of the future.

It is the immigrants who, because of their conditions of exploitation, the available forms of solidarity, and the severity of labor strife, develop the same radical forms of worker awareness that have marked the history of worker struggles in France.

REFERENCES

Adam, G., F. Bon, J. Capdevielle, and R. Mouriaux. 1971. *L'ouvrier français en 1970.* Paris: Armand Colin.
Bernoux, P., D. Motte, and J. Saglio. 1973. *Trois ateliers de O.S.* Paris: Economie et humanisme (Collection "Relations Sociales").
Bertaux, D. 1985. *La mobilité sociale.* Paris: Hatier.

Chave, D. 1985. Dix années de sociologie du travail. In *Le travail et sa sociologie: essais critiques*, 42–53. Paris: L'Harmattan.

Dubois, P., and R. Kastoryano. 1985. Recensement des recherches en cours sur le travail (1984). In *Le travail et sa sociologie: essais critiques*, 17–41. Paris; L'Harmattan.

Ecole Nationale d'Administration. 1984. *Les immigrés dans l'entreprise*. Report presented by the students of the Ecole Nationale d'Administration as part of the L. de Vinci Promotion.

Kergoat, D. 1973. *Bulledor*. Paris: Editions du Seuil.

Linhart, R. 1978. *L'établi*. Paris: Editions de Minuit.

Merckling, O. 1986. *Modification dans les politiques d'emploi des entreprises et place des phénomènes de substitution français-immigrés*. Research report. Paris: Ministère du Travail.

Noiriel, G. 1988. *Le creuset français*. Paris: Editions le Seuil.

Reynaud, J. D., et al. 1965. *Tendances et volontés de la société française*. Paris: S.E.D.E.I.S.

Thelot, C. 1982. *Tel père, tel fils? Position sociale et origine familiale*. Paris: Dunod.

Tripier, M. 1977. Concurrence et substitution. Ph.D. thesis, Université Paris X.

———. 1986. *Destins ouvriers, cultures d'entreprise, et pratiques syndicales*. Vol. 1. Paris: Centre de recherches et d'études sur la société française.

———. 1987. L'immigration dans la classe ouvrière en France. Doctorat d'Etat en sociologie, Université de Nantes, France.

Wahlraff, G. 1986. *Tête de turc*. Paris: Editions La Découverte.

de Wenden, C. Wihtol, and J. Barou. 1986. Analyse des conflits récents survenus aux usines Renault depuis 1981 au sein de la population immigrée. Contrat de connaissance C.N.R.S./R.N.V.R.: Les O.S. (ouvriers specialisés) dans l'industrie automobile.

14

SOCIOECONOMIC ATTAINMENT

Stanley Lieberson

O ne of the most impressive facts about European ethnic groups in the United States is the following: in the 1980 census, there were slightly more than 49 million people reporting themselves as partially or entirely of German ethnic ancestry. Yet the United States has fought two world wars against Germany, and this has occurred with the full and unqualified participation of the population of German ancestry. To be sure, German origin affected political positions in the period leading up to the wars—as is the case for other groups in the United States (Lubell 1956; Lieberson 1980, 106–7). Nevertheless, it is unthinkable that the United States could have been an effective participant in either war without the full participation of Americans of German origin. Indeed, either German or English is the largest single ancestry group in the nation, with arguments possible on both sides (Lieberson and Waters 1988, 37–38).

These shifts, from alien immigrant to descendants fully participating in the new society, are all the more remarkable when one considers the many nations where such changes have failed to occur, and where nations are under continuous threat of ethnic separatism. The German experience is repeated for virtually all of the groups migrating to the United States, non-European as well as European, under consideration here. This chapter, by describing and analyzing the socioeconomic positions of the white ethnic groups, obviously deals with a central issue in their adjustment and their disposition towards the society as a whole. Socioeconomic position is not only important in itself but also has significant ramifications for overall position in society.

This chapter has four parts. In the first, the current socioeconomic positions of the major white ethnic groups in the United States are examined. Second, these are contrasted with the differences that existed at the time of major immigration. Third, I suggest some of the factors that have contributed to these changes in particular, as well as to assimilation generally. Finally, I review some complicated and not entirely understood issues related to these changes.

CURRENT SITUATION

First and foremost, the present-day socioeconomic positions of the major white European ethnic groups in the United States are remarkably similar according to three central measures: educational attainment, occupation, and income. To be sure, a detailed examination of these characteristics—not possible when medians or other measures of central tendency are used—does indicate that some differences still do exist among the European groups. But the main point is that the white ethnic groups in general occupy relatively similar socioeconomic positions in the nation. Moreover, this similarity is not shared with many of the major non-European groups in the nation, who tend to occupy distinctly less advantaged positions. Blacks, American Indians, and most of the Hispanic groups occupy different and distinctly subordinate positions on these socioeconomic indicators.

Education

It is not difficult to appreciate the importance of education. As Lieberson and Waters observe:

Educational attainment is of great interest in the study of these ethnic and racial groups for three major reasons. It is one of three central variables in the study of socioeconomic attainment (along with occupation and income). First, education is itself a source of prestige and is, additionally, a factor influencing entry into various occupational opportunities. Second, education is of interest simply because it was initially seen as a major institution through which the descendants of later immigrants would be "Americanized," that is, fit the model of appropriate behavior held by those who had arrived earlier and were in control of the social institutions. Finally, the immigrant groups initially differed greatly in their educational attainment at the time of arrival—in no small way reflecting the variation within Europe in the spread of literacy and universal education. As a consequence, these differences were noted quite early in the migration of different groups to the United States. (Lieberson and Waters 1988, 105).

The average level of education varies along a relatively narrow range for the American-born adults in nearly all of the white groups in 1980 (column 1, table 14.1). Among fifteen of the groups, the medians range narrowly, from12.5 to 13.4 years of schooling for men (completion of high school being 12.0 years). Russian men are the one great exception, being distinctly highest, with 15.7 years of schooling. (United States censuses do not ask a religion question; however, there is reason to believe that a substantial part of the population reporting Russian origin in the United States are Jewish.)[1] Although among women, those of Russian origin also have the highest level of educational attainment, 13.4 years, they diverge less from other groups than do Jewish men (second panel of table 14.1). In general among women, the average educational level is less dispersed among the groups. This may reflect the greater constraints on women achieving exceptionally high levels of education, coupled with a slightly weaker propensity for women to drop out at the very lowest levels of attainment.

Measures of central tendency often hide differences between groups in their distributions among specific categories. So it is important to keep in mind that the statements about common socioeconomic attainment are true for the white ethnic groups when summarized with standard measures, but there can still be some differences underlying these averages. This is the case for education; the detailed educational data provided in the rest of table 14.1 (and summarized in the last column with the indexes of net difference) indicate that the European groups are hardly identical with respect to their percentages in each category. Inspection of the data for women, for example, shows that the percentage completing high school and stopping there is fairly similar for most of the groups. But observe how the groups still differ in the relative numbers above or below this level. The indexes of net difference (ND), shown in the last column, summarize these differences in educational attainment across all of the categories for each group compared with the entire population of the same sex who are twenty-five years of age or older. Net difference can range from +1.0 (in the impossible situation where the least educated member of a given group exceeded the most educated member of the base population) to −1.0 (at the opposite extreme, where the most educated member of a given group was exceeded by the least educated member of the base population).[2] On the one hand, Portuguese and Dutch men barely exceed the national distribution, whereas Russians are exceptionally high. But the ND indexes for the remaining groups are similar, although there is a certain amount of variation among the groups in their educational distributions. The range is

TABLE 14.1

Educational Attainment, Men/Women Born in the United States, Aged 25 and Over, 1980

Group	Median Years	High School 8 Years or Less	1–3 Years	4 Years	College 1–3 Years	4 Years	5 Year or More	ND
Men								
English	12.8	.14	.13	.30	.17	.13	.13	.14
German	12.7	.12	.12	.35	.17	.12	.12	.14
Irish	12.7	.13	.13	.33	.18	.12	.12	.12
French	12.7	.13	.13	.34	.18	.11	.11	.11
Italian	12.7	.11	.16	.34	.17	.11	.11	.11
Scottish	13.4	.09	.11	.28	.20	.15	.17	.26
Polish	12.8	.12	.13	.33	.17	.12	.14	.15
Dutch	12.6	.16	.14	.35	.16	.09	.09	.04
Swedish	13.0	.09	.10	.32	.20	.14	.16	.24
Norwegian	12.9	.12	.09	.31	.19	.14	.15	.21
Russian	15.7	.05	.07	.21	.18	.18	.30	.43
Czech	12.8	.13	.10	.33	.17	.13	.14	.17
Hungarian	12.8	.10	.12	.33	.16	.13	.15	.20
Welsh	13.4	.08	.10	.30	.21	.15	.17	.28
Danish	13.0	.09	.10	.31	.20	.15	.15	.24
Portuguese	12.5	.17	.16	.33	.18	.08	.08	.01
Women								
English	12.6	.12	.15	.37	.18	.10	.07	.08
German	12.6	.11	.13	.42	.17	.09	.07	.07
Irish	12.6	.11	.16	.41	.18	.08	.06	.05
French	12.6	.11	.15	.41	.18	.08	.06	.05
Italian	12.5	.13	.16	.45	.14	.07	.06	.01
Scottish	12.8	.07	.12	.37	.22	.13	.10	.19
Polish	12.5	.14	.15	.41	.15	.08	.07	.03
Dutch	12.4	.16	.17	.41	.15	.07	.05	−.03
Swedish	12.8	.07	.10	.41	.22	.12	.08	.18
Norwegian	12.8	.09	.09	.40	.23	.12	.07	.16
Russian	13.4	.06	.07	.34	.20	.16	.17	.30
Czech	12.6	.13	.12	.41	.17	.09	.08	.07
Hungarian	12.6	.10	.13	.42	.16	.09	.09	.10
Welsh	12.9	.06	.10	.38	.22	.14	.10	.22
Danish	12.8	.07	.09	.41	.23	.12	.08	.19
Portuguese	12.4	.17	.18	.40	.16	.05	.04	−.06

Source: Lieberson and Waters 1988, 107–8.

even more restricted for women, as shown in the second panel; Portuguese and Dutch women fall below the national distribution. In short, the white groups are remarkably similar in their average educational attainment, but a more detailed analysis does disclose that the groups still have some important differences—even if we ignore the Russians. Later we will consider whether the differences that remain are in any way remnants of historical gaps among the groups.

Income

For those born in the United States, the incomes of the largest white ethnic groups are reported in table 14.2 for both men and women. Inspection of the income categories discloses only modest differences among the groups—with the only noteworthy exceptions being Americans of Portuguese origin, who tend towards the low side, and of Russian origin (largely Jewish), who are on the high side. The reader can see this by inspecting each group's percentage in a given income category. In the lowest income category, for example, the percentages for men range between 3 and 5 percent for the European groups.[3] Russians are outstanding on the high end, with 5 percent having incomes of seventy-five thousand dollars or more, compared with 2 or 1 percent among the remaining European groups. The results in the second panel of table 14.2 describe a similar situation for women. As is the case for education, the white ethnic groups also have rather similar income distributions.[4]

Occupational Distributions

Dividing occupational activities into nine broad categories (three examples are sales; service; farming, forestry and fishing), one finds that the groups are similar in their makeup. Comparisons of each group's occupational distribution with each of the fifteen remaining groups are summarized with the indexes of dissimilarity shown in table 14.3. For each intergroup comparison, the index of dissimilarity ranges from zero (if the two groups have identical percentage distributions) to one hundred (if the groups have totally dissimilar distributions such that the occupations held by one group were not held by anyone of the other group and vice versa). The first column shows that the average index between English-origin men and each of the remaining fifteen specific groups is seven. This means that on average 7 percent of the English would have to change broad occupational categories for them to have the same distribution as the white group they are being compared with. The values for the English indexes range from only two (column 2) to twenty-five

TABLE 14.2
Income Distribution of Ethnic Groups, by Sex, 1979

Group	Under $2,000	$2,000–2,999	$3,000–3,999	$4,000–4,999	$5,000–5,999	$6,000–7,499	$7,500–9,999	$10,000–11,999	$12,000–14,999	$15,000–19,999	$20,000–24,999	$25,000–49,999	$50,000–74,999	$75,000 and over
Men														
English	.05	.02	.03	.03	.03	.05	.08	.07	.10	.17	.14	.18	.02	.02
German	.04	.02	.02	.03	.03	.04	.07	.07	.11	.19	.15	.19	.02	.01
Irish	.04	.02	.03	.03	.03	.05	.08	.07	.10	.18	.15	.18	.02	.01
French	.04	.02	.03	.03	.03	.04	.08	.07	.11	.19	.15	.18	.02	.01
Italian	.04	.02	.03	.03	.03	.04	.07	.07	.11	.20	.16	.19	.02	.01
Scottish	.03	.02	.03	.03	.03	.05	.07	.07	.10	.17	.14	.21	.03	.02
Polish	.04	.02	.02	.03	.03	.04	.07	.06	.10	.20	.17	.20	.02	.02
Dutch	.04	.02	.03	.03	.03	.05	.08	.07	.11	.18	.14	.17	.02	.02
Swedish	.04	.02	.02	.03	.03	.04	.07	.06	.11	.18	.15	.21	.03	.01
Norwegian	.04	.02	.03	.03	.03	.04	.07	.07	.10	.18	.15	.20	.02	.01
Russian	.03	.01	.02	.02	.02	.03	.06	.05	.08	.15	.14	.27	.06	.05
Czech	.04	.02	.02	.03	.03	.04	.07	.06	.10	.19	.17	.20	.02	.01
Hungarian	.04	.01	.02	.02	.03	.04	.06	.06	.09	.18	.17	.22	.03	.02
Welsh	.03	.02	.02	.03	.03	.04	.08	.07	.10	.17	.14	.21	.03	.02
Danish	.04	.02	.02	.03	.03	.05	.07	.06	.10	.18	.16	.21	.03	.02
Portuguese	.05	.02	.03	.03	.03	.05	.08	.09	.11	.19	.15	.15	.01	.01

English	.34	.08	.07	.06	.05	.07	.10	.06	.07	.06	.02	.02	.00	.00
German	.34	.07	.07	.06	.05	.07	.10	.07	.07	.06	.02	.01	.00	.00
Irish	.34	.08	.07	.06	.05	.07	.10	.07	.07	.06	.02	.01	.00	.00
French	.34	.07	.07	.06	.05	.07	.10	.07	.07	.06	.02	.01	.00	.00
Italian	.36	.07	.07	.05	.05	.06	.09	.07	.07	.06	.02	.01	.00	.00
Scottish	.31	.07	.07	.06	.05	.07	.10	.07	.08	.07	.03	.02	.00	.00
Polish	.34	.07	.07	.06	.05	.07	.09	.07	.08	.07	.03	.02	.00	.00
Dutch	.36	.09	.08	.06	.05	.07	.09	.06	.06	.05	.02	.01	.00	.00
Swedish	.34	.07	.07	.06	.05	.07	.09	.07	.08	.06	.03	.02	.00	.00
Norwegian	.34	.08	.07	.06	.05	.07	.09	.07	.07	.07	.02	.02	.00	.00
Russian	.29	.06	.06	.05	.04	.06	.09	.07	.09	.09	.05	.04	.00	.00
Czech	.33	.08	.07	.06	.05	.07	.09	.07	.08	.07	.03	.01	.00	.00
Hungarian	.34	.07	.06	.06	.05	.06	.10	.07	.07	.07	.03	.02	.00	.00
Welsh	.31	.07	.07	.06	.05	.07	.09	.07	.08	.07	.03	.02	.00	.00
Danish	.34	.07	.07	.06	.05	.07	.09	.07	.08	.07	.02	.02	.00	.00
Portuguese	.34	.07	.07	.07	.05	.07	.11	.07	.07	.05	.02	.01	.00	.00

Source: Lieberson and Waters 1988, 158–59.

(column 3). These higher occupational indexes invariably involve a comparison with Russian men. Russians have a rather unusual distribution: men of Russian ancestry have the largest percentage in three categories (executive, administrative, and managerial; professional and technical; and sales). On the other hand, they have the lowest percentage in two: the precision production, craft, repair category; and the operatives, fabricators, laborers category.[5] The comparisons in table 14.3 therefore are also done without the Russian outlier. As a consequence, the average index and the maximum are shown without the Russian group (columns 4 and 5 for men, 9 and 10 for women). A close examination of these columns shows that overall the groups are similar to each other in their broad occupational makeup. Needless to say, a more detailed analysis of occupations would yield more dissimilarities among the groups. There were and still are some sharp ethnic differences in participation in specific occupations (Hutchinson 1956; Lieberson and Waters 1988, table 5.3).

In short, the data for occupations are similar to the results obtained for education and income. There are still some differences among the groups—but general summary measures suggest that they are modest by either of two criteria: 1) in comparison with differences between these groups and some of the non-European populations (see also Neidert and Farley 1985); and 2) in comparison with differences that existed at the time of massive immigration.

PRIOR CONDITIONS

One cannot consider earlier differences among the immigrant groups without first considering when their ancestors first migrated to the United States. The European groups differ considerably in the timing of their arrival; for some groups, a substantial part of their total immigration occurred relatively early in the history of the nation, whereas for others it was more recent. Many of the Northwestern European groups and Germans (the so-called "Old" groups) started to arrive in substantial numbers earlier than did the immigrants from South-Central-Eastern Europe (the "New" groups), although, of course, there is considerable variation within each category (for example, some of the Scandinavian sources tend to be more recent); and migration from all of these sources did overlap. Nonetheless, the average number of generations in the United States for the old groups tends to be greater than for the new.

At one point, this old-new distinction was a central issue in discussions of immigration policy in the United States. The old were viewed as distinctly superior in terms of a wide-ranging set of social and cultural criteria, for example, work habits, criminality, potential loyalty to the nation, and intelli-

TABLE 14.3

Index of Occupational Dissimilarity between Specific Groups and the Average of 16 Major White Ethnic Groups, by Sex, 1980

| | Men | | | | | Women | | | | |
Group	Average (1)	Minimum (2)	Maximum (3)	Excluding Russians Average (4)	Excluding Russians Maximum (5)	Average (6)	Minimum (7)	Maximum (8)	Excluding Russians Average (9)	Excluding Russians Maximum (10)
English	7	3	25	6	10	6	3	14	5	8
German	8	3	28	6	11	5	1	16	5	8
Irish	8	3	27	7	11	5	1	16	5	9
French	9	3	29	8	12	6	2	17	5	10
Italian	9	4	26	8	11	8	5	18	7	12
Scottish	10	2	18	9	18	7	2	14	7	14
Polish	9	4	27	8	11	6	3	16	5	9
Dutch	12	4	33	10	17	10	5	21	9	15
Swedish	8	3	22	7	14	5	2	13	5	11
Norwegian	9	4	24	8	15	6	2	14	5	11
Russian	25	18	35	NA	NA	15	8	21	NA	NA
Czech	8	3	25	6	12	6	2	15	5	11
Hungarian	8	4	22	7	14	6	3	13	6	12
Welsh	10	2	18	9	18	8	2	15	8	15
Danish	9	3	22	8	15	6	2	13	5	11
Portuguese	13	4	35	12	18	10	5	21	10	15

Source: Lieberson and Waters 1988, 130.

gence. According to the thinking in vogue at the time, many of these differences were attributed to biological racial factors that were thought to generate these differences (for more details see the classic reviews by Higham 1955 and Handlin 1957). Critical to our analysis here is the fact that the group differences in the timing of arrival make comparisons somewhat difficult. Data for very early periods would yield virtually no information about later groups; comparisons for more recent periods ignore the sizable numbers from old sources who had come earlier. There is also every reason to assume that the characteristics of migrants from a given source changed through the years. Practical considerations generated by availability of data lead one to concentrate on the period after the "new" started to come in sizable numbers since there were still important numbers immigrating from most of the "older" sources.

Education

Literacy rates within Europe at the turn of the century make it clear that education spread earlier in Northwestern Europe than elsewhere in the continent. Based largely on information for army recruits, a study finds that virtually no young men were illiterate in the German Empire or in Sweden and Norway at a time when illiteracy ranged from 80 to 90 percent in new sources such as Portugal, Serbia, and Romania. Even the highest figures for old sources, respectively 12.8 and 17.0 percent in Belgium and Ireland, were lower than the most favored of the new sources, the 23.8 percent in Austria (Lieberson 1963, 71). These gaps are reflected in the educational differences among immigrants to the United States; a comparison among those arriving in 1910, prior to the introduction of a literacy test for admission, reveals almost no overlap between old and new sources (Lieberson 1980, 28). In this case, the French had the highest of the illiteracy rates reported for old groups, but this was lower than all but one of the new groups (Bohemians and Moravians combined). The variability between these immigrant groups is much greater than is found at present among their American-born descendants (see the coefficients of relative variation in Lieberson and Waters 1988, 105–16).

Wealth and Occupations

Other indicators point in the same direction. During this period, information was gathered on the amount of money brought into the country, and again there was widespread variation in the percentage bringing at least fifty dollars;

with almost no exceptions, the old Europeans exceed the new (Lieberson 1980, 28). The early occupational data for immigrants at the time of their arrival are not good, but the best indication is again that the old sources were generally far more likely to report skilled occupations during the period between 1899 and the outbreak of World War I, with Jews being the one spectacular exception (68 percent skilled of those reporting an occupation). Otherwise, the percentages of skilled (Hersch 1969, 491) reflect an almost universal advantage of the old over the new: Scottish (54); English (48); French (33); German (30); Scandinavian (21); Italian (15); Irish (14); Magyar (9); Greek (8); Polish (7); Russian (6); Lithuanian (6); Croat and Slovene (5); Slovak (4); Rumanian (3); and Ruthenian (2).

Other Considerations

Compared with immigrants from old sources, the new European groups were more segregated residentially when they first arrived in sizable numbers in the United States (Lieberson 1963, table 13). Indeed, in 1910 and to a lesser extent in 1920, a number of South-Central-Eastern European groups were more segregated from the old white stock than were blacks in the same northern cities (see the data reported in Lieberson 1963, table 42). By 1930, almost every one of these South-Central-Eastern European immigrants was exceeded in degree of segregation by blacks in the ten cities studied. (In general, black segregation increased and European immigration declined during this period.)

Finally, attitudinal dispositions clearly favored the old sources in the earlier periods. This is blatant in the Dillingham Senate Commission reports published early in the century (Handlin 1957). It is also indicated more formally in the early results for the Bogardus Social Distance Scale (see Schaefer 1984, figure 3.2).

As we can see, the gaps in attainment between the groups are not as great as they once were. Moreover, remaining differences among white groups are generally uncorrelated with earlier differences that occurred at the time of immigration—indeed, in some instances the gaps are in the opposite direction from those that existed at an earlier time. *In other words, the gaps that once existed among European groups have more than simply narrowed through the years; rather, they are uncorrelated with earlier differences and in some cases have even reversed their order.* The question then becomes, What drives this set of changes over time?

THEORETICAL ISSUES

How do we explain the fact that the relative positions of the groups are, for many key socioeconomic attributes, uncorrelated with their rankings at the time of immigration? A complete explanation for such a remarkable change is impossible to give in a single paper. However, a number of studies of ethnic assimilation through the years do suggest some important theoretical factors.

Culture

First, we have to be very cautious in using cultural or normative factors to explain group differences in socioeconomic achievement. Of course, these factors *do* matter, but there is a danger of falling into the following circular reasoning:

1. We find that groups differ in some attribute.
2. How do we explain this?
3. The answer is simple; the groups differ in their culture or values.
4. How do we know that they differ in their culture or values?
5. Very simple. Look at how they differ in the attribute in question!

It is necessary to keep in mind that cultural, normative, and personality differences among the European groups continue to persist, as witnessed by the interesting work by Salamon (1980, 1982, 1985) on ethnic differences in farming practices in the Midwest or, to a certain extent, the persistence of geographical differences (Lieberson and Waters 1987, ch. 3). A separate question is whether such differences will occur indefinitely if they have blatant consequences for attainment and prestige. For example, the extraordinary shift towards the English language in the United States is a very practical and reasonable step in a nation where the educational, economic, and social incentives for the acquisition of English are enormous. It would be a mistake simply to conclude that the values of the European immigrants favored the acquisition of English in the United States, whereas the values of other groups such as Indians in the United States and Canada, or the French in Canada (but not in New England) favored maintenance of their ancestral languages (Lieberson, Dalto, and Marsden 1975). Likewise, one should not assume that differences in values explain why compatriots living elsewhere refuse to give up their mother tongues. More about this later.

Migration

In explaining the similarities of outcomes, it is helpful to understand the role of migration. First of all, why do people choose to leave their homeland and move to a foreign place that is alien in many ways to what they are comfortable with; that is distant from their homeland, their friends, often many members of their extended family; and that entails many discomforts? There is normally only one reason for migrating—the benefits from such a move. They may take many forms: in some cases, persecution, starvation, and invasion are such severe threats to survival that virtually any other place offering a sanctuary is attractive, though even here additional factors may operate if choices exist among receiving countries. Second, in situations when the move is not "forced," migration is usually driven by differentials in the opportunities available in the sending and receiving countries for persons with given skills, education, and other relevant characteristics such as age and sex. It appears that the vast bulk of migration to the United States was driven by opportunity factors: a desire to better oneself and/or one's family through the opportunity structure available in the receiving nation.[6]

This means that the characteristics of the population migrating to the United States at a given time from a given source are influenced by an interaction among factors external to the group. The characteristics of the members of each group in the receiving country is a nonrandom sample of the population living in its homeland. The selection of migrants is affected by the characteristics of the homeland population; the differentials between sending and receiving country in the potential opportunity for each subset of the homeland population; the costs of moving (both social and economic); policies towards migration in the sending and receiving countries; and the opportunities that potential migrants have at home (including internal migration) and/or those provided by various possible receiving nations. For potential migrants with given skills and educational levels, of a given sex, age, and familial situation, options at home can be contrasted with potential gains elsewhere, coupled with the costs of the migration (which include social, psychological, and cultural costs as well as monetary expense). Each nation differs in the returns for given characteristics (i.e., skills, education, etc.), as well as in the distribution of these characteristics in the population. Likewise, each potential receiving nation also differs in both the returns to persons with different characteristics and the distribution of needs. The net effect in this simple model is striking. For it means that the market for certain skills in a given country may attract persons from one sending nation but not from another, depending on their options in their homeland and in alternative destinations.

This is what I have elsewhere called "A Theory of Intrinsic Differences":

Two important conclusions follow from these assumptions. First, there is an inherent reason for expecting differences between groups at the initial point of contact simply because the migrant groups differ in the alternatives available to them in the areas from which they are migrating. Ignoring special situations such as famine, social unrest, and oppression, emigrants from a nation with a relatively high level of living will tend to both be qualified for better jobs and have more attractions in their homeland than will those migrating from a nation with a lower level of living. Work acceptance to one group, in the sense of being a superior alternative to the opportunities available in the homeland, will not be attractive to members of another group (or to only a much smaller segment). Hence migrants from different sources will vary in their jobs and incomes not necessarily because of discrimination or work orientation but because of the alternatives available to them at home. Such groups at the initial point of contact in the United States differ not in their aspirations, but rather in the minimum they will settle for. And they differ in how little they will accept because of the alternatives at home that they must weigh them against. The second point is one well recognized in the work of Bonacich (1972, 1976), namely workers in the receiving country will view migrants from nations with lower levels of living as potential competitors willing to work for less because of the alternatives at home. (Lieberson 1980, 371–72)

Under the circumstances, one can see how the willingness of some groups to accept unattractive work might make it appear as if they are less ambitious or otherwise different in culture or norms. In point of fact, such jobs may also be less desirable to them, but nonetheless may mean substantial improvement over conditions in the homeland. Not only is the population in a more advanced nation relatively more skilled, but the opportunity gaps between their homeland and a potential receiving country are probably narrower than for those living in a very poor nation. To use a contemporary example, what would be sufficient to motivate an unskilled worker from Mexico would not be sufficient to do so for someone with comparable skills from, say, Germany or Sweden. This means that immigrant groups doing less attractive and/or poorer-paying work are not necessarily less strongly motivated or void of the ambition found among those accepting only much more attractive occupations. We can see how easily a cultural interpretation might develop to account for immigrant groups with different levels of attainment, when in fact the difference is a product of the backgrounds and options available to different groups.[7]

Types of Ethnic and Racial Subordination

Another major consideration pertains to the distinction between two types of subordination. One occurs when an indigenous population is overrun or conquered by another ethnic or racial group.[8] The second occurs when members of a group migrate to an area in which they will be socially, economically, and politically subordinate to the host population. This takes place when there are advantages for both the migrating group and the dominant receiving population in the area of settlement.[9] The migrating group enjoys advantages over its situation in the sending country, even though its members are deprived relative to the receiving population. The receiving country employs migrants to meet economic needs that cannot be filled by the population already present.[10] This is and was obviously the case for Europeans and virtually all of the other groups who migrated to the United States—with slaves being an extremely important exception. In comparison with subordinate *indigenous* peoples, subordinate *migrants* are generally more inclined towards assimilation. The dominant culture is not a symbol of conquest or earlier oppression, and the forces motivating their migration also encourage assimilation into the dominant culture, by means of learning the language, taking advantage of educational opportunities, and so forth, within a few generations. On top of this, those migrants most resistant to assimilation or most dissatisfied can often return to their homeland, an opportunity not available to indigenous peoples. In addition, the dominant population can usually set limits on the number and sources of immigrants admitted into the country (this argument is developed in Lieberson 1961; also see Ogbu 1978; and Horowitz 1985).

In reviewing the behavior of European migrants to the United States who were politically, socially, and economically subordinate at first, it should be kept in mind that we are largely considering peoples who migrated by choice and were motivated to attain in the New World that which they could not in their homeland. Their initial subordination was not simply imposed, but was accepted as an unattractive consequence. Immigrants with low skills, little education, and from cultures further from the dominant culture of the United States were no differently motivated than those arriving with more skills and education or from more appealing sources. Immigrants from South-Central-Eastern European sources, for example, were if anything quicker to become American citizens than were those from the more esteemed and better-educated Northwestern European origins (see the analysis in Gavit 1922, ch. 8; Lieberson 1963, 145–46). This commonality among migrants is a leveling factor for all of these European groups (and for many other groups as well).

Generations

For both methodological and substantive reasons, the influence of generation on ethnic behavior is vital. Obviously immigrants experience many changes after migrating to the new nation. Nevertheless, major types of change are generationally linked. In some cases, it is almost a matter of definition, for example, that immigrants will not be able to change their mother tongue (the language first learned in childhood). Similarly, adult immigrants are unlikely to take full advantage of the opportunities offered by the receiving society, such as, for example, the educational system. Immigrants' offspring born in the receiving nation are exposed to the possibilities of radically different experiences than their parents. Likewise, the grandchildren of immigrants start in a different cultural context than the American-born children of the immigrants (witness the famous Third Generation Principle of Hansen 1952). These intergenerational factors will be of declining significance with each succeeding generation.[11] Observations both of differences between ethnic groups at a given time and of changes in a group over time must take generational factors into account before any reasonable conclusions can be drawn. If, for example, one group appears to be giving up its ancestral tongue whereas another does not, the first question to ask is about the generational makeup of the two groups, particularly if there is a major immigrant component in one but not the other.

An excellent example of the importance of generational factors is provided by considering changes between 1940 and 1960 in the educational levels of the Japanese-origin population of the United States. The median attainment for men moved upward from 8.8 to 12.4 years of schooling. What accounts for this is the absence of immigration from Japan during this period. The median for foreign-born Japanese in 1960 was 8.8, a modest increase over the 8.3 in 1940; the median for the American-born component of the Japanese population also experienced a relatively small increase, from 12.2 to 12.4 during the twenty years. What accounts for the enormous increase in educational attainment from 1940 to 1960 is that the immigrant generation declined from 80 to 27 percent of the Japanese population in the United States. Almost all of the temporal shift for Japanese is due to generational differences (Lieberson 1973, 562–63).[12]

Generational effects are by no means assured. In some societies, ethnic groups are steadfastly resistant to change, and there are minimal changes between generations. But it is a critical consideration in the United States, where changes do occur in ways that are linked to number of generations in the nation. This type of analysis is particularly relevant for considering differences among migrant subordinate groups since generation influences, for example, rates of intermarriage or ties towards ancestral homelands. This means that the end of massive immigration from Europe is especially important because of the impact on the generational composition of the groups. It is possible that the decline in new immigrants affects the position of later generations in the United States.

Intergenerational Mobility

Another key factor in assimilation is the mobility system. Visualize a society in which there is simply no intergenerational mobility, regardless of ethnic or racial origin. Under such circumstances, offspring would have the same occupation as their parents and groups would continue indefinitely with favorable or unfavorable initial positions. No discrimination would be necessary on the part of the dominant group since initial group differences would be perpetuated. Visualize, at the other extreme, a system in which parental socioeconomic position had no influence on offsprings' outcome. In such circumstances, only discrimination would keep ethnic equality between the groups from occurring in one generation. From this perspective, what keeps groups from achieving identical economic positions is the lack of full fluidity within the society (i.e., the influence of parental position on life chances of offspring), coupled with the existence of discrimination, which prevents some groups from fully participating in the existing mobility system.[13] Although counterintuitive, Markov Chain analysis shows that the influence of the initial differences among the groups will have no permanent influence if each group is subject to the same mobility rates (Lieberson and Fuguitt 1967). Therefore it is clear that nondiscrimination in a society such as the United States, with its fluidity, would eliminate ethnic differences in attainment in a matter of a few generations—assuming no additional immigration of a substantial nature. The evidence gathered in large-scale analyses of intergenerational mobility for recent decades indicates that exactly this process has operated, that is, ethnic origin has virtually no influence on intergenerational mobility after parental socioeconomic origins are taken into account (Duncan and Duncan 1968; Featherman 1971; Duncan, Featherman, and Duncan 1972; Featherman and Hauser 1978).[14]

Since there clearly was discrimination against some of these groups, such as those from South-Central-Eastern Europe, this common set of mobility rates is a gratifying but still rather puzzling result. Either it means that these groups all worked harder and hence compensated for the ethnic disadvantage encountered through discrimination, or it means that discrimination was less than fully effective, or it means that the groups thwarted the discrimination. This question leads us to consider the impact of some features of the American society itself on the socioeconomic processes—features that help us understand why South-Central-Eastern groups did not fare as badly as one might otherwise expect.

Policies and Beliefs in the United States

During the heyday of immigration to the United States, assimilation was of central concern to the nation. This is easy to understand. The major cities of the nation were, to an extraordinary degree, populated by groups that were viewed with more than a small amount of antipathy and apprehension.

In Chicago, fully one-third of the residents were either immigrant or second generation members of these [South-Central-Eastern] groups; approximately 40 percent of the residents of both Cleveland and Newark belonged to these groups. In New York City, the newcomers were less than 7 percentage points away from claiming an absolute majority of the population. In other leading industrial centers of the era, Boston, Buffalo, Detroit, Philadelphia, and Pittsburgh, one-quarter of the population were South-Central-Eastern European immigrants or their immediate descendants. To be sure, there were a number of other major cities, for example, Indianapolis, Washington, D.C., Kansas City, Cincinnati, and Seattle, where the new groups were a less substantial percentage. But clearly the enormous numbers coming from these parts of Europe, coupled with the economic opportunities available in the industrial centers of the Northeast, created fear among the older white settlers about the maintenance of the American Society.

Current changes in the black-white composition of major central cities are by no means novel. If anything, the percentage of foreign white stock in many of these cities fifty years ago is far greater than the percentage of blacks currently in these centers. Not only are the patterns repeated but the current anxiety shown in some quarters about the racial composition of cities is also nothing new. (Lieberson 1980, 23–24).

The answer to this "threat" was very simple; the schools would help assimilate and Americanize the immigrants' offspring—certainly the parents could not be trusted to do this on their own. Indeed, the schools would be a counterforce to the parents. This emphasis on education fit in rather nicely with the ideology that permeated the country. As Brint and Karabel (1989, 3–9) have recently reminded us, the United States was extraordinary in its belief in education as a public good, as evident in the availability of education to the white population, the encouragement of school attendance, and the way education was seen as an avenue of mobility.[15]

Mandatory school attendance laws, a legislative matter for the states themselves rather than the federal government, were toughest in the very parts of the nation where substantial immigration was found (Lieberson 1980, 136–137). However, there was no expectation that these groups would ever equal the earlier white groups—let alone exceed them. The dominant groups were somewhat blind to the potential of these new peoples to use the opportunities provided for exceptional mobility. (Keep in mind that this was in a period when new European immigrant groups and their cultures were viewed as racial in nature. Because they were considered intrinsically inferior, all that could be done to help them maximize their potential would be to everyone's advantage and would certainly not create a threat to the Northwestern Europeans.)

In fact, there may have been an actual educational advantage for the immigrant groups because they were concentrated in that part of the nation with the best educational systems at the time, if length of school year is any indicator, and/or in large urban centers with relatively extensive and diverse offerings in their school systems.

In addition, the ideology of the nation was strongly equalitarian. Although there was no love for many of the new groups, there were limits as to what could be done against them simply because oppressive steps would clash with the prevailing principle that rights and opportunities were to be extended to all whites (Dubois 1967, 332–33 provides an excellent contrast with the situation faced by blacks). There were also special beliefs about immigration. The United States was to be receptive to immigration from everywhere in Europe. This ideology was part of the nation's mission, evidence of the superiority of the country, and also a way of helping to develop and populate a vast and expanding body of land. It was relatively easy to follow since at first the immigrants were for the most part from sources similar to those of the earlier settlers. (Even then there were anxieties about immigrants from different Northwestern European countries.) However, these beliefs were to be deeply challenged, initially by Irish Catholic migration in the 1840s and then by the enormous South-Central-Eastern European immigration flows that began towards the end of the nineteenth century. But it was not until the 1920s that really severe steps were taken to control the numbers and origins of the immigrants. In fact, the history of the nation is marred by more than a few exceptions to this ideology, but they appear *relatively* minor when one considers the treatment of blacks and the enormous numbers of immigrants who did enter. The key fact is that the oppressive movements, such as the Ku Klux Klan or the nativists or the anti-Catholics, did not get completely out of hand, as did behavior towards blacks in the United States, or behavior towards various ethnic and racial groups in many other nations of the world. (It is not possible to judge how much of the relatively positive reception should be attributed to ideology and how much simply to the vested economic interests of older Americans who benefited from large-scale immigration. There is every reason to assume that both factors operated.)

Finally, the fluid and dynamic nature of society in the United States was another factor that enabled European groups to overcome the discrimination they encountered. For those in the urban centers, there were always new niches to exploit in the continuously changing economic system. Hence many of the groups entered—if not created—new industries and new economic opportunities, where they were somewhat insulated from discrimination in the mainstream economic system. For those in rural areas, the success of immigrant groups in farming was more or less isolated from institutionalized forms of discrimination. Indeed, in many parts of the country, there was an eagerness to get immigrant newcomers to participate in agriculture and, moreover, their settlements were dense enough to avoid difficulties if any were to arise. I do not wish to minimize the obstacles encountered by these lower-ranking groups in either the country or the city—nor can one rule out the probability that many *did* have to work harder in order to overcome discriminatory obstacles—but it is the case that discrimination could be avoided or sidestepped in some cases because of the opportunities provided by the fluidity and openness of the economy itself. Moreover, the new South-Central-Eastern European migrant groups went to the areas of greatest opportunity, largely avoiding the South, with its relatively larger segment of the British population.

REMAINING ISSUES

There are a number of questions about these socioeconomic changes to be answered. One of the most important and fuzziest is the exact timing of these changes. This is important in helping us understand what factors were critical in driving them. Did the shifts in relative positions of the European groups occur gradually over the years? Are they largely a post–World War II phenomenon? If so, can one find signs in earlier periods indicating that the recent changes are an acceleration of earlier shifts that were masked by the enormous flow of new immigrants? Or did the ideology of the Allies in the war affect discrimination against the newer European immigrant groups? Did the decline in sizable immigration of these groups have a positive effect on their positions, above and beyond the generation effect? Did the economic boom after World War II simply create more openings than the more favored white groups could fill and hence provide opportunities for the descendants of the new European immigrants? There was an enormous jump in college attendance after World War II, caused in no small way by the GI Bill for veterans. Did this especially benefit the New Europeans? What about the role of blacks? Perhaps their migration to the northern urban centers where these New Europeans were concentrated had a favorable net impact on the position of the latter?

Studies of occupational attainment in earlier periods indicate sharp differences among groups, with many reporting lower attainment than that found among those of British or Yankee origin (see the research reported in the trailblazing study by Thernstrom 1973, particularly chs. 6 and 8, and the review of more recent historical studies in Bodnar 1985, ch. 6). However, in some cases the results are not entirely relevant to the question of whether intergenerational mobility is the same after taking into account group differences in parental background. Many of the historical studies are unable to measure directly the parental origins of specific subjects, but are based on cross-sectional analyses (see the cautions against such procedures in Thernstrom 1973, 116, 122). But the consistent finding that groups once differed in mobility is rather compelling. Moreover, an exceptionally elegant analysis of Providence, Rhode Island, indicates ethnic differences in mobility between 1880 and 1925, net of parental background characteristics (Perlmann 1988, 205–11). So there is reason to assume that the current uniformity in mobility rates did not always exist among white ethnic groups. In general, however, socioeconomic comparisons between earlier and later periods are handicapped by the cross-sectional problem and the fact that analyses of the earlier years tend to depend on immigrant data, as contrasted to ethnic data for the present. In addition, the census data have themselves changed over time; for example, the early years offer nothing directly on income or educational attainment (literacy being only an inadequate substitute for the latter; housing costs being an even more tenuous substitute for the former). Finally, there is no reason to assume that intergenerational progress was identical in all socioeconomic domains.

Education

We probably know more about changes in education than about the other variables.[16] There is no correlation whatsoever between the literacy levels of different immigrant groups in 1910 and educational attainment among the American-born members of these ethnic groups in 1980. When did the change occur? First, there was a certain leveling factor after literacy tests were initiated in 1917. The groups still ranked the same, but they were generally closer to one another. Apparently admission policies introduced by the United States had the effect of reducing illiteracy more for the new sources than the old—a result to be expected given that the former had higher rates to begin with. But this change of policy was probably not a key factor since much of the immigration occurred prior to 1917. Analysis of 1930 census data indicates that the second-generation differences in literacy rates were still correlated with the levels found among the foreign born in 1910. However, the differences among second-generation groups are much smaller than the differences among the immigrants. The educational system of the United States was operating as a leveler, although it did not eliminate the general advantage of the old groups. Indeed, the literacy rates of second-generation groups in 1930 are more closely correlated with the first generation twenty years earlier than with the educational levels of the ethnic groups reported in 1980. As mentioned above, there is no significant correlation between early literacy rates and recent educational attainment.

The situation is, however, rather different by 1950. For the first time, data on educational attainment, rather than on illiteracy, are available. Among the foreign born in each group, there is still an old-new difference operating. But the gap has disappeared among the second-generation members of these groups. In other words, by 1950 the old-new gap had broken down with the second generation. There is also a significant correlation between the levels of education for women in the second generation in 1950 and the levels for women in 1980. The correlation is weaker for men, albeit pointing in a positive direction. For both sexes, then, second-generation education in 1950 is a better precursor of contemporary differences in education for ethnic groups than it is a reflector of immigrant differences observed in earlier periods. This result involves age groups who had mainly completed their education before World War II. Hence, although there is every reason to believe that the gaps among ethnic groups were further reduced after the war, clearly the situation had been radically altered before then.

Second-generation birth cohort data permit a more accurate identification of the periods of change. They suggest that the patterns were not identical for all of the groups. Russians are a clear example of an early upward thrust in education, which begins with the cohort born in the United States between 1885 and 1895. By contrast, five of nine South-Central-Eastern European groups had their largest upward spurt (relative to the older-stock whites) in the youngest cohort examined, those born between 1925 and 1935. At first this might lead one to think that World War II might have played a role since many in this cohort would have completed their education after the war. However, there is reason to speculate that the war was not the trigger. First of all, it is unlikely that the GI Bill per se provides a simple explanation since the sharpest spurt among women is also found in the same cohort for four of the new groups. More significant, for most groups the two previous birth cohorts also display net improvements over the older white stock, and these include age groups whose education could not have been affected by World War II. The quality of the data does not permit reasonable speculation about what would have occurred to these groups in the absence of the war, that is, whether improvements were indeed accelerated by war. However, these broad processes of change were in evidence prior to the second war and probably would have accelerated anyway. I assume that the prolonged schooling for these groups reflects economic improvements and/or the opportunities available to those with an education (see the evidence on this in Perlmann 1987). However, as I indicate, the data are fuzzy on these points.

Other Factors

The evidence suggests that group differences were declining before World War II. However, we do not know about the influence of a number of other factors. (Indeed, we do not know whether the war per se—as opposed to the economic changes that occurred afterwards—accelerated certain trends.) Because of government restrictions, the flow of new immigrants from many European sources declined dramatically a few years after the end of World War I. Obviously this impacts on the generational makeup of the groups living in the United States and, in turn, generation affects socioeconomic attributes. Beyond this, was there an interaction between the decline of immigration and the behavior of the American-born children of earlier immigrants, as well as the behavior (discriminatory and otherwise) towards these American-born generations, when there were no longer sizable new waves of immigrants? For example, if immigrants were competing with American-born compatriots for some of the same jobs, then a decline in lower-wage competitors would affect the situation. It is hard to know from the available data, let alone to evaluate the relative importance of these various factors.

Finally, the sizable migration of blacks from the South to the urban North during World War II and the ensuing decades may have helped the European groups. This would be predicated on a queuing effect such that the South-Central-Eastern Europeans were preferred by employers over blacks. Under such circumstances, the increase of the black percentage of the labor force, in situations where the percentage of South-Central-Eastern origin remains constant, would sharply improve the occupational positions of the latter groups (see Lieberson 1980, 377–81 for the mechanisms under which this would occur). Likewise, the fear of a large black population by many whites in northern centers after the second war may have led to a minimization of the earlier emphasis on distinctions within the white population, especially since these immigrants were no longer arriving in great numbers. As noted earlier, the period after World War II was marked by an extraordinary long-time economic boom in the United States. Although it is clear that the New Europeans were moving upward prior to that period, an acceleration because of this boom cannot be ruled out. It would take better data to answer that question accurately.

What about Other Groups?

Finally, one cannot discuss these remarkable developments among the populations of European origin without at least commenting on the recent experiences of non-European groups in the United States. The data in Lieberson and Waters (1988) show that American-born segments of the black, American Indian, Mexican, and Puerto Rican groups are generally below the sixteen white groups with respect to education (107–8), occupation (131), and income (138). Although there are a few exceptions, members of these groups tend to be exceeded by even the lowest-ranking of the sixteen major white groups. The picture is largely the same for the residual "other Spanish groups" category (which does not separate Cubans and Central/South Americans from the remainder).[17] By contrast, comparisons with the leading white groups are less consistent for persons from the Indian subcontinent. But especially noteworthy is the fact that American-born men and women of Southeast Asian origin (classified as "other Asian" in the Lieberson and Waters study) fare relatively well on most comparisons with at least the bottom end of the white groups. (Sample-size problems prevented Lieberson and Waters from disaggregating this category into specific groups such as Chinese, Filipinos, Japanese, Koreans, and Vietnamese. As of this date, the 1980 census monograph giving detailed data on these groups has not yet been released. This is regrettable since there are differences among these Asian ethnic groups.)

In any case, the divergence between Asians and other non-European groups in socioeconomic attainment raises a very significant and difficult issue. Even before the growth in public awareness of Asian accomplishments in the United States, there were two competing causal interpretations of the lower achievements of the non-European groups mentioned above: 1) discrimination in some direct or indirect form; 2) cultural explanations, that is, explanations to the effect that differences in attainment reflect values, family organization, self-discipline, work habits, and other internal factors. Obviously the policy consequences for each of these interpretations differ enormously. Nevertheless, it is much easier to engage in polemics about the answer than it is empirically to determine which is valid. Indeed, it will be seen that the necessary data and information are not available for reaching a conclusion about the issues. (To analyze the historical basis for present-day gaps between South-Central-Eastern Europeans and blacks took a rather extensive monograph; see Lieberson 1980.) However, there is no reason to assume that the answer is so simple as the above either-or argument that is so frequently given.

A few guidelines may help sharpen the analysis. First, although the debate is often in the form of a cultural explanation versus a discriminatory explanation, why should it be assumed a priori that only one of these factors operates? Second, two basic types of explanations are potentially overlapping. There can be feedbacks between the two phenomena, for example, discrimination can influence normative dispositions of those who are the victims. Third, there is no reason to assume that only these two types of factors operate or that the factors producing lower socioeconomic attainment are the same for each of the groups. Fourth, the experience of European groups suggests that the relative influences of different factors may vary over time because the society itself changes. From these four considerations, it follows that only a quantitative approach can adequately assess the relative importance of different influences on the outcome for each group at a given point in time.

Nonetheless, consider the conditions of settlement for each of the non-European populations. American Indians are indigenous subordinate groups, having been conquered by Europeans (indeed their treatment as a common people, as opposed to specific distinctive tribes, is a product of European contact). As a consequence, Indian groups are more likely to maintain their old ways and less likely than migrants to assimilate into the new society. This has obvious consequences for comparisons with the attainment of European migrant groups. For example, as recently as 1900, about 40 percent of American Indians could not speak English, a far slower rate of mother-tongue shift than occurs among the migrant subordinate groups (Lieberson, Dalto, and Marsden 1975, 56). Mexicans and Puerto Ricans each include important migrant and indigenous segments. It should be noted that both groups are themselves products of ethnic contact in the New World, but their situation is still complicated, even taking into account the history of their formation as distinctive groups. Although there is still large-scale migration of Mexicans to the United States, there are Mexicans who are indigenous people in that they lived in areas of New Spain that were either conquered or purchased by the

Anglos. In the state of New Mexico, for example, which was conquered by the United States in 1846, the Spanish language was well maintained for a number of generations (see Lieberson, Dalto, and Marsden 1975, 55–56). Likewise, Puerto Ricans are migrants to the mainland but indigenous in Puerto Rico. Because they are Americans in terms of citizenship rights, they are free to move back and forth between the mainland and Puerto Rico at will, with no controls whatsoever.

By contrast, the Asian groups for the most part migrated by choice to the United States. Moreover, in recent years there is evidence of very favorable selectivity factors operating, at least among the Chinese. Whatever the attitudes towards maintaining the ancestral culture may be, their receptivity to adopting the characteristics necessary for achievement will probably be stronger than among conquered groups.

The migrant-indigenous distinction is only one of many factors that have to be considered in order to understand the lesser attainments of the different non-European groups. Group differentials in numbers and spatial concentration may well affect their ability to carve out initial occupational niches that provide toeholds for further mobility (see Lieberson 1980, 381–82). Also, the attitudes and behavior of the dominant white society towards each of these groups are not necessarily identical. (Again, it would be a mistake to assume that they are unchanging through the decades.) If one assumes that divergent interests, needs, and potential threats underlie many interethnic conflict situations, there is no reason to assume that antipathies are identical for all of the groups. If two or more groups are disadvantaged because of their common non-European origin in a society where Europeans dominate, the conclusion must not be drawn—at least without sound empirical evidence—that the handicaps are therefore identical for all such peoples, nor that the disposition of whites towards each of them are identical (see a comparison between blacks and various Asian groups in Lieberson 1980, 381–83). But observe how these become quantitative questions. If American Indians are relatively disadvantaged because they were indigenous subordinates, it does not follow that this is the only factor determining their position and that the wide range of discriminatory practices directed against them are irrelevant. Such considerations indicate the need for a thorough quantitative multivariate study before conclusions can be drawn in a responsible manner. These issues are thorny and are not yet resolved. In the absence of quantitative study they are subject to rhetorical and polemical devices that can be used to reach radically different conclusions.

However, we should not lose sight of the main point of this chapter, which is that major gaps in socioeconomic attainment between the white ethnic groups have declined through the years and that for the most part these groups are now very similar to one another. Moreover, for major socioeconomic characteristics, there is no vestige left of the original rank differences between the groups.

NOTES

1. .For an evaluation and discussion of the common practice of using these data as an indicator of Jewish patterns, see Lieberson and Waters 1988, 25–27.
2. Starting with all possible pairings between members of the group specified and the standard group, visualize three different outcomes: those in which the two people have an identical education; those in which the person from the group specified has the higher educational attainment; and those in which the person from the standard group has the higher educational level. ND gives the proportion of all cases in the second situation minus the proportion of all cases in the third. These index values provide a summary of the educational attainment of each group that is more sensitive to the overall distribution.
3. Compared with 14 for blacks, 13 among Puerto Ricans, 9 among Mexicans, and 7 for American Indians and other Spanish.
4. For a summary measure of the total income distribution of each group, see Lieberson and Waters 1988, 136–39.
5. Russians are low in farming, but there are other groups with an equally low percentage (see Lieberson and Waters 1988, appendix table 5.1).
6. There are many other reasons for migration (Lieberson and Waters 1988, 1–2), but most are not central for the groups under consideration here.
7. For a contrary view of the role of culture and the nature of migration, see the study of interethnic differences in Providence, Rhode Island, by Perlmann (1988).
8. By "indigenous" I mean not necessarily the oldest group ever to inhabit a given area that is still surviving, but rather a group sufficiently established in the area as to possess the institutions and demographic capacity for maintaining some minimal form of social order through the generations. See Lieberson 1961, 903.
9. And/or the move is viewed as temporary and hence the social and political disadvantages are accepted because of the economic rewards.
10. Or at too high a price.
11. Thus the distinctions between later generations, other than for possible prestige purposes—such as ancestry back to the American Revolution or the *Mayflower*—will be nil.
12. A similar result is also obtained for women of Japanese origin. For a different perspective on the generational influence, albeit one that this author disagrees with in terms of the validity of the analysis, see Alba 1988.
13. A third factor would be normative differences between the groups on attributes that are relevant to socioeconomic success. I am inclined to assume that the initial abilities net of class are largely the same for all of the groups.
14. Jews are an exception, with even more rapid upward mobility than can be explained by their origins.

15. Waters and Lieberson (forthcoming) observe that illiteracy was remarkably infrequent among the native white population of the United States at the turn of the century (3 percent) when compared with Europe (where the lowest rates are 14 percent in France and 17 percent in Ireland).
16. The discussion below is based largely on Lieberson 1980; Lieberson and Waters 1988; Waters and Lieberson, forthcoming.
17. For a detailed analysis of the differences between Hispanic groups and the importance of making these subdivisions, see Bean and Tienda 1987.

BIBLIOGRAPHY

Alba, Richard D. "Cohorts and the Dynamics of Ethnic Change." In *Social Change and the Life Course*, vol. 1, *Social Structures and Human Lives*, edited by Matilda White Riley. Newbury Park, CA: Sage, 1988.

Bean, Frank D., and Marta Tienda. *The Hispanic Population of the United States.* New York: Russell Sage, 1987.

Bodnar, John. *The Transplanted: A History of Immigrants in Urban America.* Bloomington: Indiana University Press, 1985.

Bonacich, Edna. "A Theory of Ethnic Antagonism: The Split Labor Market." *American Sociological Review* 37 (1972):527–59.

———. "Advanced Capitalism and Black/White Race Relations in the United States: A Split Labor Market Interpretation." *American Sociological Review* 41 (1976): 34–51.

Brint, Steven, and Jerome Karabel. *The Diverted Dream: Community Colleges and the Promise of Educational Opportunity in America, 1900–1985.* New York: Oxford University Press, 1989.

DuBois, W. E. B. *The Philadelphia Negro.* New York: Schocken, 1967.

Duncan, Beverly, and Otis Dudley Duncan. "Minorities and the Process of Stratification." *American Sociological Review* 33 (1968):356–64.

Duncan, Otis Dudley, David L. Featherman, and Beverly Duncan. *Socioeconomic Background and Achievement.* New York: Seminar, 1972.

Featherman, David L. "The Socioeconomic Achievement of White Religio-Ethnic Subgroups: Social and Psychological Explanations." *American Sociological Review* 36 (1971):207–22.

Featherman, David L., and Robert M. Hauser. *Opportunity and Change.* New York: Academic Press, 1978.

Gavit, John Palmer. *Americans by Choice.* New York: Harper, 1922.

Handlin, Oscar. *Race and Nationality in American Life.* Garden City, NY: Doubleday Anchor, 1957.

Hansen, Marcus Lee. "The Third Generation in America." *Commentary* 14 (1952): 493:500.

Hersch, Liebmann. "International Migration of the Jews." In *International Migrations*, vol. 1, edited by Walter F. Wilcox, 471–520. New York: Gordon and Breach, 1969.

Higham, John. *Strangers in the Land.* New Brunswick, NJ: Rutgers University Press, 1955.

Horowitz, Donald L. *Ethnic Groups in Conflict.* Berkeley: University of California Press, 1985.

Hutchinson, E. P. *Immigrants and Their Children, 1850–1950.* New York: John Wiley, 1956.

Lieberson, Stanley. "A Societal Theory of Race and Ethnic Relations." *American Sociological Review* 26 (1961):902–10.

———. *Ethnic Patterns in American Cities.* New York: Free Press, 1963.

———. "Generational Differences among Blacks in the North." *American Journal of Sociology* 79 (1973):550–65.

———. *A Piece of the Pie: Blacks and White Immigrants since 1880.* Berkeley: University of California Press, 1980.

Lieberson, Stanley, Guy Dalto, and Mary Ellen Marsden. "The Course of Mother Tongue Diversity in Nations." *American Journal of Sociology* 81 (July 1975):34–61.

Lieberson, Stanley, and Glenn V. Fuguitt. "Negro-White Occupational Difference in the Absence of Discrimination." *American Journal of Sociology* 73 (1967):188–200.

Lieberson, Stanley, and Mary C. Waters. "Ethnic Groups in Flux: The Changing Ethnic Responses of American Whites." *Annals of the American Academy of Political and Social Science* 487 (1986):79–91.

———. "The Location of Ethnic and Racial Groups in the United States." *Sociological Forum* 2 (1987):780–810.

———. *From Many Strands: Ethnic and Racial Groups in Contemporary America.* New York: Russell Sage, 1988.

Lubell, Samuel. *The Future of American Politics.* 2d rev. ed. Garden City, NY: Doubleday Anchor, 1956.

Neidert, Lisa J., and Reynolds Farley. "Assimilation in the United States: An Analysis of Ethnic and Generation Differences in Status and Achievement." *American Sociological Review* 50 (1985):840–50.

Ogbu, John U. *Minority Education and Caste: The American System in Cross-Cultural Perspective.* New York: Academic Press, 1978.

Perlmann, Joel. "A Piece of the Educational Pie: Reflections and New Evidence on Black and Immigrant Schooling since 1880." *Sociology of Education* 60 (1987):54–61.

———. *Ethnic Differences: Schooling and Social Structure among the Irish, Italians, Jews, and Blacks in an American City, 1880–1935.* Cambridge: Cambridge University Press, 1988.

Ryder, Norman B. "The Interpretation of Origin Statistics." *Canadian Journal of Economics and Political Science* 21 (1955):466–79.

Salamon, Sonya. "Ethnic Differences in Farm Family Land Transfers." *Rural Sociology* 45 (1980):290–308.

———. "Sibling Solidarity as an Operating Strategy in Illinois Agriculture." *Rural Sociology* 47 (1982):349–68.

———. "Ethnic Communities and the Structure of Agriculture." *Rural Sociology* 50 (1985):323–40.

Schaefer, Richard T. *Racial and Ethnic Groups.* 2d ed. Boston: Little, Brown, 1984.

Thernstrom, Stephan. *The Other Bostonians: Poverty and Progress in the American Metropolis, 1880–1970.* Cambridge, MA: Harvard University Press, 1973.

Waters, Mary C., and Stanley Lieberson. "Ethnic Differences in Education: Current Patterns and Historical Roots." To be published in *International Perspectives on Education and Society,* vol. 2, edited by Abraham Yogev. Greenwich, CN: JAI Press.

Willcox, Walter F. *International Migrations.* Vol. 1. New York: Gordon and Breach, 1969.

Yetman, Norman R., ed. *Majority and Minority: The Dynamics of Race and Ethnicity in American Life.* Boston: Allyn and Bacon, 1985.

FIVE

NATIONALITY, CITIZENSHIP, LAW, AND POLITICS

15

IMMIGRATION, REFUGEE, AND CITIZENSHIP
LAW IN THE UNITED STATES

Peter H. Schuck

In late November 1990, to the surprise of most observers, the United States Congress approved, and the President signed, the Immigration Act of 1990. The 1990 Act alters the immigration system of the United States in many important ways. For example, it significantly increases the number of legal admissions; reforms the structure of categorical preferences; adds a new category of "diversity" immigrants; changes some of the grounds and procedures for excluding and deporting aliens; establishes a temporary protected status for Salvadorans and for others who are in peril but may not satisfy the legal requirements for refugee status; authorizes administrative naturalization; and adopts special procedures for deporting certain criminal aliens.

Unfortunately, the publication schedule for this book had reached a point that made it impracticable to revise this chapter to reflect these extensive changes. Readers wanting to know more about the new Act may wish to consult the weekly U.S. publication, Interpreter Releases, which has published a series of articles analyzing the Act's provisions; the series begins with the December 3, 1990 issue. I have analyzed the new Act from a political and policy perspective in P. Schuck, "The Emerging Political Consensus on Immigration Law," Georgetown Immigration Law Journal 5: 1 (1991).

For most of America's history, the law was not much concerned with immigration. Her borders were essentially open to both entry and (with the glaring exception of slavery) exit. Patterns of migration were shaped by economic, political, ethnic, and religious developments, not by legal rules.

That changed somewhat in 1875 with the enactment of the first federal limitation on immigration (again, apart from laws dealing with the slave trade). Even so, it was not until 1917 that Congress adopted a comprehensive scheme of immigration control. That system, institutionalized in the 1924 statute, was based on national origins quotas that favored migrants from the traditional source countries (primarily the British Isles, Germany, and Scandinavia) and discriminated against those from southern and eastern Europe, Asia, and Africa. The volume of immigration to the United States under these quotas remained relatively low until the 1960s.

It was not until 1965 that the national origins quotas were abandoned. Under the powerful influence of the civil rights revolution, the system of preferences was overhauled in ways that permitted an increase in the migration from Asian, African, and Caribbean countries. With the 1965 law, the provisions relating to legal immigration assumed essentially their present form and the source country composition of the migratory stream began to shift. During the 1980s two other legal changes of great significance were adopted: the Refugee Act of 1980 and the Immigration Reform and Control Act of 1986 (IRCA).

If America's immigration law has experienced far-reaching changes, its citizenship law has exhibited remarkable stability. A naturalization statute was enacted by the First Congress (1790). Since then, however, citizenship law has changed little, with the notable exceptions of the short-lived Alien and Sedition Act (1798) and the fourteenth Amendment's Citizenship Clause (1868).

American refugee law is a rather recent phenomenon; it essentially began in the aftermath of World War II and has developed under the pressures of the Cold War and of rapid political and economic instability in the developing countries. Until 1980, refugee law was a melange of ad hoc responses to particular political crises. In that year, Congress enacted the Refugee Act, which was designed to create a more systematic, legalistic, predictable structure of control of refugee movements and determinations. The act also recognized asylum as a formal legal status, generating an unanticipated flood of adjudication and judicial lawmaking on the subject.

In this chapter, I shall discuss the immigration, refugee, and citizenship law of the United States, emphasizing the basic legal norms, ideological principles, administrative structures, policy considerations, and political constraints that animate and govern these bodies of law. I shall also note the state of public controversy about these matters and speculate about the major changes that we may expect in the future.

The chapter's structure is as follows. Part 1 is contextual; it describes the principal social, demographic, and political facts shaping the debate over American immigration, refugee, and citizenship law. Part 2 describes the system of immigration and refugee control. It consists of three sections: the legal admissions program; the new enforcement and amnesty programs created by the 1986 IRCA; and the refugee and asylum program created by the 1980 Refugee Act. Part 3 discusses the nature of membership in the American polity. It consists of two sections: the law of citizenship, and the rights associated with the principal statuses (citizenship, various legal alien categories, and undocumented aliens). Needless to say, the chapter's length requires that I emphasize the broad, general features of the American system rather than its details.

1. THE CONTEMPORARY CONTEXT

Consider the following facts: [1]

- During the decade of the 1980s, some 6.3 million people were admitted to the United States for legal permanent residence. This figure includes nearly five hundred thousand undocumented migrants who had received temporary legal status under IRCA's general, agricultural, and Cuban-Haitian amnesty programs by the end of 1989. However, it does not include more than 2.5 million others who are now in the process of receiving that status. (IRCA requires that they either adjust to permanent legal residence status within a prescribed period of time or face deportation). The total far exceeded the 4.5 million admitted during the 1970s and, if the 2.5 million who are still in the legalization process are included, approaches the almost 8.8 million who came here during the first decade of this century, when immigration was essentially unrestricted and its highest levels ever.
- As the 1980s ended, moreover, the trend was strongly upward; the 1989 figure soared to almost 1.1 million from the 1988 level of 643,000, which in turn was up from 601,000 in 1987. (The IRCA amnesty programs were responsible for 79,000 of the 1989 admissions and 69,000 in 1988). Admissions during 1989 were the highest since 1914, seventy-five years earlier.
- This new growth in legal immigration is occurring without any increase in the numerical quotas. The increases during the late 1980s were largely due to nonquota admissions and the amnesty provisions of IRCA. Several "pull

factors" are contributing to the nonquota increases. Asians and some other beneficiaries of the 1965 reforms that abolished the system of national origins quotas have naturalized at relatively high rates. Naturalization enables them legally to bring their immediate relatives to the United States without regard to quota limitations, a process known as "chain migration." Pressure to increase refugee and parole admissions in order to accommodate the large number of Jews, Armenians, and others who are now being permitted to leave the Soviet Union are growing. On the other hand, the overthrow of Communist regimes in eastern Europe and of the Sandanistas in Nicaragua may reduce those pressures.

• Unlike the turn-of-the-century influx, which was distinguished from earlier ones not only by its size but also by its geographical and ethnic sources *within* Europe, the migration of the 1980s has been for the most part from every part of the world *except* Europe. The conditions pushing and pulling people from these countries towards the United States have never been stronger. Population pressures in the Third World, most notably in nearby Latin America, are building rapidly. The labor force in Latin America alone will grow by more than 90 million workers between the years 1980 and 2000. This increase of 77 percent will make it virtually impossible to maintain even the dismal current levels of employment prevailing there. In addition, convulsive civil conflicts in Central America and other immigration source regions, such as Southeast Asia, have swollen the number of refugees to an estimated 14 million worldwide. At the same time inexpensive transportation has made it much easier for hundreds of thousands of these desperate individuals to reach our borders, where many of them claim asylum. "Pull" factors attracting migration to the United States include the expanding employment opportunities for unskilled labor, the improved prospects for attaining legal status realized in the 1986 legislation, and the critical mass of compatriots that has accumulated in the ethnic enclaves of urban America, especially in Sunbelt communities.

• Current immigration is transforming the demographic profile of the American population, particularly in large cities and in the Sunbelt region. The ethnic groups, especially Hispanics, from which most of the newer legal migrants come, have high fertility rates relative to the population generally and will account for much of America's future population growth. Immigrants tend to be younger than the population generally and more than two-thirds are now women and children, in sharp contrast to the adult male–dominated waves of immigration of the past. Six states—California, New York, Florida, Texas, New Jersey, and Illinois—were the intended residence of 80 percent of legal immigrants in 1989, a remarkable rate of concentration yet one that seems to be steadily increasing. Moreover, 37 percent planned to live in seven metropolitan areas in a single state, California.

- Immigration is also transforming America's social institutions and practices. The top ten source countries for legal (including amnestied) admission in 1989 were Mexico, El Salvador, the Philippines, Vietnam, Korea, China, India, the Dominican Republic, Jamaica, and Iran. Of these, only Filipinos, Jamaicans, and Indians are likely to be proficient in English. Widespread anxiety about linguistic and cultural fragmentation has prompted referenda establishing English as the official language in California and a number of other states. Bilingual education is a major curricular issue in public education, and dozens of languages must be used in New York City schools. The influence of Hispanic and Asian voters is growing. Certain sectors of the economy now depend almost wholly upon immigrant workers, legal and illegal.

- The politics of immigration have grown ever more complex and intense, while the pace of immigration policy formation has greatly accelerated. After enacting the Johnson Act of 1921, it took Congress over thirty years to move to the McCarran-Walters Act of 1952, thirteen more years to abandon the national origins–based quota system, and thirteen more to eliminate the hemispheric quotas in favor of a single, worldwide quota. Just since 1980, in contrast, Congress has enacted the first comprehensive regulation of refugee and asylum admissions, a sweeping set of measures directed at the problem of illegal migration, and a far-reaching scheme for the prevention of admissions based upon so-called sham marriages. Moreover, it will probably restructure the entire system of legal immigration in the early 1990s.

- During the 1980s, a cosmopolitan legal culture began to permeate the parochial bureaucratic culture of the Immigration and Naturalization Service (INS) as never before. For reasons that are not altogether clear, immigration law is shedding its shadowy reputation as a backwater legal specialty, of interest largely to marginal, low-status practitioners and the INS. More lawyers of demonstrated professional competence and high repute have been attracted to the private, "public interest," and government sectors of immigration practice. Some of the elite law schools are offering academic and clinical courses in immigration law for the first time. Legal scholars have begun to scrutinize the INS and immigration law more carefully.

- Most important, the federal courts are now intimately involved in supervising INS administration of the immigration laws. As a growing number of immigration cases have reached the federal courts in recent years, the courts have invalidated statutory provisions and INS procedures and policies with an alacrity that would have astonished the immigration lawyers of an earlier generation. Recently, for example, a lower court in California struck down on constitutional grounds a federal statute regulating access to citizenship (*Elias v. U.S. Department of State,* 1989). Such a ruling is remarkable because it contradicts a long tradition of judicial deference to Congress in matters of immigration policy in general and access-to-citizenship policy in particular, a tradition that the Supreme Court strongly reaffirmed during the 1970s.[2]

• The role of the courts in immigration and nationality law has grown significantly during the 1980s, bringing those areas closer to the mainstream of American law and government, where the symbolic and political power of courts and the robustness of judicial review have long been well established (Schuck 1989c). In this, of course, the American experience differs fundamentally from that of France and other continental nations. But given the novelty and fragility of the new judicial role in the immigration and nationality areas, its continuation cannot be taken for granted even in the United States (Schuck 1984).

2. THE SYSTEM OF IMMIGRATION AND REFUGEE CONTROL

A. The Legal Admissions Program

Broadly speaking, the immigration law authorizes the admission of three categories of aliens: (1) "immigrants" enjoy the status of permanent resident aliens; (2) "nonimmigrants" are admitted under restrictions as to the purposes and duration of their visit; and (3) "paroled" aliens are permitted to enter but legally are treated as if they stood at the border seeking entry. In this paper, I shall be concerned primarily with the first category, although the others are important to some of the themes that I shall develop: nonimmigrants because after admission many are "visa abusers" and thus become illegal; and paroled aliens because their legal status is a highly vulnerable and peculiar one.

The law permits the INS to admit 270,000 immigrants annually under the numerical quotas, this number being allocated among six hierarchically structured "preference" categories. As a formal matter, 80 percent of these preference admissions are based upon family relationships, and the remaining 20 percent are based upon labor skills. (In fact, many of the labor preferences go to people with relatives in the United States.) Most of these people were already in the United States on nonimmigrant visas; once there, they adjusted status to that of legal permanent resident.

However, the majority of legal admissions (811,000 in 1989) were admitted without regard to this preference system. Of this group more than 25 percent (217,500) were admitted as "immediate relatives" of U.S. citizens (their spouses and fiancees, parents, if the citizen is over twenty-one, and unmarried minor children). About ninety-five thousand were admitted as the result of adjustments-of-status by people who had come to the United States earlier as refugees and asylees, including twenty-eight hundred Cuban and Haitian entrants and eighty-six hundred Amerasian children born in Vietnam (as well as their families and guardians). Also, 10,500 were long-term residents admitted under the so-called registry provision (a periodically updated, pre-IRCA amnesty program) and over 480,000 aliens who had resided in the United States continuously and illegally since 1982 were granted permanent residence in their first year of eligibility under the IRCA amnesty provisions. The remainder are so-called special immigrants; this category includes former employees of the U.S. government, ministers and their families, and several miscellaneous groups.

Under the legal admissions program, each country is limited to twenty thousand quota admissions (based on the individual's place of birth) per year, and the waiting lists for the leading source countries (Mexico, the Philippines, Korea) are quite long, especially for certain preference categories. The regional origins of aliens coming to the United States under the legal admissions program is now dominated by Asia (43 percent), and to a lesser extent the Caribbean and Central America (22 percent). Europe accounts for about 10 percent and Africa 3 percent.

In 1986 Congress adopted what it then characterized as a "one-time" special preference for immigrants from countries, notably the British Isles, that were "adversely affected" by the 1965 law abolishing the system of national origins quotas (the OP-1 or "Berman" program). This change reflected the political influence of Senator Ted Kennedy, then Speaker of the House Tip O'Neill, and Irish-American groups. Since then, it has been enlarged and extended. This program is most unfortunate; it marks a return (albeit a limited one) to the long-discredited principle of preference based on national origins.

Proposals for the reform of the legal admissions program abound, and it seems likely that Congress will adopt significant changes in the near future. Recently a remarkable bipartisan consensus appears to have formed around the principle that the existing preference system, which is dominated by a concern for family unification, should be replaced by a new system that accords greater weight to labor market considerations. Although the details, numbers, and relative weightings remain very much in dispute, Congress will probably adopt a point system modeled on Canada's. It will give some preference to individuals who promise to invest in enterprises that will employ new workers, and will admit some "independent" or "new seed" immigrants who possess desired occupational, educational, and English-language skills but who lack preferential family links in the United States. In addition, Congress may establish an overall cap on admissions that would constrain one or both of the two major groups that are admitted outside the statutory ceiling: refugees and immediate relatives of citizens (Rasky 1989).

B. The Enforcement and Amnesty Programs under IRCA

The 1986 act adopted four major new programs. A brief description of each of the programs, and their current status, follows.

General Legalization. IRCA permitted aliens who had entered the United States prior to 1 January 1982 and resided there in unlawful status since that date to apply for temporary legal resident status by 5 May 1988. More than 1.75 million illegal aliens applied for this status. About 480,000 amnestied aliens were granted permanent residence in 1989, and it is anticipated that almost all of them will ultimately receive it. Virtually all of the applicants came from a few Latin American countries; almost 75 percent were Mexicans, and only four other countries (El Salvador, Haiti, Guatemala, and the Philippines) supplied more than 1 percent of the total. Under the program, aliens receiving the temporary legal status were required to apply for permanent resident status within certain time periods, demonstrating "basic citizenship skills," or they would revert to undocumented, hence deportable, status. The program is now in this "second stage."

Pressures are already building to establish another amnesty program, in addition to the IRCA programs and the registry program. Millions of undocumented workers continue to live and work in the United States under the same troubling circumstances that necessitated the earlier amnesty programs. Many of these individuals are immediate relatives of aliens who are already in, or will acquire, legal status, but were statutorily ineligible for amnesty for one reason or another. In February 1990, the INS adopted a "family fairness" program that relieves these relatives from certain risks of deportation but does not provide them with legal resident status. Political resistance to a new amnesty will be very strong.

Agricultural Labor. In the long debate over immigration reform during the 1970s and 1980s, the agricultural labor provisions became the key element in the political compromise that finally made IRCA possible by assuring a reliable labor supply to western growers. Although special immigration programs addressed to the need for agricultural labor had been on the books for decades, IRCA made three major changes. First, it revised and expanded the

H-2 program for admitting temporary workers to perform agricultural work. Second, it permitted aliens who had worked in the United States on perishable commodities for a specified period of time prior to 1 May 1986 to apply for temporary legal resident status as "special agricultural workers" (SAWs). Third, it authorized the entrance of additional "replenishment agricultural workers" (RAWs) as temporary residents after 1990 if a farm labor shortage develops. Both SAWs and RAWs may become eligible for permanent residence status.

The SAW program, which was negotiated by a handful of people without hearings, studies, or much debate, has become the wild card in the IRCA deck. Its eligibility, benefit, and evidentiary provisions are far more liberal than those in the general legalization program; and its relatively lax documentation requirements have led to persistent allegations of widespread fraud, some of which have been substantiated. No reliable data on the number of SAW eligibles existed when IRCA was enacted. Although the INS expected about six hundred thousand farm workers to apply, more than 1.3 million had done so by the time the application period closed in late November 1988; more than half of them were in California. The vast majority of these applications are likely to be granted. Beginning in 1990, this number will be further enlarged by the influx and eventual legalization of RAWs, who can be brought into the United States to replace the many SAWs who will have left the agricultural sector for more remunerative, less arduous work.

Employer Sanctions. The centerpiece of IRCA's immigration control policy is the employer sanctions program. Modeled on similar programs in some states and foreign countries, employer sanctions were intended to eliminate the principal "pull" factor attracting undocumented workers to the United States. The program was also designed to economize on scarce INS enforcement resources by conscripting employers and recruitment and referral agencies to perform the task of verifying employees' identities and authorization to work.

Implementation of the employer sanctions provision is far from being either complete or effective. In 1989, several years after IRCA's enactment, employer noncompliance due to ignorance and other reasons remained widespread. An estimated 13 percent of the employers were not aware of the law. Between 40 and 50 percent did not clearly understand one or more of IRCA's major provisions, and a large proportion of those who were aware of the law and had hired one or more employees under it had failed to complete the verification documents required for those hired (U.S. General Accounting Office 1990).

Studies conducted by RAND and the Urban Institute indicate that the employer sanctions program is having limited and decreasing effectiveness (Bean, Vernez, and Keely 1989). The INS has proceeded very gingerly, pursuing a policy of employer education and service rather than sanctions. The studies predict that if the agency does not alter this policy, the program will lose its credibility and inspire new waves of illegal entrants. They further find that while IRCA has reduced illegal border crossings below the level that would otherwise occur, the volume of entrants is still large and the demographic composition has changed in ways that create new policy dilemmas. More women and youths are entering (Bean et al. 1990), perhaps presaging longer periods of illegal residence in the United States and a greater utilization of public benefits, both matters of great political sensitivity. Finally, IRCA's initial effectiveness appears to be waning, for several possible reasons: the amnesty program has generated some illegal migration by the families of newly legalized aliens; Congress may repeal or dilute employer sanctions; hopes for a new amnesty are rising among those ineligible for the first one; and the Central American economies are continuing to deteriorate. Finally, it appears that much fraud in documenting employment authorization and identification goes undetected (Stevenson 1990).

Antidiscrimination. In the debates over IRCA, many groups predicted that the new law's employer sanctions would encourage employers to discriminate against job applicants, especially Hispanics, whose national origin or citizenship status made them more likely, as a statistical matter, to be undocumented. These groups also argued that existing remedies for such discrimination were inadequate. To mollify them and address their concerns, IRCA prohibited such discrimination and established a Special Counsel for Immigration-Related Unfair Employment Practices in the Justice Department to investigate and prosecute claims that employers, referrers, or recruiters had engaged in it. These new antidiscrimination provisions are discussed in Lance Liebman's chapter in this volume.

The existence of some job discrimination on the basis of alienage and citizenship status seems clear. In November 1988, several government agencies issued reports on this question. Governor Cuomo's Task Force on Immigration Affairs found that some New York employers were refusing to accept legally valid proof of residency, denying employment to those who experience minor delays in gathering documentation of status, and screening out applicants who look or sound foreign. Testimony to that effect was also heard by New York City's Commission on Human Rights. And a study released in March 1990 found widespread employer violations of the antidiscrimination provisions. The extent of such discrimination and its relationship to employer sanctions, however, remains a matter of some dispute (U.S. General Accounting Office 1990). Still, these findings have triggered a statutorily mandated congressional review of the employer sanctions provisions, which will probably lead to some changes.

C. The Refugee Act of 1980

The Refugee Act of 1980 creates a legal structure for the adjudication of the status of individuals who claim to be refugees. Refugees are individuals who are determined to possess a "well-founded fear of persecution" in their country of nationality or habitual residence "on account of race, religion, nationality, membership in a particular social group, or political opinion" (8 U.S.C. §1101 [a] [42]). Refugees are located outside the United States when they present their claims for protection to American officials. If they are physically present in, or at the border of, the United States when they present their claims, they are considered "asylees." In general, refugees receive more favorable treatment than asylees under American law; the major differences are mentioned below.

Before 1980, the immigration statute authorized the admission of 17,400 refugees annually and required that they have fled persecution in Communist or Middle Eastern countries. These limitations, however, were wholly inadequate to enable the United States to respond flexibly to refugee flows. Because there was no systematic legal process for the admission of refugees, the attorney general sometimes employed his largely discretionary "parole" authority to admit aliens for "emergent" or other "public interest" reasons, which were often deemed to include refugee situations. Dissatisfaction with this nonsystem by both the Congress and the Justice Department led to the enactment in 1980 of legislation designed to regularize this process.

The 1980 act contains five major innovations. First, it adopts a definition of "refugee" that tracks the language of the 1951 Refugee Convention, and establishes a legal duty of "nonrefoulement." (Goodwin-Gill 1983, ch. 4). This is a duty not to deport or return a refugee to any country "if the Attorney General determines that such alien's life or freedom would be threatened [there] on account of race, religion, nationality, membership in a particular social group, or political opinion" (8 U.S.C. §1253[h]). Second, it provides for an annual process of consultation between the president and the relevant congressional committees; this process produces annual refugee ceilings and allocates that number among the regions of the world, although both the numbers and the allocations can be changed to reflect unforeseen circumstances during that year. Third, it establishes a public-private system for providing social welfare benefits to refugees once they have been given legal protection. Fourth, it creates a regular legal status for refugees, one that enables the refugee to adjust to the status of permanent resident alien and eventually to apply for citizenship. Finally, it requires the attorney general to establish a procedure for any alien who is "physically present in the United States or at a land border or port of entry, irrespective of such alien's status, to apply for asylum."

An alien who is found to be a refugee under either program occupies an uncertain legal position initially. His or her refugee or asylee status may be revoked if conditions in the source country change in ways that eliminate the alien's fear of persecution there. Refugees automatically qualify for a variety of federal benefits, but asylees and temporary parolees (a device used to admit some humanitarian cases that cannot qualify as refugees) do not. Both categories' eligibility for state and local public benefits varies with the particular jurisdiction's law.

But in contrast to the understanding in France and other European states, the general expectation under U.S. law is that refugees and asylees will acquire a permanent legal status within a relatively short period of time, perhaps as soon as one year, and will move toward eventual citizenship. Under the 1980 act, refugees must regularize their legal status by adjusting to permanent resident status one year after their arrival if they are otherwise admissible. Asylees who would be admissible may seek to adjust to permanent resident status, but they (unlike refugees) are subject to an annual ceiling of five thousand adjustments. During 1988 Haiti and Cuba accounted for well over a third of the refugee and asylee adjustments but their prominence reflected special provisions of IRCA and is unlikely to continue. Laotian and Iranian adjustments increased sharply, and Vietnamese adjustments increased slightly.

Although the refugee program and the asylum program employ the same refugee definition, they are different in important respects. The refugee program screens and selects people overseas, usually in refugee camps, for resettlement in the United States. In practice, the refugee criteria are applied more loosely in overseas screening than they are in asylum decision making. The statutory "normal flow" ceiling is fifty thousand but the president may increase this after consulting with Congress. The 1989 ceiling is approximately ninety-five thousand. Legislation to provide special treatment for particular groups, such as individuals leaving the Soviet Union, may effectively increase this number.

There are many domestic criticisms of the refugee program. Critics argue that it distorts the refugee definition in the service of the United States's immigration policy rather than serving purely human rights goals; that it favors those fleeing from the Soviet Union and other Communist governments over those fleeing from states with whom the United States seeks friendly relations; that it fails to exert enough pressure on countries' of first asylum such as Thailand to avoid "pushbacks" of refugees; that it encourages those who are resettled in the United States to become dependent upon welfare; and that the program is too small.

The asylum program is quite different. It was essentially an "afterthought" to those who drafted IRCA; the United States had not thought of itself as a country of first asylum—two thousand applications, an all-time high, were pending then—but rather had been accustomed to screening refugees in other countries (Meissner 1988, 60). The 1980 law provides that no more than five thousand asylees per year may adjust to permanent resident status. No sooner had the legislation been signed than the Mariel boatlift occurred, bringing some 125,000 Cubans to south Florida in search of asylum. Other immediate pressures on the new asylum program arose in the wake of the Iranian and Nicaraguan revolutions and an increased flow of migrants from Haiti. An immense backlog of asylum applications quickly developed, to which the U.S. government responded with policies of detention, interdiction on the high seas, and denials of work authorization. Some of these policies were invalidated by the courts (Schuck 1991).

Aliens may apply for asylum at several different points. They may apply to a district director of the INS at any time, whereupon they are interviewed, a State Department opinion may be sought, and an administrative decision is made. INS regulations require that it issue a work authorization unless the asylum claim is deemed frivolous, but the agency has sometimes violated this policy. In addition to this administrative application process, an alien may make an asylum claim to an immigration judge (a Justice Department hearing officer) in the course of exclusion or deportation proceedings. If the claim is denied, the alien may appeal that denial to the Board of Immigration Appeals, an administrative tribunal within the Justice Department, and from there to the federal courts. The lodging of these appeals generally operates as an automatic stay of any deportation order. In 1989, 9,229 asylum applications were granted, while 31,547 were denied (Pear 1990).

From the outset the asylum program has been exceedingly controversial. It has been severely criticized on a number of grounds and from all points on the political spectrum. Some opponents (usually on the Left) argue that the executive branch of the government manipulates asylum decision making in order to support the State Department's foreign policy objectives. They emphasize, for example, that in 1987 INS district directors granted asylum to 2,213 Nicaraguans but to only thirty-nine Salvadorans. They also have challenged the logic of the government's distinction between "economic" migrants and refugees in the context of the massive social dislocations in Central America, as well as the legality of its policies of detention and interdiction, which are designed to discourage asylum seeking. Other critics of the asylum program complain that its protracted procedures lend themselves to abuse by aliens who are not fleeing persecution but who wish to avoid or forestall deportation so that they can work in the United States, and that in fact very few aliens whose asylum claims are denied are actually deported. All critics contend that the system's capacity to distinguish genuine refugees from spurious ones is seriously inadequate.

Congress and the INS have considered a number of changes in the refugee and asylum programs. In late 1989, Congress enacted provisions that would resolve the refugee claims of particular groups—Jews, Ukrainian Catholics or Orthodox, and Evangelical Christians in the Soviet Union, and certain Cambodians, Laotians, and Vietnamese—on a categorical rather than individual basis and on the basis of relaxed eligibility standards (*Foreign Operations Appropriations Act for Fiscal 1990*). Many of these people, especially the Soviet Jews who go first to Israel and are offered permanent resettlement and citizenship there, clearly would not satisfy the refugee definition.

A variant of this approach is the special "extended deferred departure" status established via executive order by the Bush administration for the forty thousand Chinese students present in the United States on 5 June 1989, whose student visas would have expired within the next year. Administration officials pledged that no students would be sent back to China while it was unsafe. Congress found the executive order inadequate and passed a measure that would have allowed Chinese students to remain for an indeterminate period, obtain work permits, and seek permanent-resident status without first returning to China as their visas required. Fearing diplomatic repercussions and insisting that he could provide the necessary relief administratively, President Bush vetoed the measure but provided the relief.

Although these approaches are being proposed as "emergency" measures, the principle that seems to underlie them may be more permanent, systemic, and far-reaching than that. These approaches accept a conception of refugee policy that is more categorical and politicized and less universalistic and individual-centered than the 1980 act appears to have intended. Whether this should be regarded as a fundamental change in the direction of U.S. refugee policy or not depends upon whether one emphasizes the 1980 act's *aspirations* or its practical *implementation*.

An even more categorical approach to reform seeks to create "temporary safe haven" as an additional form of relief designed for so-called humanitarian refugees, people who either might not qualify as refugees under the 1951 convention (and Refugee Act) definition or should qualify but for political reasons are unlikely to be accorded the protection envisioned by the convention. If adopted, the temporary safe-haven status would relieve some of the pressure on asylum policy and protection decisions could be made on a somewhat more rational, less crisis-driven basis, although it would be naive to think that foreign-policy considerations would not—or should not—continue to be relevant to such decisions. But because this proposal has been closely identified with the protection of Salvadorans, it has been made a hostage to the bitter domestic controversy over the U.S. policy in Central America. The recent repression in China has fueled new efforts in Congress to end the political impasse that has blocked this much-needed reform.

Reform of the procedures for adjudicating asylum claims has also become a focus of public discussion. Some of the impetus for reform proposals reflects concern over the growing volume of asylum claims being filed. In 1989, the INS received over 101,000 claims; in July 1990, more than seventy-seven thousand claims, many of them filed years before, were still pending with the INS (Pear 1990). Many additional asylum claims were filed—over twenty thousand in 1989, almost double the 1988 figure—with immigration judges outside of the INS. France and other western European countries have experienced a similar growth in asylum caseload in the last few years.[3]

Much of the reform sentiment, however, focuses less on the efficiency of asylum decision making than on its fairness and accuracy (although these goals are related to efficiency in important ways). The approximately seventy immigration judges who adjudicate asylum claims in the context of exclusion and deportation proceedings, while nominally independent of the INS, are closely linked to the agency by career path, organizational location, and ideology. They also lack special training in refugee law or about the conditions that exist in refugee-generating countries. Most proposals therefore have focused on the need for a corps of asylum adjudicators who would be both more independent of the INS and more expert at asylum determinations.

In April 1988, the INS forwarded to the attorney general proposed asylum regulations that would, among other things, replace the temporary procedures used since 1980 and establish a new group of specially trained asylum adjudicators linked to the INS. This proposal generated fierce opposition by some refugee advocates. In July 1990, the attorney general issued new, substantially revised asylum rules, which won the praise of many of these advocates. The new rules make it somewhat easier for applicants to establish eligibility for asylum by dispensing with the "singled out" requirement, permitting uncorroborated statements by the applicant as evidence, establishing a corps of specially trained asylum officers with access to better documentation of in-country conditions, and allowing these officers to give less weight to State Department recommendations (Pear 1990). The new procedures, however, do nothing to address the problem of asylum-related enforcement delays, and may even make that problem worse.

3. MEMBERSHIP IN THE AMERICAN POLITY

A. The Law of Citizenship

American citizenship can be obtained in three ways. The most common way —citizenship by birth in the United States—reflects the Anglo-American tradition of jus soli and is protected by the Fourteenth Amendment's Citizenship Clause. Although customary exceptions to the jus soli rule exist (e.g., children born on foreign vessels, children of diplomatic personnel), birthright citizenship has been understood to extend to the native-born children of aliens who are in the country illegally or on a nonimmigrant visa.

A second route to citizenship is through naturalization. In 1988, 242,000 individuals naturalized in the United States, a 7 percent increase over the 227,000 who naturalized in 1987, but a 14 percent decrease from the 280,000 who naturalized in 1986. In order to naturalize, a permanent resident alien must have resided in the United States with that status continuously for five years; be of good moral character; demonstrate an ability to speak, read, and write English; and demonstrate a basic knowledge of U.S. government and history. Although the vast majority of naturalizations take place under these general provisions, some people are permitted to use less restrictive procedures. Spouses of American citizens can naturalize after only three years; children who immigrate with their parents can be naturalized more or less automatically (simply by obtaining a certificate) when their parents naturalize; and adopted children of U.S. citizens can also naturalize in that fashion. Certain aliens who served with the American military during past wars may naturalize easily. Some individual or categorical naturalizations are effected by statute.

Several striking facts about aliens' attitudes toward naturalization in the United States should be mentioned. A large number of eligible aliens do not naturalize, and most of those who do naturalize do not apply until well after they become eligible. According to one analysis of the 1980 census, more than 25 percent of the foreign born who had resided in the United States for more than ten years had failed to naturalize. For "Latinos" (the term used in the study), 56 percent had failed to naturalize; even for those who had resided here for more than twenty years, the figure was 44 percent (NALEO study cited in Schuck 1989a). Naturalization rates vary considerably among different ethnic groups. Mexicans and other Central Americans, for example, naturalize at much lower rates than Asians do. In 1987, Asians naturalized on average after seven years of residency. In contrast, only 12 percent of the Canadians and Mexicans who immigrated to the United States during the 1970s had naturalized by the end of 1988 (Immigration and Naturalization Service 1988, xxxvi; North 1985, exhibit 15).

The third route to citizenship is through American parentage. The principle of jus sanguinis is codified in the statute, which identifies a number of parentage categories, sometimes augmented by residency requirements, that confer elibility for statutory citizenship on the child. Over time, these eligibility requirements have generally been liberalized.

Congress has been dissatisified with the slow pace of naturalization, and is considering legislation that would streamline the procedures. That legislation is likely to be adopted in the near future. The principal innovation would be to authorize the attorney general to naturalize administratively rather than through the courts, although the new citizen would be able to have the oath administered by a court. In addition, the legislation would permit courts to intervene to prevent the INS from delaying the processing of naturalization petitions, and would strengthen the position of petitioners appealing INS denials of naturalization. Congress has also recently considered the question of reducing the period of required residency from five to three years, the period in Canada and several European states, but there seems to be little support for this change.

Dual citizenship is increasingly common in the United States as a result of the combination of the American jus soli rule with the jus sanguinis rules of other states. Dual citizenship, although disfavored by the government, is tolerated and legally protected. The major exception is that aliens who wish to naturalize are required to renounce any prior allegiance, which may or may not be effective in terminating that foreign citizenship.

United States citizenship, once acquired, is almost impossible to lose without the citizen's expressed consent. Supreme Court decisions since the 1960s have severely restricted the government's power to denationalize a citizen for reasons of disloyalty, divided allegiance, or otherwise. Today, the government cannot prevail against a birthright citizen unless it can prove that the citizen specifically intended to renounce his or her citizenship. This standard is difficult to satisfy—as it should be. Relatively few denationalization proceedings are brought and the number of successful ones appears to be declining. Denaturalization proceedings against citizens who procured citizenship by misrepresenting their backgrounds or through other illegality are largely directed against Nazi and Soviet persecutors, and the standards that the government must satisfy to prevail are quite demanding (*Kungys v. United States* 1988).

B. The Rights of Aliens and Citizens

The distinction between legal resident aliens and citizens in the United States is today essentially a political one. There are few differences in the legal rights that the two statuses bear and those differences are relatively inconsequential.[4] Lance Liebman's chapter in this volume analyzes the constitutional standards that apply to alienage distinctions in American law.

The result is that legal resident aliens enjoy almost all of the significant rights and obligations that attach to American citizenship. Elsewhere I have referred to this fact as a "devaluation" of citizenship. By reducing resident aliens' incentives to acquire citizenship, I suggest, this devaluation may partly explain the low naturalization rates of recent years. I also argue, however, that this more uniform treatment of legal aliens and citizens is probably on balance a good thing for American society.

Be that as it may, legal aliens do suffer five disadvantages that are worth noting. Although none of these is trivial, only two of them are likely to interfere seriously with the quality of life or opportunity of many aliens. Three of the differences are political in nature; they involve the right to vote, the right to serve on juries, and the right to run for certain high elective offices and to be appointed to some high (and not-so-high) appointive ones. Each of these restrictions seems to be premised on one or more of the following assumptions: that aliens' political socialization is too fragmentary and embryonic to be trusted in matters of public choice; that confining political participation of this kind to citizens carries an important symbolic message about the value and significance of full membership; and that exclusion of aliens from such participation encourages them to naturalize as soon as possible. It is not obvious that these propositions are correct, nor does it follow that even if they were correct they would justify the kinds of restrictions being imposed. Modern tradition and political inertia, more than sound policy, account for their durability.

Although aliens enjoyed the franchise in many states during the nineteenth century, only U.S. citizens may exercise it today. This restriction certainly limits the political influence of aliens as a collectivity and as members of smaller national or ethnic groups with distinctive political identities and interests, but it is unlikely to be of great concern to an individual alien. Service on federal and many state juries is also withheld from aliens, but the practical consequences of this exclusion seem slight; indeed, many citizens regard such service as a burdensome chore of which they would just as soon be relieved. (It is, after all, commonly called "jury *duty*.")

Limitations on aliens' access to government employment present a somewhat more complex pattern. I see no merit in denying voters or elected officials the opportunity to place aliens in the kind of high elective or appointive offices from which the law sometimes bars them regardless of their ability. As a practical matter, however, few of them are likely to seek such positions. But the same cannot be said of aliens' exclusion from all federal civil service positions and from many state government jobs that are thought to involve a "political function." At a time of growing public employment, these restrictions impose a far more onerous burden on aliens, presumably affecting a significant number of individuals.

A fourth important disadvantage for many aliens concerns their lesser ability to reunite with their family members who wish to come to the United States for permanent residence. Citizens are entitled to a preferred immigration status for "immediate relatives" without regard to numerical quotas, and for their siblings and their adult children under the numerical quota system. In contrast, the spouses and unmarried children of resident aliens qualify for only a numerically limited preference, and their siblings receive no preference at all.

The other important inequality concerns the right to remain in the United States. Citizens, whether through birthright or naturalization, are not subject to deportation, but resident aliens are. The deprivations that deportation of a long-term resident can wreak upon aliens and their families and friends are potentially enormous. Although the Supreme Court has repeatedly stated that deportation is not punishment and therefore does not implicate the constitutional guarantees that surround the imposition of criminal sanctions, there can be no question that, as Justice Douglas put it, deportation "may deprive a man and his family of all that makes life worthwhile." My point, then, is certainly not that deportation is inconsequential. It is that an alien's actual risk of deportation is far lower than might be suggested by the INS's broad discretion in interpreting and applying the numerous grounds for deportation specified in the statute.

Although the immigration statute contains many grounds for deportation, a resident alien who does not engage in patently criminal behavior actually faces almost no risk of being expelled. The "due process" principle of the U.S. Constitution requires government to observe high standards of procedural fairness in adjudicating individual rights, including the qualified right of deportable aliens to remain. Aliens can also invoke extensive procedural safeguards established by statute, regulation, and judicial decision.

Statistically speaking, the risk that a long-term resident alien who has not been convicted of a serious crime will be deported is vanishingly small. In 1988, for example, fewer than twenty-three thousand aliens were formally deported out of a legal resident-alien population totalling many millions of people, and virtually all of those deportees were either illegal entrants, out-of-status nonimmigrants (i.e., temporary visitors), violators of narcotics laws, or convicted criminals. A far larger number (914,000) were expelled without formal proceedings, but almost all of these fell into the same categories (Immigration and Naturalization Service 1989, tables 60 and 66). Relatively few of those deported or expelled have been in the United States for a significant period of time (Immigration and Naturalization Service 1985, 194). In practice, moreover, the INS fails to execute many of the deportation orders that it obtains (U.S. General Accounting Office, October 1989). As a practical and legal matter, then, the right of long-term resident aliens to remain in the United States is almost as secure as a citizen's.

To say that the differences in treatment between citizens and permanent resident aliens are relatively small, however, is not to justify them. As these differences continue to diminish, as I think they generally will (Schuck 1984), the ones that remain will become increasingly obtrusive and difficult to defend. Two differences of this kind have come to light very recently: a two-hundred-year-old statute that requires owners and captains of most commercial fishing boats to be U.S. citizens (Bishop 1989),[5] and a 1988 amendment to the tax law depriving a resident-alien surviving spouse of an automatic marital deduction upon the death of the other spouse (*Technical and Miscellaneous Revenue Act of 1988*, §5033). Both are controversial and are under challenge. A resident alien's access to public benefits—cash assistance, Medicaid and Medicare, housing subsidies, food stamps, and social services—is today essentially the same as a citizen's. A recent study finds that although immigrant households are only slightly more likely to receive welfare than native households (9 percent versus 8 percent), those from certain countries have very high welfare rates; among female-based families from Cuba, the Dominican Republic, and Mexico, the rate is about 30 percent or higher (Borjas 1990).

A far more complicated and politically divisive question concerns the access of undocumented aliens to those benefits. As a purely legal matter, many undocumented aliens are entitled to claim a wide range of public benefits even under federal law. Lance Liebman's chapter in this volume describes these entitlements, and I wish to add only two points here. First, the local politics of communities with very large foreign-born populations has proved to be quite sympathetic to aliens' interests. Some of those cities have expanded the public benefits and other legal protections available to illegal aliens despite the federal government's opposition. During 1989, for example, New York City adopted a law that protects undocumented aliens, and not just legal ones, against discrimination in public services generally (Lubasch 1989),[6] while Los Angeles established a formal program to find jobs for day laborers, including those who are barred from working in the United States (Mydans 1989).

Second, the extent to which undocumented aliens actually *use* public benefits is difficult to document. The evidence that does exist suggests that many undocumented aliens who are not legally entitled to claim public benefits actually receive them, while many of the undocumented aliens who are entitled to such benefits do not in fact claim them (Lyndon B. Johnson School of Public Affairs 1984). In addition, of course, undocumented workers contribute direct and indirect taxes to public coffers.

Any realistic accounting of the burden that undocumented aliens impose on public services, especially hospitals and schools, must take note of two facts. Undocumented aliens, even more than legal ones, tend to concentrate in a relatively small number of communities, yet these high-impact communities are not the governmental units that receive the taxes that undocumented aliens pay. Thus even if undocumented aliens contribute more to the public fisc than they consume, local communities are still likely to be net losers fiscally. This local fiscal effect will be magnified if, as appears to be the case, the demographic mix of the undocumented population is changing, with a growing proportion being mothers of young children who tend to be more intensive consumers of public services.[7]

CONCLUSION

Immigration policy in the United States is now at a crossroad. Fundamental choices are about to be made concerning the shape and magnitude of legal migration to the United States. The traditional balance between family unification and labor market considerations, and the total number of new admissions that should be absorbed by American society, are now prominent public issues. Although IRCA's far-reaching policy changes directed at illegal migration are only a few years old, the continuing flow of undocumented workers raises anew the traditional concerns about national sovereignty, ethnic conflict, and labor market effects. The refugee and asylum programs are also extremely controversial because of their linkages to illegal migration, foreign policy goals, and governmental budget demands.

Only in the area of citizenship does policy seem to be settled. That stability, however, may be deceptive. At the margins of citizenship policy are fundamental disputes about the rights that ought to be accorded to individuals with varying degrees of membership in American society. And while the courts have largely settled this question with respect to citizens and permanent resident aliens, the status of undocumented aliens—especially after a reasonably generous amnesty has been concluded—remains a bitterly contested one that will surely intensify in the years ahead.

NOTES

1. The material in this part is taken from Schuck (1989b), where sources can be found, and Schuck (1991). The immigration data are found in Immigration and Naturalization Service, *1989 Fiscal Year Immigration Statistics: Advance Report* (April 1990).
2. The leading case on the scope of judicial review is *Fiallo v. Bell*, 430 U.S. 787 (1976), and the leading case on access to citizenship is *Rogers v. Bellei*, 401 U.S. 815 (1971). As discussed in part 3, the courts have been far less deferential with respect to congressional efforts to denationalize United States citizens.
3. Between 1987 and 1988, the number of asylum applications received in France increased from over twenty-three thousand to almost thirty thousand (Martin 1989, table A). The growth in Switzerland was from just under eleven thousand to almost seventeen thousand (Martin 1989, table B).
4. The discussion that follows, and the sources for that discussion, are more fully elaborated elsewhere (Schuck 1989a).
5. An appellate court has granted a temporary injunction against the statute's enforcement pending a decision on its constitutionality.
6. The bill also covers discrimination in housing and employment, although undocumented aliens are expressly excluded from the protections relating to employment.
7. See, for example, Bean et al. (1990; changing demographics); U.S. General Accounting Office (February 1989; documenting burdens on Miami social services); Belkin (1989); and Schmalz (1989).

REFERENCES

Books and Articles

Bean, F., G. Vernez, and C. Keely. 1989. *Opening and Closing the Doors: Evaluating Immigration Reform and Control.* Washington, D.C : Urban Institute.

Bean, F., T. Espenshade, T. M. White, and R. Dymowski. 1990. "Post-IRCA Changes in the Volume and Composition of Undocumented Migration to the United States: An Assessment Based on Apprehensions Data." In F. Bean, B. Edmonston and J. Passel, eds., *Undocumented Migration to the United States: IRCA and the Experience of the 1980's.* Washington, D.C.: Urban Institute.

Belkin, L. "Wave of Poor Immigrant Children Puts New Strain on Social Services." *New York Times*, 29 January, 1, col. 4.

Bishop, K. "Eighteenth-Century Law Snares Vietnamese Fisherman." 1989. *New York Times*, 26 November, A1, col. 2.

Borjas, G. 1990. *Friends or Strangers: The Impact of Immigrants on the U.S. Economy*. New York: Basic.

Goodwin-Gill, G. S. 1983. *The Refugee in International Law*. Oxford: Clarendon.

Immigration and Naturalization Service of the United States. 1985. *1984 Statistical Yearbook of the INS*. Washington, D.C.: U.S. Government Printing Office.

———. *1987 Statistical Yearbook of the INS*. 1988. Washington, D.C.: U.S. Government Printing Office.

———. *1988 Statistical Yearbook of the INS*. 1989. Washington, D.C.: U.S. Government Printing Office.

———. *1989 Fiscal Year Immigration Statistics: Advance Report*. April 1990. Washington, D.C.: U.S. Government Printing Office.

———. *1989 Statistical Yearbook of the INS*. 1990. Washington, D.C.: U.S. Government Printing Office.

Lubasch, A. "Bill to Safeguard Rights of Aliens Passed by Panel." 1989. *New York Times*, 20 June, B 3, col. 1.

Lyndon B. Johnson School of Public Affairs. 1984. *The Use of Public Services by Undocumented Aliens in Texas*. Policy Research Project Report number 60.

Martin, D. 1989. *Reforming Asylum Adjudication: On Navigating the Coast of Bohemia*. Report to the Administrative Conference of the United States.

Meissner, D. 1988. "Reflections on the Refugee Act of 1980. In D. Martin, ed., *The New Asylum Seekers: Refugee Law in the 1980's*. Boston: Kluwer Academic Publishers.

Mydans, S. 1989. "Los Angeles Project Aids Illegal Aliens in Challenge to U.S." *New York Times*, 26 October, A1, col. 1.

North, D. 1985. *The Long Gray Welcome: A Study of the American Naturalization Program*. NALEO Educ. Fund.

Pear, R. 1990. "U.S. Issues Asylum Rules Praised as Fairer to Aliens." *New York Times*, 19 July, A16, col. 5.

Rasky, S. 1989. "Senate Debates Overhauling the Laws Governing Legal Immigration." *New York Times*, 13 July, A18, col. 3.

Schmalz, J. 1989. "Miami Students: Future's Hope, Today's Crisis." *New York Times*, 21 March, A1.

Schuck, P. 1984. "The Transformation of Immigration Law." *Columbia Law Review* 84:1.

———. 1989a. Membership in the Liberal Polity: The Devaluation of American Citizenship. In W. Brubaker, ed. *Immigration and the Politics of Citizenship in Europe and North America*. Lanham, Md.: University Press of America.

———. 1989b. "Introduction: Immigration Law and Policy in the 1990's." *Yale Law & Policy Review* 7:1–6.

———. 1989c. "The Civil Liability of Judges in the United States." *American Journal of Comparative Law* 37:655.

———. 1991. "The Emerging Political Consensus on Immigration Law." *Georgetown Immigration Law Journal* 5:1.

Stevenson, R. 1990. "Growing Problem: Aliens with Fake Documents." *New York Times*, 4 August, 8, col. 1.

U.S. General Accounting Office. February 1989. Report B-234489.

———. October 1989. Report B-232893.

———. 1990. Report B-125051.

Cases, Statutes, Regulations

Elias v. U.S. Department of State, 721 F. Supp. 243 (N.D. Cal. 1989).

Fiallo v. Bell, 430 U.S. 787 (1976).

Kungys v. United States, 485 U.S. 759 (1988).

Rogers v. Bellei, 401 U.S. 815 (1971).

Foreign Operations Appropriations Act for Fiscal 1990, Pub. L. No. 101–167, 103 Stat. 1261–1264 (1989).

Refugee Act of 1980, Pub. L. No. 96–212, 94 Stat. 102 (1980).

— 8 U.S.C. §1101 (a) (42); I.N.A. §101 (a) (42).

— 8 U.S.C. §1253 (h); I.N.A. §243 (h).

Technical and Miscellaneous Revenue Act of 1988, Pub. L. No. 100–647, 102 Stat. 3342 (1988).

16

HISTORIC ELEMENTS OF THE POLITICS OF NATIONALITY IN FRANCE (1889–1989)

André-Clément Decouflé

The history of the politics of French nationality—its substance and successive orientations—is not well known.[1] There are at least two key explanations for this.

The first explanation is found in French researchers' traditional lack of interest in studying public policy and evaluating its effects, although this observation should be qualified in more recent times for certain policy areas (for example, labor; see Decouflé 1989).

The second explanation is doubtless that nationality policy, more than other policy areas, has traditionally been considered only in legal terms. This limited view certainly diminishes its importance. G. Noiriel urges those studying foreign populations to use "analytical devices less faithful to legal logic" (1988, 50) than to history, but he is reassuring about the legal aspects. For example, Noiriel points out that now a foreigner in France is officially subject only to a permit requirement (residence permit, work permit, etc.) and the code (of naturalization law).

We must clarify for American readers, but also for our own benefit, an essential feature of French treatment of nationality. In the United States and Canada access to nationality (obtaining both naturalization and full citizenship) naturally follows from being an immigrant—a foreigner settled in the country in question. In France, access to nationality[2] comes principally from being an "outsider," a nonnational (foreigner or stateless person).

In fact, in at least two situations French law allows a foreigner to become French without any residency requirements or proof of adoption of the "habits and customs of France" (for example, by proving a fair knowledge of the French language): thus a foreigner marrying a French person who lives outside of France and continuing to live in his/her own country can become French. The only requirement this foreigner must fulfill is to prove to the French consulate nearest his/her home that he/she has lived with his/her French spouse for at least six months from the date of their marriage (article 37-1 of the French nationality code). This is very easy to prove, and foreigners obtain French nationality simply by making the proper declaration as soon as the legal requirements have been met. This is also the case with the foreigner who can request French nationality through naturalization, even though living outside of France, if "he is fulfilling a public or private professional activity for the French State or for an organization whose activities benefit the French economy or culture" (article 78-1 of the French nationality code).[3]

Naturalization policy has only recently taken into account two requirements: first, immigration must not be reduced to a strictly legal matter; and second, both the legal and the cultural dimensions of the population concerned—foreigners and immigrants alike—must be considered.

In the day-to-day administration that is so important in these matters, however, old habits remain and new doors must be opened.

The history of naturalization policy in France is recorded in a succession of writings that reflect the main changes that have occurred over two centuries in the nation's demographic patterns, defense politics, and colonial politics—but also in often-forgotten domestic politics. I will limit this discussion to some of the most important developments during the past century, the era in which France, with the 26 June 1889 law, established what is generally considered its first naturalization legislation.[4]

The 1889 law offers a precise example of why we need varied interpretations of laws. This law appears to be completely responsive to the need to "enforce obligatory military service for all French" (Niboyet 1938) by noticeably relaxing the requirements for acquiring French nationality at birth as well as by naturalization. A bit less than twenty years after the 1870 defeat, France had found a way to subject almost every young man born on its soil to military service.[5]

Certainly a preoccupation with national defense was the central factor in the plans of the legislature at the time. We would be wrong, however, not to point out at least two other relevant considerations: colonial developments and domestic politics.

The 1886 census in Algeria clearly showed a European population at least half non-French: Spanish, Maltese, and Italian. This made it necessary to "Frenchify" the non-Muslim people of the colony. The process was already underway under the clauses in the senatus-consultum of 14 July 1865[6] and above all in the 24 October 1870 decree (the Cremieux decree) concerning the automatic naturalization of "Israelites indigenous to Algerian departments."

In addition to colonial politics, domestic politics were a factor. The years from 1886 to 1889 were characterized by the turmoil caused by an authoritative and conservative populist faction rallying around a military figure who turned out to be without substance: General Boulanger.

This movement exacerbated a nationalist push such as France had not seen since the revolutionary wars: the institution of "equality with respect to military service" was a response to fear of the masses by the republican political leaders that was both real and symbolic. They overestimated the power of the masses to bring an insignificant person into power. The 1889 laws (the 26 June naturalization law is in fact inseparable from the 15 July law concerning army recruitment) set the stage for universal conscription; but the law endeavored to avert an internal threat to the republican order rather than to satisfy a desire for revenge against Prussia, by showing fidelity to the revolutionary message at the time of the first centennial celebration of 1789. Exactly the opposite happened in 1940.

The law of 10 August 1927, which further relaxed the conditions for obtaining French nationality through naturalization, authorized "French nationality for French women who marry foreigners, which then permits their children to be declared French" (Lagarde 1975, 28). This law appeared to be filling the demographic gap created by World War I,[7] but it also reflected domestic politics. The period 1926–1927 marked the end of the government's effort to form a "national union," to which Raymond Poincaré, council president, gave his support—after already having been president of the Republic under the "sacred union" of the war years. The 1928 elections witnessed a return to the traditional Right and to its extremely nationalistic and jingoist (for lack of a better word) values.

These elections occurred in the depths of an economic crisis, between the brutal recession of 1926–1927 and the beginning, in 1931, of the interwar period of extensive industrial unemployment. Entire communities of immigrant workers paid the price for this situation. This was particularly the case for the Polish miners in the North and in Pas-de-Calais, who were required to return to their country in large numbers between 1931 and 1936. Janine Ponty, who studied their case thoroughly, drew this heart-wrenching conclusion: "France sent back anyone, at any time," even forcing repatriation, with their Polish parents, of "children who were French by birth,[8] as well as of

Polish people who had just turned in a request for naturalization thinking that this would protect them" (1988, 313–14).

Jingoism (see appendix A) is particularly strong in France in times of national identity crises; we therefore should not be surprised that such jingoism was the hallmark, to an excessive degree, of the Vichy period (1940–1944), an equally important period in the recent history of naturalization policy in France.

In fact, the Vichy regime decreed and put into practice legislation that permitted:

— retroactive withdrawal of French nationality from some beneficiaries of the 10 August 1927 law with the 22 July 1940 law, which was applied to about fifteen thousand people, including many Jews;[9]
— forfeiture of French citizenship, affecting exiles who had been hostile to the regime—especially Gaullist Resistance workers.[10]

History played an unusual trick on France; at one point, being deprived of French nationality was one of the highest forms of French patriotism. We cannot help noticing that these changes, fortunately unique in the history of the law and politics of nationality, were among the primary preoccupations of the political regime that rose out of the 1940 defeat. It was as if what was called for was a reaction to the defeat, which one of the experts on the subject of Vichy, American historian Robert O. Paxton, quite aptly called a "defense xenophobia," inspired by the slogan "France for the French" (1973, 167).[11]

The period immediately following the war is significant for two important advances in law and in practice. The first was the publication of new naturalization legislation (19 October 1945), the essential purpose of which was to restore the prior naturalization law by erasing the crimes that had been committed in its name.[12]

The second was an affirmation of the political desire to associate naturalization policy with immigration policy. This was accomplished:

— in the legislature, by publication of the first major ordinance (2 November 1945) concerning foreigners' entry and residence in France, and in particular by the creation of the National Office of Immigration; and
— in the administration, by joining the Office of Naturalization, henceforth called the Subdepartment of Naturalization, and the Office of Population of the Ministry in charge of Social Affairs and Population, which became responsible for supervising the newly created National Institute for Demographic Studies (INED).[13]

The 1945 ordinances facilitated management of the major migratory phenomena associated with the era of reconstruction and strong economic growth, from 1946 to 1973. In particular they permitted the integration of these foreign communities traditionally dominant in immigration (Italians and Spanish but also Polish and Belgian) by easing access to French nationality.

The period from the postwar era to the 1960s is significant for two major phenomena affecting the politics of nationality. The legislation of 1945 obviously could not anticipate them and in fact would have little influence over them.

The first was the decolonization of the French Empire in Africa and Asia. France had to meet the problems this raised with new laws, such as the 21 July 1962 ordinance about Algerians (who had become independent a few days earlier). The second was the reform of certain fundamental historic principles of our civil law, such as the preeminence of the father's status in the family or the inequality of a child's rights, depending on whether the child is legitimate or natural.

The 1945 legislation had to be brought up to date. In the end, a complete overhaul of the entire naturalization code was begun with the 9 January 1973 law. "[F]or the first time in history, our laws about nationality are being revised at a time when our country is feeling no outside menace" (Lagarde 1973, 431). Furthermore, it should be noted that the new legislation was being instituted (mostly thanks to an important memorandum that went out on 12 February 1974) on the eve of a decisive change in immigration policy: the closing of frontiers to most candidates for entry and settlement in France (July 1974).[14] The migratory aspect of nationality policy was thus brought to the attention of the political powers that be, while in 1973 it had been basically absent from legislative preoccupations.

Domestic politics would, from the 1980s on, reappear in the most traditional way. They reflected the resurgence, for the first time since the end of the war, of a jingoist and racist ideology, in an extremely right-wing political party, the National Front.[15] So, the moderate-right government formed after the spring 1986 legislative elections introduced a proposal to reform the naturalization code. This reform limited the right to acquisition of French nationality to those who could prove to have fulfilled the legal conditions necessary for the exercise of this right (acquisition by declaration and, less frequently, by reintegration), reinstating official preference for those who otherwise had proven a clear desire to become French.

Several provisions of the reform proposal were revised by the State Council (Conseil d'Etat). Generally, the bill was opposed by the leftists. The government, to avoid a debate similar to the one on school issues that the Left had to confront in the period 1983–1984, was adept enough both to withdraw its bill and to create a first in the annals of contemporary France's politico-administrative history: a "committee of wise men," outside of the legislature and independent of the government. It was given the responsibility of "carrying out a thorough study of the problems posed by the possibility of a nationality code reform" and invited, in doing so, to "clarify without a priori a subject that has been debated with passion and to leave no stone unturned" (Commission de la nationalité 1988, 13).

The committee functioned both as "a typical administrative committee" (Schnapper 1988, 10) and as a parliamentary inquiry panel, "American style," going through public hearings, ordering expert testimony, etc. Made up of representatives of the major branches of political persuasion in France (excluding the extreme Left and Right), the committee completed a high-quality, well-thought-out analysis, and succeeded at what might appear to be an impossible task: achieving the consensus of its members on how crucial it was not to undermine the principles that inspire the current French laws of nationality. These principles follow the dictates of two main concerns: that many ways be open to candidates to acquire French nationality, and that there be a strict processing of those applications for nationality. Especially in France, the politics of nationality is constantly threatened by two apparently contradictory temptations: being too discriminatory and being too easy. It is by its very nature the object of "politics for its own sake," both from the Right/extreme Right, always ready to denounce indulgence and carelessness, and from the Left/extreme Left, always happy to uncover strains of racism and jingoism.

Since the French Revolution, the politics of French nationality has always illustrated a singular view of French-style nationalism: belonging to the national community does not just mean supporting patriotic principles but also supporting universal values that were symbolically expressed and historically embodied in the French nation by the Revolution.[16]

This is a specifically French version of the "founding myth" that G. Noiriel discusses (in his 1988 work and in this volume). As a citizen of the French Republic—that is, the universal republic, French-style (see below)—the foreigner who acquires French nationality is stripped of memories or roots; this is of course why for so long his/her integration and "assimilation" were considered problems with an obvious solution, and even more, a solution that was just a matter of time. We now know that the reality is not so simple. Immigration is not a hidden question; it has an historic depth and dimension that determines its future. The "old country" does not realize yet that it is already a new country.

Like the United States, and unlike most other large countries, France welcomes people from the entire world and makes them citizens of a universal republic as well as of France, through the process of allowing them to be French. But the United States grants this universality through its "American way of life": [17] the American naturalization law creates only American citizens, even though any person has the opportunity to become American. The French nationality laws create world citizens at the same time as French citizens—soldiers of the universal republic whose values were expressed by the 1789 Revolution.

In other words, American naturalization creates citizens of a new republic, who build that republic together. French naturalization consecrates citizens, bringing them into a universal republic already completed once and for all at its origin (the mythical origin of the republic, the Revolution).

This reminder also broadens somewhat the traditional problem in analyzing French politics of nationality, usually considered in the context of a nation-state that was slowly formed over centuries and found its final form in the Revolution, the turning point between the old way of building up a nation (the "ancien régime") and the birth of a potentially universal republic.

This traditional view is not completely unfounded; it simply confuses the process of state formation with that of nation formation, all the while giving too much attention to what should have been just a natural transition between the old regime and the republic formed by the Revolution.[18]

It is thus essential to remember that the formation of the French state was completed in 1789, in the sense that from that point on an indispensable alliance was worked out between political power (whatever the symbolic form —kingdom, republic, empire, the "French State" of 1940–1944) and the administrative management of civil society. The principal function of a state should always be to assure its own future. The French nation is, on the other hand, in continual flux, with a long past and extending into the future.[19] Because of the reproductive history of the "original" French population, the nation cannot get along without an influx of nonnative populations to support its growth.[20]

We are therefore not being very daring in conjecturing that the nature and the destiny of naturalization policy in France, as well as the law on which it is based, will continuously be faced with making adjustments: in the future may history not ignore this.

APPENDIX: A FRENCH VERSION OF NATIONALISM—JINGOISM

A "jingo" is someone who, according to the meaning popular in the era of the First Empire and referring to Napoleon's military exploits, expressed "exaggerated and ridiculous beliefs about patriotism and war" (Littre dictionary). As an important journalist from the Paris Commune said, in France we see this type of jingoism traditionally as a "narrow sense of patriotism with neither justice nor common sense" (Dubois 1962, 244). French jingoism is both a caricature of nationalism—in that it is based on hatred and rejection of foreigners, while the true nature of French nationalism is universal openness—and a perversion of patriotism, in the sense that the "values" it supposedly exalts are the most "jingoist," nationalist, and militaristic. One can see just how hard it is to define jingoism by how hard it is to translate the French words.

The best guide through the confused history of traditionalism, patriotism, and jingoism in France from 1870 to 1940 is Henri Guillemin (1974), who reminds us that jingoism was not always restricted to the traditional political Right; there were several periods of leftist jingoism in France, sometimes hidden behind pseudointernationalism. The story of the symbols and values associated with the idea of "nation" is still to come.

Suzanne Citron's recent study (1987) is an interesting contribution to the subject's historiography.

NOTES

1. The last full study on naturalization (general acquisition of French nationality) was by Pierre Depois, in 1942, a somber era in the politics of nationality. Cf., however, R. Robin (1973) and A. Lebon (1987).

2. Remember that until 1983 (law of 12 August 1983) French nationality law made a distinction between a national and a citizen by placing certain restrictions on the newly naturalized person's civil rights. The distinction between a national and a citizen was applied rigorously at the time when France ruled a colonial empire.

3. On the more general problem see G. Noiriel (1988), who highlights effectively the "invisible" character of the traditional image of a French migrant worker. See also Donald L. Horowitz: "In France . . . official classifications have traditionally referred only to 'French' and 'foreigners'. Citizenship should simply make one French. . . . The American Revolution was seen as a beginning, not an end. In some sense, however, French civilization was regarded as completed by the Revolution of 1789, and the immigrant was not necessarily viewed as a prospective citizen in the way he was in the United States."

4. Strictly speaking, it wasn't until the 19 October 1945 ordinance that we had a nationality code conforming to the typical definition of the term. The 1889 law can, however, be considered as a nationality code before the 1945 "letter of the law," as it put forth for the first time a coherent classification of provisions, consisting of a relatively complete group of texts.

5. We are reminded of Niboyet's statements, published on the eve of the second

defeat (1940): "From this era (1889) on, our legislation about nationality was consistently influenced by the issue of military service. We can say that from now on the shadow of the recruiting office hovers over our documents, and is the only explanation and justification for them" (1938, 154).

6. "The foreigner who can prove three years' residence in Algeria can enjoy all the rights of French citizenship" (article 3). The Muslim native is a French national, but not a citizen, (unless he renounces the Muslim religion.)

7. Remember this figure: 1,357,000 military deaths, which represent 27 percent of males aged eighteen to twenty-eight (Guillemin 1974, 154).

8. According to the terms of article 3 of the 10 August law.

9. According to a recent study, 15,154 (Laguerre 1988), which appears to be supported by indirect sources; 14,712 according to the numbers in the statistical report of the Ministry of Justice's service of naturalization for the period 1941–1947 (unpublished—available at the archives of the Subdepartment of Naturalization).

10. The laws of 23 July and 10 September 1940, and 28 February and 8 March 1941. One of the first people to whom the legislation was applied was De Gaulle himself, stripped of French nationality by the law of 23 July by a decree of 8 December 1940 (Journal Officiel of 10 December 1940), which puts the date of deprivation at 2 August 1940, less than six weeks after the 18 June appeal to join the Resistance. A total (according to the same source as in note 9) of 378 people were deprived of their citizenship under the legislation from 1940 to 1943. The archives of the Subdepartment collected and kept the names and the documents relevant to these two sets of "legal" provisions, which were declared null and void in 1945: but even today the Subdepartment is questioned at times by some previous victim of the legislation who wants to know whether he/she is French or not. This is a particularly eloquent example of the possible implications of the principle that states that no one should be ignorant of the law.

11. The French historian Robert Aron, who published in 1954 a first, courageous history of Vichy, explains this "nationalism" delirium well by waxing ironic on the theme of the "homo nationalis" of Vichy and his companions, the "virgo nationalis" and the "mater nationalis" (Aron 1954, 237).

12. Certain lawyers seem to want, even now, to minimize or even erase the significance of the Vichy politics concerning this subject: "We had to end this xenophobic excess from the preceding era," wrote one of them soberly (Lagarde 1975, 28); the 1945 ordinance, another noted, is, among other objectives, "destined to remedy certain xenophobic excesses of the interwar era" (Mayer 1987, 529). Yvon Loussouarn and Pierre Bourel (1988, 814) are the only contemporary authors to clarify the necessary references. Remember that the 1940–1941 legislation was not secret legislation applied by a shadowy bureaucracy—it was legislation that the administration applied, at least at first, with zeal, and publicized through pamphlets and newsletters "from the new France," etc.

13. Even though the Subdepartment of Naturalization has been, since 1945, the main naturalization agency, it is not the only administrative institution involved. The ministerial services of the Ministry of Justice (Chancellerie) have a prominent role in creating nationality laws and controlling some of the applications. The Ministry of the Interior, mostly through the intermediary of police headquarters, plays a

decisive role in the preliminary investigation of applications for naturalization. The Ministry of Foreign Affairs is also expected to take care of certain aspects of naturalization. We are far from the standardized treatment of applications that (at least on paper) characterizes American and Canadian law.

14. Remember that similar measures were taken at the same time by West Germany (November 1973) and Belgium (August 1974).

15. It is not surprising that the National Front's slogan with respect to nationality, "To be French you've got to earn it," copies "word-for-word a 1930's slogan taken up by Raphael Alibert, Vichy's prime minister of "justice" in July 1940 (*Le Journal des Débats* 1940), justifying the only law that ever established the criteria for withdrawing nationality from naturalized citizens" (Laguerre 1988, 3). Donald Horowitz (1989) points out, with good reason, that in spite of the racist history of some of its states, the United States has never had a political party that ever came close to the National Front.

16. It is upsetting to discover, in the *Journal Officiel* of 1976, a reproach like this about American nationalism: "The Americans who have not been to Europe yet will not be able to avoid, after walking through the international displays (of the 1876 Philadelphia Expo), confirming their jingoist idea that the Yankee is a universal being, superior to all others" (cited by Littre as an example of his definition of *jingoist* in the *Dictionnaire de la langue française*).

17. This expression is sometimes misunderstood by the French, who see in it the generic image of a civilization ruled by the dollar. Alexis de Tocqueville, to whom the French must refer when we want to understand the United States, clearly explained in 1831: "The idea of the possibility of doing better, of a successive and continuing improvement of social conditions, is impressed on him (the American) constantly, from every direction" (1865, 233).

18. Remember that Tocqueville, quite some time ago, refuted this illusion (1865).

19. Well before Fernand Braudel, whose works are required reading on this subject, Charles Seignobos, a classic and somewhat outdated historian, clearly expressed a subtle association between the nation's debt to immigration and the universalist tradition of the French concept of belonging to a nation:

> The French nation is more heterogeneous than any other European country; it's a truly international mix of people. This explains the international orientation of the French spirit and the universal character of French literature. In this mixture of peoples, who have nothing in common, national unity could not come naturally from shared origins, customs, or language. There has never been a common law or a common language for everyone, and only someone who knew nothing of anthropology would speak of a "French race." France has therefore never had ethnographic or linguistic boundaries. Its boundaries are only geographic and political; they have been formed slowly and often accidentally. (Seignobos 1946, 3)

20. This is an unresearched issue. The only example of a strictly indigenous reproduction of a French population is in the French community of Quebec, between the middle of the eighteenth century and the end of the 1960s. This was "nurtured" by spectacular growth during the "baby boom," which ended with the arrival, in the 1960s, of the consumer society associated with an advanced system of social services. Quebec thus found itself confronted by a new challenge: to encourage francophone immigration (see the Entente between France and Quebec on 9 July

1989, which gives preferential treatment to "French nationals or foreigners normally residing in France, for temporary or permanent entry into and employment in Quebec").

REFERENCES CITED

Aron, R. 1954. *Histoire de Vichy, 1940–1944*. Paris: Fayard.

Braudel, F. 1988. *L'identité de la France*. Paris: Arthaud-Flammarion.

Citron, S. 1987. *Le mythe national*. Paris: Editions ouvrières.

Decouflé, A. C. 1989. *Quarante ans d'histoire des politiques de l'emploi en France (1946–1986)*. Vigneux: Editions Matrice.

Depoid, P. 1942. *Les naturalisations en France (1870–1940)*. Paris: Imprimerie nationale.

Dubois, J. 1962. *Le vocabulaire politique et social en France de 1869 à 1872*. Paris: Larousse.

Commission de la nationalité. 1988. *Etre français aujourd'hui et demain*. Paris: Union Générale d'Editions.

Guillemin, H. 1974. *Nationalistes et nationaux (1870–1940)*. Paris: Gallimard, Collection "Idées."

Horowitz, D. L. 1989. Europe and America: a comparative analysis of "ethnicity." *Revue européene des migrations internationales* 5, no. 1: 47–61.

Lagarde, P. 1975. *La nationalité française*. Paris: Dalloz.

———. 1973. La renovation du code de la nationalité par la loi du 9 janvier 1973. *Revue critique de droit international privé* 112, no. 3: 431–69.

Laguerre, B. 1988. Les "denaturalisés" de Vichy. *Vingtième siècle* 20: 3–16.

Lebon, A. 1987. Attribution, acquisition, et perte de la nationalité française: un bilan, 1973–1986. *Revue européene des migrations internationales* 3, nos. 1 and 2: 7–34.

Loussouarn, Y., and Pierre Bourel. 1988. *Droit international privé*. Paris: Dalloz.

Mayer, P. 1987. *Droit international privé*. Paris: Montcrestien.

Niboyet, J. P. 1938. *Traité de droit international privé français*, vol. l, *Sources; Nationality; Residence*. Paris: Sirey.

Noiriel, G. 1988. *Le creuset français*. Paris: Le Seuil.

Paxton, R. O. 1973. *La France de Vichy*. Paris: Le Seuil.

Ponty, J. 1988. *Polonais méconnus*. Paris: Publications de la Sorbonne.

Robin, R. 1973. Bilan de dix années de naturalisation (1962–1971). *Revue française des affaires sociales* (January–March): 39–56.

Schnapper, D. 1988. La commission de la nationalité, un instance singulière. *Revue européene de migrations internationales* 4, nos. 1 and 2: 9–28.

Seignobos, C. 1946. *Histoire sincère de la nation française*. Paris: P.U.F.

Tocqueville, A. de. 1865. *Mélanges. Fragments historiques*. Paris: Michel Lévy.

17

IMMIGRATION STATUS AND AMERICAN LAW: THE SEVERAL VERSIONS OF ANTIDISCRIMINATION DOCTRINE

Lance Liebman

1. INTRODUCTION

As it has been through most of its history, the United States is a country of immigration. In the period of greatest immigration, 1880–1930, about six hundred thousand persons entered the United States every year, then about 0.8 percent of the population.[1] Today legally sanctioned immigration brings in about the same number of new residents each year—representing an annual population increase of only 0.25 percent. In 1890, 14 percent of the United States population was foreign born. Today the figure is less than 5 percent. In addition, an unknown number of persons is now in the country without legal sanction; sober estimates are between 4 and 6 million (after 2.5 million previously "illegal" persons were legitimized by the Immigration Reform and Control Act of 1986). By one estimate, 130,000 new undocumented aliens enter the country every month.[2] Experts suggest that the United States, with an aging domestic population and a large young population south of its borders seeking economic opportunity, will be employing many persons of Mexican and other Latin American heritage over the next quarter-century.[3] If so, legal rules and institutions will be pressed to accommodate to this economic and social reality.

Immigration into the United States has never been a simple matter. It forms a part of this country's complex history of relationships among a wide variety of ethnic groups: from the Native Americans, French, British, and Dutch of colonial times to today's Vietnamese and Salvadoran arrivals; with black slaves from about 1620 and freed blacks from as early as 1696. Some of our most important and difficult political and legal issues concern the relations among these groups. The series of 1989 Supreme Court decisions concerning employment discrimination (Wards Cove Packing Co. v. Atonio 1989; Martin v. Wilks 1989)—and congressional debate over whether to amend the laws in response to those judicial decisions—is only one example.

Immigration is a key ingredient in the stew that is American group politics and group-based law. Of all the people in the world who might prefer to live in the United States, who will be admitted? What will be their rights if they arrive without permission; if they are legally present but not yet citizens; if they are recent citizens? How do determinations of eligibility for immigration and of the legal rights and responsibilities of different categories of new arrivals affect people already living in the United States? On all these topics, the ground is legally and politically in flux.

2. JOB RIGHTS

A. Citizens and Lawful Aliens

1. Private Employers. Until 1964, United States law did not restrict private employers' decisions about whom to hire.[4] Decisions of government employers—national, state, and local—were subjected to the Fifth and Fourteenth Amendments to the Constitution, assuring due process of law and equal protection of the laws. But even as to public sector jobs, little judicial intervention had taken place.

Enactment of Title VII of the Civil Rights Act of 1964 changed all that. The country undertook massive legal rearrangement of the distribution of jobs among groups, in the process confronting directly such controversial issues as the validity of standardized tests,[5] the "essence" of various jobs,[6] and—most divisive—the use of "affirmative action" or even "reverse discrimination" to alter past results of the job allocation system (Wygant v. Jackson Board of Education 1986; Johnson v. Transportation Agency 1987). Civil rights advocates are now calling on Congress to overturn new decisions by the Supreme Court, most of them decided by a five-to-four vote of the justices, that they believe have undermined this redistribution.

Title VII of the 1964 law prohibits discrimination "because of such individual's race, color, religion, sex or national origin." Title VII's prohibitions against discrimination by race or sex were originally interpreted by the Supreme Court to bar employer use of neutral criteria having an adverse impact on protected groups. Thus an employer could not use a high school diploma requirement or a standardized intelligence test that had the result of reducing the number of blacks hired or a height or strength requirement that reduced the number of women hired unless the job criterion could be shown "to bear a demonstrable relationship to successful performance of the jobs for which it was used."[7]

Courts have been less expansive in interpreting Title VII's provisions regarding national origin. In Espinoza v. Farah Manufacturing Co. (1973), the Supreme Court held, eight to one, that a private employer in Texas could limit hiring to American citizens. In this case, the San Antonio, Texas, employer's workforce was overwhelmingly composed of U.S. citizens of Mexican origin, and the Court left open the possibility that in a different case, a citizenship requirement might be held to have an unlawful impact on the national origin composition of the workforce. The *Espinoza* decision spawned thirteen years of lower-court actions that overturned employer decisions only when direct and intentional discrimination because of national origin could be proved. For example, the courts did not use the "national origin" provision to extend job rights to non–English speaking persons. They allowed employers to require English of prospective employees (Mejia v. New York Sheraton Hotel 1978) and even allowed an employer to enforce a rule prohibiting employees from conversing with each other in Spanish, justifying the rule by the need for non–Spanish speaking supervisors to understand what workers are saying to each other.[8]

IRCA, the 1986 immigration law, provides a new framework for legal consideration of employment discrimination on the basis of national origin. A primary motivation for IRCA was public perception that porous borders were permitting too many unauthorized entries. But the United States political process has also revealed public recognition of the economic contributions of immigrant (even unlawful immigrant) labor, as well as concern and support for recent immigrants legally present in the country. With Hispanic political power growing (especially in the immensely important states of California, Florida, and Texas), Congress is hesitant to take any action perceived as hostile to or discriminatory against recently arrived Spanish-speaking residents. The 1986 law thus represented a compromise between these two strands of public sentiment. As enacted, the law sought tougher enforcement at the borders (though later funding decisions may not have reflected the same congressional commitment); it gave citizenship as a form of amnesty to persons who entered the country unlawfully and were here continuously since 31 December 1981; it sought to discourage hiring of ineligible immigrants by imposing a legal duty on employers to check documents and the possibility of sanctions for employers who fail to do so; and it sought to prevent this new employer duty from resulting in discrimination against lawful aliens.

The latter is a real risk. If an employer can be fined (or even, in some circumstances, imprisoned) for hiring illegal immigrants, what is to prevent employers from taking the easy way out and hiring only citizens (or discriminating against everyone who looks foreign or speaks with a foreign accent)? Discrimination on the basis of race or national origin was already illegal, but discrimination against all aliens may have been lawful.[9] Thus one provision of IRCA, codified at 8 U.S.C. sec. 1324B, declares it to be

an unfair immigration-related employment practice for a person . . . to discriminate against any individual (other than an unauthorized alien) with respect to [employment] . . . (A) because of such individual's national origin, or (B) in the case of a citizen or intending citizen . . . because of such individual's citizenship status.

A new category is therefore devised: "intending citizens."[10] Aliens who declare that they intend to become citizens are legally protected against employment discrimination on the grounds of their current status as noncitizens. In an odd (and interesting) provision, not present in any of the other American antidiscrimination laws, subsection 4 of this law says that the alien can legally be dispreferred if the employer regards the qualifications of the citizen and the alien as "equal."[11] Among the few IRCA cases reported so far is United Latin American Citizens v. Pasadena Independent School District (1987), where a judge ruled that undocumented aliens were likely to prevail on their claim that IRCA was violated when they were terminated for providing false Social Security numbers. The judge said that some of them would turn out to be eligible for citizenship under the amnesty provision in IRCA.

2. Government Employment. Many laws of the United States, the states, and municipal subdivisions have restricted employment to U.S. citizens.[12] In a series of cases, the Supreme Court has held that the U.S. Constitution prohibits many such laws.[13] In re Griffiths (1973) invalidated a state statute that excluded aliens from eligibility for membership in the New York bar.[14] In Sugarman v. Dougall (1973), the Court held that the Fourteenth Amendment prohibited barring aliens from a broad range of state jobs. A similar holding in Hampton v. Mow Sun Wong (1976), based on the due process clause of the Fifth Amendment, invalidated across-the-board bans on hiring aliens for permanent positions in the civil service, while recognizing that there is a compelling governmental interest in barring aliens from some positions. In Foley v. Connelie (1978), the Court held that a state could require citizenship for "important nonelective positions" held by "officers who participate directly in the formulation, execution, or review of broad public policy." Subsequent cases have further defined the parameters of *Foley,* generally limiting the broad holdings of *Sugarman* and *Hampton.* In Ambach v. Norwick (1979), the Court upheld a Connecticut statute prohibiting aliens from teaching in the public schools, although they could teach in private schools or be elected to the school board. In Cabell v. Chavez-Salido (1982), the Court upheld a California statute requiring probation officers and their deputies to be citizens, although an alien could be appointed as chief probation officer, could serve as attorney in a case before the probation board, or could serve as a state superior court judge or Supreme Court justice. In Bernal v. Fainter (1984), the Court struck down a Texas statute that prohibited aliens from becoming notaries public, stating:

> As a general matter, a State law that discriminates on the basis of alienage can be sustained only if it can withstand strict judicial scrutiny, . . . [except for] laws that exclude aliens from positions intimately related to the process of democratic self-government. . . .
>
> [A] State may . . . limit the right to govern to those who are full-fledged members of the political community. . . .
>
> [Aliens can be barred only from offices which] "participate directly in the formulation, execution, or review of broad public policy" and hence "perform functions that go right to the heart of representative government." (Bernal, quoting Sugarman v. Dougall, 1973)

The net effect of these cases would seem to be that aliens are a protected class for purposes of constitutional adjudication, that state rules barring aliens from particular occupations will be scrutinized carefully by courts to see whether it is appropriate that a particular job be restricted to persons with the commitment to the policy that citizenship suggests, and that even federal restrictions are constitutionally dubious unless enacted by Congress and justified by significant national needs.

It is fascinating that these judicial revisions of legal doctrine (like other similar revisions reported later in this paper) occurred in a period of growing national concern over excessive immigration and over illegal immigration. The lesson, it appears, is that nativist and pro–law-and-order sentiments coexist with a positive image of the United States as a nation formed by successive waves of immigration and with the sentiment, so powerful in the recent period, that improper discriminations of all sorts should be combatted by law. The consequence has been the seeming anomaly of statutory changes attempting to discourage illegal entry and domestic judicial decisions making alien status more desirable.

B. Undocumented Aliens

The Immigration Reform and Control Act of 1986 established a new legal regime designed to control illegal immigration by restricting access to employment. Previously, some states had attempted to stop employers from hiring undocumented workers.[15] And federal laws had attempted to bar hiring of undocumented workers in agriculture (e.g., Federal Migrant and Seasonal Agricultural Worker Protection Act).

The 1986 immigration law applies to all employers, regardless of size or industry. It prohibits employers from hiring undocumented workers and provides civil penalties of $250 to $2,000 for each undocumented worker hired. For a "pattern or practice" of violations, a six-month term of imprisonment is possible. Employers are required to ask job applicants for documents but are not required to check the authenticity of the documents they are shown.

IRCA authorized legalization for undocumented aliens in the country continuously since 1981.[16] It thus assures that persons who arrived in 1982 or later will remain in illegal status, as will close relatives or legalized aliens who arrived after 1981. Since the border has not been sealed and the pulls and pushes that have created postwar undocumented migration to the United States, especially from Latin America, continue, it is certain that the United States will have a large undocumented population for many years to come.[17] It is a matter of great significance that employers commit no IRCA offense when they continue to employ an undocumented alien first hired before 1986 but that they commit a crime if they hire a new undocumented alien. Thus the post-1981 arrivals can keep jobs they had before 1986 but cannot legally obtain a new job. They are therefore at the mercy of their current employers, and presumably must accept whatever wages and terms are offered.

Very much uncertain after IRCA are various questions about unlawful immigrants who do work, notwithstanding the statutory policy of seeking to prevent such labor. Sure-Tan v. NLRB (1984), decided prior to IRCA, permitted the National Labor Relations Board to conclude that the NLRA was violated when an employer discriminated against undocumented aliens because of union activity. Since IRCA is such a clear statement that undocumented aliens should not be in the labor force, it is possible to argue that when they do work, labor statutes should not protect them. In the first important post-IRCA case, a federal district judge refused to award back pay to an undocumented alien from India who had worked for Indian-owned motels and had not received the pay to which minimum wage laws entitled him.[18] The judge said that granting such rights would encourage persons to enter the country unlawfully in search of work, and added that because Mr. Patel had had legal training in India, he should have known better than to expect legal relief as an undocumented alien in the United States. But the *Patel* decision was reversed by the court of appeals, which saw no contradiction between granting Fair Labor Standards Act protection to undocumented workers and the purposes of IRCA (see Patel v. Sumani Corp.). The appellate decision said that granting minimum wage protection to illegal immigrants who do work is in fact consistent with the purposes of IRCA:

> [I]t offsets what is perhaps the most attractive feature of such workers—their willingness to work for less than the minimum wage. If the FLSA did not cover undocumented aliens, employers would have an *incentive* to hire them.[19]

The court did not discuss, but was undoubtedly influenced by, the argument that a polity in which human beings are without legal entitlements—to pay, to freedom from harrassment, to safe working conditions, to promised fringe benefits, and to an absence of racial discrimination—is a society tolerating relationships very close to serfdom. Indeed, a strong argument is available that making it criminal for employers to hire undocumented aliens means that offending employers should be liable under all worker protection statutes. Why immunize an employer for violations of the Fair Labor Standards Act or the Occupational Safety and Health Act or the Civil Rights Act because the employer committed the crime of hiring an undocumented worker? IRCA seeks to halt, not encourage, the continuation of work under substandard conditions by employees deterred from complaining.

C. Conclusion

Thus U.S. law now seeks to draw a clear line between persons unlawfully in the country (or lawfully in the country without legal permission to work) and, on the other hand, citizens and aliens authorized to work. Employers may be fined or imprisoned for hiring illegal workers. Regarding their legal employees, private employers must make decisions on bases that do not discriminate according to citizenship or national origin. Government can discriminate in favor of citizens, but only when a job's responsibilities include the "formulation, execution, or review of broad public policy." In practice, as some of the cases show, the distinction between those eligible for work and those ineligible is not very clear. Many "illegal" immigrants, for example, apply for refugee or asylum status, and from the moment of that application are in an uncertain status. Congress has recently considered legislation that would grant a right to work to the forty thousand or more citizens of China now in the United States on student visas.

3. RIGHTS TO GOVERNMENT SERVICES AND BENEFITS

As Schuck and Smith (1985) saw clearly, issues of immigration status are today entwined with legal issues posed by the contemporary welfare state. Once the United States was a giant frontier. Most citizens benefited when immigrants crossed the ocean to labor in the cities or cultivate new land. Indeed, the continent was populated by importing blacks as slaves and whites as indentured workers. Breeding slaves and selling them to work in the West was a major American industry (Morgan 1986). Today, there is no single political consensus. Some believe that, especially with the domestic birthrate low and the population aging, young immigrants contribute to national prosperity by accepting low-wage jobs and by contributing entrepreneurial zeal (Simon 1989). Others see immigrants as rivals for a limited number of desirable jobs and as competitors for the limited supply of pension and medical benefits.

Legislative and judicial consideration of the rights of aliens to various services and benefits reflects these points of view. Some rules result from a sense that immigrants should have to prove themselves before becoming eligible to share in the American bounty. Other outcomes are based on a perception that immigrants contribute to the economy as their predecessors did and that equality of rights among those in the country is an important policy goal.

In reviewing federal policies, the Supreme Court has exhibited substantial deference to Congress. Mathews v. Diaz (1976) held that Congress did not violate the Constitution when it provided that Medicare Part B benefits, which reimburse elderly persons for physicians' expenses, could be extended only to those aliens who have been lawfully admitted and have been in the United States for five years. Writing for a unanimous court, Justice Stevens said that "a legitimate distinction between citizens and aliens may justify attributes and benefits for one class not accorded to the other." He also said that "the class of aliens is itself a heterogeneous multitude of persons with a wide-ranging variety of ties to the country," and that therefore it is reasonable for Congress to have provided that "citizens and those who are most like citizens qualify. Those who are less like citizens do not."[20]

The most controversial development in this field was the decision of the Supreme Court, by a five-to-four vote, in Plyler v. Doe (1982), that Texas violated the federal Constitution when it sought to refuse state payments for the education of children illegally in the country.[21] The majority held that the equal protection clause protects all persons "within [the state's] jurisdiction," whether or not legally present; that because these individuals are not lawful aliens, a law discriminating against them must meet only a test of rationality; but that the Texas law failed that test. Justice Brennan's opinion was eloquent about the policy consequences of denying education to young persons likely to spend their lives within the country:

> This situation raises the specter of a permanent caste of undocumented resident aliens, encouraged by some to remain here as a source of cheap labor, but nevertheless denied the benefits that our society makes available to citizens and lawful residents. The existence of such an underclass presents most difficult problems for a Nation that prides itself on adherence to principles of equality under law.

The law is unconstitutional because of "its costs to the Nation and to the innocent children who are its victims."

The four dissenting justices suggested that as legislators they would vote to educate these children but that the Texas law did not offend constitutional requirements. (It is quite possible that with today's post-Reagan Supreme Court membership, the dissenting position in Plyler v. Doe would be the majority.)

One year later, in Martinez v. Bynum (1983), the Court permitted Texas to deny public education to children who were U.S. citizens but who came to the state for the purpose of obtaining free schooling. This, the Court said, was a requirement imposed neutrally on all children, and thus no special discrimination against these children, whose parents were in Mexico and who sought to stay with relatives or friends in Texas so as to attend school. The consequence apparently is that one can attend school if one comes to Texas for some other purpose but not if one comes specially in search of education.[22]

The most interesting and challenging disputes arise when several government policies point in different directions. One important income support program, AFDC-UP, makes payments to families when parents are unable to obtain work. The program is administered by states, but about half the expenditures are reimbursed by the federal government. Families qualify only if parents are attempting to get work, an effort usually demonstrated by participation in a training and placement program called Work Incentive Program (WIN). When parents are undocumented but children are citizens or legal aliens, the law is clear that the family can get benefits on behalf of the children but not the additional money to support parents that would be available if the parents were citizens or legal aliens. But if the parent does not meet the work-effort test, the entire family is denied benefits. In Doe v. Reivitz (1987) a court of appeals held that the federal and state governments were in violation of the Social Security Act when they denied benefits to these families on the basis of the parents' legal inability to participate in the WIN program. The court decided to prefer Congress's purpose of supporting needy children to its purpose of denying benefits to entire families when the parents are not in compliance (because their immigration status does not permit them to be) with the program's requirements for seeking work.[23]

Essentially, these judicial decisions assign benefit eligibility decisions to the national legislature. Congress has been given broad leeway to draw distinctions between aliens and citizens, and also to subdivide the noncitizen population. Although legal aliens are a protected class for purposes of constitutional interpretation, and discrimination against them must survive strict scrutiny, nonetheless courts have allowed Congress to employ a great variety of arrangements for determining eligibility of lawful aliens under various social welfare programs. These arrangements range from full eligibility to noneligibility and include a variety of waiting periods. For example, lawful aliens are eligible for Social Security and Aid to Families of Dependent Children benefits; only some aliens receive Medicare benefits; aliens cannot receive certain farm loans. Clearly, the national government can deny benefits to unlawful residents. It does so in food stamps, in Supplemental Security Income, in Medicare Part A, and in Medicaid.[24]

What may seem odd to persons from countries with less fragmented policy-making institutions than those of the United States is that Congress has not made a comprehensive effort to shape this variety of arrangements. Congress could define the various categories along the immigration continuum: illegal residents, children of illegal residents, legal short-term workers, aliens intending to become citizens, and so on. It could then establish standards of eligibility for the various social welfare programs providing income and public services. Congress might well conclude, for example, that emergency medical care should be provided to everyone physically in the country; that all children should be educated; that legal alien workers who pay the Social Security tax should be eligible for all Social Security benefits; and so on. The current state of things is not so different from the probable results of such an overhaul. But the system is unnecessarily complex for those subjected to it, and contains many specific rules that would be altered if subjected to a general review.

4. HUMAN DIGNITY

It has long been American jurisprudence that even persons unlawfully within the country are entitled to basic human rights. For a recent example of this tradition see Lynch v. Cannatella (1987),[25] which allowed stowaways to sue state officials for beating them. The lawsuit was permitted under section 1983 of the Judiciary Act, which authorizes suits against government officials for violating constitutional rights. The judge said the constitutional standard, even for those attempting to enter the country by unlawful means, is "humane treatment."

A. Uninvited Refugees

This commitment was put to the test in the last decade when two great waves of Caribbean immigrants arrived in the United States. About 125,000 so-called Mariel Cubans arrived in a short time in 1980. About thirty-five thousand Haitians came over a more extended period. Some of those who arrived from both Cuba and Haiti were ill; others had criminal records. Soon thousands of these immigrants were in refugee camps, as bureaucratic institutions were established to decide who could stay, who should be sent elsewhere,[26] and who should be in an American prison.

In a series of cases, American courts reviewed the systems established by the executive branch for coping with these uninvited persons, testing policies and procedures for their conformity with the constitutional requirement of due process of law. In some instances, rules and procedures of the executive branch were rejected, and the government was forced to revise its systems.[27]

Only one stage in these many legal disputes has so far reached the United States Supreme Court. In Jean v. Nelson (1985), a class of undocumented and unadmitted aliens from Haiti sued the commissioner of the Immigration and Naturalization Service, alleging that INS officials had denied them parole because of their race and their national origin. The issue arose because the Immigration and Nationality Act of 1952 says aliens without entitlement to enter the country "shall be detained" but that "in his discretion" the attorney general may "parole" such persons and thus let them enter the country temporarily. This privilege was routinely given until mass arrivals of Haitians and Cubans engendered domestic political opposition. An en banc panel of the Eleventh Circuit held that even racial discrimination by the attorney general in making parole decisions would not violate the Constitution, because the government has plenary power to decide who can enter the country (Jean v. Nelson 1984).

The Supreme Court could hardly accept so blunt a statement of executive authority to discriminate according to race (although many cases decided over the country's history would lend support to the court of appeals' statement of law). Instead, the Supreme Court held that there was no need to reach that issue at the present stage in the litigation, and instead the case should be returned to the trial court. By the time the litigation reached the Supreme Court, the attorney general had issued regulations specifying the grounds on which parole into the country should be granted or denied. The regulations did not authorize consideration of either race or national origin.[28]

Jean v. Nelson shows a Supreme Court understandably hesitant to decide either that the Constitution permits the executive branch to discriminate at the borders on the basis of race or that the discrimination in immigration policy on the basis of race and national origin that has been part of American immigration law for two hundred years and continues (in many aspects of the immigration system) today no longer meets constitutional requirements. We may expect courts to continue seeking to avoid that choice for some time.[29]

The Cuban and Haitian experiences highlight the inevitable difficulties that face an immigration system that acknowledges (yet is uncomfortable with) the geopolitical significance of decisions made as to individuals. For the United States today, about 70 percent of the six hundred thousand annual lawful immigrations are granted because of a family connection between the immigrant and someone already in the United States. About 25 percent of the places go to refugees.[30] The U.S. government's support of certain Central American regimes (Guatemala, El Salvador) leads it to deny refugee status to persons from those countries, even though at least some of those seeking refuge in the United States would be at political risk in their home country. Before the Nicaraguan elections, a larger percentage of Nicaraguans who applied were admitted, because of United States hostility to the Sandinistas.[31] Those seeking economic refuge (which is how the United States government classifies most Haitians) are ineligible.[32] Are Soviet Jews and Armenians now to be denied admission to the United States because of the political transformation of the Soviet Union and the revolutions in Eastern Europe and because more want to come than the United States can conveniently accept? The Reagan and Bush administrations have sought to avoid answering the legal question whether married Chinese couples are eligible for refugee status because in China they would be encouraged (or coerced) to abort fetuses once they have met their quota under the one-child policy.[33]

In 1990, the Bush administration announced major changes in INS rules governing asylum and withholding of deportation procedures. The new regulations ease the burden of proof on aliens seeking asylum and provide for the adjudication of initial applications by a corps of asylum officers specially trained in international relations. In keeping with a basic guiding principle of the 1980 Refugee Act, which is that "the granting of asylum is inherently a humanitarian act distinct from the normal operation and administration of the immigration process," all initial applications for asylum or withholding of deportation will be adjudicated by the asylum officers in a nonadversarial setting.[34]

The new rules also allow an applicant to establish refugee status—that is, prove that he or she has been a victim of past persecution or has a "well-founded fear" of future persecution on the basis of race, religion, nationality, social group, or political opinion—without corroboration of the applicant's testimony if that testimony is "credible in light of general conditions" in his or her country. An asylum applicant no longer has to prove he or she would be singled out for persecution if the applicant can show that there exists a pattern or practice of persecuting a group of persons of which the applicant is a member. In addition, an applicant may obtain work authorization while his or her case is pending if an asylum officer determines that the application is not "frivolous," "frivolous" being defined as "manifestly unfounded or abusive."

Some advocates of the new rules believe not only that they will make it easier for some applicants to gain asylum but also that they will help to eliminate disparities in the granting of asylum status for refugees from those countries with whom the U.S. government is friendly and those towards whom the United States is hostile.

B. Search and Seizure

Enforcement of immigration laws poses difficult questions concerning the interpretation of constitutional provisions protecting privacy and assuring due process of law. The Fourth Amendment protection against unreasonable searches and seizures applies even to undocumented aliens present in the country,[35] but the courts have consistently held the INS to a looser constitutional standard than that required of domestic police in criminal prosecution of citizens.

To a significant extent, the courts—led by the Supreme Court—have responded to the public perception that the INS has an immensely difficult task to perform, and that the country has "lost control of its borders." In 1975, for example, the Supreme Court sanctioned use by INS roving patrols of a motorist's ethnic appearance as a partial basis for suspecting that the motorist was an unauthorized alien (United States v. Brignoni-Ponce 1975). And in Blackie's House of Beef, Inc. v. Castillo (1981), a court of appeals upheld the constitutionality of an INS workplace search warrant that lacked particularized suspicion. In yet another case, the Supreme Court found that a series of raids in which armed agents surrounded factories and blocked all exits did not amount to a violation of the workers' Fourth Amendment rights, despite substantial evidence that some of them were coerced to answer questions (INS v. Delgado 1984). A majority of the court said that no seizure had occurred because the workers could move around inside the surrounded factory, and because the encounters between the four litigants and the INS agents were "classic consensual encounters." Finally, in INS v. Lopez-Mendoza (1984), the Supreme Court held, five to four, that evidence obtained as a result of an unconstitutional arrest could be admitted in a deportation proceeding.

The Court's opinions in the *Lopez-Mendoza* case mirrored debates about Fourth Amendment rights in criminal proceedings. Justice O'Connor's majority opinion said that immigration proceedings are civil, not criminal, matters and that excluding evidence obtained through unconstitutional procedures is not necessary to deter future illegal behavior by INS agents. In his dissent, Justice White demonstrated that the logic of excluding illegally obtained evidence from criminal prosecutions of citizens should also apply to immigration proceedings. White argued that the alternative means of deterrence identified by the majority are unlikely to be effective. For example, the INS was unable to identify a single instance in which it had disciplined an agent for an illegal search or arrest. And filing suit against the erring government officials, he noted, is hardly a serious option for persons who have been deported.

But the majority would not accept responsibility for what it suspected would be a major detriment to INS enforcement efforts. A system in which officers apprehend *1 million* deportable aliens per year, the Court seemed to imply, cannot be held to strict constitutional norms. Rather, deportable aliens are entitled to "a streamlined determination of eligibility to remain in this country, nothing more." And so allegedly illegal aliens do not receive so-called Miranda warnings,[36] they can have involuntary confessions introduced against them, and they can be deported on the basis of "clear and convincing" evidence, not evidence "beyond a reasonable doubt."

Enactment of the Immigration Reform and Control Act of 1986 will bring reconsideration of many of these issues. Now that employing an illegal immigrant can be a crime, it will be harder to continue the fiction that immigration enforcement is a civil, not a criminal, matter. But if an employer consents to the search of a workplace, can individual workers protest?[37] American law requires search warrants for safety and health inspections of businesses (Marshall v. Barlow's, Inc 1978) but not for welfare "visits" to the apartments of poor families (Wyman v. James 1971). Will the law be that warrantless searches infringe the property rights of factory owners but not the human rights of those for whom the consequence can be deportation? The process of reconsidering search and seizure law in light of IRCA has only begun.[38]

5. WORLD BUSINESS

Legal issues concerning international migration of workers do not affect only poor persons traveling from developing to developed countries in search of economic opportunity. The internationalization of business means that executives and professionals regularly work outside their home country. America's complicated immigration rules have recently generated growth in immigration law practice on behalf of multinational companies seeking to move their managers in and out of the United States. The laws that make this difficult may need to be revised.

A related issue is the attempt by the United States to apply its official norms, especially those that concern nondiscrimination, to hiring for positions to which the laws and customs of other nations are also relevant. One court, for example, held that an American medical college violated U.S. law when it excluded Jewish physicians from participating in a program that sent cardiovascular surgical teams to Saudi Arabia (Abrams v. Baylor College of Medicine 1986). Another court allowed a helicopter pilot to be recruited in the United States for work in Saudi Arabia on condition that the person hired convert to Islam (Kern v. Dynalectron Corporation 1983). The court was influenced by the apparent fact that a non-Moslem flying into Mecca would be beheaded. Other issues arise when an American is recruited by the wholly owned foreign subsidary of a U.S. corporation (Lavrov v. NCR Corporation 1984); when discriminatory employment practices occur outside the United States but the employer also does business in the United States (Boureslan v. Aramco 1988); when a foreign employer recruits for foreign work with an advertisement in American media; and when foreign companies doing business in the United States impose conditions of employment that are normal in the company's home culture (usually Japan) but unlawful under American law.[39] These issues will increase in importance as the internationalization of the American economy continues. Before long, negotiated bilateral or multilateral agreements will be required.

6. CONCLUSION

Law concerning immigration and immigrants must confront conflicting themes in American public life. First, the United States has always been a large, sparsely populated country that imports its citizenry. The nation declares a belief, captured in the Declaration of Independence, in equality before the law for all of its residents. The United States cannot accept as new citizens all those from around the world who would be happy to immigrate, however, and so difficult choices must be made. Plainly also, there is not true equality within the United States, and current citizens and voters will pay a limited price to give opportunity to new citizens.

Nevertheless, the country does seek a principled basis for selecting immigrants and for defining the category of eligible refugees. Proposals to end the practice of citizenship by birth receive little attention. The United States supplies many public benefits to resident aliens. There is still room in the United States, the birthrate among current residents is low, and the economy needs the diligent labor that immigrants are willing to provide. Also, American culture is dynamic and diverse in its sources. Many Americans respond positively to the Hispanic and Asian influences that have become a part of the larger culture.

Courts and legal arguments play a central role in the debate and resolution of issues of this sort in the United States. As this chapter shows, a great deal about American immigration policy is told in the language of judicial opinions. Political authority in the United States is decentralized; states and municipal governments play important roles in shaping public policy. The president and the Congress share responsibility for foreign affairs, and the boundaries between their respective responsibilities are not delineated in the Constitution. Congress does not coordinate its statutes. It considers immigration policy in one year, refugee policy in another year, and programs for financing medical care at a third time. Thus it is inevitable that important problems will arise as to which the overlapping legal rules are silent or in conflict. Only courts, exercising their jurisdiction over specific disputes, can bring even a degree of coherence to the tangle of American rules. The American system assumes that legislative and executive action must satisfy constitutional requirements and that judges should be trusted to give contemporary meaning to the ambiguous eighteenth-century language of the Bill of Rights. The result is that important political struggles are fought over the appointment of judges and for the minds of those judges after they assume the bench.

De Tocqueville understood all of this. America, still a land of immigration and of law, is the country he described.

NOTES

1. Between 1880 and 1930 the total population grew rapidly, from about 50 million to almost 125 million. The percentage in the text fits the 1900 population of about 75 million.
2. For the early history of United States immigration policies see Kettner (1978). For the entire history see Harwood (1986). For discussion of United States immigra-

tion policies in an international context see Piore (1979); Zolberg (1983). See generally Pozo (1986).

3. Sassen (1988); Bosniak (1988). For a different view of the social process see Lopez (1981):

> Where there is substantial economic disparity between two adjoining countries and the potential destination country promotes, *de jure* or *de facto,* access to its substantially superior minimal wage, that promotion encourages migrants reasonably to rely on the continuing possibility of migration, employment, and residence, until a competitive economic alternative is made available in the source country.

The Lopez view provoked Schuck's extended nautical metaphor:

> Once society's duty to aliens is no longer moored to the classical norms of mutual consent and compliance with publicly sanctioned legal procedures but is derived from vague, even circular, notions of social expectations and relationships, the legal order is cast adrift upon a sea whose ungovernable tides may carry it to realms unknown, unimagined, and fraught with danger (Schuck 1984).

4. Beginning in 1945, several states enacted laws banning some forms of employment discrimination.

5. See, for example, Sharif v. New York State Education Department (1989), holding that New York cannot give out college scholarships according to scores on the standardized Scholastic Aptitude Test because males score higher on the test than females.

6. See, for example, Diaz v. Pan American World Airways (1971), holding that Pan Am must hire men as flight attendants because customer preference for female "stewardesses" is not a legally valid basis for selection.

7. Griggs v. Duke Power Co. (1971). The validity of this statement of the law is in question after Wards Cove Packing Co. v. Atonio (1989).

8. Garcia v. Gloor (1980). But refusal to hire an individual because of his accent may violate Title VII (Berke v. Ohio Dept. of Public Welfare 1980).

9. In Bhandari v. First National Bank of Commerce (1987), an en banc panel of the court of appeals held *by a seven-to-six vote* (with one judge not participating) that 42 U.S.C. sec. 1981, an 1866 law saying that "all persons . . . within the jurisdiction of the United States shall have the same right . . . to make and enforce contracts . . . as is enjoyed by white citizens," bars discrimination against aliens by government but not by private companies. The *Bhandari* decision was reinstated after reconsideration (1989).

10. For the argument that IRCA is unconstitutional because it does not protect applicants for political asylum—many of whom are allowed to work while the government considers their applications—from discrimination, see Scaperlanda (1988). A related issue is the standard used to evaluate the applications for asylum and work authorization of those awaiting a decision on their applications. Such people are granted permission to work unless the INS decides that their application is "frivolous." At least one judge, William Wayne Justice of the federal district court in Tyler, Texas, has decided that the INS violated the law in its application of the term "frivolous" when it placed too great a burden of proof on the applicant in establishing the merit of the application. The judge ruled that the INS must determine that an application is "indisputably meritless" before dismissing it as

frivolous (*New York Times*, 26 July 1989). And in New York, where about 150,000 people await decision on their applications, a group of applicants from El Salvador and Afghanistan also filed suit against the INS for wrongly classifying their applications as frivolous.

11. For a comprehensive summary of the IRCA legislation see Fox (1987).
12. See the discussion of federal provisions in Espinoza v. Farah Manufacturing Co. (1973).
13. The earliest Supreme Court decisions establishing constitutional rights of aliens were Yick Wo v. Hopkins (1886) and Truax v. Raich (1915).
14. Very occasionally, there is constitutional litigation about national-origin distinctions drawn among citizens. Hirabayashi v. U.S. (1943) and Korematsu v. U.S. (1944) permitted the U.S. government, during World War II, to intern U.S. citizens of Japanese ancestry (see Rostow 1945). Recently, a federal district court at a preliminary stage in litigation was extremely skeptical of the constitutionality of a Defense Department regulation denying security clearance to persons recently naturalized if they had lived in one of twenty-nine countries (Huynh v. Carlucci 1988).
15. See, for example, De Canas v. Bica (1976), upholding the constitutionality of a California law.
16. However, aliens who enroll in the legalization program must give up for five years their right to obtain benefits under Aid to Families of Dependent Children, the major income-protection program for needy families.
17. For the argument that IRCA should be amended to permit legalization by those who entered after 1981 and before IRCA was enacted in 1986 see Merino (1988).
18. Patel v. Sumani Corporation (1987). See also Hernandez v. M/V Rajaan (1988), allowing an undocumented immigrant to obtain tort damages when injured even though the damages are compensation for future U.S. wages he had no legal right to collect; In re Reyes (1987) (Fair Labor Standards Act); and NLRB v. Ashkenazy Property Management Corporation (1987) (National Labor Relations Act). Issues needing resolution include whether undocumented aliens after IRCA can be "available" for work under statutes (such as unemployment insurance laws) so requiring, and whether they can be reinstated when that is the regular legal remedy as after determinations of illegal discrimination because of union activity or on the basis of race or sex. See Bosniak (1988) at 1020.
19. This question is analogous to ones that arise in the extensive jurisprudence concerning the legal consequences of leases granting occupancy to tenants in apartments that do not meet housing code standards. See Haar and Liebman (1985).
20. For the very different judicial approach to decisions about medical benefits by state and local governments see Memorial Hospital v. Maricopa County (1974), which struck down an Arizona county's attempt to limit health benefits to persons who had been living there for one year. See also Lewis v. Gross (1986), finding that the relevant federal statute did not authorize the secretary of Health and Human Services to limit the group of aliens eligible for Medicaid benefits.
21. The issue would not have arisen as to the different category of children born in the United States to unlawfully resident parents. The law seems quite clear that the United States follows a rule of citizenship by birth (INS v. Rios-Pineda 1985; Plyler v. Doe 1982). Schuck and Smith have argued vigorously and effectively that

this is bad law, and not a necessary interpretation of the Fourteenth Amendment. Many other countries would not grant citizenship in this situation (Schuck and Smith 1985). But there is little evidence that the arguments of Schuck and Smith have so far been heeded.

22. See also Nyquist v. Mauclet (1977), prohibiting New York from denying resident aliens state financial aid for higher education. That case was decided by a five-to-four vote, and changes in composition of the Supreme Court since it was decided suggest it might come out differently today.

23. See also Sudomir v. McMahon (1985), permitting denial of Aid to Families of Dependent Children benefits to individuals awaiting a decision on their asylum applications.

24. This list is from Plyler v. Doe (1982) at 251 (Burger, C. J., dissenting). While federal statutes denying eligibility to undocumented aliens or to noncitizen permanent residents are likely to be upheld, state decisions have fared badly, except where the states have been specially authorized by Congress to deny benefits on these bases.

25. However, in Medina v. O'Neill (1988), the court of appeals found that the INS did not have a statutory duty to provide appropriate detention facilities for excludable aliens (as opposed to deportable aliens) and that absent allegations of civil treatment maliciously inflicted, or gross physical abuse, the INS did not violate the aliens' due process rights.

26. The Cuban and Haitian situations were different in a number of ways. One important difference is that Haiti was willing to accept emigrants if they returned. Most or all of the Mariel travelers would not have been permitted to return to Cuba.

27. See, for example, Rodriquez-Fernandez v. Wilkinson (1981); Garcia-Mir v. Meese (1986) (reversing the district court's conclusion that Mariel Cubans had legal rights based on a speech by President Carter stating that Mariels would be welcomed "with open hearts and open arms"); Bertrand v. Sava (1982); Student Note 1986; and Student Note 1983.

28. While the Supreme Court did not consider the issue of the constitutionality of race discrimination in this case, the district court awarded the plaintiffs nearly $1 million in attorneys' fees as "prevailing parties" under the Equal Access to Justice Act. This award was challenged by the government, and in Jean v. Nelson (1988) the court of appeals held that the Haitian refugees were entitled to attorneys' fees because there had been sufficient legal and factual reasons to support the district court's finding that the government's departure from established policy of paroling undocumented aliens was "not substantially justified." In Commissioner, INS v. Jean (1990; see Jean v. Nelson), the court held that an additional award of fees under EAJA for the fee litigation itself did not require a second finding on the same set of issues.

29. Compare the constitutional validity of decisions to exclude individuals because of the political views they would express if allowed admission (Kleindienst v. Mandel 1972). See also cases upholding immigration discrimination against homosexuals. (Matter of Longstaff 1983). Of course U.S. law permits discrimination against citizens who are homosexual as well (Bowers v. Hardwick 1986). See also Fiallo v. Bell (1977), which permitted Congress to deny family status to the relationships

between children and illegitimate fathers. Discrimination on the basis of illegitimate birth has been held to be unconstitutional in domestic law (Trimble v. Gordon 1977). The Immigration Reform and Control Act denies legalization rights to families of amnestied residents. For the argument that this failure violates the Helsinki Accords of 1975, see Sanger (1987).

30. Under U.S. law, refugee status is given to someone applying from outside the country and asylum status to someone in the country.

31. One expert has shown that Nicaraguans were five times more likely than Salvadoreans to win approval as refugees (Anker 1989); see also Bosniak 1988 at 971 n 48).

32. Under the 1980 Refugee Act an applicant must demonstrate a "well founded fear of persecution on account of race, religion, nationality, membership in a particular social group, or political opinion." The statute bars refugee or asylum status to persons who "ordered, incited, assisted, or otherwise participated in the persecution of any person." The act is substantially based on article 1 of the United Nations Protocol Relating to the Status of Refugees (1967). See INS v. Cardoza-Fonseca (1987) ("well-founded fear of persecution" does not require showing that it is "more likely than not" that an alien will be persecuted in home country).

33. On the broad discretion of the attorney general in these matters see Hotel and Restaurant Employees Union v. Attorney General (1986); Dwomoh v. Sava (1988) (reversing denial of asylum status even though the applicant participated in a *coup d'état* against the government of Ghana).

34. Adjudication of the same issues for those applicants who are in exclusion or deportation proceedings will continue to be adversarial and in front of immigration judges, however.

35. See, for example, Flores v. Meese (1988) (can't strip-search undocumented juveniles absent reasonable suspicion that search would yield weapons or contraband).

36. Miranda v. Arizona (1966), is the foundation for a body of law about the rights of persons detained by the police. For example, if the police do not tell the suspect that he or she is entitled to remain silent and to consult a lawyer, the suspect's confession cannot be admitted into evidence at his or her criminal trial.

37. See also the issue posed in Rojas v. Richardson (1983) of whether a jury can be told that a tort plaintiff is an illegal alien. The court of appeals first held that a jury verdict for defendant-employer should be reversed, but on rehearing declared that although the reference was "highly prejudicial and [a] blatant appeal to jury bias," the judgment should be affirmed because the ranch hand's lawyer did not object at trial. And see United States v. Gomez (1986), which allowed a sentencing court to take notice of the fact that a defendant convicted of drug offenses was an illegal alien from Colombia.

38. See Student Note 1987.

39. See, for example, Sumitomo Shoji America, Inc. v. Avagliano (1982), holding that the 1953 Friendship, Navigation, and Commerce Treaty between Japan and the United States provides no defense to an action against the U.S. subsidiary of a Japanese company for allegedly hiring only Japanese male citizens to fill executive, managerial, and sales positions.

REFERENCES

Books and Articles

Anker, Debra. 1989. "The Legal Position of Foreigners: United States Immigration and Alienage Law." Paper delivered at International Association of Legal Science, Belgrade.

Bosniak, Linda S. 1988. "Exclusion and Membership: The Dual Identity of the Undocumented Worker under United States Law." *Wisconsin Law Review:* 955.

Fox, Wendy D. 1987. "Aliens and the Right to Work: Congress Comes to Terms with the Problem of Employment Discrimination Against Aliens." *University Law Quarterly* 65: 193.

Haar, Charles M., and Lance M. Liebman. 1985. *Property and Law.* 2d ed. Boston: Little, Brown.

Harwood, Edwin. 1986. *In Liberty's Shadow.* Stanford, Cal.: Hoover Institution Press, Stanford University.

Kettner, James H. 1978. *The Development of American Citizenship, 1608–1870.* Chapel Hill: University of North Carolina Press.

Lopez, Gerald P. 1981. "Undocumented Mexican Migration: In Search of a Just Immigration Law and Policy." *U.C.L.A. Law Review* 28: 615.

Merino, Catherine L. 1988. "Compromising Immigration Reform: The Creation of a Vulnerable Subclass." *Yale Law Journal* 98: 409.

Morgan, Edmund S. 1986. *American Slavery, American Freedom.* New York: Norton.

Piore, Michael J. 1979. *Birds of Passage.* New York: Cambridge University Press.

Pozo, Susan, ed. 1986. *Essays on Legal and Illegal Migration.* Kalamazoo, Mich.: W. E. Upjohn Institute for Employment Research.

Rostow, Eugene V. 1945. "The Japanese American Cases: A Disaster." *Yale Law Journal* 54: 489.

Sanger, Carol. 1987. "Immigration Reform and Control of the Undocumented Family." *Georgetown Immigration Law Journal* 2: 295.

Sassen, Saskia. 1988. *The Mobility of Labor and Capital: A Study in International Investment and Labor Flow.* New York: Cambridge University Press.

Scaperlanda, Michael A. 1988. "The Paradox of a Title: Discrimination within the Anti-Discrimination Provisions of the Immigration Reform and Control Act of 1986." *Wisconsin Law Review:* 1043.

Schuck, Peter H. 1984. "The Transformation of Immigration Law." *Columbia Law Review* 84: 1.

Schuck, Peter H., and Rogers M. Smith. 1985. *Citizenship without Consent.* New Haven: Yale University Press.

Simon, Julian L. 1989. *The Economic Consequences of Immigration.* New York: Blackwell.

Student Note. 1986. "The Constitutional Rights of Excludable Aliens: History Provides a Refuge." *Washington Law Review* 61: 1449.

Student Note. 1983. "Developments in the Law: Immigration Law." *Harvard Law Review* 96: 1286.

Student Note. 1987. "Reexamining the Constitutionality of INS Workplace Raids after the Immigration Reform and Control Act of 1986." *Harvard Law Review* 100: 1979.

Zolberg, Aristide R. 1983. "The Political Economy of Immigration." In *America's New Immigration Law: Origins, Rationales, and Potential Consequences*, edited by W. Cornelius & R. Montoya. La Jolla, Cal.: University of California at San Diego Press.

Cases, Statutes, and Regulations

Abrams v. Baylor College of Medicine, 805 F.2d 528 (5th Cir. 1986).

Ambach v. Norwick, 441 U.S. 68 (1979).

Berke v. Ohio Department of Public Wefare, 628 F.2d 980 (6th Cir. 1980).

Bernal v. Fainter, 467 U.S. 216 (1984).

Bertrand v. Sava, 684 F.2d 204 (2d Cir. 1982).

Bhandari v. First National Bank of Commerce, 829 F.2d 1343 (5th Cir. 1987), reinstated after reconsideration, 887 F.2d 609 (5th Cir. 1989), cert. denied, 110 S. Ct. 539 (1990).

Blackie's House of Beef, Inc. v. Castillo, 659 F.2d 1211 (D.C. Cir. 1981), cert. denied, 455 U.S. 940 (1982).

Boureslan v. Aramco, 857 F.2d 1014 (5th Cir. 1988), adopted en banc, 892 F.2d 1271 (5th Cir. 1990).

Bowers v. Hardwick, 478 U.S. 1039 (1986).

Cabell v. Chavez-Salido, 454 U.S. 432 (1982).

De Canas v. Bica, 424 U.S. 351 (1976).

Department of Justice. "Final Rule on Aliens and Nationality; Asylum and Withholding of Deportation Procedures." *Federal Register 55*, 145 (27 July 1990): 30,674.

Diaz v. Pan American World Airways, 442 F.2d 385 (5th Cir. 1971).

Doe v. Reivitz, 830 F.2d 1441 (7th Cir. 1987), modified, 842 F.2d 194 (7th Cir. 1988).

Dwomoh v. Sava, 696 F. Supp. 970 (S.D.N.Y. 1988).

Espinoza v. Farah Manufacturing Co., 414 U.S. 86 (1973).

Federal Migrant and Seasonal Agricultural Worker Protection Act, 29 U.S.C. sec. 1816.

Fiallo v. Bell, 430 U.S. 787 (1977).

Flores v. Meese, 681 F. Supp. 665 (C.D. Cal. 1988).

Foley v. Connelie, 435 U.S. 291 (1978).

Garcia v. Gloor, 618 F.2d 264 (5th Cir. 1980), cert. denied, 449 U.S. 1113 (1981).

Garcia-Mir v. Meese, 788 F.2d 1446 (11th Cir. 1986), cert. denied sub nom. Ferrer-Mazorra v. Meese, 479 U.S. 889 (1986).

Griggs v. Duke Power Co., 401 U.S. 424 (1971).

Hampton v. Mow Sun Wong, 426 U.S. 88 (1976).

Hernandez v. M/V Rajaan, 848 F.2d 498 (5th Cir. 1988), cert. denied, 109 S. Ct. 530 (1988) and 109 S. Ct. 837 (1989).

Hirabayashi v. U.S., 320 U.S. 81 (1943).

Hotel and Restaurant Employees Union v. Attorney General, 804 F.2d 1256 (D.C. Cir. 1986), affirmed en banc, 846 F.2d 1499 (1988).

Huynh v. Carlucci, 679 F. Supp. 61 (D.D.C. 1988).

In re Griffiths, 413 U.S. 717 (1973).

In re Reyes, 814 F.2d 168 (5th Cir. 1987), cert. denied, 108 S. Ct. 2901 (1988).

INS v. Cardoza-Fonseca, 480 U.S. 421 (1987).

INS v. Delgado, 446 U.S. 210 (1984).

INS v. Lopez-Mendoza, 468 U.S. 1032 (1984).

INS v. Rios-Pineda, 471 U.S. 444 (1985).

Jean v. Nelson, 727 F.2d 857 (11th Cir. 1984) (en banc), modified, 472 U.S. 846 (1985), fees awarded, 863 F.2d 759 (11th Cir. 1988), affirmed sub nom. Commissioner v. Jean, 110 S. Ct. 2316 (1990).

Johnson v. Transportation Agency, 480 U.S. 616 (1987).

Kern v. Dynalectron Corporation, 577 F. Supp. 1196 (N.D. Texas 1983), aff'd, 746 F.2d 810 (5th Cir. 1984).

Kleindienst v. Mandel, 408 U.S. 753 (1972).

Korematsu v. U.S., 323 U.S. 214 (1944).

Lavrov v. NCR Corporation, 591 F. Supp. 102 (S.D. Ohio 1984).

Lewis v. Gross, 663 F. Supp. 1164 (E.D.N.Y. 1986).

Lynch v. Cannatella, 810 F.2d 1363 (5th Cir. 1987).

Marshall v. Barlow's, Inc., 436 U.S. 307 (1978).

Martin v. Wilks, 109 S. Ct. 2180 (1989).

Martinez v. Bynum, 461 U.S. 321 (1983).

Mathews v. Diaz, 426 U.S. 67 (1976).

Matter of Longstaff, 716 F.2d 1439 (5th Cir. 1983).

Medina v. O'Neill, 838 F.2d 800 (5th Cir. 1988).

Mejia v. New York Sheraton Hotel, 459 F. Supp. 375 (S.D.N.Y. 1978).

Memorial Hospital v. Maricopa County, 415 U.S. 250 (1974).

Miranda v. Arizona, 384 U.S. 436 (1966).

NLRB v. Ashkenazy Property Management Corp., 817 F.2d 74 (9th Cir. 1987).

Nyquist v. Mauclet, 432 U.S. 1 (1977).

Patel v. Sumani Corp., 660 F. Supp. 1528 (N.D. Ala. 1987), reversed, 846 F.2d 700 (11th Cir. 1988), cert. denied, 109 S. Ct. 1120 (1989).

Plyler v. Doe, 457 U.S. 202 (1982).

Refugee Act, 8 U.S.C. sec. 110l(a)(42)(A).

Rodriquez-Fernandez v. Wilkinson, 654 F.2d 1382 (10th Cir. 1981).

Rojas v. Richardson, 703 F.2d 186 (5th Cir. 1983), rehearing denied, 713 F.2d 116 (5th Cir. 1983).

Sharif v. New York State Education Department, 709 F. Supp. 345 (S.D.N.Y. 1989).

Sudomir v. McMahon, 767 F.2d 1456 (9th Cir. 1985).

Sugarman v. Dougall, 413 U.S. 634 (1973).

Sumitomo Shoji America, Inc. v. Avagliano, 457 U.S. 176 (1982).

Sure-Tan v. NLRB, 467 U.S. 883 (1984).

Trimble v. Gordon, 430 U.S. 762 (1977).

Truax v. Raich, 239 U.S. 33 (1915).

United Latin American Citizens v. Pasadena Independent School District, 662 F. Supp. 443, 672 F. Sup. 280 (S.D. Tex. 1987).

United States v. Brignoni-Ponce, 422 U.S. 873 (1975).

United States v. Gomez, 797 F.2d 417 (7th Cir. 1986).

Wards Cove Packing Co. v. Atonio, 109 S. Ct. 2115 (1989).

Wygant v. Jackson Board of Education, 476 U.S. 267 (1986).

Wyman v. James, 400 U.S. 309 (1971).

Yick Wo. v. Hopkins, 118 U.S. 356 (1886).

18

DISCRIMINATION AGAINST FOREIGNERS
UNDER FRENCH LAW

Danièle Lochak

As in many countries today, French legislation oscillates between a universalist principle of equality, which condemns discrimination against foreigners by nationals, and a realistic principle of state sovereignty—and protectionism—which results in reserving a certain number of rights and prerogatives for French citizens only. Although legislation is heading, indubitably, in the direction of increasing judicial assimilation of foreigners with nationals, significant discrimination continues to exist in French law. This discrimination raises two questions. The first is practical and quantitative and refers to discrimination that inevitably has an effect on the fate of those concerned. The second question is theoretical and refers to the legitimacy of different treatment for different people based on nationality, understanding that the word "legitimacy" is meant here in the juridical sense and not in the philosophical or political sense. Thus, by "legitimate" I mean that it conforms not only to the universal and humanist moral philosophy that states that "all men are born and live free and equally under the law," but more specifically, that it conforms to international positive law and to the general principles of domestic French law.

It is in the framework of the answer to the second question, discussed in part 1 of this chapter, that part 2 will examine the manifestations of discrimination against foreigners that still exist in French law.

I

The question of the lawfulness of discrimination based on nationality can be looked at either with regard to discriminatory actions of individuals or public institutions, or in relation to standards currently in force.

1. Protection against Discriminatory Behavior

Since the adoption of the 1 July 1972 statute related to the fight against racism, discriminatory behavior falls within the domain of the Criminal Code, whether the behavior is practiced by a private individual or by a representative of the government. Article 416 of the Criminal Code punishes by imprisonment of two months to one year and a fine of two to twenty thousand French francs anyone who refuses to provide goods or services, or who refuses to hire or who fires someone because of origin or affiliation or nonaffiliation to a particular ethnic group, nation, race, or religion, or who binds an offer to a discriminatory condition. Article 187-1 punishes by imprisonment of two months to two years and a fine of three to forty thousand French francs "any public servant or citizen fulfilling a public service" who, for the same reasons, knowingly refuses the benefit of a right a claimant was entitled to. And finally —it is important to be reminded of this because it makes it possible for these provisions not to remain just idle words—the law gives antiracist associations the power to act as plaintiffs in civil lawsuits filed on the basis of these articles.

These provisions make unlawful, and enable one to fight against, the many types of discrimination frequently encountered in everyday life: refusal of service in a café, restaurant, or business establishment, refusal to rent an apartment, refusal to hire, etc. These provisions protect foreigners on two grounds: as potential victims of racial discrimination in the strict sense, that is, on the basis of their affiliation to a particular ethnic group, race, or religion (in actuality, the majority of the victims of racial discrimination are foreigners); and as victims of discrimination based specifically on their nationality or on the fact that they are foreigners ("their affiliation or nonaffiliation to a particular nation"). The law prohibits both of these practices.

Case law states, in effect, that refusing to extend a job offer or service to someone for the sole reason that the individual is not French constitutes the offense provided for and punished in the Criminal Code. Regarding employment, the Labor Code goes even further: not only does it prohibit discrimination in employment, but it also prohibits adopting as internal policies provisions that would penalize salaried employees on account of nationality, opinions, or religion (article L 122-35), and prohibits penalizing or firing a salaried employee on account of origin, affiliation to an ethnic group, nation, or race, or religious convictions (article L 122-45).

The symbolic scope of these provisions surpasses their practical effectiveness, which appears fairly limited because those concerned are often dissuaded, beforehand, from instituting an action, or because these cases are often dismissed for lack of grounds for prosecution.[1] As an example, prosecutors are often unwilling to institute proceedings because such individual complaints are almost always filed and closed whereas the civil law suits combined with those complaints when brought on behalf of an association have some chance of succeeding. We must also remember that article 416 of the Criminal Code, in its original wording, and until recently, made it possible for the perpetrator of the discriminatory act to exonerate himself or herself by putting forward a "legitimate motive" for refusing to provide goods or services or refusing to hire, or to fire someone. This option, as one might suspect, was widely used and often constituted effective grounds for defense by those being prosecuted.[2] We can hope that recent reforms, which have wiped out the provision allowing for the exception of "legitimate motive," will strengthen the protection of victims.[3]

Another obstacle, often nullifying the provisions of this text, is a problem of proof. It is difficult, as one can imagine, for victims of discrimination to prove that the refusal that they met was indeed motivated by their nationality or national or ethnic affiliation. Even when the discrimination is overt and obvious one must be able to provide witnesses; and most often, prudence leads perpetrators of discrimination to put forward a thousand justifications for their refusal to rent an apartment or to allow someone into a nightclub. In matters of job discrimination, in addition, how does one prove that there was discrimination when an employer is free to hire whomever he chooses and is under no obligation to justify his choice? And if the employer wants to fire a foreign employee, he would hardly have trouble finding a "valid" reason to justify the dismissal. In spite of all of these obstacles, however, one could say that the law, although imperfectly, fulfills its duty, in so far as perpetrators of discrimination are sometimes convicted, on the basis of the provisions of either the Criminal Code or the Labor Code.

On the other hand, it is exceedingly rare to obtain a conviction based on article 187-1 of the Criminal Code, which forbids, even more severely, discrimination perpetrated by persons acting on behalf of a public entity. The number of cases where this provision could be applied are more numerous than one can imagine, whether they concern access to public housing, discriminatory offers of employment circulated by the ANPE (National Employment Agency), or most recently, obstacles put forth by certain municipalities regarding foreign children's access to public schools.[4]

Is it fear of public authority or abdication that dissuades those concerned from acting? In any case, complaints in incidents like these are rare. Those complaints that are filed almost always result in a dismissal, notably because the judge in the case, applying the law in a very restrictive manner, refuses to convict the agent who was responsible for the refusal or who rejected the demand if said agent was not the person legally qualified to make the decision.

2. The Lawfulness of Discriminatory Legislative Provisions or Regulations

The more delicate problem is knowing whether—and to what degree—the legislature and the government can insert in statutes and regulations provisions that result in the differential treatment of foreigners and nationals. The question of the lawfulness of discriminatory legislative provisions or regulations arises in relation to France's international commitments, and even more in relation to constitutional principles or the general principles of law.

The Principles of International Law. Under international law, discrimination based on nationality is not necessarily unlawful: it is considered unlawful only if it deprives a foreigner of the "minimal civilized treatment" that the state is required to grant, or if it is specifically prohibited by international convention. However, many international conventions either do not mention distinctions based on nationality, or they put forth principles of nondiscrimination that are valid only in a limited area.

The major international conventions on human rights confirm the universality of fundamental rights but also the limits in applying these rights to foreigners. The European Convention for safeguarding human rights compels states to acknowledge the rights and liberties that it sanctions "to every person falling under their jurisdiction," foreigners or nationals, whether or not they are nationals of one of the subscriber states. However, if one looks at how this particular provision has been interpreted in case law, it does not prohibit all differential treatment between foreigners and nationals: only "arbitrary" distinctions are prohibited. In the same way, the international agreement related to civil and political rights compels states "to respect and to guarantee all individuals in their territory and under their jurisdiction" all rights acknowledged in the agreement. States, therefore, cannot establish discrimination in areas of fundamental rights, barring two very significant exceptions.

First is the exception of political rights. Not only is the acknowledgement of political rights strictly reserved for citizens (article 25 of the agreement), but the European Convention does not prohibit states from "imposing restrictions on the political activities of foreigners" (article 16).

Second is the exception of the right of access or entry. None of these conventions questions a state's sovereign prerogative to refuse a foreigner access into, or to deport them from, their territory, which strongly compromises and clearly makes precarious a foreigner's ability to exercise his or her acknowledged rights.

We should remember that discrimination based on nationality is not a form of racial discrimination within the meaning assigned by the convention on the elimination of all forms of racial discrimination: "distinctions, exclusions, restrictions or preferences, established by a party state to the Convention," and depending on whether those involved are or are not its own nationals, do not constitute prohibited discrimination (articles 1–2).

In the domain of social and economic rights the principle of nondiscrimination becomes weaker still, no doubt because "inalienable and sacred rights" are harder to set forth, but especially because states are concerned with protecting the economic activities of their nationals against foreign competition. Also, social rights, as opposed to traditional liberties, cost the state money. Thus, the International Agreement of 1966, concerning economic, social, and cultural rights, is not as explicit as its twin agreement regarding civil and political rights, when referring to how its provisions apply to nonnationals. The French government has specified that the clauses regarding the right to work, social security, an adequate standard of living, and education must be interpreted as not being obstacles "to the provisions regulating a foreigner's access to work or to setting conditions of residency in assigning certain social benefits." This clearly and seriously limits the agreement's scope.

Convention No. 97 of 1949, regarding the migrant workers and concluded under the aegis of the ILO, sets forth a general principle of nondiscrimination to be applied to labor and social security legislation. However, in addition to having a more restricted coverage, it states that this principle does not forbid a state from limiting a foreigner's access to employment in order to protect national manpower. Convention No. 111 of 1958, regarding employment and occupational discrimination, does not include in its list of prohibited activities discrimination based on nationality, but only discrimination based on national ancestry. These two conventions were completed by the even more protective provisions found in Convention No. 143 of 1975, which compels the states to promote and guarantee equal opportunity and treatment, in matters of employment, occupation, social security, union and cultural rights, and personal and collective freedoms, to all migrant workers and to members of their families who are legally in their territory. However, this convention was ratified by only a limited number of states. There remains Convention No. 118, on equal treatment in matters of social security, which forbids all discrimination based on nationality but, here again, in a very limited domain.

The contribution to matters of nondiscrimination of the two conventions adopted under the aegis of the European Council, the European Social Charter, and the European Convention on the legal status of migrant workers is very limited. The first, while asserting the principle of equal treatment in allowing the exercise of a profitable activity and in social protection, also recognizes a state's right to enact restrictions "based on serious economic and social grounds," which basically makes the first assertion nothing more than a pious wish. The guarantees that this convention sets forth are, in addition, reserved for nationals of states party to the convention. The second convention also provides for equal treatment with nationals in matters of social security, social and medical assistance, and exercising the right to join a union. But, like the preceding convention, based on the principle of reciprocity, it only binds the six states that have ratified it, that is, France, the Netherlands, Portugal, Spain, Sweden, and Turkey. Further, since only three of the six are countries with a large emigrant population, two of which are members of the EC, the impact of this convention is reduced to almost nothing.

What remains are the often more favorable bilateral conventions, which provide that in certain areas, such as access to a profession normally reserved for the French, a national of another state would enjoy the same rights and equal treatment as a French citizen. We see this especially in the Treaty of Rome, which by proclaiming the principles of free movement for workers and their right of establishment and by prohibiting all social and economic discrimination based on nationality, has made more equivalent, in many areas, the position of Community nationals and citizens. Without a doubt, Community law, demonstrating that exclusions based on nationality are not inescapable, could prompt us to reexamine the question of how discrimination strikes foreigners and to ask whether it is lawful. But, at present, the Treaty of Rome, like bilateral conventions, concerns, by definition, only certain categories of foreigners. These categories, later found in domestic legislation, appear more like exceptions to discrimination based on nationality than a complete prohibition of the principle of discrimination. One must, therefore, go back to domestic law and to the question of the lawfulness of discrimination under the constitutional principle of equality.

3. The Lawfulness of Discrimination and the General Principles of Domestic Law

Paradoxically, the question of knowing whether—and to what extent—foreigners in France can demand the benefits of the rights and freedoms sanctioned by the law is much less clearly addressed in domestic law. In fact, this question has never been explicitly posed, at least not completely or under the form of a question of principle, as it has been in the United States before the Supreme Court.

First of all, the question has never been settled by the texts. The 1789 Declaration of the Rights of Man and Citizen, which utilizes the terms "men" and "citizens" alternately as if they were perfectly interchangeable, is of no help here. Nor does the Preamble of the 1946 Convention contain any precise indication allowing one to assert with certainty that the principle of nondiscrimination that it sets forth also applies to foreigners; however, nothing points to the conclusion that foreigners are excluded from the benefits of the rights proclaimed, which seem to be general in scope: "Every person has the duty to work and the right to obtain employment. . . . All men can defend these rights and interests through unions, etc." If one goes beyond declarations of principle—which the Conseil Constitutionnel (Constitutional Council) considered as being part of the positive law, with recognized constitutional standing—one finds in the legislation a series of provisions that, within their respective areas, directly respond to the question, at times equating foreigners with nationals and at other times, to the contrary, subjecting them to separate rules or subordinating a certain right to a condition of nationality. But the basic question remains: does differential treatment based on nationality conform to the Constitution and to the general principles of French law?

Case law provides only partial answers. If the highest jurisdictions have affirmed, on several occasions, that foreigners must benefit from the rights accorded to nationals, they have done so each time with respect to a particular right, but without taking a position on the problem in its entirety. Thus, both the Conseil Constitutionnel, in 1980, on the matter of detaining foreigners pending deportation, and the Cour de Cassation (Supreme Court), in 1985, on the matter of identity checks, ruled that article 66 of the Constitution prescribes that "no one can be arbitrarily detained" and holds the courts responsible for assuring that this principle is respected and applied to foreigners. The Conseil d'Etat (State Council, France's highest administrative jurisdiction and advisory body to the government in matters of legislation), in a famous decision—the GIST case of 8 April 1978—drew from the phrase in the 1946 Preamble, "the nation assures an individual and a family the necessary conditions for their development," a general principle, applicable alike to foreigners and nationals: the right to lead a normal family life.

In a recent decision, dated 22 January 1990, the Conseil Constitutionnel went even further, asserting that "the legislature can take specific measures, with regard to foreigners, provided they respect international obligations subscribed to by France and the fundamental constitutional rights and freedoms recognized for all of those who reside on the Republic's territory." On these grounds, it was ruled unconstitutional to exclude foreigners normally residing in France from the benefits granted to needy, elderly persons. So we can deduce, in general terms, that nationality should not constitute legitimate grounds for discrimination in matters of social protection. The decision leaves open, however, the question of knowing which are the "fundamental constitutional rights and freedoms" that cannot be denied to foreigners.

The Conseil Constitutionnel does not assert, then, that all discriminatory activities are unconstitutional. In fact, it does not take a stand on the principle of equality. Without a doubt, the Conseil Constitutionnel acknowledges the principle of equality, proclaimed in the Declaration of 1789 as well as in the Preamble of the 1946 Constitution, as a constitutional principle binding on the legislature, just as the Conseil d'Etat has always considered the principle of equality as a general principle of rights binding on the government and the administration. But, the principle of equality does not compel equal treatment for all people, or equal application of the laws. It only prohibits establishing arbitrary discrimination, not justified, for example, by a difference in circumstances. The question is, therefore, to what degree can foreigners demand the same treatment as nationals, based on this principle of equality?

In certain areas, the fact that one is a foreigner justifies applying a different standard from the one applied to nationals, whereas, in other situations, taking into account one's nationality would be considered unlawful discrimination. Thus, neither the existence of specific legislation regarding the right of foreigners to enter and reside in the country nor the condition of nationality placed on the right to vote poses a constitutional problem because there are, undeniably, in these areas different standards applied to foreigners and nationals.

On the other hand, a law that interfered, without legitimate grounds, with liberties as fundamental as the freedom of movement, the right to safety, and the right to privacy would certainly be presumed unconstitutional. Between these two hypothetical extremes exists an important margin of uncertainty. It is fitting, then, when looking at the discrimination remaining on the books today, to ask whether it is justified by the principles formulated by the Conseil Constitutionnel and the Conseil d'Etat.

II

The dialectical argument between the principle of equal treatment and the principle of discrimination, which underlies the situation for foreigners, can be explained by the fact that a foreigner is sometimes regarded as a person who should enjoy all of the fundamental liberties acknowledged to apply to everyone without distinction of nationality, and sometimes as a noncitizen who is refused not only political rights but a whole series of rights and prerogatives that enable a person to take part in the exercise of public authority. The dividing line between what conceptually constitutes human rights and what constitutes a citizen's prerogatives is, in practice, difficult to draw with certainty. The solutions provided by positive law are not always consistent. Moreover, a right as fundamental as that of earning a living, which conflicts with the interest in protecting a national's economic well being from competition, is subject to barriers that are not compatible with the principle of economic freedom.

1. The Private Sector

In terms of the more fundamental human rights, aimed at guaranteeing an individual personal autonomy and protection from the central government, it stands to reason that one would not subordinate them to a condition of nationality. Therefore, foreigners enjoy, in principle, the same conditions as nationals regarding the freedom of movement, of safety, of the right to privacy, the freedom to do what they want with their own bodies, the right to property, and freedom of conscience and opinion. And as I stated before, any law that would restrict, without legitimate grounds, one of these rights would be a priori unconstitutional.

Unless—and here lies the ambiguous status of a foreigner and of the case law—these restrictions are justified by the particular situation of a foreigner who, unlike a national, never has an absolute right to enter and to reside on French territory. Thus, the Conseil Constitutionnel, while affirming that foreigners have the same rights as the French with respect to individual freedoms, has also adopted the principle of governmental retention, aimed at ensuring the deportation of foreigners under a "remove from territory measure," provided that the principle of retention is placed under the control of the courts.[5]

As for the Conseil d'Etat, did it not rule the right to lead a normal family life inconsistent with abridging this right with several conditions and forbidding the local legal settlement of families?[6] Generally speaking, we must acknowledge the fact that foreigners are subjected to constraints to which nationals are not: their freedom to come and go can be shackled by prohibitions regarding length of stay or where to reside. And unlike the French, they are obliged to declare changes of residence and to present, upon police request, proof of their right to reside, etc.

Outside of the strictly private sector, discriminatory practices between nationals and foreigners have a tendency to multiply in economic and social matters.

2. The Economic and Social Sphere

In the sphere of economic and social rights there is a clear contrast between economic freedom, on one hand, understood as the right to engage in profitable activity, which is highly controlled by a series of constraining regulations and is therefore very limited, and social rights, on the other hand, where the equal treatment with nationals is the rule with very few exceptions.

Access to Employment. Today, the most widespread discrimination is exercised, although largely unrecognized, in the area of employment. Despite the assertion in the 1946 Preamble, according to which "every person has the right to obtain employment," the right of a foreigner to exercise the profession of his or her choice was, paradoxically, more guaranteed a century ago than it is today. The number of professions and jobs that are forbidden to foreigners has increased since the end of the nineteenth century.

The development in this area has been against the common trend. Whereas in general the legal status of foreigners has tended to come close to that of nationals, here the opposite is occurring. Moreover, this phenomenon is not unique to France. All industrialized countries, since the latter part of the nineteenth and even more so in the first part of the twentieth century, have taken part in a progressive, steady narrowing of the field of professional activities accessible to foreigners.

The reasons are well known: fear of a foreigner's influence in allegedly sensitive fields (for example, the fabrication of war materials), but more often simply the desire to protect nationals' economic activities from foreign competition, in other words, for protectionist and Malthusian reasons.

The right to work, therefore, is not the rule for foreigners, if one admits that a right subject to regulation is not really a right. In order to engage in a salaried profession, a foreigner must obtain a work permit, which the French administration decides to issue or not and then to renew according to the situation of employment. Further, foreigners cannot take a nonsalaried job without prior authorization, that is, if they do not possess permits to engage in agriculture, artisanry, or commerce. It is true that many constraints have been considerably alleviated for the great majority of foreigners residing in France, since this severe system is no longer applicable to holders of permanent resident cards, nor to nationals belonging to the EC, nor, regarding unpaid jobs, to nationals of countries with which France has an Alien Residency Convention. And yet, the result of this liberalization is still only a limited freedom since foreigners continue to be excluded from professions more often than one would like to think. In fact, the jobs and professions from which they are excluded number in the millions.

First, they are excluded from civil service jobs. Access to public service employment is considered, as we know, a civic right and an essential characteristic of citizenship. Consequently, it is reserved for nationals. The practical scope of this exclusion is enormous. To the 2.3 million French military and civil servants, add the six hundred thousand civil servants in all the territories and the six hundred thousand public service hospital workers (caretaking staff such as nurses or administrative personnel); thus, 3.5 million jobs are reserved for nationals, counting only those officially entitled to their jobs. The large numbers lead one to question the justifications generally invoked for such exclusion. Although one can understand, within the framework of the nation-state, the refusal to entrust a foreigner to an office associated with state authority (police, army, law, taxes), this explanation is no longer valid when one considers that the majority of civil servants perform tasks that do not grant them any particular prerogatives. The real reason for this exclusion, no doubt, lies elsewhere: to reserve an area for nationals where they will be sheltered from competition, or better yet, to blatantly refuse to allow foreigners from benefiting from the (relative) advantages connected with civil-service employment.

From this arises a series of paradoxes. Paradox number one: the development of the welfare state through the multiplication of the number of public service positions, and thus the number of jobs closed to foreigners, has increased the scope of discrimination, despite the fact that civil servants, more and more, are performing the same jobs as wage earners in the private sector. Paradox number two: we refuse to recruit foreigners for civil-service positions, yet we accept recruiting them, to perform the same tasks as contract or part-time or adjunct employees, for lower-paying jobs without the advantage of job security. In sum, they are used to plug holes. To provide an illustration, foreign students are recruited as auxiliary teachers in disciplines where there are shortages (for example, we have used them to teach math in schools in northern France), even though it's well known that these students do not have full legal status or even work permits.

The situation is so illogical that it cannot be maintained indefinitely. Furthermore, the legislature has introduced a loophole in the system that allows people of foreign nationality to be recruited and integrated in higher education and research just as are the French.[7] It is, no doubt, a narrow loophole; however, it bears witness to the fact that excluding foreigners from public jobs is not inescapable and that it does not result from any categorical constitutional mandate. Consequently, it is difficult to find reasons to oppose the widening of this loophole to secondary education and, in due time, to all teaching positions (which represent almost half of the public-service positions).

What could help promote change is the Treaty of Rome. It is true that article 48 of the treaty does exclude from equal treatment access to employment in the public service. But, with regard to this principle of equal treatment we also know that the European Community Court of Justice has interpreted this exception restrictively. In its judgment, the exclusion only applies to jobs that involve direct or indirect participation in the exercising of public power and to positions whose purpose is to protect the general interests of the state and other public entities.[8] In other words, the fact that a job falls within the public service is not reason enough to reserve access to it for nationals. And that is how the Court appraised, as being against the spirit of the Treaty of Rome, the exclusion of community nationals in Belgium from access to municipal jobs such as nursing, child care, plumbing, carpentry, and electricity; in Germany from the teaching profession; and in France from nursing jobs in the public hospitals.[9]

France, like its European partners, is therefore going to be forced to modify its domestic legislation so that it conforms to its European obligations. In due time, a good number of civil service jobs should become available to nationals of member states in fields such as research, teaching, and health care. Directives to that effect are currently being prepared in Brussels.[10]

Again, this development affects, by definition, only a limited number of foreigners, those with rights under the Treaty of Rome. Still, it leads us to question again the well-established tradition of excluding foreigners from public service since, once the loophole is opened, the legitimate and natural character of these exclusions can no longer compel recognition as clearly as before.

Beyond public service itself, this principle of exclusion spread to most of the jobs in the public and in the nationalized sectors, meaning that approximately 1 to 1.5 million more jobs are closed to foreigners. If one considers that there are about 18 million wage-earning jobs in France, a quick calculation leads to the conclusion that approximately one-third of these jobs are reserved for the French. The main nationalized businesses, based on the statutes currently in force, can only hire persons of French nationality, as is the case at EDF (France's national electric company) and GDF (France's gas company), whose personnel are subject to a legal status going back to 1946. This is also true for the SNCF (the French national railway system) (Status of Railway Employees); the RATP (the Paris transport authority); Air France, in regards to both air crew and ground personnel (the Civil Aviation Code requires that all professional pilots be of French nationality, but Community nationals are, henceforth, to be treated as French nationals); the Atomic Energy Commission; etc. On the other hand, French nationality no longer pertains to miners (coal miners and laborers working for hydrocarbon production companies such as Elf Aquitaine.)

The explanation for these exclusions has been that the jobs in question imply that the employees are in a position to exercise some public authority. But this explanation is inadequate, because how then does one justify the hiring of foreigners as auxiliary agents in administrative jobs, where they in fact do participate in the exercising of public authority? The fact is that many find repugnant extending to foreigners the privileges or benefits of a legal status. The best evidence is that public enterprises do recruit wage-earning foreigners, but only to perform underling tasks and without giving them the same benefits as other employees.

Foreigners are not, after all, excluded only from public service jobs. In the private sector there is also a neverending list of professions reserved for the French. Foreigners are sometimes excluded from salaried occupations (foreigners cannot be employed in gaming rooms, nor become pilots, even for a private company, except if they are nationals of a member state of the EC). But more often independent professions are reserved for the French, although they do accept foreigners in driblets, and only then based on international conventions—notably, the Treaty of Rome—or by a discretionary decision from the public authority.

Except under certain favorable provisions of an international convention, foreigners cannot run liquor stores[11] or tobacconist shops,[12] nor operate game rooms or casinos,[13] nor devote themselves to the manufacture and sales of arms and munitions.[14] They cannot manage entertainment businesses nor private technical schools. They cannot be managers or directors of private research agencies, nor can they perform privately or as agents of a private business surveillance, security guard, or money transportation firm. They cannot be directors of a periodical[15] or of an audiovisual communication service, and they cannot serve on the editorial staff of a publication for children. They are excluded from a number of jobs in transportation,[16] insurance, [17] stock market, and business.[18] They cannot be granted concessions of public services or hydraulic energy.[19] And, as one might suspect, the above-mentioned do not even make up the entire list.

As for professions, exclusion here is also the rule. Concerning the health profession, the regulations require that doctors, surgeons, dentists, and midwives be of French nationality and that they possess a French diploma, subject to the restrictions in reciprocal agreements with foreign states, to individual dispensations granted by the minister of health within an annually established quota, and/or subject to Community provisions.[20] Similar rules govern who can practice pharmacology and veterinary medicine. Subject to the same restrictions, architects, surveyors, and accountants must also, in theory, be of French nationality, as must members of the legal profession. In this last case, the argument is made conveniently rather than convincingly that they participate in the public administration of justice. Also required to be of French nationality are notaries, bailiffs, and auctioneers, as well as trustees in bankruptcy, authorized liquidation agents, and also lawyers. Foreign lawyers can practice their profession in France only if they benefit from a reciprocity agreement or if they are nationals of a member state of the EC.

How many of these exclusions are based on legitimate grounds? If certain exclusions can be linked to a preoccupation with national independence or with law and order—foreigners, by definition, are suspected of being a threat to one or the other—most translate as simply the desire to protect nationals from foreign competition. In addition, these restrictive measures often have been relatively recently enacted—either between the two wars, or after the war—because of pressures applied by the professional communities concerned. Today, this concern by members of certain professions to protect themselves against competition, is not sufficient reason to justify, in terms of constitutional principles, differential treatment between nationals and foreigners. And since foreigners have been authorized to live and work in France they must, therefore, be able to claim for themselves the principles set forth in the Preamble of the 1946 Constitution: "Every person has the right to obtain employment" and "no persons can be harmed, in their work or profession, by reason of their nationality."

Social Protection. Therefore, there is a clear contrast between the absence of a basic right to work, which is eminently discriminatory in societies claiming economic freedom, and the progressive equalization of the treatment of foreigners and nationals under social legislation. The tendency toward equal treatment is relatively old with regard to the strict application of work conditions: length of work day, weekly time off, paid vacations, compensations, etc., where a foreigner's interests are not the only ones at stake. It is in the interest of nationals not to have to compete with workers who would accept less favorable working and salary conditions. The Labor Code does not distinguish between nationals and foreigners; moreover, it sets forth the principle of equal treatment and condemns all discrimination by an employer in this matter.

This same trend is evident in the realm of "social rights" in the broad sense. What is mainly targeted here are the acknowledged prerogatives of wage earners to protect their interests and to participate in the business world, as well as the right of workers to be protected against various "risks," such as sickness, old age, unemployment, etc. During the 1970s foreign workers obtained the right to sit on labor-management committees, to be elected to the position of personnel representative, and to become a union leader or representative; and the law of 28 October 1982 did away with all remaining restrictions in this area by completely equalizing the conditions of foreign workers with those of nationals. Finally, foreign employees and employers were given the right to participate in elections for the Conciliation Board of Employers and Wage Earners (the responsibility of the board is to rule on disputes between wage earners and employers; the board is composed of elected representatives of both groups). Foreigners, however, are barred from becoming board members on the grounds that those who dispense justice "on behalf of French people" must necessarily be French.

As for family and social assistance, foreigners, in theory, are eligible for the same benefits as the French. This principle clearly only applies to foreigners and their families who regularly reside in France. The residence requirement, which guarantees the payment of benefits only to persons residing on French territory who have regular legal status, is required in some but not all cases and can curtail a foreigner's access to social benefits. Yet, types of assistance subject to conditions of nationality have become increasingly scarce. This is true for assistance that is funded by taxes rather than by contributions and that is paid to foreigners only if they come under the jurisdiction of an international agreement. However, by declaring such discrimination unconstitutional, in its decision of 22 January 1990, the Conseil Constitutionnel implicitly invited the legislature to remove the condition of nationality whenever found in the area of social protection.

The same principles apply to public assistance programs set up by municipalities or departmental bodies. In fact, when a group of mayors claimed that the benefits under certain special programs created at the municipal level were reserved for the French, the judge, in every instance, censured their decision on the grounds that their actions constituted illegal discrimination. Such was the case regarding unemployment relief that the Office of Public Assistance in Châtillon had subjected, without valid grounds, to a condition of nationality. In another incident, which caused quite a stir because it involved Paris, foreign families were excluded from the benefits of the Parental Educational Leave grant, created by the city of Paris for the benefit of families with three children. In the latter case, the Conseil d'Etat confirmed the decision rendered first by the Paris Administrative Court, for once with a vigorously well-grounded order, after recalling that in the case of the cost of a child's education, no condition based on the parents' nationality existed. The Conseil d'Etat rejected the City of Paris's arguments, pointing out "that taking into account the purpose of the grant for Parental Educational leave, which is to encourage the growth of the Parisian population, and to that end, to allow parents to devote themselves more easily to the care of their young children, the concerns invoked by the city, about preserving the demographic balance of the city, and the desire to remedy the insufficiency of funds for large French families, cannot be regarded as essential to the purpose of this grant" and do not justify differential treatment among Parisian residents based on their nationality. By its generality, this court decision seems to outlaw in advance all provisions, not only from local authorities but from public authorities in general, authorizing differential treatment based on nationality in matters of public assistance.[21]

3. The Public Sector

The political disqualification of foreigners in France is, at this moment, an absolute rule that allows for no exceptions. Article 3 of the Constitution reserves the right to vote as an expression of national sovereignty, "for men and women who are French nationals and of full age, enjoying their civil and political rights." It follows that foreigners are not allowed to participate in the elections for senators or deputies or for referendums, nor in the election for the president of the French Republic. In addition, the Election Code reserves for the French the right to vote for and be elected as municipal, regional, and national councilor (representative). Thus, deprived of civil rights, foreigners are not allowed, as stated above, to hold public positions.

The coming to power of the Left in 1981 revived the controversy over granting foreigners the right to vote at the local level. This demand, supported by the majority of opinion, ran counter not only to the unfavorable political atmosphere but also to deeper ideological reticence, resulting from the traditional view linking civil rights to nationality, which the Left, almost as much as the Right, has a hard time breaking away from, so solidly engrained is it.

This political disqualification has repercussions on the exercise of rights other than the right to vote, notably on freedom of expression in all forms. If foreigners did obtain, in 1981, freedom of association, they are not always granted freedom of the press, since foreign publications are subjected to exceptional treatment, and can be forbidden by a simple order from the minister of the interior.

Generally speaking, freedom of expression is limited by the requirements of law and order, which are traditionally invoked with much more vigor when they involve foreigners rather than nationals. Although nothing in positive law limits foreigners' freedom of expression or their right to belong to a political party or group, the ability to exercise these rights remains severely restricted by the burdensome threat of deportation. In fact, a foreigner whose behavior is judged injurious to law and order risks deportation at any time. It is true that, although in the past this option was widely used by public authorities, current regulations that forbid deportation of a foreigner who would not have been condemned to a year in prison for a criminal offense now limit this power to exceptional cases (an attack against state security, for example). There is, after all, an increased tolerance by public authorities regarding the political activities of foreigners, at least as long as they do not affect France's diplomatic relations.

Nevertheless, foreigners do not remain totally deprived of all aspects of citizenship. The first field open to a form of citizenship independent of nationality is that of the place of business, as I stated earlier. Through the years, foreigners have also acquired rights equal with those of the French in fields where the participation of beneficiaries or users is organized. Thus they are now electors and are eligible to serve on boards of social security establishments, public housing authorities, and teaching institutions, whether of grammar, elementary, or secondary schools, or at any level of management in a university. Only the president of a university must be of French nationality.

On the other hand, the tradition of excluding foreigners from managing public service agencies has not, for the moment, been questioned with respect to professional and business organizations. Only French citizens can be members of chambers of commerce and industry, chambers of agriculture, and trade guilds. And, in general, foreigners are excluded from the administrative boards of professional societies, to which, it is true, they are allowed access in very small numbers.

CONCLUSION

The optimism one might feel after reading the preceding observations needs to be tempered. In spite of the progress in granting foreigners equal treatment in more and more fields under French legislation, foreigners never benefit from legal guarantees as completely as do nationals. The indomitable seed of discrimination still exists. Judicial equality is, in effect, still incomplete since entire sections of national legislation are excluded from the principle of non-discrimination; the most radical exclusion concerns, of course, the political rights and prerogatives linked with being a citizen (notably, access to civil service).

Judicial equality remains precarious, since a suspensive or resolutory condition is always implied. Only foreigners who are allowed to live in French territory, and only for as long as they are allowed to reside there, can exercise the rights acknowledged for nonnationals by domestic legislation. The state's right to refuse any person who is not a national the right to visit, reside in, work in its territory, as well as the right of the state to return to the border or deport someone when it is judged convenient—subject to international obligations that may curtail this right—appears, therefore, a fundamental component of the discrimination between nationals and foreigners, even though the latter would see themselves as having the same rights and privileges as the former.

NOTES

1. For an analysis of the case law and the effectiveness of this provision, see George Pau-Langevin's articles, "L'Etat du droit positif en matière de lutte contre le racisme" (The state of positive law in the struggle against racism), *Droit Ouvrier* (Worker's Rights), May 1984, 171, and "La loi française contre le racisme" (French law against racism) *Actes No. 51* (Acts No. 51), September 1985, 51, as well as the MRAP (Movement against Racism and for Friendship between People) piece, *Chronique du flagrant racisme* (Chronicle of Flagrant Racism), La Découverte (Discovery), 1984.
2. However, neither the fear of seeing a business collapse because of too many foreigners, nor the demands of the clientele, nor the Muslim religion of one applicant (under the pretext that the restaurant served pork) who applied for a job as a dishwasher, were considered as legitimate grounds for refusing to hire someone.
3. The law of 25 July 1985, regarding job discrimination, and the law of 30 July 1987, regarding discrimination in supplying goods and services.
4. In February 1988, the MRAP (Movement against Racism and for Friendship

between People) did obtain a conviction for racial discrimination against a mayor who refused to register children of foreign families in the schools in his community.

5. According to the Conseil Constitutionnel, a violation of article 66 of the Constitution, which asserts that "no one can be arbitrarily detained" and that "the judicial authority, guardian of individual freedoms, assures that this principle is respected," occurs only if the intervention by the presiding judge is not expeditious (decision of 9 January 1980) or if the person has been retained too long (decision of 3 September 1986).

6. C.E. (Conseil d'Etat), "GISTI," 26 September 1986.

7. The decree of 6 June 1984 regarding the status of teachers and researchers in higher education, applying the law of 26 January 1984, expressly provides for the recruiting of foreign lecturers and professors. The decree of 30 December 1983, based on the law of 15 July 1982, has similar provisions permitting hiring of foreigners by research groups as directors of research, research engineers, and project engineers.

8. CJCE (European Court of Justice), 17 December 1980, *Commission c/ Royaume de Belgique* (Commission vs. the Kingdom of Belgium), *Affaire 149/79, Recueil 1980-88,* 3881.

9. CJCE (European Court of Justice), 3 June 1986, *Commission c/République Française* (Commission vs. the French Republic), *Affaire 304/84,* "Actualité juridique —Droit administratif" (Judicial News—Administrative Law) 1987, 44.

10. Consequently, Community nationals in France have the right to be medical doctors and to compete for positions in medicine, odontology, and biology (decree of 24 February 1984, on the legal status of medical doctors).

11. This restriction was introduced by the decree-law of 29 July 1939.

12. The management of tobacconist shops, part of the state monopoly, is considered to be a public service.

13. Article 3 of the law of 15 July 1907, modified by the law of 9 June 1977.

14. Decree of 14 August 1939.

15. Article 6 of the law of 29 July 1881 (modified on several occasions).

16. Employment in air, road, and river carriers is reserved for the French, subject to the conditions of international conventions.

17. Brokers and general agents must be French according to the terms of article R 511-4 of the Insurance Code.

18. In the past, regulations required that stockbrokers be of French nationality. That was before the profession was restructured pursuant to the law of 22 January 1988, which now entrusts their services to the stock exchange. French nationality is required for certain specialized brokers and for managers of investments.

19. The decree-law of 12 November 1938 and article 26 of the law of 16 October 1919, respectively. However, the decrees of 15 April 1970 and of 12 May 1971 have given Community nationals equal access with the French in these two areas.

20. The example of the medical field perfectly illustrates the xenophobic protectionist tendencies that limit a foreigner's access to these professions. Until 1933, the practice of medicine in France was dependent on the possession of a diploma of Doctor of Medicine. Foreigners could obtain schooling and exam waivers and present equivalent diplomas. In 1933, a law was passed, under pressure from

doctors worried about competition from foreigners, that reserved the practice of medicine to the French and, in addition (in order to bar naturalized citizens), required that medical studies be completed in French universities. Today, discriminatory measures against naturalized citizens have disappeared, but others remain.

21. C.E. (Conseil d'Etat) 30 June 1989, *BAS de Paris c/ Levy* (BAS of Paris vs. Levy) reprinted in *Droit Social* (Social Law), November 1989, 767, with commentary by X. Prétot.

19

NATIONAL AND LOCAL POLITICS AND THE DEVELOPMENT OF IMMIGRATION POLICY IN THE UNITED STATES AND FRANCE: A COMPARATIVE ANALYSIS

Sophie Body-Gendrot and Martin A. Schain

INTRODUCTION

By the mid–twentieth century, the immigrant heritage of the United States had been fully legitimized. The "melting pot" image was largely replaced by the representation of America as a nation of "enduring subcultures, through which amicable diversity would and should prevail" (Higham 1990, 12). It has now become commonplace for American policymakers to identify the United States as a nation of immigrants or, as John F. Kennedy phrased it (quoting Walt Whitman), a "nation of nations."

The interaction of disparate cultures . . . gave America a flavor and a character that make it as unmistakable and as remarkable to people today as it was to Alexis de Tocqueville in the early part of the nineteenth century. The contribution of immigrants can be seen in every aspect of our national life. . . . There is no part of our nation that has not been touched by our immigrant background. Everywhere immigrants have enriched and strengthened the fabric of American life. As Walt Whitman said,

"These States are the amplest poem,
Here is not merely a nation but
   a teeming Nation of nations."

... We must know how they met the new land and how it met them, and, most important, we must know what these things mean for our present and for our future (Kennedy 1964, 3).

France has never reveled in its immigrant heritage, nor have French policy-makers ever depicted France as a nation of nations. Nevertheless, since the period of the Third Republic France has welcomed, and at times encouraged, successive waves of immigration. The French pattern of high immigration has been unique in Europe and is related to birth rates, which began to decline in France a full century earlier than in the rest of Europe, as well as to resulting labor shortages. France is the only European country that has imported man-power since 1850. For more than a century, France has recruited not only its workers but also its engineers and its soldiers from beyond its frontiers (Long 1988, 23). Almost 10 percent of the French population in 1982 was foreign born, a percentage that is considerably higher than that of any other European country, and 30 percent higher than the foreign-born population of the United States.

Thus, both the United States and France are countries of high immigration. In this chapter we will focus on policy development on immigration in two very different political environments. Although it will be clear in this chapter that the very different structure of political institutions in each country has constrained the way policy is developed and implemented, our primary interest is the reverse relationship: the impact of the policy process on the structure of, and relationships among, political institutions. Here the impact has been similar if not the same.

In the first section we will examine the construction of immigration as a political issue. In both countries the issue as we now understand it was defined and developed by political actors under pressure of rising levels of immigration. We will argue that the process of developing the issue was certainly constrained by the structure of each political system, but that the process generated by immigration also had an impact on the relationship between center and periphery that was similar in each country. The political construction of the issue of immigration in the United States and France occurred in different time periods. Nevertheless, as Ira Katznelson has argued, "social time" can be fruitfully compared, even in two different countries, if the characteristics of each event are "close enough to be studied together" (Katznelson 1973).

In the second section we will analyze the dynamics of the process of policy development as they have emerged in the 1980s. Once again, we find that the principal actors are different in each country, but that there are surprising similarities between the dynamics and the tensions between center and periphery.

1. THE EMERGENCE OF THE IMMIGRATION ISSUE: THE CHANGING ROLE OF CENTER AND PERIPHERY

In the United States and France we can usefully differentiate between the local and national political arenas, each of which tends to structure the policymaking process in a different way. Although the national arena has generally been dominant in the centralized French system, and the balance in importance has been far closer between the two in the American system, in both countries the arenas of local politics have been important for the development of immigration policy. Moreover, the emergence of immigration as a political issue has tended to increase the role and importance of the national arena in both countries. In the United States the emergence of political issues of immigration at the turn of century—both the regulatory issue and the integration issue— provoked the expansion of the national arena at the expense of local political authority. In France, where the unitary structure *formally* placed both kinds of issues in the hands of central authorities, considerable policymaking authority remained *informally* in the local political arena until the 1980s. During the past decade, there has been a shift of decision making for immigration policy from the local to the national levels, provoked by changing perceptions and definitions of the issues involved.

How can we account for this movement of issues from one arena to the other, and what are the consequences? In each case, the shift of arenas is related to changing definitions of the immigrant problem, to the development of new formal institutional arrangements, to the structure and behavior of political parties, and/or to the role of interest group politics.

The United States

The increased role of the national government in policymaking on immigration is related to the growing politicization of the immigration issue. We can see this pattern emerging as early as the turn of the century. Until the 1880s, the function of the federal state in the United States was very limited regarding entrance regulations and integration policies for immigrants. At the beginning, institutions oscillated between openness toward immigration, expressed in terms of universalism and respect of particularities, on one hand, and protectionist local practices on the other. For Lincoln and Jefferson, civil religion and loyalty to the democratic values of the Constitution were the essential conditions to citizenship. That cultures, religions, and habits belonging to the private sphere subsisted was for them a secondary political matter. The only duty for the state was to filter out dangerous individuals to protect the survival of the institutions.

Because of numerous factors linked to the circumstances of the birth of the American nation, to the spread of its territory, to federalism and to the local importance of political parties, it was possible for immigrants, encouraged by local party organizations, to develop an ethnic space in the public domain, to avoid military service, identity cards, and all those regulations imposed by the centralized state in France in order to get a job, to get a place to live, to receive benefits and schooling. For one hundred years, immigrants were regulated only by the police power of the states.

Occasionally, the Supreme Court tried to limit the power of the states when they infringed on the role of the federal government. As early as 1849, in the "Passenger Cases," the Court refused to the states the power to collect special taxes from immigrants.[1] Only much later did the federal government take advantage of this power. However, it was only in 1876 that the Supreme Court attempted to put some order in scattered state procedures, noting that from that point on, treatment of immigration was no longer a state matter (under the police power) but that it fell within the competence of the federal government to regulate interstate commerce. Although Congress could have used this decision to develop a broad immigration policy, it refused to commit itself on this issue for more than ten years. This demonstrates a conception of "laissez faire" very different from the French approach, an approach characterized by Theodore Lowi's description of "the automatic society," in which the federal government refuses to intervene in social dynamics that should remain autonomous (Lowi 1969, 4).

The move to the national level was caused by the rapidly growing volume of "new" immigrants from Southern and Eastern Europe that began to enter the United States in the 1880s. In 1888, immigration committees were created in the House and in the Senate, while the Bureau of Immigration in the executive branch widened its function. These new federal institutions rapidly came under the influence of groups hostile to immigration. The success of the restrictionist trend can be explained by several factors: the numerical and qualitative change in immigration and in the larger population (between 1880 and 1924 the population of the United States increased from 50 to 100 million inhabitants), the end of territorial expansion, labor dissatisfaction, and economic depression. All those factors provoked a civic crisis (Schain 1989, 19) and brought into question the inclusive principles that had governed the long period of national construction and the values expressed by Thomas Paine: "America had to prepare over time an asylum for human kind" (Paine 1983, 110).

Between 1880 and 1924, immigration became a critical political issue that brought into question the definition of the political community, of its limits, and therefore of acceptable and accepted alternatives. Until then, Congress had simply enumerated criteria that made certain individuals undesirable on American territory. As early as the end of the nineteenth century, as in Europe, a more structured filtering system was established. In the United States, this process used political criteria (refusal of individuals deemed to be subversive), as well as national/racial criteria (exclusion of Chinese and Japanese). It was no longer sufficient to desire to belong to the political community; now the political community would make the judgment about who was worthy of belonging. The state would choose and refuse those who could not belong to the national family (Body-Gendrot, d'Hellencourt, and Rancoule 1988).

These views were clearly expressed by a majority of the justices on the Supreme Court in the *Elk v. Wilkins* decision in 1884: to acquire citizenship, individuals take an oath of allegiance to the nation; nevertheless, "no one can become a citizen of a nation without the nation's consent." "The nation has the arbitrary power to create the law that it considers the most appropriate to forbid entrance on its territory," the Supreme Court added in 1892, in a series of court cases brought by citizens and residents of Chinese descent following the passage of the Chinese Exclusion Act.

Times seemed to demand selection and in a variety of ways citizenship was limited on the basis of race. In addition to effectively limiting the citizenship rights of freed Blacks beginning in the 1890s, refusing citizenship rights to Native Americans until 1924 and to the Chinese until 1952, not to mention the treatment of the Japanese, an ethnocultural exclusion of White members of Southern and East European "races" began to appear as early as 1880. Restrictionist campaigns were gradually legitimated by Congress and the Supreme Court. Through the campaign for literacy tests for potential immigrants, there was an attempt to reconstitute a nation that never actually existed, to obliterate the tensions of its creation (particularly the ambiguities of the place of Blacks and Native Americans), and to establish a clear line between the "in-group" and the "others." Three times Congress voted literacy restrictions on immigration that were vetoed by the president, partly because of the opposition of immigrants' associations, before being finally adopted at the eve of the entrance of the United States into World War I (Zolberg 1983, 27).

The hysteria of the 1920s, which J. Higham dubbed the "tribal years," was not without precedent (Higham 1985). Indeed, nativist local reactions appeared with each immigration wave: Irish, German, Chinese, Jewish, Italian, Mexican. On the eve of the Civil War, the xenophobic and virulently anti-Catholic "Know Nothing" party was able to attract a majority of the vote in five states. After its decline, a new anti-Catholic organization, the American Protective Association, emerged in Clinton, Iowa, in 1887, with the objective of eliminating Irish political influence. The association was eventually supported by 2.5 million members in the Midwest and the West. Later, the Ku Klux Klan (its second manifestation), created in 1917 in Georgia, became one of the most xenophobic political organizations in the country. Even today, campaigns to impose English as a national language have a similar nativist flavor.

The efforts of nativists in the 1880s to prevent foreigners from voting remained scattered and limited to certain regions. They also provoked the establishment of immigrant defense groups that were quite active during restrictionist campaigns. Moreover, nativist efforts could not counter the willingness of local parties to attract the vote of new immigrants. Until the beginning of the twentieth century, a dozen states granted voting rights to foreigners providing they made a commitment to become citizens. In 1924 Arkansas was the last state to abolish immigrant voting.

The conflict between policies of openness and exclusion is still current in the sense that it represents the continuing tension about concerns for national integration and the danger presented by foreign "races" for institutions and the American society. Racial thinking was reinforced and institutionalized by the quota system that was established after World War I, and this thinking influenced the way political institutions evolved in the twentieth century.

The process of establishing immigration policy also reinforced the structure of the national state. The federal government took over from the states the function of regulating immigration, and important new structures were established at the national level both to develop new policy (the House and Senate immigration committees) and to implement this policy (the Bureau of Immigration). Thus, increased concern with immigration also meant increased centralization and nationalization of immigration policymaking. At the same time, the growth of administration of immigration also meant increased activity of pressure groups and political parties at all levels.

France: The Emerging Crisis of Immigration

In France, the central state has always been important in the regulation of immigration, as well as in the process of establishing policies by which immigrants would be integrated into the national community.[2] What is frequently less appreciated has been the significant role that has been played by institutions other than the central state, especially local governmental institutions, in defining, establishing, and implementing policy relevant to immigration and immigrants. Indeed, we will argue here that the 1980s was a critical period, during which the definition of the immigrant problem was tacitly changed to one of ethnicity (although the term was never used) and, at the same time, the focus of policymaking moved from the local arena to the national arena in France.

Until immigration became a nationally divisive political issue in the 1980s, local officials played a considerable role in defining public policy on immigration. Officially, the French population has been divided between Frenchmen and citizens, on one hand, and immigrants (by definition noncitizens) on the other, but in the local political arena careful public policy differences were formulated towards groups, based broadly on racial/cultural/religious (i.e., "ethnic") criteria, regardless of citizenship. For purposes of public policy, immigrants from European countries were considered different from those from Third World countries, and continental White citizens were treated differently from non-White citizens from the overseas departments and territories; Moslems from all origins were treated differently from non-Moslems.

The best-documented examples of local policymaking that depended on these criteria come from municipalities that were governed by the Left from the late 1960s to the early 1980s. This is related to the fact that a disproportionate number of non-European immigrants had settled in these municipalities during this period, but these examples of local policies can be extended to municipalities with high concentrations of Third World populations, regardless of political orientation.[3] Moreover, policymaking in the local arena involved quiet collaboration with departmental and national administrative officials.

For example, the municipal government of Vénissieux (an inner suburb of Lyon) took an initiative to exclude immigrant families from a massive housing development, Les Minguettes, in 1977, but with the approval and collaboration of the Lyon regional (COURLY) authorities, state urban renewal authorities (FAU), and departmental authorities, as well as the various public and private companies that were among the eleven participants that constructed and administered the complex. The exclusion of immigrant families from Les Minguettes, however, was only a more extreme example of a general policy to limit the presence of immigrants in both housing and schools.

Virtually every town in the Lyon region, in collaboration with departmental and state authorities, made the same kinds of decisions during the late

1970s to limit the availability of housing for immigrant families based on a commonly accepted notion of a "threshold of tolerance" (Grillo 1985, 125–27). On the initiative of local governments, the state also collaborated in establishing quotas for immigrant children in primary schools (Schain 1985, 176–81). Local governments in the Paris region expanded the notion of quotas by also limiting and excluding immigrant children from summer camp programs, as well as winter ski schools sponsored by the municipalities. The implied definition of "immigrants" generally included those from North Africa (rather than Europe) and, at least in the Paris region, Black French citizens from the overseas territories.

Local governments, by their actions, generally formulated public policy towards immigrants in exclusionary terms. They tended to define the "immigrant" problem as one of ethnic relations between native White Frenchmen against nonwestern immigrants, a problem of how to approach integration of people who were racially and (especially) culturally different, rather than a problem of how to deal with temporary labor. One indication of this definition of the issue is the fact that citizens from the overseas territories were frequently included as part of the problem. Thus, communications that dealt with the imposition of quotas in housing or schools frequently made reference simply to "north Africans," without differentiating between those who were citizens (as many second-generation Algerians were) and those who were not. Other restrictions were directed more specifically against French citizens from the overseas departments:

the administrative council [of public housing in St. Denis] has decided to house only native families . . . [because of] the saturation in our district of applications by foreign families and families from the overseas departments and territories.[4]

Not all of the policies developed at the local level were hostile and exclusionary during the 1970s, but even more positive policy initiatives tended to deal with immigrants in terms of their ethnicity, rather than their immigrant status. For example, the city of Grenoble planned parts of its urban renewal in the 1970s by consulting with, and considering the needs of, its North African (as well as other immigrant) inhabitants; consideration was given to collective social needs, as well as architectural style. In other towns, mosques were constructed, with local approval, in response to demands of an increasingly settled Moslem population.[5]

The construction of prayer rooms had begun in workers' dormitories under private auspices in the early 1970s. By the end of the decade, however, mosques were being constructed in hundreds of cities and towns throughout the country, generally with broad-based support, but sometimes in spite of strong local opposition.[6] The construction of the mosque in Mantes-la-Jolie, for example, was begun in 1979, supported by the mayor as well as a broad-based committee that included Catholics, Protestants, trade unions, and the Socialist Party (Bekouchi 1984, 58–62). Although the mosques were usually understood as a way of stabilizing and controlling an immigrant community, they rapidly became centers for large numbers of Moslems, whether or not they were immigrants.[7] After the Iranian revolution, opposition to the construction of mosques became more intense, but this also coincided with a growing opposition to non-European immigrants in other areas of French life, to increasing acts of violence against North Africans, as well as to the politicization of the immigration issue in the national arena (see below). Thus the number of "racial" attacks against "immigrants" registered by the Ministry of the Interior suddenly jumped four times between 1979 and 1980, and continued to increase during the 1980s (Costa-Lascoux 1989, 112).

Therefore, by the time the government of the Left came to power in 1981, a great deal of policy had been made at the local level, by local elected officials (usually the initiators) in collaboration with the field services of national ministries. In general, policy decisions targeted non-Europeans, both immigrants and citizens, and focused on modes of integration for a settled rather than a migrant population. Migration policy was formulated in the national arena, but the arena for integration policy was the locality.

The constraints of the local political-administrative system tended to limit the politicization and the intensity of ethnic conflict by restricting access to decision making and by separating local decision making (administrative) from the more global considerations of the political parties of local officials. Access was limited first by the minimal political opposition at the local level that was widespread in the 1970s. Even in larger towns there was a tendency towards political consensus building that was reinforced by the electoral law in place between 1965 and 1983, a law that virtually assured that there would be no institutionalized opposition in municipal councils of larger towns.[8] Therefore, even if local decisions did come before the municipal council, a great deal of institutionalized conflict had already been precluded.

Second, local decisions about immigrants were generally dealt with through an administrative process, with local officials participating as administrators rather than as elected officials (although the former were clearly dependent on the latter). Mayors participated in the formulation of housing policy as members of the boards that governed low-income housing (OHLM); the decision to limit the number of immigrant families with children in certain areas of the Lyon region was made by the prefect of the Rhône, but with the support and even at the initiative of local political authorities.[9] While some of the important decisions concerning immigrants and integration policy did come before city councils (decisions concerning the building of mosques, for example), many did not. Because so many of these important decisions were defined as administrative, consultations with interested groups, especially immigrant groups, were restricted, or simply took place after decision had already been made.[10] This process further limited political mobilization.

However, within the local arena there were also dynamics for rapidly elevating issues to the national level, particularly when conflict could not be contained by the local system. This is more or less what happened to the issue of ethnicity and immigrant integration in the 1980s. The "emergence" of ethnicity as a national issue in French politics during the past decade is related to the inability of the local system to deal with very real problems of ethnic integration, the outbreak of urban riots, and the dynamics of the party system. But the way that the issue emerged was constrained by the formal and informal structure of center-periphery relations.

The centralized administrative system greatly facilitated the movement of issues involving education and housing, for example, from ad hoc decision making at the local level to more general policy development at the national level. In both cases, policy formulation rested on assumptions about ethnic differences and definitions of policy that had been developed at the local level. In education, problems of rising dropout rates and student failures were behind the establishment of zones of education priority (ZEP) in 1981. The designation of such zones—which meant more money, more teachers, and more experimental programs—rested upon criteria that focused on the ethnic composition of an area, and gave additional support to programs that in some cases had already been begun by local authorities.[11]

Urban riots in the Lyon region during the summer of 1981, which were concentrated in Les Minguettes, were widely reported, and were largely responsible for the establishment of an Interministerial Commission on the Social Development of Neighborhoods and the Commission of Mayors on Security. The Neighborhood Commission was chaired by the (then) Socialist mayor of Grenoble (Dubedout), and focused a great deal of attention on problems of housing in the region. Its reports confirmed the essential problem of immigrant (really ethnic) concentration, and eventually it advised the demolition of part of Les Minguettes (its advice was taken); it also recommended more long-term national support for efforts at the local level (*Les Minguett* 1982, 44).

Consideration by administrative authorities at the national level of problems of ethnic integration was encouraged by the perception of real problems, but was facilitated by the structural links between localities and the central state: the centralization of the administration, and the overlap between local and national political office holding *(cumul des mandats)*. Over 80 percent of the deputies in the National Assembly hold local offices at the same time (about half of these are mayors), and the Senate is elected by an electoral college that consists overwhelmingly of local office holders. Thus, mayors who feel that their local problems need national help have easy access to the national arena. Marcel Houël, for example, the Communist mayor of Vénissieux in the early 1980s, was also a deputy, as were a large number of his colleagues with urban problems.

However, until the early 1980s, the focus for the formulation of integration issues and policy remained on the local level, even with increased national intervention. Restricted access to decision making in the local political-administrative system tended to limit local political mobilization and conflict around immigrant-ethnic issues. Of course, this process also mitigated the influence of opponents to the kinds of exclusionary policies that were frequently developed at the local level.

2. THE DYNAMICS OF NATIONAL POLITICS

The processes of policymaking with regard to immigration at the national level in France and the United States are quite different. The important actors are different, they appear at different historic moments, and the dynamics of their relationships are different in each country. In addition, local actors continue to play a more important role in the United States than in France, because of the dispersed way that the issue of immigration is treated in the United States. Nevertheless, given the differences between the systems, there are some surprising similarities. Both in France and in the United States the dynamics of center-periphery relations are important for policy development and implementation. While overall policy changes in both countries have been debated and processed at the national level, many of the initiatives for change have taken place at the local level and have been influenced by local problems and local political forces. In France, these local initiatives have quickly worked their way into the national political debate (indeed—have often *provoked* a national debate and moved policy considerations different from what they had been before), while in the United States, many local initiatives have been contained by the American federal system.

The United States: Federalism, Pressure Groups, and Dispersion

Since 1965, American society has had the difficult task of integrating new pieces into an already complicated ethnic mosaic. Four-fifths of new immigrants have come from the Third World, and they are quite different from one another. One approach of public policymaking has been to attempt to integrate these diverse people by creating a new kind of ethnicity, while acting as if only the gap between American society and the immigrants is important and that differences among immigrant groups do not exist. This approach, which does not clearly differentiate "immigrants" from "minorities," has influenced the range of political choices that immigrants have, as well as the way they themselves organize politically.

The federal government, in the way that it counts population, classifies students and workers, spends public aid, and develops affirmative action programs for minorities, has produced a three-part classification and has placed in the same category populations fragmented by ethnicity, race, and class. These classifications have also been adopted by local authorities and by voluntary mutual aid societies that dispense help to new immigrants, as well as by immigrant groups themselves. "Recent immigrants," notes P. Ireland, "have become conscious of the obvious tripartite division of multi-ethnic movements supported by the state—Black, Hispanic, and Asian—as a result of explicit approaches and categorizations [by the state] that aggregate citizens and immigrants" (Ireland 1989, 321). To have political weight, to defend their interests, Chinese, Filipinos, Vietnamese, Koreans, and others have joined together in "Asian" organizations, such as the Asian Law Caucus. This may seem peculiar, since these groups do not share the same language, and because native populations such as Native Americans have also demanded to be reclassified as "Asian." In the same way Chicanos, refugees from Central America, and the citizens from Puerto Rico (an American "commonwealth") find that it is advantageous to unite as "Hispanics" for political purposes. At the national level, the permanent or temporary political cooperation within these new categories carries considerable weight, and enables them to gain special access to the caucuses that Black, Asian, and Hispanic congressional representatives have developed into important pressure groups within the federal government.

One consequence of the imposition of these categories by the federal government, and the minority coalition building that has resulted from it, has been the magnification of the importance of immigrant issues. The alliance of minorities led by Jesse Jackson has had an important impact on the electoral registration of these groups, and, in various places, on voting turnout. In five states of the Southwest, which account for a fifth of the votes necessary for the victory of a presidential candidate, a massive "Hispanic" vote can tip the balance by 10 percent. Political parties are also conscious of the implications of multiethnic solidarity, and when no particular national group is dominant, politicians have sometimes developed a broader Asian or Hispanic image, rather than one that is more narrowly Korean or Cuban. The political benefits of this kind of minority coalition building tend to be broadly communal, and therefore extend to immigrants as well as citizens and voters.

The debates on immigration legislation also indicate the effectiveness of multiethnic lobbies. In 1986, the "Hispanics" were able to prevail on key points over the representatives of agroindustry and the trade unions. Every legal reform of immigration must, from now on, take into account "the voice" of these political participants, who are aided in the defense of their interests by powerful groups. Thus, policy has been a result of a political process that has linked the state with groups that have emerged out of society, groups whose structure and organization have been influenced by policy decisions of the state.

We find a similar relationship in policy implementation, which is defined by widespread devolution of authority for policy implementation from the national government to churches, unions, associations for the defense of the rights of immigrants and refugees, and groups of civil rights lawyers. When Congress decided to grant amnesty to undocumented immigrants in 1986, it also permitted these organizations to deal with individual cases, to act as legal advisors, and to conduct information campaigns. The unions were subsidized for giving English courses and civic instruction to candidates for naturalization. (At the same time, they socialized immigrants into the political system.) The directives came from Washington, but were carried out at the local level, in different ways in different states and cities.

Of course, this also weakens the state when it becomes the target of these partners. With the strength of legitimacy granted by the state, these groups pressure elected representatives as advocates for immigrants. They direct their attention towards problems of discrimination for which the state is responsible, towards protection for immigrants, and towards violations of human rights that are in conflict with methods of expulsion of families of undocumented aliens (separated from their children, for example), and they do not hesitate to go to court to enforce policy decisions that are slow in coming (Body-Gendrot 1990b).

These same uneasy partners, financed by the federal government, have also pressured for further reforms when political conditions were favorable, generally at the local level. One example is the creation of a bureau responsible for immigration in the office of the mayor of the city of New York; another is the decision to establish sanctuary cities under the insistent pressure of centers for the defense of immigrant and refugee rights and civil rights lawyers.

San Francisco, Oakland, Chicago, and New York are sanctuary towns, meaning that these cities do not follow the immigration policies enacted by Washington that deny political asylum to refugees from San Salvador or Guatemala. By refusing, for instance, to denounce illegal aliens to the INS, those cities are accused of disobedience and could face financial sanctions. Of course, the INS does not recognize the power of these cities to enact their own immigration policies. These grass roots organizations, in turn, have frequently found advocates within the system, since commissions for civil rights are integrated into municipal institutions by law, and because elected representatives from immigrant neighborhoods are effective advocates on the state and national levels.

Thus, in various localities, these federally financed organizations occupy a place that is more or less institutionalized (or, in more current terminology, neocorporatist). In functional terms, they have often taken the place that in other times was filled by political machines in providing everything from welfare to information on naturalization to a means of political expression for immigrants. Outside of the South, churches, unions, and immigrant defense organizations play important roles in dealing with both immigration policy and policy implementation.

This emphasis on the relationship between the national and local levels should not obscure the central fact that policy *implementation* is generally decentralized, fragmented, and tends to focus on only certain categories of immigrants. As a result, the various representatives of immigrant interests rarely question immigration laws enacted by Congress, and even less what is an often illusory "immigration policy," except at the initiative of Congress.[12] Nevertheless, the basic elements of the immigration debate in 1990 are produced by those watchful advocates of immigrant and racial minorities who are anxious to demonstrate, for example, that sanctions against employers of illegal work force have discriminatory consequences. In the case of immigration, local efforts culminate in a debate that takes place in Congress, but the dynamics of grassroots initiatives are essentially local.

Most of the issues that in France would pertain to a *national* debate under the label "immigration" and would attract the attention of politicians and media, such as voting rights and their consequences, or labor rights and illegal aliens, are processed in a decentralized manner in the United States, and are intimately linked to questions of civil rights. For instance, a 1972 amendment extended the benefits of the Voting Rights Act of 1965 to Latino and Asian citizens. Nevertheless, real change can come only from the capacity of those groups and of their advocates to engage in legal action to change electoral systems alleged to dilute the impact of their vote.

In Texas, when sixty-two cities changed districting, representation of racial minorities as council members more than doubled. In California, in 1985, the city of Los Angeles was forced by legal action by civil rights activists to modify its districts. The result was the unprecedented election of two Latinos to the city council (among fifteen members). At the county level, with a Republican majority, a 28 percent Latino population had not been represented at all because of the districting system, but because of recent legal action, mandated redistricting now seems to guarantee Latino representation (Colin 1988). In Florida, another state with a strong immigrant concentration, "Anglos" resist attempts to alter districting in Dade County, which includes Miami.

Political exclusion of minorities and immigrant groups is also facilitated by the localism of, and the weak linkages within, American political parties. Areas of the Southwest where large numbers of immigrants have settled often have strong reform traditions and nonpartisan elections, and the decentralized organization of parties tends to reflect local culture and local bias. In localities in which, in France, M. Le Pen would obtain results that would trigger a counterattack by leftist parties, the two major U.S. parties are often not present. The result is both a lack of access of immigrant groups as well as a localization of policymaking. Consider the difference in the way similar local actions were dealt with in Monterey Park, California, and Montfermeil in France.

In 1983, Monterey Park was selected by *USA Today* as a symbol of racial and ethnic harmony, with the election to City Hall of the first Asian-American woman. Latino families had followed Jewish families in settling there. Later, new immigrants from Hong Kong and Taiwan arrived in large numbers, and soon became a numerical majority. As early as 1986, a strong nonpartisan campaign by Barry Hutch expressed the uneasiness of native "Anglos" who were facing sudden change. With the new Asian immigration, the economic growth of the city seemed unlimited. Almost $43 million had been invested there. However, Hutch captured Monterey Park City Hall on the basis of an anti-immigrant campaign. The drastic decisions of the new city government— declaring English as the "official language," forbidding bilingual education, imposing a minimum of two-thirds English letters in public signs in restaurants and stores—have been challenged in court as infringements of the constitutional rights of citizens of Asian descent, but attempts by opponents to recall Hutch from office through a recall campaign have failed. By and large, the issues have remained local, and the case did not even make it to the state level. Asian leaders have understood this and have already begun a registration and organization drive for the 1990 (nonpartisan) local election.

Similar decisions of the xenophobic mayor of Montfermeil attracted the attention of the national media when he denied schooling to new immigrant students in public schools, and quickly became a point of contention among national political parties and the national teachers' unions (two teachers had been fired by the mayor for admitting immigrant children to infant schools in violation of local directives). In the end, most of the mayor's actions were reversed by the prefect and administrative courts (*Le Monde*, 28 March 1990, 8). As we shall see, the nationalization of the immigration issue in France in the 1980s has meant that actors such as political parties and national administrative structures have become central in linking local initiatives to national politics.

Although, in American ethnic communities, the interests of citizens and immigrants are clearly linked both by government and the communities themselves, concentrations of immigrants within these communities have an impact on community political behavior. Thus, first-generation Asian and Latino immigrants are under severe economic pressures, and they avoid political involvement because of the distrust for politics they acquired in their native countries under the political regimes they left. Moreover, Latinos, because of the proximity of their native countries, and their desire to return, naturalize at half the rate of other immigrants. A study by the Urban Institute on the political adaptation of Latino immigrants reveals that first- and third-generation Mexican immigrants tend to concentrate on their private lives and to get less involved in politics than Anglos and Blacks. On the other hand, the second (and fourth) generations are inclined to compensate for the absence of political participation by their parents. Their experience with discrimination and their growing familiarity with the functioning of the U.S. society promotes their political involvement and their willingness to be recognized as a component of this society. Here, as everywhere else, education and socioeconomic status are also decisive determinants for participation (Goodis 1988). However, new generations tend to enter the political arena by adopting arbitrary preexisting classifications, in order to build on the advances obtained by former generations. Many immigrants, whether legal or illegal, live in districts already represented by one of their group in the city council, a school board, the state assembly, or Congress.

The political relations between immigrants and government institutions have also been fluid and changing. These changing relations produce diversified strategies and political styles among different groups and between the same groups over time.[13] The mode of operation of Cubans in Miami (pampered by the federal government as refugees who arrived in a time of prosperity) has been very different from that of the Mexicans of Los Angeles or San Antonio (themselves internally divided along generation lines, social class, and immigration types). The low-keyed political attitude of the Chinese already living in Chinatown, San Francisco, is itself very different from that of Chinese residents who have just arrived from Hong Kong, many of whom are friends of the mayor and of important financial investors in downtown San Francisco. This attitude again is very different from diverse political relationships one can observe in other Chinatowns in the United States. The political socialization process that influences immigrants varies with the length of their stay, their command of English, the citizenship of their spouse, and specific local conditions that in turn are influenced by immigrants, and this process is different for each successive wave of immigration (Portes and Rumbaut 1989).

Finally, immigrant strategies themselves evolve over time. Philip Kasinitz demonstrates convincingly how in New York, immigrants from the Caribbean, who used to be an elite among minorities, complicate the political situation of the city, and the political situation of Blacks in particular, because of the power they derive from their strength of numbers and of the resources they draw from their ethnic militancy. They number roughly three to six hundred thousand (when illegal aliens are included). They are settled in the heart of Brooklyn, and they have taken control of most community institutions. They held important political offices in the city as "Blacks" even before they were so numerous as "Caribbeans" (i.e., with a separate Caribbean identity).

Between 1930 and 1960, the educational achievements of Caribbean immigrants and their competence made them natural leaders of the Black community (not without friction). However, with the rise of Black political power in the 1970s, they were pushed aside. Currently, they choose to focus on their Caribbean[14] identity rather than racial solidarity. This places them in a pivotal position that enables them to tip the balance in favor of a Black candidate or another White candidate, to choose whether or not to follow political parties' directives, and to negotiate party support. Some people accuse Caribbeans of having been coopted, but in fact they follow a strategy that has proved effective. Candidates for public office have adapted their campaigns to these communities by appearing in carnivals and calypso clubs.

This political approach, deliberately ethnic and not racial, derives from the territorial concentration of recent immigrants from the Caribbean. The geographical nature of the US political representation tends to structure political interest according to the neighborhood. (Kasinitz 1987, 55)

In 1985, Caribbean voters were responsible for Mayor Koch's success in their neighborhood; in 1987, on the other hand, they chose Jesse Jackson and in 1989, after much hesitation, they supported the Black candidate David Dinkins. The territorial concentration of those people, combined with particularly skillful leadership, enabled them to influence the outcome of the election. The future of this strategy will depend therefore on several factors: the willingness of recent immigrants to secure citizenship, their success in registering new voters, the decrease of the number of illegal aliens, and the capacity of this community to avoid territorial and political divisions.

France: The Dynamics of Party Politics and the National Focus of Policymaking

In France, the changing dynamics of the party system provide us with the key for understanding the emergence of political issues of immigration and ethnicity at the national level in the 1980s. The party system that developed in France during the first two decades of the Fifth Republic was far stronger than that of the United States: far more able to control local candidacies, far more able to impose party loyalty in legislative voting, and far more capable of presenting policy choices. However, because so many members of parliament and government ministers have strong local bases, national parties have been open to considerable local influence. Therefore, as in the United States, issues of local concern find their way into national politics rather easily, but are transformed by the dynamics of the national arena.

In contrast with the local arena, where local politicians of different political persuasions frequently work with field administrators of the state to develop "practical" policy, alliances and policies that emerge in the national arena are far more constrained by party interests and ideology. For example, at the same time when numerous towns and cities governed by Socialists and Communists were imposing quotas on immigrant families, with the cooperation of state administrators, both parties were vehemently opposing government efforts to expel and control the same immigrants.[15] The issue of immigrants in national politics during the 1970s focused on limiting immigrant labor and attempting to expel immigrant workers without valid papers, and it divided the Conservative government from the Left opposition.

This changed abruptly during the presidential campaign of 1980–1981, when the candidate for the Communist party supported a coordinated campaign in a number of Communist-governed towns against Black (both immigrants and citizens from overseas departments) and North African immigrant families. Although there had been many incidents before, the series of actions by Communist local authorities undertaken in December 1980 attempted to tap what the PCF perceived as a rising opposition to non-White ethnics for national electoral purposes. The Communist campaign was widely condemned, but not universally; it was supported by the Socialist group in the town where the campaign began (Vitry), as well as by some other local Socialists (*Le Monde,* 30 December 1980, 23). The campaign proved to be a poor electoral tactic, and by 1985 the party had substantially changed its position on immigrants and ethnicity in France. Nevertheless, by linking Third World immigrants (and Frenchmen) to more general social and economic problems, the party did succeed in altering the terms of the immigrant issue at the national level.

Three trends have assured that the immigrant issue, defined in terms of ethnic danger to the French nation, would remain on the national political agenda. The first was the rapid decline of the Communist party that first became evident in 1981, but in many respects had begun in the 1970s. Although the PCF had played a key role in politicizing the immigrant/ethnic issue at the national level, its growing organizational and electoral weakness was not entirely compensated for by the growing strength of the Socialists during the same period. This meant that even when the party moved away from its position of 1980–1981, the Left in general would be less effective in mobilizing against a resurgent Right that based its appeal on an anti-immigrant stance. The organizational and electoral decline also finally ended the role of the PCF as an important (perhaps the most important) institution through which successive waves of immigrant workers had been integrated into French society. This role of the party had been least effective for North Africans (whom the PCF came to view as citizens of their home countries, rather than fellow workers); nevertheless, the party had in fact performed valuable services for individual North Africans (particularly legal services) that it was now increasingly less able to perform (Leveau 1989, 247–62).

The second trend has been a declining number of voters who are strongly attached to a political party. This trend, which has been evident since 1978, is indicated by a rising tide of voter volatility, voters who switch parties from election to election.[16] Although relatively few voters cross the left-right ideological divide, this trend has created a mass of available voters, who can be mobilized around emerging issues. Thus, because of the emergence of the National Front (FN), the established parties of the Right have been unable to gain as many votes in *any* election in the 1980s as they gained in 1978 (35 percent of the registered voters); in 1986, when they won the legislative elections on a wave of antigovernment sentiment, the two established parties of the Right received only 31 percent of the registered vote.

The third trend has been the electoral rise of the anti-immigrant National Front. Although the party has existed since 1972, it was not able to attract a significant percentage of the electorate until 1984 (the elections for the European parliament), when weakened party ties, voter volatility, and the electoral weakness of the established parties of the Right established a pool of available voters that the National Front was able to mobilize around its anti-immigrant positions. Party spokesmen and propaganda deal extensively with immigration, but what they most emphasize is the danger of cultural and racial differences for the future of France. What clearly differentiates the roughly 10 percent of the electorate that have voted for the National Front is their overwhelming concern for issues of law and order and immigration (which have become related in French political perceptions). Moreover, the National Front has succeeded in sustaining the altered terms of the political debate.

Through the dynamics of party competition it has forced other political parties, especially those of the Right, to place these issues of immigrants and ethnicity high on their political agendas, and the debate has mobilized interest among all voters. With each succeeding election the percentage of voters who claim to be concerned with these issues increases: among all voters concern with law and order has increased from 15 to 31 percent from 1984 to 1988, and concern for immigration has increased from 6 to 22 percent (Schain 1990, table 1).

Political parties on both the Right and the Left have struggled, without great success, to undermine the ability of the National Front to sustain the initiative in defining these issues. The RPR is torn between competing with FN for voters frightened by the problems of a multiethnic society, and attempting to destroy the party through isolation and acceptance of their issues in more moderate terms. Each time that RPR feels that it has succeeded in outmaneuvering the National Front (the legislative elections of 1988 and the municipal elections of 1989), it is reminded that the challenge will not disappear (the by-election victories of the FN in Marseilles and Dreux in December 1989).

As for the Socialists, they have struggled to defuse the rhetoric of the National Front by a variety of approaches: by strengthening border controls at the same time that they have tried to develop a policy of integration, when they have controlled the government; by agreeing with the established Right that "the National Front poses some real questions" (the Fabius-Chirac debate in 1985), when they have been opposition; and, more generally, by alternating between a pluralist "right to difference" approach to immigrants (in December 1989) and an individualistic "right to indifference" approach (February 1989) (*Le Monde*, 11 February and 7 December 1989).

Despite the confusion, the dynamics of party competition have resulted in redefinition of the issue of immigration, from a labor market problem to a problem that touches on the structure of French society—problems of education, housing, and law and order, as well as the requirements for citizenship. A case has also been made that there is a developing consensus among the established parties of the Right and Left, if not about specific policies then about a general approach to policy, that goes back to the Fabius-Chirac debate in 1985—a policy of integration "respecting our laws, our customs and our values," that limits any substantial increase in immigrants but that also excludes recourse to forced return (Leveau 1989, 258–61).

However, within the relatively open national arena it has been difficult to arrive at a policy of integration. The National Front continues to maintain pressure on the Right, while the Socialist government is now challenged by more politicized North Africans born in France ("beurs"), who are now well organized, as well as by more assertive Moslems who are less hesitant about questioning French laws, customs, and values. Thus, the Rocard government wanted to downplay the issues of immigration when it first arrived in office. Nevertheless, it found that, because of the challenge of the "Islamic scarf" crisis in the fall of 1989, as well as the subsequent electoral victories of the National Front, it was unable to avoid the pressure that moved the issue to center stage. In the United States, a comparable crisis would have been largely contained within specific localities, and if it reached the national level at all, the route through the courts would have been long and difficult.

These incidents centered on the case of several girls who were wearing traditional Moslem scarves that covered their hair, head, and neck, were refused entry into secondary schools, and were seen by local school authorities as a challenge to the secular public school. Within days, the national press, major organizations representing immigrants (SOS-Racisme and France Plus —which sharply disagreed on both the interpretation of the issue and the proper policy that should be followed), and numerous political leaders had issued statements about the incidents, and had reinterpreted them in terms of historic conflicts over church-state relations, ethnic pluralism and integration, Islamic fundamentalism, and women's rights. Thus, this "affair" very quickly became the concern of the minister of education, as well as an issue of parliamentary debate. The minister's decision to compromise and to permit the girls to wear the scarves if they insisted was hotly debated in parliament, and eventually considered by the highest administrative court in France. The Conseil d'Etat decided to turn the decision back to local education authorities, which could decide one way or the other according to local circumstances and criteria established by the ministry. A decade earlier, such incidents might have been dealt with more quietly within the local arena, in the same way that it dealt with housing and other school problems. By 1989, however, local school problems that involved integration could no longer be contained by the local political-administrative system, and were rapidly transformed into a national political issue.

The pressures of party competition within the national arena were all played out in the spring of 1990, when the Rocard government made an attempt to develop a consensus around immigration. Using as a pretext a disturbing report by the National Consultative Committee on the Rights of Man, the prime minister called a meeting of all political leaders, except those of the National Front, to develop a program to combat racism. The opposition, however, rejected this definition of the problem and organized their own meeting the weekend preceding the meeting with the prime minister to discuss problems of immigration. When they met with the government, the opposition came armed with four propositions for changing immigration policy. They were able to extract from the Rocard government a commitment for a second meeting that would deal with their initiatives, preceding a general parliamentary debate on racism and immigration in May 1990.[17]

Thus, in the spring of 1990, the question of immigration and integration was once more on political center stage and, given the proliferation of propositions, was likely to remain there for some time. It was also likely to remain there because behind this activity was the growing pressure of the National Front, which was holding its national congress while the government and the opposition were developing their positions. The opposition groups had never come closer to agreement on a unified approach to the politics of immigration, and their propositions tentatively approached those of the National Front. The clearest statement was made by former president Valéry Giscard d'Estaing, who was quoted as saying, "The foreigners can live in France with full rights [dans le respect des droits de l'homme] but they cannot change France." Giscard promptly launched a national petition to hold a referendum to make naturalization legislation more restrictive (one of the proposals agreed to by the opposition).

What began as local initiatives in the fall of 1989 were magnified by the electoral success of the National Front, and seem to have exacerbated divisions between the government and the opposition over immigration—or rather, over how to define and treat foreigners on French soil. The far Right has benefited from growing national concern about immigration (between September 1989 and February 1990, the issue moved from seventh to second place among the concerns of French voters) but has also mediated and defined that concern within the party system. In this kind of environment, it seems unlikely that any kind of consensus will develop, despite the fact that it is frequently reported that "political leaders are convinced that the issue is too important for partisan quarrels. . . . They vie with each other to accentuate their divergences as if to mask their agreements" (*Le Monde,* 3 April 1990, 12).

Therefore, it appears that the separation of different issues of immigration between the local and national arenas in France that was still operating a decade ago, no longer exists. Both the labor market issues of immigration and issues of integration are dealt with and structured within the national arena.

Nevertheless, the local arena continues to play an important role in the development of policies related to immigrants. First, because of the structural links between the local and national arenas, through administration, political parties, and parliament, issues initiated at the local level frequently generate national politics. This was clearly the case in the Islamic scarves affair, where the decisions of local school authorities in a few localities forced a national political debate that changed the political agenda of the government and every major political party. But this case is not an exception.

At the same time that this vast debate was going on, at least two mayors (one in suburban Paris, the other in southern France) were creating a new school issue by refusing to permit North African students to register for the new school year. Their stated purpose was to get the "attention" of national authorities and to protest the influx of North Africans into their towns (*Le Monde,* 17 October and 26 October 1989). It is not clear whether the decision of the Conseil d'Etat will defuse the school issue by pushing it back into the local arena, or exacerbate it by reaffirming the power of local authorities to initiate policy that will ignite new issues in the national arena.

Moreover, other approaches to ethnic integration, which have been quietly initiated within the local arena for many years, are also potential national issues. On the basis of agreements concluded with all Mediterranean countries, as well as Portugal, between 1974 and 1987, local education authorities have permitted teachers from these countries to teach language and culture courses that include religious instruction. Although fewer than 20 percent of the students who come from immigrant families from these countries participate in these programs, they have been quietly established in about 10 percent of primary schools in France. Until now, they have existed parallel to the secular school and have been questioned only by scholars and some administrators concerned with their impact on the integration of immigrant children. Now, however, they have become a potential concern of the national debate on integration policy, as have other policies that have been established through the administrative process, such as the important role played by North African governments in directing and paying for the construction of mosques (Costa-Lascoux 1989, 88–93; Leveau 1989, 259; and *Le Monde,* 23 November 1989).

CONCLUSION

There are clearly many differences between the United States and France with respect to immigration policy and the process through which this policy has been developed. There are, however, two aspects of this problem that have been similar in both countries. The first is the impact of immigration on the centralization of policymaking; and the second is the definition of the problem that has slowly emerged.

In the United States, immigration was dealt with, both legally and administratively, on the state level until national political elites reformulated the problem in racial/ethnic terms at the turn of the century. In the process of dealing with what was understood as a problem of national identity and citizenship, new structures were created at the federal level that generated both political debate and new national policies. Once the major lines of policy on entry were set at the national level, however, the local arena became the focal point for policy implementation and policy development on integration.

National policy became the impetus for the organization of a multitude of interest groups, many of them linking immigrants with citizens through ethnic heritage. By the 1960s, the sons and daughters of the immigrants of the turn of the century had organized sufficiently to change the exclusionary legislation of the 1920s, but they had also changed the process through which national legislation is developed. Legislation on entry was now the product of complex group interaction, and policy on integration was now directly related to the broader politics of ethnic policy. By the 1980s, interest groups were directly involved in the implementation of national policy at the local level, and were therefore well positioned to initiate changes in that policy.

In France, policy on both entry and integration had always been formally developed at the national level. Nevertheless, the implementation of integration policy at the local level has also implied a considerable range of policy development. The emergence of immigration as a national political issue in the 1980s, and pressures to develop more exclusionary policies, have resulted from changes in the party system. Indeed, political parties have become the motor force behind the movement of policy initiation from the local to the national level. As in the United States at the turn of the century, as immigration has become increasingly politicized, the national state has become increasingly involved in both policy development and policy implementation. As in the United States, the more informal aspects of French policy on integration in the 1980s have made the traditional line between immigrants and ethnic groups less clear. As a result, immigrants and some ethnic Frenchmen have begun to organize, bringing into question the nature of French nationality and citizenship.

French commentators have frequently contended that the French model of individual integration is very different from the American model of integration through the recognition of ethnic pluralism.[18] However, the American recognition of the legitimacy of ethnic pluralism is a post–World War II phenomenon that was the result of political pressures set in motion by ethnic organization after 1924. During the period before World War II, the operating model of immigrant integration in the United States, which stressed White Protestant middle-class values, was close if not identical to the French. The symbol of "Our ancestors the Gauls" had its equivalent in the Founding Fathers for American school children[19] (Olneck 1990; Mohl 1981). The challenge to and the change in the operating model of integration was the result of a political process that has hardly begun in France, but that can be seen in the present debate over the nature of French nationality. Thus, in the American experience, if there is a lesson to be learned, it is probably the process through which well-organized immigrant/ethnic groups were able to alter the model of American national identity. Until now, immigrant pressure groups have not been able to exert comparable influence on the political process in France.[20] It is still the state that chooses its negotiating partners, and the state itself takes the initiative to generate these partners if they do not yet exist.

NOTES

1. The "Passenger Cases" are *Smith v. Turner*, consolidated with *Norris v. City of Boston*, 48 US (1849). One previous Supreme Court decision, *Mayor, Aldermen and Commonalty of the City of New York v. Miln*, 35 US (1837), had upheld a state immigration statute against a constitutional attack based on federalism. Miln, however, was later qualified by *Holmes v. Jennison*, 39 US (1840), and has never significantly influenced subsequent Supreme Court decisions in this area. In the 1849 decision, referred to as "Passenger Cases," five of the justices held the Boston taxation unconstitutional on the ground that it usurped an exclusively federal power.
2. See, for example, the contributions of André-Clément Decouflé and Gérard Noiriel in this volume, as well as Singer-Keriel (1989).
3. By 1977, 55 percent of cities (over thirty thousand population) governed by Communist mayors had immigrant populations greater than 10 percent, compared

with 23 percent for towns governed by Socialists and 21 percent of towns governed by the Center-Right. In 1977, 82 percent of the larger towns with more than 10 percent immigrant population were governed by the Left, and more than two-thirds of these were governed by the PCF (see Schain 1985).

4. Letter from the Office of Public Housing of St. Denis, 28 November 1980, to applicants from public housing from the overseas department of Guadaloupe.

5. The process of developing plans for urban renewal projects is described in the city magazine *Grenoble,* no. 2 (November 1980): esp. 57–62.

6. Gilles Kepel estimates that there were about a thousand prayer rooms or mosques in France in 1987 (see Kepel 1987, 17 and ch. 3).

7. The mosque in Mantes, for example, welcomed all Moslems in the area, including Harkis (Algerians who had sided with the French during the Algerian revolution), except for Turks, who established their own mosque (see Bekouchi 1984).

8. A list that received a majority of the votes in the first round, or a plurality in the second round, gained all of the seats in the municipal council. The tendency for opposition in local councils to disappear is analyzed by Becquart-Leclercq 1976, 117–207.

9. The first Arreté was on 15 June 1970 (see Grillo 1985, 126).

10. This was complicated by the fact that immigrants groups could not formally organize their own associations until 1982. Thus, consultations about immigrant issues often took place with representatives of North African governments.

11. For more details on the Z.E.P.s, see Costa-Lascoux 1989, 93–95.

12. The situation is quite different in France, where immigration policy as a whole is hotly debated by interested groups (see Weil 1990).

13. For a discussion of the interplay between structures and subjects, see Body-Gendrot 1990a.

14. This term refers to inhabitants of the Caribbean islands and to those of English-speaking nations (Belize and Guyana), as well as to English-speaking inhabitants of Afro-Creole enclaves within Spanish-speaking countries of the Caribbean.

15. We are referring here to the Fontanet-Marcellin *circulaires* of 1972 (struck down by the Council of State in 1975) and the Bonnet Law of 1980. Martin Schain has elaborated on this in Schain 1985.

16. Schain has analyzed these trends in "Immigration and Changes in the French Party System," in Schain 1988. The analysis of voter volatility in this article ends in 1986, but Philippe Habert and Alain Lancelot demonstrate continuing voter volatility through the 1988 legislative elections, in Habert and Lancelot 1988.

17. The initiatives of the government and the opposition are reported in *Le Monde,* 3 and 4 April 1990.

18. Michael Wieviorka writes, for example, in a *Libération* editorial of 14 April 1990 entitled "U.S. multi-ethnicity and France": "Even in extrapolating the darkest trends, nothing indicates that French society is approaching the American model."

19. For an analysis of Americanization programs before 1924, see Maris A. Vinovskis's chapter in this volume.

20. During the first half of 1990, Pierre Joxe, minister of the interior (responsible for the police and law and order), established an advisory council of fifteen widely respected French and foreign Moslems from the various Moslem ethnic commu-

nities. This organization will have the status that other churches have when they bargain with the state, and as a result, will diminish the impact of foreign Moslem states in French affairs.

REFERENCES

Becquart-Leclercq, J. 1976. *Paradoxes du pouvoir local.* Paris: Presses de la FNSP.

Bekouchi, M. H. 1984. *Du bled à la Z.U.P. et/ou la couleur de l'avenir.* Paris: CIEM l'Harmattan.

Body-Gendrot, S. 1990a. "Migration and the Racialization of the Post-modern City in France." In M. Cross and M. Keith, eds., *Racism, the City, and the State.* London: Unwin Hyman.

———. 1990b "Deux approches contrastées de l'immigration: la France et les Etats-Unis." *Revue Migrants-formation* (April).

Body-Gendrot, S., B. d'Hellencourt, and M. Rancoule. 1988. "Entrée interdite: la législation sur l'immigration en France, au Royaume-Uni et aux Etats-Unis." *Revue française de science politique* 39 (February).

Christopher, W., J. Corbett, and J. Stack. 1990. "Hispanic Ascendancy and Tripartite Politics in Miami." In R. Browning, et al., eds., *Racial Politics in American Cities.* New York: Longman.

Colin, M. 1988. "For Latinos, Immediate Object Is City Council Membership." *New York Times,* 4 September.

Costa-Lascoux, J. 1989. *De l'immigré au citoyen.* Paris: La Documentation Française.

Goodis, T. 1988. "The Political Adaptation of Hispanic Immigrants to the United States." Urban Institute, Policy Discussion Paper.

Grillo, R. D. 1985. *Ideologies and Institutions in Urban France.* London: Cambridge University Press.

Habert, P., and A. Lancelot. 1988. "L'emergence d'un nouvel électeur." In *Elections législatives 1988.* Paris: Le Figaro/Etudes Politiques.

Higham, J. 1985. *Strangers in the Land.* New York: Atheneum.

———. 1990. "The Pot That Didn't Melt." *New York Review of Books,* 12 April.

Ireland, P. 1989. "The State and the Political Participation of the 'New' Immigrants in France and in the U.S." *Revue française d'études américaines* 41 (July). Special issue on immigration.

Kasinitz, P. 1987. "The Minority Within: The New Black Immigrants." *New York Affairs* 10 (Winter).

Katznelson, I. 1973. *Black Men, White Cities: Race Politics and Migration in the United States, 1900–1930, and Britain, 1948–1968.* London: Oxford University Press.

Kennedy, J. F. 1964. *A Nation of Immigrants.* New York: Harper and Row.

Kepel, G. 1987. *Les Banlieues de l'Islam: naissance d'une religion en France.* Paris: Seuil.

Leveau, R. 1989. "Les partis et l'intégration des 'beurs'." In Y. Mény, ed., *Idéologies, partis politiques et groupes sociaux.* Paris: Presses de la FNSP.

Long, M. 1988. *Etre français aujourd'hui et demain.* Rapport de la Commission de la Nationalité, présenté par M. Marceau Long, président, au Premier ministre, vol. 1.

Lowi, T. 1969. *The End of Liberalism*. New York: Norton.

Les Minguettes. 1982. Rapport présenté à la Commission pour le Développement Social des Quartiers. Lyon: COURLY-Ville de Vénissieux.

Mohl, R. 1981. "Cultural Assimilation versus Cultural Pluralism." *Education Forum* (March).

Olneck, M. 1990. "Americanization and Education of Immigrants, 1900–1925: An Analysis of Symbolic Action." *American Journal of Education*.

Paine, T. 1983. *Le sens commun*. Translated by B. Vincent. Paris: Aubier.

Portes, A., and R. Rumbaut. 1989. *Immigrant America: A Portrait*. Berkeley: University of California Press.

Schain, M. 1985. "Immigrants and Politics in France." In J. S. Ambler, ed., *The French Socialist Experiment*. Philadelphia: ISHI.

———. 1988. "Immigration and Changes in the French Party System." *European Journal of Political Research* 16.

———. 1989. "Immigration, Race, and the Crisis of Citizenship in the United States (1880–1924)." Paper delivered to the Annual Workshops of the ECPR, Paris, April.

———. 1990. "Immigration and Politics." In P. Hall, J. Hayward, and H. Machin, eds., *Developments in French Politics*. London: Macmillan.

Singer-Keriel, J. 1989. "Foreign Workers in France, 1890–1936." Paper delivered at the University of Glasgow, 15 September.

Weil, P. 1990. "La politique d'immigration: au-delà du désordre." *Regards sur l'actualité* (March).

Zolberg, A. 1983. "Contemporary Transnational Migrations in Historical Perspective: Patterns and Dilemma." In M. Kritz, ed., *U.S. Migration and Refugee Policy*. Lexington, Mass.: Lexington Books.

20

INTERNATIONAL POPULATION MOVEMENTS: IMPLICATIONS FOR FOREIGN POLICIES AND MIGRATION POLICIES

Myron Weiner

Foreign policies and immigration policies are intertwined. This truism was painfully demonstrated to Americans, French, and other Europeans when the government of Iraq announced that it was holding Western migrant workers as hostages to ensure that there would not be a military assault to liberate Kuwait from Iraqi occupation. In this instance it was the policies of another country toward *our* migrant workers that constrained our foreign policies. But more often it is the presence of third world migrants in the West that constitutes a constraint upon policies. Immigrants and their descendants have frequently influenced American foreign policies and in recent years Latin American countries have argued that since U.S. policies on trade, aid, and investment shape their population flows, then the regulation of migration between the United States and its neighbors is a matter for wide-ranging negotiations.

In France, too, immigration policies are intertwined with foreign policies. Refugee, asylum, and migration policies must be harmonized with those of other members of the European Community if European borders are to be open, and the question of intra-European migration for noncitizen migrant workers is also a matter for international negotiation. Even the questions of how immigrants should be treated, what religious rights they should have in the schools, and whether they should be permitted to organize themselves to influence either the foreign policies of their host society or the domestic politics of their home societies are no longer purely domestic matters.

Is there then a convergence between France and the United States in the relationship between foreign policies and migration policies, notwithstanding their different histories and attitudes toward migration? At one level, some differences remain: migrants and their ethnic descendants play an active, legitimate, and influential role in shaping American foreign policies and migration policies, but not (yet?) in France or elsewhere in Europe. However, in both countries migrants can and do attempt to influence the politics of their home countries. And in both countries immigration policies are increasingly shaped by foreign policy considerations.

It is the argument of this essay that these convergences are the result of global changes in the patterns of international migration, in the linkage between population movements and other international flows, in the changing determinants of population movements, in the character of international communications, and in the economic interdependence of countries. The result is increasing pressure upon states to establish bilateral, regional, and even international rules with respect to immigration, refugee, and emigration policies as well as in the treatment of immigrants and refugees. To develop these arguments I shall first briefly describe how and why international migration has been changing, and how and why there is now a global category of people with dual identities, then turn to some of the implications for formulating foreign policies and migration policies.

1. THE NEW TRANSNATIONALS: EXILES, REFUGEES, MIGRANT WORKERS, NATURALIZED CITIZENS, AND ETHNICS

Our era has produced a new class of people who live in a country other than the one in which they were born. They have migrated in search of employment, to join their families, or to escape from oppression and violence. They can be refugees, temporary migrants, permanent residents, or naturalized citizens. They live and work in Western Europe, North America, and the Persian Gulf and in refugee camps in Ethiopia, Sudan, Thailand, Hong Kong, and Pakistan. Their numbers are legion. The United Nations high commissioner for refugees reports that in 1988 there were 13.3 million refugees in need of protection and/or assistance. In the past decade their numbers dramatically increased: 4.6 million in 1978, 9.8 million in 1981, 11.6 million in 1985. In 1980 one hundred thousand sought asylum in Western Europe. Since 1986 the number of annual asylum seekers has been over two hundred thousand (*World Refugee Survey* 1989). In 1990 six hundred thousand applied for asylum in Western Europe (*The Economist,* March 15, 1991).

These numbers refer to current flows and stocks. Several·times that number are settled and no longer count as refugees. Twelve to 15 million people permanently crossed the borders between India and Pakistan between 1947 and 1950. A million Indochinese settled in the United States and France. Numerous *pieds noirs* moved to or returned to France. Several million Jews from European concentration camps and from Arab countries migrated to Israel. Large numbers of Arabs in Israel fled to neighboring countries. Much of the population of Hong Kong migrated from the mainland, as did a significant portion of the population of Taiwan. Indians and Pakistanis fled Uganda, Kenya, and Burma in the 1950s to settle in the United Kingdom, the United States, Canada, and India. Hungarians, Czechs, Cubans, and Soviet Jews rebuilt their lives in the United States or Western Europe. While some settled refugees remained as exiles, most became naturalized citizens.

Millions more moved across international borders for employment or to join their relatives. More than 10 million Indians live in the United Kingdom, the United States, and the Persian Gulf. Four million Indians have settled in Nepal, Sri Lanka, Malaysia, and Singapore, many in the last thirty years. Twelve million Chinese live in Southeast Asia, and another million in the United States. Twelve million Turks, Algerians, Yugoslavs, Moroccans, Greeks, and other migrant workers and their dependents live in Western Europe. Three to 4 million Asians and Arabs work in the Persian Gulf in countries where they are often more numerous than local nationals. Between 1950 and 1981 10.8 million migrants moved to the United States, 2.5 million to Canada, and 2 million to Australia, mostly from developing countries (Klein 1987; Alonso 1987; Reimers 1985). In the 1980s over six million legal migrants entered the United States.

In search of work or land millions have moved to their neighboring country: Colombians to Venezuela, Portuguese to France, Mexicans to the United States, Indonesians to Malaysia, Nepalis and Bangladeshis to India, Indians to Nepal, Ghanaians to Nigeria, Malawis to South Africa, Italians to Switzerland, Jordanians to Kuwait. Political conflicts have produced new diasporas: Lebanese, Palestinians, Iranians, Tamilians, Ethiopians, Central Americans.

2. WHY HAVE POPULATION MOVEMENTS INCREASED?

There has been a quickening of all international flows—trade, capital, investment, information—and the movement of people is a part and often a consequence of these flows. Individual migrant decisions are part of a larger network of interstate relations. More than ever before countries are linked to one another through trade, investment, cultural and educational exchanges, political and security relations. American investments in the Caribbean and in Latin America created a network of ties that facilitated the flow of migrants to the United States. The expansion of U.S. relations with Japan, South Korea, and Taiwan necessitated an end to long-standing Oriental exclusion policies. U.S. political and military involvement in Vietnam created a set of moral obligations that led the United States to open its borders to refugees. France's colonial involvement in Algeria and other North African states, its need for oil and gas, investments by the French business community, and a network of cultural ties facilitated the movement from the Mahgreb to France. The United Kingdom attracted migrants from the Commonwealth, from South Asia and the West Indies, while people from Surinam and Indonesia migrated to Holland. "We are here, because you were there," said the protest poster of a black migrant in the United Kingdom.

The end of colonialism and the worldwide expansion of trade and investment after World War II brought an end to Eurocentric immigration policies in North America and in Western Europe. Ethnocentropathic sentiments—a concern for members of one's own race, religion, and nationality—did not end, but the definition of what is "one's own" people became broader as immigration became more diverse. France accepted migrants from Francophone regions of Africa as earlier it had accepted Italians, Poles, Ukrainians, and Czechs. As the racial composition of migrants to the United States became more diverse, America's conception of itself expanded.

International communication—films, television, radio, print media, telephone, and now the fax machine—heightened awareness of national economic differences and opportunities, and provided potential migrants with information as to how to move. Tamils in Jaffna quickly learned that the route to West Germany is via an Aeroflot connection to East Berlin and a train trip across the open border to West Berlin. East Germans learned that the route to the West is not across the wall, but through Czechoslovakia and Hungary to Austria. The Irish learned that the United States had established a lottery for admission. Turkish migrants learned that family allowances were larger if their children joined their fathers in the Federal Republic of Germany.

Labor shortages created a demand for migrant workers. The story of the decision by West European countries to fill temporary labor shortages after World War II by importing labor is well known. The story is similar in the American Southwest during World War II, when *braceros* were imported from Mexico. In the 1970s the oil-rich, low-population countries of the Gulf were in need of labor as a result of the rise in oil prices. Each new initial migration influx created a migration chain as migrant workers found employment opportunities for friends and relatives. Family unification laws permitted grandparents, parents, children, sisters, and brothers to migrate. Migrants sent remittances home to help friends and relatives join them. Migrants created businesses, opened restaurants, built temples, and started newspapers, which in turn created a demand for migrant accountants, restaurant workers, priests, and journalists.

The costs of international migration declined. A (discounted) airticket can be repaid out of savings after a few months of work abroad. Convenient flights are easily available between Puerto Rico and New York, Algiers and Marseille, Ankara and Munich, Colombo and Berlin, Cochin and Dubai. Labor contractors and travel agents help with no-objection certificates, work permits, passports, visas, photos, foreign exchange clearances, airplane tickets —the seemingly endless paperwork and bureaucratic hurdles that migrants must overcome.

Bureaucratic regulation notwithstanding, some barriers are down. Even when governments have not increased quotas for admission, they have become less restrictive as to race and national origin. The annual legal flow to the United States is of the same magnitude as it was in the latter part of the nineteenth century, but the sources of migrants are more diverse. Chinese, Japanese, Koreans, Indians, and other Asians are no longer excluded. Australia, New Zealand, and Canada have become more open. For Europeans, refugees once meant other Europeans; now they mean Tamils, Iranians, Ethiopians, Cambodians, Lebanese, Laotians, Vietnamese.

Above all, internal wars, violence, and repression are a cause of worldwide migration (Zolberg, Suhrke, and Aguayo 1986; 1989). Civil conflicts and human rights violations are rampant in the third world. Yesterday it was Nigeria, Bangladesh, Uganda, Brazil, Argentina; today it is Angola, Kuwait, Sudan, Ethiopia, Mozambique, Lebanon, Afghanistan, Cambodia, Nicaragua, El Salvador, Vietnam, and Sri Lanka. Tomorrow?

3. EARLY WARNINGS

There are signs of impending new international flows. Tiananmen Square increased the already-high anxieties in Hong Kong, and the British foreign minister has given assurances that Britain would join with others in providing refuge if need be after 1997. Ethnic strife and greater opportunities to emigrate are new factors in Eastern Europe and the Soviet Union. Minorities and dissidents see exit as their ultimate freedom. How many Armenians, Jews, Lithuanians, Estonians, Latvians, or Moldavians and other national minorities will leave the Soviet Union, especially if the movement toward autonomy is halted? In a fragmented Soviet Union would Russians flee non-Russian republics? How many people would exit if Eastern European countries failed in their reform efforts, or if a reversal in political democratization took place?

After 1992 will there be an increase in the movement from the less developed regions of Europe—Greece, southern Italy, Portugal, Spain, and Ireland —to the more developed regions, and from declining industrial regions and areas of high youth unemployment into economically expanding regions? A movement of new financial resources to these regions could slow the flow, but they could also attract outsiders with skills not readily available locally.

Regional wars and internal strife in the third world seem unlikely to abate. Some of the conflicts that have produced these flows have subsided, but other countries are on the edge. One could imagine strife within Burma, Iran, Pakistan, Southern Africa, or between India and Pakistan, Thailand and Vietnam, Jordan and Syria, Syria and Iraq, Libya and Chad. The easing of tensions among the great powers may well be accompanied by a rising tide of nationalism among third world countries, a growth in their military capabilities, and regional expansion. The Iraqi invasion of Kuwait led to a flight from Kuwait, and the exodus of hundreds of thousands of Asian, Arab, and European migrants. The third world remains a dangerous place. Wars between states, ethnic strife, aborted democratic movements, droughts, floods, famines, and economic collapse in debt-ridden countries will increase the flight of people across national boundaries.

With the slowdown in the world economy, labor shortages no longer appear to be as significant a factor in international migration as they once were. Even so, the combination of low economic growth in low-income countries and the availability of jobs in developed countries that local people do not want attracts migrants to illegal crossing of international borders. Employer sanctions notwithstanding, the United States continues to pull migrants from Mexico. Japan, which bars all migrants, now has a steady stream of illegals from the Philippines and other areas of southeast Asia. Even the high-unemployment Mezzogiorno region attracts illegals from North Africa. No amount of capital flows, no amount of international assistance, no amount of debt relief, no amount of technology transfers will end economic differences among countries. And as long as large differentials in wages and employment opportunities continue, as they invariably will, people will move across international borders.

4. PLURALISM AND DUALISM

Pluralism refers to the multiethnic character of societies. Dualism refers to the dual identity of individuals within those societies. International population movements transform both the social structures of the receiving societies and the character structures of those who migrate.

I asked an Israeli Arab from Haifa, a visiting scholar at MIT, how he identified himself. "I am," he replied, "an Israeli citizen and a Palestinian national." To the same question my downstairs neighbor in Brookline, a naturalized American citizen from Korea, replied, "a Korean-American." So are his children, all born in the United States. A Parisian friend, an academic who came to France from Rumania as an adolescent, describes himself simply as French. So here we have three very different notions of the relationship between nationality and citizenship.

For most Western Europeans it is inconceivable that one could have, as my Palestinian colleague does, the nationality of one country or people and the citizenship of another. Nor could one be an Algerian-French, or Turkish-German, or Yugoslav-Swiss in the hyphenated American style, with its implications of a dual nationality.

There are a variety of ways in which migrants and their children can live in a country and have a relationship to the state that is different from that of the natives. There is nothing sacrosanct about the relationship between citizenship and nationality (Brubaker 1989; Carens 1989). Let us consider a variety of relationships that those accustomed to the notion of a common citizenship and nationality find anomalous.

- There reside in the United States several million illegal aliens, mainly from Mexico. They have no right of residence and, if discovered, can be expelled. The Immigration Reform and Control Act (IRCA) made it illegal for employers to hire illegal migrants. Yet because the American Constitution guarantees due process to all *persons* (not only citizens), illegal migrants have the right to send their children to public schools, have access to medical care in public hospitals, and are entitled to a variety of public benefits. Moreover, notwithstanding their own illegal status, their children born in the United States automatically become citizens. They remain foreign citizens and nationals, but their children are American citizens and Mexican-Americans (Schuck and Smith 1985; Schuck 1989).
- Migrant workers in Europe retain their Algerian, Turkish, and Yugoslav citizenship and nationality, but have the right of residence, can obtain benefits provided by the welfare state, are free to live and work where they

choose, and in some countries can vote in local elections. They have many
of the benefits of citizenship without being citizens.

- Many migrant-sending countries follow the law of jus sanguinis so that
European-born children of migrants continue to retain the citizenship and
nationality of their parent's country. Some European countries follow the
principle of jus soli, or citizenship by birth, while others subscribe to jus
sanguinis. Thus, the country in which the young person has *never* lived may
bestow citizenship, while the country in which the individual is born may
deny citizenship.
- In North America and in France many exiles from the third world have
become naturalized citizens, but even after acquiring citizenship many retain
their sense of identity with their country of origin and dream of returning
after the government falls. Like Israeli Arabs, they have citizenship in one
country, but retain the nationality (or national identity) of another.
- After 1992 there will be easier movements within Europe across national
boundaries. The Irish, Italians, Portuguese, Spaniards, Greeks, and other
people who migrate will retain their nationality and citizenship even as they
have the right to reside and work in another country. Should they stay on,
their children may become citizens, but what national identity will their
children acquire? That of their parents, or that of their citizenship?
- Finally, there is the situation of minorities who flee to another country,
change their citizenship, but continue to have a sense of national identity
with their own people at home—Kurds, Sri Lankan Tamils, Armenians,
Lebanese, Palestinians, Timorese, Tibetans.

The world is full of people away from home, their legal status often in
limbo, their national identities uncertain. They are denizens or naturalized
citizens of one country, but do not choose, or may not be permitted to choose,
the national identity of their host. The anomalies are partly the result of the
policies of governments that admit people to work but do not grant citizenship. Often they are the preferences of the migrants themselves, who want to
retain the culture of their homeland and to transmit that culture to their
children but seek the right of permanent residence or citizenship in another
country. The anomalies also result from the toleration of ethnic diversity and
dual identities in the United States, Canada, Australia, and Western Europe.
Finally, sending countries contribute to the anomalies by forcing patriotic
opponents into exile or regarding those who left for employment abroad as
potential benefactors. Indians abroad, said Prime Minister Rajiv Gandhi,
"should not be considered as a brain drain but as a bank on which the country
could draw from time to time" (*Hindustan Times,* 23 November 1988).

5. MIGRATION POLICY AND FOREIGN POLICY

The new circumstances and characteristics of international migration—its global character, its association not only with differentials in income and employment among states but also with political violence and repression within states, the separation of citizenship and denizenship, and the strong linkages between migrants and their country of origin—have made migration policies matters of foreign policy. Moreover, the presence of migrants also influences the foreign policies of states. Each of these international relations consequences of migration will be considered in turn.

The immigration and emigration policies adopted by states—their entry and exit rules—shape interstate relations. Countries prevent, restrict, permit, encourage, or force emigration. Other countries prohibit, limit, permit, or encourage immigration. Countries may have compatible rules: both the People's Republic of China and the Soviet Union forbid emigration and immigration across their shared borders, thus making the largest border in the world (dividing countries with unequal incomes) nonconflictual with respect to migration. Where rules are incompatible, extensive bargaining may ensue. East Germany forbade emigration to the West, but permitted its citizens to visit countries in Eastern Europe. The Hungarian decision to open its borders to Austria resulted in the exodus of large numbers of East Germans to the West through Hungary. East Germany sought, unsuccessfully, to pressure Hungary to restrict exit. Failing that, it had to consider whether to seal its borders to East European countries in order to prevent further emigration. Instead, it opted for the strategy of opening its borders to West Germany in the hope that its citizens, now free to travel, would not emigrate. (Thus, the creation of the wall and its removal were motivated by the same goal: to discourage emigration.)

As with other elements of foreign policy, issues of reciprocity and compatibility enter into the migration policies adopted by governments (Weiner 1985). To minimize conflict, the entry policies of receiving states must be compatible with the exit policies of sending states. Where one state seeks immigration of a specific group and another state prohibits emigration of that group (e.g., Soviet Jews in the 1970s and early 1980s, who sought to emigrate to the United States and Israel), conflicts arise. Some states permit themselves to be the country of first asylum (e.g., Thailand and Austria) on the condition that other states will thereafter grant refugee status. One state opened its borders to another (the Federal Republic of Germany toward the German Democratic Republic), assuming that its neighbor would restrict emigration. Still other states tightened border controls because too many of their neighbors sought illegal or unwanted admission (the United States and Mexico, India and Bangladesh, Malaysia and Vietnam).

Domestic considerations are not the sole basis for formulating migration policies. Governments may be guided by manpower considerations, by a concern for enabling families to unite, by notions of fictive kinship, or by humanitarian concerns for those in distress, but these considerations are weighed against the effects that migration decisions must have upon relations with sending countries as well as with the domestic political consequences.

Migration policies of receiving countries not only entail decisions as to who and how many people can enter. They also include (1) decisions concerning the economic rights of migrants to change employers, to purchase land, and to start a business; (2) education policies, especially the question of whether migrants and their children can attend schools where their mother tongue is the medium of instruction, and whether the curriculum is monocultural or multicultural; (3) social welfare policies, including access to medical care, entitlements for children, and sundry welfare benefits; (4) political rights, including the right to join unions and create ethnic associations, access to the media, freedom of assembly, and other civil liberties; and finally, (5) access to citizenship itself, both for migrants and for locally born children of migrants. While these decisions are substantially shaped by a country's history, traditions and culture, legal norms, and internal political considerations, they are also shaped by foreign policy considerations. Decisions to admit, reject, or expel, and policies and actions affecting migrants, have foreign policy *determinants* because they have foreign policy *consequences*.

The decision to grant asylum to a head of state in exile, or to opponents of a regime, are matters of international politics at the highest level. President Carter's decision to admit the Shah of Iran for medical treatment had profound consequences for United States-Iranian relations and, indeed, for his own political future. The granting of asylum to high officials or dissidents from Iran, Haiti, Tibet, the Philippines, and elsewhere raises the issue of whether a government-in-exile is contemplated, or whether the host country will become a base for efforts to change the regime from which the asylees fled. Moreover, to grant asylum under the international convention of 1951 that defines a refugee as a person who flees "owing to well-founded fear of being persecuted for reasons of race, religion, nationality, membership of a particular social group or political opinion" is to declare that a particular government is engaged in persecution (Gordenker 1987).

The narrowly defined international legal norm for granting asylum has proven to be inadequate for enabling states to make decisions solely on humanitarian grounds. But governments are also reluctant to substitute for the word "persecution" the words "killed, injured or incarcerated" because the refugee door would then be too widely opened. To admit individuals because of violence in their home country or because of the generally repressive character of their government would mean that the number of potential refugees would then include the entire population of some countries.

An important exception, however, has been the willingness of the United States to provide refugee status to those who fled Communist regimes without regard to whether the individual has a fear of persecution. For many Americans, the exodus from Cuba, Vietnam, Laos, Cambodia, the Soviet Union, Hungary, Czechoslovakia, and Nicaragua demonstrated the illegimate character of these regimes. That the United States was less generous in providing refugee status to those who sought to flee from non-Communist autocratic regimes demonstrates how enmeshed refugee policies are in foreign policy (Kritz 1983; Nicholas 1988; Teitelbaum 1988; Zucker and Zucker 1987).

In time, however, the U.S. government recognized the double-edged element in granting refugee status to dissidents from Communist countries. The United States was, in effect, enabling Communist regimes to painlessly remove their critics (Bach 1987; Mitchell forthcoming; Keely and Tucker 1990). Communist regimes engaged in dumping policies—by discharging prisoners from Cuban jails, by exporting entire social classes and ethnic groups, and by exiling critics. The U.S. government subsequently took a more restrictive view toward potential refugees from Communist countries. In contrast to the open-door policy adopted by the U.S. government during the earlier Soviet repression in Czechoslovakia and Hungary, President Bush urged Polish and Hungarian dissidents to remain in place to take part in the reform movement. The Bush administration has adopted a similarly cautious policy toward Chinese students, granting asylum in a few individual cases but otherwise merely extending visas in the hope that Chinese students, most of whom support democratization, will eventually return home. The Bush administration—with much dissent from the U.S. Congress, which wanted to grant de facto asylum to Chinese students— is concerned with the impact of granting asylum on U.S. relations with the Chinese government.

Paradoxically, the ease of exit from the Soviet Union and Eastern Europe has been accompanied by a tightening of entry into the United States. So long as exit was restricted the United States regarded those who were able to leave as refugees. As these states opened their borders, the U.S. government concluded that they should no longer be regarded as refugees unless as individuals they had a fear of persecution. Thus, Soviet Jews and other emigrants from the Soviet Union are finding it increasingly difficult to enter the United States.

The decision by some governments to reject those who seek refugee status is often a matter of disapprobation by other governments. Relations between the United States and Malaysia and Thailand have been strained by the decisions of those governments to turn away Vietnamese, while both governments in turn attributed their decisions to the unwillingness of the United States adequately to expand its refugee quota. Thailand adopted a first-asylum policy on the assumption that the United States and other countries would then take the bulk of the refugees; as the United States reduced its quota for Indochinese, the Thais questioned the wisdom of maintaining their first-asylum policy. The United States initially agreed to expand the year's quota for refugee admissions by an additional fifteen thousand, mostly for Armenians, Soviet Jews, and other East Europeans, so as to prevent a cut in the number taken from Southeast Asia. (Subsequently, this was cut back as well.) But the United States also adopted a new screening procedure to determine whether Vietnamese boat people qualified for refugee status or were economic migrants.

There has also been much international criticism of the British government's unwillingness to grant entry rights to holders of United Kingdom passports in Hong Kong; the British policy of forceful repatriation of Vietnamese refugees to Hong Kong; and of the unwillingness of the U.S. government to grant refugee status to people fleeing from Central America in a violent conflict with which the United States is associated.

As the number of requests for asylum and refugee status increases, governments tighten their entry rules by requiring more rigorous proof from those who claim to be persecuted. Western governments do not want to admit people who flee because of deteriorating political and economic conditions. The result is that acceptance rates are down, from 40 percent in France in 1986 to 32 percent in 1988, and for Switzerland from 70 percent acceptance in the 1970s to 7 percent in 1988.

As part of the rejection process a number of governments engage in a deterrence policy. The U.S. Immigration and Naturalization Service regards many of the claims for asylum as economic claims. (In 1988 the INS received 60,736 petitions for political asylum, mostly from Central America.) When a majority of detainees temporarily released by the INS pending hearings never turned up at their hearings and quietly slipped into the American labor force, the INS responded by establishing detention camps in south Texas, with dormitories, compulsory uniforms, and a camp atmosphere, all intended to deter would-be immigrants from entering the United States to seek political asylum. A similar deterrence policy has been adopted by the British in Hong Kong toward boat people from Vietnam, most of whom are regarded as economic migrants. The West German government, reluctant to create refugee camps that would be characterized by the media as concentration camps, confined Tamils to dormitory facilities in hotels and denied them access to employment pending decisions as to their refugee status. The harshest deterrence policies have been in Southeast Asia, where Vietnamese boat people have not been permitted to come ashore.

Expulsion of illegal migrants and would-be refugees is often constrained by foreign policy considerations. To push a large number of people across the border is to stir conflict with one's neighbors. The U.S. government was unwilling to expel several million illegal Mexicans, choosing instead to grant amnesty to illegal migrants who had resided in the United States for an extended period. Nor has France or other governments of Western Europe been prepared to expel migrant workers, having instead offered financial incentives to return and the right of residence to those who remain (Rogers 1985). On the other hand, Nigeria ignored international criticism when it expelled Ghanaians and other foreign workers when the oil boom ended.

The selection process for immigrants may also generate international criticism. The most dramatic and bitterly contested issue was when the Arab states successfully persuaded a majority of the members of the UN General Assembly to condemn Israel for its right-of-return migration policy under which Jews anywhere in the world were entitled to Israeli citizenship. The "Zionism is racism" resolution embittered Israelis, who noted that a number of countries (the Federal Republic of Germany and the Republic of Ireland among others) also have citizenship and migration rules based upon the principle of descent.

Governments are often critical of one another for their exit policies. While the "right" of emigration raises the policy question of who will receive those who choose to leave, the right to exit is regarded by liberal democracies as the ultimate freedom from tyranny. The United States made emigration rights a feature of its bilateral relations with the Soviet Union and with Rumania by linking emigration to trade policy.

Finally, the ways in which citizens treat immigrants have foreign policy implications. Attacks against Algerians in Marseille, Pak-bashing in Brighton, "dot busting" of Indians in New Jersey alert the embassy and foreign office of the sending country. Sensitive issues pertaining to the religious beliefs of migrants easily spill over into foreign relations: whether Muslim girls should be required to attend the same schools as boys, whether Muslim girls should be permitted to wear a veil in school, whether books regarded as blasphemous by Muslims should be published, widely advertised, and displayed in store windows, and whether the Italian government should permit the construction of a mosque in the heart of Rome. Security concerns by the host government toward migrants also put a strain on relations with the migrants' country of origin. What to the police of the host country is a prudent check against potential terrorists is for another government harassment of its citizens or an unwarranted restriction on tourists. Third world governments are generally more critical of the treatment of their citizens or former citizens by governments and employers of developed than of developing countries. Arab governments, for example, have been more sensitive to how their citizens are treated by the government of France than by, say, the governments of Saudi Arabia or Kuwait. Similarly, the governments of India and Pakistan are more sensitive to how their nationals or former nationals are treated in the United Kingdom than in the United Arab Emirates.

In summary, migration policies have become foreign policies in the following ways: (1) governments attempt to influence the immigration, refugee, and emigration policies of other states; (2) in making their own immigration and refugee policies many governments take into account the emigration policies of other states; (3) in making emigration, immigration, and refugee policies and in their treatment of immigrants governments recognize that these decisions have an impact on their relations with others so that foreign policy considerations shape migration and refugee policies.

6. FOREIGN POLICY, IMMIGRANTS, AND ETHNICS

Foreign policy, as we have noted, shapes migration policy. This section examines how migrants (including refugees) and their descendants attempt to influence the foreign policy of their host country and the domestic politics of their home country.

The mode of *political incorporation* of a migrant community into the host society will influence whether and how it will seek to play a role in foreign policy issues. It clearly makes a difference as to whether or not migrants have become naturalized citizens, whether they can vote, form their own community organizations, be integrated into class organizations such as trade unions, and become office holders.

It particularly makes a difference as to whether a society regards as legitimate efforts by immigrants, naturalized citizens, and their native-born children to express their ethnicity through group action. At one end of the continuum is the United States, which legitimizes ethnic identities. Near the other end of the continuum is France, which assumes that in time migrants and their children settled in France will in every respect be French, without a hyphenated identity. These differences are reflected in the role migrants and their descendants play in matters of foreign policy.

In the United States, four types of group action by ethnic groups are commonplace: (1) to influence policies and programs that affect the well-being of the ethnic community; (2) to influence migration and refugee legislation; (3) to influence American foreign policy so as to affect the country of origin; and (4) to influence the domestic politics of the country of origin.

Immigrants are sympathetic or hostile to the government of their country of origin depending in part on whether they came as refugees. In the United States, those who came from the Soviet Union, Hungary, Czechoslovakia, Poland, Cuba, Vietnam, Laos, Cambodia, Nicaragua, Ethiopia, and Afghanistan are usually hostile to their regimes. These communities have advocated strong defense budgets and are often conservative Republicans.

Immigrants who came in search of employment may also be critical of their home government. Where there have been movements against authoritarian governments, a considerable part of the migrant community in the United States has supported the forces of democratization. Thus, Filipino-Americans supported the opposition to the Marcos regime and actively lobbied in Washington on behalf of efforts to dislodge him. Sections of the South Korean and Taiwanese communities supported democratization movements, and Asian-Indians, normally supportive of the Indian government, were critical of Prime Minister Indira Gandhi when she imposed a national emergency and suspended civil liberties.

Chinese mainlanders are the newest community critical of their home government. Chinese students in the United States early in the century identified themselves with the May Fourth Movement; today their symbol is Tiananmen Square. Chinese students at American universities have held national conventions and openly demonstrated against Deng Ziaoping and the Chinese government. They have had access to the American media and to Congress and while they generally support the U.S. government's position toward China, they are less constrained than the Washington administration, which is concerned with not disrupting relations between the two countries.

Chinese dissidents abroad have begun to seek help from the 30 million overseas Chinese around the world, as Sun Yat-sen did early in this century. In July 1989 student leader Wu-er Kaixi and other prominent emigres formed the Chinese Democratic Front (known as the "Paris Group") in Paris. (France has a long history of hosting Chinese exiles, including Zhou Enlai and Deng Xiaoping in the 1920s.) New York has the Chinese Alliance for Democracy (or Minlian), which publishes the monthly magazine *China Spring*, and London has the Chinese Students and Scholars Association (CSSA). During the summer of 1989 Chinese students met in Chicago in an attempt to create an umbrella association. It is reported that many of these associations are receiving financial support from Hong Kong and from the Republic of China (*Far*

Eastern Economic Review, 24 August 1989). The overseas Chinese (the *hu-agiao*) have a long history of involvement with their mother country; the infusion of thousands of post-Tiananmen exiles into this community is having a major political impact on the *huagiao,* which in turn affects the politics of the host country and its relationships with the People's Republic of China.

While some ethnic groups in the United States have lobbied against their home governments, other ethnic groups have pressed the United States to take foreign policy positions to benefit the security and well-being of the country to which they are attached by birth, descent, or ethnicity (Keely and Tucker 1990). Greek-Americans lobby against U.S. aid to Turkey and in support of Greek claims upon Cyprus; American Jews support Israel and oppose arms sales to Arab states; Asian-Indians campaign against arms sales to Pakistan. With an increase in the number of Arab-Americans, there is now a lobby on behalf of the Palestinians and in opposition to Israel.

Until the 1970s the major ethnic lobbies in the United States were largely concerned with European affairs: Czechs, Hungarians, Poles, Italians, Jews, Greeks, and Irish lobbyists were known on Capitol Hill. With the diversification of migration to the United States since 1965, the old lobbies are joined by new ones from the third world (Daniels 1988; Jensen 1988; Heisler and Heisler 1986; Miller and Papademetriou 1983). A good example is the increasingly active role played by Asian-Indians. The National Federation of Indian-American Associations (NFIAA) has been attempting to influence U.S. policy toward South Asia. In November 1986, when the Reagan administration proposed providing $4.2 billion in military aid to Pakistan, the NFIAA launched a campaign against the aid among congressmen and senators, and representatives of the Indian community testified before the Senate Foreign Relations Subcommittee on the Near East and South Asia.

Where cordial relations exist between migrants and their country of origin, the home government may actively seek their support. Several governments — the People's Republic of China, South Korea, Taiwan, and India, among many others — have turned to their citizens or former citizens abroad for assistance in the acquisition of technology, for investment and trade, and for support in dealing with the host government. To maintain these ties governments may create cultural centers abroad, establish special banking arrangements, including convertible accounts, and instruct their embassies and consulates to keep in close touch with their emigrants and their children born abroad (Fitzgerald 1972).

Ethnic groups that identify with another country are not necessarily unqualified or united in their support of the country to which they are, by birth, descent, or ethnicity, attached. American Jews, for example, are divided in their views of Israel's position with respect to the West Bank, one group advocating a land-for-peace solution through negotiations with Palestinians, another group opposed to the creation of a Palestinian state under any conceivable circumstances. Migrants are often sharply divided from other migrants from their home country when they differ along ethnic lines. Differences at home are often reflected in differences abroad. Indian Sikhs, Sri Lankan Tamils, Kurds, Lithuanians, Latvians, Estonians, Armenians, Northern Irish Catholics, Soviet Jews, and Palestinians identify with their ethnic kinfolk, not with the country from which they come. Where there are civil conflicts at home, the migrant community may be active in Washington, lobbying against the home government. The community may also raise funds and participate in clandestine efforts to provide arms for militants at home.

Migrants and their descendants may attempt to influence the politics of their country of origin. The role played by Korean-Americans in Korea's last presidential elections provides us with a good example. Korean-Americans actively participated in efforts to influence the Korean presidential elections in 1988, with supporters of the two rival candidates, Kim Young Sam and Kim Dae Jung, competing for support. Though the 1 million Koreans in the United States could not vote by absentee ballot, they were organized to write or phone home in support of their candidates, to raise funds, to place political advertisements in the Korean press, and to distribute leaflets, bumper stickers, and other campaign materials. Korean-Americans for Kim Dae Jung carried out a telephone and letter campaign from their offices in Manhattan, Chicago, Los Angeles, and Portland as a continuation of their earlier efforts to support the democratization movement in Korea. A delegation of prominent Korean-Americans visited Korea during the elections to volunteer in Kim Dae Jung's campaign. Similarly, supporters of Kim Young Sam held campaign rallies in Flushing, Queens, and launched a door-to-door campaign to collect funds.

What Americans may regard as an acceptable involvement of an ethnic community in the politics of its country of origin may be regarded by another government as interference in its domestic affairs. American television and newsweeklies, cassettes, and now fax machines provide immigrants and ethnic groups in the United States with an opportunity to reach back to their country of origin. At a less benign level ethnic groups may, as noted earlier, send money and arms to dissidents at home, and engage in clandestine activities to overthrow their former government. Indeed, the United States and other Western governments have often provided a haven for dissident exiles and revolutionaries and permitted ethnic groups to use the liberal political environment provided by their host to conspire against their home government. The list of leaders who used their stay abroad to mobilize opposition and then returned home to replace or overthrow their government is impressive: Benigno Aquino, Corazon Aquino, Benazir Bhutto, Ayatollah Ruhollah Khomeini, Andreas Papandreou, and earlier Syngman Rhee, Sun Yat Sen, Vladimir Ilyich Lenin, Zhou Enlai, Deng Ziaoping, and Mohandas Karamchand Gandhi.

7. DO TRANSNATIONALS UNDERMINE NATIONAL SOVEREIGNTY?

The Swedish scholar Tomas Hammar has proposed that governments reverse their historic antipathy to dual citizenship (Hammar 1985; 1989). He writes that the number of persons holding more than one citizenship has already increased substantially, in part because some countries grant citizenship to children upon birth while the country of their parents grants them citizenship on the basis of descent. A woman who marries a man of another nationality often acquires her husband's citizenship without losing her own. Refugees often become naturalized citizens without renouncing their previous citizenship. Moreover, even governments that oppose dual citizenship have become tolerant towards it.

Hammar argues that a more liberal attitude toward dual citizenship would increase the rate of naturalization and thereby more quickly incorporate migrant workers into the society and polity of the country in which they are permanent residents. But whether or not states permit their naturalized citizens to hold another citizenship, a very large proportion of those who are naturalized and their native-born citizen children will remain attached to another country. For Muslims, Jews, Sikhs, and members of Eastern Orthodox churches the bonds of religion serve to strengthen a dual identity (Williams 1988). And for Koreans, Chinese, Japanese, Vietnamese, Asian-Indians, Sri Lankans, Pakistanis, Ethiopians, Nigerians, and Jamaicans it is the bonds of race. Moreover, the new technologies of communication and transportation enable the bonds to be sustained in ways not possible only a few decades ago. The governments of sending countries often nurture these ties, while host countries, though by no means all of them, have become more tolerant of dual identities if not dual citizenship.

It distresses some people to see naturalized citizens and ethnics take on the causes and conflicts of another country to which they remain attached. Let it be noted that these attachments are not confined to migrants and ethnics, but have been present among "native" English, French, and Americans who, by virtue of their ideologies, have identified with another country. At various times leftists have identified with the Soviet Union, China, Cuba, or Vietnam, and rightists with Nazi Germany. Still, there is an understandable concern when the conflicts that go on within and between countries are fought within one's society and thereby constrain policy makers from adopting policies they believe reflect the nation's best interests. Today, the struggles within and over Beirut, East Jerusalem, Ramallah, Teheran, Belfast, Amritsar, Srinigar, and Nicosia may also be fought in Paris, London, New York, and Washington. The weapons in these struggles are debates in the media, petitions, testimonies before government bodies, public demonstrations, electoral contests. They can also be assassinations and terrorist attacks on airplanes, airports, restaurants, and synagogues.

Efforts to obliterate these identities seem unlikely to succeed. The issue is how to channel the concerns and claims of immigrants and their descendants into the democratic framework by accepting as legitimate the efforts of ethnic groups to express their ethnicity through group action. For the United States, which regards itself, to use the language of Lawrence Fuchs, as a land of pluralism with a single civic culture (Fuchs 1990), the political incorporation of millions of migrants from the third world is within a political culture that permits migrants to voice their own views on foreign affairs. Americans do not regard the foreign policy claims of Greek-Americans, Jewish-Americans, Korean-Americans, Asian-Indians, and Chinese-Americans as a threat to national security so long as these claims are made within the democratic political process. Even France, its more homogeneous sense of identity notwithstanding, has become more tolerant of its own minorities speaking out on foreign affairs, as demonstrated by the protest of French Jews on radio stations, in newspapers, and in television interviews at a visit of Yasir Arafat to France. Moreover, France has a long history of providing a haven for exiles and permitting them to use French soil to build a revolutionary movement against the home government.

The claims, protests, and clashes of the new transnationals—the exiles, refugees, migrant workers, naturalized citizens, and ethnics—that make up the United States, France, and other countries of Western Europe seem likely to persist and grow. That they will increasingly speak out on matters of foreign policy as well as on migration policies seems likely. What is less certain is how governments will react and whether domestic political groups will regard their lawful assertions as legitimate.

8. IS AN INTERNATIONAL REGIME FOR INTERNATIONAL MIGRATION POSSIBLE?

Attempts to create unified rules with respect to international migration—or, to use the current jargon of international relations theory, "international regimes" or "sets of implicit or explicit principles, norms, rules, and decision-making procedures around which actors' expectations converge in a given area of international relations" (Krasner 1983)—have not been particularly successful (Gordenker 1987). International regimes with respect to international trade have been more successful partly because of the hegemonic trade position of a small number of states, but also because there is a strong case for arguing that all states are better off in a world of freer trade. No such case can be made for a world of borders open to the free movements of people. A massive movement from country A to country B may relieve country A of its political opponents, its unwanted ethnic minorities, and its unemployed and poor to the detriment of country B. Prosperous and economically expanding countries can usefully gain from immigration, but the marginal utility declines and becomes negative as the numbers increase, the quality of migration goes down, and ethnic conflicts arise between migrants and the indigenous population.

In international trade there are market mechanisms to correct an imbalance. Countries with a trade imbalance must increase their imports or decrease their exports. No such market mechanism exists with regard to international population movements. Countries have no need to balance immigrants and emigrants. Moreover, the number of individuals who want to or are forced to move from their country is well in excess of the willingness of states to admit migrants and refugees. Given the imbalance of supply and demand and the absence of self-correcting market mechanisms, receiving states impose rules to restrict entry. How states, singly or collectively, can set entry rules that are just when the supply is so much greater than states are willing to accept remains one of the most difficult contemporary moral problems in international relations.

The difficulties in creating such norms notwithstanding, there are growing pressures upon states to develop compatible entry and exit rules. For one thing, as we have noted, the immigration policies of states have become contingent upon the immigration and emigration policies of other states. West Germany's policy on freely admitting East Germans was based upon an assumption of limited migration, since the GDR borders were virtually closed. Moreover, the Berlin Wall itself as a barrier to emigration was only meaningful so long as Hungary and Czechoslovakia closed their borders to Austria. When those borders were opened the GDR had to choose between closing its borders to the East or opening its borders to the West.

States often put pressure upon one another to change their policies. At the most extreme, countries have even gone to war or militarily intervened because a neighboring state was engaged in behavior that resulted in an exodus of refugees: Tanzania's armed intervention in Idi Amin's Uganda, India's intervention in East Pakistan, and Vietnam's intervention in the Kampuchea of the Khmer Rouge. In each case repression by a government resulted in a refugee flight that imposed a burden on a neighboring state, which then intervened to protect its own security as well as to ensure the security of its neighboring population.

Western Europe migration policies have moved from unilateralism to bilateralism and, as 1992 grows near, to regionalism. Members of the European Community are now attempting to make uniform their migration and refugee policies. If refugees and migrants admitted into one country are permitted to live and work anywhere in Western Europe, then entry policies must be uniform. Just as the removal of barriers to the movements of goods within the European Community leads to the adoption of common policies toward imports, so does the removal of barriers to the movement of people imply the adoption of common entry policies. With 1992 rapidly approaching, attention has largely been given to reaching an agreement upon the rules of entry, but in time many other elements of migration policies and policies toward migrants and their children will have to be collectively addressed. How these will be resolved, given the special ties that each country has with countries of emigration and different policies toward the migrants themselves growing out of national traditions, will itself involve a complicated set of international negotiations.

The still larger issue remains of whether an international refugee and migration regime is possible. Some elements of such a regime are in place—the international refugee convention of 1951 and other conventions of the UNHCR regarding refugees; ILO conventions regarding the treatment of migrant workers: the UN Declaration of Human Rights; the Helsinki agreement; ad hoc international arrangements to deal with Vietnamese refugees; sundry agreements among international private voluntary organizations. But these are fragmentary, inconsistent, and without enforcement procedures.

Any effort to create a coherent international refugee and migration regime would have to deal with some or all of these issues: (1) the establishment of rules of entry for asylees, refugees, migrant workers, family members, and other classes of migrants; (2) the establishment of norms concerning the rights of denizens; (3) the establishment of legal rules involving the granting of citizenship; (4) the establishment of a mechanism for collective action toward states that produce refugees; and (5) the creation of procedures and collective financial arrangements for assisting low-income countries that provide a haven for refugees.

The barriers to creating such international norms are formidable. To the extent, however, that the European Community is able to create some norms for itself, there is likely to be a ripple effect on the United States and Canada as well as upon others. But the benefits to migrants, refugees, and their children are considerable. And international norms may be necessary if international conflicts, even wars, over refugees and migration are to be reduced.

BIBLIOGRAPHY

Alonso, William, ed. 1987. *Population in an Interacting World.* Cambridge: Harvard University Press.

Bach, Robert L. 1987. "The Cuban Exodus: Political and Economic Motivations." In Barry B. Levine, ed., *The Caribbean Exodus.* New York: Praeger.

Brubaker, William Rogers, ed. 1989. *Immigration and the Politics of Citizenship in Europe and North America.* Lanham, MD: University Press of America.

Carens, Joseph H. 1989. "Membership and Morality: Admission to Citizenship in Liberal Democratic States." In Brubaker.

Daniels, Roger. 1988. *Asian America: Chinese and Japanese in the United States since 1850.* Seattle: University of Washington Press.

Fitzgerald, Stephen. 1972. *China and the Overseas Chinese: A Study of Peking's Changing Policy, 1949–1970.* Cambridge: Cambridge University Press.

Fuchs, Lawrence H. 1990. *The American Kaleidoscope: Race, Ethnicity, and the Civic Culture.* Middletown, CT: Wesleyan University Press.

Gordenker, Leo. 1987. *Refugees in International Politics.* London: Croom Helm.

Hammar, Tomas. 1985. "Citizenship, Aliens' Political Rights, and Politicians' Concern for Migrants: The Case of Sweden." In Rogers.

Hammar, Tomas. 1989. "State, Nation, and Dual Citizenship." In Brubaker.

Hammar, Tomas, ed. 1985. *European Immigration Policy: A Comparative Study.* Cambridge: Cambridge University Press.

Heisler, Martin O., and Barbara Smitter Heisler, eds. 1986. "From Foreign Workers to Settlers? Transnational Migration and the Emergence of New Minorities." *The Annals of the American Academy of Political and Social Science* 485.

Jensen, Joan M. 1988. *Passage from India: Asian Indian Immigrants in North America.* New Haven: Yale University Press.

Keely, Charles B., and Robert Tucker, eds. 1990. *Immigration and U.S. Foreign Policy.* Boulder, CO: Westview.

Klein, Sidney, ed. 1987. *The Economics of Mass Migration in the Twentieth Century.* New York: Paragon.

Krasner, Stephen D., ed. 1983. *International Regimes.* Ithaca: Cornell University Press.

Kritz, Mary M., ed. 1983. *U.S. Immigration and Refugee Policy.* Lexington, MA: Heath.

Miller, Mark J., and Demetrios G. Papademetriou. 1983. "Immigration and U.S. Foreign Policy." In Demetrios G. Papademetriou and Mark J. Miller, eds., *The Unavoidable Issues: U.S. Immigration Policy in the 1980s.* Philadelphia: Institute for the Study of Human Issues.

Mitchell, Christopher, et al. Forthcoming. *Immigration Policy and U.S. Foreign Relations with Latin America.*

Nicholas, J. Bruce. 1988. *The Uneasy Alliance: Religion, Refugee Work, and U.S. Foreign Policy.* New York: Oxford University Press.

Pastor, Robert A., ed. 1985. *Migration and Development in the Caribbean: The Unexplored Connection.* Boulder, CO: Westview.

Reimers, David M. 1985. *Still the Golden Door: The Third World Comes to America.* New York: Columbia University Press.

Rogers, Rosemarie, ed. 1985. *Guests Come to Stay: The Effects of European Labor Migration on Sending and Receiving Countries.* Boulder CO: Westview.

Schuck, Peter. 1989. "Membership in the Liberal Polity: The Devaluation of American Citizenship." In Brubaker.

Schuck, Peter H., and Rogers M. Smith. 1985. *Citizenship without Consent: Illegal Aliens in the American Polity.* New Haven: Yale University Press.

Teitelbaum, Michael S. 1988. "Right versus Right: Immigration and Refugee Policy in the United States." *Foreign Affairs* 59:21–59.

Weiner, Myron. 1985. "International Migration and International Relations." *Population and Development Review* 11(3):441–55.

Williams, Raymond Brady. 1988. *Religions of Immigrants from India and Pakistan: New Threads in the American Tapestry.* Cambridge: Cambridge University Press.

World Refugee Survey: 1988 in Review. 1989. New York: U.S. Committee for Refugees.

Zolberg, Aristide, Astri Suhrke, and Sergio Aguayo, 1986. "International Factors in the Formation of Refugee Movements." *International Migration Review* 20(2):151–69.

———. 1989. *Escape from Violence: The Refugee Crisis in the Developing World.* New York: Oxford University Press.

Zucker, Norman L., and Naomi Flink Zucker. 1987. *The Guarded Gate: The Reality of American Refugee Policy.* San Diego, CA: Harcourt Brace Jovanovich.

CONTRIBUTORS

SOPHIE BODY-GENDROT is Professor of American Civilization at Paris-Sorbonne, and at l' Institut d'Etudes Politiques, Paris, and editor-in-chief of *La Revue Française d'Etudes Américaines*. Author of numerous articles and books on American cities, black Americans and cultural differences between France and the US, her most recent book is *La nouvelle immigration aux Etats-Unis* (1991).

DANIELLE BOYZON-FRADET is with the Ecole Normale Supérieure de Fontenay-St. Cloud and the Centre de Recherche et d'Etude pour la Diffusion du Français. She has written extensively on education of the children of immigrants in France.

ANDRÉ-CLÉMENT DECOUFLÉ is with the Ministère de la Solidarité, de la Santé et de la Protection Sociale, in the population and migration division. His most recent book is *Quarante ans d'histoire de politiques du travail et de l'emploi en France (1946–1986)*.

VÉRONIQUE DE RUDDER does research on migration and society with the Centre National de la Recherche Scientifique. She has written on immigrants and multiethnic housing and urban settlement.

LAWRENCE H. FUCHS is Meyer and Walter Jaffe Professor of American Civilization and Politics, Brandeis University, and served as executive director of the Select Commission on Immigration and Refugee Policy, whose recommendations served as the basis for recent immigration reform legislation. He is author of several books on immigration and ethnicity in the US; the latest is *The American Kaleidoscope: Race, Ethnicity and the Civic Culture* (1991).

NATHAN GLAZER is Professor of Education and Sociology, Harvard University, and co-editor of *The Public Interest*. Author of many publications on ethnicity, urban affairs, and public policy, his recent books include *The Limits of Social Policy* (1988), *The Public Face of Architecture* (1987), and *Ethnic Dilemmas, 1964–1982.* (1983).

PHILIP GLEASON is Professor of History, University of Notre Dame. He is author of *Speaking of Diversity: Essays on the Language of Ethnicity* (forthcoming), *Keeping the Faith: American Catholicism Past and Present* (1987), and *The Conservative Reformers: German-American Catholics and the Social Order* (1968), as well as of numerous articles on immigrants.

DONALD L. HOROWITZ is Charles S. Murphy Professor of Law and Professor of Political Science, Duke University. He is author of *A Democratic South Africa? Constitutional Engineering in a Divided Society* (1991), *Ethnic Groups in Conflict* (1985), and other works on ethnic and racial pluralism in the U.S. and elsewhere.

STANLEY LIEBERSON is Professor of Sociology, Harvard University. He has written extensively on many facets of ethnic and racial relations in the U.S. and other nations. His books include *Ethnic Patterns in American Cities* (1963), *Language and Ethnic Relations in Canada* (1970), *A Piece of the Pie: Blacks and White Immigrants since 1880* (1980) and others.

LANCE LIEBMAN is Dean and Professor of Law, Columbia University School of Law. He has written on urban issues and race and ethnic relations, and is author of *Employment Law* (2nd ed. 1991) and editor of *Ethnic Relations in America* (1982).

DANIÈLE LOCHAK is Professor of Law, University of Paris X-Nanterre, and president of Groupe d'Information et de Soutien des Travailleurs Immigrés (GISTI). She has written extensively on citizenship, discrimination and the rights of foreigners in France.

GÉRARD NOIRIEL is Professor of Social History, Ecole Normale Supérieure. He has done pathbreaking work on the history of immigration in France, including *Le creuset francais* (1985), *Workers in French Society* (1990), *La* *tyrannie du national* (1991); and *Les lieux de mémoire*, ed. P. Nora (forth-coming).

MICHEL ORIOL is with the Institute d'Etudes et de Recherches Interethniques et Interculturelles, Université de Nice. His research has been on the sociological and cultural aspects of immigration in Western Europe.

MARTIN A. SCHAIN is Professor of Politics and Associate Director of the Center for European Studies, New York University. He is the author (with Henry Ehrmann) of *Politics in France* (1991); *French Communism and Local Power* (1985); and (with Philip Cerny) *Socialism, the State and Public Policy in France* (1985). He has written extensively on the politics of immigration and the emergence of the National Front in France and is currently engaged in research on the politics of immigration in France and the U.S.

PETER H. SCHUCK is Simeon E. Baldwin Professor of Law, Yale Law School. His most recent books include *Agent Orange on Trial: Mass Toxic Disasters in the Courts* (1987) and *Citizenship Without Consent: Illegal Aliens in the American Polity* (with Rogers M. Smith) (1986).

ROXANE SILBERMAN is a research scholar with the Centre National de la Recherche Scientifique, Laboratoire Analyse Secondaire et Méthodes Appli-quées à la Sociologie. Her special fields are immigration, the methodology, sociology and politics of nationality statistics in France, and the study of immigrants and ethnic groups.

WERNER SOLLORS is Henry B. and Anne M. Cabot Professor of English Literature and Professor of Afro-American Studies, Harvard University. His publications include *Amiri Barake/LeRoi Jones: The Quest for a "Populist Modernism"* (1978) and *Beyond Ethnicity: Consent and Descent in American Culture* (1986). He is currently working on a study of the theme of black-white families in literature.

STEPHAN THERNSTROM is Winthrop Professor of History, Harvard Univer-sity. A pioneer in the quantitative history of social mobility in 19th century America and of ethnic groups in the US, his books include *Poverty and Progress: Social Mobility in a Nineteenth Century City* (1964), *The Other Bostonians: Poverty and Progress in the American Metropolis, 1880–1973* (1970) and, as editor, *Harvard Encyclopedia of American Ethnic Groups* (1980).

MARYSE TRIPIER is a sociologist, University of Paris VII, and the Centre National de la Recherche Scientifique, IRESCO. Her research is on immigrants in the labor force and the role of labor unions.

MARIS A. VINOVSKIS is Professor of History and research scientist in the Institute of Social Relations, University of Michigan. He recently published *The Origins of Public High Schools: A Reexamination of the Beverly High School Controversy* (1985) and *An Epidemic of Adolescent Pregnancy? Some Historical and Policy Perspectives* (1988), and has edited *Towards a Social History of the American Civil War: Exploratory Essays* (1990).

MYRON WEINER is Director of the Center for International Studies and Ford International Professor of Political Science, Massachusetts Institute of Technology. He is author of *Sons of the Soil: Migration and Ethnic Conflict in India* (1978) and *The Child and the State in India: Child Labor and Education Policy in Comparative Perspective* (1991). He is now studying the international relations implications of international population movements.

INDEX

Abrams, Jacob, 220–21
Abrams v. Baylor College of Medicine, 382
Access, right of, 395
Access-to-citizenship policy (U.S.), 338
Acculturation: in France, 23, 29; in Germany, 13; through schools, in U.S., 7, 132, 142, 147
Achievement, disparate: sources of, 26–28
Adam, G., 294
Adamic, Louis, 46, 223, 225–26, 230, 236 n7
Adams, John Quincy, 41
Adaptation (France), 265–66
Administrative classifications (France): based on socioprofessional categories and nationality, 72, 77 n12, 116
AFDC-UP, 376–77
Affirmative action (Great Britain), 16
Affirmative action (U.S.), 26, 56, 90, 369, 422; and self-classification of ethnicity, 97–98, 99–100
Afghanistan, 443, 453
Africa, 10, 334, 339, 361
African-Americans (Afro-Americans), 29, 49–50, 168; education and income, 27; number of, 208; *see also* Blacks
African immigrants (France), 13, 19, 257; *see also* North African immigrants (France)
Agricultural Confederation of Devastated Regions (France), 155
Agricultural labor program (U.S.), 340–41
Aguayo, Sergio, 443
Aid to Families of Dependent Children (U.S.), 377, 385 n16, 386 n23
Air France, 403
Alabama, 48
Alaskan Natives, 99
Alba, Richard M., 21, 102

Aldrich, Thomas Bailey, 214–15, 216, 219
Alexander, Daryl Royster, 58
Alger, Janet Merrill, 8
Algeria, 120–21, 156, 195, 358–59; French colonial involvement in, 443; independence of, 361
Algerians, 191, 441; in France, 6, 19, 119, 418; academic performance, 28; discrimination against, 264, 451; housing, 253, 254
Algerian war, 19
Alibert, Raphael, 366 n15
Alien and Sedition Act (U.S.), 334
Alien Residency Convention(s) (France), 401
Aliens (U.S.), 339, 349; applying for asylum, 345, 346; attitudes toward naturalization, 348–49; categories of, 338; children of, 348; deportable, 381; exclusion and deportation of, 333; job rights of, 369–73, 374; political participation by, 50–51; as protected class, 15, 372, 377; rights of, 335, 350–53, 375–77, 383; *see also* Illegal aliens; undocumented aliens
Allen, Walter R., 104, 138
Allen v. Board of Elections, 17
Alonso, William, 441
Alsace, 119, 120
Alsatians, 121
Ambach v. Norwick, 372
Amerasian children, 339
America: antebellum, 127, 129–32, 141; ethnic literature and redefinitions of, 205–44; immigration and group relations in, 3–35; redefinition of, 225; *see also* United States
American (term), 209–11, 220, 221, 223, 224, 228–29, 235; redefinition of, 233, 234–35
American-Americans, 221
American Character, The (Brogan), 180